A Synopsis
of American
History

A Synopsis of American History

★ ★ ★ ★

Eighth Edition

NEIL R. McMILLEN
with Charles C. Bolton

University of Southern Mississippi

Originally Under the Authorship of
Charles Sellers and Henry F. May

IVAN R. DEE, PUBLISHER

Chicago

A SYNOPSIS OF AMERICAN HISTORY. Copyright ©1997 by Ivan R. Dee, Inc. All rights reserved, including the right to reproduce this book or portions thereof in any form. For information, address the publisher at 1332 North Halsted Street, Chicago 60622. Manufactured in the United States of America and printed on acid-free paper.

The Library of Congress has cataloged the single-volume edition of this book as follows:
McMillen, Neil R., 1939–
     A synopsis of American history / Neil R. McMillen with Charles C.
Bolton. — 8th ed.
          p.   cm.
     Includes bibliographical references and index.
     ISBN 1-56663-160-2 (acid-free paper)
     1. United States--History.   I. Bolton, Charles C.   II. Title.
E178.1.M46   1997
973--dc21   97-1450

ISBNs for the two-volume edition:
Vol. 1, ISBN 1-56663-161-0
Vol. 2, ISBN 1-56663-162-9

CONTENTS

CONFLICTING HISTORICAL VIEWPOINTS

SPECIAL TABLES

MAPS

PREFACE

A Synopsis of American History, now in its eighth edition, provides students with a brief introduction to a complex subject. Our object in writing this comparatively slender volume is not to reduce the amount that students read but to liberate them from the traditional oversize textbook so that they may pursue their own historical inquiries in primary sources and specialized accounts. By design, then, the *Synopsis* is concise but chronologically inclusive.

This edition of a textbook first published nearly forty years ago emphasizes political history, which in our opinion affords the clearest organization of the nation's past. Yet we have defined *politics* broadly, and have endeavored to link it to the larger environment in which it functioned. Thus, while our focus is generally political, we also analyze the social, cultural, economic, intellectual, and diplomatic currents that give added dimension to American history.

In reducing a long and complicated story to a relatively few pages, we have found it neither possible nor desirable to avoid a point of view. While we have tried to be fair and judicious, we have not been reluctant to offer historical judgments. Appropriate reading in other books—the whole purpose of our synoptic approach—should enable students to accept or reject our interpretive statements. "For Further Reading" sections at the ends of chapters, though generally restricted to books that are readily available in college libraries, introduce students to the literature of each period. The sixteen essays called "Conflicting Historical Viewpoints" supplement the text and remind students of the subjectivity of the historian's craft; the Viewpoints highlight enduring scholarly controversies and suggest the development of scholarly thought through the years. Other pedagogical aids include nineteen time charts, which give a chronological summary of political and other important events. Three photo essays cover the Republic's early days, the Civil War and Reconstruction, and the Depression and New Deal era.

We wish to thank the many colleagues who, in one edition or another, read all or parts of this book and made many valuable suggestions. We tried to follow their suggestions insofar as they were consistent with the philosophy of the book.

In its first two editions, the *Synopsis* was the work of Charles Sellers and Henry May. Neil McMillen joined the enterprise in 1974 and, while he assumed responsibility for all revisions after that date, he shared coauthorship with Sellers and May in the third through the seventh editions. Although this book in many ways still bears their conceptual thumb prints, Sellers and May are no longer authors of record. Charles Bolton wrote the new material for the eighth edition.

N. R. M.

A Synopsis
of American
History

1

★　★　★　★　★　★

Beginnings, 1607–1700

WHEN Christopher Columbus broke through the water barrier to the New World and became the first European to set foot on San Salvador, he opened a momentous chapter in the history of the Old World as well as the New. Already, a static and status-bound Europe was responding to new intellectual stirrings, growing trade, and competition among emerging nation-states in overseas exploration and commerce. The dramatic European discovery of the New World frontier accelerated these beginning currents of change into a 400-year revolution. The very knowledge of the existence of seemingly limitless space and resources in America set off a prolonged economic boom, quickened the spirit of enterprise, generated mounting pressures against the rigidities of the social order, and hastened Europe's entrance into the modern world of individualism, capitalism, and liberal democracy.

The development of America took place in the midst of this profoundly important transformation of the Atlantic world. The central characteristics of the emerging "modern" epoch, as the term is used here, were the increasing importance of individual autonomy and the growing faith that human beings could win secular salvation — wealth and "happiness" — through individual enterprise. By the nineteenth century, when modernity in this special sense reached its fullest development, this emphasis on the individual had given rise to the social philosophy known as *liberalism*. In its original meaning, liberalism was the conviction that the good of everyone would be served if all were left as free as possible to pursue their individual ends. In the economic sphere, liberal doctrines lent support to *laissez-faire* capitalism. In the political sphere, liberal doctrines encouraged a majoritarian democracy with some protection for the rights of minorities.

EUROPE DISCOVERS THE NEW WORLD

Although October 12, 1492 is the traditional date for the discovery of the Americas, Columbus was a relative latecomer to the New World. Many centuries before the Italian adventurer sailed west from Spain in search of trade routes to the Orient, Asian nomads entered the North American wilderness. The combined work of geologists, archeologists, and anthropologists suggests that this migration from the east was possible as early as the beginning of the Ice Age (perhaps 50,000 years ago). The mainstream of migration to the Americas, however, began some 11,000 years ago and continued for several centuries. Very likely these earliest discoverers traveled the "land bridge" across the Bering Strait; some may have entered the New World by crossing the Pacific Ocean to other points of entry. But however they came, the New World's first settlers were dispersed in a relatively brief time throughout the western hemisphere, from Alaska to Tierra del Fuego.

In our own millennium, the New World was rediscovered by eleventh-century Scandinavian sailors. Although the exploits of these colorful Northlanders are also largely unknown, there is substantial evidence that Viking explorers sailed brightly painted, high-prowed ships from their settlements in Greenland to the North Atlantic coast of the Americas. About the year 1000, Leif Ericson led an expedition to "Vinland," a location possibly near Cape Cod but more likely in Newfoundland. During the next 10 to 20 years — four centuries before the French "discoverer" Jacques Cartier gave the region its name — other Viking parties probably scouted the vast reaches of the Gulf of St. Lawrence. These tentative Viking probings, however, had no lasting impact on North America. Whatever settlements the Norse established quickly disappeared. Theirs was an apparently isolated adventure without direct implication for future explorations in the great age of discovery.

Curiously it was Spain and not seafaring Portugal that was in the forefront of the bold exploration of the New World. Pioneers in the use of ships for trade and exploration, Portuguese mariners under the patronage of Henry the Navigator directed their swift, seaworthy caravels south along the coast of western Africa in search of gold and a passage to India. Some 25 years after Henry's death and 5 years before Columbus's first voyage to America, Bartholomeu Dias rounded the Cape of Good Hope. In 1498 Vasco da Gama reached India, and two years later India-bound Pedro Cabral was blown off course and happened upon the coast of Brazil. By that time, however, Spain had already seized the initiative in New World exploration. In fact Columbus, who had developed his considerable navigational skills in the service of the Portuguese, turned for the support of his first New World voyage to Ferdinand and Isabella of Spain only after being refused by the King of Portugal. Buoyed by the success of Columbus, the Spanish crown soon dispatched Vasco de Balboa, who discovered the Pacific (1513), and Ferdinand Magellan, whose expedition completed the first circumnavigation of the globe (1519–1522). By the early years of the sixteenth century, fully a century before the founding of the first permanent English colonies to the north, Spanish settlers occupied portions of Haiti, Cuba, Puerto Rico, Jamaica, and Panama. Soon thereafter (1519–1521), the resourceful Hernando Cortés, in the name of the Spanish crown, subdued the Aztec empire of

Montezuma to claim the vast treasure of Mexico. In the 1530s, Francisco Pizarro, following a nine-year seige, defeated the Incas to give Spain the even richer prize of Peru.

Initially, when the explorations of Juan Ponce de Leon, Francisco Coronado, and Hernando de Soto uncovered no gold or silver, the Spanish showed little interest in the region north of Mexico. Yet by the time the French and English began planting their North American colonies, the Spanish had already staked out Florida and present-day New Mexico and Arizona. A century later Spain added Texas, and in the eighteenth century extended its missions and fortresses (*presidios*) to California. Always secondary to Peru and Mexico in the Spanish scheme of things, these northern outposts served largely as buffers against hostile Indians and rival European powers. As the coming years would prove, these settlements were the most vulnerable New World possessions of an Old World nation rapidly declining in power and wealth.

The empire of New Spain in the south had its French and Dutch counterparts in the north with New France and New Netherland. Although the French and Dutch also sailed west in search of riches, they found it not in gold and silver but in fish and furs. Following the failed efforts of explorers Giovanni da Verrazano (1524), Jacques Cartier (1534), and Henry Hudson (1609), both nations abandoned their hope of a short cut to China and turned early in the seventeenth century to the less spectacular enterprise of colony building. In 1655 New Netherland managed to absorb a tiny Swedish outpost (New Sweden) along the Delaware River, but the colony soon became New York when the Dutch lost out to their commercial and colonial rivals, the English. The French proved more tenacious, but they too were to be driven from the continent in the eighteenth century.

The English also looked westward for a water route to the East. From the fifteenth-century voyages of John Cabot and John Rut to the eighteenth-century adventures of James Cook and Alexander Mackenzie, Britain searched for the elusive Northwest Passage. Failing here, the English became colonizers. Oddly, the area they eventually exploited was the last major segment of the New World frontier to attract Europeans. In the sixteenth century, while the Portuguese concentrated on Brazil, the Spanish on Central and South America, and the French on Canada, most of the intervening expanse of temperate and fertile country lay untouched while England slowly readied herself for overseas expansion.

English colonization in American differed in character and consequences from that of other European nations. England was closer to having a tradition of individual rights and social mobility, and the English exhibited earlier and more fully that spirit of individual enterprise that was to be a major force in the modernization of the European world. Henry VII and Henry VIII had destroyed the power of the feudal nobility, already weakened by the War of the Roses, and had established a strong centralized state. In so doing, the Tudor monarchs had encouraged the growth of the business middle classes, the merchants and entrepreneurs who were to be major agents of the modernizing process. Moreover, Henry VIII had welcomed the Protestant Reformation in England, and Protestant theology, with its spiritual individualism, reinforced the individualistic, enterprising spirit of English middle-class life. All of these influences culminated in a burst of national vigor and creativity in the late sixteenth century under the last of the Tudors, Elizabeth I. It was at this point that the English turned their eyes toward the New World.

A second crucial difference between England and the other major colonizing nations was that England entered into her colonizing ventures as a poor country. Though the Elizabethans dared to challenge the might of Catholic Spain, they were only on the threshold of holding major-power status, and the Queen's treasury had insufficient funds to support the New World ventures that seemed vital to England's grand strategic design. Private enterprise had to be enlisted, and the English responded to this national purpose with a mixture of patriotism, Protestant religious zeal, thirst for adventure, and greed.

Sir Humphrey Gilbert, one of the first individual colonizers, died in his effort to found a colony in Newfoundland in 1583. Gilbert's half-brother Sir Walter Raleigh then took up the task of establishing a colony in America. In 1585, he sent 108 male colonists, who landed on heavily wooded Roanoke Island in present-day North Carolina. They were unsuccessful in their search for gold and a route to the Pacific Ocean; instead, they encountered hostile Indians and experienced food shortages. Coming upon the colony during his explorations, Sir Francis Drake, the first Englishman to sail around the world, returned them to England the following year. Another group, composed of 117 men, women, and children, was sent out in 1587. Under circumstances that still remain a mystery, they had all disappeared from Roanoke when a supply ship arrived in 1591. These failures demonstrated that a colonizing venture was beyond the financial capacity of any one individual. The polished and daring Raleigh, a favorite of Queen Elizabeth, solved this problem by organizing a syndicate of London merchants, a profit-seeking "joint-stock company," to finance his second colonial venture in Virginia. The joint-stock device, forerunner of the modern corporation, dated back to the time of Henry VIII when English merchants had pooled their capital and shared the risks of trade with Russia by buying shares in the "stock" or capital of the self-governing Muscovy Company. Applied to America, this device not only made English colonization possible, but insured that it would be carried out under the direction of private entrepreneurs seeking private profits as well as national ends.

The private entrepreneurial aspect of English colonization and the individualistic character of English society interacted with the New World environment to produce important consequences. Everywhere in the New World, the absence of established institutions left people free to build new social orders, and abundant natural resources afforded a field for enterprise that led English Americans toward individualism and modernity.

The ready source of gold and silver that the Spanish found in their America reinforced the authoritarian social structure they had brought with them.

The fur trade played a like role in French America. The English colonizers at first also sought gold or a northwest passage that would open to them the Pacific and the riches of the fabled Orient. They, too, attempted to impose on their colonies a rigid form of social organization designed to promote corporate rather than individual ends. But the English New World, the temperate zone of North America, yielded no ready riches. Instead, it proved superbly fitted for the humbler pursuits of farming, fishing, and trade, tasks better adapted to individual than corporate enterprise.

Paradoxically, the English colonies flourished because they failed in their original corporate aims and thus left fields of enterprise open for individual English colonists. It was under these circumstances that English America surged into the forefront of the Atlantic world's drift toward modernity. This movement, with interesting variations, can be seen in the two colonial societies established in the first half of the seventeenth century, one on Chesapeake Bay and the other in New England.

THE CHESAPEAKE COLONIES: VIRGINIA AND MARYLAND

Following Queen Elizabeth's death in 1603, her successor, James I, made peace with Spain, thus freeing English human and economic resources for overseas ventures. Although this text focuses on the region destined to become the United States, England's seventeenth-century imperial reach was global; it stretched west from Ireland to Newfoundland and Nova Scotia, southward to Bermuda, and eastward to the subcontinent of India. It was to the west in the New World in 1606 that King James issued charters to two joint-stock companies to colonize the land that Raleigh had named Virginia in honor of the virgin Queen Elizabeth. The more important of the two Virginia companies, with headquarters at London, promptly sent out an expedition of 144 people aboard the *Sarah Constant*, the *Goodspeed*, and the *Discovery*. They reached Chesapeake Bay in April 1607 after an arduous voyage of four months. The 105 surviving English men and boys proceeded up a great river, which they named for King James, and founded Jamestown on a marshy peninsula — the first permanent English settlement in North America.

Hunger, hostile natives, and malaria took many lives in the early years before the settlers learned to cope with their alien and densely forested environment. All but 38 of the first arrivals died in the first year. Although the colony's numbers were replenished in 1609, out of some 500 inhabitants just 60 survived the "starving time," the fearsome winter of 1609–1610. Only the arrival of 300 reinforcements with a new governor, Lord De la Warr, persuaded the dispirited remnant not to abandon Jamestown and return to England.

Much of the settlement's early difficulties can be traced to the Englishmen's inexperience with farming and the unrealistic commerical aims of the enterprise itself. The colonists were eager to find instant riches in gold and silver, or a northwest passage to the Pacific. Many of them were gentlemen unaccustomed to physical labor and slow to do the mundane agricultural work necessary for survival. Placed under great pressure to produce profits for investors, initially the settlers planted few crops and failed to prepare for life in the wilderness. Those who lived through the first difficult winters did so because of the Indians of the Powhatan Confederation, from whom the English learned much New World lore, and with whom they exchanged knives and hatchets for corn.

Gradually, as both settlers and investors recognized that the area held no undiscovered short-cuts to the Orient and no quick profits from precious minerals, the policies of the Virginia Company shifted to develop trade. To make the colony more attractive to immigrants, the famous "headright" system was inaugurated in 1618. Under it, 50 acres were awarded to any individual who paid for the transportation of a settler who would agree to cultivate the land and pay an annual *quitrent* (or tax payable to a superior) of one shilling to the company. Although the system proved more beneficial to speculators who bought the land claims of settlers than to the settlers themselves, it did stimulate immigration. Toward the same end, the early "cruell lawes," which imposed a rigid military discipline on the colonists, were replaced by the "free lawes" of England. The settlers were also permitted to send delegates to the House of Burgesses, (Virginia Assembly); in 1619, as the first representative body in the New World, the Virginia Assembly organized itself on the model of the English House of Commons and claimed the right of local self-government.

The shift in company policy was a graceful adaptation to social fact: the fortunes of the colony were increasing only as people found opportunity to pursue their individual ends rather than the corporate ends of the company. John Rolfe, best known as the Virginian who helped gain peace with the Indians by marrying Pocahontas, daughter of the local chieftain, made a greater contribution to Virginia by developing, around 1613, a strain of Indian weed tobacco that achieved instant popularity in England. As the craze for tobacco in England created a flourishing market and high prices, Virginians poured all their energies into growing tobacco for individual profit, and company enterprises were left to languish.

The company made one final effort to recruit immigrants to staff its corporate enterprises, but the cost of promotion was too great, and the lure of tobacco quickly drew the new workers away. The company fell into factional bickering, and in 1622, after the death of Pocahontas's father, a new and more bellicose chieftain led the Indians in a massacre of the English farmers along the James River. About one-third of the settlers (347) were killed, and the devastation came up to the gates of Jamestown. The disaster, followed by bloody reprisals and a crop failure, so discredited the company that the King revoked its charter in 1624, and Virginia became a royal colony ruled by a governor appointed by the king. The headright system was continued, however, as was the House of Burgesses. Despite King James's reluctance to concede the principle of colonial self-rule, the crown interfered in Virginia's affairs less than the company had.

The high profits from tobacco brought quick recovery from the effects of the Indian massacre and made Virginia a land of opportunity for the disadvantaged and discontented. Gripped by such demographic and economic forces as rapid population growth, inflation, and the commercialization of agriculture with its need for fewer farmers, England teemed with farm and town workers available for colonial emigration. The poorest of English farm workers could emigrate as indentured servants of a Virginian who would pay their ocean passage. Labor was so dear and land so cheap in the New World that when the three to five years of servitude were completed, a servant could often buy a farm, plant tobacco, and perhaps acquire indentured servants of his own. The most enterprising and affluent of the early settlers accumulated both labor and land in abundance by importing indentured servants and acquiring headrights in the process. While these more successful planters filled the offices of colony and county government, Virginia society remained so fluid during most of the seventeenth century that the planters could not be said to constitute an aristocracy or ruling class.

For one category of immigrants, the Virginia environment produced not self-fulfillment but enslavement. In 1619, the year of the first representative assembly in British North America, a Dutch trading ship dropped anchor at Jamestown with the first cargo of Africans. The original English settlers had brought with them the traditional European prejudice against blacks, but there was no provision in English law for treating Negroes differently from other indentured servants. However, it was easier to take advantage of blacks. Torn forcibly from their African cultures and languages, they had few means of resisting oppression in the alien culture of Virginia. Conspicuously distinguishable from European servants, they could not run away and melt into the free population. Even as the conditions of servitude became less onerous for whites, masters gradually began holding black servants for life and claiming the labor of their children. By the middle of the seventeenth century, Virginia law was modified to define a separate status of permanent and absolute slavery for Africans. When the colony's evolving slave laws were first codified in 1705 and bondsmen were "adjudged to be real estate," blacks numbered perhaps 10,000 in a population totalling about 85,000. This was to be a land of opportunity for Europeans only. Indeed, it was through the exploitation of cheap black labor in the tobacco fields that some white Virginians began to amass great fortunes in the later seventeenth century.

While whites flourished in Virginia, a similar pattern of colonial life was being established under very different auspices farther up the shores of Chesapeake Bay. In 1632, King Charles I, successor of James I, granted to Cecilius Calvert, second Lord Baltimore, proprietorship (theoretically, personal ownership) of the feudal domain of Maryland lying between the Potomac River and the 40th parallel. The Calverts were a noble Catholic family who envisioned Maryland as a refuge for their fellow Catholics from Protestant England. The first settlement was established at Saint Mary's in 1634, when some 200 colonists, most of them Protestants, arrived aboard the *Ark* and the *Dove*. Soon both Protestants and Catholics were emigrating to Maryland to become tobacco growers like the Virginians. But unlike the early Virginians, they enjoyed peace with their Indian neighbors and experienced no starvation.

Due to a remarkable royal charter, Lord Baltimore had absolute political power and personal ownership of the land. In order to attract settlers and make the colony a success, the young Lord Proprietor shared both soil and power with them. Large grants of 3,000 to 6,000 acres were made to some colonists, mostly Catholics; they presided as manorial lords over large numbers of servants and tenants and came to constitute a kind of gentry. Most of the population were yeoman farmers, perhaps employing a few servants and leasing their lands from the proprietor on a basis nearly equivalent to ownership in return for a nominal tax or quitrent. The Calverts appointed a governor, but eventually allowed the inhabitants to elect an assembly that soon asserted its right to initiate legislation. The most notable piece of legislation was the Act of Toleration of 1649. This act promised less tolerance than is commonly believed; it applied only to orthodox trinitarian Christians and assured neither separation of church and state nor universal freedom of worship. Yet the act assured a measure of religious liberty to Protestants and Catholics. Within three decades of its founding, the colony had perhaps 13,000 inhabitants.

NEW ENGLAND: PLYMOUTH AND MASSACHUSETTS BAY

Meanwhile, far to the north of the Chesapeake colonies, a different kind of English colonization was taking place on the less hospitable coast of New England. The New England colonies were a direct outgrowth of a renewal of religious conflict in England. The more intense Protestants had never been satisfied with the moderate English Reformation as it was institutionalized in the Church of England. Calling themselves Puritans, they wanted to rid the English church of Roman Catholic practices and to "purify" it by eliminating the hierarchy of bishops and simplifying church ritual. The Puritans shared with Anglicans the predestinarian doctrines of the Swiss cleric John Calvin: a heightened sense of an inscrutable God's sovereignty and goodness and a recognition of depraved humanity's dependence on divine grace for salvation. The Puritans strove to live strictly in accordance with God's will and to create a community modeled on that of the earliest Christians.

Queen Elizabeth's astuteness had prevented the growing Puritan spirit from causing trouble during her reign, but her successors, the Stuart monarchs James I (1603–1625) and Charles I (1625–1649), invited conflict. James bluntly told the Puritans that they would either conform to the usages of the Church of England or be "harried out of the land." His son Charles married a French Catholic princess and supported efforts to compel religious conformity.

Early on, James harried one little band of particularly fervid left-wing Puritans out of England, and they took refuge in Holland. They were known as Separatists because they sought to separate from the Church of England and not merely to purify it. Although they were able to worship as they wished, after several years in Holland these Pilgrims, in order to preserve their identity, turned their eyes toward America. With support from a group of London merchants, they and additional recruits from England, totalling 101 men and women (87 of them either Separatists or members of Separatist families), set out for Virginia in the *Mayflower* in September 1620. Poor navigation brought them to the American coast at Cape Cod, north of the company's territory, and rather than brave further winter storms on the Atlantic, they established nearby the settlement of Plymouth. Half of this ill-prepared band died of illness and malnutrition during the first winter. The remaining Pilgrims were spared largely through the timely appearance of Squanto, a friendly Indian who spoke English, having spent some time in England after being kidnapped by a ship's captain. He taught them to fish and to grow corn. Thus, Plymouth Plantation endured, if it did not grow rapidly, as a "sweet communion" of simple and pious souls who eked out a living from poor New England soil and from trade in fish and furs. The first English community in New England, it was soon overshadowed and eventually absorbed (1691) by the larger, more prosperous Puritan colony of Massachusetts Bay. Its place in the American imagination, however, was assured by the eloquent history, *Of Plymouth Plantation*, left by its long-time governor, William Bradford, and by the first Thanksgiving, its celebration of the first harvest in the new colony. Not least of all, New England's first permanent settlement is remembered for the Mayflower Compact. This first American "constitution" was a self-governing agreement inspired by radical Puritan notions of church government; 41 adult males signed it on shipboard before the Pilgrims landed at Cape Cod. Under its terms, the colonists formed a "civill body politic" to govern themselves by majority will and promised "all due submission and obedience" to the "just and equall lawes" of the colony.

The main Puritan migration to New England was made possible when a group of well-to-do and influential leaders obtained from King Charles in 1629 a charter for the Massachusetts Bay Company authorizing settlement in the area north of the Plymouth colony. In a bold move, the leaders resolved to make this charter of a joint-stock company the constitutional basis for a holy commonwealth beyond the King's reach by moving charter and company officers across the Atlantic. All over England, Puritans subscribed funds and volunteered themselves, and in the summer of 1630, a fleet of 17 vessels carried nearly 1,000 people to establish a series of towns around Boston harbor. As conditions for Puritanism worsened in England, these original settlers were followed by thousands more. Within little more than a decade, New England had 20,000 people.

However foreign the Puritans' ideals may seem to later generations, their enterprise for a holy commonwealth was certainly one of humanity's nobler dreams. If one accepts the Puritans' premises that God is sovereign, that one's primary duty is to do His will, and that the major issue of life is whether one receives God's grace or salvation then it is hard to resist their conclusion that society should be constructed around a divine plan for human redemption.

The Puritans' theory of civil government was similar to their congregationalist theory of church government, and both were based on the idea of covenant. A true church was a group of the "visible elect" (those who appeared by their lives to be true recipients of God's grace) who had entered into a sacred agreement or covenant with God and each other to obey the divine will and establish a church to preach His word. It was then the business of the church members to choose as minister a man especially qualified by character and education to interpret divine will. (Women were, of course, generally denied education and were not eligible for the clergy.) This theory contained an element of democracy in that all members participated in the holy covenant, the choice of a minister, and the admission of new members; an element of aristocracy in that the minister once chosen should be accorded the authority due his special qualifications for interpreting God's will; and an element of monarchy in that God's will was sovereign.

The Puritans similarly believed that their holy commonwealth was founded on an implicit covenant with God and each other and that civil magistrates derived their authority from their special qualifications for interpreting God's will for the society. The Puritan commonwealth took its form from the corporate charter of the Massachusetts Bay Company. The stockholders or "freemen" of a joint-stock company met annually as a "Great and General Court" to decide major company policies and to elect the company's executive officers, a governor and a board of assistants or magistrates. When the Puritan leaders transferred the charter of the Massachusetts Bay Company from England to New England in 1630, only a handful of magistrates — the governor, John Winthrop, and a few freemen (stockholders) of the company who were also assistants — went along.

In their zeal to protect the religious objectives of the holy experiment, these few magistrates sought at first to make all rules, judge all cases, and govern alone. But within a year, a number of the leading settlers demanded a voice in government, and the magistrates decided that henceforth all adult male church members could be considered freemen and be allowed to attend the annual General Court to elect the governor and assistants. By 1632, three years after settlement, the General Court had forced the magistrates to concede it a share in the lawmaking power. As the population increased and the General Court became unwieldy, the practice was adopted of having the freemen in each town elect two deputies to represent them in the General Court. The evolution of the General Court as a representative legislative body was completed in 1640 when the elected deputies and the governor and magistrates began meeting separately, thus forming a bicameral legislature.

The Puritan commonwealth was theocratic in the sense that God's will was law, but not in the sense that ministers were given direct political power. The real power of the clergy arose from their authority as interpreters of God's will. With respect to civil matters, this function was ordinarily performed by the magistrates, but when they disagreed with the deputies, the magistrates could usually call the powerful authority of the clergy to their support. Nearly everyone believed that it was the duty of the state to support the church, to require church attendance by members and non-members alike, to enforce a strict morality, and to do anything else that would increase the chances of salvation for every member of the community.

The pattern of settlement reflected the religious aims of the holy commonwealth. Individuals were not permitted to buy land wherever they wished. The General Court, in a practice quite unlike that of Virginia or Maryland, insisted on compact settlement in contiguous towns. When warranted by population increases, the General Court would authorize a group of people to settle a new town adjacent to one already established. Thus, in orderly and controlled fashion, the original settlement at Salem was followed by ones at Charlestown and Boston and subsequently at Haverhill, Concord, and Sudbury, and then by others well beyond the Boston Bay area. Families were assigned house lots (the sizes of which were generally determined by social rank) in a compact village within the town's boundaries, and they worked the outlying agricultural lands they were allotted. The church was located in the village center, and villagers and the town and church officials were encouraged to guard, warn, and reprove each other against moral lapses. Freeman and nonfreeman alike were allowed to participate directly in the town meeting, which elected town officials and decided local policy.

Deeply believing that a trained intelligence was required to discern God's will, the Puritans were zealous advocates of education. The family was the basic unit of instruction. Although male dominance was an accepted principle and women were expected to regard their men with "a reverend subjection," the mother exercised considerable, at times decisive authority within the home. Day-to-day child-rearing, like most domestic matters, were her responsibility. Technically, at least, the father was responsible for educating his dependents; he saw to it that his children and servants mastered the rudiments of reading, writing, and arithmetic and that his sons learned a trade. Fathers were responsible, too, of course, for the religious and moral training and behavior of their families. In 1647, the General Court ordered every town of 50 houses to maintain an elementary school, and some of the larger towns supported public secondary schools as well.

Puritan theory required not only a decently educated general population but also a highly educated magistracy and clergy. More than 100 graduates of Oxford and Cambridge came to Massachusetts Bay in its first decade to fill this need. In 1636, the General Court established at Cambridge a college modeled on the English universities and named after John Harvard, a young English clergyman who bequeathed to it his library and half his estate. Bright boys from ordinary farm families attended Harvard, and about half of the graduates became ministers.

RHODE ISLAND, CONNECTICUT, NEW HAMPSHIRE

It was inevitable that the holy commonwealth's efforts to maintain social discipline and a uniform doctrine would lead to friction in a population filled with gifted, intense, and devout individuals. The most embarrassing troublemakers in the early days were Roger Williams and Anne Marbury Hutchinson, both of whom challenged the principle of religious uniformity. A brilliant young minister, Williams was a radical Puritan who arrived at the modern principle of separation of church and state on the not so modern ground that enforcement of religious uniformity impeded the soul in its search for religious truth. Such a view clearly threatened the commonwealth, and Williams's close friend Governor Winthrop warned him of his impending arrest in time for him to escape. Banished from the colony, he made his way south with some of his followers to Narragansett Bay in 1636. He established the town of Providence, and then the colony of Rhode Island, where he proclaimed the policy of complete religious freedom and inaugurated a democratic system of self-government. Receiving a charter from the English government in 1644, Rhode Island attracted dissenters from Massachusetts and Europe, flourished as a farming and trading community, and was a thorn in the sides of its orthodox Puritan neighbors.

Soon after Williams's exile, Anne Hutchinson, a gifted lay theologian and an uncommonly assertive Puritan woman, was also banished from Massachusetts to Rhode Island. She had been holding meetings in which she stressed the covenant of grace, which appealed to many Puritans. Because she believed that the continuing process of divine revelation could supplant orthodox scriptural interpretation, she was accused in the colony's General Court of disrespect for the clergy and the heresy of Antinomianism, which emphasized the primacy of inner faith and direct communion with God over outward religious observance and other good works. In today's more secular age, her doctrinal differences with the Puritan leadership seem small — matters of degree, not kind. Yet her outspoken criticism of established clerical authority — and her intrusion into affairs that the Puritan fathers thought were better left to men — assured her conviction as "a woman not fit for our society." After a brief imprisonment she along with her family and some followers fled to Rhode Island; she was killed in 1643 by Indians.

Another New England colony came into being when the strong-minded Reverend Thomas Hooker and members of his congregation in Cambridge became excited over the fertile Connecticut River Valley, 100 miles inland from the Massachusetts Bay settlements. Rivalry between Hooker and the other leaders probably figured in the fact that the magistrates departed from their rule of compact settlement and allowed the Cambridge people to go. Traveling overland in 1636, Hooker's followers founded Hartford and organized their own colony of Connecticut on the model of Massachusetts Bay. Other Puritan groups founded settlements at Saybrook and New Haven on the coast and maintained an independent status for a quarter of a century before merging with Hooker's valley settlements as the united colony of Connecticut.

Massachusetts Bay sought to maintain control over the sporadic settlements that grew up to its north. In 1679, the towns beyond the Merrimac River obtained a charter making them the separate royal colony of New Hampshire, but the Maine area beyond continued to be ruled from Boston.

ENGLISH STRIFE AND AMERICAN AUTONOMY

The Stuart monarchy of Charles I had little liking for the stiff-necked independence of Puritan New England, but Charles had his hands too full with Puritanism in old England to undertake any punitive measures across the broad Atlantic. English Puritans had become increasingly important leaders in Parliament's struggle against the arbitrary policies of the Stuarts. The long and bitter conflict culminated in civil war in the 1640s. Oliver Cromwell's Parliamentary army defeated the royalist forces, King Charles was beheaded in 1649, and Cromwell became the dominant figure in a Puritan Commonwealth.

Under these circumstances, the English colonies on the Chesapeake Bay and in New England had been left to develop as they pleased. The Virginians cared little who ruled in England so long as they were left alone to grow tobacco and pursue their individual fortunes. In Maryland, however, the Protestant majority took advantage of the English Civil War to overthrow the Calverts and the Catholic ruling class and to repeal the Act of Toleration.

The New Englanders became more independent than ever. The leaders of Massachusetts Bay regarded their holy commonwealth as a model for England and indeed for all humanity, "a Citty Upon a Hill, the eies of all people upon us." The early success of the Puritan cause in the English Civil War reinforced their faith that they were leading the way to a world organized under the will of God. With redoubled zeal to maintain a pure and undefiled commonwealth, they sought to eliminate religious error wherever it appeared. The Quakers caused the Puritans the greatest trouble. These adherents of the Religious Society of Friends represented a kind of radical Puritanism of lower-class origin that enjoined each person to follow the divine promptings of the "Inner Light" in his or her own soul. The antiauthoritarian Quakers felt impelled to bear witness to their faith in the most hostile places, and many of them came to Massachusetts Bay for this purpose. Although they were banished, they returned at the first opportunity. The authorities tried whipping, then cutting off ears, then the threat of hanging, but still the banished Quakers returned. Finally four were hanged.

But suddenly New England lost its sense of cosmic significance. The Puritan Commonwealth collapsed in England, and the Stuart monarchy returned to power in the Restoration of 1660. The new Stuart king, Charles II, restored Maryland to the Calverts and sought to strengthen his control over the other colonies, but the habit of independence had become so deeply ingrained that he encountered strong resistance. Though the New England magistrates and clergy ceased their persecutions and grudgingly began to tolerate Quakers, Anglicans, and other dissenters, they stubbornly sought other ways to maintain their autonomy and power in loyalty to the ideal of the holy commonwealth. But by now, this ideal was being weakened from within as well as from without.

PURITANISM IN A SECULARIZING SOCIETY

The Chesapeake colonists had reacted to the New World environment and the lure of profits from tobacco culture by moving easily toward a society of merchants and staple-crop producers, based on individual enterprise and liberal institutions. In New England, an equally autonomous society had developed, but here institutionalized Puritanism was a brake against the pull of the New World environment toward modernity.

In emphasizing God's sovereignty and humanity's dependence, Puritanism (only somewhat more forcibly than Protestantism generally) was profoundly antagonistic to the modern spirit of optimism and confident individualism. Yet at the same time, Puritanism gave a powerful psychological impetus to individual striving. The Puritans were "moral athletes" who believed that "right living" was the best evidence (although no guarantee) that one enjoyed God's grace. Right living included working as hard and being as successful as possible in whatever worldly calling or business God had placed one. With these convictions, it was not surprising that Puritans were highly successful in their temporal pursuits, especially under the favoring circumstances offered by the New World environment.

Despite its scarcity of fertile soil, New England prospered from the beginning. Although fur trapping flourished only briefly and failed as game supplies dwindled, cod fisheries were developed early and remained a source of steady profit. Lucrative opportunities arose in trade with the English colonies in the East Indies and, to a lesser degree, with England and Spain. The Caribbean Islands produced only two crops — tobacco and sugar — for the European market, and New England colonists began to supply the islanders with food and other items they needed — fish, grain, staves, and livestock. These northern merchants also traded New World goods for manufactured products at Glasgow, Bristol, and London. Sometimes they exchanged rum for slaves on the coast of West Africa. Between the New World, the Caribbean Islands, and the Old World, a trading pattern, imprecisely called *triangular*, was established by the New Englanders. To facilitate their maritime endeavors, they built a flourishing merchant marine, which in turn stimulated a shipbuilding industry in New England.

By the middle of the seventeenth century, the Puritan colonies contained a growing class of successful and wealthy merchants and entrepreneurs, second-generation Americans with no memory of the persecutions once visited upon their forebears. Such people found it increasingly more difficult to maintain the fervid piety of the first settlers. Some could not put the search for salvation before worldly prosperity, and some did not feel helplessly dependent on the grace of an omnipotent God. There was no conscious parting from orthodoxy, no open rebellion against Puritan rule, but the religious fervor of the early commonwealth gradually ebbed. This became apparent when the children of the first generation of church members increasingly failed to give sufficient evidence of God's grace to be received into full membership themselves. Stubbornly retreating before the relentless tides of heterodoxy and secularism, the churches compromised; to retain influence, they opened their membership under a "half-way covenant" to those baptized children of church members who led exemplary lives and accepted the orthodox doctrines, but who were still unable to testify to a "saving faith," a convincing subjective experience of grace. Having blurred the distinction between the elect and the merely devoted, some churches soon went even further by permitting communion without public confession of faith.

Meanwhile, some of the more successful and less pious New Englanders began to argue that religious intolerance discouraged immigration and hampered growth and prosperity. These settlers also chafed under the orthodox leadership and disapproved of the continued defiance of royal authority. Thus when the British government finally lost patience with Massachusetts Bay, it found some allies among the Puritans. In 1684, Charles II annulled the Massachusetts charter, and the following year his brother and successor, James II, placed all the New England colonies, along with recently acquired New York and New Jersey, under the new and singular jurisdiction of the Dominion of New England. All legislative bodies were suspended, and the Dominion was arbitrarily ruled by a royally appointed governor, Sir Edmund Andros, and his council. But James's equally arbitrary rule at home was arousing opposition. When the King was overthrown in the "Glorious Revolution" of 1688, a series of popular demonstrations ousted the Dominion authorities in the American colonies.

In 1691, the Massachusetts Bay authorities had to accept from the new English monarchs, William and Mary, a charter that assured further secularization and seriously compromised the ideal of the holy commonwealth. The legislative power of the General Court was restored, but henceforth the governor was to be royally appointed, and property ownership replaced church membership as a qualification for voting. Under the new charter, the anticlerical elements gained increasing political influence and finally succeeded even in taking control of Harvard College.

The clergy sought to stem the ebbing of their spiritual and political authority by ever more fervent reminders of God's power and wrath and unwittingly contributed to the Salem witchcraft hysteria of the early 1690s. Before this frenzy subsided, 2 dogs and 19 innocent people died on the gallows, an old man was pressed to death by rocks, and some 150 others awaited (but would not suffer) a similar fate. Although belief in witches was almost universal throughout Christendom and although the Salem witch mania was modest and restrained compared to those of Scotland and Germany, the revulsion against the outrages in New England further undermined the prestige of the orthodox leadership. In all likelihood, the hysteria owed more to tensions resulting from a changing social, economic, and political order than to clerical excesses, but the tragic episode was another major setback for the Puritan hierarchy. By the turn of the century, the social and political leadership of the Puritan colonies was clearly passing into the hands of the enterprising commercial class that constituted the vanguard of modernity.

The Puritans have too often been viewed through the dark window of the witch trials. Until recently, much has been made of the somber, more repressive, and self-denying tendencies of these extraordinary people. Although their piety seems extreme to a more secular age, the Puritans were not necessarily the grim, self-righteous prigs of popular imagination. In a threatening and uncertain world, theirs was a purposeful community that proved immensely appealing to uprooted, discontented, and otherwise "unredeemed" Englishmen, that attracted an uncommon number of subtle minds, and that produced great intellectual vigor. Their modern critics have faulted their "hell-fire and damnation" religion, yet their ministers were well-educated men whose sermons were often models of lucidity. Nor were the Puritan faithful necessarily more stuffy or abstemious than other Anglo-Americans of the period; preferring moderation to total abstinence, they used tobacco and alcohol in moderation. Church records reveal that premarital sex could be forgiven the repentant Puritan, and that divorce was permitted for cruelty, adultery, and impotence. Marriage was often marked by tenderness and based on deep love between partners, who took pleasure in what one approving Puritan divine called the "Use of the Marriage Bed." In sum, these were appealing folk, sober and human, God-fearing and practical. They were not libertines, but they were probably no more puritanical than other seventeenth-century Englishmen on either side of the Atlantic.

FOR FURTHER READING

Samuel Eliot Morison's *The European Discovery of America* (1971) is a notable introduction to English explorations, and Wallace Notestein describes *The English People on the Eve of Colonization, 1603–1630* (1954). Gary Nash's *Red, White, and Black* (1992) explores the interactions between native Americans, Europeans, and Africans in colonial North America. The authoritative account of the early colonies is Charles M. Andrews's *The Colonial Period of American History* (4 vols., 1934–1938). The early history of the Chesapeake colonies is traced in James Horn's *Adapting to a New World* (1994), J. A. Leo Lamay's *The American Dream of Captain John Smith* (1991), and Wesley Frank Craven's *The Southern Colonies in the Seventeenth Century* (1949). Good recent explorations of colonial New England include Stephen Innes, *Creating the Commonwealth* (1995), and William Cronon, *Changes in the Land* (1983). Darrett B. Rutman, in *American Puritanism* (1970), provides a good introduction to early New England faith and practice; Perry Miller's classic two-volume study ably details *The New England Mind* (1939, 1953); and T. H. Breen's *The Character of the Good Ruler* (1970) examines Puritan political thought. Both Edmund S. Morgan's *Visible Saints* (1963) and Richard Gildrie's *Salem, Massachusetts* (1975) help explain the transformation of the Puritan commonwealth into a Yankee province. Important biographical and family studies include Edmund S. Morgan's brief study of Governor Winthrop, *The Puritan Dilemma* (1956); Morgan's *Roger Williams* (1967); Kenneth Silverman's *The Life and Times of Cotton Mather* (1984); and John Demos's analysis of Plymouth colony, *A Little Commonwealth* (1970). The best account of the social and economic context of the witch trials is Paul Boyer and Steven Nissenbaum, *Salem Possessed* (1974). John Demos, in *Entertaining Satan* (1982), places the Salem tragedy in broader perspective. In this period (as in all others) the student is advised to examine contemporary accounts, particularly Governor William Bradford, *Of Plymouth Plantation, 1620–1691* (1966) and John Winthrop, *Winthrop's Journal* (1908).

MAP 1: EUROPEAN SETTLEMENTS AND INDIAN TRIBES IN AMERICA, 1650

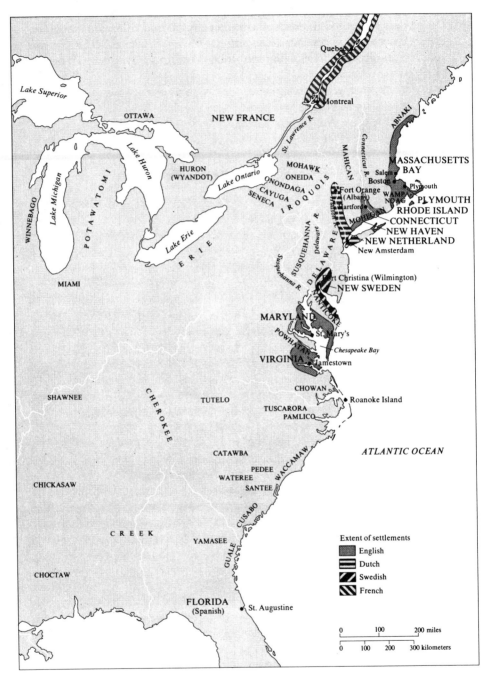

Source: Redrawn by permission of the Smithsonian Institution Press from B. A. E. Bulletin 145, *Indian Tribes of North America,* John Swanton, Smithsonian Institution, Washington, D.C., 1952.

2

★ ★ ★ ★ ★ ★

Britain's North American Empire, 1660–1763

BEFORE 1660, the English had little or no conception of a colonial empire. The isolated American settlements were rarely thought of, and the British government had been too distracted by political chaos to devise any systematic scheme of beneficial relations between colonies and mother country. The end of civil strife brought a new interest in America. Under the Stuart Restoration, the whole North American seaboard, from Maine south to Spanish Florida, was organized for settlement and exploitation, and an emerging theory of empire began to be embodied in a set of colonial policies.

THE PROPRIETARY COLONIES

The expansion of English settlement in North America was prompted partly by a desire to gain strategic advantages against other colonizing nations and partly by a desire to reward favored courtiers who had sided with the Stuarts during the Civil War. In 1663, Charles II granted a group of eight English noblemen the vast domain stretching south from Virginia to the borders of Spanish Florida and westward across the continent from sea to sea. This grant of Carolina was modeled on the proprietary grant of Maryland to the Calverts, and the eight Lords Proprietor were given title to the soil as well as political authority over the area. Carolina already contained a small population that had spilled over from Virginia into the area of Albemarle Sound. In 1670, an expedition from the British West Indies colony of Barbados established another settlement several hundred miles down the coast at Charles Town (Charleston); a contingent of French Huguenots (Protestants), Scots, and Germans augmented the English group.

Anxious to encourage immigration and make profits from rising land values, the proprietors promised religious toleration and adopted a liberal land system, including headrights. Settlers in the two sections (later to become the colonies of North and South Carolina) were allowed to elect an assembly and make laws in conjunction with a governor and council appointed by the proprietors. The northern settlements in the Albermarle district were blocked off by coastal sandbars from good ocean transportation, so this area came to be populated by small landowners whose isolation and independence made them difficult to govern. The southern settlements around Charles Town, on the other hand, quickly developed an export trade through profitable staple products — first deerskins and naval stores, and then rice and indigo. Brought to work the plantations, blacks outnumbered whites by the turn of the century, and a particularly brutal form of bondage based on the slave code of British Barbados became fully entrenched. Great plantations grew up on the tidal estuaries, and the planters came to constitute a tightly knit ruling class. They had their headquarters in Charleston, where they spent the malarial summer months in breeze-swept town houses.

While Carolina was emerging as a buffer against the Spanish to the South, the British were eliminating another competitor farther north: the Netherlands, the European nation most like England in the enterprising qualities of its people. Early in the sixteenth century, the Dutch merchant marine dominated the Far Eastern spice trade. Though their Far Eastern ventures absorbed so much of their slender resources and work force that they had little left for the New World, the Dutch were interested in finding a more direct water passage to the spice islands through North America. It was the search for such a northwest passage that led Henry Hudson in 1609 up the river that bears his name.

The Hudson River proved to be no northwest passage, but it did lead into the heart of the fur-rich Iroquois country, and by 1624, the Dutch had established trading posts that grew into the colony of New Netherland. New Amsterdam at the tip of Manhattan Island became a cosmopolitan trading center; a scattering of Dutch farmers spread out over Long Island, Staten Island, and across the Hudson from Manhattan; along the Hudson, vast manors were granted to wealthy patroons who exercised feudal authority over their tenants. Yet the preoccupation of the Dutch with the Far East, their authoritarian patroonship system, and the petty tyranny of its governors prevented New Netherland from flourishing like its English neighbors.

The English resented this Dutch intrusion into what they regarded as their domain. In 1664, Charles II granted the area between the Delaware and Connecticut rivers to his brother, the Duke of York (who ascended the throne in 1685 as James II). James promptly organized a fleet and sailed for New Amsterdam, which surrendered without a shot. He found his proprietary domain, which he renamed New York, to be larger than he desired, and he transferred some 5,000,000 acres between the Delaware and the Hudson rivers to two of his favorites as the proprietary grant of New Jersey. The New Jersey proprietors encouraged settlement by promising land and religious tolerance. Large numbers of Puritan New Englanders, Dutch New Yorkers, English Barbadians, and colonists from Scotland and England responded, making the region one of Anglo-America's most ethnically and religiously diverse colonies. In 1674 the grant was divided into eastern and western sections, and the original proprietors sold their rights to others. West Jersey eventually came into the hands of a Quaker group, which included William Penn.

Penn was responsible for filling one of the last gaps in the continuous band of English settlement along the Atlantic Coast of North America. The son of a British admiral, Penn had been a convert to Quakerism, a radical separatist fringe that carried Puritan doctrines of religious purification to the extreme of rejecting a clergy and the Sacraments. Reviled by Anglicans and Puritans alike, the passionate Children of the Light were often persecuted, and Penn himself spent time in prison for his religious convictions. While on missionary tours of continental Europe, he envisioned a political and religious refuge in America where not just Quakers but the persecuted and poor of all sects and countries could live in peace. The reigning Stuarts had owed Penn's father a large sum of money; in 1681, this debt and perhaps a desire to be rid of the Quakers led Charles II to grant William Penn the vast region between Maryland and New York — 29,000,000 acres, nearly the size of England. Penn later added to this tract by purchasing the former Swedish colony of Delaware. Penn arrived in the New World in 1682 and laid out Philadelphia between the Schuylkill and the Delaware rivers. Thus, the Quaker paradise was built not in New Jersey, but in what was called Pennsylvania.

Penn promptly began advertising his province, offering complete religious freedom, representative government, and the most generous land policy of any of the American colonies. The quick response from English Quakers, the Welsh, and persecuted German sects made Pennsylvania the most rapidly growing and populous area in British America. Penn himself spent several years there, and inaugurated a government that enforced the most humane code of laws in the world. Separate assemblies were provided for the Philadelphia area and the area of the "Three Lower Counties" of Delaware below Philadelphia; both had the same governor who was appointed by the proprietor. The preponderant Quakers continued for decades to govern the province in the generous spirit of Penn's "Holy Experiment," and Pennsylvania became for European liberals the pre-eminent symbol of a tolerant and prosperous New World society.

Thus, by 1682, Great Britain's North American empire had been almost completely rounded out. Georgia, the last remaining American colony of Great Britain, was not established until 1732. In that year, a group of English philanthropists persuaded the British government to appoint them trustees of the area south of the Savannah River, which was to be used as a refuge for imprisoned debtors and other deserving paupers. The leading trustee and first governor, James Oglethorpe, sailed with a contingent of settlers in 1733 and founded Savannah. The benevolent trustees tried to ensure a moral society of small farmers by limiting each settler to 50 acres and prohibiting the importation of rum and slaves. When this southern-most colony proved not to be the New World Eden that its promoters had advertised, these restrictions were relaxed to enable it to compete for settlers with its prosperous neighbor South Carolina. Yet Georgia remained for many decades a tiny outpost against Spanish Florida.

The failure of the Georgia restrictions was merely the final demonstration that corporate purposes, however high-minded, could not survive among the English in the New World. This lesson was forced upon the Virginia Company early, and the holy commonwealth of the Puritans resisted it only a little longer. The proprietary colonies founded after 1660 all promised religious toleration, representative government, and cheap land — policies designed to attract settlers by guaranteeing individual rights and opportunity. The characteristics of the English and the free environment of the New World led irresistibly toward a society permeated with the spirit of individual enterprise.

THE NAVIGATION ACTS AND THE COLONIAL ECONOMY

While the proprietary colonies were eschewing corporate purposes in the New World, officials in London were developing a series of policies designed to implement the larger corporate purposes suggested by an emerging concept of British empire. These policies were based on the theory of political economy known as *mercantilism*. Although the term was not coined by Adam Smith until 1776, mercantilism was widely practiced throughout Europe during the preceding century. This economic doctrine presupposed that nations were engaged in a continuous struggle for supremacy. Economic strength was valued for the military and strategic advantages it yielded, and was to be measured primarily by the accumulation of *bullion* (uncoined gold or silver). As nations lost gold and silver by buying things from other nations, the most self-sufficient nations were considered the strongest and healthiest.

Colonies held an important place in mercantilist thinking. England, like Spain, France, and the Netherlands, turned to empire in order to make itself economically less dependent on others. Colonies could also contribute to the prosperity of the mother country by providing a market for its manufactures. Finally, an extensive trade with colonies would support a large merchant marine, and in a period when merchant ships and seamen were easily converted to naval purposes, this increased the fighting strength of the mother country.

England with its scanty resources and abundant labor was ideally suited to gain from mercantilism. Although slow to develop consistent colonial policies, the British government under Oliver Cromwell attempted to exclude foreign shipping from its New World possessions. Following the Restoration, Charles II and Parliament sought additional control of colonial economic activity through a series of Acts of Trade and Navigation, enacted between 1660 and 1672 and augmented by subsequent legislation. The Navigation

Acts contained three major requirements. First, all trade between England and her colonies was to be carried in ships built, owned, and operated by the British or British colonials. Second, all European goods imported into the colonies — with a few exceptions — were to pass through England and were thus subject to British import duties. Finally, certain "enumerated articles" produced by the colonies (primarily tobacco at first but later nearly every export) were to be shipped first to England, even if destined for ultimate resale in other European countries. Ultimately, the colonies were forbidden to produce certain finished goods that competed with those made in the mother country.

The exclusion of Dutch merchants from the Chesapeake tobacco trade and the loss of the direct European market for North American tobacco contributed to a period of stringency in Virginia and Maryland in the late seventeenth century. The Navigation Acts clearly subordinated colonial trade to England's, but their effects were by no means uniformly negative for the Americans. Mercantilist policies were more easily legislated than implemented, and at least until the end of the French and Indian War (1763), the colonists were generally agreed that the advantages of the loosely administered British imperial policy outweighed its disadvantages. The British colonies were given a monopoly of the tobacco market in the mother country, and bounties were paid to colonial producers of indigo and naval stores. The exclusion of foreign-built and foreign-owned ships from the trade between England and the colonies was a great boon to the New England shipbuilding industry and merchant marine. Indeed, the Navigation Acts were the "cement of empire," a positive force that bound colony to mother country.

Certainly by the first half of the eighteenth century, the colonial economy was in a highly prosperous state. European demand for tobacco, sugar, rice, indigo, and naval stores rose even faster than the production in the southern and West Indian colonies could expand. As these colonies grew and concentrated ever more exclusively on the profitable staples, they provided an ever greater market for wheat, flour, ground vegetables, salt fish and meat, lumber, and livestock from the middle colonies and New England. Philadelphia and Baltimore became flour milling and exporting centers, and New York exported the furs brought into Albany by the far ranging Iroquois.

New England produced few or no staples for the mother country and at first did not seem to fit the mercantilist prescriptions for usefulness. But the New Englanders quickly made themselves indispensable to the operation of the imperial economic system. Carrying provisions from the mainland to the West Indies, they picked up cargoes of sugar and then proceeded to England where they loaded their vessels with manufactured goods for America. In another variation of this "triangular trade," they brought molasses from the West Indies to New England, manufactured it into rum, took the rum to West Africa and traded it for slaves, and then carried the slaves for sale to the West Indies or the southern colonies. Similarly they carried Chesapeake tobacco or Carolina rice to England, bringing back manufactured goods. Prospering greatly from this trade and from shipbuilding and fisheries, New England also became the heaviest consumer of British manufactured goods.

As the colonial economy matured, British officials found additional regulations necessary to maintain mercantilist aims. To prevent New England rum makers from importing their supplies from non-English sources, Parliament passed the Molasses Act in 1733, levying a prohibitive duty on foreign molasses or sugar imported into British possessions. But New England evaded the duty by systematic smuggling, and the rum trade continued to flourish. To prevent colonial producers from competing with British manufacturers, Parliament passed a series of acts between 1699 and 1750 forbidding colonists to export woolen cloth and beaver hats or to expand their production of finished iron products.

The most serious economic problem of the colonies — money supply — was greatly aggravated by British restrictions that grew out of the mercantilist preoccupation with bullion for the mother country's treasury. Because gold and silver coin was the only recognized money and because the colonists could neither import British coin nor mint their own, they had to rely on Spanish coin acquired in the West Indian trade. Even this was an unstable money supply for it was constantly drained away to offset colonial trade deficits with England. Thus, there was never an adequate money supply for an intercolonial exchange of goods and services.

Under these circumstances, the colonial governments finally resorted to issuing paper money. These issues were to be redeemed within a certain period and were accompanied by new taxes designed to yield a sufficient fund to pay for redemption. But if too much paper money were issued or if redemption were delayed, the paper money depreciated in value and creditors complained. Moreover, colonial paper money was worthless in England and caused trouble to English merchants who tried to collect from American debtors. The British government first sought to remedy the situation by instructing the colonial governors to veto all but the most soundly backed paper money issues. This failing, Parliament in 1751 forbade the New England colonies, where the worst abuses occurred, to issue any further paper for payment of debts.

ADMINISTERING THE EMPIRE

While British officials were groping toward a concept of empire, administrative agencies for colonial planning and control were haphazardly evolving in the British government. Soon after the Restoration, the king's principal advisory body, the noble Privy Council, designated a committee known as the Lords of Trade to consider colonial matters. But not until the Glorious Revolution of 1688 and the accession of William and Mary did colonial officials in London seriously consider the creation of a centralized empire of politically uniform and dependent colonies directly supervised by the imperial government. A supplementary Navigation Act in 1696 set up a system of admiralty courts in America to enforce commercial regulations and punish smugglers. This same legislation created in England a Board of Trade and Plantations (a group of bureaucratic experts on colonial matters) to advise the Privy Council through the Lords of Trade. While the Board of Trade had little direct power, it did attain considerable importance as the one agency of the British government that systematically considered all colonial matters. Gradually and over many years, the Board of Trade was able to implement some consistent policies of colonial control.

One basic aim of the Board was to convert all the corporate and proprietary colonies into royal colonies. This process, begun with Virginia in 1624 and New Hampshire in 1679, became a deliberate objective upon the accession of William and Mary. Massachusetts Bay, Plymouth, and Maine were organized into the province of Massachusetts under a royal governor in 1691. That same year the Calverts' Maryland proprietary was royalized, and in 1692, Penn's Pennsylvania and Delaware suffered the same fate. But the new policy was too weak to withstand the political influence of such powerful proprietors: Penn's domain was restored within two years, and the Calverts finally got theirs back after being converted to Protestantism in 1715. Despite these setbacks, the colonial reorganizers persevered, extracting East and West Jersey from their proprietors and uniting them as the royal province of New Jersey in 1702. The Carolina proprietors gave up South Carolina in 1719 and North Carolina ten years later, and in 1752 Georgia fell under royal control. Only the strong English respect for property and charter rights enabled Connecticut and Rhode Island to maintain their corporate status and Penn and the Calverts to regain their domains.

The British government had several means of control over a royal colony. Most important was appointment of the governor, who was sent out with a set of detailed instructions drafted by the Board of Trade and who had an absolute veto over the acts of the colonial assembly. Moreover all colonial legislation was sent to the Board of Trade for careful scrutiny, and anything objectionable could be disallowed by the Privy Council. The Privy Council was also a court of appeal from decisions of colonial courts.

Through these means, the Privy Council and the Board of Trade sought to restrain the provincial governments from acts harmful to either English merchants or the royal prerogative. But this restraint was not burdensome. Sir Robert Walpole, who became the king's chief minister in 1721, believed that it was in England's interest to let the colonies flourish without interference; his policy of "salutary neglect" continued until the 1760s.

Under these circumstances, the provinces became virtually self-governing. All had a similar form of government. Except in Rhode Island and Connecticut, which continued to elect all their officials, and in Massachusetts, where the assembly elected the council, the governor and council were appointed by the king or the proprietor for indefinite terms. The council and an elected lower house formed a bicameral assembly. The assembly could convene only when called by the governor, who could suspend its sessions or dissolve it at will. The governor's veto could not be overridden. But whatever the governor's legal authority, he had practical difficulties in resisting the assembly's will. Lax imperial administration, either through design or neglect, permitted colonial assemblies gradually to exercise powers and privileges that in practice, though not by law, shifted the center of colonial control from the executive to themselves. Although intended to be dependent assemblies, they became, in effect, little Houses of Commons and claimed broad Parliamentary authority over local affairs. They particularly insisted on the well established English principle that citizens could be taxed only by consent of their representatives. The governors were paid by the colonies, and an assembly's refusal to levy taxes or appropriate funds for the governor's salary was a powerful political weapon.

Disputes between governors and assemblies were legion. Often incompetent and invariably caught between the conflicting demands of the London officials and the local assemblies, the governors could satisfy neither group. The ablest among them achieved some success only through the astute distribution of favors and by horsetrading with leaders of the assembly. At times, a governor could fill the council with influential provincials who would side with him against the lower house. But except in the few areas of special concern to the Privy Council, the assemblies usually had their way.

As the decades wore on, Americans increasingly assumed that they had an inalienable right to self-government through their assemblies. The recurrent disputes with the governors taught them political sophistication and political skills that were to be invaluable when this right was challenged. Serious conflict with Crown and Parliament was to be avoided only so long as imperial authorities did not demand that colonial practices coincide with imperial policies.

THE ANGLO-FRENCH WARS

While the English colonies were growing strong and prosperous along the eastern seacoast of North America, the French were developing a different kind of empire to the north and inland. In 1608, one year after the founding of Virginia, Samuel de Champlain began a French settlement at Quebec on the St. Lawrence River. For years Champlain devoted himself to exploring the interior far up the St. Lawrence and into the Great Lakes country and to developing a flourishing fur trade with the Algonquin and Huron Indians of the region. The French fur traders were soon joined by a band of dauntless Jesuit missionaries who ranged far and wide over the wilderness of the north country preaching Christianity to the Indians. By the middle of the seventeenth century, there was a narrow zone of agricultural settlement along the St. Lawrence where humble French *habitants* worked peasant-style on the manorial grants of a rather down-at-the-heels class of feudal *seigneurs*.

Despite the fewer numbers of the French in America, their vigorous exploration and the good relations they had achieved with their Indian allies made them a formidable barrier to English westward expansion. Only the powerful Iroquois confederation in upper New York, hostile to the French-oriented Huron and Algonquin tribes, shielded Dutch New Netherland and the English colonies from contact with the French. But after the rise of Louis XIV in the 1660s, the French pushed their Canadian enterprise more vigorously and assisted their Indian allies in making war on the Iroquois. Meanwhile Louis sought to make France the dominant power in Europe as well as to expand its colonial empire in America and other parts of the world. England joined a series of alliances designed to block French ambitions, and the result was a series of four great wars (1689–1763) fought mainly in Europe but also between the French and English in America.

In the first three encounters — King William's War, 1689–1697; Queen Anne's War, 1702–1713; King George's War, 1744–1748 — the French and their Indian allies raided the New England and New York frontiers. Beginning with Queen Anne's War, the Spanish were allied with the French, so that there was skirmishing along the southern as well as northern British frontier. The only American territorial change that resulted from the first three wars was the transfer of Nova Scotia, Newfoundland, and the Hudson Bay country in the far north from France to England in 1713.

Meanwhile, during the intervals of peace, the French moved into the Mississippi Valley behind the English settlements. Around 1700, they set up posts in the Illinois country on the northern Mississippi and established themselves at Biloxi and Mobile on the Gulf Coast near the great river's mouth. New Orleans was founded as the capital of French Louisiana in 1718.

The final phase of the conflict between Britain and France in North America was the French and Indian War (known in Europe as the Seven Years' War). This conflict began when a group of Virginians sent agents across the Appalachians and into the upper Ohio Valley for the purpose of Indian trade and land speculation. The French responded by building a chain of small forts on the upper Ohio. Young George Washington, sent out in command of a force of Virginia militia in 1754, arrived barely too late to prevent construction of Fort Duquesne at the forks of the Ohio on the future site of Pittsburgh. He was driven off by the French, and the war began — though it was not officially declared for two more years.

All the major European powers were quickly drawn into the fighting. At first things went badly for the British in America and elsewhere. General Edward Braddock's army was routed within a few miles of Fort Duquesne, throwing the whole frontier open to several years of pounding by the French and Indians. The British seemed to have no overall strategy, and the colonies could not be persuaded to contribute very loyally or enthusiastically to the war effort. Delegates from eight of the colonies, meeting at the so-called Albany Congress in 1754, approved Benjamin Franklin's farsighted plan for intercolonial defense and unity, but this early plan for voluntary union failed to win the support of either the crown or the colonial assemblies. (Its implications, however, were not lost on a later generation of rebels who, during the imperial crisis that followed the war with France, would again entertain plans for a closer union.)

The situation changed dramatically in 1757 when the vigorous William Pitt assumed direction of the British war effort. Making the conquest of Canada his paramount aim, Pitt organized a series of offensives that culminated in the capture of Quebec by General James Wolfe in 1759. By the time the war ended in Europe, the British were victorious everywhere. In the Peace of Paris (1763), Britain gained French Canada and Spanish Florida, as well as acquisitions in India and elsewhere. The ownership of Louisiana was transferred from France to Spain.

No one had more reason to rejoice than the British Americans. Suddenly freed from the greatest threat to their security, they now looked west upon an unbounded arena of opportunity lying open to their enterprise. It did not yet occur to them that their new security and confidence might weaken their attachment to the mother country whose emergence as the world's most powerful nation they were now so loyally celebrating.

FOR FURTHER READING

The final volume of Charles M. Andrews's *The Colonial Period of American History* (4 vols., 1934–1938); Richard R. Johnson's *Adjustment to Empire* (1981); and Robert M. Bliss's *Revolution and Empire* (1990) are significant analyses of British policy and administration. Jack P. Greene has studied the struggles between colonial governors and assemblies in *The Quest for Power: The Lower House of Assembly in the Southern Royal Colonies, 1689–1776* (1965). Wesley Frank Craven describes *The Colonies in Transition, 1660–1713* (1968). The 13 volumes in the *History of the American Colonies* series, edited by Milton M. Klein and Jacob E. Cooke, are designed for both the serious student and the lay person. See, for example, Michael Kammen's *Colonial New York* (1975), and Joseph E. Illick's *Colonial Pennsylvania* (1976). *The Middle Colonies* (1938) are described by Thomas J. Wertenbaker. Mary Maples Dunn has written a good biography of *William Penn* (1967); Frederick B. Tolles deals with the changing role of Philadelphia's Quaker merchants in *Meeting House and Counting House* (1948); and Oliver A. Rink provides a useful survey of Dutch New York in *Holland on the Hudson* (1986). Francis Parkman's *France and England in America* (8 vols., 1851–1892) is still a useful account of the development of French Canada and the great struggle for empire in North America, but it should be read in conjunction with the more recent *France in America* (1990) by William John Eccles. The final phase of the French-English struggle in North America and the period after the French and Indian War are delineated authoritatively in Lawrence Gipson's *The British Empire Before the American Revolution* (15 vols., 1936–1970). Fred Anderson's *A People's Army* (1984) provides a vivid look at the American colonial contribution to the British war effort against France.

3

★ ★ ★ ★ ★ ★

A New Society,
1600s–1700s

Within the loose institutional framework of Britain's North American empire, a distinctly new kind of society had been taking shape. Inside this new society, the typical European was being subtly altered. "What then is the American, this new man?" the French immigrant Hector de Crèvecoeur was asking by the 1770s.

THE AMERICANS

De Crèvecoeur's American, in the first place, belonged to a numerous and rapidly multiplying people. The American population grew from about a quarter of a million in 1700 to two-and-a-half million by 1775, roughly one-third the population of England and Wales. The majority of these Americans were of English origin. But English immigration slowed in the latter part of the seventeenth century, and the continuing predominance of English stock owed much to the fecundity of Anglo-American parents.

The spectacular population increase of the eighteenth century was also based on a quickening of non-English immigration, much of it with little affinity for English culture and even less liking for British political control. From the founding of Pennsylvania in the 1680s, Penn's advertising attracted a steadily mounting flow of impoverished peasants from the war-ravaged states of the German Rhineland. By the 1770s there were around 200,000 industrious German farmers in the North American colonies. These so-called Pennsylvania Dutch (from the word *Deutsch*, meaning *German*) constituted a third of the population of that middle colony.

An even larger tide of immigration began flowing in the first decades of the eighteenth century from Ulster, the six counties of northern Ireland.

These Protestants of Scottish origin are called Scotch-Irish by their descendants, to distinguish them from the indigenous Roman Catholic population of the rest of Ireland; they had been transplanted to Ulster in the early seventeenth century as part of the campaign to subdue Ireland, the first overseas English colony. By the beginning of the eighteenth century, they were suffering from English restrictions on Irish trade and industry, increasing farm rents, and various civil disabilities against their staunch Presbyterianism. Under these circumstances, Scotch-Irish by the thousands, perhaps as many as a quarter million, crossed the Atlantic. Concentrated along the frontier as pioneer farmers and aggressive Indian fighters, they made up from one-twelfth to one-tenth of the entire population by the 1770s. Like Pennsylvania's Germans, the Scotch-Irish proved to be unwilling subjects of British rule.

Smaller groups from Europe included the Dutch and the French Huguenots. New Netherland had 8,000 Dutch residents at the time of its transfer to English control, and their descendants remained a substantial segment of New York's population. The Huguenots, or French Protestants, began leaving France when the revocation of the Edict of Nantes in 1685 ended religious toleration in that predominantly Catholic country. They did not come to America in large numbers, but their enterprising qualities made many of them successful and prominent. Probably the largest number came to South Carolina, where they were quickly assimilated to Anglicanism and emerged as a major element of the mercantile-planting elite.

Whether English or non-English, the European immigrants of the eighteenth century came mainly from the lower or middling orders of Old World society. Probably half or more of the settlers in the middle colonies crossed the Atlantic as indentured servants. Some were actually kidnapped and sold to America by dealers in human merchandise. Thousands more — orphans, pauper children, and prisoners — were sent abroad by public authorities. Not a few of them chose emigration as a welcome alternative to long imprisonment or execution for minor offenses. Some 40,000 English convicts were transported to North America in the six decades before the Revolution, and in Maryland, convicts made up the bulk of the servant class.

But whatever their legal status, most Europeans who embarked on the long voyage to America were the younger and more vigorous people from their home communities. Once free of indenture, even the lowliest among them was free to rise. Colonel John Lamb, a wealthy merchant and prominent political leader in New York in the 1770s, was the son of a man who had been taken from the gallows in England and transported to America, where he established himself as a solid citizen and laid the basis for his son's later success.

The African slaves, however, more than one in five of all Americans by 1775, came most unwillingly and had no chance to rise, whatever their vigor or ability. By the late seventeenth century, the very prosperity of the European immigrants was creating a growing demand for cheap and easily exploited labor. Yankee and European ship captains hastened to supply this demand, shuttling tightly packed cargoes of "black ivory" from the West

Coast of Africa and the West Indies for sale in British North America. Slavery became established in all the colonies, New York and Rhode Island as well as South Carolina and Georgia, but the readiest market for the black men and women who survived the horrors of slave ships was found in the southern states. There a privileged but growing class of planters depended on slaves to do the exhausting but routine plantation tasks of tobacco, rice, and indigo culture. By the eve of the Revolution, British North America held about 600,000 sons and daughters of once flourishing West African civilizations such as Ghana, Mali, and Songhai. In South Carolina blacks made up two-thirds of the population; in Virginia, nearly half; in New York, around one-seventh. Blacks contributed to the cultural and economic development of the emerging American society and in time developed a resilient and adaptive Afro-American subculture of their own. Unlike the other ethnic groups mentioned in this section, they were stigmatized by color, held down by the degradation of slavery, and shut off from the advantages enjoyed by others in the comparatively fluid New World order.

AMERICAN ENVIRONMENTS: NEW TOWNS AND THE OLD WEST

The acceleration of immigration and economic activity in the eighteenth century created a diversified society in the American colonies. Although the colonial population in 1775 was almost entirely rural, towns began to play an increasingly important role in colonial life. The early upsurge of commercial activity in New England was accompanied by a trend toward urbanization as Boston, Newport, and Salem became flourishing trading centers. Later, Philadelphia and New York emerged as major urban centers, and they eventually outstripped their predecessors. By the 1770s, Philadelphia's population of nearly 40,000 made it the largest American city or the second largest city in the British empire. New York was the second biggest city of British North America followed by Boston, Charleston, and Newport, the last having a population of around 7,000. The Chesapeake tobacco country, where oceangoing ships could sail directly up to the individual planter's wharf for trade, was the only area that did not develop a major urban center.

The colonial cities were scarcely more than overgrown villages compared to the older, larger, and more developed cities of Europe. Fewer than one out of twenty colonists living in 1700 and 1776 made their homes in cities. But the newspapers, pamphlets, and almanacs that formed the means of communication in the colonies were published in these cities, and in them flourished shoemakers, weavers, hatters, cabinet-makers, and artisans of countless other trades who satisfied most of the colonists' needs. The principal courts were found in cities, and in these urban centers lawyers emerged as an influential professional group. In short, the seaboard cities became dynamic sites of growth and change, sites of much of the evolving economic, intellectual, and political life of the colonies.

While towns were developing along the coast, the pressure of the population increase was forcing a line of settlement far inland. In this hinterland, or "Old West," a new society took shape by the middle of the eighteenth century. The distinguishing characteristic of this settlement was that it lay beyond the "fall line," the point where the rivers descended over rapids into the level coastal plain and became navigable. In the absence of good roads or other transportation facilities, the Old West lay too far inland to produce goods for market and thus became an area of pioneer subsistence farming, isolated from the coastal settlements and the Atlantic world. Nevertheless, to those who peopled it, the Old West seemed an agrarian paradise where the ease of acquiring farms of their own promised a degree of security, well-being, and independence that would have been unthinkable in the land-hungry Europe they had left behind.

New England's Old West included the northern and western hill towns and lay away from the coast and the deep inland extension of coastal society along the navigable Connecticut River. The old Puritan pattern of town planning broke down in New England as the provincial governments began disposing of blocks of new towns to land speculators who in turn sold farms to actual settlers.

South of New England, New York's Hudson River was a magnificent highway north into the interior. The Mohawk River, flowing east from the Great Lakes country into the Hudson at Albany, afforded the colonies their only easy avenue through the Appalachian mountains to the Ohio and Mississippi valleys. But fur-trading interests blocked settlement along the Mohawk until the early eighteenth century when the British government sponsored the resettlement of Germans above Albany.

The main current of German settlement flowed through Philadelphia and on inland to fill the broad and fertile lower valley of the Susquehanna. Beyond the Susquehanna, it washed up against the series of Appalachian ridges that run from the northeast through central Pennsylvania. Diverted down the valleys to the southwest, the Germans settled interior Maryland and crossed the Potomac into Virginia. Here some drifted southeast of the first great Appalachian range, the Blue Ridge, into the rolling Virginia Piedmont, but the main current moved on southwest up the Shenandoah Valley behind the Blue Ridge. By the 1750s, some Germans were pushing southeast from the upper Shenandoah across the Blue Ridge and down into the North Carolina Piedmont.

The German migration was followed and overlapped by the migration of the more aggressive Scotch-Irish. The Scotch-Irish filled in the gaps left by German settlements and then surged beyond them to the west and south. In Pennsylvania these hardy Indian fighters crossed ridge after ridge and filled valley after valley until by the 1770s they were on the waters of the Ohio occupying the area around Pittsburgh. Farther south, in the Carolinas, the Scotch-Irish pushed the Piedmont frontier up against the mountains; while in Virginia they pressed southwest through the mountain valleys toward the headwaters of the Tennessee River.

COLONIAL SOCIETY

The people of the Old West — the Yankee farmers of the New England hill towns, the Germans on the Mohawk, and the Germans and Scotch-Irish in the great curve southwest against the Appalachians from the Susquehanna to Georgia — soon complained of grievances against the older colonial settlements along the coast. The older areas continued to dominate the provincial governments by refusing to give the new settlements the representation to which their population entitled them. In Pennsylvania, the three oldest counties had only one-third of the province's population but elected two-thirds of the assemblymen. The frontier people complained that unrepresentative, Quaker-dominated assemblies were indifferent to such western problems as the need for an aggressive policy against the Indians. The most extreme case of indifference to frontier needs occurred in South Carolina where the new settlements were separated from the old coastal planting society by a wide belt of sandhills. Though the up-country people in the new settlements came to be a majority of the free population, the low-country people not only refused them any representatives whatever in the assembly, but also neglected to provide them with courts or local law-enforcement officers.

Not remarkably, the failure to give representation or consideration to the rapidly growing frontier settlements led to sporadic tensions and occasional outbreaks of violence. As early as 1676, Nathaniel Bacon led an armed rebellion in Virginia against the governor, Sir William Berkeley, who had ruled the province autocratically for 25 years in alliance with the wealthiest planters. Similar tensions among New Yorkers figured in Jacob Leisler's rebellion at the time of the Glorious Revolution. Great landlords periodically faced mob violence from their tenants in New York, New Jersey, and elsewhere. There was a bitter struggle between debtor and creditor interests in Massachusetts over an inflationary Land Bank scheme in the 1740s. In 1764, the Paxton Boys, an armed mob of frontier men, marched on Philadelphia in anger at the pacific Indian policy of the eastern-dominated Pennsylvania assembly. The most spectacular of these outbreaks occurred in North Carolina where the oppressive policies of the local ruling class finally goaded the people of the interior into systematic mobbing of the courts. The governor had to march an army against the insurgents, or the Regulators, as they called themselves, and in a ragged engagement at Alamance in 1771 dispersed them.

The tension between the old and new settlements was only a phase of a more general tension that accompanied the emergence of somewhat sharper class distinctions in the eighteenth century. The English who came to the New World in the seventeenth century had brought with them the traditional European notion that people should defer to their betters in a society of ranks and orders. Old World distinctions, however, made little sense in a fluid society of mobile individuals, and, consequently, class and property qualifications for voting were almost unknown in the early assemblies. Yet the very atmosphere of equal opportunity that eroded Old World notions made for new forms of inequality. In an environment of growing wealth and expanding opportunities, social and economic disparities widened as some inevitably became more successful than others. Eventually, a disproportionate share of wealth from trade and commercial farming fell into the hands of the most enterprising New England merchants and southern planters. As a result, the relatively simple society of roughly equal yeomen in the seventeenth century became a more highly stratified and differentiated society in the eighteenth.

This process of stratification was abetted by the British government, which actively encouraged the growth and political influence of a colonial elite. After the Glorious Revolution, London authorities replaced religious qualifications for voting with a property qualification in the new Massachusetts charter, and property qualifications became general in the colonies. Usually a voter had to be a "freeholder," the owner of 50 acres or a town lot. Royal governors generally sought to secure the support of the wealthiest colonials by bestowing important appointments and other favors on them. The provincial councils became the political strongholds of the very rich, while the assemblies were usually controlled by the merely well-to-do. Thus the eighteenth-century provincial governments were generally dominated by a local ruling class, the wealthiest members of which sometimes sided with the governors in disputes with the assemblies.

Too much can be made of socioeconomic conflict in eighteenth-century America. Unquestionably, this was a "deferential society." Marked by extremes in standards and styles of life, fundamentally elitist and class-conscious in character, American society was governed by men of privilege. Their starched ruffles and powdered wigs, their bearing, speech, and dress differed strikingly from those of ordinary folk, and their influence was usually derived from wealth and property. But prerevolutionary American society presented those outside the power structure with more opportunities for advancement than the older and more highly structured societies in Europe. Although hardly democratic by twentieth-century standards, this highly mobile New World society offered remarkably broad economic opportunities, relatively little poverty, and much class fluidity. Except for the anomaly of slavery and pervasive restrictions on the rights enjoyed by women, there was no real social stratification in the Old World sense. Even the property restriction on suffrage was hardly restrictive in a society of extensive land ownership. In some colonies, where the franchise was open to a vast majority of free male adults, there is evidence to suggest that suffrage was more widespread than the willingness to use it. To be sure, this remarkable breadth of franchise owed much to the availability of inexpensive land and very little to either constitutional theories or modern democratic notions. Even in a society that readily acquiesced to government by aristocrats, colonial rulers could not entirely ignore the needs and aspirations of the general population. Certainly, few historians would argue today that class tension was a principal, or even an important, cause of the Revolution. By the 1760s and 1770s, most scholars now agree, the Americans had already made significant progress toward a more representative social and political order for men. It would be some two centuries, however, before American women won even token admission to this circle of privilege.

COLONIAL WOMEN

With rare exceptions, women in colonial America were confined to the household sphere — child-rearing, home-making, and the moral instruction of servants and off-spring. The overwhelming majority of white women were married and lived on small farms, and in small and poorly lighted homes. Their days were crowded with the endless seasonal routine of colonial life: gardening and preserving food; spinning, weaving, knitting, and sewing clothes; making candles, soap, butter, and cheese; and laundering, cleaning, and cooking. Slave women typically worked in the fields, but on substantial southern plantations they also served as seamstresses, cooks, or midwives. Female indentured servants, who normally could not marry, devoted their hours to working for their masters. In towns a few women, usually widows, became shopkeepers or innkeepers; others worked as laundresses, nurses, or even skilled laborers; and some women operated "dame schools." Those women who found employment outside the home inevitably earned less than men.

Although colonial families were paternalistic, child-rearing was a shared responsibility. Children were required to be obedient to their parents. Wives were their husbands' "helpmeets" — not their slaves, but also not their equals. Husbands were the heads of their households, though marriages were often marked by affection and mutual respect.

Colonial women married at about the same age as American women do today: whites in their early twenties; blacks in their late teens. In an agricultural era when large families were an economic asset — and the means of birth control primitive — women commonly had 5 to 7 children, and not infrequently 10 or more. Throughout their years of fertility, the pattern for women was to be either nursing or pregnant, a fact that contributed both to their premature aging and to rapid population growth. The high mortality rate of children also fostered the desire to have large families.

Regional variations within colonial America make generalizations about life expectancy hazardous. In New England, with its healthful climate and pure drinking water, adults were remarkably long lived. A seventeenth-century New Englander who survived infancy could expect to live more than 60 years. In the malarial Chesapeake colonies, on the other hand, the death rate was frightful. Fully half the population died before the age of 20; the life expectancy was perhaps 45 years for men, less for women.

By law and by custom, a colonial woman's status was lower than a man's. Under the English common law of coverture, a wife's legal personality was submerged in her husband's. Under most circumstances, her income and her personal and real estate were not her own. She could not make a contract or a will; she had no legal control over her children; except in New England, she could not obtain a divorce. Women could not vote, rarely influenced economic decisions, and were legally subject in most colonies to physical punishment by their husbands. Perhaps their relative scarcity — not until the mid-eighteenth century did women constitute half of the population — gave them slightly more freedom than their English sisters. But even so, they were denied places in most professions, including the ministry, politics, and literature. Although Anne Dudley Bradstreet (1612–1672) distinguished herself as the first American poet, she was published anonymously. Some daughters of the colonial elite were taught social competencies in female seminaries, and a few were educated in European schools. More typically, young American women were encouraged to cultivate the practical arts, not their intellects. Except for domestic matters, education beyond the most basic rudiments was widely regarded as a male prerogative.

THE ENLIGHTENMENT

By the eighteenth century, the Atlantic world's advance into modernity had produced a new climate of thought known as the Enlightenment. The people of this optimistic age believed that a benevolent Creator had laid down certain "natural laws" regulating all phenomena for the purpose of producing human happiness. Human beings, it was believed, had been endowed by the Creator with powers of observation and reasoning that would enable them to understand and live by these natural laws and thus achieve happiness.

This faith of the Enlightenment received a strong impetus from Sir Isaac Newton's description of the physical world as a harmonious system of bodies regulated by simple natural laws (*Principia Mathematica*, 1687). Another English thinker, John Locke, persuasively applied the Newtonian kind of analysis to the moral and political spheres. In *An Essay Concerning Human Understanding* (1690), Locke analyzed the processes of observation and reasoning that enabled human beings to understand what kinds of behavior were conducive to happiness or, in other words, consistent with the Creator's natural laws for human behavior. Following Locke, thinkers of the Enlightenment exalted "reason" as the faculty that could lead humanity toward virtue, happiness, and perfection. Analyzing politics (*Two Treatises on Government*, 1689), Locke maintained that natural law ordained a government that rested on the consent of the governed and that respected the inherent "natural rights" of all.

Enlightenment thought was the theoretical expression of the emerging spirit of modernity. In British North America, society was too young and too busy with the processes of wresting a living from this new land to give much attention to metaphysical speculation. Indeed, how far any formal thought reaches into popular consciousness is problematic. Yet many thoughtful colonists gladly embraced Lockean ideas as explanations of what already seemed to them obvious. The better educated individuals often drifted from the tenets of orthodox Christianity toward the rationalism of *Deism*, the belief in an impersonal God, whose revelations came through natural law — not miracles.

The influence of Enlightenment thought can be seen in eighteenth-century American life. The esthetic principles of rational simplicity, order, and balance, for example, were exemplified in the colonial or Georgian architecture of the period. American writers imitated the simple elegance of the English authors Joseph Addison and Sir Richard Steele and sought to persuade their readers by rational argument.

The Enlightenment gave a great impetus to the maturing cultural and intellectual life of the colonies. Beginning with the Boston *News-Letter* (1704), newspapers sprang up everywhere; by 1765 there were 25, and every colony except Delaware and New Jersey had at least one. A hungry market developed for pamphlets on every conceivable topic. Artisans organized clubs for discussion and intellectual self-improvement. Booksellers flourished, many wealthier persons developed fine private libraries, and following the example of an enterprise launched by Benjamin Franklin in Philadelphia, subscription libraries were established in most towns.

By placing such a high value on intellect, the Enlightenment reinforced the religious impulse toward higher education. This combination of influences resulted in the creation of nine colleges by the 1770s. Harvard (1636) was joined by Virginia's William and Mary (1693), Connecticut's Yale (1701), and the Philadelphia Academy, which was originally founded as a secondary school by Benjamin Franklin and became in the 1750s the most modern and secular of the colonial colleges. Five other new colleges owed their founding most immediately to a great religious movement that seemed at first to oppose the spirit of the Enlightenment and modernity.

THE GREAT AWAKENING

The drift toward modernity had steadily eroded the seventeenth-century piety that the settlers had brought to all the early colonies and of which Puritanism was merely the most intense form. Religious observances were as strictly enforced in early Anglican Virginia as in New England, but the prosperity from tobacco soon converted Anglicanism into a bland and undemanding adornment of Virginia's genial country life. It was this kind of Anglicanism that became the established or official religion, supported by public taxation, in all the southern colonies and the three lower counties of New York. Anglican religious zeal was apparent only where the missionaries sent out by England's Society for the Propagation of the Gospel were at work and in New England where the Anglicans were an unpopular minority. Perhaps the most conspicuous example of the erosion of piety in the New World was the quick conversion of the Huguenots, those French counterparts of the Puritans, to the polite Anglicanism of the South Carolina planter class. Even the Pennsylvania Quakers, growing wealthy as a result of godly industry, frugality, and honesty, arrived at a point where the counting house seemed to overshadow the meeting house.

The decline of piety can be clearly traced among the theologically sophisticated and articulate Puritan Congregationalists of New England. By the end of the seventeenth century, the Reverend Cotton Mather, the last great defender of the orthodox order, was talking more about the necessity of right living in this world than about humanity's dependence on God for salvation in the next. The wealthy Boston merchants who founded the Brattle Street Church in 1699 did not require an account of conversion for full membership and chose a minister who preached a "free and catholic" version of Christianity emphasizing morality over piety. As the eighteenth century advanced, the most influential ministers in Boston, Charles Chauncy and Jonathan Mayhew, drifted into the "Arminian" heresy, which diminished human dependence on God by regarding human beings as capable of contributing to their own salvation by right living.

But a people conditioned to piety did not adjust easily to the clear, rather bland atmosphere of the dawning Enlightenment. The embers of the old intense faith still smoldered and, in the 1730s and 1740s, were fanned into a bright blaze of religious enthusiasm that burned up and down the length and breadth of the colonies. This American Great Awakening was only part of a general movement in the Protestant world including such parallel phenomena as an upsurge of Pietism in Germany and the Wesleyan revival in England. Beginning as an effort to reassert the earlier extreme piety against the rationalism and optimism of the Enlightenment, these awakenings appealed frankly to the emotions and ended by unconsciously accommodating Christianity to the modern spirit.

The American Great Awakening began in different places. As early as the 1720s, the Reverend Theodore J. Frelinghuysen touched off emotional revivals of religious feeling among the Germans in New Jersey's Raritan Valley. Nearby a group of ardent Presbyterian ministers began trying to stimulate intense religious feeling in place of the cold formalism of Calvinist orthodoxy. And at Northampton, Massachusetts in 1734, a gifted Congregationalist minister, Jonathan Edwards, stirred up a series of revivals by his powerful appeals to the religious emotions. All these streams merged into a general revival movement throughout the colonies when England's spellbinding evangelist, George Whitefield, swept through on his triumphant American tour of 1739–1740, leaving spiritual anguish and ecstatic conversion in his wake.

The Great Awakening was emotional, popular, and anti-intellectual. The revivalists were often poorly educated, and their fervent exhortations sometimes touched off extravagant reactions — barking, writhing, swooning — by their audiences. Revivalists maintained that a heart open to the divine spirit was more important than a highly trained intellect. The least temperate among them, the inflammatory James Davenport of New England, stirred up strife by accusing conservative, educated clergy to be the "dead husks" and "Old Lights" of spiritual emptiness. Sophisticated observers alleged that the "beastly brayings" of these "shouters" produced more hysteria than holiness. But in large towns and the countryside, and particularly in frontier areas and the South, more common folk responded with enthusiasm to the new evangelicalism. The more popular Protestant denominations — the Baptists, the "New Light" Presbyterians, and later the Methodists — grew enormously, and a religious pluralism swept the colonies. In appealing for an emotional response to God's grace and a commitment to an exemplary Christian life, the revival preachers often unconsciously suggested that salvation was available to all, not merely to the elect, and that the individual played an important part in the process. The Methodists came to espouse these Arminian (and modern) "heresies" quite consciously.

Paradoxically, despite its emphasis on sentiment over reason, the Awakening had as a major leader the most gifted colonial intellectual and perhaps the most creative of American theologians: Jonathan Edwards. This brilliant Congregationalist minister burned with a personal sense of God's majesty and power that would have been exceptional even among the first-generation Puritans. But he also had an understanding of the intellectual implications of Newtonian-Lockean thought that was equaled by few if any of his generation in Europe or America. In a series of impressive treatises, he turned the Enlightenment against itself, using the most advanced thought of his day to reconstruct the old Puritan vision of an omnipotent and inscrutable God. In a very real sense, this remarkable theologian was a transitional figure, a bridge between two ages, who sought to recast and modernize Puritanism in the light of eighteenth-century rationalism.

Few in his generation understood what Edwards was trying to do. His fellow revivalists gladly adopted his highly charged rhetoric and his advanced principles of human psychology, which recognized the importance and legitimacy of emotion. But most Americans had moved too far into modernity to share, even in seasons of religious exaltation, his vision of the beauty and fitness of God's awful sovereignty and the sinner's helpless dependence on the miracle of divine grace.

Finally, historians have also found political consequences in the fervid evangelicalism of Edwards's time. Spreading like a religious epidemic, the Great Awakening transcended political boundaries and thereby strengthened intercolonial ties. It has aptly been called the first truly American event. Perhaps it is too much to claim, although some scholars have, that without the Awakening there would have been no revolution, no independence. Yet this "great and extraordinary outpouring of the Spirit" touched more than the souls of enraptured colonists. By emphasizing the personal dimensions of salvation and undermining established religious institutions, the Awakening not only encouraged spiritual diversity and paved the way to the separation of church and state, but it also nourished the egalitarian colonial temper and the developing sense of American distinctiveness and thus hastened the break with Great Britain.

The Awakening prompted the establishment of three colonial colleges designed to train ministers for revivalist wings of the sponsoring denominations: the Presbyterians' College of New Jersey (Princeton, 1746), the Baptists' College of Rhode Island (Brown, 1764), and the Dutch Reformed Rutgers (1766). Two other colonial colleges were founded under nonrevivalist church auspices: Anglican King's College in New York (Columbia, 1754) and Congregationalist Dartmouth (1769), which began as an Indian school in New Hampshire. For all of its anti-intellectualism, this eighteenth-century resurgence of religious enthusiasm contributed mightily to the nation's educational development.

"THIS NEW MAN"

De Crèvecoeur's "new man," then, was a product of New World opportunity, whether the opportunity to acquire a farm of one's own in the Old West, to grow rich planting tobacco, to trade with the West Indies, or to achieve dignity and independence as an artisan in one of the growing colonial towns. According to de Crèvecoeur, Americans welcomed the optimistic tendencies of Enlightenment thought as something their New World experience revealed. In politics, they stoutly defended the English tradition of individual rights and aspired to control the representative institutions of provincial government in the interest of their group. In religion, they tended consciously toward Deism or Arminianism if educated; otherwise they reveled in the emotionalism of the Great Awakening while moving less consciously away from the orthodox piety of their ancestors.

"The American, this new man" took a fully developed form in the *Autobiography* of Benjamin Franklin. This son of a Boston candlemaker sat in Cotton Mather's congregation as a boy, assimilated Enlightenment thought while working on his brother's newspaper and while sowing wild oats in London, and returned to win wealth and prestige as a Philadelphia printer. Retiring from business while still in his early forties, he spent the rest of his life in scientific experiments that explained the nature of electricity, in developing a host of practical devices and projects for the benefit and improvement of his fellow citizens, and in public service culminating with attendance at the birth of a new nation.

Wise, humane, and practical, Franklin reflected the spirit of a people who preferred mobility to nobility, who, to quote Franklin, characteristically inquired of a stranger not *"What is he?* but *What can he do?"* Franklin was the quintessential American, simple, vigorous, independent, and uncorrupted by supposed Old World decadence. He embodied American self-awareness, that sense of an evolving new people, politically linked to the English, yet identifiably American, distinctive in character and culture.

The fascination with Franklin lies in the fact that he personified so many traits characteristic of his compatriots. De Crèvecoeur wrote that an American leaves "behind him all his ancient prejudices and manners, receives new ones from the new mode of life he has embraced, the new government he obeys, and the new rank he holds. . . . Here the rewards of his industry follow with equal steps the progress of his labor. . . . Here religion demands but little of him. . . . The American is a new man, who acts upon new principles; he must therefore entertain new ideas, and form new opinions. From involuntary idleness, servile dependence, penury, and useless labor, he has passed to toils of a different nature, rewarded by ample subsistence. — This is an American."

FOR FURTHER READING

J. Hector St. John de Crèvecoeur recorded his impressions of eighteenth-century American life in *Letters from an American Farmer* (1782). A readable overview of the period is Daniel J. Boorstin's interpretation of emerging New World attitudes and institutions, *The Americans: The Colonial Experience* (1958), but James A. Henretta and Gregory Nobles's *The Evolution of American Society, 1700–1815* (1987) is a more up-to-date survey of colonial society. European immigrants to America are described in Marcus Lee Hansen's *The Atlantic Migration, 1607–1860* (1940) and David Hackett Fischer's *Albion's Seed* (1989); Abbott Emerson Smith's *Colonists in Bondage* (1947) deals with indentured servants; and Herbert S. Klein's *The Middle Passage* (1978) describes the African slave trade. Winthrop D. Jordan's *White over Black* (1968) examines the development of white racial attitudes; Peter Wood's *Black Majority* (1974) examines black life in colonial South Carolina; and Gwendolyn Midlo Hall looks at *Africans in Colonial Louisiana* (1992). Carl Bridenbaugh's *Cities in the Wilderness, 1625–1742* (1938) is the standard study of early American urban life; he deals with the mechanic classes of the towns in *The Colonial Craftsman* (1950). Related works include such model social histories as Phillip Greven, *Four Generations: Population, Land, and Family in Colonial Andover, Massachusetts* (1977); Richard I. Melvoin, *New England Outpost: War and Society in Colonial Deerfield* (1989); Gary Nash, *The Urban Crucible: Social Change, Political Consciousness, and the Origins of the American Revolution* (1979); and Michael Zuckerman, *Peaceable Kingdoms: New England Towns in the Eighteenth Century* (1970). Daniel Blake Smith's *Inside the Great House* (1980) is an important analysis of eighteenth-century Chesapeake family life, and Allan Kulikoff's *Tobacco and Slaves* (1986) describes the development of colonial Chesapeake society. Studies of the southern colonies and backcountry include Carl Bridenbaugh's *Myths and Realities: Societies of the Colonial South* (1952), A. Roger Ekirch's *"Poor Carolina"* (1981), Richard R. Beeman's *The Evolution of the Southern Backcountry* (1984), and Daniel Usner's *Indians, Settlers and Slaves in a Frontier Exchange Economy* (1992). Wilcomb Washburn's *The Governor and the Rebel* (1957) is an interpretation of Bacon's rebellion; Richard M. Brown examines the *South Carolina Regulators* (1963). Laurel Thatcher Ulrich's *Good Wives* (1983) and Carol Berkin's *First Generations* (1996) explore the lives of colonial women. The intellectual and theological transformation of New England Congregationalism may be followed in Conrad Wright's *The Beginnings of Unitarianism in America* (1955). Jon Butler explores the importance of Protestantism in the development of American society in *Awash in a Sea of Faith* (1990), and Henry May examines the nature, development, and impact of *The Enlightenment in America* (1976). Norman Fiering looks at *Jonathan Edwards's Moral Thought and Its British Context* (1981). Carl Van Doren has written the best biography of *Benjamin Franklin* (1941), but Franklin's quality shines forth in his fascinating *Autobiography* (many editions).

4

★ ★ ★ ★ ★ ★

Toward Revolution, 1763–1775

AT THE CLOSE of the French and Indian War in 1763, the inhabitants of British North America considered themselves patriotic and loyal British subjects. Under British rule, the colonies had become flourishing and prosperous societies, affording to ordinary individuals well-being and opportunities without parallel in Europe and perhaps anywhere in previous human history. The British navigation laws had, by and large, fostered colonial prosperity; British fleets and armies had defended colonials against their Spanish, French, and Indian enemies; and a benevolent (or careless) home government had allowed them to develop representative institutions and to regulate their domestic affairs with only minor interference. Nourished on the British Whig tradition of limited monarchy stemming from the Glorious Revolution of 1688, the American colonists thought of their political rights and liberties as British rights and liberties.

Yet within 12 years, these same loyal British subjects were at war with the mother country. Although their relations with Britain until 1763 were relatively harmonious, the crisis of the next dozen years taught them that they had long since developed a deep attachment to the society they were creating in the colonies. Somewhat to their own surprise they learned that they valued the British connection only as far as, and as long as, it was compatible with their desire to preserve and perfect their free and semiautonomous American society. In one of history's most notorious instances of bad timing, British officials had chosen to tighten the lax administration of the Empire at the very moment when American colonials were beginning to feel their own separate identity. Colonial cries of imperial despotism and oppression were doubtless overdrawn, but the stiffening of British policy was at best untimely. The result was not only a deepening hostility to Great Britain, but a heightened sense of common purpose that would turn colonists into Americans.

TABLE 1. EVENTS LEADING TO THE REVOLUTION, 1735–1776

Year	British Actions	American Actions
1735		John Peter Zenger tried for libel and acquitted.
1764	Revenue (Sugar) Act — duties for revenue. Currency Act.	James Otis, Jr., *The Rights of the British Colonies*
1765	Quartering Act. Stamp Act.	Crowd action. Sons of Liberty formed. Nonimportation agreements.
1766	Repeal of Stamp Act. Declaratory Act — asserting right of Parliament to legislate for colonies in all respects.	Nonimportation suspended.
1767	Townshend duties — revenue duties on various articles.	Crowd action. Nonimportation agreements. John Dickinson, *Letters of a Pennsylvania Farmer*
1770	Repeal of Townshend duties, except duty on tea.	Boston Massacre. Suspension of nonimportation.
1772		Committees of correspondence organized. *Gaspée* burned.
1773	Tea Act — giving East India Co. monopoly on colonial tea trade.	Crowd action. Boston Tea Party.
1774	Intolerable acts: 1. Closing port of Boston. 2. Restricting self-government in Massachusetts. 3. Allowing royal officers to be tried in England. 4. Allowing royal troops to requisition private buildings for quarters. Quebec Act — continuing nonrepresentative government in Quebec, tolerating Roman Catholicism in Quebec, and incorporating Ohio Valley in Quebec.	First Continental Congress: 1. Rejects Galloway's plan of union. 2. Adopts Continental Association, establishing committees of safety to enforce commercial nonintercourse with England. 3. Encourages Massachusetts to establish revolutionary government and prepare for military defense.
1775	Lexington-Concord — British troops skirmish with Massachusetts militiamen.	Committees of safety seize control. Second Continental Congress — appoints Washington to commmand continental army at Boston.
1776		Thomas Paine's *Common Sense* published.

THE NEW IMPERIAL POLICY

When Britain emerged victorious from the great Anglo-French wars, there were conditions that supported a new and more vigorous imperial policy. First, King George III, enthroned in 1760, was an ambitious and conscientious monarch who desired to play a larger role in governmental affairs than had his predecessors. Through manipulation of royal patronage and maneuvering of parliamentary elections he tried to re-establish the royal influence that earlier monarchs had exercised by right. Unfortunately, the king and his ministers proved to be less flexible and astute in dealing with the colonists than their easygoing predecessors had been. Yet probably any British ministry would have sought to strengthen the inefficiently managed imperial system at this time. During the war, the colonists had irritated the British by their reluctance to furnish troops, supplies, and money and in too many cases had actually prospered by trading with the enemy. Moreover, the empire had been greatly enlarged, and more efficient regulation seemed necessary everywhere if the colonial territories were to serve their purpose of benefiting the mother country.

The most pressing immediate problem was that of revenue to pay off the crushing debt incurred during the war and to support the increased costs of defending and administering the enlarged empire, costs that had multiplied fivefold since the war with France. Compared with English landowners, the colonists were virtually untaxed, and in London it seemed only fair that they should bear some of the heavy tax burden required for the defense of American territory.

The new and tighter imperial policy that grew out of these conditions was inaugurated by the ministry of George Grenville during 1763–1765, and it provoked colonial hostility. After Chief Pontiac's rebellion (an effort by the Ottawas and their allies to block English expansion into the trans-Appalachian region), the British had issued the Proclamation of 1763, which restricted colonial settlement on the new western frontier. The proclamation's intent was to minimize conflict with the Indians and to promote orderly disposition of crown lands. But the Americans, some of whom had settled beyond the Appalachians and were now ordered back, resented this British land grab and soon forced major revisions in the proclamation. The Currency Act (1764), which forbade the already hard-pressed colonies to issue paper money, and the Quartering Act (1765), which required them to provide shelter and supplies for British troops, also stirred American indignation. And the Revenue Act (better known as the Sugar Act) of 1764 met with colonial rage. This measure marked the first British attempt to levy import duties on colonial trade for the purpose of revenue rather than regulation.

Although the Sugar Act applied also to wine, coffee, silk, and linen, the duty on molasses seemed the most onerous. For years New England merchants had evaded an earlier levy under the Molasses Act of 1733 by smuggling molasses from the French West Indies for manufacturing rum. The new molasses duty was only half of the old, but it was rigorously enforced and crippled New England commerce. Shocked by the sudden vigor of imperial control after decades of salutary neglect, and squeezed by a postwar depression, the infuriated colonists protested that they could not rightfully be taxed except by their own elected representatives.

Either underestimating the strength of colonial opposition or not caring how strong it was, Grenville pushed through Parliament in 1765 the even more provocative Stamp Act. This measure required the colonists to purchase revenue stamps and affix them to all kinds of legal and commercial documents, newspapers, almanacs, playing cards, dice, and liquor licenses. This was taxation in a highly visible and odious form. Moreover, it most offended those who were most influential in shaping colonial opinion — merchants, lawyers, printers, and tavern keepers. An explosion of protest indicated not only how averse the colonists were to taxation of any kind, but also how attached they were to the representative tradition of British Whiggery and to the home rule that they had enjoyed with so little interference.

At question was the relationship of the colonial assemblies to Parliament. Claiming precedence over colonial lawmakers, Parliament denied that Americans were subject only to self-imposed taxes, and Grenville denied that Americans were being taxed without their own consent. As British subjects, he averred, they enjoyed "virtual," if not precisely direct, representation in Parliament. For the moment, few colonists were prepared to challenge Parliament's regulatory or legislative authority within the British Empire. But a growing number agreed that as British citizens, under the protection of the English Bill of Rights, they could be taxed only by their own assemblies — the only legislative bodies in which they were represented.

Colonial protest took many forms. Pamphleteers, including Massachusetts's James Otis, Jr. (*The Rights of the British Colonies asserted and proved*) and Maryland's Daniel Dulaney (*Considerations on the Propriety of Imposing Taxes*), argued in print the American case against the constitutionality of parliamentary taxation. From New Hampshire to South Carolina, resistance groups emerged. Often calling themselves the Sons of Liberty, these secret bands of artisans and small merchants burned effigies of Grenville, blocked the sale of stamps, besieged and sometimes destroyed the homes of crown officials, and intimidated agents of the British government in other ways. Colonial legislatures called for the repeal of the hated measures, and representatives from 12 colonies (all but Georgia) met in New York at the so-called Stamp Act Congress in October 1765. At this first intercolonial assembly since 1754, the representatives pledged loyalty to the king and "all due subordination" to Parliament, but denied Parliament's right to tax the colonists. The most effective protest against taxation without representation, however, was a nonimportation agreement sponsored by the colonial merchants that led to a boycott of British goods. This had such an effect on British manufacturers and exporting merchants that Parliament was persuaded in 1766 to repeal the Stamp Act. But Parliament did not surrender its claim to tax the colonists, for repeal was accompanied by a Declaratory Act asserting Parliament's right to legislate for the colonies in any and all respects.

That this was no idle claim was shown the very next year, 1767, when Charles Townshend, Chancellor of the Exchequer, pushed through Parliament the so-called Townshend Acts levying duties for revenue on a new class of previously untaxed articles. The new taxes were rendered more unpalatable by provisions for further strengthening the enforcement and collection machinery and by the stipulation that revenues from the act would be used to pay the salaries of royal officials in the colonies, thus robbing the colonial assemblies of their most potent weapon, the power to withhold salaries from uncooperative royal officers. The Americans, of course, protested. In his *Letters from a Farmer,* John Dickinson, a cultivated Philadelphian and a member of the Stamp Act Congress, rallied colonial support for a second boycott of British goods. Colonials protested, newspapers attacked British policy, and merchants employed the proven weapon of nonimportation agreements. And once again, in 1770, Parliament softened its stand, repealing all the duties except the one on tea.

Most colonists were willing to accept this action as settling the controversy, and the next few years brought a period of prosperity and relative peace between colonies and mother country. Except for New England merchants and, later, wealthy Virginia planters — two of the most powerful and articulate segments of the population — the trade regulations adopted after 1763 imposed no significant hardship on the colonial economy. Yet the British ministers were badly deceived if they supposed that imperial relations were as cordial as they had once been. During the seven years of controversy over parliamentary taxation, the Americans analyzed their relationship with the mother country and became increasingly conscious of their separate identity and the colonies' common interest. They had successfully defied what they viewed as the tyranny of the home government, and they were now more committed than they perhaps realized to republican principles of self-government.

THE RADICALS AND THE URBAN CROWD

Especially dangerous to continued harmony was a small but well organized and ably led group of American radicals. Since the 1760s, they had opposed any British effort to tax or regulate colonial affairs. Most of these radicals had led the more militant agitation against the Stamp Act and the Townshend duties; their hostility toward the British was often combined with a democratic resentment of elitist politics and aristocratic pretensions. In Virginia, for example, Patrick Henry's radical opposition to the Stamp Act simultaneously challenged control of the House of Burgesses by the most conservative wing of the planter oligarchy. In Charleston, though the radical group was led by the young aristocrat Christopher Gadsden, its rank and file was drawn largely from artisans, manual workers, and others from poor and middle segments of colonial society. In economically hard-pressed Boston the radical leader Samuel Adams, though backed by the wealthy merchant John Hancock, drew most support from socially immobile artisans and shopkeepers who welcomed an opportunity to strike at Bostonians with close royal ties. Anti-elitist sentiment was particularly apparent among the disfranchised and otherwise politically inarticulate classes: the propertyless working poor, apprentices, slaves, and women. These made up the crowds that contributed to the hellish fury of the 1765 Boston street demonstrations and that followed the impoverished shoemaker and war veteran, "Captain-General" Ebenezer MacIntosh, and burned Lt. Governor Thomas Hutchinson's elegant house. In such crowd actions, anti-British sentiment and class resentments melded, as the "unthinking multitude," including many not entitled to participate in organized politics, found purposeful and coordinated ways to influence events.

American men and women of every social level were politicized by changing imperial policy and joined in the protest against the Stamp Act and Townshend duties. The wealthier and more conservative among them, however, were dismayed by the excesses of the "lower ranks." These more conservative American Whigs (not a few of whom would become Loyalists) were satisfied when Parliament repealed all the offensive duties except the one on tea, while the radicals insisted on continuing to agitate against it.

The most dangerous radical leader was that superb organizer, agitator, and propagandist Samuel Adams, this self-styled "Populus" who had deep roots in the artisan class, despite having a Harvard degree. Through his control of the town meeting, Adams kept Boston in an uproar, though quiet returned to other areas. Adams exploited incidents like the Boston Massacre of 1770, in which an angry crowd goaded a small party of British soldiers into firing; they killed five persons, including the runaway slave Crispus Attucks. Adams's propaganda maintained the colonists' alarm over British "tyranny." In addition, Adams and his allies — notably such outspoken critics of wealth and power as William Molineux and Thomas Young — were creating a radical organization that joined Boston's merchant and laboring classes in an uneasy union.

Operating from his base in the Boston town meeting, Adams induced other Massachusetts towns to establish "committees of correspondence" to promote intercolonial resistance to imperial policy. The idea spread and, shortly, dissident Virginians urged the establishment of a provincial committee of correspondence in every colony. Naturally these committees came to be dominated by those with relatively radical attitudes. While the radicals were unable to dispel the complacency that prevailed in the comparatively prosperous years from 1770 to 1773, they created an organization that could seize the initiative whenever an opportunity arose.

THE SECOND CRISIS

Opportunity came when the British ministry of Lord North, in all innocence, undertook to aid the British East India Company by pushing through Parliament the Tea Act of 1773. The company was given the exclusive privilege of selling its tea directly to American consumers without paying the English export tax, thus increasing the company's profits, lowering the price of tea to Americans, eliminating widespread smuggling, and depriving American importing merchants of any share in the tea trade. But the cheap tea was still subject to tax under the Townshend duty.

The resentment of the conservative American merchants drove them again into alliance with the radicals, and the radicals made the most of this opportunity to renew violent agitation. Convinced that the British were using lower tea prices to seduce Americans into surrendering their liberties, again the radicals organized and resorted to mob action. In New York, Philadelphia, and other cities, the Sons of Liberty and committees of correspondence found a broad base of support. In the South, East India tea was locked in warehouses by Charleston patriots. In Boston in December 1773, colonists, ill-disguised as Mohawk Indians, boarded British vessels and dumped some 45 tons of East India tea in the harbor. Coming as it did only one year after angry Rhode Islanders had burned the British customs vessel *Gaspée*, the defiance of the Boston Tea Party shocked many Americans, but patriot leaders and the public in general agreed that to accept the Tea Act was to risk conceding Parliament's right to tax the colonies for revenue.

The British government, on the other hand, was now convinced that only punitive action could bring the rebellious colonists to heel. Promptly, Parliament passed a series of four "Coercive Acts" (known to Americans as the "Intolerable Acts"), closing the port of Boston until the Bostonians paid for the tea they had destroyed, drastically reducing the representative and self-governing features of the Massachusetts provincial government, allowing royal officials to be tried in England when accused of crimes in the colonies, and permitting the British army to requisition American buildings as quarters. However logical and necessary these measures appeared to a London government faced with colonial insubordination, they confirmed American suspicions of Britain's despotic designs. A fifth measure followed that, although not punitive in nature or actually one of the Coercive Acts, proved no more tolerable to the colonists. Through the Quebec Act of 1774, Parliament added to the Canadian province western territory claimed by several colonies, continued the autocratic rule in Quebec that had prevailed under the French, and afforded complete religious toleration to the province's Catholic population.

These measures threw the radical propaganda machine and committee organization into high gear. "The cause of Boston is the cause of all British America" was the message trumpeted everywhere during the spring and summer of 1774. Food, fuel, and money were collected for the relief of the beleaguered Bostonians, local nonimportation agreements sprang up on all sides, and a proposal for a continental congress to coordinate resistance won quick endorsement from the assemblies or from extralegal meetings of the assemblies in most of the colonies.

THE FIRST CONTINENTAL CONGRESS

In September 1774, an extralegal Congress of delegates from every colony except Georgia assembled in Philadelphia's Carpenters' Hall. Although sharing common anti-British sentiments and a commitment to the "cause of Boston," the 55 delegates were strangers to one another and not of one mind on the constitutional relationship of the colonies to England. The most radical among them embraced the doctrine of natural rights, denied parliamentary jurisdiction over the colonies, and argued that the colonists were subject only to the laws of their respective assemblies. Others did not assert the eighteenth-century doctrine of the rights of man, but their rights as English citizens instead; they recognized Parliament's power to regulate imperial trade, but denied its right to tax or otherwise interfere with internal colonial affairs. After some debate, the delegates unanimously adopted the defiant Suffolk Resolves, which condemned virtually all British trade regulations; they narrowly defeated a conciliatory plan for colonial government presented by Joseph Galloway of Pennsylvania, which was closely patterned after the Albany Plan of 1754. The first Continental Congress also created a "Continental Association," a detailed plan for nonimportation, nonconsumption, and nonexportation of goods between the colonies and Great Britain. To enforce the boycott, the delegates authorized every county or town to elect extralegal committees of safety. These committees were to circulate the Association among all citizens for endorsement and then to single out violators for boycott and for denunciation as "enemies to the rights of British America." Goods imported in violation of the Association could be seized, and the work of the local committees was to be coordinated in each colony by a provincial congress and a provincial committee of safety.

During the winter and spring of 1774–1775, the radicals began vigorously implementing this revolutionary scheme in every colony. A drastic decline in British imports quickly demonstrated the Association's effectiveness as an instrument of economic warfare; it was probably even more important as an instrument of political persuasion and coercion.

While nearly all Americans favored efforts to secure concessions from the British government, perhaps only a minority supported the aggressive tactics of the radicals. Many colonists were decidedly hostile to any action that threatened to break the British connection, and many more were simply confused or indifferent. But the Association and its committee system gave the organized and purposeful radicals a highly efficient means of committing the passive and often hostile majority to their program.

Though the committees were supposed to be elected, they were frequently in fact self-constituted bodies of the local radical leaders and in some cases were merely the old committees of correspondence continued under a new name. Where public denunciation failed to secure compliance with the Association, committees did not hesitate to employ threats and even physical violence. As the revolutionary crisis deepened, the committees increasingly assumed the powers of government, fixing prices, levying fines, and taking charge of local militia units.

Yet radical control was far from complete by the spring of 1775. The mercantile and officeholding aristocracy put up strong opposition in the northeastern port towns; up-country Carolina farmers were disposed to side with the royal governors against the provincial politicians who had oppressed them in the past and who were now leading the radical movement; and everywhere there were wide areas still so unexcited over British oppression that the radicals had made little headway. An additional impulse was needed and once again Samuel Adams's Massachusetts radicals supplied it.

WAR

British "despotism" was anything but a remote and idle threat to the Massachusetts radicals during the winter and spring of 1774–1775. As part of the British plan to crush the spirit of insubordination in Massachusetts, additional troops were sent to Boston, and their commander, General Thomas Gage, was designated military governor of the province. With the endorsement of the Continental Congress, the radicals took the momentous step of establishing a revolutionary provincial government under the old suspended charter and began training troops and collecting military supplies.

The inevitable clash came on the morning of April 19, 1775, when General Gage sent a detachment of British soldiers from Boston to seize the powder and arms that had been collected at nearby Concord and to arrest Samuel Adams and John Hancock. Warned by Paul Revere and William Dawes, the farmer "minutemen" (so-called because they were expected to "Stand at a minute's warning") challenged the British regulars at Lexington and Concord. Shots were exchanged, and by the time these surprised "redcoats" had run the 16-mile gauntlet of farmers' muskets on the road back to Boston, they had lost 273 dead, wounded, and missing. About a hundred patriots also were casualties in this bloody, first encounter of the Revolution.

Instantly the radicals sent special riders flying through the colonies with exaggerated accounts of the massacre of innocent Massachusetts farmers by British soldiers. Everywhere there was a burst of patriotic indignation, enabling the radical-dominated committees of safety to gain complete control. Royal governors were driven from their posts, troops were drilled, and royal forts and powder magazines were seized.

On May 10, a Second Continental Congress hastily assembled in Philadelphia. As a gesture to the timid, this radical-dominated body sent an "Olive Branch Petition" to the king as a final appeal for a peaceful settlement. When this petition was refused, the last vestiges of loyalty to the crown dissolved. Rapidly, a once-respected monarch was becoming, in Tom Paine's memorable words, a "royal brute." With all other acceptable avenues of resistance closed, Congress prepared for war. The thousands of armed New Englanders who had rushed to besiege Gage's redcoats by taking positions on the hills overlooking Boston were taken under the aegis of the Congress. And George Washington, who came to Philadelphia in the blue uniform of the Virginia militia, was named to command the emerging continental army. As resistance became rebellion, the 2.5 million British subjects in 13 New World colonies were awash in sentiments that would rapidly make them a single and independent people — Americans.

CONFLICTING HISTORICAL VIEWPOINTS: NO. 1

What Caused the American Revolution and How Revolutionary Was It?

Nineteenth-century historians rarely quarreled about the origin and nature of the Revolution. The war for American independence, they concluded, was a just and truly revolutionary struggle against the tyrannical and reactionary British imperial system. The colonial triumph ushered in a new era of human liberty, fraternity, and democracy. Indeed, to George Bancroft, author of the authoritative and justly celebrated History of the United States *(12 vols., 1834–1882), the Americans were God's chosen people and their revolution was part of the "grand design of Providence," a noble prelude to the "regeneration" of humankind.*

In the 1890s the patriotic distortions of this traditional view were challenged by two schools of historical interpretation: the imperialist and the progressive. Influenced by a turn-of-the-century spirit of Anglo-American accord, such imperialist historians as Charles McLean Andrews (The Colonial Background of the American Revolution, 1924) were more critical of colonial behavior than English policy. The quarrel with England, they argued, could be interpreted correctly only within the broad context of the British empire as a whole. Examining the imperial as well as the colonial point of view, they sympathetically concluded that the British Trade and Navigation Acts were not oppressive and that Parliament's efforts to tax the Americans were justifiable.

While imperialistic scholars sought the origins of the Revolution in political and constitutional issues within the empire, the progressives focused on social and economic issues within the colonies themselves. Products of the reform mentality of the late nineteenth and early twentieth centuries, these liberal scholars addressed not only the question of home rule but the question of who should rule at home. As Carl Becker, the greatest of the progressive historians, expressed it in The History of Political Parties in the Province of New York *(1909), the American Revolution was actually two revolutions in one. The first, an external revolution, involved a conflict of economic interests between Great Britain and the American colonies. The second, an internal revolution, involved a class conflict between the haves and have-nots of colonial society. More recently, such distinguished historians as Lawrence Gipson (The British Empire Before the American Revolution, 15 vols., 1936–1970) and Merrill Jensen (The Founding of a Nation, 1968) still analyze the Revolution from the imperialist and progressive persuasions, and echoes of the progressive theme of colonial class tensions can be found in Gary B. Nash's* The Urban Crucible *(1979), a provocative analysis of the social and economic processes that shaped the Revolution.*

But in recent decades, new directions in historical thought have challenged earlier viewpoints. In the 1950s, for example, so-called consensus historians, apparently mirroring the conservatism of the Cold War pe-

riod, disputed progressive notions of class conflict. Arguing that American society was far more democratic, affluent, and fluid than the progressives had believed, such consensus histories as Robert E. Brown's Middle-Class Democracy and the Revolution in Massachusetts (1955) and Daniel J. Boorstin's The Genius of American Politics (1953) concluded that the Revolution was essentially a conservative movement waged to protect traditional American rights and liberties from a changing and increasingly arbitrary British policy.

Edmund S. Morgan (The Birth of the Republic, 1956), Bernard Bailyn (The Ideological Origins of the American Revolution, 1967), and other scholars who stress the causal importance of ideas have also discounted internal social and economic cleavage theories. Colonial patriots, Bailyn wrote, although not unmindful of their pocketbooks, were genuinely alarmed by the changing course of imperial policy and deeply affected by the anti-authoritarian tradition of English thought. Possessed of "real fears, real anxieties, [and] a sense of real danger," they viewed their opposition to parliamentary taxation as a struggle of liberty against the corrupting force of power. Thus the new intellectual history has returned to the nineteenth-century conclusion that constitutional rights and lofty values lie at the heart of the American Revolution. Although embracing neither Bancroft's patriotic and religious excesses nor his undue criticism of British policy, it finds the old master correct when he argued that the colonists revolted in the name of liberty and republican ideals.

Radical or New Left scholars, such as those who contributed essays to Alfred E. Young's The American Revolution (1976) or Edward Countryman, author of A People in Revolution (1981), have added yet another dimension to the debate. Not without justification, they indict their fellow historians for overemphasizing the attitudes and behavior of social and economic elites to the neglect of the great mass of human society. In the radical view, the Revolution can be correctly interpreted only from "the bottom up," the vantage point of colonial nonelites. Regardless of the perspective, however, there is little likelihood of unanimity of historical opinion.

FOR FURTHER READING

Edmund S. Morgan's *The Birth of the Republic* (1977) is an excellent introduction to the period from 1763 to 1789, and John C. Miller's *Origins of the American Revolution* (1943) offers a narrative overview of the events leading to conflict. John R. Alden has assessed the role of *The South in the Revolution, 1763–1789* (1957); Rachel Klein's *Unification of a Slave State* (1988) explains the coming of the Revolution in South Carolina. Arthur M. Schlesinger, Sr., *The Colonial Merchants and the American Revolution* (1918) is dated but still commands attention, while John W. Tyler's *Smugglers and Patriots* (1986) updates Schlesinger's account. Pauline Maier's

From Resistance to Revolution (1972) provides a synthesis of the role of colonial radicals in the development of hostilities; Rhys Isaac's *The Trans-formation of Virginia, 1740–1790* (1982) demonstrates how religious con-flict helped shape revolutionary political culture; and Marc Egnal's *A Mighty Empire* (1988) examines the range of opinion on British imperial policy among the American colonial elite. Bernhard Knollenberg traces *The Origins of the American Revolution* (1961); Edmund S. and Helen M. Morgan bril-liantly analyze *The Stamp Act Crisis* (1953); Hiller B. Zobel surveys *The Boston Massacre* (1970); Benjamin W. Labaree details *The Boston Tea Party* (1964); Peter D. G. Thomas examines *The Townshend Duties Crisis* (1987); and Robert A. Gross surveys *The Minutemen and Their World* (1976). Both John C. Miller's *Sam Adams* (1936) and Bernard Bailyn's *The Ordeal of Thomas Hutchinson* (1974) are readable biographies, and Pauline Maier's *The Old Revolutionaries* (1980) is a collective portrait of five first-genera-tion patriot leaders.

5

★ ★ ★ ★ ★ ★

Independence Achieved, 1775–1783

THE FIRST YEAR OF WAR

The military struggle began slowly, and during the first year no really decisive engagements occurred. In June 1775, shortly before Washington arrived to take command of the poorly organized American forces on the hills surrounding Boston, General Gage managed to drive his besiegers from one of their strongest positions, Breed's Hill. But the misnamed Battle of Bunker Hill cost the British some 40 percent of their force, and these frightful losses demonstrated that the Americans, though outnumbered, could not easily be dislodged. During the months that followed Washington methodically converted his untrained militia into a disciplined army and tightened the ring around the British.

With Gage's army encircled in Boston, the ebullient Americans undertook, during the winter of 1775–1776, a two-pronged offensive against Canada. The forces led by Richard Montgomery and Benedict Arnold surmounted great hardships and won some early successes, but in the end the reluctance of the Canadian population to join the rebellion forced a retreat.

In the first year of the war, perhaps the most important struggle was among the colonists themselves. Because neither the British nor the American leaders were prepared to compromise, few people doubted that the issue could be resolved by means short of full-scale war. But only two-fifths of the colonial population actively supported the Revolution. Perhaps one-fifth of all whites — from every social class and ethnic group — remained loyal to the British. Some 55,000 American Tories actively joined the British cause. Another 80,000 went into exile in Canada, the Bahamas, or England. Other neutral or potentially subversive elements included pacifists, apolitical western frontiersmen, indentured servants, slaves, and Indians.

MAP 2: THE AMERICAN REVOLUTION

CANADA
(British)

L. Superior

MASS.

L. Huron

L. Michigan

N.H.
Lexington-Concord
April 1775

Mar. 1776

Saratoga
Oct. 1777

N.Y.

Breed's Hill
June 1775

MASS. Boston

Claimed by Mass.

CONN. R.I.

Claimed by Conn.

L. Erie

L. Ontario

Trenton-Princeton
Dec. 1776

New York

PENN.

July 1776

Philadelphia

V I R G I N I A

Ohio Valley
claimed by N.Y.

N.J.

MD.

DEL.

LOUISIANA
(Spanish)

Yorktown Oct. 1781

Guilford Courthouse,
Mar. 1781

ATLANTIC OCEAN

Kings Mt.,
Oct. 1780

N. CAROLINA

Cowpens,
Jan. 1781

Camden, Aug. 1780

S. CAROLINA

Claimed by Spain 1783-95

Charleston

May 1780

GEORGIA

Savannah

Dec. 1778

New Orleans

FLORIDA
(Spanish)

GULF OF MEXICO

- - - Boundary of the U.S. by
the Treaty of Paris, 1783

Disputed or uncertain
boundary areas

← Routes of main British armies

☆ Major battles

0   200   400 miles

0   200   400 kilometers

For the most part, the revolutionists managed to neutralize British efforts to exploit these indifferent or resentful peoples. But several thousand slaves cast their lot with the British in the hope of freedom; a greater number capitalized on wartime confusion by running away. However, the much-feared wholesale enlistment in the black army of John Murray, Lord Dunmore, last royal governor of Virginia, did not occur. Prodded by British actions, General Washington lifted an initial ban on black enlistment and initiated active recruiting. Some 5,000 blacks (slave and free, mostly from the northern colonies) joined the Continental army, serving in both integrated and all-black units. Similarly, though most Native American tribes had legitimate grievances against the colonists, Indians (with some exceptions) generally chose to remain neutral, rather than to ally with the British.

Faced with these actual and potential internal divisions, Congress and the colonies imposed severe penalties on those suspected of loyalty to the crown: censorship, ostracism, disfranchisement, loss of public office, confiscation of property, and detention. Those women believed to be aiding the British cause were treated as harshly as their male counterparts and received "disrespectful Indignities." Though excesses and wrongful persecutions did occur, the American Revolution produced none of the wholesale imprisonments or executions of dissidents that have tarnished some other revolutions. Given the dangers posed by so many subversives, real and imagined, the penalties imposed on the Loyalists do not seem disproportionate.

In March 1776, General Gage finally abandoned the increasingly difficult task of holding Boston and sailed away with his army and hundreds of Loyalists to the British stronghold at Halifax, Nova Scotia. His departure did not mark a decisive American victory, but rather the end of a year of stalemate in which each side had consolidated its position and prepared for the real struggle yet to come. During that fortunate year of respite a new American nation animated by fresh and exciting ideals had been coming to birth.

"CONCEIVED IN LIBERTY"

Few Americans admitted that they sought independence from England until months after the Revolutionary War had begun. Yet the pressure of events increasingly forced them into independent acts and steadily prepared them for an open break.

The question of independence was connected in an indirect, but important way with the acceleration of democratic tendencies inherent in the revolutionary movement. While home rule was the primary issue in the Revolution, a political upsurge of the lower orders of the social hierarchy raised the important secondary issue of "*who* should rule at home?" The Liberty Boys who rioted against the Stamp Act or the Townshend duties were making a bid for political status. Perhaps more important, the revolutionary agitation opened an avenue by which ambitious persons of the "middling sort"

(Samuel Adams, Patrick Henry, and their counterparts in other colonies) could rise to influence. The revolutionary movement offered such "new men" an opportunity to gain power by espousing radical measures and appealing indirectly to the inchoate democratic aspirations of those heretofore without influence in government.

The success of these "new men" was due in considerable measure to a favorable climate of ideas. The revolutionary era was one of those periods in history when ideas had great consequences. All Americans, including the most conservative and aristocratic, believed that the Glorious Revolution of 1688 and its great Bill of Rights had guaranteed to every British citizen certain rights — especially rights of liberty and property — upon which no government could rightfully infringe. In the British tradition of dissent dating to the Civil War (1642–1649) and the Commonwealth (1649–1653), Americans believed that government — power and authority — was naturally aggressive and tended to go beyond legitimate boundaries at the expense of liberty. In the spirit of that tradition, Americans distrusted government and were eager to restrict it lest force and compulsion dominate liberty and virtue. Their opposition to the new imperial policy was based on the claim of Britain's Whig party that this was an arbitrary exercise of power, a violation of this heritage of English rights. "Liberty and Property" became the slogan of the Revolution; a fear of the transgressions of authority became the controlling concept of an emerging American republicanism.

The ideas of British Whigs carried democratic implications that could be applied to government within as well as outside of the colonies. When the colonial leaders argued for the Whig principle of "no taxation without representation" in imperial relations, inadequately represented Americans required no great imagination to apply the same argument to domestic affairs or even to expand it into the more general principle that government should be representative of the governed, meaning *all* the governed.

These democratic implications of seventeenth-century British libertarianism were refined and reinforced by the larger stream of Enlightenment thought. Confident that the Creator desired human happiness, the people of the eighteenth century were drifting toward the notion that all people were equal in their "natural rights" and that the only just end of government was to maintain a state of society in which all could enjoy their rights to the fullest possible extent. Since liberty was the most precious of these rights, government should be restricted to the smallest possible compass that would enable it to keep individuals from invading each other's liberty, and since all persons were potentially rational, government should rest on the consent of the governed. The second of John Locke's *Two Treatises on Government* (1689) was a most trenchant justification of revolution on the basis of the natural-rights argument.

During the later stages of the revolutionary crisis, the colonial leaders broadened the basis for their claim to autonomy from their rights as British citizens, according to the Whig tradition, to their rights as human beings, according to the natural-rights tradition. Directly or indirectly, Americans were thinking in Lockean terms as they decided for revolution, drafted their

Declaration of Independence, and established a republican system of government.

Americans did not rebel against England, as conservative Tories often charged, to overthrow the established social order and advance the leveling spirit of democracy at home. Compared to subsequent European revolutions, the American Revolution was essentially conservative, begun for limited political and constitutional purposes and accomplished without major internal upheaval. Unlike the toppling of anciens régimes in France (1789) and Russia (1917), the overthrow of royal tyranny in America was followed by no shattering changes in class, economic, or property arrangements. Yet large segments of the population rallied to the movement for colonial autonomy because they were aroused by the logic of rebellion. Moreover, while creating broad support for their movement, revolutionary leaders sought out new groups that had previously played little part in public life. Consequently, the new provincial congresses organized at the war's start encompassed a more diversified membership than the previous colonial assemblies and councils.

This rise of the lower orders affected how the colonial ruling group reacted to the Revolution. Many gentry were alarmed into being Loyalists by their fear of having a government "independent of rich men." A larger number (conservative Whigs) continued to furnish leadership to the revolutionary movement but resisted independence. They hoped to win colonial autonomy while restoring the British connection as a means of preserving the dominance of the aristocrats within the colonies. A third segment of the gentry (radical Whigs) was so deeply infected with the revolutionary ideology that they worked closely with the new men who spoke for the lower orders, espousing independence and paving the way for a new distribution of political power.

It was this last group, especially Richard Henry Lee of Virginia and Samuel and John Adams of Massachusetts, who controlled the Continental Congress in the early war years. On the question of independence, they were aided by the drift of events. The British government showed little disposition to conciliate the Americans and every disposition to wage vigorous war against them. The importance of aid from Britain's ancient enemy France became increasingly apparent, and it was hoped that independence might pave the way for a French alliance. Finally, Americans of all classes were gradually beginning to sense the exciting possibility of building a new and independent society based on natural rights and the implicitly democratic principles of revolutionary rhetoric. How rapidly this feeling had spread was demonstrated by the tremendous public response to Thomas Paine's anonymous pamphlet *Common Sense*, a spirited defense of the American cause, published in January 1776. Advocating both independence and democracy, Paine's slashing document sold several hundred-thousand copies.

A new American, who emigrated from England only in 1774, Paine did not create the sentiment for independence; he merely crystallized an often unspoken but rapidly growing attitude. Once catapulted into the arena of open debate, the idea of independence rapidly overcame conservative opposition. On July 2, the Continental Congress resolved that "these United States are, and of right ought to be, free and independent states"; two days later the Declaration of Independence was adopted.

Drafted by Thomas Jefferson, with the help of Benjamin Franklin and John Adams, this remarkable document was for the most part a long and exaggerated catalog of British violations of American rights. Designed in large part as propaganda for world consumption, the Declaration offered no subtle interpretations of events. It was the hapless George III — not Parliament, the source of most colonial grievances — who was made the villain of the piece. What made the Declaration a momentous factor in history, however, was its opening section, which distilled in a few sentences of enduring prose the essence of the Lockean, natural-rights theory of government: "We hold these truths to be self-evident, that all men are created equal, that they are endowed by their Creator with certain inalienable Rights, that among these are Life, Liberty, and the pursuit of Happiness. That to secure these rights, Governments are instituted among Men, deriving their just powers from the consent of the governed. That whenever any Form of Government becomes destructive of these ends, it is the Right of the People to alter or abolish it." Much of subsequent American history was to be a working out of the implications of the principles so ringingly enunciated here.

THE NEW STATE CONSTITUTIONS

As the colonies became states, they adopted explicitly republican charters — documents that not only expunged what the Americans thought to be British tyranny, but assured protection against future infringements on liberty. The object of the present controversy, Jefferson said in the spring of 1776, was the reordering of the American polity, the shaping of a virtuous society of independent men living in harmony and equality under republican institutions. By the time the Declaration of Independence was adopted, four colonies had already applied its idealistic principles in drafting their state constitutions. Directed by the Continental Congress to create new governments "under the authority of the people," the other states followed suit, except for Rhode Island and Connecticut, which continued to operate under their unusually liberal colonial charters. The writing of constitutions was unprecedented (Britain's consisted of laws and custom and was not written) and significant — unmistakable evidence that Americans wanted the limits of governmental power and citizens' rights clearly delineated. With British authority destroyed, Americans were free to perform the act that lay at the root of all legitimate government according to Lockean theory: they entered into a "social contract." The new state constitutions were conceived of as voluntary compacts among all the people, creating governments of limited and explicitly defined powers. In several states, the people elected special conventions to draft the fundamental compacts; in several others, the constitutions were submitted for popular ratification; but in a majority of cases, the existing provincial congresses themselves drafted and promulgated the new constitutions.

However adopted, the new constitutions uniformly reflected the distrust of governmental power — especially "ever restless, ambitious, and ever grasping" executive or gubernatorial power — that arose from the Enlightenment's liberalism and from the colonists' experience with British authority. To prevent the encroachment of power upon liberty, most states followed Virginia's constitution, including a bill of rights specifying in detail the rights of citizenship (freedom of speech, freedom of the press, trial by jury, and the like) that no government could rightly abridge. All the constitutions sought to minimize the danger of arbitrary power by building "checks and balances" and a "separation of powers" into the very structure of government. The executive, legislative, and judicial functions were exercised by separate bodies, and except in the unicameral states of Pennsylvania, Georgia, and Vermont (which became a state in 1777), the legislatures were divided into two houses that were expected to act as checks on each other. The senates, by common consent, were designed to represent society's wisest and best, and were to serve as checks on excesses of the popular will, as reflected in the lower houses of representatives.

The checks and balances principle, however, was tempered by memories of the long struggles between the colonial assemblies and the royal governors. The new constitutions made the legislatures dominant and the governors relatively impotent. Governors in most cases were elected annually by the legislatures, were denied veto powers, and were subject to impeachment. Moreover, the awesome power of appointment, the most dangerous threat to free government, was given to most state legislatures, rather than to governors.

Along with restrictions on the governmental power, the new constitutions also tended toward more representative government, toward *actual* as opposed to *virtual* representation. These impulses toward closer supervision of legislators were reflected in annual elections, residential requirements for lawmakers as well as for voters, and (in five states) proportional electoral districts that gave representation to back country settlements. Although the state constitutions did not grant *universal* white male suffrage (Massachusetts raised its property qualifications for voting), and no state granted female suffrage, these charters generally extended the privilege of voting, either by reducing the colonial freehold (property) requirement or by opening the polls to most taxpayers. As a result, men of moderate means, petty entrepreneurs, and farmers gradually joined the well-to-do gentry in the conduct of public affairs.

The Revolution thus weakened the social hierarchy, opening new opportunities, both economic and political, for enterprising men outside of the aristocratic and wealthy elite. Yet incongruities in the ideal of human rights remained. It may have been true, as a French traveler observed in 1788, "that the Americans more than any other people are convinced that all men are born free and equal." But that doctrine applied only to white males. For blacks, the revolutionary ideology of republicanism did contribute to the gradual abolition of slavery in northern states, where the institution was least profitable. The nation's free black population grew dramatically, and even in the South more liberal manumission statutes were adopted. However, race distinctions were all but universally applied, and slavery (a truly "peculiar institution" in any republic) survived the Revolution by many decades.

The condition of women improved marginally, and only in such areas as educational opportunity and less stringent divorce laws. Along with these, perhaps there was a greater freedom to select marriage partners and slightly more reciprocity within matrimony. The origins of American feminism can be traced to the remarkable Abigail Adams's oft-quoted plea of 1776 — "Remember the Ladies" — and to the wartime emergency that temporarily enlarged the woman's sphere. Yet during the War for Independence and for many decades thereafter, General Washington's view of the female patriot's proper role — "passive, admiring, and quietly suffering" — was widely, if not universally, shared. The revolutionary generation seemed oblivious to the sexual implications of republican thought.

THE ARTICLES OF CONFEDERATION

As the Continental Congress still had no regular constitutional authority, it began working on a plan for a confederation that would provide sufficient powers to conduct the war and to unite the states once victory was achieved. After protracted debate, the Articles of Confederation were finally approved by Congress in 1777, though a dispute over the western lands claimed by some of the states delayed final ratification until 1781.

The Articles of Confederation established not a government, but a confederation of sovereign states. Because the Revolution was being fought to abolish central control and because liberty was deemed safe only when government was kept close to where the governed could watch it, the Confederation was given only the powers to: (1) conduct foreign affairs by negotiating treaties and making war and peace; (2) control Indian affairs; (3) set standards of coinage, weights, and measures; (4) settle disputes among the states; and (5) conduct a postal service. Although an improvement over the voluntary arrangement under the Continental Congress, the Confederation was a less than perfect instrument of national unity. It could not raise money or troops except by requisitions on the states. It had no power to make laws binding individual citizens and no means of enforcing its will on either citizens or states. Each state was to have a single vote in the Confederation Congress, the votes of nine states were required to approve all important measures, and the Articles could be amended only with the approval of Congress and the legislature of every state. The Articles did not provide a separate judicial branch or an executive division to carry out policies Congress might adopt. Yet the Articles did represent a move toward national unity;

for the first time, there was a permanent agency that could speak for the citizens of the 13 American states.

THE CAMPAIGNS OF 1776–1777

The Declaration of Independence had just been adopted and the constitution-making process was well under way in the states and the Congress when the British launched the American war in earnest. In July 1776, the greatest military force Britain had ever sent abroad sailed into New York harbor; hundreds of ships carried 32,000 soldiers under the command of Sir William Howe. Anticipating the British strategy, Washington had moved his army to the vicinity, but his greatly outnumbered forces were easily pushed off Long Island, out of Manhattan, steadily through New Jersey, and across the Delaware River into Pennsylvania.

The 43-year-old Washington was a leader of imposing presence and command, but he had little combat experience and was probably no military genius. Indeed he lost more battles than he won. Yet his courage and tenacity kept his army intact and the American cause alive. When he assumed command, his troops were largely without uniforms and without a semblance of unified command. Pay was low; both enlistments and rations were short. The men were eager to return to family and farms. The officers were often elected and poorly qualified for leadership. War materials, always in short supply in this undeveloped country, had to be captured or imported from Europe. Yet by good fortune and force of will, this sober, aristocratic Virginian prevailed. With the assistance of such foreign advisers as the Count Casimir Pulaski, the Baron von Steuben, and the Marquis de Lafayette, he built a force of some 8,000–10,000 regulars. (There were an additional 7,000 short-term militiamen.) Wisely avoiding decisive engagements, he waited until the British ceased offensive operations for the winter, and on Christmas night, 1776, he daringly ferried his troops back across the icy Delaware and fell upon unsuspecting British forces at Trenton and nearby Princeton, New Jersey. With these small but brilliant victories to buoy American hopes, he went into winter quarters at Morristown.

The following summer of 1777 was the time of greatest military peril for the infant American nation. From Canada, General John Burgoyne launched a British offensive by way of Lake Champlain toward Albany and the lower Hudson Valley. Sir William Howe had the opportunity to move up the Hudson from New York City to join Burgoyne and cut the colonies in two. Instead, the indecisive Howe succumbed to the temptation of occupying the rebel capital at Philadelphia, brushing aside what resistance Washington's outnumbered army was able to offer at the Battle of Brandywine.

Freed from the threat of Howe to their rear, the American commanders in the Hudson Valley, Horatio Gates and Benedict Arnold, were able to put up a stubborn resistance against Burgoyne's advance from the north. Far from his base of supply and harassed on every side by farmer militia, the British commander was finally forced to surrender his entire army at Saratoga in October 1777. The importance of this victory and the narrowness of the American escape from a crushing military catastrophe cannot be exaggerated. Thanks to a combination of British lethargy and American determination, it now appeared for the first time that the patriot bid for independence might succeed.

THE FRENCH ALLIANCE AND THE SOUTHERN CAMPAIGNS

Even the victory at Saratoga could not make up for the feebleness of the American war effort. Driven from Philadelphia to York, Pennsylvania, Congress struggled ineffectually during the winter of 1777–1778 with the problems of supply and funds, as inflation rose sharply and paper money issued to finance the war became increasingly worthless. Meanwhile, cold and hunger in the winter camp at Valley Forge decimated Washington's ragtag army. Often local American farmers and merchants traded their goods for British coin and supplied enemy forces encamped in the relative comfort of nearby Philadelphia. But the patriot cause saw its share of profiteering, official corruption, provincial rivalries, disaffection, and desertion, though subsequent generations remembered only the gallantry and sacrifice of the revolutionaries.

Across the Atlantic, the Saratoga victory was bearing fruit. From the beginning of the conflict, Americans had hoped that France would avenge her recent defeat by Britain by giving them aid. As soon as independence was declared, Congress sent the engaging and inimitable Franklin (who affected a fur cap and homespun airs for the occasion) to seek an alliance in Paris. The French government proved willing to furnish supplies and funds secretly, but before siding with them openly, it wanted assurance that the Americans had a real chance of winning. Saratoga furnished this assurance, and in February 1778, the treaty of alliance was signed. As a result, France's ally Spain was also pulled into the war with Britain, and soon afterwards the Netherlands were drawn into the conflict because of their insistence on continuing trade with the French and the Americans. Spain and the Netherlands furnished much needed loans for the American war effort, but France became the main source of both the money and the munitions that enabled the Americans to keep fighting. In addition, the French sent an army and a powerful naval force, without which victory would have been impossible.

Military activity was at a stalemate for a year following Saratoga as the British prepared for another offensive, this time aimed at the southern colonies. Landing at Savannah, Georgia, in December 1778, the British army under the aggressive Lord Cornwallis easily took Charleston and occupied most of South Carolina. When the Americans finally marched against him in August 1780, they were soundly defeated at Camden, and Cornwallis was able to push his invasion northward. By this time, however, the American forces in the South were under the able command of Nathanael Greene. At King's Mountain and at Cowpens, severe defeats were inflicted on contingents of Cornwallis's army, and in March 1781, the British army sustained heavy losses in a hard fought but inconclusive battle at Guilford Court House, North Carolina. Cornwallis, despairing of subduing the vast and hostile southern interior, withdrew his seriously weakened army to Yorktown on the peninsula between the York and James rivers in tidewater Virginia, where his forces waited to be evacuated by the British fleet.

But it was not the British fleet that appeared. By a miracle of good fortune and good timing, Washington and the French commanders were able to march the combined Franco-American army down from the north just as the French fleet appeared off the Virginia coast. Thus caught between a hostile army and a hostile navy, Cornwallis had no alternative but to surrender his 7,000 British and Hessian troops on October 17, 1781. As he did so, legend has it, a British military band played "The World Turned Upside Down."

THE TREATY OF PEACE

Cornwallis's surrender finally convinced the British government that the effort to subdue the Americans was too difficult and too expensive to continue. Despite considerable advantages in population (11 million to 2.5 million), economic resources, diplomatic alliances, and military experience, Britain suffered from disadvantages in pursuing the war. Its problems included maintaining communications with, and providing supplies to fighting forces who were 3,000 miles away; it took some two to three months to send messages or to convey arms and men to the colonies. Able to raise only one-third of its troops in Great Britain, the crown relied heavily on German mercenaries and American Tories, in roughly equal numbers. These British troops, though often skilled in formalized European-style warfare, were ill-prepared to fight in a remote and savage wilderness without major industrial or population centers and without adequate roads. (As in later wars of colonial liberation, the imperial power found it easier to control the towns than the countryside.) Although the British navy — the world's largest — controlled the seas until 1781, and the well-trained Redcoats usually defeated American armies when they could catch them, these advantages brought little ultimate success. The country was too vast, the population too deeply committed to resistance, the indigenous guerrilla forces too elusive, and the costs too great to be borne indefinitely. In the end, a once-confident and often blundering Britain was outlasted by militarily weaker, but more resourceful and determined colonial forces.

Following the debacle at Yorktown, Lord North resigned his ministry, and a new ministry came to power prepared to negotiate with the Americans. Although John Adams, Benjamin Franklin, and John Jay were already in Europe for such purposes, a peace settlement was delayed for some time by the crosscurrents of international politics. The Franco-American alliance committed each party to continue fighting as long as the other was fighting, and the Franco-Spanish alliance committed France to continuing the war until Spain won Gibraltar from England. This seemed to mean that the

Americans could not make peace with England until Spain regained Gibraltar. But when the American commissioners uncovered evidence that the French were arranging that the Spanish and British control the northern and southern portions of the American land between the Allegheny Mountains and the Mississippi, the Americans felt absolved of their obligation to negotiate in concert with the French.

Seeing an opportunity to detach the Americans from French influence, the British accepted an American proposal for separate Anglo-American negotiations. By thus playing off one power against the other, the American commissioners won an exceedingly favorable treaty. Besides recognizing the independence of the United States, the British also acquiesced in giving up a generous extent of territory, stretching from the Atlantic to the Mississippi and from the Canadian border on the north to the Florida border on the south. These terms were agreed upon by late 1782, but peace did not come officially until Spain and France ended hostilities in early 1783. In this general settlement, Florida was transferred from Britain to Spain to compensate for Spain's failure to win Gibraltar.

FOR FURTHER READING

Gordon S. Wood's *The Radicalism of the American Revolution* (1992), Edward Countryman's *The American Revolution* (1985), and Robert Middlekauff's *The Glorious Cause* (1982) are the best overviews of the American Revolution, but John R. Alden's older *A History of the American Revolution* (1954) is still useful. A good general military history of the war is Marshall Smelser's *The Winning of Independence* (1972). Don Higginbotham, *The War of American Independence* (1971), and John Shy, *A People Numerous and Armed* (1976), analyze the unconventional character of the armed conflict; and R. Arthur Bowler examines *Logistics and the Failure of the British Army in America* (1975). Also excellent for military and naval history are two biographies: Don Higginbotham, *George Washington and the American Military Tradition* (1985), and Samuel Eliot Morison, *John Paul Jones: A Sailor's Biography* (1959). Diplomatic histories of the period include William C. Stinchcombe's *The American Revolution and the French Alliance* (1969), Lawrence S. Kaplan's *Colonies into Nation* (1972), and Reginald Horsman's *The Diplomacy of the New Republic* (1985). James Henderson's *Party Politics in the Continental Congress* (1975) closely examines congressional politics during a crucial period. For the political thought that influenced the development of new political institutions during the revolutionary years, see Morton White's *The Philosophy of the American Revolution* (1978) and Carl L. Becker's *The Declaration of Independence* (1922). Studies of loyalists in the American Revolution include: Robert S. Lambert's *South Carolina Loyalists in the American Revolution* (1987), Philip Ranlet's *The New York Loyalists* (1986), and Robert M. Calhoons's *Loyalists in Revolutionary America, 1760–1781* (1973). Peter S. Onuf in *The Origins of the Federal Republic* (1983) describes the conflicts surrounding the formation of the new state governments; Jackson T. Main analyzes *The Upper House in Revolutionary America* (1967); and Merrill Jensen offers a controversial analysis of the drafting of *The Articles of Confederation* (1940). Important contributions to an understanding of the republican ideology of the Revolution include Bernard Bailyn's *The Ideological Origins of the American Revolution* (1967), J. G. A. Pocock's *The Machiavellian Moment* (1975), and Gordon S. Wood's *The Creation of the American Republic* (1969). The social effects of the war are explored in J. Franklin Jameson's pioneer study *The American Revolution Considered as a Social Movement* (1926) and in James K. Martin's *In the Course of Human Events* (1979). The black experience during the Revolution is covered in Sylvia R. Frey, *Water from the Rock* (1991), and Benjamin Quarles, *The Negro in the American Revolution* (1961). David Brion Davis's *The Problem of Slavery in the Age of Revolution* (1975) is a landmark study that explores the context for an emerging abolitionism. Mary Beth Norton in *Liberty's Daughters* (1980) and Linda K. Kerber in *Women of the Republic* (1980) offer differing perspectives on the impact of the developing republican ideology on women's rights.

6

★ ★ ★ ★ ★ ★

A Nation Emerges, 1780–1788

THE NEW NATION brought into being by the Revolution covered a thinly populated but vast expanse of territory six times the area of England and Wales combined. Ninety-five percent of its 3 million people lived in the countryside. Most of them were near the seacoast, but even here they were so dispersed that there were only six cities with more than 8,000 inhabitants. Philadelphia, with fewer than 40,000, was largest, followed by New York, Boston, Charleston, Baltimore, and Salem. (By contrast, contemporary London had 750,000 people, and Paris, 500,000.) Transportation facilities from one part of this far-flung republican empire to another were rudimentary, and communication was so infrequent that the letters carried by the postal service amounted to only one per capita per year.

Nevertheless, the shared experience of the Revolution had given Americans a sense of national pride and optimism about the future of their experiment in liberty. But because not all Americans agreed about what that future should be, the decade of the 1780s was one of conflict. It was also, as time would prove, the richest and most intense period of American political and constitutional thought.

THE AGRARIAN-MINDED AND THE COMMERCIAL-MINDED

One fundamental division was between what might be called the *agrarian-minded* and the *commercial-minded* portions of the population. The great majority of the people were small farmers. Measured against the Europe that they or their peasant forebears had left behind — the Europe of arbitrary government, heavy taxes, military conscription, state churches, and rigid social distinctions — America seemed a virtual paradise. In America, the dream of land ownership — the key to security, independence, and dignity — could be realized by the great majority.

To these small landowners, secure on their acres, far from cities, often illiterate or semiliterate, the American utopia w\s already at hand. Provincial and typically adhering to the more orthodox brands of Protestantism, they regarded the farmer's way of life as morally superior to all others. They were deeply suspicious of cities, of change, and of those ambitious and probably evil urban people who grew rich by commercial manipulations. This agrarian mystique was also shared in good part by many southern planters and by many of the great landlord families in New York's Hudson Valley.

Less numerous but equally influential were the people who saw America's future in terms of general economic growth and national strength. This commercial-mindedness was centered in the cities and especially among the merchant and professional classes, the best educated and most cosmopolitan parts of the population. Included also were a good many farmers and planters who lived close enough to transportation and cities to produce commercial crops for foreign and domestic markets.

The division between the commercial-minded and the agrarian-minded merged into the other major political division of the 1780s: there was a tendency for the agrarian-minded to be democratic-minded and for the commercial-minded to resist democratic tendencies. However, the two alignments did not coincide completely. Thomas Paine, for example, was among the most effective advocates of both democracy and commercial expansion, while much of the leadership for the agrarian forces was provided by elitist gentry from the great landholding families.

With some important exceptions, then, the political struggles of the 1780s involved two rough groupings. On one side were those who favored leadership by the gentry, vigorous and more centralized government, and policies designed to foster national strength and economic growth through encouragement to entrepreneurs. On the other side were persons resentful of any pretensions to superiority, deeply suspicious of all government, and mistrustful of even their own elected representatives. They consequently wanted government kept as decentralized as possible, as inactive and inexpensive as possible, and subject to the check of frequent and democratic elections.

CONFLICT WITHIN THE STATES

The state governments were the principal arenas of conflict between the two groups. The conflict was in part a straight struggle for control, as in Pennsylvania where displaced conservatives warred unrelentingly against the ultrademocratic constitution of 1776 and the power it gave to western farmers and the lower orders of Philadelphia.

Religion was frequently another divisive issue. In New England (outside Rhode Island where religious freedom had always prevailed), the Congregationalists were persuaded to surrender only part of the exclusive privileges they had enjoyed by law before the Revolution. But in New York and the southern states, the members of the formerly established Anglican church were reduced to an equal footing with those other denominations. In Virginia, the Anglicans of the wealthy and conservative tidewater area managed to stave off this movement until 1786 when James Madison's coalition of liberal gentry, back-country Baptists, Methodists, and Presbyterians pushed through the legislature Jefferson's Statute for Religious Freedom.

The greatest cause of alarm to conservatives was the democratic legislatures' apparent disregard for property rights. In some states, property-minded persons fought against wholesale confiscations of the property of Loyalists, and they were even more alarmed by the movement for debtor laws and state-issued paper money.

Paper money had been used during the colonial period with both good and bad results, but the collapse of the Continental currency during the Revolution had utterly discredited the whole idea with merchants and creditors. Yet the return to a specie (gold and silver) currency at the end of the Revolution, the collapse of the brief boom that followed, and the ensuing depression of 1785–1786 produced a severe deflation. People who had borrowed money during inflationary times found that they had to repay their debts in money that was worth much more than the money originally borrowed and at a time when money of any kind was hard to obtain.

Under the pressure of desperate debtors, seven state legislatures authorized issues of paper money, while in several other states, creditors and merchants barely averted such demands. The paper issues were relatively beneficial where taxes were levied to support them, but in other instances, the old story of rapid depreciation was repeated. Some states tried to compel creditors to accept the paper money in payment of debts, and creditors were said to flee the state of Rhode Island to avoid payment in depreciated paper.

The conflict became most violent in Massachusetts, where debtors and small farmers of the interior simply could not find enough of the scarce specie to pay their debts and heavy state taxes. As the courts began imprisoning large numbers of defaulting debtors or foreclosing on their farms, armed mobs started breaking up sessions of the courts. By the winter of 1786–1787, the interior was swarming with a virtual insurrectionary militia of several thousand debt-ridden farmers whose principal leader was a Revolutionary veteran named Daniel Shays. Finally, a state army of 4,000 marched into the area and quelled the disorders after a series of minor skirmishes. Meanwhile, accounts of "Shays's Rebellion" had further alarmed property-minded conservatives in all the states, convincing many of the need for revising the Articles.

PROBLEMS OF THE CONFEDERATION

In the early 1780s, conservatives were already seeking to guard against the localism and democratic irresponsibility of the states by strengthening the Confederation government. Under the leadership of the "financier of the Revolution," Robert Morris, a Philadelphia merchant who had grown wealthy from war contracts, they had persuaded Congress to appoint full-time executives to superintend departments of finance, war, foreign affairs, and marine. Morris himself became superintendent of finance and exercised great influence in all areas. His primary concerns were economic stability and the attachment of monied interests to the central government. Toward those ends, Continental paper money was abandoned, and Morris sought to finance the government by borrowing, partly from American citizens. In the process, he encouraged the creation of a powerful class of public creditors (bond buyers) who had a vested interest in a government that would be strong enough to pay its debts.

But the Confederation government could neither pay its debts nor effectively carry on its ordinary operations as long as it had to depend for income on voluntary contributions by the recalcitrant states. Morris's whole program hinged on getting the states to approve the "Impost of 1781," a proposed amendment of the Articles of Confederation that would give Congress the power to levy limited import duties to pay the Confederation debt. But Rhode Island refused to ratify, and all further efforts to give Congress any taxing power failed to get the required unanimous approval of the states. Meanwhile, the coming of peace dissipated the atmosphere of emergency, and the drive to add vigor to the Confederation government stalled.

Through the mid-1780s, national-minded persons could only grumble helplessly at the impotence of the Confederation in many areas. Lacking any means of enforcing its policies either on the states or directly on their citizens, the Confederation was unable to deal effectively with unseemly quarrels among various states over boundaries, western lands, and state-levied tariffs and trade restrictions.

The Confederation's weakness was most evident in foreign relations. Partly because the United States could not enforce uniform commercial regulations in its own territory or threaten uniform retaliatory regulations against other countries, it was unable to secure favorable commercial treaties with the leading European powers. More serious, Spain and Great Britain threatened the territorial integrity of the new nation in the Southwest and Northwest respectively.

Spain had lost Florida to Great Britain at the end of the Seven Years' War in 1763 but had gained formerly French Louisiana (the entire western watershed of the Mississippi and the "island" of New Orleans east of the river). Then, in 1783, Spain regained Florida, making her the dominant power on the southwestern borders of the United States. Moreover, Spain would not be bound by the 31° northern boundary of Florida specified by the Anglo-American treaty, but occupied territory north of that line and claimed the greater part of the Southwest. These claims she actively buttressed in the 1780s by gaining control over the southwestern Indians and restricting the Mississippi River trade through New Orleans. When the Confederation proved powerless to protect new settlements in the Tennessee-Kentucky area against the Indians or to secure them a right to trade down the Mississippi, many settlements sought the protection of Spain, and for a time there was a serious danger that the western settlers would cooperate in making the entire Southwest a Spanish territory.

Great Britain understandably treated her former subjects with great contempt, closing her West Indian possessions to American trade, restricting American trade with England, and refusing to enter negotiations for a commercial treaty or even to send a minister to the new nation. Most threatening of all, she continued to occupy military posts along the northern frontier within territory she had ceded to the United States, and from these posts she retained dominion over the Indians of the northern Ohio Valley and encouraged them to resist the advance of American settlement.

The British found justification for these actions in the failure of the American states to live up to their obligations under the Treaty of Paris. Congress technically complied with the treaty by urging the states to restore confiscated property to Loyalists, but it could not force the states to do so. Nor could it prevent the states from violating the treaty by impeding the collection of debts that Americans owed to British merchants. The Confederation authorities could counter British complaints on these points only by demanding payment for several thousand slaves that the British armies had carried away from the southern states.

THE CONFEDERATION AND THE WEST

For all its weaknesses, the Confederation had one magnificent achievement to its credit: the creation of a great national domain west of the Appalachian Mountains and the formulation of a system for land sales and territorial government by which this West and later Wests would become a spectacularly expanding "empire for liberty."

Even before the Revolution, pioneers had crossed the mountains to form pockets of settlement in a few areas. New Englanders had moved up and across the Connecticut River to populate the green hills of Vermont. Resisting the claims of New York and New Hampshire to the area during the Revolution, Ethan Allen and his "Green Mountain Boys" created an independent republic that was not admitted as one of the United States until 1791.

Farther south, other pioneers had established themselves on the upper waters of the Ohio River in the Wheeling-Pittsburgh area, and still others had pushed southwestward through the valleys of the Virginia mountains to found the Watauga settlement on the headwaters of the Tennessee River in what was to become the northeastern corner of Tennessee. During and immediately after the Revolution, these outposts became staging areas for further advances of settlement into the country north of the Ohio, through Cumberland Gap into the Bluegrass region of what would later be central Kentucky, and over the Cumberland Plateau into the Nashville basin of what would later be middle Tennessee.

Seven states laid claim to various parts of the trans-Appalachian empire. Virginia, making the most of the vague boundaries specified by its colonial charter, claimed Kentucky and all the territory north of the Ohio River. New York had a shadowy claim to the Ohio Valley resting on Indian treaties, while

Massachusetts and Connecticut argued that their boundaries extended indefinitely westward, cutting across the Virginia claim. Farther south the two Carolinas and Georgia asserted that their boundaries extended all the way to the Mississippi.

Even before the war was over, under heavy pressure from landless states, Congress had urged that these western claims be ceded to the Confederation to create a great common domain. Virginia led the way in 1781 by offering its lands north of the Ohio, and by the end of the 1780s all except one of the landed states had followed suit. Georgia finally ceded its western lands in 1802, while, in 1792, Virginia passed the sovereignty over its remaining western territory directly to the new state of Kentucky that was created from it.

Congress lost no time in providing for land sales and a governmental system in the new public domain. The Ordinance of 1785 established a "rectangular" system of survey. Land was to be divided into squares one mile from north to south and one mile from east to west. "Townships" six miles square were to be laid off, each of which would contain 36 one-mile-square (640-acre) "sections." As the line of settlement advanced, these sections were to be auctioned off to the highest bidders, with a minimum price of two dollars an acre.

A year earlier, in the Ordinance of 1784 (drafted by Thomas Jefferson), Congress had declared that territorial governments in the public domain should evolve as quickly as possible into new states fully equal to the original states. The process by which this was to happen was altered by the so-called Northwest Ordinance of 1787, adopted to meet the wishes of the Ohio Company, a group of New England land speculators who were promoting a settlement in the Muskingum Valley of what was to become southeastern Ohio. The Ordinance of 1787 established a Northwest Territory in the area north of the Ohio and east of the Mississippi rivers; this area was to be administered first by a governor appointed by Congress. When the population of the territory reached 5,000, the people were to elect a representative assembly and a nonvoting delegate to Congress. Eventually the Old Northwest was to be divided into not less than three and not more than five states, and when the population of any of these proposed states reached 60,000, it could be admitted to the union on an equal footing with the original states. During the territorial stage, civil liberties and religious freedom were guaranteed, a system of free public education was called for, and slavery was excluded. Thus Congress laid down the pattern of territorial evolution by which the United States was to become a continental nation of equal states.

THE MOVEMENT FOR A STRONGER GOVERNMENT

Many Americans — particularly subsistence farmers — were generally satisfied with the Confederation. Indeed, it often functioned reasonably well. But, amid a growing awareness that the Articles could not meet important national needs, others grew more impatient with its weakness and more determined to secure a strong national government in its place. The unpaid public creditors constituted a standing lobby for change. Merchants wanted a uniform commercial policy that could force concessions from the great trading nations. The artisan class and infant industrial sector wanted a uniform tariff policy that would protect them from the competition of British manufactures. The elite of many states dreaded the possibility of irresponsible popular control of state politics. Creditors and wealthy persons cried out for protection against debtor legislation, paper money, and the assaults of the unpropertied on property. Frontier people demanded more vigorous defense against the Indians and their British and Spanish abettors. And the more cosmopolitan and national-minded patriots wanted their country to assume a position of greater strength and dignity among the nations of the world. Quite obviously the reasons for the discontent were nearly as numerous as the people who advocated a stronger government. The pressures for revising the Articles could be traced as much to dissatisfaction with state government as to deficiencies in the Confederation. But overriding all considerations was a pervasive fear among the nation's political leaders that the Confederation, as originally constructed, could not adequately protect American interests in a hostile world and that the excesses of the Revolutionary era threatened the interests of authority and stability in the name of popular liberty.

As the 1780s wore on, events pushed some of these national-minded elements into an almost revolutionary mood. Robert Morris's drive to strengthen the Confederation from within had stalled when the urgency of war was removed in 1783; all further attempts to remedy the inadequacy of the Articles by amendment failed. More important, the brief economic boom that followed peace collapsed into a commercial and financial depression in the mid-1780s, and inevitably merchants, financiers, and artisans began to think that their distress was related to the Confederation's weakness. As a result of the depression, the panic of conservatives over paper money and debtor legislation reached its peak. In the autumn of 1786, the conservatives' worst fears of the lower orders and anarchy seemed confirmed by the exaggerated accounts of Shays's Rebellion.

By this time, a concerted movement was under way to bypass the prescribed method for amending the Articles and to create a stronger government through constitutionally questionable means. The movement was initiated by a small group of national-minded people, particularly George Washington and James Madison in Virginia and Alexander Hamilton in New York. Unlike such older revolutionaries as Richard Henry Lee of Virginia and Samuel Adams of Massachusetts, these nationalists were less concerned with popular liberty than with social stability and economic growth, and less alarmed by central authority than by majoritarian tyranny. Washington shared the fears of anarchy held by other members of the upper classes, but his nationalism was more than a class prejudice. His views reflected his position as the pre-eminent personal symbol of American nationality, and he cared deeply about the strength, dignity, and perpetuity of the nation he had done so much to bring to birth.

Hamilton and Madison were younger men. After serving as Washington's aide-de-camp during the Revolution, Hamilton had become a highly successful lawyer in New York, where he had married into one of the leading families and had proved himself a staunch defender of property rights. But Hamilton was not primarily a servant of propertied interests. Instead he was obsessed with the need for vigor and strength in government and sought to ally wealth with government in the interest of strong government rather than of wealth.

Madison was a nationalist on more theoretical grounds. A close friend and correspondent of Jefferson and like him a member of the liberal wing of Virginia's planting gentry, the frail, youthful (36 in 1787), scholarly Madison, had combined the study of ancient and modern governments with a quiet but increasingly influential role in Virginia politics. His nationalism was a matter of intellectual conviction, stimulated by his association with Washington and buttressed by his wide reading and disinterested reflection on political problems. Although, until his death in 1836, he generously and accurately protested that the Constitution was not "the offspring of a single brain" but "the work of many heads and many hands," he, more than any other framer, was the father of that document.

In 1785, on Madison's initiative, a conference of commissioners from Virginia and Maryland met at Mount Vernon and Alexandria to consider improving navigation of the Potomac. Madison and Washington persuaded the commissioners that other states should be brought into the consultation, and the Virginia legislature invited all the states to send delegates to a convention at Annapolis in 1786 to deliberate on "a uniform system in their commercial regulations." When delegates from only five states appeared at Annapolis, Hamilton, a delegate from New York, persuaded the convention to send out a call for another convention in Philadelphia in May 1787, to "devise such further provisions as shall appear . . . necessary as to render the constitution of the federal government adequate to the exigencies of the union."

The call for the Philadelphia convention was grudgingly endorsed by the Confederation Congress with the explicit stipulation that any amendments it proposed must be endorsed by all the states as the Articles required. During the spring, delegates were selected by the legislatures of every state save debtor-dominated Rhode Island. With only a few exceptions, those who were satisfied with the Articles as they stood refused to serve as delegates, thus permitting people who were inclined to a stronger government to represent even those states where they were in a minority. The legislature of Hamilton's New York, dominated by his opponents, permitted him to be a delegate only as a member of a three-man delegation controlled by two staunch opponents of change. More typically, Richard Henry Lee and Patrick Henry, who "smelt a rat," pointedly stayed home, though they were chosen to serve by the Virginia legislature. Also conspicuously absent was the old and ailing Samuel Adams, who would in time reluctantly support the Constitution but preferred a "Federal Union of Sovereign States" to a "National Government." John Adams and Thomas Jefferson, who would both support ratification of the Constitution, were in Europe on diplomatic assignments and could not participate.

THE CONSTITUTIONAL CONVENTION

Except for scattered opponents, the convention was composed of delegates from the national-minded side of the political spectrum. In Hamilton's telling phrase, they were numbered among the Americans "who think continentally." Predominantly lawyers, merchants, and planters, the 55 male delegates were drawn principally from urban and seaboard areas and from the upper classes; no women were selected to serve as delegates. These men made an impressive showing of youth, education, ability, political experience, and wealth. Due to the circumstances of their selection, the crucial decision facing the convention — whether the government should continue as a decentralized confederated government with some additional powers to raise revenue and regulate commerce, or whether it should become a stronger, more centralized national government directly affecting the states and their citizens — was settled before the delegates met.

Had this not been the case, Madison could never have scored such a resounding victory for a national plan at the very outset of the convention. The Virginia delegation arrived in Philadelphia some days before the convention opened, and Madison had his fellow Virginians hard at work on a "Virginia Plan" that became the basis for the convention's early deliberations. By accepting the Virginia Plan as its basis for deliberation, the convention made the momentous decision that it would propose not simply amendments to the Articles but an entirely new frame of government. It also indicated that it favored a government radically different from the Confederation.

The two principal features of the Virginia Plan were its grant of sweeping powers to the central government and its requirement that representation in the national legislative body be in proportion to population. It was the second feature that raised the only fundamental disagreement in the convention's proceedings, for delegates from the small states rightly feared that basing representation on population would allow the large states to control the new government. Consequently the small-state delegates presented a "New Jersey Plan" to amend the Articles rather than to draft an entirely new constitution. The heart of the New Jersey Plan was the continuance of a one-house Congress in which each state would have one vote. By adhering to the form of the Articles, the small-state delegates were also proposing a confederated government of limited powers, though their plan did give Congress the power to levy import duties, regulate commerce, and admit new states. Yet it was the matter of representation rather than the question of nationalism that was at the bottom of the disagreement, and a compromise was finally effected by proposing a two-house Congress where representation in the lower house was apportioned by population and where the influence of the small states was safeguarded in an upper house composed of two senators from each state. Once the small states won this concession, their delegates showed less zeal in defending a confederated structure. From this point on, the convention was able to work out the detailed powers and structure of the new government without serious disagreement.

Though the delegates were predominantly nationalists and though many of them feared the influence of popular majorities, they were also political realists who recognized that whatever they proposed would have to be accepted by a society that was considerably more confederationist and democratic than the convention itself. Consequently, and to Hamilton's discomfort, the document that resulted from their deliberations was a compromise between the two poles of political thought. Its basic feature was the creation of a "federal" system in which powers and responsibilities were distributed between the state and national governments. While the powers given Congress were specified with the implication that only these powers could be exercised, the specified powers were quite ample. The new government was to have virtually unlimited authority to levy taxes, borrow money, regulate domestic and foreign commerce, conduct foreign relations, and maintain an army and navy. Moreover, the states were specifically forbidden to engage in diplomatic negotiations, maintain armies, or — closing the door on debtor legislation and paper money — "emit Bills of Credit, make any Thing but gold and silver Coin a Tender in Payment of Debts; pass any . . . Law impairing the Obligation of Contracts. . . ." Finally and most important, the new national government was to operate directly upon the citizens rather than upon the states, and the proposed national constitution and laws and treaties made in pursuance of it were declared to be "the supreme Law of the Land."

Following the eighteenth-century doctrine of separation of powers and fearful of a concentration of power anywhere in government, the convention was at pains to create, in addition to Congress, a strong and independent executive and judiciary so that the three branches would act as checks and balances on each other. The vesting of the executive function in a single and relatively strong president, independent of the legislative branch and eligible for re-election, was a remarkable departure from existing practices in the states and the Confederation. The president was given a veto over congressional legislation (unless repassed by two-thirds of both houses); he was to appoint judges and other officers (with consent of the Senate); he was given primary responsibility for foreign relations and the making of treaties (with the advice and consent of two-thirds of the Senate); and he was to be commander in chief of the armed forces.

The convention spent much of its time working out the methods for choosing the personnel of the legislative, executive, and judicial branches. Nearly all the delegates recognized that popular majorities must have a voice somewhere in the governmental structure they were planning, but they were equally anxious to erect ample safeguards against the workings of popular passions and temporary enthusiasms. Popular majorities were allowed direct sway in the House of Representatives, whose members were to be elected every two years by those who were qualified to vote for the popular branches of the legislatures in the respective states. But laws passed by the House of Representatives also had to be approved by the Senate, and the senators were to be chosen for six-year terms by the state legislatures. Even after passage by both houses of Congress, laws still needed the approval of the president, and the convention worked long and hard before devising a method of selecting the president that would leave him independent of state legislatures, Congress, and popular majorities. The result was that famous invention, the electoral college. Each state was to appoint, as its legislature directed, as many electors as it had members of Congress, and the electors were then to elect a president who was to serve for four years. Finally, the members of the judiciary were to be appointed by the president for life.

The system as a whole seemed admirably contrived to frustrate direct popular control of all branches of the government at any one time and to ensure that the various branches would pull in such different directions as to hobble effective government. The convention did not foresee that the rise of political parties would quickly subvert its intentions in both respects, and indeed the government under the Constitution would probably have proved unworkable if it had operated exactly as its architects intended that it should.

RATIFICATION

In September 1787, nearly four months after it convened, the convention lifted the veil of secrecy with which it had covered its debates and presented its handiwork to the country. Only then did people outside the convention discover that the delegates had vastly exceeded their authority. Not only had they drafted a substantially new framework for government, instead of a revision of the existing Articles, but they provided for its ratification by only 9 of the 13 states.

The work of a relatively small but vigorous and talented group of continental-minded leaders who called themselves "Federalists" (rather than the more straightforward "Nationalists"), the Constitution won quick and decisive ratifications in the small states of Delaware, New Jersey, and Connecticut, whose powerful neighboring states had taken advantage of them under the Confederation, and in the small and exposed frontier state of Georgia. Two states, Rhode Island and North Carolina, were so well satisfied with the virtually independent course they had been pursuing that they refused even to consider ratification until after the new government was in full operation.

The crucial struggles occurred in the great states of Pennsylvania, Massachusetts, Virginia, and New York, which had been able to take care of themselves under the confederated system. Anti-Federalist delegates were probably in a majority when the ratifying conventions of several of these states opened — certainly overwhelmingly so in New York — but ratification finally carried in all of them. Rhode Island, the last to approve, did so in 1790. Federalist superiority in initiative, organization, and debate counted heavily in these close contests as did the strategy of agreeing to recommend whatever amendments the Anti-Federalist delegates wished to propose. Most of all, the Federalists had the advantage of a concrete proposal. Their opponents were forced, as one conceded, to ratify "this or nothing." Nor were Federalists opposed to unscrupulous tactics: in New York, Governor John Hancock was cynically won over by the implied promise of high national office; in Pennsylvania, Anti-Federalist legislators were physically dragged to their seats in a quorum-shy Assembly so that a ratification convention could be called. Thus not only was the Constitution adopted by extraconstitutional means, without the test of a mass plebiscite or even of Congressional ratification, but the Federalists' tactical advantages may well have given them victory over a potentially opposed but ineffectively organized majority in the country.

Allowing for the multitude of particular interests affecting people's attitudes toward the Constitution, there seems to have been a general pattern of division. The urban and seaboard areas were almost solidly in favor of the document, not just because particular interests were stronger here, but because in these wealthier, more commercial, more cosmopolitan areas, general commercial and elitist concerns were more prevalent. Conversely, the Constitution tended to be strongly opposed in the more provincial back-country areas of small farms because of the greater prevalence of agrarian and democratic concerns. The numerically predominant small farmers, who comprised the backbone of Anti-Federalism during the ratification controversy, saw little need for stronger government.

The Federalist leaders tended to be the younger generation of nationalists — the John Jays, Alexander Hamiltons, James Madisons — who served their political apprenticeships with the emergent republican institutions of the independence movement and grew up with the Revolution. Many of their prominent critics, on the other hand, were the "old Revolutionaries" — the Richard Henry Lees, Patrick Henrys, Mercy Warrens — who came of political age combatting crown and Parliament and who often equated government with tyranny. There were exceptions, of course: Benjamin Franklin, 81 in 1787, was a strong supporter of the Constitution; Washington, the convention president, was 55. Certainly, the sides were not neatly drawn by generations. Yet among the leaders of the debate, age, or at least experience, was apparently a factor.

Until fairly recently, the Anti-Federalists were often described as small-minded, provincial obstructionists who in their petty, self-interested particularism lacked the continental vision of the Federalists. Recent scholarship, however, suggests that for all their political weakness and disunity, the Anti-Federalists should not be so easily dismissed. To be sure the Anti-Federalists were very often more state-centered, less cosmopolitan, and less educated than their opponents, and they were usually more suffused with the traditions of localism. Yet because they chose to align themselves against some of the nation's most formidable and revered political thinkers — the Founding Fathers: Washington, Franklin, Madison, Hamilton, Marshall, and Jay — it does not follow that they were "men of little faith," that they lacked virtue, or that their arguments were not well-founded.

Despite the centralizing pressures of the 1770s and 1780s, fears of concentrated governmental authority and loss of individual liberty remained central to popular American thought. It was in this tradition, then, that the Anti-Federalists opposed the Constitution. They were traditionalists, the conservators of a national heritage and were truer than the Federalists to the "wisdom of '76." Often their leaders, the old patriots, had been more committed to the struggle for independence than their Federalist opponents. In their fear of tyranny from centralized authority, in their fidelity to localism, in their belief that republicanism could survive only in a small and homogeneous society, the Anti-Federalists had their roots firmly planted in revolutionary assumptions. Some of them recognized the need for some revision of the Articles, but the Constitution, as they understood it, represented a profound departure. Patrick Henry, their principal spokesman, thought it "horribly frightful," "incompatible with the genius of republicanism," and "a revolution as radical as that which separated us from Great Britain." Richard Henry Lee believed that it turned back the clock, once again placing "Civil Liberty . . . at the mercy of Rulers." Yet if the Constitution did not "squint toward monarchy," it did create a strong executive office whose powers would, from time to time, be abused. Compared to some European nations, the regime crafted by the Constitution's framers was relatively decentralized. Yet in the context of the American experience, the Constitution represented, as the Anti-Federalists believed, a leap toward national consolidation and a radical erosion of state power.

Finally, it should be noted that the agrarian- and democratic-minded majority might have defeated the Constitution had it been effectively mobilized. The fact that the majority did not mobilize suggests that the opposition was not terribly intense. Politics beyond the local and state level was still a matter of indifference to most farmers. Only a small proportion of the eligible voters bothered to vote at all for delegates to the ratifying conventions, and when the Constitution went into effect, it was readily accepted by all elements of the population. Within little more than a decade, under a Constitution whose operations had been transformed by political parties that the framers did not envisage, the hitherto apathetic agrarian- and democratic-minded majority would come into its own.

CONFLICTING HISTORICAL VIEWPOINTS: NO. 2

How Democratic Was the Constitution?

American exceptionalism has been one of the basic presuppositions of our national experience. America was a land peculiarly blessed; its people were God's chosen people, the embodiment of the promise of human perfection.

In the words of John Adams, the nation's founding marked "the opening of a grand scheme and design in Providence for the illumination and emancipation of the slavish part of mankind all over the earth." More particularly, the Constitution was an instrument of heaven's will; its framers, Jefferson said, were themselves "demi-gods." Early students of American history were in full agreement. In fact, no article of American faith was more sacred to nineteenth-century nationalist historians than the document of 1787. In his History of the Formation of the Constitution *(2 vols., 1882), pious, patriotic George Bancroft concluded that the nation's fundamental law fulfilled the promise of the Revolution. It was inspired by the scriptures, he believed, and drafted with providential blessings. Much the same conclusion was reached by John Fiske, who portrayed the document as one of the supreme achievements of human intelligence. In full agreement with Bancroft, his older contemporary, Fiske viewed the Articles of Confederation as an unfit instrument for national government. In his* The Critical Period of American History *(1893), he described the half-dozen years following the Revolutionary War as "the most critical moment in all of the history of the American people." The period of national crisis passed, he believed, only upon the creation of a strong central government. To both Bancroft and Fiske, the Founding Fathers were men of noble purpose and unquestioned devotion to the national welfare.*

A later generation of scholars was more critical of both the Constitution and its framers. In his path-breaking study An Economic Interpretation of the Constitution *(1913), the progressive historian Charles Beard offered the then shocking argument that the Founding Fathers were not selfless patriots but self-serving plutocrats: "men whose property interests were immediately at stake." The product of their labor represented not the culmination of the democratic revolutionary spirit of 1776 but a counterrevolution. Thus, through the instrument of the Constitution, Beard averred, a few conservative men of property effected a coup d'état to protect their economic self-interest and check the growth of popular democracy. Samuel Adams and Patrick Henry could not have said it better!*

Although Beard confessed that his work was fragmentary and his conclusions tentative, his neo-Anti-Federalist interpretation won prompt and almost universal acceptance. Among the many latter-day Beardians, none did more to fill out and document the Columbia University scholar's interpretation than Merrill Jensen. In The Articles of Confederation *(1940) and* The New Nation *(1950), Jensen carefully supported Beard's contention that the Confederation government was not one of "stagnation, ineptitude, bankruptcy, corruption, and disintegration." In his view, the democratic radicalism that waxed with the Declaration of Independence waned with the Constitution. The framers engineered a "conservative counterrevolution" that served to "thwart the will of 'the people.'"*

More recently, Beard's critics have all but discredited his economic interpretations. Robert E. Brown (Charles A. Beard and the Constitution, *1955) and Forrest McDonald* (We the People, *1958), for example, have questioned Beard's use of the evidence and nearly all of his conclusions.*

Neither scholar accepted his class-conflict theories, and Brown argued cogently that the Constitution was an essentially middle-class democratic document ideally suited for essentially middle-class democratic America. Other scholars have offered different conclusions, and both Jackson Turner Main (The Antifederalists, *1961) and Lee Benson* (Turner and Beard, *1960) have found elements of Beardian conflict in the alignment of mercantile capitalists versus agrarians during the period of struggle over the Constitution. Yet most historians of the present generation (Main and Benson included) agree that Beard's thesis is seriously deficient. As the intellectual historian Gordon Wood writes in his important* The Creation of the American Republic *(1969), the notion that the ideas and behavior of the founders were determined by material consideration is "so crude that no further time should be spent on it." Wood does not reject the progressive view of the Constitution as an intrinsically aristocratic document designed to curb the democratic excesses of the Revolution. But he does suggest that the struggle between Federalist and Anti-Federalist was actually a struggle over what kind of democracy America would have — an elitist, nationally oriented democracy or a popular, locally based democracy.*

The founders, then, may not have been Jefferson's demigods nor Bancroft's agents of providential will, but modern scholars find little merit in the Anti-Federalist charge that they were "avaricious adventurers" and partisans of aristocracy. Rather, recent historians agree that the product of their labors was basically democratic and that they themselves were people of great stature and vision whose devotion to nation transcended pocketbook concerns. It should be noted, however, that democracy in this context did not apply to blacks, the "slavish part" of John Adams's own nation, or to women. The creative energies of the framers were lavished on the foundation of a republic for white males, not on extending the benefits of liberty to blacks or women. A half-century after ratification, when the abolitionist William Lloyd Garrison proposed to burn the Constitution in the name of liberty, he did so on the unassailable ground that it perpetuated slavery. Although later generations of Americans celebrated the framers' work as a charter for political freedom, it should not be forgotten that in 1787 it was not such a charter for blacks, women, or native Americans.

FOR FURTHER READING

An excellent starting point for any study of the political and constitutional significance of the American Revolution is R. R. Palmer's *The Age of the Democratic Revolution* (2 vols., 1959–1964). Jack N. Rakove, *The Beginnings of National Politics* (1979) examines the Continental Congress, and David P. Szatmary offers a fresh interpretation of *Shays' Rebellion* (1980). The classic interpretation of the Constitution itself is found, of course, in *The Federalist* (many editions), essays by Hamilton, Madison, and Jay. But several modern-day studies — Clinton Rossiter, *1787: The Grand Convention* (1966); Calvin C. Jillson, *Constitution Making* (1988); and Forrest Mc-

Donald, *Novus Ordo Seclorum: The Intellectual Origins of the Constitution* (1985) — may prove more useful to the student. The second and third volumes of Irving Brant's biography of *James Madison* (6 vols., 1941–1961) give an excellent detailed view of both the Confederation period and the constitutional convention; Robert J. Morgan also provides a valuable look at *James Madison on the Constitution and the Bill of Rights* (1988). Robert Allen Rutland traces *The Birth of the Bill of Rights* (1983), and in *The Ordeal of the Constitution* (1966) explains the battle over ratification. Michael J. Lacey and Knud Haakonssen have collected essays that examine the Bill of Rights from a variety of perspectives in *A Culture of Rights* (1991). David Brion Davis's *The Problem of Slavery in an Age of Revolution* (1975) and Staughton Lynd's *Class Conflict, Slavery and the United States Constitution* (1968) offer differing perspectives on a common problem. Both E. James Ferguson in *The Power of the Purse* (1961) and Forrest McDonald in *E Pluribus Unum* (1965) develop the financial dimensions of union.

TABLE 2. PRESIDENTIAL ELECTIONS AND MAJOR POLITICAL EVENTS, 1789–1800

1789	**George Washington** elected without opposition.
1790–1791	Hamiltonian program enacted.
	Funding the national debt.
	Assumption of state debts. Bargain involving location of the national capital.
	First Bank of the United States.
	Excise taxes.
1792	**George Washington** reelected without opposition.
1793	Wars of the French Revolution begin.
	Washington's Neutrality Proclamation.
1794	Whiskey Rebellion.
1795	Jay's Treaty with Great Britain.
1796	Pinckney's Treaty with Spain.
	John Adams (Federalist) elected over Thomas Jefferson (Republican).
1797–1798	American commissioners to France insulted.
1798	Undeclared naval war with France begins.
	Alien and Sedition Acts.
1798–1799	Virginia and Kentucky Resolutions.
1800	Convention of 1800 resolves differences with France.
	Thomas Jefferson (Republican) elected over John Adams (Federalist).

7

★ ★ ★ ★ ★ ★

Federalists and Republicans, 1789–1800

THE NEW Constitution as written and ratified was merely a grand outline of government. An actual government was created only as the Constitution was put into practice, through adaptation and conflict, in the 1790s. During this stormy decade there were three major developments that lastingly affected the nature of the federal government. First, precedents were set with regard to the composition and functioning of the various branches of government. Second, the real and potential scope and authority of the new government were enormously broadened by Alexander Hamilton's vigorous program of exercising to the limit every power granted or even implied by the Constitution. Finally and most important, Hamilton's policies provoked a growing opposition around which a political party formed. By the decade's end a two-party system was well established, and it profoundly influenced how the new government operated.

LAUNCHING THE NEW GOVERNMENT

It was only natural that friends of the Constitution should be chosen to put it into effect. To no one's surprise, the first electoral college agreed unanimously on Virginia's George Washington for president. To provide geographical balance while avoiding the suspect Samuel Adams and John Hancock, the electors turned for vice-president to that sturdy patriot and nationalist, Massachusetts's John Adams. When the first Congress tardily assembled in New York's City Hall in April 1789, both houses were dominated by Federalists.

While the senators squabbled behind closed doors about titles and ceremonial procedures, James Madison was pushing through the House of Representatives a series of laws that would put the new government into practical operation. Income was provided by a tariff act levying import duties at a moderate rate, designed for revenue purposes only. An organization for the executive branch was provided by the creation of departments of state, treasury, and war. The Judiciary Act of 1789 specified that the Supreme Court should consist of six justices, that there should be a district court for each state, and that two Supreme Court justices sitting with a district judge should constitute an intermediate court of appeals. The act also provided for an attorney general and explicitly specified that any decision in the state courts that questioned federal, as opposed to state, powers could be appealed to the Supreme Court, thus authorizing the Supreme Court to pass on the constitutionality of state laws.

Finally, this first Congress considered the 78 amendments to the Constitution that had been proposed by the state ratifying conventions. Somewhat reluctantly, the House approved 17 of these, the Senate approved 12 of the 17, and by 1791, a sufficient number of states had ratified 10 of the 12. These first 10 amendments, now known as the Bill of Rights, guaranteed citizens that the federal government would not invade such rights as trial by jury and freedom of religion, speech, and the press. All proposed amendments that substantially modified the powers of the federal government had been carefully omitted from the approved list, and disgruntled Anti-Federalists could take only small comfort from the Tenth Amendment, which "reserved to the States respectively, or to the people" all powers not mentioned by the Constitution.

Meanwhile President Washington was enhancing the dignity of the new government through formal and ceremonial behavior that some critics thought too high-toned, perhaps too aristocratic, for a republic. In fact, some wished to address him as "His Elective Majesty" or "His Highness the President"; in the end the more democratic "Mr. President" was adopted. Also, during the first years of his administration, Washington contributed to the popularity of the new regime by taking exhausting tours through all parts of the country. The president influenced the course of events most by his appointments, especially of Alexander Hamilton as secretary of the treasury and Thomas Jefferson as secretary of state, enormously talented figures having antithetical convictions and personalities. Washington consulted with them regularly along with his secretary of war and attorney general, and soon the cabinet, nowhere mentioned in the Constitution, emerged as an important governmental institution.

THE HAMILTONIAN PROGRAM

Alexander Hamilton had no sooner taken office than he became the master spirit of the administration; indeed he thought of himself as Washington's prime minister. This ambitious and controversial man burned with a vision of national greatness. Aiming at a unified nation, he opposed the localistic tendencies of the states. Convinced that vigorous leadership by the able few, especially in the executive branch of the government, was the only way to

The Early Days of the Republic

The site for the permanent capital of the new Republic was chosen in the middle area of the eastern seaboard. The plans for the city were drawn by the engineer Pierre L'Enfant. This engraving of Washington made in 1826 by J. W. Steel shows its undeveloped, rural aspect, with cows grazing in the foreground. *(Library of Congress)*

In a cartoon drawn in the mid-1790s, George Washington gazes down at the Federalist-Republican struggle. He says, "I left you a precious casket of choicest blessings [Peace & Plenty; Liberty & Independence] supported by three pillars — Desist my sons from pulling at them. Should you remove one, you destroy the whole." The man tugging at the Federalism column is saying: "This pillar shall not stand — I am determined to support a just and necessary war." The other man says, pulling at the Democracy support, "This pillar must come down — I am a friend of Peace." *(Library of Congress)*

The Louisiana Purchase from France doubled the land area of the new nation. This depiction of the historic purchase shows James Monroe and Robert Livingstone completing negotiations with Tallyrand, the French foreign minister, on April 30, 1803. *(Library of Congress)*

The optimistic tenor of the Republic's first days appears in this engraving showing an Allegory of America resting her shield to engage in art, education, agriculture, and naval commerce. This is from the title page of *The Universal Asylum and Columbian Magazine for 1790. (Library of Congress)*

American society was not classless. The wealthy and powerful followed European fashions and purchased goods from Europe. This detail from "The Tea Party," a painting by Henry Sargent, shows the dress and gracious living of the well-to-do. *(Courtesy, Museum of Fine Arts, Boston)*

During the early days of the struggle for independence from England, Americans of the Second Continental Congress passed the Articles of Confederation and Perpetual Union Between the States in 1777. Under this document the former colonies became a confederation of sovereign states. *(Library of Congress)*

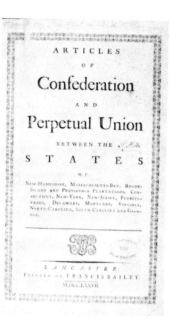

The growth of commerce and trade in the United States contributed to the expansion of the coastal cities. In the pre-mass production days, artisans were often entrepreneurs as well. *Nos. 168–172 Fulton Street, New York, showing the Shop and Warehouse of Duncan Phyfe,* 1816–17, is attributed to John Rubens Smith. From the left, the buildings are the workshop, shop, and warehouse of the famous furniture maker. *(The Metropolitan Museum of Art, Rogers Fund, 1922)*

As the nation grew, more and more people began to celebrate the anniversary of the adoption of the Declaration of Independence on July 4, 1776. In this painting, the 1819 Fourth of July celebrants congregate for the festivities, which at this time included not only fireworks but commemorative sermons. *(Historical Society of Pennsylvania)*

WE OWE ALLEGIANCE TO NO CROWN.

The freedom of the seas and cessation of impressment of American seamen by the British navy became rallying points for the War of 1812. In this painting by John Woodside, a sailor loosed from shackles crushes the crown with his foot. *(American Heritage)* build a powerful nation, he distrusted human nature and feared what he viewed as the turbulence and irresponsibility of the democratic masses. Astutely aware of the relationship between political power and economic power, he was determined to promote the country's rapid economic growth and to forge political and economic ties between the government and the rich and well-born.

Hamilton was far from satisfied with the Constitution as an instrument for national power and economic growth. Yet he recognized that it was the best that could be secured, and he came into office resolved to strengthen it by an expansion of its provisions and by vigorous administration. Seizing from Congress the initiative for public policy, he outlined in a series of four reports a brilliant, tightly integrated program for the achievement of his objectives.

Hamilton first proposed that the long unpaid continental debt, having a face value of over $50 million, he funded at par — that is, that the old and greatly depreciated securities be called in and exchanged for new federal bonds on which interest would be regularly paid and which upon maturity would be redeemed at full value. This would not only dramatically restore American public credit, but would at the same time bolster the private credit of American entrepreneurs and make it easier for them to obtain the European capital needed for a rapidly growing economy. Gilt-edged federal bonds could form the basis for investment capital. Moreover, the whole class of wealthy investors (or speculators) in continental securities would be greatly enriched, for many of them had obtained their securities from the original holders for as little as 20 or 25 cents on the dollar. On all these grounds, funding would have the political effect of attaching the wealthy to the idea of a strong federal government.

Hamilton next proposed that the federal government assume, in similar fashion, over $20 million in unpaid debts incurred by the various states during the Revolution. This would have the advantage of attaching the large class of state creditors to the federal government rather than to the states, thus strengthening the prestige of the former at the expense of the latter.

Funding and assumption of debts required additional revenue, and Hamilton recommended that this be raised by increasing tariff duties and by levying a direct excise tax on spirituous liquors. He frankly advocated the latter tax both as a means of increasing the government's power to collect a tax and of demonstrating that power to the fiercely independent whiskey-making farmers of the interior.

The capstone of Hamilton's financial system was his proposal for a national bank. The bank was to be chartered for 20 years as a mixed public-private corporation controlled by private investors who were to purchase four-fifths of the $10 million worth of capital stock. Investors could pay three-fourths of their stock subscriptions in the form of federal bonds and one-fourth in gold or silver coin (specie). On the basis of this capital the bank was to issue specie-redeemable bank notes for loans to borrowers. The fact that these notes were to be receivable for all dues to the government would tend to keep up their value. Such an institution, Hamilton argued, would provide an ample and uniform circulating medium, a source of credit for businesses, and a profitable investment for capitalists. More particularly it would convert into fluid and expandable capital the funded Continental and state securities. In all these ways, it would be another instrument for binding the wealthy to the federal government. A final advantage of the bank, Hamilton believed, was that it was nowhere authorized in the Constitution; it could be chartered only under a "broad construction" of that instrument and would help to establish a doctrine of "implied powers."

One major element in Hamilton's economic vision remains to be mentioned. As a pioneer student of what today would be called the economic growth of underdeveloped countries, he was far ahead of his time in recognizing the importance of promoting manufacturing. A major factor in his financial proposals was the desire to provide capital for industrial development and make the new nation less dependent on foreign markets. The last of his four great reports was devoted wholly to this subject, calling for tariff rates that would give "infant industries" a competitive advantage in the domestic market until they could become well established.

To win congressional support for these proposals Hamilton fought with every political weapon at his command. The more agrarian-minded sections of the country had taken immediate alarm, and the first battle came over funding the Confederation debt. Critics objected particularly to the windfall profits of speculators who had acquired Continental securities at greatly depreciated rates. Indeed the opposition was so strong in Virginia that Madison parted with Hamilton, proposing that current holders be paid at only the depreciated rate with the remainder going to the original holders. Nevertheless, Hamilton's will prevailed. The commercial-minded Federalists in the first Congress passed the measure as originally proposed.

Assumption of state debts aroused even stronger opposition, especially from states like Virginia that had already paid off many of their own debts, and again Madison was in opposition. This time the measure was stalled, until Hamilton adroitly connected it with the simultaneous controversy among New York, Pennsylvania, and the southern states over the permanent location of the national capital. At a dinner with Hamilton, Jefferson agreed that he and Madison would draw off some of the opposition to assumption and that in return the national capital would be moved for 10 years to Philadelphia and then permanently to a 10-mile-square tract to be selected by Washington on the Potomac River between Virginia and Maryland.

Hamilton's revenue proposals met their strongest opposition not in Congress but among backcountry farmers who violently resisted the tax on whiskey, their only easily transported and salable product. By 1794 this resistance culminated in a Whiskey Rebellion in Pennsylvania, and only when Washington sent an army of some thousands into the disaffected area were the armed mobs dispersed and order restored.

The serious constitutional objections to the national bank gave even Washington pause, and before signing the bill he requested written opinions from members of his cabinet. Embracing a doctrine of implied power, Hamilton pointed out that the Constitution authorized Congress to "make all laws which shall be necessary and proper for carrying into Execution" the specifically enumerated powers. "Necessary" should be construed as meaning "*needful, requisite, incidental, useful, or conducive to,*" and he argued that powers "ought to be construed liberally in advancement of the public good." Jefferson, an opponent of centralized, concentrated national authority, on the other hand, argued from a "strict construction" point of view, contending that all powers not expressly granted were reserved by the Tenth Amendment to the states or the people. Restricting "necessary" to the narrowest sense, he asserted that the bank was unconstitutional. Washington, after some temporizing, followed the loose constructionism of Hamilton and signed the bank bill, thus foreshadowing his future political alignment with the Hamiltonians.

Hamilton's proposals for encouraging manufacturing were the only part of his program that failed in Congress. Manufacturing was still in an infant state in the country, most of it carried on by independent artisans and in people's homes, and there was no strong interest group to back Hamilton's plans. Indeed, the wealthy mercantile capitalists who were his strongest supporters on other measures were opposed to tariff barriers that would impede the flow of international trade.

On the whole, Hamilton had been successful, and his policies gave to the new government a vigor and direction that profoundly affected its future development. Combative, opinionated, and often imperious, Hamilton also had helped provoke a rising opposition from agrarian-minded people. By 1791 there was a group in Congress opposed to Hamiltonian policies, and Madison and Jefferson began to organize resistance to the New Yorker's influence. American politics was polarizing along lines of ideology and economic interest, and some observers already spoke of a Republican or Anti-Federalist interest in contrast to the Federalist interest of the Hamiltonians and the followers of the more moderate John Adams. Despite the confusion of names and some overlapping membership, the two political groupings are not successors to the pro- and anti-Constitution factions of the later 1780s. Some original Federalists, such as Madison, became latter-day Anti-Federalists, or Republicans, and some opponents of the Constitution, Patrick Henry, for example, became Federalists once the party system developed. (At Washington's re-election in 1792, this nascent Republican party — also known as Democratic-Republican and Jeffersonian — was strong enough to garner 50 electoral votes for New York's George Clinton for vice president against 77 votes for John Adams.) Though Washington disliked political controversy and tried to remain above the partisan storm, he found Hamilton's ideas more congenial than Jefferson's and may properly be called a Federalist.

THE WARS OF THE FRENCH REVOLUTION

The outbreak of the French Revolution in 1789 was greeted with enthusiasm by most Americans for it confirmed their faith that their own Revolution had blazed a trail to liberty that all humanity would eventually follow. But widespread "Bastille fever" lasted only so long as the revolution in France remained relatively moderate. As the great upheaval moved into a new and more somber phase, American ardor cooled and public opinion divided sharply. The people who tended toward Federalism in domestic politics were shocked by the execution of Louis XVI and the wholesale guillotining of political opponents. When the revolutionary agitation spread to other countries, followed by French revolutionary armies, conservative Americans were driven into hysterical fears of mob rule, atheism, and Jacobinism at home. On the other hand, more democratic-minded Americans, those who tended toward Republicanism in domestic politics but often deplored the worst excesses of the "reign of terror," remained steadfast in their support of the goals of the French Revolution. Jefferson, for one, did not applaud the beheadings, but he believed that "the liberty of the whole earth" depended on the triumph of *liberté, égalité,* and *fraternité* in France. To Jefferson and his followers, the conservative reaction was proof that their Federalist opponents were really monarchists.

The French Revolution precipitated a great European war, lasting with brief interruptions from 1793 until 1815 and pitting France against a series of European coalitions headed by Great Britain. American leaders of all persuasions agreed that their infant nation should avoid becoming directly involved on either side, but there were sharp differences in sympathies. The Hamiltonians favored the British, partly because they preferred British conservatism as opposed to French radicalism and partly because the large trade with Great Britain enriched the merchant class and provided 90 percent of the tariff revenues essential to Hamiltonian financial policies. Jefferson and his friends, more sympathetic to French aims, argued that the country owed its independence to the Franco-American alliance of 1778, which was still in force, and urged a neutrality that would be benevolent toward France.

Actually France did not want to invoke the alliance to bring the United States into the war as a belligerent. The powerful British navy was sweeping French merchant ships from the seas, and the French hoped that if the United States remained neutral, American merchant ships could supply her with foodstuffs and raw materials. Britain, too, as she devoted more of her resources to war, relied increasingly on American shipping. As a result, commercial interests and producers of exports in the United States entered upon a period of unparalleled prosperity.

Washington's proclamation of American neutrality in 1793 made considerable sense economically, but it did not begin to solve all the problems created by the European war. Existing American grievances against Great Britain over the northwest posts, incitement of the northwestern Indians, and discrimination against American trade were compounded in 1794 when Great Britain moved to cripple the newly flourishing American commerce on the high seas. Determined to starve France into submission, the British navy suddenly seized some 300 American ships under newly promulgated rules that forbade neutrals to carry grain or flour to France, to carry any French-owned goods whatever, or to engage in trade with the French West

Indies. Adding insult to injury, British naval commanders began stopping American merchant ships and forcibly taking off crew members thought to have deserted from the British navy, including some American citizens.

Despite a storm of indignation, Hamilton was determined to avoid a break with Great Britain at all costs. Jefferson had already resigned in disgust at Hamilton's domination of the administration and interference in the affairs of the State Department, leaving no one in the cabinet strong enough to oppose the iron-willed treasury secretary. The only diplomatic weapon against the British the United States had was the threat to join the Armed Neutrality of smaller European trading nations that was forming to resist British restrictions on international trade. Chief Justice John Jay was sent to London to negotiate, but Hamilton undercut his mission by assuring the British minister that the United States would not join the Armed Neutrality.

As a result Jay had to accept whatever terms the British offered. The British did agree to pay indemnities for seized American shipping and to withdraw by 1796 from their posts within the northwestern boundary of the United States. In return, Jay had to agree that the United States pay old claims of British merchants against American citizens and tacitly accept the restrictive British definitions of the rights of neutrals in international trade. Not a word was said about British impressment of American sailors, British interference with the northwestern Indians, or indemnity for the slaves carried away by British armies.

Hamilton's outraged opponents charged that these terms were a humiliating surrender to British power; in the violent debate over Jay's treaty during 1795, the emerging line of division between Federalists and Republicans finally crystallized. The only alternative to accepting the treaty, argued the Hamiltonians, was war with England. Ratification of the treaty by the Senate guaranteed a return of commercial prosperity and gave the young nation a further period of freedom from European embroilments, during which it could further strengthen its independence and institutions.

In another area of diplomacy, the Washington administration was able to capitalize on Spain's involvement in the European wars to achieve a brilliant diplomatic triumph. When Spain shifted in 1795 from the British to the French side and when the Jay Treaty appeared to align the United States with Great Britain, the Spanish authorities recognized that their possessions on the southwestern border of the United States had become exceedingly vulnerable. Consequently, the American minister Thomas Pinckney had little difficulty negotiating a treaty, ratified in 1796, that granted all the American demands: the fixing of the Florida boundary at the 31st parallel, free navigation of the Mississippi and a right of "deposit" (the right to bring goods down the Mississippi and land them while awaiting oceangoing ships) at New Orleans for American citizens, and a Spanish promise to restrain the Indians along the frontier.

Thus by the end of Washington's second term, the Jay and Pinckney treaties had eased America's difficulties with two of the three European powers with which the United States was dangerously involved. Washington's policy of preserving American neutrality had strengthened the nation's independence and yet afforded it opportunities to capitalize on the involvements of European nations. Whether this policy could be pursued in the face of difficulties with a third European power, France, was the major problem facing Washington's successor, John Adams.

THE TRIALS OF JOHN ADAMS

Washington's determination to retire at the end of two terms inopportunely deprived the Federalists of their greatest political asset just as the Jay Treaty controversy unfolded. Consequently the election of 1796 was the first hard fought and closely contested presidential election. Hamilton, the "High Federalist," had made too many bitter enemies to be a successful candidate; his ultracommercial and elitist views were too extreme for many Federalist voters. Vice President John Adams, to whom the party leaders turned, represented a more moderate Federalism. The Republicans, almost without discussion, accepted Jefferson, spokesman for the agrarian-minded majority, as their candidate. After a vituperative campaign, Adams narrowly edged Jefferson, 71 electoral votes to 68. According to electoral college procedure, Jefferson became vice president, thus dividing the Adams administration. Once friends and allies, Jefferson and Adams soon became antagonists; they were only reconciled late in life, largely through Abigail Adams.

At the time of Adams's election, the French were enraged by the Jay Treaty. When they ordered seizure of American ships carrying British goods, the Hamiltonians took exception, reversing the stand they had taken when the British stopped American ships. Resisting Hamiltonian pressure, however, Adams sent a special commission of three men to Paris to try to settle the difficulties. When French officials treated the commissioners insultingly and set impossible conditions, including the demands of French agents "X, Y, and Z" for a bribe of $250,000, the commissioners allegedly cried, "Millions for defense, but not one cent for tribute." And the war spirit again flamed high in the United States. By the spring of 1798, President Adams and Congress were making preparations for war, and an undeclared naval war broke out between French and American vessels on the high seas. Yet Adams was never quite swept away by the war fever, and in early 1799, against bitter Hamiltonian opposition, he resolved to make one last effort for peace. Another three-man commission was sent to France and this time an agreement was reached that recognized American principles of neutral rights and abrogated amicably the Franco-American alliance of 1778.

John Adams must be credited with courage and disinterestedness for single-handedly resisting the war hysteria at the cost of his own popularity and the political success of his party, but there was one respect in which he went along with the Hamiltonian extremists. As in other periods of national crisis, the populace was suspicious of political dissenters and foreigners, and the Federalists regarded the Republicans as disloyal — sympathizing with, if not acting as agents of, the nation's enemies. (The ideas of free speech, a free press, and the legitimacy of partisan opposition were not yet firmly established.) In the name of national security, Adams and the Federalists capitalized on the war hysteria and the furor caused by the XYZ Affair by pushing through Congress in 1798 four measures designed in large part to crush the political opposition. Known collectively as the Alien and Sedition Acts, three of these laws lengthened from 5 to 14 years the minimum residence requirements for new citizens (a great many of whom were pro-Republican) and authorized the president to deport or imprison any alien he thought dangerous. The fourth, the Sedition Act, prescribed fines up to $5,000 and imprisonment up to five years for persons who opposed the government's measures, who promoted riots or unlawful assemblies, or who uttered, wrote, or published "any false, scandalous, and malicious" statements against the government or its officials.

No aliens were deported under these extraordinary measures, although many left the country in fear of prosecution. But partisan Federalist district attorneys and judges used the Sedition Act to secure indictments against 15 Republican newspaper editors; 10 were convicted, one of them a Vermont congressman who had printed that Adams possessed an "unbounded thirst for ridiculous pomp, foolish adulation, and selfish avarice." The congressman sought re-election while in jail and won handily.

No one was more alarmed by the Alien and Sedition Acts than civil libertarian Thomas Jefferson. To arouse popular protest, he drafted a set of resolutions and sent them to Kentucky where they were adopted by the legislature. Meanwhile, Madison secured adoption of similar resolutions by Virginia lawmakers. Claiming for the states the power to determine the constitutionality of federal law, these Kentucky and Virginia resolutions of 1798 took the position that the Alien and Sedition Acts violated the First Amendment and were therefore null and void. Although largely ignored by the other states, these resolutions became part of a tradition of southern state-rights thought that would ultimately threaten the Union.

THE "REVOLUTION" OF 1800

The Kentucky and Virginia resolutions opened the campaign for the return match between Adams and Jefferson in the presidential election of 1800. Again there was a close, hard fought contest. The Republicans had been greatly weakened by the charge of Francophilism during the war hysteria, but with the passing of the threat of war, the reaction against the Alien and Sedition Acts gave hope of a Republican comeback. Moreover, the Federalists were weakened by the increasingly rancorous split between the Adams and the Hamilton wings of the party. The death in December 1799 of Washington, the party's chief political asset and unifying presence, compounded their problems, as did popular resentment of the taxes levied to support the war-preparedness program. This time Jefferson edged Adams, 73 electoral votes to 65. Nevertheless, the election had to be decided in the House of Representatives because Jefferson's vice presidential running mate, Aaron Burr, received as many electoral votes as Jefferson. The Constitution did not as yet specify separate balloting for the two highest offices. Ironically, although the Federalist majority in the House favored the unscrupulous Burr, the "high Federalist" Hamilton gave his support to Jefferson, who won on the 36th ballot. The procedural imperfection in the Constitution was corrected in 1804 with the ratification of the Twelfth Amendment.

This "revolution of 1800" inaugurated no revolutionary change in public policy, nor even a revolutionary shift in the balance of strength between the emerging parties. In fact, it was hardly a revolution at all. But the working of the constitutional system had been transformed beyond the intention of the framers by the growth within it of a system of two opposing political parties, representing divergent constituencies, holding divergent ideologies, and proposing divergent policies. The potentially overwhelming majority of the Republicans was not yet fully mobilized for political action in pursuance of its democratic- and agrarian-minded objectives. But already that party had overcome the great initial advantages of its competitor and won a majority. Meanwhile the Federalists, though often out of tune with the awakening majority and insensitive to popular yearnings for equality and personal liberty, had given the new government a vigorous start, had avoided international war, and had turned over a thriving and intact country to the Republican party of Thomas Jefferson. Thus the principle of peaceful competition and transfer of power between parties was established.

FOR FURTHER READING

A good analysis of the political thought of the 1790s can be found in Joyce O. Appleby's *Capitalism and a New Social Order* (1984). The rise of the legitimate opposition is perceptively traced in Richard Hofstadter's *The Idea of a Party System* (1969). John C. Miller's *The Federalist Era* (1960) is a brief and sympathetic overview of the Federalists, while Stanley Elkins and Eric McKitrick offer a more comprehensive look at *The Age of Federalism* (1993). John R. Alden's *George Washington* (1984) and James T. Flexner's *George Washington and the New Nation* (1970) are excellent studies. Manning J. Dauer distinguishes between two wings of the Federalist party in *The Adams Federalists* (1953). Recent biographies of the second president include Joseph J. Ellis's *Passionate Sage* (1993) and John Ferling's *John Adams* (1992). Jacob E. Cooke has provided a brief and readable biography of *Alexander Hamilton* (1982). On the Republican side, Noble Cunningham has analyzed the development of the Republican party organization in *The Jeffersonian Republicans* (1957), and Lance Banning focuses on the evolution of party ideology in *The Jeffersonian Persuasion* (1978). John F. Hoadley has suggestively analyzed the *Origins of American*

Political Parties, 1789–1803 (1986), and sociologist Seymour M. Lipset in *The First New Nation* (1963) has made a suggestive comparison between the problems faced by American leaders in the 1790s and the problems faced by leaders of the new nations of the twentieth century. James M. Smith in *Freedom's Fetters* (1956) focuses on the Alien and Sedition Acts, and Thomas P. Slaughter explores *The Whiskey Rebellion* (1986). Charles R. Ritcheson's *Aftermath of Revolution* (1969) offers a bold interpretation of early British policy toward the United States; Daniel G. Lang explains *Foreign Policy in the Early Republic* (1985); and William C. Stinchcombe examines *The XYZ Affair* (1980).

TABLE 3. PRESIDENTIAL ELECTIONS AND MAJOR POLITICAL EVENTS, 1800–1823

1800	**Thomas Jefferson** (Republican) elected over John Adams (Federalist).
1803	*Marbury* vs. *Madison*. John Marshall's Supreme Court declares a law of Congress unconstitutional. Louisiana Purchase.
1804	**Thomas Jefferson** (Republican) re-elected over Charles C. Pinckney (Federalist).
1804–1806	Lewis and Clark expedition.
1805–1807	Mounting seizures of American shipping under British Orders in Council and Napoleon's Decrees.
1807	*Chesapeake-Leopard* affair. Embargo Act.
1808	**James Madison** (Republican) elected over Charles C. Pinckney (Federalist).
1809	Nonintercourse Act replaces Embargo Act.
1810	Macon's Bill No. 2 replaces Nonintercourse Act.
1811	Recharter of First Bank of the United States defeated. Power of northwestern Indians broken at Tippecanoe.
1812	**James Madison** (Caucus Republican) re-elected over DeWitt Clinton (Independent Republican).
1812–1815	War of 1812.
1814–1815	Treaty of Ghent.
1816	**James Monroe** (Republican) elected over Rufus King (Federalist).
1817	Rush-Bagot Agreement with Great Britain demilitarizes the Great Lakes. Andrew Jackson invades Spanish Florida.
1818	Convention of 1818 settles outstanding differences with Great Britain.
1819–1821	Transcontinental Treaty with Spain acquires Florida.
1820	**James Monroe** (Republican) re-elected without opposition.
1823	Monroe Doctrine enunciated.

8

★ ★ ★ ★ ★ ★

The Jeffersonian Republic in a Threatening World, 1800–1823

THOMAS JEFFERSON wisely recognized the political foolhardiness, if not the practical impossibility, of trying to erase the legacy of Hamiltonian measures that he inherited. The national bank was allowed to run its course undisturbed until its 20-year charter expired in 1811, and the funded federal debt continued to be honored. Yet there was a significant shift in the tone and direction of public policy. The government had just moved to the new Washington City. In sharp reaction to the formality and ceremony that his more aristocratic predecessors had cultivated, the egalitarian Jefferson invested the muddy little capital on the Potomac with a studied casualness, an almost ostentatious simplicity. This lack of pretension symbolized his deliberately negative policy: to avoid ambitious measures, to keep the federal establishment as plain and simple as possible, to practice the most frugal economy, and to reduce as rapidly as possible the federal debt that Hamilton had apparently designed as permanent.

In taking this line, Jefferson was not only following his own agrarian and democratic preconceptions, but also proving himself a shrewd reader of the country's mood. The Hamiltonian system, for all its brilliant success, had been premature, resting on the transitory and fortuitous ascendancy of a commercial-minded minority that was out of tune with the bulk of the population. Even in the Federalist stronghold of New England, religious and sectional considerations had contributed more to that party's strength than commerical-mindedness, and the Adams brand of Federalism was more popular than the Hamilton brand. Despite a flourishing overseas commerce that was gradually pulling more farmers and planters into producing staples for market, the country as a whole remained wedded to the vision of a simple, unprogressive, democratic utopia, dominated by self-sufficient and, therefore, independent and virtuous farmers. Jefferson's reasonable behavior in office and the eloquence of his statements and policies in behalf of the agrarian, democratic ideal won him overwhelming political strength, even in New England.

During these Jeffersonian years Americans appeared to believe that their utopian republican order might endure without change forever. They failed to realize that history will not leave societies, much less utopias, alone. The only problems that most of them saw were those arising out of the continuing international conflict. These were indeed to be severe problems for Jefferson and his successor Madison and would lead ultimately to war. Yet it was not war that was to undermine the republican utopia, but the unsuspected forces of westward expansion and economic change that were already gaining momentum.

VESTIGES OF FEDERALISM

Jefferson's disciplined majorities in Congress had moved promptly to repeal the whiskey tax, the unpopular war-preparedness taxes, and the parts of the Alien and Sedition Acts that had not already expired. Those imprisoned under the latter measures were freed, and their fines were refunded. The only serious battle over remnants of Federalism arose in connection with the judiciary.

The federal courts were staffed entirely by Federalists serving for life, and some judges had conducted themselves with flagrant partisanship. In the last days of the Adams administration, the Federalists had sought to strengthen their judicial bastion with an act establishing a series of new courts, and President Adams had spent his last hours in office signing commissions for the "midnight judges" and other officials to staff the new courts. Adams had made his most important contribution to perpetuating Federalist principles a month earlier by appointing as Chief Justice of the Supreme Court John Marshall, a Virginian of the Washington rather than the Jefferson-Madison stamp, whose nationalistic ideas were to dominate the Court from 1801 until 1835.

The Republicans had no sooner assumed power than they repealed the act establishing the new courts, and Jefferson ordered Secretary of State James Madison to withhold the commissions of Adams's midnight appointees. The stage was set for a showdown when one of these appointees applied to the Supreme Court for a *writ of mandamus* ordering Madison to deliver his commission. Chief Justice Marshall's famous decision in the case of *Marbury* vs. *Madison* was handed down in 1803. Marshall knew that he had no means of forcing Madison to deliver the commission so he skillfully sidestepped a direct confrontation with the administration while he gained an advantage in another quarter. Declaring that the petitioner was entitled to his commission, he contended nevertheless that the Supreme Court was not empowered to act in this kind of case. It had been given such jurisdiction by the Judiciary Act of 1789, but Marshall argued that in this respect the Judiciary Act contradicted the constitutional definition of the Supreme Court's jurisdiction. Therefore, said Marshall, this section of the Judiciary Act was unconstitutional and consequently void. The Court for the first time asserted the power, nowhere explicitly given it, to invalidate an act of Congress on constitutional grounds.

Even before Marshall's decision, the Republicans had begun a campaign to neutralize the Federalism of the judiciary. Incensed by the prosecutions under the Sedition Act and fearful of keeping any branch of the government from popular control, Jefferson favored making the judiciary amenable to political influence. This he thought might be accomplished by congressional impeachment of the more notorious judges. The Republicans had little difficulty getting one drunken and incompetent district judge removed from office. In a key case, however, they failed to get enough votes to impeach Supreme Court Justice Samuel Chase. This failure preserved the principle of an independent judiciary and left Chief Justice Marshall free to develop the Supreme Court into a fortress of nationalistic and anti-Jeffersonian influence.

AN EMPIRE FOR LIBERTY

Early in Jefferson's administration, the exigencies of international war again presented the United States with a splendid diplomatic opportunity. Napoleon had just forced Spain to return Louisiana (in Spanish hands since 1763) to France, hoping to use it as the granary for a growing French empire in the Western Hemisphere. Under Spanish control, Louisiana had been no great threat to the United States, but the prospect of having Napoleonic France astride the Mississippi with an economic stranglehold on the whole interior of the country was another matter. Promptly, Jefferson sent James Monroe to aid the American minister in Paris, Robert R. Livingston, in securing American interests at the mouth of the Mississippi. If possible, they were to purchase the isle of New Orleans, that small portion of Louisiana that lay east of the lower Mississippi. (See map on page 109.)

By the time the negotiations opened in 1803, the collapse of the French expeditionary force in the West Indies and the resumption of the European war after a brief truce had caused Napoleon to abandon his plans for a French empire in America. To the astonishment of the American negotiators, the French offered to sell not only New Orleans but the whole of Louisiana, the entire western watershed of the Mississippi. A price of $15 million was quickly agreed upon, although the Americans were exceeding their instructions. When the news reached Washington, Jefferson, the strict constructionist, worried briefly about the lack of specific constitutional authorization for such purchases of territory, but his philosophical doubts were dissipated in his pragmatic enthusiasm for so vast an extension of his agrarian "empire for liberty." Advising Congress to ratify quickly lest Napoleon change his mind, Jefferson seemed to embrace the Hamiltonian doctrine of implied powers.

Even before the Louisiana Purchase was consummated, Jefferson had evinced his interest in the western country by beginning preparations for the exploration led by Meriwether Lewis and William Clark. Between 1804 and 1806, Lewis and Clark's party ascended the Missouri River to its sources, crossed the Rocky Mountains, and descended the Columbia River to the Pacific, returning with a wealth of information about the vast domain the United States had acquired.

During these years, a strong tide of migration was running westward out of the original states; the line of regular settlement had not yet reached the Mississippi River. The first of the new states (Vermont, 1791; Kentucky, 1792; Tennessee, 1796; and Ohio, 1803) were becoming populous common-wealths, while the French-Spanish settlements around New Orleans were attracting sufficient immigrants from the older states to enter the Union as the state of Louisiana in 1812.

Thomas Jefferson and his party showed a special solicitude for the agrarian, democratic West. One demonstration of this solicitude was the provision made that a percentage of the public land proceeds from the new state of Ohio would be used to construct a great National Road from Cumberland, Maryland, on the Potomac River across the mountains to Wheeling, Virginia, on the Ohio. From there, the National Road was eventually extended through Ohio and Indiana and surveyed as far as St. Louis.

The new western states returned Jefferson's solicitude with overwhelming support for the Republican party. And so, increasingly, did the other states. In 1804, Jefferson was elected to a second term by a resounding victory over Charles Cotesworth Pinckney, 162 electoral votes to 14.

THE PERILS OF NEUTRALITY

During Jefferson's second administration the European war entered a more desperate phase. Napoleon's authority was extending over the whole of continental Europe, while the British were achieving unchallenged supremacy on the high seas. As the great land power and the great naval power moved into their final mortal struggle, each increasingly sought to cripple the other through economic warfare, and Americans, the leading neutral traders, were caught in the middle.

Out of self-interest and principle the United States had asserted an advanced doctrine of neutral rights, claiming the right to trade unmolested with all belligerents. This doctrine had been tenable in connection with the limited warfare of the sixteenth and seventeenth centuries, and it was supported by the code of international law that won considerable acceptance during that period. But the wars of the French Revolution brought a new kind of general warfare, precursor of the total war of the twentieth century, ranging populations against populations. This new warfare was waged by mass armies with sweeping ideological and nationalistic objectives, in place of the earlier small professional armies seeking limited national goals.

Under these circumstances, it was not realistic to expect belligerents to respect the doctrines of neutral rights that the United States sought to maintain. The Federalists had earlier recognized the realities of the world power situation in accepting Jay's Treaty as an alternative to war. Faced with these same realities, Jefferson was just as anxious as the Federalists had been to avoid American involvement in the war but more reluctant to compromise American principles of neutral rights. Believing that the belligerents needed American trade too much to risk war with the United States, he embarked on the difficult task of using American commerce (the strength of which he overestimated) as a weapon to coerce the belligerents into respecting neutral rights.

During Jefferson's first administration, American shippers had been able to pile up such tremendous profits as to more than offset their losses from seizures under the temporarily relaxed British and French restrictions. But in 1805, in the *Essex* case, the British admiralty courts outlawed the most lucrative part of this trade, involving goods shipped from the French West Indies to France by way of the United States. This was but the first in a series of British decisions blockading Europe to stem the flow of commodities useful to the French war effort. As a result, seizures of American shipping mounted alarmingly. Even more intolerable to American pride was an increase in British impressments of sailors from American ships.

Congress responded in 1805 by barring certain British goods from American ports, and the Jefferson administration sought to use this Nonimportation Act as a counter in negotiations in London. The British were willing to relax their restrictions on the French West Indian trade, but since they refused to renounce altogether the right of impressment, Jefferson would not submit the resulting treaty to the Senate for ratification. British indignities culminated in 1807 when the British naval vessel *Leopard* opened fire on the unsuspecting American naval vessel *Chesapeake*, stopped her, and at cannon's mouth impressed four seamen.

Like Adams before him, Jefferson had to resist the clamor for war, meanwhile pushing through Congress the Embargo Act of 1807. This extreme measure of economic coercion forbade American ships to sail for Europe. Jefferson hoped, of course, to force the British to terms by denying them desperately needed American goods and shipping. Unfortunately the effects of the embargo were felt more severely by American commercial and exporting interests than they were by the British. New England, its economy prostrate and its people bitter, moved back into the Federalist orbit. Finally even Jefferson concluded, just before he left office in the spring of 1809, that the embargo could no longer be sustained. Congress repealed the act, and it was left to James Madison to seek some better solution to the prickly problem of neutral rights.

MADISON TRIES HIS HAND

By the time of Madison's election, French depredations on American commerce were becoming as serious as those by the British. Napoleon had responded to the British blockade of the Continent with a series of decrees declaring the British Isles blockaded. Though he did not have the naval power to enforce a blockade, he could and did order the seizure of American ships reaching French ports after having submitted to British regulations. Such seizures reached wholesale proportions early in the Madison administration.

Shifting from one expedient of economic coercion to another, Madison and his congressional followers tried supplanting the embargo with a Nonintercourse Act (1809), freeing American shippers to trade with all nations except France and England and promising to resume trade with whichever of these nations would first remove its restrictions. Profits of trade were so high, however, that American shippers preferred to take their chances on the British and French trade even under the restrictions, and in 1810 Congress supplanted the Nonintercourse Act with a measure known as Macon's Bill No. 2. This overingenious measure reopened the whole world to American trade but declared that whenever either of the major belligerents rescinded its restrictions on neutral shipping, nonintercourse would be reinvoked against the other.

American embarrassment was compounded by the pathetic eagerness of the Madison administration to seize upon any indication that its policy of economic coercion was working. Under the Nonintercourse Act, the president used favorable negotiation with a too pliable British minister as a pretext for announcing resumption of trade with Great Britain, only to have to eat his words when the British minister's work was disavowed in London. Napoleon exploited Macon's Bill No. 2 with even greater cynicism. A carefully ambiguous French promise to rescind the obnoxious decrees against neutral shipping hoodwinked Madison into reinvoking nonintercourse against Great Britain, whereupon the French resumed seizing American ships.

Thus by 1811, the pacific, agrarian-minded diplomacy of economic coercion had been tried in every way that could be imagined, all to no avail. The nation had never seemed so powerless to avert indignities, and the only alternatives seemed to be humiliating submission or war.

THE WAR OF 1812

Submission was utterly unacceptable to a remarkable group of vigorous young men who were elected to the Congress that convened in December 1811, and who came to be known as the War Hawks. Led by the captivating Henry Clay of Kentucky and the intellectually impressive John C. Calhoun of South Carolina, the War Hawks represented a new generation of Republican politicians who were eager to wrest leadership from the tired hands of Madison and his dispirited companions of the Revolutionary generation.

These new Republicans were nationalistic, not only in their patriotic love of country but also in their freedom from the agrarian localism that animated the companions of Jefferson. This was especially true of Clay, whose Kentucky Bluegrass constituency had been drawn into flourishing hemp production for the international market by way of New Orleans, and Calhoun, whose South Carolina up-country was undergoing a heady transformation into a land of cotton plantations. Such areas of recent economic boom shared the cosmopolitanism, progressivism, and nationalism of the older commercial-minded areas and might be characterized as agrarian-commercial in spirit; they were increasingly emanating a new style of Republican nationalism.

It was no accident that the advocates for the agrarian-commercial areas were War Hawks in 1811 and 1812. In the older, strictly commercial areas of the Northeast, merchants and shipowners could run the risk of British and French seizures and still make great profits; they opposed both the Republican measures of economic coercion and the talk of war. But in the agrarian-commercial enclaves of the South and West, exhilarating booms had been stalled by the disorganization of international trade. As loyal Republicans, people in these areas had been willing to give the policies of economic coercion a trial, but their patience had run out. Only war could save the national honor and enable the march of progress and prosperity to resume.

Embarrassingly, Great Britain and France had been equally obnoxious, and the United States could hardly take on both. There were special reasons for hostility to Great Britain. The British officials in Canada were thought to have encouraged Indian unrest in the Old Northwest and the organization of an ominous Indian confederacy, headed by Tecumseh and his brother the Prophet, to oppose the advance of American settlement. Though a frontier army destroyed Tecumseh's power at Tippecanoe in 1811, the bumptious Republicans of the Ohio Valley clamored for the conquest of Canada.

Similarly southwestern Americans were calling for the conquest of Spanish Florida, and Spain was again allied with Great Britain in the European war. Through Spanish Florida ran the rivers on which the people of the Georgia, Alabama, and Mississippi country depended for trade. The Spanish authorities were also suspected of encouraging Indian hostility, and their territory was a haven for the runaway slaves of the Americans. The United States asserted a doubtful claim under the Louisiana Purchase to West Florida, roughly the territory between Mobile Bay and New Orleans. Already by 1810, the Madison administration had taken advantage of a "revolution" by immigrants from the United States to annex part of this area. War with Great Britain would provide an opportunity to complete the conquest of Florida.

Thus the stalling of economic booms in several agrarian-commercial areas, resentment of British tampering with the Indians, and a desire for Canada and Florida made the war fever especially intense in a great arc running along the frontier from northern New England out through Kentucky and Tennessee to South Carolina and Georgia. Yet more important than any of these specific grounds for war was the widespread desire, especially among younger Republicans of the War Hawk stripe, to avenge the national honor and dignity. The callous impressments of American sailors made Great Britain the inevitable enemy.

By the spring of 1812, the Madison administration, not knowing what else to do, was ready to go along with the agitation for war. In June, on the President's recommendation, a declaration of war was pushed through a seriously divided Congress. Two days before the declaration, the British government in London decided to repeal all its restrictions on neutral trade. The Republican diplomacy of economic coercion had finally accomplished its purpose. The moralistic Republican diplomacy that had escalated issues of commercial rights and neutral rights to a question of national honor had left no alternative to war.

The War of 1812 was a military debacle. But for British preoccupation with Napoleon, it would have been an utter disaster. Feeble administration in Washington and feebler generalship in the field brought defeat after defeat. Grandiose western boasts about the easy conquest of Canada eventuated in the surrender of the American army at Detroit. In 1814, the defeat of Napoleon enabled the British to pay serious attention to the American war. One invading army easily captured Washington and burned the public buildings. Another, marching down from Canada to cut the country in two along the line of the Hudson, would have succeeded if its timid general had not been unduly discouraged by the success of a small American flotilla in maintaining naval control of Lake Champlain along his line of march. A final formidable force, fresh from victories over Napoleon, was sent to seize New Orleans with the aim of wresting much of the West from the United States. This seasoned army was annihilated by Andrew Jackson and his western militia in the only significant American triumph of the war. Americans were able to take pride in the naval victories of individual ships, but these could not prevent the mighty British navy from establishing unquestioned control of the seas along the American coasts.

Much of the American weakness arose from internal dissension. Southerners had little enthusiasm for the conquest of Canada, and Northerners had little for the conquest of Florida. The whole war was bitterly opposed in commercial areas, especially New England. New England banks and capitalists would not lend money to rescue the bankrupt federal treasury, the New England governors refused to supply troops, and in December 1814, a convention of the New England states met at Hartford to seek redress against the tyranny of the federal government. Some participants advocated the secession of New England, but the more moderate majority contented itself with proposing constitutional amendments that would protect the interests of their section.

The war had hardly started when the Madison administration began efforts to end it, but it was 1814 before a group of British and American commissioners got down to negotiating in earnest at Ghent in Belgium. The treaty they finally agreed on in December simply restored the state of things existing at the beginning of the war without mention of neutral rights, impressment, or any of the other questions that had been in dispute between the two countries. The United States escaped without loss of territory only because the British were too war weary at the end of their long struggle with Napoleon to go on fighting. Indeed, had the British defeated Jackson as expected at New Orleans in January 1815, two weeks after the peace terms were agreed upon at Ghent, they would probably have insisted on territorial concessions before ratifying the treaty.

THE CENTURY OF SECURITY

However ignominious the War of 1812 seemed at the time, the independence of the United States was not really secure until it had been fought and, by great good luck, the country had survived. Thus began a century such as no other western nation has ever had the good fortune to enjoy, a century in which the United States would develop free from any external threat.

This security was guaranteed primarily by British domination of the seas. By the end of the War of 1812, Great Britain was ready to accept the permanence of the United States and to look for advantage in encouraging trade between the two countries. Seeing great commercial opportunities throughout the Americas, British ministries observed with satisfaction the crumbling of the Spanish Empire, the last great colonial empire in the New World, and resisted any efforts by other European powers to extend their influence across the Atlantic.

This happy turn in British-American relations was signaled by the amicable settlement of the outstanding questions between the two countries shortly after the War of 1812. The Rush-Bagot Agreement of 1817 provided for demilitarization of the Great Lakes, and in the Convention of 1818, American fishing rights in Canadian waters were specified, the northern boundary of the United States was set at the 49th parallel from the head of the Mississippi to the Rocky Mountains, and the two countries agreed to joint occupation of the Oregon country beyond the Rockies for a period of ten years. In 1827 the joint occupation agreement was extended indefinitely until such time as either nation should give a year's notice for terminating the arrangement.

The Anglo-American rapprochement facilitated another diplomatic achievement of this period: the liquidation of American difficulties with Spain through the acquisition of Florida. After acquiring West Florida as far east as the Pearl River (the area now a part of the state of Louisiana) through "revolution" in 1810, the Madison administration took advantage of the war to annex, in 1813, another chunk extending beyond Mobile Bay east to the Perdido River (the coastal areas of the present states of Mississippi and Alabama). Following the war, Spain was wracked by political turmoil at home and revolution in her South American colonies. Forays on American territory by Florida Indians intensified southwestern demands for annexation and furnished the pretext that Spain was not living up to her obligations under Pinckney's Treaty. When Andrew Jackson was sent to pacify the Indians along the Florida border in 1817, he moved on into Florida and seized the whole northern Gulf Coast area.

The administration in Washington could not sanction this rash and unauthorized occupation, but Secretary of State John Quincy Adams (son of President John Adams) finally persuaded his Cabinet colleagues that Jackson should not be censured. Instead Adams told the Spaniards that the incident revealed their inability to maintain their treaty obligations along the Florida boundary, indicating the propriety of ceding Florida to the United States. Under this implied threat of forcible seizure, Spain yielded. By a treaty signed in 1819 but not ratified until 1821, Florida was ceded to the United States in exchange for the sum of $5 million. In the process, the Americans won undisputed control of the territory to the Rocky Mountains as well as a window on the Pacific. Sometimes called the Transcontinental Treaty, this remarkable agreement defined the boundary between the United States and the Spanish possessions to the southwest as running from the Gulf of Mexico up the Sabine River (the western boundary of the state of Louisiana), then west and north of the Rockies, then west along the 42nd parallel to the Pacific coast. The Florida treaty was consummated during the administration of James Monroe, who had succeeded Madison in 1817.

During his presidency, Monroe defined America's diplomatic position of hemispheric separation and avoidance of foreign entanglements. Called the Monroe Doctrine, the policy was declared in the president's last message to Congress in December 1823. He asserted that the American continents were no longer open to colonization by European powers, and he warned against any European interference in the revolutionary new nations of Latin America and against extension of European political systems into the Americas. In return for such nonintervention, the president pledged the United States to noninterference in the "internal concerns" of Europe. An expression of self-confident American nationalism, Monroe's unilateral declaration recognized the existence of spheres of influence and, by implication, claimed one in Latin America for the United States.

In part, recent scholarship suggests, the document was the product of domestic politics, of Secretary of State John Quincy Adams's concern with the forthcoming presidential elections. But international considerations very likely predominated. The noncolonization declaration was prompted by an expansion of the spheres of Russian activity down the northwest American coast from Alaska, and in 1824, the Russians agreed to limit their interests to the area north of 54°40', leaving the United States and Great Britain as the only claimants of the Oregon country between that line and the Spanish-Mexican boundary at 42°.

The *nonintervention* statement in the Monroe Doctrine was prompted by the fear that major European powers might unite to subdue Spain's rebellious American colonies and by the growing American commercial interests in Latin American markets. Great Britain also opposed European takeover and intervention in Latin America, so earlier the British foreign secretary had suggested that the United States join his country in opposing such action. But Secretary of State Adams and Monroe decided that the United States should act independently. But, in fact, it was British seapower that enforced the policy, not American. The doctrine had little effect in the short term. Though irritated by this "arrogant" American "blustering," the European powers had no enthusiasm for the reconquest of Spanish America against British opposition. But the doctrine did clarify the American view of the relationship between the Old World and the New, and it expressed the U.S. claim of dominance in the Western Hemisphere. Although it had no standing in treaty arrangements or international law — and was forgotten after its declaration for a generation — the Monroe Doctrine remains a cornerstone of twentieth-century American foreign policy.

CONFLICTING HISTORICAL VIEWPOINTS: NO. 3

What Caused the War of 1812?

The American war cry of 1812, "Free trade and sailors' rights," moved the eccentric Virginian John Randolph to quip: "Men shall not live by bread alone, but mostly by catchphrases." The phrase nevertheless appealed to the people of Randolph's generation, who believed that the second Anglo-American war was fought for national honor and neutral maritime rights. With their president, James Madison, they traced the origins of conflict to "the continued British practice of violating the American flag on the great highway of nations, and of carrying off persons sailing under it." Actually, in his war message to Congress, Madison had mentioned other causes as well, but the maritime interpretation captured the American imagination. Throughout the century, lay persons and scholars alike believed that British commercial interference lay at the heart of the conflict. Historians as diverse as John Bach McMaster (History of the People of the United States, 8 vols., 1883–1913) *and Alfred T. Mahan* (Sea Power in Its Relation to the War of 1812, 1905) *stressed impressment of sailors, interruption of trade, and the Royal Navy's blockade. Even Henry Adams* (History of the United States, 9 vols., 1889–1891), *who found the exclusive emphasis on maritime matters oversimple, offered only a slightly modified version.*

Following World War I, however, a generation of scholars, disillusioned by the failures of American wartime idealism, looked for causes less lofty than patriotism and principle. For example, Louis Hacker (Mississippi Valley Historical Review, March 1924), *then an economic determinist, identified conflict in the War Hawks' lust for Canadian land. Julius Pratt* (The Expansionists of 1812, 1925), *on the other hand, emphasized southern yearnings for the Floridas and a western desire to drive Britain from Canada as a solution to the Indian problem. A third scholar, George Taylor* (Journal of Political Economy, 1931), *linked westerners to seaboard grievances by noting that the farmers of the interior, hardly less than New England merchants, were economically dependent on foreign trade.*

More recently, pocketbook and sectional considerations have fallen from favor. After World War II, during a period of domestic conservatism and

Cold War, a number of scholars returned to arguments of national honor and free seas. Bradford Perkins (Prologue to War, 1961), Reginald Horsman (The Causes of the War of 1812, 1962), and Norman Risjord (William and Mary Quarterly, April 1961), with varying degrees of emphasis, led us back to the maritime causes stressed by nineteenth-century historians. Indeed, most historians today agree that England's policies of impressment and commercial restriction left its former colonies with but two alternatives: submission or war. As Risjord put it, "War was the only alternative to national humiliation and disgrace."

FOR FURTHER READING

Henry Adams's *History of the United States During the Administrations of Jefferson and Madison* (9 vols., 1889–1891) is a classic of American historical writing. Much material that has come to light since Adams wrote is utilized in two distinguished multivolume biographies: Irving Brant, *James Madison* (6 vols., 1941–1961), and Dumas Malone, *Jefferson and His Time* (6 vols., 1948–1981). Merrill D. Peterson's *Thomas Jefferson and the New Nation* (1970) is an excellent one-volume biography; Marshall Smelser's *The Democratic Republic* (1968) views Jefferson as a "Whiggish moderate"; Noble Cunningham's *In Pursuit of Reason* (1987) examines Jefferson's political career; Forrest McDonald's *The Presidency of Thomas Jefferson* (1976) offers a latter-day Hamiltonian critique; and Leonard Levy's *Jefferson and Civil Liberties* (1963) savagely explores "the darker side" of the sage's life. Noble Cunningham has written a study of *The Jeffersonian Republicans in Power* (1963); Drew McCoy's *The Elusive Republic* (1980) examines the political economy of Jeffersonian America; and Richard E. Ellis's *The Jeffersonian Crisis* (1971) carefully analyzes judicial politics and reform in the young republic. David H. Fischer's *The Revolution of American Conservatism* (1965) probes Federalist efforts to adapt to a more popular style of politics; Robert L. Clinton explains *Marbury v. Madison and Judicial Review* (1989); and Linda K. Kerber's *Federalist in Dissent* (1970) assesses Federalist ideology in the period of Republican ascendancy. For the Lewis and Clark expedition and western development during the Jeffersonian era, see Stephen Ambrose's *Undaunted Courage* (1996) and Gary E. Moulton's edition of *The Journals of the Lewis and Clark Expedition* (7 vols., 1986–1991). On the coming of the War of 1812, see J. C. A. Stagg's *Mr. Madison's War* (1983) and Roger Brown's *The Republic in Peril: 1812* (1964). Donald R. Hickey's *The War of 1812* (1989) is a good general history of the conflict. The Treaty of Ghent and postwar diplomacy are splendidly delineated in Samuel Flagg Bemis's *John Quincy Adams and the Foundations of American Foreign Policy* (1949); Dexter Perkins's *A History of the Monroe Doctrine* (1955) is the standard account of that subject; and Ernest R. May's *The Making of the Monroe Doctrine* (1975) emphasizes the role of domestic politics in external policy. R. David Edmonds explains *Tecumseh and the Quest for Indian Leadership* (1984), while Laurel Thatcher Ulrich, in *A Midwife's Tale* (1990), uses the richly detailed diary of one woman to paint a vivid portrait of the lives of women in the early republic.

MAP 3:   WESTWARD EXPANSION, 1800–1860

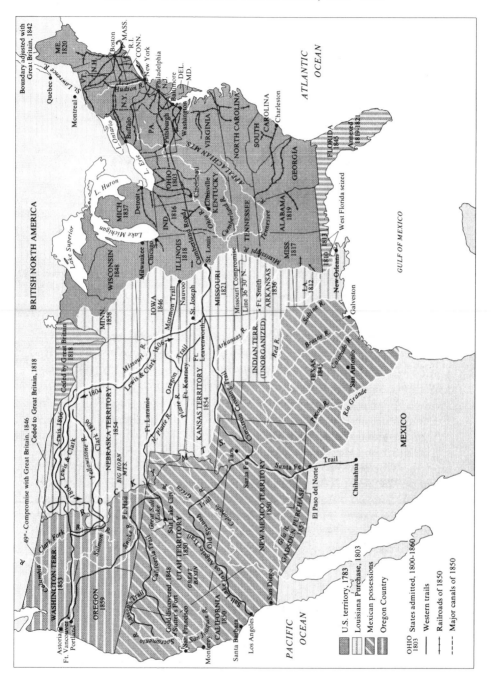

9

★ ★ ★ ★ ★ ★

The Market versus the Agrarian Republic, 1800s–1850s

THE CENTURY of Security into which the Republican leaders ushered the country was also a century of exceptional growth and development in the United States. Freedom from all entanglements with the Old World, except a free and peaceful trade, was deemed essential to the simple, and therefore virtuous republic that Jefferson and his colleagues sought to perfect. Yet this freedom and security helped to foster a spirit of enterprise and rapid change that undermined the agrarian ideal.

The spirit and direction of American life became so strikingly different after the War of 1812 that the period around 1815 must be regarded as a major turning point in American history. The change was not quite so abrupt as it may appear — war has a way of temporarily damming up latent tendencies in a society and accelerating others so that they all seem to burst forth at the end of the conflict and as a result of it. In this case, economic changes were primary.

THE MARKET REVOLUTION

The American economy has developed through three main stages: the staple-exporting, national market, and industrial stages. The economy of the colonial period was a *staple-exporting economy,* in which people either concentrated on production of tobacco, grain, and other staples for overseas markets or on the carrying trade, or were largely self-sufficing in their economic activities. About the middle of the eighteenth century, population flowed heavily into the interior where poor transportation prevented staple

110

production, and the self-sufficing sector of the economy began to grow relative to the staple-exporting and, therefore, commercial sector. This development set the stage for the struggle between commercial-mindedness and agrarian-mindedness in the last quarter of the century.

From the viewpoint of economic development, the important thing about the staple-exporting economy was its static quality, its lack of any tendency to self-acceleration or change. The overseas markets for American staples were seriously disturbed by the Revolution, and with the steady growth of the self-sufficing sector toward the end of the century, the economy was becoming, if anything, more set in its ways. This unprogressive, staple-exporting economy with its sizeable self-sufficing sector supported the stable agrarian utopia of Thomas Jefferson.

How, then, did this economy become a dynamic *industrial economy?* The "industrial revolution" that brought factories, large-scale enterprises, and rapid technological change did not really gain full momentum in the United States until after the Civil War. But the critical shift in the pace, direction, and spirit of the economy had occurred decades before as a result of the "market revolution," which brought most American economic activity into the orbit of an intricately intermeshed national market system. Between the *staple-exporting economy* of the eighteenth century and the *industrial economy* of the late nineteenth century there intervened a *national market economy*, which did not until the 1850s become significantly industrial.

The essence of the market revolution was a vast extension of the division of labor or, in other words, specialization of economic activities. Areas and individuals who had formerly been self-sufficing or who had engaged in mixed enterprises began to concentrate on the one product or service they could produce most efficiently, selling it for money and then buying with that money the other goods and services they needed. Areas and individuals engaged formerly in only barter or limited local trade were inexorably drawn into a national and international market system, linked together by the mysterious mechanisms of money and credit. Overnight the resulting gains in efficiency and productivity jolted the formerly static economy into rapid growth. And it was in this atmosphere of rapid growth and ready profits that an economically conservative population became deeply infected with the spirit of enterprise, progress, and economic individualism.

The market revolution seemed to spring full blown from the War of 1812. With a staple-starved Europe paying high prices for American products, a long dammed-up flood of European imports pouring into American harbors, and settlers swarming over the newly opened lands of the West, the country was swept into an unprecedented four-year boom (1815–1818). Lured by high profits and easy credit into venturing their all on enterprises ranging from farms to steamboats, countless Americans were drawn for the first time into the money-market nexus. This spectacular boom ended in the even more spectacular bust of 1819 and the depression of the 1820s, to be followed by another boom-bust cycle in the 1830s.

The short-term boom-bust cycle of 1815–1819 arose immediately out of war and peace, but it had roots in the market revolution and in the greater interdependence of the economy that the market revolution produced. The market revolution itself was rooted in certain long-term developments that began before, and continued long after the War of 1812. One of these was the accumulation of investment capital from the high profits of the American carrying trade during the Napoleonic Wars. Others will be discussed in the following sections.

THE ADVANCE TO THE MISSISSIPPI

A major stimulus to the growth of the American economy after 1815 was the rapid settlement and economic development of the West up to, and across the Mississippi River. Much of this area was not open to settlement until William Henry Harrison destroyed the Indian power in the Old Northwest and Andrew Jackson crushed the Creeks and Cherokees of the southwestern areas during the War of 1812. Following the war, the broken tribes yielded to repeated demands for additional cessions of territory. In the 1820s, John C. Calhoun, Monroe's secretary of war, inaugurated a policy of resettling the remaining Indians beyond the Missouri River, and by the middle 1830s, this objective had been substantially accomplished.

With the return of peace in 1815, a flood of settlers poured west to take up rich lands under the liberal Harrison Land Act of 1800. A tract of as little as 160 acres could be bought for $2.00 an acre, with a minimum down payment of 50 cents an acre and four years to pay the remaining $1.50. Overnight, great plantations appeared on the fertile river lands of Alabama and Mississippi as planters from the worn soils of eastern Virginia, the Carolinas, and Georgia moved west with slaves, stock, and plantation gear. Along the line of the Mohawk Valley and the Great Lakes came a torrent of refugees from the stony hill farms of northern and western New England, blanketing the productive plains of northern Ohio, Indiana, and Illinois with townships, churches, and school houses on the New England pattern. The older western states of Kentucky and Tennessee became thickly settled, and from them and from farther south and east a stream of immigrants moved into southern Ohio, Indiana, and Illinois, establishing a pattern of life that differed from the New England-based style in the northern sections of those states.

During the boom years, this migration attained staggering proportions. Annual federal land sales, which had risen from 67,800 acres in 1800 to over 500,000 acres in 1813, abruptly shot to 1,306,400 acres in 1815 and reached a peak of 3,491,000 acres in 1818. Even during the depressed 1820s, the tide continued to run strongly. The population of the country beyond the Appalachians doubled between 1810 and 1820 and again between 1820 and 1830. In quick succession, five new states came to be: Indiana (1816), Mississippi (1817), Illinois (1818), Alabama (1819), and Missouri (1821). The typical western migrant was no solitude-loving Daniel Boone, but a person of enterprise, bent on self-improvement through shrewd investment, hard work, and a ride on a rising market. The market revolution in its early stages fostered the western boom that stimulated migration, and the great migration in turn accelerated the market revolution.

COMMERCIAL AGRICULTURE

The most important feature of the market revolution was the spectacular expansion of commercial agricultural production, with cotton leading the way. The development in England during the latter part of the eighteenth century of machinery that could manufacture cotton cloth cheaply had created a heavy demand for cotton. Cotton production was restricted for a time by the difficulty of separating the fibers from the seeds, but after Eli Whitney perfected in 1793 a gin that performed this task, cotton plantations mushroomed across the interior of Georgia and South Carolina. Checked for a time by the embargo and the War of 1812, the cotton boom roared ahead with the return of peace and the opening of the rich southwestern lands to cultivation. Production rose from 146,000 bales in 1814 to 209,000 bales in 1815 and 349,000 bales in 1819. Within a few years after 1815, a wide belt extending from North Carolina around to Louisiana had been converted into the world's largest cotton-producing area, and cotton was the country's leading export.

Unlike the staple-exporting sector of the colonial economy, the new cotton sector was intimately tied to the national as well as the international market system. The bulk of the cotton shipped from New Orleans, Mobile, and Charleston went to Europe, much of it by way of northeastern ports, especially New York. The crop's proceeds paid for European imports that found their way back to all parts of the United States through northeastern mercantile houses. Importations from Europe were financed to a great extent through the services of merchants in the Northeast in shipping and selling the South's cotton crop, through the South's purchases of northeastern manufactures, and through the foodstuffs and livestock shipped by the farmers in the Northwest to southern cotton planters. For some decades after 1815, the ever-mounting cotton exports were the most important factor in the economy's growth.

Cotton production was merely the biggest segment of an expanding commercial agriculture. Tobacco cultivation in the old tidewater area of Virginia and Maryland never recovered from its post-Revolution slump, but new tobacco belts developed along the North Carolina-Virginia border and in sections of Kentucky, Tennessee, and Missouri. Not until the 1840s, however, did tobacco production flourish and become highly profitable. Rice culture benefited from improved seed selection and methods of cultivation, but did not expand beyond its long-established locale in the coastal region of South Carolina and Georgia. The development of an improved variety of ribbon cane fostered a booming sugar-plantation economy in Louisiana following the War of 1812; hemp, used especially for baling cotton, afforded a similarly profitable commercial crop for areas in Kentucky and Missouri.

While the great export staples were concentrated in the South, other sections were not lacking in an extensive commercial agriculture produced at first for the national market. Areas of commercial wheat production expanded steadily west from Pennsylvania's Susquehanna Valley to New York's Mohawk and Genesee valleys to Ohio, Indiana, and Illinois. In the decade after 1815 a mounting stream of wheat, flour, corn, pork, beef, and livestock began pouring from the Old Northwest into the East and South. Cincinnati became the country's leading center of flour milling and meat packing, and by the 1840s the flood of cheap wheat and flour from the fertile Northwest was becoming a major item in American exports to Europe.

Farmers on the less productive soils of the Northeast, forced out of cereal and meat production by the cheap western products, turned to producing perishables — fruits, vegetables, poultry, and dairy products — for the growing eastern cities. Improved breeds of wool-bearing sheep and increased demand from an expanding woolens industry made wool production a profitable enterprise in many parts of the Northeast as well as the Northwest.

Thus within a brief space of time, mainly following the War of 1812, countless self-sufficing or general farmers had responded to the lure of cash returns held out by a mushrooming national and international market system and were concentrating on those staples that they could produce most efficiently. Little of this would have occurred, however, had it not become possible to transport bulky products cheaply from one part of the country to another.

THE ONSET OF INDUSTRIALIZATION

Commercial agricultural products did not represent the only bulky items requiring transportation; as the century wore on, manufactured items grew in volume. But during the first quarter of the nineteenth century, despite the early appearance of cotton textile mills and iron works in New England and Pennsylvania, most American manufacturing was still of the domestic variety — spinning, weaving, shoemaking, hatmaking, and countless other enterprises carried on in the homes, mills, or small shops of artisans who marketed their goods locally. Thereafter, though independent craftsmen survived longer in some trades than in others, household manufacture declined rapidly, as factory growth, development of modern transportation, and a spreading market economy sped the transition from hand to machine production.

The movement from domestic manufactures to the factory system came first to the Northeast. Lacking the fertile soil required for successful, large-scale agriculture and blessed with ready access to raw materials, a growing home market, and an abundance of water power, Yankee merchant-investors (particularly New Englanders) turned easily from commerce to manufacturing. Thus, the American factory had its beginning in 1790 at the cotton-spinning mill of Almy, Brown, and Slater in Pawtucket, Rhode Island. The mill, powered by waterwheel, was based on British technology pirated by the gifted mechanic and immigrant Samuel Slater, and produced cotton yarn for markets throughout New England and the middle states. Soon there were a number of these small enterprises putting out their yarn to individuals to be woven into cloth on hand looms in their homes. When imports of English cloth were cut off during the War of 1812, the infant American textile industry expanded to meet the demand.

In Waltham, Massachusetts, in 1813, Francis Cabot Lowell's Boston Manufacturing Company introduced the first successful American power loom and built the world's first self-sufficient textile plant, which brought all steps in cotton cloth production under one roof. The rapidly expanding firm marketed its coarse sheeting nationally and soon opened factories in the new town of Lowell, where women operated the machines. The "Lowell System" employed unmarried Yankee farm girls in their late teens and early twenties, who lived in comfortable but tightly regulated surroundings. The women worked long hours (72 per week) for low wages ($2.50 to $3.00 per week, less room and board). Never the "philanthropical manufacturing college" it was often called, the Lowell experiment in industrial paternalism was briefly imitated and widely celebrated. But it was shortly abandoned by cost-conscious managers, who turned in the 1840s to cheaper, more compliant, and abundant, unskilled immigrants for laborers.

Periodic depressions (1819, 1837, 1857) caused working conditions to worsen steadily not only in Lowell, the "Manchester of America," but throughout New England's textile industry. As competition for jobs mounted with the rising numbers of immigrants, and demand for cotton cloth fluctuated with the business cycle, managers came to regard workers as commodities to be bought at the lowest price. Production rates increased, factories became more dangerous places to work, hours were extended, and wages were slashed below already low levels. By the 1840s the drab and blighted factory town, once thought to be a post–Civil War development, was already a fixture of New England life. A substantial urban industrial class — including not only women but a growing number of children — was already inured to the rigorous demands of machines. Even as Alexis de Tocqueville was celebrating the principle of equality in America, the cities of the Northeast were marked by growing inequality between classes, especially as the pre-industrial artisan class began to decline to wage-earner status.

The textile factory system found ready application: first in woolen goods and then by the 1850s in clocks, firearms, farm implements, footware (rubber and leather), glass, iron, sewing machines, and other consumer goods. Deriving power successively from the waterwheel, the water turbine, and after 1860 the steam engine, these industries were based on the nation's uniquely rich natural resources and on borrowed British technology, particularly machine-tool technology. But Yankee ingenuity must not be discounted. Much of the nation's initial industrial success, perhaps even its ultimate economic leadership, can be traced to early mastery of manufacturing principles essential to mass-production. Based on the late eighteenth-century innovations of Delaware flour miller Oliver Evans and Massachusetts inventor Eli Whitney, the so-called American system of continuous-process manufacture (assembly-line production) and interchangeable parts became the model of the industrial world.

THE CONQUEST OF DISTANCE

So important were the dramatic improvements in transportation facilities in the early nineteenth century that some historians have called the market revolution a transportation revolution. Like the great westward migration, the transportation revolution was part cause and part effect of the broader market revolution.

During the colonial period, production for market had been confined to areas along navigable waterways, and at the beginning of the nineteenth century, almost the only other transportation was by wagon or pack team over primitive dirt roads. As late as 1816, a ton of goods could be shipped 3,000 miles from England for what it cost to transport the same goods 30 miles overland in America. The cost of moving a bushel of wheat from Buffalo to New York City in 1817 was three times the market value; the cost of moving corn was six times the market value for corn; and the cost for oats was twelve times the market value. Cheaper transportation was an obvious prerequisite to a national market economy.

The first attempts to solve the problem were through improved roads. In 1794 a company chartered by the Pennsylvania legislature opened between Lancaster and Philadelphia the first major turnpike, or graded and paved road on which tolls were charged. So dramatically did it lower wagoning rates and stimulate commercial development and so profitable did it prove that a wave of turnpike construction followed. By the War of 1812, most major cities in the Northeast were connected by turnpikes; after the war the turnpike craze reached its peak and spread into the West. One major turnpike led west from Baltimore to Cumberland, Maryland; from here, the federal government began constructing the National Road. By 1818 this great highway had reached Wheeling, Virginia, on the Ohio River, and by 1833 it extended to Columbus, Ohio. The National Road quickly became a major artery of east-west trade, while elsewhere the turnpikes reduced transportation costs and brought previously isolated areas into the market.

More important than better roads, especially in the West, was the introduction of the steamboat. From the early days of settlement, flatboats going down the Ohio and Mississippi rivers to New Orleans had transported some production to market, but this mode of transportation was extremely slow even downriver while upriver shipping by oar-driven keelboat was so slow, backbreaking, and expensive as to inhibit any extensive commerce. A new era was predicted when Robert Fulton operated the first commercially successful steamboat, the *Clermont,* on the Hudson River in 1807. By 1812, a few forerunners of the classic shallow-draft sternwheeler had appeared on the Mississippi. The development of western steamboating came with a rush at the end of the war, and by 1820 there were 60 steamboats on the Mississippi-Ohio system (by 1860 there would be more than 1,000) and others on the river systems of Alabama and Mississippi. Steamboat freight rates were only 5 to 10 percent of what keelboats had charged to haul goods upriver and only 25 to 30 percent of what it had cost to flatboat goods down river; there were also gains in shipping time. Able to operate far up the network of tributaries that laced the West, the shallow-draft sternwheeler made possible the commercial production of cotton, wheat, and other bulky commodities in widespread areas that could not otherwise have entered the national market.

While the steamboat was accelerating commercial development in the West — and nourishing such river cities as Cincinnati, Louisville, and St. Louis — another transportation development was providing a direct water link between East and West. In 1817 the New York legislature, prodded by Governor DeWitt Clinton, authorized the construction of a canal from Albany on the Hudson River west along the Mohawk Valley to Buffalo on Lake Erie, and by 1825 the 364-mile Erie Canal was completed. Traffic on the new canal was so heavy that tolls equaled its construction cost within nine years. Given cheap water communication with New York City and Europe, a flood of commodities from the Great Lakes region soon flowed eastward along the canal, meeting a return flow of eastern and European goods destined for the entire West.

The success of the Erie Canal (operating today as the New York State Barge Canal) prompted Pennsylvania to build a competing system linking Philadelphia with Pittsburgh on the Ohio, and in the 1830s and 1840s the states of the Old Northwest completed a series of canals connecting the Great Lakes with the Ohio and the Mississippi rivers.

The development of a railroad network in the 1840s and 1850s gave added efficiency to a transportation system that had already succeeded in bringing most parts of the country within the orbit of the irresistible market. Baltimore began constructing its railroad west toward the Ohio River in 1828, and in the next decade several thousand miles of short lines were built. Not until the 1850s, however, did the railroad boom reach its height. In this decade the great trunk lines connecting East and West were completed, and by 1860 the country had more than 30,000 miles of railroad.

In a parallel development, Samuel F. B. Morse perfected the electric telegraph, which revolutionized the nation's communication system. Often literally parallel, wires were strung beside the railroad tracks wherever practical. The innovation spread rapidly, carrying news, building markets, and transforming business and financial patterns. By 1860 there were 50,000 miles of telegraph wire in use.

Measuring the economic benefits of these changes in transportation and communication is impossible, but their impact was vast. In 1815 it took more than 50 days to ship a cargo from Cincinnati to New York by keelboat and wagon. By 1850 the same commodities could be shipped from and to the same cities by barge in 18 days, and by railroad in 6 to 8 days. Overland freight rates by wagon ranged from 30 to 70 cents per ton per mile in 1815. By the 1850s the cost dropped: 2–9 cents per ton-mile by railroad, and about 1 cent per ton-mile by canal barge. Similarly, a message sent overland from the nation's midsection to the West Coast could take six months by wagon, a month by stage coach, 7 to 10 days by the fabled (and briefly operated) Pony Express, and scarcely an instant by magnetic telegraph.

ENTERPRISE AND PUBLIC POLICY

The transportation revolution, the market revolution, and the onset of industrialization would have come much more slowly if the Americans of the early republic had followed the *laissez-faire* notions of political economy that are often mistakenly ascribed to them. Instead, as the market advanced and the spirit of enterprise quickened, entrepreneurs demanded that their governments ally themselves with private interest to speed progress.

The most notable alliance of public and private enterprise at the state and local level was in the field of transportation, where progress demanded undertakings too vast for individuals or even groups of individuals. The early turnpike companies raised much of their capital from stock subscriptions by the states and towns through which they ran. The great canals, including the Erie, were built directly by state tax money, while other states spent large sums of public revenue on improving navigable rivers. Congress financed the first telegraph line, the Washington–Baltimore line, before turning it over to private enterprise in 1847; the first transcontinental telegraph line, completed in 1861, was subsidized generously by the federal government. Public aid to transportation reached its peak in the construction of railroads; many were subsidized by local, state, and federal grants, and a few were built entirely with state money. How many million dollars of public funds spent on these projects is not known, but the revolutionizing transportation and communication networks could certainly not have grown so without governmental aid.

The turnpike, steamboat, and railroad companies were the forerunners of the modern corporation. These early corporations were born out of the theory of "mixed enterprise" — the idea that government should ally itself with private enterprise to accomplish ends beneficial to the public. In the simple days of the staple-exporting economy, all enterprise had been carried on by individuals or partnerships. Economic combinations of many individuals or their capital in large enterprises were thought to be dangerous to the public interest and were frowned upon by the law. Only where some great public purpose was to be accomplished were these corporations thought to be justified, and then only when chartered by special act of a legislature.

Such corporate charters usually facilitated the raising of capital by granting the privilege of "limited liability," making stockholders in the corporation (unlike members of partnerships) liable for debts of the corporation only to the extent of the stock they held. Charters also usually granted, either explicitly or implicitly, monopolies or semimonopolies — for example, when a company was given the exclusive right to develop a certain transportation route. Thus the early corporate charter was thought of as a privilege conferred by government in order to enlist private enterprise for the accomplishment of a public purpose.

The corporate device found much of its early use not only in transportation but in banking, and the rapid growth of banking was another major factor in the acceleration of economic development. The banking system before the War of 1812 had consisted of the Hamiltonian national bank, chartered by Congress, and a small number of private banks that were called *state banks* because they were chartered by state legislatures. In theory at least, stockholders bought stock in these banks by paying in gold and silver. On the basis of this specie capital, the banks made loans; the interest they collected from their borrowers provided profits that could be paid back to the stockholders as dividends. What made the banks extremely profitable was the fact that they could safely lend out more than their capital. Instead of lending specie, a bank gave borrowers *bank notes*, or pieces of paper resembling modern paper money, each bearing a promise that the issuing bank would redeem the note on demand with a specified sum of specie. These bank notes then circulated as money in the vicinity of the bank and, as long as people had confidence in the bank, were not returned for redemption in specie. Thus the bank could safely print, lend, and collect interest on considerably more bank notes than it had specie to cover.

Though at first conservatively managed and restrained by the national bank, the state banks were potentially capable of expanding the supply of credit and investment capital almost infinitely and, thus, of stimulating feverish economic activity. This began to happen when the national bank's demise in 1811 and the war's economic stimulus prompted enterprising politicians and businesses to secure legislative charters for a large number of new state banks designed to operate on more generous and lucrative principles than their predecessors. The bank mania reached its peak after the war, and the rapid multiplication of banks and bank credit contributed greatly to the boom-and-bust cycle of 1815–1819. Bust was again followed by boom, and the expansion of bank credit reached even greater heights than in the 1830s. In spite of the violent short-term fluctuations that the banks fostered, they also contributed greatly to the spectacular, long-term prosperity of the economy through their active stimulation of its growth.

REPUBLICAN NATIONALISM

The spirit of enterprise was strong in the new generation of Republican leaders who had pushed Madison into war in 1812 and who dominated a transformed Republicanism after the war. Federalism, despite a momentary comeback in embargo days, was so weakened by the steady swelling of the Republican electorate and so discredited by secession discussion at the Hartford Convention before the war that in 1816 only three states voted for the Federalist presidential candidate. To succeed Madison, the Republicans picked James Monroe, the last prominent Virginian of the Revolutionary generation, and in 1820 Monroe was re-elected without opposition.

Monroe himself retained some of Jefferson's agrarian-minded and strict-constructionist scruples and rejoiced that the death of Federalism had ushered in an "Era of Good Feelings" when parties should no longer be necessary. In truth, the younger men surrounding the president had moved, in the enterprising atmosphere of the boom years, so far toward the nationalist and commercial-minded views of the Federalists that Federalism had become superfluous. Monroe's State Department was headed by the ardent nationalist John Quincy Adams, who had deserted his father's party over the embargo issue. Monroe's Secretary of the Treasury, William H. Crawford of Georgia, worked for a new national bank. Presiding over the War Department was John C. Calhoun, vigorous champion of a strong army, protective tariffs, and federal road and canal construction. And in Congress, the dominant figure was Speaker of the House Henry Clay, who for a generation would symbolize a broad program of federal action — he would call it the "American System" — to aid enterprise and speed progress.

These people were preaching Hamiltonianism shorn of its elitist overtones. The onrushing market revolution was democratizing business, and the rapid spread of the entrepreneurial spirit through all levels of society made the new Republican nationalism more dynamic than the old Federalist nationalism of conservative merchants and financiers.

The war was no sooner over than several problems growing out of wartime developments were attacked in the spirit of Republican nationalism. The overexpansion of state banks had led to a financial crisis early in the war. Outside New England, the overextended banks had had to "suspend specie payments" (stop redeeming their bank notes in gold or silver coin on demand), and their notes had depreciated; the resulting financial chaos had contributed greatly to the government's difficulties in carrying on the war. To get the federal government out of its financial troubles and to furnish a sound paper currency and credit system as a basis for orderly business growth, the younger Republicans pushed through Congress in 1816 a charter for a Second Bank of the United States.

This institution, with headquarters in Philadelphia and branches elsewhere, was to have a capital of $35 million as compared with the $10 million of Hamilton's national bank. It was to be the depository for all federal funds, and its bank notes were declared receivable for all sums due the government. The bank was to serve public purposes by making loans to the government and also by regulating the state banks, aiding them to resume specie payments at the earliest possible moment, and thereafter keeping them on a sound basis by sustaining them in periods of financial stringency and by restraining them in periods of boom. Power to do this came from the bank's large capital base and from the fact that it was constantly receiving large quantities of state bank notes in its role as federal depository. By promptly presenting these notes to the state banks for redemption during booms, it could force them to curtail their issues, while by expanding its own loans and note issues during bust periods, it could ease any pressure on the state banks. Yet this was to be essentially a private, profit-making institution with the government subscribing only one-fifth of its capital and designating only one-fifth of its directors.

Beginning operation in 1817, the Second Bank helped secure a general resumption of specie payments and then succumbed to the boom spirit itself. Inefficient and often dishonest officers so overextended the bank's own loans and note issues that it lost all power to restrain the expanding state banks. The inevitable reaction, the Panic of 1819, was much more severe than it might otherwise have been because the national bank suddenly reversed its policy and saved itself by ruthlessly applying pressure against its debtors and the state banks. Not until Nicholas Biddle became the bank's president in 1823 did it begin to realize its great potential as a balance wheel and regulator for the economy as a whole.

A second problem growing out of the war was the desperate situation of American industry. As we have seen, the War of 1812 — by cutting off imported European goods — stimulated a rapid growth in this manufacturing activity. But when the war had ended, British manufacturers dumped on the American market their stored-up surplus of products at cut-rate prices, an act that threatened the promising American manufacturing establishment with sudden death.

In the mood of generous nationalism that followed the war, Republican members of Congress from all areas responded to the plight of the beleaguered northeastern manufacturers by passing the first tariff act designed primarily to protect American producers from foreign competition. The Tariff of 1816 required foreign imports that competed with such leading American manufactures as cotton, woolen cloth, and iron to pay import duties ranging around 20 to 25 percent of their value. Additional protection was granted to iron and textiles in 1818 and 1819.

One great ambition of the national-minded Republicans was frustrated by the lingering constitutional doubts of Presidents Madison and Monroe. In the closing days of his administration, Madison vetoed as unconstitutional Calhoun's Bonus Bill of 1817, a measure reserving $1.5 million, which the new national bank paid the government for its charter, for beginning a great national system of roads and canals. Although he recognized that internal improvements were necessary to encourage national expansion and to cement the national union, Madison's strict-constructionist background asserted itself. While Calhoun found justification for the measure in the "general welfare" clause, Madison reluctantly concluded that without a constitutional amendment, federal expenditures for internal improvements were unlawful. With this judgment, his successor, solemn, middle-of-the-road James Monroe, agreed fully.

JUDICIAL NATIONALISM

In the congenial atmosphere of Republican nationalism following the War of 1812, the Federalist nationalism of Chief Justice John Marshall and the Supreme Court he dominated came to full fruition. Having asserted the court's authority on constitutional questions in *Marbury* vs. *Madison* back in 1803, Marshall now used this authority in a series of remarkable decisions to establish his Federalist and nationalist views on questions of property rights, constitutional interpretation, and federal and state powers.

In *Dartmouth College* vs. *Woodward* (1819), the Supreme Court overruled an attempt by the New Hampshire legislature to change the college's colonial charter. Marshall's court had already made itself the defender of property rights against state legislatures in an earlier case, and now Marshall declared that charter rights, too, were sacred. This decision was to become increasingly significant with the growing importance of chartered corporations in American economic life.

The biggest corporation of Marshall's day, the Second Bank of the United States, was involved in his most far-reaching decision, *McCulloch* vs. *Maryland* (1819). This case arose from Maryland's attempt to tax out of existence the bank's branch at Baltimore. The power to tax was the power to destroy, he argued, and no state could be allowed to destroy an instrument of the federal government. Perhaps the most important part of this decision was Marshall's argument, based on the doctrine of implied powers, that Congress had acted constitutionally in chartering the bank. Here he echoed Hamilton's argument to President Washington at the time the first national bank was chartered, maintaining that if the end Congress sought to attain was sanctioned by the Constitution, then "all means which are appropriate, which are plainly adapted to that end" are constitutional.

Among various other decisions affirming federal over state powers, one may be singled out as particularly important. In *Gibbons* vs. *Ogden* (1824), the court invalidated a monopoly that New York had granted over steamboat service between New York and New Jersey. In giving Congress the power to regulate interstate commerce, Marshall declared, the Constitution meant that *only* Congress should have such power. Furthermore he defined interstate commerce so broadly as to include the carrying of passengers or any other variety of commerce between states. Marshall's sweeping extension of the commerce clause not only invalidated the New York monopoly as an invasion of Congress's exclusive power to regulate, but also laid the basis for the great future extensions of federal regulatory powers. The antimonopoly implications of Marshall's decision in *Gibbons* vs. *Ogden* were carried further by Marshall's Jacksonian successor, Chief Justice Roger B. Taney. In *Charles River Bridge* vs. *Warren Bridge* (1837) Taney diminished the vested rights of monopolistic corporate charters in a decision that created the opportunity for a more venturesome corporate capitalism to open up new markets.

Thus in the first flush of the market revolution, the spirit of enterprise and nationalism seemed pervasive in American life — in the entrepreneurial undertakings of countless citizens, in the states' efforts to hasten progress through transportation projects and corporate charters, in the tariff and banking legislation of Congress, in the diplomacy of President Monroe's doctrine, and in the Supreme Court's decisions. The only jarring note seemed to be the doubts of old-fashioned Virginia presidents about federal appropriations for roads and canals, and even this slight barrier to progress would be removed when one of the younger, national-minded Republicans entered the White House in 1825. Yet an unprogressive, agrarian society had not — could not have — changed so totally and quickly as this one momentarily appeared to have done. Two decades of crisis and conflict were to elapse before Americans would be at ease in the new world of enterprise.

FOR FURTHER READING

A good introduction to American economic history is Stuart Bruchey's *The Roots of American Economic Growth, 1607–1861* (1965). Other general surveys for this period include Douglass C. North's somewhat technical but rewarding analysis of *The Economic Growth of the United States, 1790–1860* (1961); Thomas C. Cochran's *Frontiers of Change* (1981); and Charles Sellers's *The Market Revolution* (1991). These may be supplemented with detailed accounts of specific aspects of the economic revolution in the following: George R. Taylor, *The Transportation Revolution, 1815–1860* (1960); Christopher Clark, *The Roots of Rural Capitalism* (1990); Robert Albion, *The Rise of New York Port, 1815–1860* (1939); Robert W. Fogel, *Railroads and American Economic Growth* (1964); Paul Wallace Gates, *The Farmer's Age* (1960); and Ronald Shaw, *Erie Water West: A History of the Erie Canal* (1966). Useful community studies include Steven Hahn and Jonathan Prude's collection of local studies on *The Countryside in the Age of Capitalist Transformation* (1985); Jonathan Prude's *The Coming of Industrial Order: Town and Factory Life in Rural Massachusetts, 1810–1860* (1983); Thomas Dublin's *Women at Work: The Transformation of Work and Community in Lowell, Massachusetts* (1979); and Anthony Wallace's *Rockdale: The Growth of an American Village in the Early Industrial Revolution* (1978). For western development, see Frederick Jackson Turner's *The Frontier in American History* (1920), Ray A. Billington and Martin Ridge's *Westward Expansion* (1982), and Richard White's *"It's Your Misfortune and None of My Own"* (1992). Malcolm Rohrbough's *Land Office Business* (1968) and *The Trans-Appalachian Frontier* (1978) are important works on early white settlement of the West. Reginald Horsman's *The Frontier in the Formative Years* (1970) is a skillful synthesis of developments on the Old Northwest and Old Southwest frontiers. *Flush Times of Alabama and Mississippi* (1853) by Joseph Baldwin is an absorbing contemporary account of the boom years in the Old Southwest. George Dangerfield's *The Era of Good Feelings* (1952) is an account of the political history of the era of Republican nationalism.

TABLE 4. PRESIDENTIAL ELECTIONS AND MAJOR EVENTS, 1816–1828

1816	**James Monroe** (Republican) elected over Rufus King (Federalist). Tariff of 1816, the first deliberately protectionist tariff act.
1816	Second Bank of the United States chartered. Madison vetoes Calhoun's Bonus Bill for internal improvements.
1817–1825	Erie Canal constructed.
1818	National Road reaches the Ohio River.
1819	*Dartmouth College* vs. *Woodward*. John Marshall's Supreme Court defends charter rights against state legislation. *McCulloch* vs. *Maryland*. John Marshall's Supreme Court upholds the constitutionality of the national bank. Panic of 1819 forces a general suspension of specie payments and inaugurates a long and severe economic depression.
1820	Land Act of 1820. Lower land prices and abolition of credit system. Missouri Compromise. **James Monroe** (Republican) re-elected without opposition.
1824	Tariff of 1824. Higher protection. *Gibbons* vs. *Ogden*. John Marshall's Supreme Court extends the federal power to regulate interstate commerce. **John Quincy Adams** (Republican) elected over Andrew Jackson, William H. Crawford, and Henry Clay (all Republicans).
1826	Anti-Masonic movement begins.
1828	Tariff of Abominations. Extremely high protective duties. **Andrew Jackson** (Democratic Republican) elected over John Quincy Adams (National Republican).

10

★ ★ ★ ★ ★ ★

Depression Decade: Sectionalism and Democracy, 1819–1828

THE PANIC of 1819 was the first severe economic crisis that affected the American people as a whole. Part of an international economic dislocation following a long period of war, it was especially intense in the United States because of the reckless expansion of banks, credit, and entrepreneurial investment that preceded it. When the prices of cotton and other commodities suddenly plummeted on the world markets, countless Americans faced the loss of their homes, farms, workshops, and other property because they could not meet the debts they had incurred to finance their ventures. The banks suspended specie payments, and bank notes, the only circulating medium, skidded toward worthlessness in their holders' hands. Merchants went bankrupt, city workers lost their jobs, and the economy ground to a standstill. The paralysis maintained its grip through the early 1820s, and not until after mid-decade did prosperity return.

The economic effects of the Panic were no more momentous than its psychological and political effects. In rapid succession, the American people had been drawn from the settled ways of the old agrarian order into a national market economy of dizzying prosperity, unlimited optimism, and headlong change; then they were suddenly plunged into privation and despair. The shock of this experience made the 1820s a decade of soul-searching and tension. The postwar mood of generous nationalism evaporated as sections and interest groups became narrowly concerned with their own welfare and jealous of rival sections and interest groups. There was a striking revival of Jeffersonian orthodoxy as prodigal agrarians gave up the fleshpots of the market and resolved to return to the old ways of frugality and honest toil. Class antagonisms sharpened as impoverished farmers and urban workers blamed political and business leaders — above all, the banking fraternity — for the disaster. And finally, there was a growing interest in politics, a dissatisfaction with the political leadership that had allowed hard times to come, and a demand for new leaders who would be more responsive to the popular will and use government to relieve the distress.

POLITICAL SECTIONALISM

The resurgence of sectional rivalries was dramatically demonstrated by the heated congressional controversy in 1820 over admitting Missouri as a slave state. Slavery had been a source of conflict in the constitutional convention and on several later occasions, but it had not yet become a major issue. The Quakers had been bearing testimony against human servitude for some time, and by 1804 every state north of Delaware had provided for the ultimate emancipation of slaves within its borders. But there was no strong general movement against slavery as a moral and political evil, for most persons of goodwill, both North and South, continued to indulge Jefferson's hope that it would eventually disappear everywhere through the gradual operation of economic and moral forces.

Thus when northern members of Congress sought to amend the Missouri admission bill to require the gradual emancipation of Missouri slaves, they were acting less from moral repugnance at the institution than from a revival of the traditional northeastern resentment at southern political domination. Much of the South's political power was derived from the constitutional provision that three-fifths of its slaves be counted in apportioning congressional representation and electoral votes. Northeasterners seized upon the Missouri question as a means of blocking the extension of this political injustice throughout the Louisiana Purchase. Southern members of Congress, on the other hand, reacted violently to this attack on their vulnerable system of labor. Admission of Missouri as a free state would upset the even balance between slave and free states and destroy the protection that this gave the South in the Senate against any future antislavery measures.

A Missouri Compromise was finally reached because of the simultaneous movement to make the geographically separate eastern appendage of Massachusetts (now Maine) a separate state. Maine was admitted as a free state, Missouri was admitted as a slave state, and no further slave states were to be created from that part of the Louisiana Purchase lying north of latitude 36°30′ (the latitude of the southern boundary of Missouri).

What many northern members of Congress had in mind when they opposed the admission of any more slave states was illustrated at this same session of 1820 by the fate of a bill to extend further tariff protection to the hard-pressed manufacturers. Representatives from slave-holding states voted almost five to one against this measure in the House and provided most of the votes that killed it in the Senate. By 1824, when the manufacturers tried again for higher duties, the South was opposed 57 to 1 in the House. This time the Northeast was heavily in favor, the only opposition there coming from representatives of international merchants and shippers, who resisted any diminution of international trade. Western representatives provided the margin by which the tariff bill squeaked through Congress, because western farmers had become convinced that the growth of manufacturing might create a flourishing home market for their unprofitable products. The Tariff of 1824 raised duties on textiles to 33.3 percent, sharply increased the rate on iron, and won rural support with duties on raw wool and hemp.

RELIEF AND DEMOCRACY

Manufacturers were not the only ones who had learned from the doctrines of Republican nationalism to look to government for aid. Thousands of western settlers were now unable to complete their payments for public lands under the credit system inaugurated by the Land Act of 1800. In response to their outcries, Congress forgave interest charges, extended payment periods, and allowed delinquent purchasers to retain an amount of land proportionate to the payments they had made. At the same time the Land Act of 1820 abolished the credit system and lowered the minimum price of public lands from $2.00 to $1.25 an acre. The minimum tract that could be purchased had recently been reduced to 80 acres, and all these changes enabled a settler to buy a farm for as little as $100 cash.

But people looked to the state governments for relief from the most desperate problem created by the Panic, the disappearance of money and the collapse of the pyramid of debt that had been built up during the boom. People could neither collect debts owed them nor pay the debts they owed, property could not be sold, and a sweeping liquidation through foreclosures and bankruptcies threatened many Americans.

Legislatures, especially in the hard-hit South and West, responded to the demands of their aroused constituents by various schemes to circumvent the constitutional prohibition against issuing paper money or making anything except gold and silver legal tender. Some states established "banks" or "loan offices" to print state-backed paper money for loan to desperate debtors. Usually these measures were coupled with "stay laws" requiring creditors who refused to accept the state-backed paper money to delay executions on their debtor's property. Relief was also provided through "property laws" whereby a "disinterested" jury composed of the debtor's neighbors set a minimum value below which property could not be forcibly sold to satisfy a debt.

The violent political struggles over debtor relief laws and the closely related banking question accelerated the drift toward a more democratic political system in many states. A few socially complex states like New York and Pennsylvania were already far along the road toward a well-developed two-party or bifactional system in which evenly matched candidates campaigned against each other, aided by party newspapers and stable party organizations expert in the techniques of garnering votes. Under such circumstances, voter interest and participation were high, and public policy was responsive to majority wishes.

In most of the country, however, widespread interest in politics had appeared only sporadically before the 1820s. Having little sense that government — at least the remote state and national governments — affected them much anyhow, most people were willing to leave politics to those well-to-do and socially superior men in their communities who had something to gain from political power, whether land grants or bank charters or simply offices. This resulted in a *personal-factional* political system in which a group of leaders allied through personal or family ties normally maintained unchallenged predominance in a county or other district. In the legislatures, representatives from the various local oligarchies formed shifting alliances, again based on personal or family ties.

This system was sanctioned by Jeffersonian political theory. Jefferson had never maintained that the people as a whole should decide public policy, but only affirmed that the people were wise enough and virtuous enough to select the wisest and most virtuous among them as political leaders. Candidates pretended that they did not seek office and certainly did not electioneer; they only reluctantly consented to serve when called upon by their fellow citizens. The voters did not tell their chosen representatives — who were, of course, always male — what to do once elected, and certainly the representatives did not seek votes by promising to do thus and so. Instead, according to Jeffersonian theory, these unusually wise and virtuous men should be left free to reach wise and virtuous decisions through rational debate and compromise with each other in legislatures and Congress.

The personal-factional system was best adapted to homogeneous communities where conflicts of interest were not very important. It mustered enough genuine wisdom and disinterestedness to function satisfactorily until the market revolution began multiplying the number of specialized economic roles and competing interest groups in the community, while at the same time making people more conscious of the connection between enterprise and public policy. This caused no difficulty during the boom years when there seemed to be enough for everybody. But the Panic made people suddenly aware of their separate and competing interests at the very moment that they began looking to government for mutually contradictory kinds of aid. With debtors clamoring for stay laws and loan offices while creditors denounced them, the Jeffersonian notion of a harmony of interests served by wise and virtuous leaders could no longer be sustained. Voters wanted to know where candidates stood on questions of vital concern to them, and the more alert politicians began telling the voters what they thought a majority wanted to hear.

As elections began to be transformed into popular referenda on public policy, discontent with the established political leadership appeared. The main target of popular resentment was the banking system, which was blamed for causing the collapse by its reckless overexpansion of credit. While the banks were refusing to pay their own debts by not redeeming their notes in specie and while the depreciation of bank notes was the most conspicuous source of loss to the whole community, the banks were foreclosing on the property of their debtors, continuing to pay dividends, and extending special accommodations to their favored borrowers. The state banks managed to shift some of the resulting resentment to the national bank, against which they had similar complaints. But in the eyes of many newly aroused voters, the blame belonged to the banking system as a whole, along with the politicians and business people who had fostered and profited from it. Moreover, these same politicians and business people were often leading the opposition to debtor relief.

As voters came to the polls in increasing numbers to repudiate the established leaders, a new style of democratic politics began to supplant the personal-factional system. The new-style democratic politicians not only promised what the voters wanted, but also portrayed themselves as fighting the battle of the plain people against a group of unscrupulous aristocrats. The old loose and shifting factional groupings in state politics began to stabilize as "democratic" and "aristocratic" alignments. In Kentucky, and to a lesser extent in some other southern and western states, something very like a two-party system developed out of the violent conflict over debtor relief.

In the East, where debtor relief was not such a pressing problem, other issues led to similar results. In New York, DeWitt Clinton capitalized on some high-handed maneuvers by the long entrenched "Albany Regency" candidates to make a smashing political comeback as gubernatorial candidate for the "People's Party." In the same state in 1826, the disappearance and presumed murder of a man who had revealed the secrets of the Masonic order caused an astonishing anti-Masonic outburst, which became a political movement and eventually a short-lived political party. Since Masonic lodges were usually composed of the most prominent men in their communities and since many dominant politicians were Masons, the anti-Masons attacked the order as an aristocratic conspiracy against the rest of the community.

The urban counterpart of anti-Masonry was the labor movement that began to flourish late in the 1820s. By fostering larger and more specialized units of production, the market revolution was making it more difficult for artisans to follow the traditional progression from apprenticeship through the wage-earning journeyman status to independent proprietorship. The depression and unemployment highlighted the insecurity of the permanent wage-earning status in which more and more workers were finding themselves. Journeyman workers organized labor unions and called strikes against the 10-hour day. On the political front, they joined with small entrepreneurs, whose middle-class status was likewise threatened, to form workers' parties in Philadelphia and New York City. Under the banner of "Equal Rights," these parties advocated free public education, opposed imprisonment for debt, and agitated against banks and other monopolies through which a favored few could exploit the many.

Amid the frustrations and conflicts of the 1820s, the long drift toward popular sovereignty in the United States was reaching its culmination. From the beginning of settlement, the cheapness of land and the demand for labor had created an atmosphere of universal opportunity and rough social equality that was quickly reflected in the quasi-democratic political institutions of the colonies. The Revolution, consigning the destiny of Americans to their own hands, had cut off elitist tendencies and firmly established the ideal of equal political rights, but only for white males. In the following decades, state after state had alleviated restrictive male suffrage requirements and other denials — often more symbolic than real — of the Revolutionary ideal. Meanwhile, the egalitarian tendency of American life had been reinforced by the process of western settlement, and the new western states had been free to adopt constitutions reflecting the increasingly democratic tone of the country.

Yet it remained for the market revolution to democratize enterprise, to give a final push to the egalitarian tendency, and to arouse a hitherto apathetic electorate to the importance of public policy and politics. The boom-bust cycle made this popular political awakening more abrupt than it might otherwise have been. Appearing first at the local and state levels, the new-style democratic politics began to manifest itself at the national level in the presidential election of 1824.

THE ELECTION OF 1824

An institutional symbol of the established personal-factional system was the presidential caucus. Every four years, the Republican senators and representatives met in caucus at Washington to designate their party's presidential candidate, and since 1800 the caucus designation had been tantamount to election. As the election of 1824 approached, the foreordained choice of the caucus was William H. Crawford of Georgia, Monroe's secretary of the treasury and a favorite in areas that had been relatively immune to the postwar boom and the Republican nationalism accompanying it. He ran as the candidate of a resurgent Jeffersonianism.

This time, however, the caucus system itself was challenged by the sectional and personal rivalries that had rendered Monroe's second term anything but an "Era of Good Feelings." Secretary of State John Quincy Adams was the choice of New England, Speaker of the House Henry Clay was the favorite of the West, and Secretary of War John C. Calhoun found his backers in the South. All these anti-Crawford candidates, in fact, were champions of Republican nationalism. Calhoun led them in attacking the caucus as undemocratic, and their supporters' refusal to attend it resulted in Crawford's being nominated by only a minority of the Republican congressmen.

The beneficiary of these rivalries was Andrew Jackson, hero of the Battle of New Orleans. Although not thought of initially as a serious candidate even by his home state (Tennessee) politicians, "Old Hickory" demonstrated remarkable appeal. Though no one knew where the general stood on public issues, to those disenchanted with the old leaders it was enough that he was a popular hero — the people's man against the established leadership.

When the election took place, Jackson had the most popular and electoral votes, but none of the candidates won a majority. The Constitution directed that the House of Representatives, voting by states, should choose among the three highest candidates. This eliminated Clay, low man in electoral votes; Crawford was also removed from serious contention by a physical collapse; and Calhoun had withdrawn before the election. Clay had the opportunity to wield his great influence in the House on behalf of either Jackson or Adams. He chose Adams, who was narrowly elected.

THE TRIBULATIONS OF THE
SECOND ADAMS

John Quincy Adams was among the ablest and most patriotic presidents but was also one of the least successful. Partly through circumstances and partly through insensitivity to public sentiment, he defied and was overwhelmed by the most powerful political currents of the 1820s.

The Jackson supporters regarded Adams's election as a flouting of the people's will. But when he appointed Henry Clay as secretary of state, traditional stepping-stone to the presidency, their fury knew no bounds. The cry of "Bargain and Corruption" rang throughout the land, touching off a four-year campaign to vindicate popular sovereignty by placing Jackson in the White House.

Adams compounded his difficulties by underestimating the depression-bred reaction against Republican nationalism. Adams and Clay sought to build a National Republican party, based on a coalition of the Northeast and the Ohio Valley and dedicated to Clay's "American System" of protective tariff, national bank, and internal improvements. In addition, the president's first annual message called for a national university and federally sponsored scientific research and exploration, while cautioning Congress against being "palsied by the will of our constituents."

The Adams-Clay program outraged the neo-Jeffersonian Crawford supporters, now led by New York's Martin Van Buren, and drove them into alliance with the Jackson and Calhoun factions. Calling itself the Democratic Republican party, this Jacksonian coalition for four years blocked the president's program in Congress and harassed him in every way possible. The only significant legislative product of these four years was a tariff act passed in 1828. With both parties trying to win presidential votes by juggling complicated tariff schedules, this "Tariff of Abominations" pushed duties on both manufactured and agricultural products to absurdly high levels and satisfied almost no one.

The presidential election of 1828 was marked by the return of the two-party system to national politics and by an abusiveness on both sides that was unmatched since the last closely contested two-party election in 1800. Questions of public policy were hardly discussed, the real issue being whether the people's man Jackson should prevail over the seasoned statesman and old-style political leader Adams. This was enough to produce a substantial increase in the number of voters and a substantial majority for Jackson.

FOR FURTHER READING

Murray N. Rothbard focuses on *The Panic of 1819* (1962). The best general account of the 1820s is Frederick Jackson Turner's *The Rise of the New West, 1819–1829* (1906), but see also George Dangerfield's *The Awakening of American Nationalism, 1815–1828* (1965). Although it deals only with the southern states, Charles S. Sydnor's *The Development of Southern Sectionalism, 1819–1848* (1948) is also suggestive. Glover Moore has carefully examined *The Missouri Controversy, 1819–1821* (1953). Some idea of the political transformations going on in the states in the 1820s may be gained from Shaw Livermore, Jr.'s *The Twilight of Federalism* (1962); from Thomas E. Jeffrey's *State Parties and National Politics* (1989); and from Charles Sellers's *James K. Polk, Jacksonian: 1795–1843* (1957). The entire political career of John Quincy Adams is splendidly narrated by Samuel Flagg Bemis in *John Quincy Adams* (2 vols., 1949–1956), while Mary W. M. Hargreaves focuses specifically on *The Presidency of John Quincy Adams* (1985). Robert V. Remini has written a lively scholarly account of *The Election of Andrew Jackson* (1963).

TABLE 5. PRESIDENTIAL ELECTIONS AND MAJOR EVENTS, 1828–1840

1828	**Andrew Jackson** (Democratic Republican) elected over John Quincy Adams (National Republican). Tariff of Abominations.
1830	Jackson vetoes the Maysville Road Bill. Indian Removal Act.
1831	*Cherokee Nations* vs. *Georgia.*
1832	Tariff of 1832 remedies worst abuses of the Tariff of Abominations but fails to satisfy South Carolina Nullifiers. Black Hawk War ends Indian resistance in Northwest. Jackson vetoes Second Bank of the United States recharter bill. **Andrew Jackson** (Democratic-Republican) re-elected over Henry Clay (National Republican). South Carolina nullifies tariff laws.
1833	Compromise Tariff gradually reduces all tariff duties to 20%. Force Act authorizes president to use military to enforce the laws. Jackson transfers the federal deposits from the national bank to selected state-chartered deposit banks.
1835	Seminole resistance to removal begins.
1836	Jackson issues Specie Circular requiring specie for purchase of federal lands. Distribution Act distributes the federal surplus among the states. **Martin Van Buren** (Democrat) elected over William Henry Harrison, Daniel Webster, and Hugh Lawson White (all Whigs).
1837	Panic of 1837 forces a general suspension of specie payments and initiates a severe and prolonged economic depression. Van Buren proposes the independent treasury system.
1838	New York Free Banking Act is a forerunner of general incorporation laws: one of the many efforts by the states to reform and regulate banking. Cherokee removal to Oklahoma.
1840	Independent treasury system finally approved by Congress after three years of debate. **William Henry Harrison** (Whig) elected over Martin Van Buren (Democrat).

11

★ ★ ★ ★ ★ ★

The Jacksonian Era, 1828–1840

WITH Andrew Jackson's inauguration, the forces of egalitarianism swept over the federal government. Though Jackson had risen to become master of a large plantation and one of his state's leaders, he had never abandoned the egalitarian habits of his earlier surroundings in small-farmer North Carolina and frontier Tennessee. On Inauguration Day, he opened the White House reception to an unruly mob of the high and the low, shocking the older official society but unmistakably announcing the new regime's conviction that common people were as good as aristocrats.

The same point was made with more substantial effect by Jackson's extension of the "spoils system" and his frank advocacy of "rotation in office." The new president was accompanied to Washington by a host of new-style democratic politicians demanding office as a reward for their support. Jackson took the position that any honest citizen could discharge the duties of a government office as well as any other. Furthermore, public offices should not be the property of their holders for life. They should be passed around, with a preference shown for friends of the administration that the people had elected. The numerous removals and appointments that Jackson made on these principles somewhat impaired the efficiency of government service but also made it more representative of, and responsive to the country as a whole. Moreover, the spoils system helped make possible the new-style political parties through which the popular will could be translated into public policy.

Jackson was the first president to operate on the principle that the people themselves should decide public policy. Arguing that the president was the only federal official elected by the people as a whole, he was supremely certain that his policies represented the popular will. So great was the popular confidence he inspired that the people, or a majority of them, usually agreed.

By assuming this role of democratic tribune, Jackson greatly increased the power of the presidency relative to Congress. All his predecessors combined had vetoed only 9 congressional measures, usually on the grounds that they were unconstitutional. Old Hickory used the veto 12 times, against legislation he thought inexpedient as well as legislation he thought unconstitutional. By taking his differences with Congress to the voters, he was highly successful in making recalcitrant legislators compliant or in replacing them.

JACKSONIAN POLICIES

Though the people's candidate had been elected, it was by no means clear what policies a people's administration would follow. Jackson himself had little political experience, and it was supposed that much would depend on whether Calhoun or Van Buren controlled the administration and became the heir for the presidential succession. Calhoun wanted to base the Jacksonian Democratic-Republican party (which gradually came to be called simply the Democratic party) on an alliance between the South and the West, which would reduce tariffs for the South and liberalize federal land policy for the West. A most embarrassing issue for Calhoun's plans was that of internal improvements, which the West favored and the South increasingly opposed.

Van Buren, on the other hand, wanted to resurrect the old Jeffersonian coalition between southern planters and the "plain Republicans" of the Northeast. Such a coalition could unite on neo-Jeffersonian grounds to oppose internal improvements (New York wanted no federally financed competition for its Erie Canal) and the national bank (New Yorkers resented the bank as a Philadelphia institution that gave New York City's rival an undeserved financial dominance). The one issue dangerous to Van Buren's plans was tariffs, over which northerners and southerners were disagreeing with mounting vehemence.

Although the Calhoun supporters seemed to have the upper hand in the party, Jackson's inauguration produced a sudden reversal. Calhoun's friends were almost frozen out of the cabinet, while Van Buren himself was made secretary of state. Van Buren astutely used information that Calhoun, while a member of Monroe's cabinet, had advocated punishing Jackson for his rash invasion of Spanish Florida. The New Yorker was aided, too, by the "Eaton imbroglio," when the socially prominent women of Washington tried to ostracize the somewhat disreputable wife of Jackson's old friend and Secretary of War John Eaton. Calhoun's wife, Floride, was among the ladies who angered the president by snubbing Peggy Eaton, while the widower Van Buren was free to treat her with conspicuous gallantry. Relations between Jackson and Calhoun steadily deteriorated until the South Carolinian was finally driven from the party.

Jackson found Van Buren more congenial than Calhoun, both personally and in political outlook. Though Jackson came to Washington without a very well-thought-out position on the major issues, he did have some deeply rooted political instincts that he trusted implicitly. These determined his administration's policies. His instinctive egalitarianism has already been noted. Joined to this was an instinctive neo-Jeffersonian agrarian-mindedness.

Jackson himself had once engaged in extravagant land and commercial speculations based on credit. The bankruptcy that ended these operations and the long struggle to pay off his debts and regain solvency through farming were experiences decisive for his political outlook. Thoroughly chastened, advocating the virtues of agriculture, hard work, and economy, abhorring debt, and fearing the get-rich-quick atmosphere fostered by easy credit, he interpreted the boom-bust cycle of 1815–1819 as reproducing his own personal experiences on a national scale. Consequently, when he assumed the presidency, his one clearly defined objective was to administer a simple, economical government and to pay off the national debt as rapidly as possible.

Jackson's mood agreed more with Van Buren's neo-Jeffersonianism than with the Republican nationalism that had heretofore been Calhoun's trademark. The influence that this gave Van Buren became most apparent over an improvements matter. The advocates of a nationwide federal road system managed to push through Congress the Maysville Road Bill in 1830. Though this bill only provided that the federal government should buy stock in a company building a turnpike from Maysville to Lexington in Kentucky, it was regarded as the test measure for the whole internal improvements program. Such expenditures would delay Jackson's cherished project for paying off the national debt, and Van Buren had little difficulty persuading him that the measure should be vetoed. The veto message not only condemned the Maysville project, but suggested that all federal expenditures for internal improvements were perhaps either unwise or unlawful — showing that the Jacksonians favored not only frugal government but limits on federal powers. Though the veto did retard for several decades the dream of a nationally financed transportation network, the effect of the Maysville veto was more symbolic than practical. Jackson himself authorized some $10 million in improvement bills, including some for local projects.

THE TARIFF AND NULLIFICATION

Clearly, Jackson and Van Buren were not ready to assault all the works of Republican nationalism. To undertake a thorough downward revision of the Tariff of Abominations would be to delay payment of the public debt and to disrupt the North-South alliance that Van Buren sought to perfect. Consequently, the president urged his first Congress to handle the question with "utmost caution," and the resulting tariff revisions of 1830 hardly touched the more abominable features (the outrageously high duties) of the system.

At this point South Carolina exploded. No state had enjoyed a more uninterrupted prosperity from colonial days to 1819 than South Carolina. Rice, indigo, and sea island cotton first had created a wealthy ruling class in the low country, and then the upland cotton boom had spread comparable riches through the rest of the state. No state, except perhaps Kentucky, was harder hit or more permanently damaged by the depression of the 1820s. The disruption of business coincided with the rise of more efficient cotton-producing areas in the Gulf states, and to make matters infinitely worse, a growing anxiety over the slavery issue made South Carolina particularly sensitive about state rights. South Carolina's reaction to its economic prostration was the more violent because a long period of heady prosperity had preceded it and because no state had developed a prouder or touchier group of political leaders.

Until the depression, the Republican nationalism of Calhoun and his friends had been ascendant in South Carolina. The hard times enabled a rival state-rights faction to blame Calhoun's favorite policies for all the state's woes. By the mid-1820s, the state-rights advocates had stirred up a storm of resentment against the protective tariff and were close to winning political control of the state. Calhoun and his friends were forced to retreat from Republican nationalism as rapidly and unobtrusively as possible. When Congress passed the Tariff of Abominations in 1828, the Calhoun supporters confounded their state rights rivals by outdoing them in violent agitation against protection and by adopting an even more radical version of the state rights doctrine.

The famous Doctrine of Nullification was announced in the South Carolina Exposition and Protest of 1828, secretly written by Calhoun and issued as a report of a legislative committee. The Nullifiers maintained that the Constitution was a compact among states that retained their essential sovereignty and had delegated only limited and clearly specified powers to the federal government. The states themselves were the only proper judges of whether their common agent, the federal government, had exceeded the powers delegated to it by the constitutional compact. If a state judged that some federal law was a violation of the compact, it could declare it null and void, whereupon the federal government must desist unless and until three-fourths of the states, through the amending process, explicitly granted it the nullified power.

The South Carolinians counted on the Jackson administration to push tariff reform, and only after failure to do so in 1829–1830 did Calhoun's friends begin a campaign in the state for actual nullification. The Jacksonian Congress responded by eliminating some of the worst excesses of the Tariff of Abominations in 1832, but the rates were still decidedly protectionist. Meanwhile, Calhoun had openly broken with Jackson and put himself at the head of the Nullifiers; the Nullifiers won the two-thirds majority in the state legislature necessary to call a state convention; and in November, 1832, the state convention declared the tariff laws null and void and forbade their enforcement in South Carolina.

When Congress met in December, Jackson called for thorough tariff reform but at the same time announced his determination to enforce all federal laws throughout the land, by military means if necessary. This situation produced the Compromise Tariff of 1833. Snatching from the Jackson party the credit for tariff reform, Clay and Calhoun united to push through a measure by which all tariff rates were to be reduced by gradual steps over a 10-year period to a uniform rate of 20 percent. Congress also complied with Jackson's demand that it simultaneously pass a Force Act, authorizing him to use the armed forces to uphold the laws. The South Carolina convention then reassembled and rescinded its nullification of the tariff laws, but got in the last word by nullifying the Force Act.

The seemingly inconclusive outcome should not obscure the important long-range effects of this dangerous crisis. The fact that the Nullifiers could claim victory — the tariff had been reformed — heightened their uncompromising attitude toward the federal government and gave them complete dominance over South Carolina. From this time on, the state and its magnetic leader Calhoun sought to unite the South in radical resistance to "federal tyranny," and the incessant agitation from this source was a major factor in producing the eventual secession of the southern states.

In the shorter run, nullification and disunion were discredited. Every other southern legislature denounced the South Carolina doctrine, the aged Madison denied that it derived from the Kentucky and Virginia resolutions of 1798, and the country as a whole responded enthusiastically to the nationalistic sentiments that Jackson expressed in opposing the Nullifiers. In fact, Jackson's zeal for preserving the Union led him to embrace a nationalistic interpretation of the Constitution that greatly embarrassed Van Buren and other state-rights Jacksonians. Heretofore the state-rights idea had been associated with democratic-mindedness in American politics, but now that the people's candidate was in the White House proclaiming federal pre-eminence over the states, federal power seemed less threatening. Perhaps the most significant result of the nullification crisis was the decline of state-rights sentiment in the face of a rising democratic nationalism.

INDIAN REMOVAL

Jackson was not always a single-minded champion of federal prerogatives, as indicated by his handling of claims of the Cherokee nation, one of the Five Civilized Nations. A practical westerner and renowned Indian fighter who was not inclined to romanticize the "noble savage," the Tennessee president winked at Georgia's expropriation of Cherokee lands in defiance of a federal court ruling. In *Cherokee Nation* vs. *Georgia* (1831) and *Worcester* vs. *Georgia* (1832), the Marshall court sided with the Indians and invalidated the state's claim to Cherokee territory. But Jackson refused to enforce the ruling, reportedly saying, "John Marshall has made his decision, now let him enforce it."

That which followed — the enactment of the Indian Removal Act of 1830 and the relocation at gun point of these Native Americans to territory beyond the Mississippi — is one of the darker chapters in the nation's history. Amid scenes of indescribable suffering, some 4,000 of the 16,000 refugees died in 1838 and 1839 of cold, hunger, and disease along the 800-mile-long route known in Cherokee memory as the "Trail of Tears." One witness, the young Frenchman Alexis de Tocqueville, watched as "the wounded, the sick, newborn babies, and the old men on the point of death" passed near Memphis and feared he could never forget the "solemn spectacle." By 1839, three more of the remaining Five Civilized Nations — Choctaw, Chickasaw, and Creek — had been forcibly removed to the West under congressional authorization. In 1843, the fifth nation, the Seminoles of Florida who under the leadership of Osceola had resisted removal efforts since 1835, were all but exterminated by federal troops. Meanwhile, the Black Hawk War (1832) had ended effective Indian resistance to white settlement in the Old Northwest.

Through relocation, about 100,000 Indians were forced onto western lands that were pledged to them "forever." Their evacuation opened some 100 million acres of fertile eastern agricultural land to land-hungry whites. In return, they received $68 million, 32 million acres, and empty promises of federal protection from future white encroachment. Emerging as it did at the peak of the nullification crisis, the federal restraint implicit in Jackson's Indian policy may have confused some Jackson watchers. But Southerners, Westerners, and land speculators were delighted to find a president who shared their views of the Indian's place in an expanding nation. In fairness to Jackson — who, as nearly all historians agree, was no champion of Native American rights — the policy of dispossession and relocation that he so vigorously enforced was begun well before his election. Moreover, given the social values of the age and a context of growing conflict between Indian nations and eastern states, it did not appear an unreasonable solution to the "Indian problem." Convinced that assimilation was impossible and that autonomous Indian enclaves were impractical, if not unconstitutional, Jackson seems genuinely to have believed that his was a "just and humane policy" that placed the Indian "beyond the reach of injury or oppression." That it proved to be none of these things is indisputable; that other, more enlightened alternatives were open to him is less certain.

THE BANK WAR

Simultaneously with the nullification controversy, another great conflict had begun to take shape, this one between Andrew Jackson and the Second Bank of the United States. Jackson's experience with debt and depression had made him distrustful of all banks. On the bank question, his democratic-mindedness merged with his agrarian-mindedness to produce the conviction that banks fostered an unhealthy atmosphere of speculation, created boom-and-bust cycles, and transferred wealth from the many to the few. The national bank was open to special objection because it concentrated so much power in private hands and because it violated the Jeffersonian principles of strict construction and limited government. Jackson's views in all these respects reflected the resurgent agrarian-mindedness and neo-Jeffersonianism produced by the depression, as well as the antibank animus of the emerging workers' movement.

Actually, since Nicholas Biddle had become president of the bank in 1823, it had acted to restrain the numerous state-chartered banks from the tendencies Jackson feared, and most businesses and politicians had become convinced that the bank was indispensable to a soundly growing economy. Yet the opponents of banking in general saw the national bank as the head of the whole odius system and as the only part of the system that the federal government could readily reach. As a new boom gathered strength in the early 1830s, they were aided by an incongruous ally — entrepreneurial democracy.

As in the boom years following the War of 1812, the glittering promise of profits held out by a rapidly expanding market economy was creating a host of new entrepreneurs. For these business people, easy credit was the key to success, and the more reckless of the state-chartered banks became the citadels of the entrepreneurial spirit. By restraining the state banks from overexpansion, the national bank curtailed the profits and dimmed the prospects of the state banks and their borrowers. Consequently, the new entrepreneurs, the more speculative elements of the economy, regarded the bank as an aristocratic and repressive institution, representing established wealth and using its privileged position to hobble newcomers who attempted to join the race for success.

Both the entrepreneurs and the agrarian-minded had been heavily attracted to Jackson's Democratic party. Both groups opposed the bank on somewhat egalitarian grounds, but their common hostility to Biddle's institution could not indefinitely conceal the fact that their ultimate objectives were diametrically opposed.

When Jackson became president, Biddle was already thinking about getting a bill passed to renew the bank's charter, which was due to expire in 1836. Jackson dismayed the bank's supporters when he questioned its constitutionality and expediency in his first message to Congress. Their dismay turned to alarm when it became clear that Jackson would be a candidate for re-election in 1832. The old Adams-Clay alignment, calling itself the National Republican party, was planning to run Clay against Jackson, and Clay was urging Biddle to press for recharter before the election. Clay argued that this would force Jackson to approve a recharter bill, for a veto would be a damaging issue against him in the election. Biddle finally agreed, and in July 1832 a recharter bill passed Congress by substantial majorities.

Jackson promptly returned the measure to Congress with a veto message declaring the bank unconstitutional and demagogically denouncing the foreign ownership of much of the bank's stock. At the heart of his message was an eloquent paragraph expounding the Jacksonian social philosophy. The president granted that natural inequalities existed in every society. "But," he said, "when the laws undertake to add to these natural and just advantages artificial distinctions, to grant titles, gratuities, and exclusive privileges, to make the rich richer and the potent more powerful, the humble members of society — the farmers, mechanics, and laborers — who have neither the time nor the means of securing like favors to themselves, have a right to complain of the injustice of their government."

Jackson's hostility to the bank was genuine, but his veto message was at least in part designed to make the bank an election issue. The bank supporters did not have the votes in Congress to override the veto, but they confidently expected that both the veto and its author would be repudiated in the ensuing presidential election. When the returns were in, Jackson's estimate proved to be the shrewdest as he won 219 electoral votes to Clay's 40.

Yet the bank was far from dead. Jackson rightly feared that Biddle was determined to use the bank's great economic and political power to push a recharter bill through Congress over his veto. Equally determined to cripple the bank, the president resolved to remove the government's mounting deposits from its vaults. Federal receipts were booming along with the economy, the national debt had been paid off, and a federal surplus of millions of dollars was beginning to accumulate. These surplus federal deposits greatly extended the bank's lending ability, profits, and power. It took the administration a year to find a way of removing surplus deposits from the bank. After discharging two consecutive uncooperative secretaries of the treasury and after protracted negotiations with nervous state bankers, Jackson announced in September 1833 that henceforth the Treasury would deposit the federal funds in selected state banks, so-called deposit banks or pet banks.

Enraged by the removal of deposits, Biddle recklessly threw the full economic power of the national bank against the government. Deposit removal and Jackson's hostility made some contraction of the bank's loans necessary, but Biddle resolved to force such a severe loan contraction and to create such widespread distress that Congress would be compelled to restore the deposits and eventually recharter the bank. As a result, the "Panic Session" of Congress was under intense pressure during the winter of 1833–1834 to restore the deposits to relieve the country from mounting bankruptcies, unemployment, and distress. But Jackson's antibank majority held firm. Biddle was finally forced to relax the pressure, and the bank's doom was sealed — partly because Biddle's panic helped to prove Jackson's case against the bank's immense power.

BOOM AND BUST AGAIN

The destruction of the national bank was only a Pyrrhic victory in the Jacksonians' larger campaign to reform banking in general. Jackson and many of his principal followers were "hard-money" people who wanted all bank notes driven from circulation, leaving only gold and silver coin as a circulating medium. Their attack on the national bank was only the first step in their deflationary, agrarian-minded program, and they hoped to use the state-bank deposit system to reform the state banks. The deposit banks would be required, as a condition for receiving the deposits, to cease issuing notes in denominations under $5 or accepting such notes in their transactions with other banks. Gradually the prohibition would be extended to notes under $10 and then $20. Driving small notes from circulation would create a steady demand for specie for small transactions, and all banks would have to reduce their loans and note issues in order to have enough specie on hand to meet the demand.

But this scheme did not have time to get under way before it was overwhelmed by a massive inflation. The Jacksonians had destroyed the national bank's stabilizing influence on the economy just at the moment when powerful inflationary forces were pushing the country into a boom even more wildly speculative than the one that followed the War of 1812. With the national bank's restraining influence removed, the state banks expanded their loans, note issues, and profits; new state banks were chartered by the hundreds; the deposit banks themselves got out of control; and the wave of inflation and speculation rolled ominously higher toward its inevitable cresting and crash.

The hard-money supporters could only shout futile warnings. Their Jeffersonian constitutional scruples prevented them from attempting direct federal regulation of the state banks. Regulation at the state level was equally impossible because the uneasy alliance between hard-money (or agrarian-minded) Democrats and enterprise-minded Democrats began breaking down as soon as their common enemy, the national bank, was finally defeated.

Nevertheless, in 1836, Jackson attempted a drastic remedy with his Specie Circular. The flood of bank notes had stimulated an especially frantic speculation in public lands, and the Circular directed that thenceforth lands must be paid for in specie or specie-redeemable bank notes. Coming too late, the Specie Circular succeeded only in putting a strain on the vastly overextended structure of credit. The strain was increased by the Distribution Act that Jackson had reluctantly signed a few weeks before. Congress had decided to distribute the bulging federal surplus (approaching $40 million) among the states; the federal deposit banks were suddenly called upon to transfer vast sums to the state treasuries. Finally, in the spring of 1837, only weeks after Jackson left office, a financial crisis in England set off a wave of bankruptcies in the United States. The banks suspended specie payments, and the Panic of 1837 brought the whole towering pyramid of credit crashing down.

Jackson's hand-picked successor Van Buren was left to cope with a severe and prolonged depression. Aligning himself with the hard-money wing of the Democratic party, Van Buren proposed that the government sever its connections with all banks and keep its funds in its own "independent treasury" offices. He further proposed that the government accept and pay out only gold and silver coin, which would have some deflationary effect by creating a constant demand for specie. But in the main the proposal meant that the federal government would wash its hands of responsibility for the economy. Because of the split between hard-money and soft-money Democrats, Congress wrangled over the independent treasury throughout Van Buren's term. The bill was finally passed in 1840.

Meanwhile, the depression had forced most state legislatures to attempt some kind of banking reform. A few states prohibited banks entirely, others gave a monopoly of the banking business to a state-owned or mixed public-private bank, and most states adopted stricter regulations to prevent an overextension of credit by private banks. New York's widely imitated Free Banking Act of 1838 sought to provide state regulation and at the same time to divest banks of the monopolistic special privileges they enjoyed through their legislative charters. Foreshadowing general incorporation laws for all kinds of enterprises, the act provided that anyone who complied with certain regulations could engage in the banking business. Thus by the early 1840s, the country had reached a practical compromise on the banking question: banks would continue to stimulate economic growth, but they would be restrained through free competition and state regulation rather than through a national bank.

The long and hotly contested struggle over banking was important in two respects. On the most obvious level, it reflected the efforts of an economy newly swept forward by the market revolution to develop a credit and currency system that would sustain growth and broaden opportunity without causing disastrous boom-and-bust cycles. At a deeper level, it reflected the psychological ambivalence of a conservative, agrarian society toward the world of rapid change and growth into which it had suddenly been thrust.

The boom-bust cycle experience made its mark on the people. During the first great boom, 1815–1819, the country as a whole succumbed with uncritical enthusiasm to the new spirit of enterprise. The depression of the 1820s produced an equally decided reaction in the other direction — against banks, easy credit, paper money, and entrepreneurial ambition. Thus the return of prosperity and the second great boom, 1834–1837, evoked more ambivalent reactions. Some Americans again saw unlimited opportunity and clamored for unlimited credit; others, the neo-agrarians who remembered the 1820s, championed hard money, took seriously Jackson's Bank Veto plea for equal-rights, and contrasted the self-interest of privileged corporations (especially banks) with old republican virtues. The great depression of 1837 and its long aftermath increased neo-agrarian fears of the collusion of legislatures and corporations. New midwestern state constitutions of the 1840s placed restrictions on both legislative and corporate power. Ideological differences, dating to the conflicts of Jefferson and Hamilton, remained, despite the new politics of the second party system.

THE NEW POLITICS

Just as the Jacksonian era saw the evolution of financial institutions and practices to serve the emerging spirit of enterprise, so did it see the evolution of political institutions and practices to serve the emerging spirit of egalitarian democracy. The basic feature of the new politics was the two-party system, which had flourished briefly and imperfectly around 1800 and which re-emerged to reach its full development only in the 1830s.

Carrying to the national level the new-style democratic politics that had emerged in the states during the 1820s, the Jacksonians created a strong political party and forced their opponents to imitate their organization and techniques for wooing a mass electorate. The anti-Jacksonians were at first an ill-organized coalition of Clay-Adams National Republicans, Nullifiers, and — out of hostility to the Van Buren organization in New York — the democratic-minded anti-Masons. These elements were unable to unite to stem the Jacksonian tide in the presidential election of 1832, but they were already beginning to learn the lessons of Jacksonian politics. In fact the anti-Masons had anticipated the Democrats in calling a national party convention representing the grass-roots elements of the party to replace the discredited caucus method of nominating candidates.

A powerful, unified opposition party developed only in 1833–1834 when Jackson's removal of deposits caused the defection of many business-minded Democrats and enabled his opponents to unite on the platform of resistance to executive tyranny. Taking the name *Whigs* to identify themselves with earlier defenders of liberty, they stood for sound business enterprise and a program of Republican nationalism. Though the Whigs drew increasing support from all sections and classes, they appealed especially to the wealthier and more established members of the business community, to the manufacturing interests, and to the larger southern planters whose staple crops involved them extensively in the commercial network. Calhoun's Nullifiers cooperated with the Whigs for a few years, but after 1837 returned to the Democratic party.

In 1836 the new Whig party sought to capitalize on political sectionalism by running three presidential candidates, hoping to throw the election into the House of Representatives. But the magic of Jackson's popularity was sufficient to win his candidate, Van Buren, a slim majority over all three Whigs. The Whigs' day finally came in 1840 when the Democrats were discredited by the depression and when the Whigs outdid the Democrats at the game of democratic politics. Running the popular old Indian fighter William Henry Harrison as the people's candidate against the "aristocratic" Van Buren, the Whigs whipped up enthusiasm with monster rallies, torchlight parades, songs, and log-cabin symbolism to win a sweeping majority.

The presidential election of 1840 also produced by far the largest outpouring of voters yet seen. Only 27 percent of the estimated eligible voters had voted for president in 1824; the Jackson-Adams contest of 1828 had raised the figure to 56 percent; but the contest of 1840 brought out 78 percent of the eligible electorate, a proportion that may never have been equaled since. This dramatic rise in political interest was a result of the full development of the two-party system. By 1840 the two parties were almost equally strong not only at the national level but also in every section, in most of the states, and in a majority of counties. This meant closely contested elections for all offices from sheriff to president with no efforts being spared to woo hesitant voters. Each party maintained an elaborate network of stridently partisan newspapers in Washington, the state capitals, and countless villages and towns. Rival orators stumped every neighborhood for months before every election. Competing systems of party committees at county, state, and national levels issued a constant stream of broadsides and pamphlets, organized parades and rallies, and made sure that no voter stayed away from the polls on election day. This incessant political activity not only brought voters to the polls in droves, but also made politics a leading form of American recreation, while providing the population with a massive political education.

But the parties were as much affected by the voters as they affected the voters. The new-style democratic politicians of both parties developed an acute sensitivity to shifts in public opinion and became expert in building coalitions that would yield a majority or near-majority. The Whigs continued to appeal more strongly to business interests, the well-to-do, manufacturers, and large planters, while the Democrats attracted smaller farmers, workers, and frontier areas. But both parties needed additional support to achieve a majority, and both quickly learned the techniques for constantly adjusting their positions to changing public moods. As a result the parties tended not to differ sharply in normal times and to maintain a nearly even balance of strength. From Jackson's day to our own, with only brief interruptions, this two-party system has remained a reasonably sensitive instrument for translating majority opinion into public policy while moderating the sharpness of conflict among the diverse groups that compose American society.

CONFLICTING HISTORICAL VIEWPOINTS: NO. 4

What Was Jacksonian Democracy?

In his Life of Andrew Jackson *(3 vols., 1860), the nineteenth-century historian James Parton concluded that the seventh president was "a patriot and a traitor. . . . A democratic autocrat. An urbane savage. An atrocious saint." On this note of paradox, scholarly investigation of Jacksonian politics began, and the Jacksonian era remains among the most controversial in American history.*

Parton, the earliest and most distinguished nineteenth-century Jackson scholar, represented the patrician school of historians. Sons of affluent and often aristocratic eastern families, deeply suspicious of popular democracy and the common folk, these early historians viewed Jacksonianism as the degradation of American government. Jackson, they affirmed, was an illiterate backwoods barbarian, the agent of the unwashed and ignorant masses.

Soon after 1900, a generation of reform-minded scholars challenged this decidedly conservative interpretation. Countering the anti-democratic beliefs of the patricians with pro-democratic views, these progressive historians celebrated Jackson as the champion of the popular will. Thus, in his distinguished Life of Andrew Jackson *(2 vols., 1911), John Spencer Bassett* praised the rustic Tennessee president for his *"brave, frank, masterly lead-ership"* of a broad democratic movement. Although generally agreed on the nature of Jacksonian democracy, the progressives often argued about its origins. In The Frontier in American History *(1920) and* The United States, 1830–1850 *(1935), Frederick Jackson Turner emphasized the influence of frontier democracy in the development of Jacksonianism. In Turner's view, Jacksonian Democracy was a sectional, rather than a class, movement. It was inspired and sustained, he believed, by the pioneer societies of the new states of the West and Southwest. To Arthur M. Schlesinger, Jr., on the other hand, Jacksonianism was "a problem not of sections but of classes." In his* Age of Jackson *(1945), the younger Schlesinger included eastern wage earners as well as western farmers among the Old Hero's supporters. The movement, he argued, pitted "noncapitalist groups, and laboring men, East, West, and South" against "capitalist groups, mainly Eastern."*

By the 1950s and 1960s the critics of the progressive interpretation, par-ticularly of Schlesinger's labor thesis, were numerous. Bray Hammond (Banks and Politics in America, *1957) and Edward Pessen (*Jacksonian Amer-ica, *1969), for example, denied that Jackson's was a working-class move-ment. Arguing that his supporters were not common people at all but incipient entrepreneurs, Hammond characterized the Jacksonians as "newer, more aggressive businessmen" who clashed with "an old and conservative merchant class." According to Pessen, Old Hickory was anti-labor, and workers opposed him at the polls. Marvin Meyers (*The Jacksonian Persua-sion, *1957) and John W. Ward (*Andrew Jackson, Symbol for an Age, *1955), on the other hand, fastened on symbolism and psychology to explain the Jacksonian phenomenon. In differing though complementary studies, these scholars concluded that in Jackson, Americans found not a champion of class or section but the embodiment of old-fashioned republican virtues. The ultimate refutation of the Schlesinger interpretation, however, came from Lee Benson, who argued in* The Concept of Jacksonian Democracy *(1961) that Jacksonianism existed only as a figment of the historical imag-ination. Benson's argument that ethnic and religious differences were more important than class or section in determining voting behavior seemed to invalidate the need for the concept of Jacksonian Democracy altogether.*

While Benson's ethnocultural thesis attracted numerous followers and de-stroyed forever any notion that Jacksonian Democracy had a purely class or sectional basis, over the last two decades scholars have sought to restore some meaning to the concept of Jacksonian Democracy by focusing on the ways Jacksonian politics were a response to the social, economic, and cul-tural changes of the era. Harry L. Watson has synthesized much of this re-cent work in his Liberty and Power *(1990). Watson argues that Jacksonian politics represented "a serious policy debate about the future of the Re-public and the nature of its society," as Whigs and Democrats offered dif-ferent positions on how best to respond to the most sweeping change of the day, the emerging market revolution. At the same time, while "ethnocul-tural tensions" affected voters' choices, such conflict did not necessarily override concern about more substantive economic and social issues. Other scholars, while also emphasizing the centrality of the market revolution to Jacksonian politics, have noted that political change during the era sometimes came from actors outside the formal party system, such as the working-class radicals of New York City during the 1830s, brilliantly detailed in Sean Wilentz's* Chants Democratic *(1984).*

While the Old Hero is no longer the focus of studies of Jacksonian America, debate over the nature of the political party system launched by his election in 1828 continues to rage.

FOR FURTHER READING

Robert V. Remini's *Andrew Jackson* (3 vols., 1977–1984) is both a comprehensive and flattering portrait. Glyndon Van Deusen's *The Jacksonian Era* (1959) provides a generally Whiggish overview of the entire period. John Ashworth's *"Agrarians" and "Aristocrats"* (1983), Ronald P. Formisano's *The Transformation of Political Culture* (1983), and Harry L. Watson's *Jacksonian Politics and Community Conflict* (1981) describe party formation in the Jacksonian era. Robert V. Remini has analyzed *Andrew Jackson and the Bank War* (1967); James Roger Sharp's *The Jacksonians Versus the Banks* (1970) follows the controversy in the states; and Edward Pessen's *Riches, Class, and Power Before the Civil War* (1973) provides a valuable social portrait of the era. In *The Political Culture of the American Whigs* (1979), Daniel Howe considers some of the nation's most influential political losers; in *Prelude to Civil War* (1966), William Freehling observes the nullification controversy in South Carolina; and Charles Wiltse focuses on *John C. Calhoun: Nullifier, 1828–1839* (1949). Other important biographies of Jackson's contemporaries include Merrill D. Peterson, *The Great Triumvirate: Webster, Clay, and Calhoun* (1987), and Robert V. Remini, *Henry Clay* (1991). Ronald N. Satz outlines *American Indian Policy in the Jacksonian Era* (1975); the consequences of those policies may be traced in Thurman Wilkins's *Cherokee Tragedy* (1970) and Arthur DeRosier's *Removal of the Choctaw Indians* (1970). Bernard W. Sheehan's *Seeds of Extinction* (1973) thoughtfully analyzes the evolution of pre-removal white attitudes; and in *Fathers and Children* (1975), Michael Rogin ranges widely, draws upon both Marx and Freud, and explains the dispossession of the Indians. Richard White examines the *Roots of Dependency* (1983) for the Choctaws and compares their experience with that of two other tribes — the Pawnees and the Navajos — removed from their lands later in the century. A firsthand impression of Martin Van Buren can be gained from his *Autobiography* (published in the *Annual Report of the American Historical Association*, 1918); and Donald B. Cole examines *Martin Van Buren and the American Political System* (1984). The analyses of Jacksonian America by European observers are highly illuminating. The classic is Alexis de Tocqueville's *Democracy in America* (2 vols., 1835–1840). Also fascinating are Michael Chevalier, *Society, Manners, and Politics in the United States* (1839); Francis J. Grund, *Aristocracy in America* (1839); Harriet Martineau, *Society in America* (1837); and Frances Trollope, *Domestic Manners of the Americans* (1832).

12

★ ★ ★ ★ ★ ★

Romanticism, Reform, Slavery, 1800s–1850s

THE COUNTRY had no sooner developed a two-party system for reflecting the majority will while moderating conflict than it ran head-on into the one conflict that could neither be resolved by majority will nor be moderated: the conflict over slavery. The age of enterprise and egalitarianism that produced the two-party system had also brought Americans to their highest pitch of confidence about the possibilities for individuals and for optimism about the future of their society. It was a reforming age, abounding in schemes for wiping out the remaining blemishes that marred the full perfection of humanity. It was a utopian age, spattered with perfectionist communities and looking forward to the early perfection of the whole society. Such an age was bound to find intolerable the most glaring affront to the liberal principles of the Declaration of Independence. Yet slavery of blacks was so deeply rooted as a social and economic institution that the slaveholders, though themselves heirs of the American liberation tradition, could not surrender it.

ROMANTICISM

Underlying the reformist spirit of the age was a new configuration of ideas and attitudes called *Romanticism*. A vast and complicated movement in the intellectual and literary history of the western world, Romanticism took different forms and suggested different conclusions for different countries, periods, and individuals. As used here, the term denotes the central tendencies of thought in the United States in the first half of the nineteenth century.

Romanticism grew out of the eighteenth-century Enlightenment and was akin to it. Both movements assumed that the world was designed for human happiness, emphasized human ability, and had little concern for the rights of women. In America at least, both movements led in the direction of optimism, individualism, and liberal political principles. But Romanticism was a reaction against the Enlightenment's mechanical view of the natural world and its emphasis on intellect. Where Enlightenment thought ascribed human competence to the ability through reason to understand the natural laws by which a watchmaker Creator regulated both the physical and moral universes, Romanticism distrusted intellect and valued human emotional and intuitive qualities. Regarding the natural world as the embodiment of a divine spirit, Romanticism held that the natural and the spontaneous were good and that the highest truth was derived not through reason but through the instantaneous spiritual intuition of the individual.

American Romanticism reached its most sophisticated and self-conscious form in the Transcendentalism of Ralph Waldo Emerson and the New England intellectuals who shared his belief in a philosophical system that exalted the spiritual over the natural, the intuitive over the empirical. Most of Emerson's contemporaries were probably unaware of Transcendentalism or Romanticism as an explicit body of doctrine, but the pervasive Romantic assumptions were apparent in every aspect of American life. The overwhelming theme of popular literature and the popular stage was the primacy of feeling over intellect. In more serious writing, James Fenimore Cooper celebrated the moral perfection and superior wisdom of the "natural" but untutored woodsman Leatherstocking and the "noble savage" Chingachgook, and from a Romantic standpoint, Nathaniel Hawthorne *(The Scarlet Letter, The House of the Seven Gables,* and *The Blithedale Romance)* and Herman Melville *(Moby Dick* and *Billy Budd)* explored the problem of evil and some darker implications of Romantic doctrine. Landscape painters of the Hudson River School, notably Thomas Cole and Asher B. Durand, sought to capture on canvas the emotion of the "sublime" evoked by the unspoiled majesty of American river valleys and mountains. Architects turned from the intellectually satisfying simplicity, harmony, and proportion of the eighteenth century's colonial or Georgian style to exotic and more titillating models — Gothic, Moorish, and Egyptian. Even in laying out gardens and parks, Americans abandoned formal patterns and tried to reproduce nature in its wild state, as in Frederick Law Olmsted's design for Central Park in New York City.

The influence of Romanticism extended far beyond intellectuals, writers, and artists. Jacksonian egalitarianism was reinforced by some widely accepted Romantic assumptions. The Enlightenment's emphasis on reason and education, with its insistence that reason was more highly developed in some people than in others, had prevented even the more liberal people of the eighteenth century from endorsing full egalitarianism and popular sovereignty. Thus, Jefferson had relied on a "natural aristocracy" to rule, trusting the people to elect the natural aristocrats to office, yet not trusting the people to dictate public policy. But when intuition rather than reason was seen as the source of truth, the situation changed. The Romantic doctrine of democracy was expounded most boldly by the Jacksonian politician and distinguished historian George Bancroft: "If the sentiment of truth, justice, love, and beauty exists in every one, then it follows, as a necessary consequence, that the common judgment in taste, politics, and religion is the highest authority on earth." Indeed, by Jackson's time, the semiliterate farmer who lived simply and close to nature was often regarded as being superior in virtue and wisdom to a city dweller whose "natural" impulses had been stifled by the artificialities of education and culture.

Jackson's enormous popularity may be attributed in considerable measure to the prevalence of such attitudes. The contest between Jackson and John Quincy Adams in 1828 was widely interpreted as pitting a natural man of virtue, a product of the American frontier, against the well-educated, highly cultured (and therefore suspect) Adams, who had the additional disadvantage of having spent much of his early life in the artificial surroundings of an overcivilized and decadent Europe. To Harvard-trained John Quincy Adams, Jackson was "a barbarian who could not write a sentence of grammar and hardly could spell his own name." But the people found in him the embodiment of all the natural wisdom of the common folk. In the presidential election of 1840, the Whigs turned the tables by using, in naked parody, the Jacksonian political formula. Deftly exploiting a hard-cider and log-cabin symbolism, they presented William Henry Harrison, "the Ohio Plowman," as the representative of the "hardy yeomanry" whose "primitive" qualities contrasted sharply with the city-slicker airs of the Jacksonian candidate, Martin Van Buren. The voters who responded enthusiastically to these appeals had never heard of Romanticism as a body of doctrine, but the smashing victory they gave Harrison at the polls demonstrated their unconscious conversion to some key Romantic assumptions.

ROMANTIC CHRISTIANITY

Apart from political behavior, extensive popular acceptance of Romantic assumptions was most evident in religious behavior. Well into the nineteenth century, the story of religion in the United States was a story of the gradual erosion of the originally dominant Puritan-Calvinist strain of Protestant Christianity. In an increasingly self-reliant, optimistic, and individualistic society, it continually became more difficult to sustain a view of life that emphasized the awful sovereignty of God, the sinfulness and helplessness of humanity, and the necessity for salvation by God's miraculous and arbitrary grace.

Under the impact of the eighteenth-century Enlightenment, some members of the more sophisticated classes had abandoned the inscrutable, omnipresent God of the Calvinists for Deism's remote and kindly Creator. Others had moved in the same direction more gradually, retaining the outward forms and language of orthodox Christianity but coming to believe that a reasonable God was favorably disposed toward all people, that people were sufficiently endowed with reason to be capable of goodness, and that the objective of a religious life ought to be goodness in this world rather than

God's arbitrary salvation in a world to come. Such opinions spread rapidly even among the direct descendants of seventeenth-century Puritanism, the New England Congregationalists. However, violent controversy broke out between the liberal and orthodox factions. By the end of the century, the liberal Congregationalists — representatives of the often wealthier, better educated "rational" wing of American Protestantism — were breaking off to form separate churches and taking the name Unitarians. Replacing the God of Vengeance with the God of Benevolence, Unitarians stressed the basic goodness of human beings and the mercy of God. Heavily influenced by Enlightenment thought, they rejected trinitarianism and what they thought to be the irrational side of Christian orthodoxy for a doctrine of God in one person.

Though Unitarianism and even its more popular offshoot, Universalism, remained minority movements — too intellectual, perhaps too optimistic for the great mass of Americans — religious orthodoxy was unquestionably at a low ebb in the last quarter of the eighteenth century. The mighty orthodox counteroffensive, the Great Awakening of the 1730s and 1740s, had spent its force; the Revolution had brought with it the spiritual and moral laxity usual in wartime; Deism was growing popular and militant; and the orthodox themselves had become listless and had begun to acquiesce in compromises with the spirit of the age.

It was under these circumstances that the orthodox clergy resorted to the emotional techniques of the Great Awakening to launch another vigorous counteroffensive known as the Great Revival, or the Second Great Awakening. Really a series of revival movements beginning around the turn of the century, the Great Revival kept the country in religious ferment for 25 years, obliterating the last traces of Deism and bringing a majority of Americans into the Protestant churches. America did not return to Calvinism, for in the process of capturing America, Protestant Christianity was itself captured and transformed by the Romantic optimism and individualism of American culture.

One phase of the Great Revival began with spectacular open-air camp meetings led by James McGready in Kentucky. These week-long extravaganzas of religious enthusiasm spread rapidly over the West and spawned a host of poorly educated but effective revivial preachers, including famed Methodist circuit rider Peter Cartwright. These traveling revivalists left in their wake many new churches, which were mainly of such evangelical and popular groups as Baptists and Methodists who won converts at the expense of the often staid Presbyterians, Congregationalists, and Episcopalians.

Meanwhile President Timothy Dwight of Yale and his protégé Lyman Beecher were showing the conservative clergy in the East how to use a more restrained revivalism as a technique for combating Unitarianism and maintaining the hegemony of orthodox Congregationalism. At the same time, the Congregationalists were cooperating with the Presbyterians in a joint campaign to evangelize the frontier areas of western New York and the Old Northwest. The revival movement and the western missionary effort both culminated in the 1820s in the spectacularly successful evangelism of Charles Grandison Finney, "father of modern revivalism" and precursor of later religious spell-binders like Dwight Moody, Billy Sunday, and Billy Graham. A former lawyer, Finney combined emotional intensity with some shrewdly devised new techniques: cottage prayer meetings preceding his protracted revival meetings, the full participation of women, the "anxious bench" where sinners sat directly under the gaze of the exhorter, the "holy band" of zealous young helpers to pray individually with the religiously smitten. His approach produced an explosion of emotional piety that entrenched a revivalistic "Presbygationalism" in the western regions. Although he was ordained a Presbyterian minister, Finney's "New School" Calvinism led him far from the belief in original sin and the hell fire and damnation of traditional American Protestantism. He embraced the optimistic doctrine of free will and laced his sermons with a call to perfectionism that urged social reform as well as personal salvation. Because Finney's doctrine, like the ones of a number of evangelists including Peter Cartwright, required "work as well as belief," it suggested that the redemption of American society could accompany the moral perfection of the individual. It was no accident, then, that among Finney's disciples were Theodore Dwight Weld and Arthur and Lewis Tappan, abolitionists who combined religious enthusiasm with moral reform.

Most revivalists started from positions they would have regarded as theologically orthodox, but like Finney they were more interested in the effectiveness, the preachability, of what they were saying than in its theological correctness. They quickly found that it was easiest to evoke the desired emotional response by preaching that God was anxious to save sinners, that sinners need only accept God's love. Many Presbyterians and the more conservative Protestants of all denominations in the South resisted this tendency, but the main body of American Protestantism moved gradually and unconsciously toward a Romantic theology. Love was viewed as the essence of the Christian life. God was love, freely offering his love to all who would accept it. Conversion was the emotional experience of acceptance and loving response. In some versions, as with many Methodists and in the theology that Finney himself taught, conversion was viewed as carrying with it a kind of spiritual perfection. The tone of this Romantic Protestantism was clearest perhaps in hymns like "O Love That Will Not Let Me Go" and its juvenile counterpart "Jesus Loves Me."

UTOPIANISM AND HUMANITARIANISM

Wherever the Great Revival burned — and especially in the frequently ravaged "burned-over district" of western New York — it left behind a bed of glowing embers ready to be fanned into varied reform, perfectionist, and utopian movements. Many were millennialist, expecting Christ's early return to establish the Kingdom of God on earth. When the Reverend William Miller calculated from biblical prophecies the time a Second Coming would take place, his followers reacted by disposing of their worldly possessions and expectantly gathering together at the appointed time. But they were disillusioned when the event did not occur, either in the originally predicted spring of 1844, or (after Miller had corrected his calculations) on October 21 of that year.

Various groups that looked forward to an early millennium sought in the meantime to assemble those who had been "perfected" through conversion and to form communities that would be without sin or blemish. Because they emphasized the primacy of love in all relationships and the freedom from sin that comes with salvation, these perfectionist utopians had particular difficulty with conventional notions about the proper relations between the sexes. One group, led by John Humphrey Noyes, established a flourishing community at Oneida, New York; its members rejected both private property for common ownership, and exclusive marriage for a carefully regulated system of "complex marriage" in which the men were husbands to all the women, and the women wives of all the men. A more long-lasting group, Mother Ann Lee's Shakers, solved the problem of exclusive love by practicing celibacy in their many communities. The most durable of all these groups was the Mormons; founder Joseph Smith claimed that he was God's prophet and that in upstate New York he had discovered some buried golden plates containing new divine revelations, which were translated and published as the Book of Mormon. Formed in New York in 1830, the community of Latter-Day Saints met persecution and moved to Ohio and Missouri for a brief time and then settled for a somewhat longer period in Nauvoo, Illinois. In the face of violent opposition to its developing practice of polygamy, the group moved in 1847–1848 to the virtually uninhabited Mexican territory of the Great Salt Lake Valley, where it thrived under the forceful leadership of Brigham Young.

In addition to the religiously oriented utopian movements, the Romantic age produced many secular utopian communities. Perhaps the best known was short-lived Brook Farm (1841–1847), founded at West Roxbury, Massachusetts, by the Unitarian minister George Ripley. A cooperative community of intellectuals, Brook Farm enjoyed the support of many people on the fringes of the Transcendentalist movement and such writers as Nathaniel Hawthorne and Margaret Fuller. A more ambitious socialist community at New Harmony, Indiana, was founded in 1825 by Robert Dale Owen, son of the English textile manufacturer and social reformer Robert Owen. The most extensive movement in secular communitarianism was inspired by Charles Fourier, a French social philosopher who had calculated the optimum size and organization for the ideal socialist community, which he called a "phalanx." Attracting the support of the prominent New York editor Horace Greeley, the Fourierists established some 40 or 50 phalanxes in the United States. In general, the secular utopias did not fare as well as those that had a religious motivation to keep their members loyal to the communitarian ideal. Many of the latter survived late into the nineteenth century, dwindling away only as the ebbing of religious revivalism dried up their source of recruits.

The perfectionist impulse that produced the utopian communities also inspired a broader series of movements aimed at wiping out every individual and social evil that the age could identify. Much of this reform activity was devoted to previously neglected classes of unfortunates. Dorothea Dix led the crusade that persuaded state legislatures to establish institutions for the care of the mentally ill. A related movement induced a number of states to undertake extensive programs of penal reform, emphasizing rehabilitation rather than merely punishment of criminals. For the first time, facilities were developed for educating the deaf, dumb, and blind. Indeed, the great movement for publicly supported common schools for all children got its real start in this perfectionist age, with Horace Mann's ambitious program in Massachusetts leading the way.

The reform movements that had the greatest impact were those most closely associated with the Great Revival. In the early stages of his revivalist campaign in Connecticut, Lyman Beecher devised the technique of organizing through local churches voluntary societies of lay members to promote various moral and evangelical objectives. By the late 1820s, these local societies had developed into a group of regional and national federations with paid agents to organize new local societies, raise funds, and carry out the various objectives of the federations. The American Home Missionary Society, which hired evangelists to carry the Great Revival into the West, was one of the first of the national federations. It was soon joined by other national societies that devoted themselves to such religious objectives as foreign missions, distributing Bibles and religious tracts, promoting Sunday schools, and saving sailors. Leadership and financing for all these societies came from the same group of revivalistic "Presbygational" ministers and philanthropists led by Beecher and Finney.

The developing Romantic theology of the Great Revival soon inspired a reform impulse that went beyond the evangelical objectives of the earliest societies. Finney in particular was preaching that conversion caused a disposition of "disinterested benevolence" in the converted, and his revivals left behind numbers of converts anxious to find some object on which to lavish their disinterested benevolence. The first object to be discovered was the drunkard.

The remarkable consumption of whiskey, hard cider, and rum in the early Republic constituted a serious social problem. The national liquor bill in 1810 ($12 million) exceeded the federal budget; in 1823 the annual per capita consumption of spirits was estimated to be 7.5 gallons, up from the 2.5 gallons consumed by each American three decades earlier. The problem prevailed even among the clergy — one beer was named Ordination Brew — and in 1816 the Methodists forbade their preachers to sell alcohol. Moved by the evangelical spirit of the age and alarmed by the widespread misuse of "demon rum," reform-minded Lyman Beecher inspired the organization of local temperance societies, which aimed at moderation in the consumption of alcohol. When this tactic proved ineffective, Beecher began campaigning for total abstinence, and in 1826 the American Society for the Promotion of Temperance was organized. Sending evangelists through the country to persuade people to sign a pledge of total abstinence, the Society's Temperance Union claimed 5,000 local branches with one million members by 1834.

Turning to politics to secure legal prohibition, temperance forces gained a local option law in Massachusetts in 1838, and the first statewide law prohibiting the manufacture and sale of liquor was passed in Maine in 1851. Soon most of the northern states had legislated against alcohol. In contrast to twentieth-century prohibitionism, the nineteenth-century movement was much weaker in the South, where only the border states of Delaware and Tennessee resorted to legislative prohibition.

Temperance was merely the first of the reform movements inspired by the Great Revival. By the 1830s, the headquarters for the benevolent societies had shifted from Boston to New York City, where Finney had been established as pastor of a great "free" church (charging no pew rents) for the poor and where the two leading financial angels of the general benevolence movement, the merchant brothers Arthur and Lewis Tappan, resided. New societies were continually being organized: to foster the pseudoscience of phrenology, to promote international peace, to encourage healthier diets, to stop the carrying of the mails on Sunday, or to prohibit the wearing of corsets. Into New York every May poured an army of the benevolent-minded from every part of the country to attend a series of annual conventions of all the societies.

WOMEN'S RIGHTS

Animated by the same humanitarian and moral impulses as men, women played significant roles in reform movements. Very often, however, their effectiveness was severely limited by the fears and prejudices of the men with whom they sought common cause. Angelina and Sarah Grimké, for example, left their South Carolina home and went north to aid in the anti-slavery cause. But their efforts to speak in its behalf were frequently opposed by male abolitionists and howled down by audiences unaccustomed to such "unladylike" endeavors. In 1840, Lucretia Mott, Elizabeth Cady Stanton, and a half-dozen other American women traveled to London to attend the World Anti-Slavery Convention only to be excluded because of their sex. In the 1850s, Susan B. Anthony had much the same experience in the temperance movement, where "ladies" were expected to be seen but not heard. The irony of such discrimination by men and by organizations dedicated to humanitarian causes was not lost on this generation of women. With Angelina Grimké, not a few of them would ask: "What can a *woman* do for the slave when she herself is under the feet of man and shamed into silence."

The sexual prejudices of the male reformers were mirrored and magnified by the larger society they sought to uplift. In the eyes of the law, women were perpetual minors, the wards of male guardians without whom they had no separate legal identity. Although often idealized by men for their tenderness and purity, women could not vote, hold office, sit on juries, or speak in public. They enjoyed few property guarantees, suffered gross education and job discriminations, and had no legal claim to their own incomes. Women found divorce laws stringent and prejudicially administered. They were legally subject to their husbands, even to corporal punishment by them; until 1850, nearly every state permitted wife beating "with a reasonable instrument" (defined by one Massachusetts judge as a "stick no bigger than my thumb"). Men also enjoyed a virtual monopoly on property rights. Except in Mississippi (after 1837) and New York (after 1845), women who owned real estate — generally only single women could — did so only through the authority of a male guardian.

Confronted by such disabilities, women (usually of the upper-middle class) organized for their own relief, often combining women's rights with temperance, abolition, public education, and prison reforms. Except for some highly significant breakthroughs in the fields of literature and education, their successes were few; throughout the period, feminism remained little more than an attitude shared by a few intrepid social pioneers. Sarah Grimké's *The Equality of the Sexes* (1838) and Margaret Fuller's *Women in the Nineteenth Century* (1844) were important early women's manifestoes. Amelia Bloomer's sensible but much ridiculed crusade for dress reform, Lucy Stone's repudiation of marriage laws that gave a husband "injurious and unnatural superiority" over his wife, and Stanton and Mott's Seneca Falls declaration (1848) of women's independence ("We hold these truths to be self-evident: that all men *and women* are created equal") symbolized a heightening feminist consciousness. But the work of these early feminists scarcely touched the lives of the vast majority of women. Sisterhood was not powerful in antebellum America. For all the vigor of their protest, the Susan B. Anthonys and the Angelina Grimkés of that era organized more effectively for causes other than their own. Despite the reform enthusiasms of the age, nineteenth-century concerns were nearly always restricted to the rights of *men*, not women.

ABOLITION

While the women's movement probably owed little directly to evangelical Christianity, religion was clearly a principal engine of abolition. The unfocused impulses of disinterested benevolence fostered by the Great Revival found their great and absorbing object in the institution of human bondage. Before 1830, the organized antislavery movement had been small and ineffectual, drawing its support mainly from those persons, notably Quakers, with strong religious scruples against the institution. A scattering of manumission societies, principally in the upper South, encouraged owners to free their slaves. Since 1821, Benjamin Lundy had published *The Genius of Universal Emancipation*, a newspaper dedicated to "olive-branch" abolitionism: genteel persuasion, gradual manumission, and compensation to slave owners. In addition, the American Colonization Society had been promoting (without much success) the migration of free blacks to Africa; this conservative approach to the problem aroused the suspicion of both the defenders and the critics of slavery.

Only after the British Parliament's widely publicized debates over emancipation came to the attention of the leaders of the American benevolence movement did antislavery become a major force on this side of the Atlantic. In 1830 the Tappan brothers, caught up in the religious fervor of the Great Revival, helped organize an antislavery society in New York. The next year in Boston, young, radical William Lloyd Garrison left Benjamin Lundy's employment to set up his own militant antislavery newspaper, *The Liberator,* which was "harsh as truth," "uncompromising as justice," and untainted by moderation. In the following years, Garrison and the small group of zealous antislavery reformers he inspired in New England furnished an uncompromising ideology of "immediatism" — emancipation without delay, condition, or compensation — for the growing antislavery movement, while the Finney-Tappan benevolence movement committed its substantial support, stretching west from New York, to the cause.

At first, antislavery was only one among many causes espoused by the Tappans and their associates. A turning point came when one of Finney's ablest young converts and apprentice evangelists, Theodore Dwight Weld, shifted his energies from temperance to become wholly devoted to abolitionism. In 1833, Weld enrolled at Lane Seminary in Cincinnati, a school that had just been established under Lyman Beecher's presidency to train Finney's converts for the ministry. Proselytizing among his fellow students, Weld provoked the famous Lane Debate, a revivalistic discussion of slavery that lasted for 18 days and nights and ended with the conversion of virtually the entire student body to the abolitionist cause. Meanwhile the Tappan and the Garrison groups had come together in uneasy alliance to form the American Anti-Slavery Society, which now employed Weld and his fellow Lane converts as agents. During the mid-1830s these and others conducted a whirlwind evangelistic campaign through New England, New York, Pennsylvania, and the Old Northwest, which resulted in the conversion of some whole communities to antislavery and the organization of over 1,000 local antislavery societies with more than 100,000 members.

The abolitionism preached by Weld and his associates emphasized the moral evil of slavery and the religious duty of good people to align themselves against it. In fact, most abolitionists were intensely pious people, driven by religious sentiments that portrayed good works as the result of salvation. At first they naively hoped to persuade slaveholders to abandon the institution by sending into the South tons of pamphlets portraying the sin of holding human beings in bondage. The slaveholders countered, however, with religious arguments of their own, for the proslavery argument, too, found its moral base in biblical texts.

Although the leadership of the antislavery movement remained largely white, blacks were vitally active in its ranks from the beginning. Before 1800, the Free African Society of Philadelphia and such black spokesmen as the astronomer Benjamin Banneker and the church leader Richard Allen had denounced slavery in the harshest terms. By 1830 there were 50 black-organized antislavery societies, and blacks participated in the formation of the American Anti-Slavery Society in 1833. In a movement notable for impassioned oratory, black speakers on the antislavery circuit were among the most compelling. Isabella, an illiterate former slave better known as Sojourner Truth, moved audiences in New England and the West, while the brilliant fugitive slave Frederick Douglass emerged as the foremost abolitionist orator, lecturing to audiences throughout the North and England. Blacks also helped run the Underground Railroad; Harriet Tubman, its most notable "conductor" and herself an escaped slave, was said to have led more than 300 blacks to freedom.

Generally, black abolitionists shared the nonviolent philosophy of the Garrisonians. But black anger could not always be contained. Both David Walker's *Appeal* (1829) and Henry Highland Garnet's address to a Convention of Colored Citizens (1843) urged the slaves to arms. "Strike for your lives and liberties," Garnet commanded. "Rather die freemen than live to be slaves."

Not the least of the black abolitionists' frustrations was the racism they found within antislavery ranks. Moved by both tactical considerations and race paternalism, white abolitionists tried to limit their black counterparts to peripheral roles and sometimes either assigned them to separate-but-equal auxiliaries or excluded them from local organizations. The deeds of the ambivalent white abolitionists, Garrison and Weld included, did not always match their egalitarian rhetoric. Outside the movement, the mood was less simplistic. Despite the rapid spread of antislavery sentiment, abolitionism remained highly unpopular in much of the North, particularly in Indiana and Illinois. Deeply infected with the same race prejudice that bolstered slavery in the South, many Northerners feared that abolitionism threatened established racial practices. Others with no great fondness for slavery were still afraid that antislavery agitation imperiled the Union. Abolitionists had to face hostile mobs, official indifference, and police hostility; one white editor, Elijah P. Lovejoy, was killed in 1837 for his antislavery views.

The abolitionists, however, gained support far beyond their own ranks when they moved into politics in the mid-1830s with a petition campaign asking Congress to abolish slavery and the odious slave trade in the District of Columbia. Many Northerners who shied away from the constitutionally difficult question of abolition in the slave states were glad to support the abolitionist petitions with reference to the national capital over which Congress had unquestioned jurisdiction. Northern opinion was generally indignant when Congress responded to southern pressure in 1836 by adopting a "gag rule" refusing to consider petitions related in any way to slavery. At this point, ex-president John Quincy Adams, who served in the House of Representatives, took up the cause. Originally not an abolitionist, "Old Man Eloquent" was infuriated by this denial of the constitutionally guaranteed right of petition. Supported by a growing body of northern opinion, he carried on a dogged fight against the gag rule until it was eventually repealed in 1844. Though the North was still far from abolitionized, the steady agitation of the question was gradually conditioning increasing thousands of voters to view the slaveholding section of American society with hostility.

THE SOUTH AND SLAVERY

Meanwhile white Southerners were being forced to re-examine their attitudes toward their "peculiar institution." Christianity and the liberal principles of the Declaration of Independence affected Southerners just as much as Northerners. During the latter part of the eighteenth century, many of the South's outstanding leaders had emancipated their slaves, denouncing slavery as incompatible with the ideals of the Revolution. Thomas Jefferson and other liberal Southerners had counted on the gradual operation of economic forces to eliminate slavery in the South as was already being done in the North. As late as the Missouri debate in 1820, southern members of Congress refused to defend slavery in the abstract, arguing instead that the unfortunate institution had been inherited and was difficult to eradicate.

Southern opinion had already begun to shift in a direction that would ultimately lead to civil war. The fundamental cause for change was the market revolution. Until the end of the eighteenth century, the stronghold of slavery had been in the Chesapeake tobacco region of Virginia and Maryland. The economic depression in this region following the Revolution had encouraged the spread of antislavery sentiment and afforded some grounds for Jefferson's hope that the institution might wither away. But farther down the coast the great plantations of South Carolina had continued to flourish; with the perfection of the cotton gin in 1793, high profits stimulated the rapid spread of plantation slavery into the up-country. South Carolina was the only state that permitted a resumption of the barbarous foreign slave trade before its prohibition by Congress in 1808.

The most spectacular expansion of plantation slavery came during the boom years following the War of 1812 when it flooded over the newly opened lands of Alabama, Mississippi, and Louisiana. Taking deep root as a flourishing economic system, the chief source of wealth, and a spur to enterprise, slavery became increasingly impossible for white Southerners to surrender. The cotton boom in the lower South dampened antislavery tendencies in the upper South by creating a heavy demand at high prices for the surplus slaves of the declining tobacco kingdom. Nonslaveholders, too, came to feel that they had a stake in the institution. Only about one-fourth of the white families in the South ever owned slaves, and even among the slaveholding minority only 12 percent owned as many as 20 slaves. But the South was as deeply infected as any other part of the country with the spirit of enterprise that the market revolution generated, and in the South the acquisition of slaves was becoming the primary and almost the exclusive means of raising one's economic and social status.

At the same time, another factor was reinforcing the white South's growing economic attachment to slavery. Thomas Jefferson had assumed that deep antipathies between whites and blacks would make emancipation unthinkable without some plan for removing the emancipated slaves from the United States. This conviction that the two races could not live side by side in freedom received a powerful impetus in the 1790s when the slaves of the nearby French West Indian island of Santo Domingo rose in rebellion, murdering or forcing into exile thousands of their former masters. From this time on, the more the white South became attached to slavery as an economic institution, the more it feared its slaves and, consequently, the more it insisted on slavery as an institution for controlling this dangerous population. Alarms over threatened slave insurrections became more frequent, some with a basis in fact and others arising more from imaginations made excitable by fear and guilt.

A real insurrection finally came in August 1831, when a slave named Nat Turner led an uprising in Southampton County, Virginia. Over 60 whites were killed before the rebels were crushed. A wave of hysteria washed over the whole domain of slavery, and the Virginia legislature was frightened into the Old South's only full and free debate over the peculiar institution. Not a voice was raised to justify slavery in the abstract, and proposals for gradual emancipation were barely defeated.

The entire South sensed that a fateful choice had been made. The fears of slave insurrection had culminated just at the time when slavery was becoming too entrenched as an economic institution to be surrendered and at the very moment when the American antislavery movement was launching a massive propaganda barrage against slavery, appealing to Christian and liberal values that white Southerners shared. Slowly and reluctantly, Southerners faced the fact that, if slavery were to be retained, they could no longer ease their consciences with hopes for its eventual disappearance or tolerate the expression of such hopes in their midst. Southern minds must be nerved for a severe struggle in defense of the institution to which they now saw themselves committed. So southern leaders of the Calhoun school began trying to convince themselves and others that slavery was not merely a "necessary evil" but a "positive good," while southern legislatures abridged freedom of speech and the press, made manumission difficult or impossible, and imposed tighter restrictions on both slaves and free blacks.

Proslavery arguments never succeeded in relieving the majority of white Southerners from varying degrees of moral uneasiness or feelings of guilt. Like all people unsure of their ground but unable to change it, Southerners responded to attacks on slavery with mounting vehemence. Even in the 1830s, when both Southerners and Northerners were still preoccupied with the Jacksonian political issues, the abolitionists' petitions provoked such violent congressional debates that the gag rule had to be imposed. Within another decade, the explosively emotional quarrel over slavery would move to the center of the political stage, there to remain until blood was shed.

CONFLICTING HISTORICAL VIEWPOINTS: NO. 5

How Brutal Was Slavery?

In his monumental studies American Negro Slavery *(1918) and* Life and Labor in the Old South *(1929), Ulrich B. Phillips set forth the classic defense of slavery as a labor system beneficial to both master and slave. A tireless re-*

searcher and a prolific writer, Phillips uncovered a wealth of new material and contributed enormously to our factual knowledge of the "peculiar institution." But the work of this Georgia-born scholar was seriously flawed by racial prejudice. The slave, he believed, was innately inferior and naturally submissive. In his view the plantation was a school in which primitive and uncouth blacks were purged of their African savagery and offered the blessings of western civilization and Christianity.

This sympathetic interpretation of a benign and paternalistic institution dominated American historical writing for almost three decades before World War II. But in the increasingly enlightened climate of racial opinion following the war, historians began reassessing traditional assumptions about the antebellum South's labor system. In American Negro Slave Revolts (1943), Herbert Aptheker, a Marxist historian and a passionate civil rights advocate, portrayed a rebellious and discontented slave work force that contrasted sharply with the carefree darky of Phillips's idyll. The most sweeping revision, however, was Kenneth Stampp's broad synthesis The Peculiar Institution (1956). A distinguished liberal scholar who argued that "Negroes are, after all, only white men with black skins," Stampp viewed slavery as a harshly cruel system degrading to both exploiter and exploited. The typical slave, he concluded, hated both the institution and the master.

Not all of Phillips's critics agreed with Stampp. In Slavery (1959), Stanley Elkins, for example, offered a controversial study that blended Stampp's harsh criticism of slavery with Phillips's view of the slave as contented Sambo. Using social science and comparative history techniques, Elkins concluded that the labor system of the Old South was so brutal and dehumanizing that it infantilized its victims. According to this interpretation, the typical slave was thus childlike, docile, and convinced of self-inferiority.

During the 1970s historians rejected Elkins's conclusions and moved beyond Stampp's. Increasingly the direction has been away from studying slavery as an institutional problem toward analyzing day-to-day life in slave quarters. Masters now attract less scholarly attention than slaves, and though the physically and emotionally coercive side is not discounted, the emphasis has shifted to the vigorous black culture largely independent of white influence. John Blassingame's study of plantation life and labor from the slaves' vantage point, The Slave Community (1972), for example, describes the evolution of a remarkable, semi-autonomous black community and culture that inhibited white control and gave plantation blacks the means to survive an otherwise brutal and dehumanizing system. Eugene Genovese's Roll, Jordan, Roll (1974) also portrays (as its subtitle promises) "the world the slaves made." A leading Marxist historian who views American slavery as an essentially feudal, pre-bourgeois system of class exploitation, Genovese describes the slaves' deft manipulation of the two-edged sword of paternalism, "a doctrine of reciprocal obligations," of patronage and dependence, of mutual rights and mutual duties. He argues that by creating their own religion and maintaining strong family ties and a separate cultural identity, slaves "rendered unto Caesar," but they managed to fix the limits of white authority, to "assert manhood and womanhood in their everyday lives," and to resist the "moral and psychological aggression" of slavery and white supremacy. Although differing in important particulars, Herbert Gutman's The Black Family in Slavery and Freedom, 1750–1925 (1976) also focuses on the autonomy, rather than the dependence, of black society. Examining the black family and extended kinship network, Gutman finds close multi-generational ties, settled monogamous unions, and little evidence that African-American institutions were shattered by the slavery experience. A final example is Lawrence Levine's Black Culture and Black Consciousness (1977). Imaginatively examining the folk expressions of a creative slave society that was anything but degraded or pathological, Levine concludes that slaves were not wholly powerless to influence the patterns of their own lives — they were not "perfect victims." "For all of its horrors," he writes, "slavery was never so complete a system of psychic assault that it prevented slaves from carving out independent cultural forms." Although not completely ignoring the unjust and often unspeakably cruel dimensions of slavery, these scholars concluded that slaves' lives were often joyful, exuberant, and personally meaningful. Most of all, these writers appreciated the adaptive and creative capabilities of a people who, within an exploitive system, found a measure of cultural and personal autonomy. In recent years, however, some historians have suggested that the slave studies of the 1970s and 1980s overstated the theme of slave autonomy. In American Slavery (1993), Peter Kolchin argues that while the focus on slave culture and community has greatly expanded our knowledge of slave life, the emphasis on slave autonomy fails to convey adequately the reality that slavery ultimately oppressed and degraded those held in bondage.

Another and far more controversial approach to the institution of slavery is in Robert Fogel and Stanley Engerman's Time on the Cross (1974). Emphasizing the more salutary dimensions of the slave economy, the book attracted much public interest and scholarly criticism. This computer-based analysis contends that slave labor was more efficient and productive than free labor and that slaves lived comparatively well-provisioned, secure, and comfortable lives. "Over the course of his lifetime," the authors argue, "the typical slave field hand received about 90 percent of the income he produced." These conclusions, although less novel than the authors claim, provoked a storm of controversy. Many blacks found them offensive, and many scholars — including most historical quantifiers — faulted the data and research procedures upon which they were based. An example of scholarly criticism of Time on the Cross can be found in Herbert Gutman's Slavery and the Numbers Game (1975), which finds particular fault with Fogel and Engerman for their neglect of the beliefs and behavior of the slaves themselves.

FOR FURTHER READING

In the absence of an adequate general account of Romanticism in American thought, much can be learned from the splendid segment of a study left uncompleted by Perry Miller, *The Life of the Mind in America from the Revolution to the Civil War* (1965). An older work by Octavius B. Frothingham is still the fullest account of *Transcendentalism in New England* (1876), but Anne C. Rose offers a good portrayal of *Transcendentalism as a Social Movement* (1981). General accounts of antebellum reform can be found in Alice Felt Tyler's *Freedom's Ferment* (1944) and Ronald G. Walter's *American Reformers, 1815–1860* (1978); Russell Nye's *Society and Culture in America* (1974) examines antebellum cultural and intellectual life. For the Great Revival and its impact on perfectionism and reformism, see Whitney Cross, *The Burned Over District* (1950); William McLoughlin, *Revivals, Awakenings, and Reform* (1978); Timothy Smith, *Revivalism and Social Reform* (1957); and Robert H. Abzug, *Cosmos Crumbling* (1994). David Rothman in *The Discovery of the Asylum* (1971) argues that antebellum reformers were moved less by humanitarianism than by a desire for social control. For other perspectives on antebellum social conditions and the reform impulse, see Ellen Du Bois, *Feminism and Suffrage* (1978); Nancy Cott, *The Bonds of Womanhood* (1977); Nancy Hewitt, *Women's Activism and Social Change* (1984); Stephen J. Stein, *The Shaker Experience in America* (1992); Paul E. Johnson, *A Shopkeeper's Millennium* (1978); W. J. Rorabaugh, *The Alcoholic Republic* (1979); and Ian Tyrrell, *Sobering Up* (1979).

Important studies of the Old South include Bertram Wyatt-Brown, *Southern Honor* (1982); James Oakes, *Slavery and Freedom* (1990); Elizabeth Fox-Genovese, *Within the Plantation Household* (1988); John Hope Franklin, *The Militant South* (1956); J. William Harris, *Plain Folk and Gentry in a Slave Society* (1985); and Mills Thornton, III, *Politics and Power in a Slave Society* (1978). Aspects of the peculiar institution are analyzed in Deborah Gray White, *Ar'n't I a Woman?* (1985); Barbara J. Fields, *Slavery and Freedom on the Middle Ground* (1985); William Scarborough, *The Overseer* (1966); and Charles B. Dew, *Bond of Iron* (1994). Ira Berlin's *Slaves Without Masters* (1974) portrays the life of the free black. Differing views on the origins of abolitionism are offered by Gilbert Barnes in *The Anti-Slavery Impulse* (1933) and by Louis Filler in *The Crusade Against Slavery* (1986). William S. McFeely's *Frederick Douglass* (1991) details the life of an important black abolitionist; Bertram Wyatt-Brown is the author of *Lewis Tappan and the Evangelical War Against Slavery* (1969); Gerda Lerner examines *The Grimké Sisters from South Carolina* (1967); Aileen Kraditor in *Means and Ends in American Abolitionism* (1969) emphasizes variety and conflict within the abolitionist movement; Robert H. Abzug in *Passionate Liberator* (1980) considers the life of radical abolitionist Theodore Dwight Weld; and Richard Sewell's *Ballots for Freedom* (1976) is a history of antislavery politics. The interpretations of a number of scholars on various aspects of abolitionism are presented in a volume of essays collected by Martin Duberman, *The Anti-Slavery Vanguard* (1965).

TABLE 6. PRESIDENTIAL ELECTIONS AND MAJOR EVENTS, 1840–1852

1840 William Henry Harrison (Whig) elected over Martin Van Buren (Democrat).

1841 Vice President **John Tyler** becomes President on death of Harrison.
Whig Congress repeals the independent treasury system.
Land Act of 1841: Pre-emption principle allows settlers to buy public lands they occupy at minimum price.
Tyler vetoes successive bills chartering a national bank and is disowned by the Whig party.

1842 Tariff of 1842, a Whig measure, extends substantial protection to American manufactures.
Webster-Ashburton Treaty with Great Britain settles the Maine boundary and other disputed matters.

1844 Tyler's treaty for the annexation of Texas defeated in the Senate.
James K. Polk (Democrat) elected over Henry Clay (Whig).

1845 Texas annexed by joint resolution of Congress.

1846 Democratic Congress reinstitutes the independent treasury system.
Tariff of 1846 substantially reduces rates.
Polk's veto of Rivers and Harbors bill checks policy of internal improvements.
Oregon controversy with Great Britain compromised.
Polk precipitates Mexican War by insisting on extreme Texas boundary claim.
Wilmot Proviso proposed to bar slavery from any territories acquired from Mexico.

1848 Treaty of Guadelupe Hidalgo ends Mexican War, with the United States paying Mexico for a vast cession in the Southwest.
Zachary Taylor (Whig) elected over Lewis Cass (Democrat) and Martin Van Buren (Free Soiler).

1849 Gold Rush to California.

1850 Vice President **Millard Fillmore** becomes president on death of Taylor.
Compromise of 1850: (1) California admitted as free state; (2) Utah and New Mexico territories organized on principle of squatter sovereignty; (3) Texas surrenders claims to area in New Mexico, and United States assumes Texas debt; (4) slave trade abolished in the District of Columbia; (5) a more stringent Fugitive Slave Law enacted.

1852 **Franklin Pierce** (Democrat) elected over Winfield Scott (Whig).

13

★ ★ ★ ★ ★ ★

Manifest Destiny and Sectional Conflict, 1840–1852

THOUGH the Whig and Democratic leaders continued to battle each other in the early 1840s over tariffs, the national bank, and internal improvements, these old issues no longer excited Americans as they had in Jackson's day. The market revolution had completed its psychological conquest of the country, and with hard times receding, an enterprising generation was engrossed in the pursuit of wealth and status.

For countless thousands, the pursuit led west toward the perennial American goal of cheap land and a fresh start. But now, for the first time in the American experience, there seemed a limit to the supply of cheap, fertile land. In the South the tide of settlement rolled up to the boundary of the Mexican province of Texas. Farther north it was nearing the treeless Great Plains, which were thought unfit for cultivation.

Yet neither political nor geographical boundaries were to halt the 200-year advance of the American frontier. Since the 1820s, American settlers had been pouring into Texas, where in 1836 they rebelled against Mexican authority, defeated a Mexican army, and set themselves up as an independent republic looking toward union with the United States. During the same period, wagon trains from the Missouri frontier had been crossing the plains along the northern borders of Texas and pushing on to trade with the ancient Spanish-Mexican settlement of Santa Fe on the upper Rio Grande. Still farther north, fur traders had followed in the tracks of Lewis and Clark, exploring the Rocky Mountains and bringing back tales of new promised lands beyond in the Oregon country and Mexican California. Meanwhile, the enterprising merchants of Boston and Salem and New York were sending their ships around Cape Horn at the southern tip of South America to pick up hides on the California coast and were becoming excited about the possibility of dominating trade with the Orient from the magnificent Pacific harbors at San Diego, San Francisco, and Puget Sound.

While Americans were discovering the far West, romantic assumptions were intensifying their faith in the superiority and glorious destiny of their free institutions. Rapidly the idea grew that it was the "manifest destiny" of these free institutions to spread over all the vast, thinly inhabited, and lightly held territories between the Mississippi Valley and the Pacific Ocean.

The growing enthusiasm for territorial expansion further confused an already tangled political situation, while raising an ominous question. The decade of the 1840s opened with the Whigs and Democrats still battling inconclusively over old issues that no longer stirred the voters, and both parties were for different reasons somewhat demoralized. Under these circumstances the issue of expansion was a godsend to ambitious politicians with various axes to grind. But it was a dangerous issue. The controversy over slavery was making the country edgy. The mounting hostility between North and South was becoming too apparent to be wished out of consciousness. A great crusade to fulfill the manifest territorial destiny of the United States might reunite Americans in enthusiastic patriotism. But it could also incite a disastrous sectional conflict over the territorial spoils.

TIPPECANOE — AND TYLER TOO

Such possibilities were still far from most people's minds as the Whigs took over the national government following their great victory in the presidential election of 1840. President Harrison called a special session of Congress to pass the traditional Whig program — repeal of the independent treasury system, a new national bank, a higher protective tariff, and a scheme for distributing the federal land revenues among the states. Yet the Whigs were the unluckiest of the major political parties. Within a month after his inauguration, "Old Tippecanoe" died, leaving the Whig program at the mercy of the vain, stubborn vice-president, John Tyler of Virginia (see Table 6, p. 165).

Tyler had left the Democratic party when Jackson threatened to coerce the South Carolina Nullifiers in 1832, and he retained much of the old-fashioned Virginian attachment to state rights. He went along with Clay in repealing the independent treasury system, but after indicating a willingness to approve a national fiscal agency, he vetoed two successive bills chartering a new national bank. By other vetoes, Tyler made it clear that Clay could have either a higher protective tariff or distribution but not both. Clay chose increased protection for manufacturers, and the Tariff of 1842 raised duties generally to the levels that had existed before the Compromise Tariff of 1833. Meanwhile, in a futile effort to secure distribution, the Whig Congress included in the Land Act of 1841 the principle of *pre-emption*. Pre-emption enabled any head of a family to settle on 160 acres of the public domain before they were offered for sale at the customary auction and then to bid them in at the minimum price of $1.25 an acre.

Thus the stubborn Virginia president frustrated every part of the Whig program except the higher tariff and caused Clay to accept a pre-emption system for which he had no great enthusiasm. The overwhelming majority of the Whig members of Congress, both northern and southern, turned on Tyler in fury and read him out of the Whig party. Every member of his cabinet resigned, Secretary of State Daniel Webster tarrying only a little longer than the others. Webster's delay was partly to enable him to complete the negotiations with England that led up to the Webster-Ashburton Treaty of 1842, compromising a dispute over the boundary between Maine and Canada. Bereft of party support, Tyler took up the issue of expansion, hoping that it might enable him to run for president in 1844. Secretly, his administration began negotiating with the Texas authorities for a treaty of annexation.

The Texas question had long been regarded as a threat to the delicate sectional balances that held the two parties together as national organizations. From the moment of the Texas Revolution in 1836, antislavery people had been denouncing it as a plot by southern filibusterers to extend the area of slavery, and even Jackson, despite his warm friendship for the Texas leader Sam Houston, had delayed recognition of the new republic until after Van Buren was safely elected. Van Buren had similarly avoided the question of annexation during his administration as being too dangerous to the harmony of the Democratic party.

Thus, by pushing the Texas question to the fore, Tyler hoped to embarrass the old party leaders and either to run for president as the candidate of a pro-Texas third party or to displace Van Buren as the Democratic nominee. The potential for sectional conflict over the Texas issue was increased when Tyler brought in Calhoun as his Secretary of State to complete the secret negotiations for an annexation treaty. The treaty was signed and sent to the Senate in April 1844. Along with it, Calhoun sent a copy of a dispatch he had written to the British minister, Richard Pakenham, denouncing British interference in Texas, defending slavery as a positive good, and justifying annexation mainly as a measure in defense of slavery. Calhoun's Pakenham letter, irritating even moderate antislavery people, doomed the treaty to defeat in the Senate and produced violent political turmoil on the eve of the presidential nominating conventions.

THE PRESIDENTIAL ELECTION OF 1844

Clay and Van Buren had both seemed assured of nomination by their respective parties, and both wished to keep the Texas issue out of the campaign. At the end of April, hard on the heels of Calhoun's Pakenham letter, they published simultaneous letters opposing immediate annexation. Shortly thereafter, Clay was nominated by the Whig convention, but Van Buren's Texas letter aroused a storm of opposition against him at the Democratic convention.

Although a majority of the delegates to the Democratic convention had originally been instructed for Van Buren, the late developing Texas excitement had produced, especially in the southern and western states, a decided popular reaction in favor of a pro-Texas candidate. Van Buren's Texas letter was the signal for pro-Texas and anti-Van Buren factions to join forces in a last-ditch fight to block his nomination. Their strategy was to insist on a two-thirds majority for nomination. Many delegates who felt bound by their instructions to vote for Van Buren on the early ballots were nevertheless able to vote for the two-thirds rule that made his nomination impossible.

But if Van Buren could not muster a two-thirds majority, neither could his leading rival, Lewis Cass of Michigan. The deadlock might have destroyed the Democratic party if the convention had not finally hit upon a compromise candidate. James K. Polk had recently suffered two successive defeats in campaigns for governor of Tennessee, but he was almost the only Democrat of any prominence who could command the confidence of all the feuding factions. The hard-money Van Buren wing of the party respected him as a protégé of Jackson and able leader of the Democratic forces in the House of Representatives during the Bank War, while as a slaveholding Southerner and outspoken advocate of immediate annexation, he was acceptable to the expansionist, anti-Van Buren wing.

Having nominated Polk by acclamation, the convention adopted a platform calling for "the reoccupation of Oregon and the reannexation of Texas, at the earliest practicable moment." The Oregon question had recently generated considerable enthusiasm in the Northwest, but even there it had been overshadowed by the Texas question. The Oregon plank seems to have been included primarily to remove the sectional sting from the inescapable Texas issue.

The ensuing election reflected the nearly equal division of popular strength that the matured two-party system had by this time produced. In the closest presidential race to this time, Polk received 49.6 percent of the popular votes to 48.1 percent for Clay. Polk's majority margin in the electoral college was provided by New York, where the diversion of a small number of normally Whig votes to an antislavery third-party candidate swung the balance in favor of the Democrats.

The pro-Texas people interpreted this narrow victory as a mandate for annexation. Just before Polk's inauguration in early 1845, Congress approved, by joint resolution rather than treaty, the admission of Texas as one of the United States.

THE POLK ADMINISTRATION

Polk was one of the hardest working and most effective men ever to occupy the White House. Unimaginative, undramatic, and without much prestige when he entered office, he was nevertheless spectacularly successful in getting what he wanted from a deeply divided Democratic party and Congress and from other countries. And he wanted a great deal.

Polk was first of all an old-fashioned, doctrinaire Jacksonian Democrat. He wanted an independent treasury system reinstituted, and from his first Congress in 1846, he got it. He wanted a drastic downward revision of the tariff, and the same Congress gave him a tariff act incorporating the antiprotectionist principle of moderate rates designed chiefly for revenue and expressed in uniform percentages — with only moderate discrimination in favor of the most important American manufactures. He wanted an even further reduction in the already circumscribed federal expenditures for internal improvements, and his vetoes of long sanctioned appropriations for river and harbor improvements were sustained. Thus, under Polk, the traditional Democratic policies were finally established, to remain substantially unchanged until the Civil War.

While cleaning up this unfinished Democratic business, Polk was simultaneously moving aggressively along the new line of expansionism. With the Texas issue settled, he wasted not a moment in turning his attention to the Oregon country. This vast expanse of territory — stretching from the Rockies to the Pacific and from the border of Mexican California at 42° on the south to Russian Alaska at 54°40' on the north — had been jointly occupied by the United States and Great Britain with the proviso that either nation could terminate the joint occupation by giving one year's notice. In the early 1840s, American settlers began finding their way to Oregon in substantial numbers and disputing possession of the land with the well-established British posts of the Hudson's Bay Company. This migration had created considerable interest in Oregon in the states of the upper Mississippi Valley, northwestern Democrats had begun agitating for a more vigorous assertion of American claims to the country, and the Democratic platform had declared that "Our title to the whole of the Territory of Oregon is clear and unquestionable."

Polk's inaugural address echoed the Oregon plank in the Democratic platform, but he felt bound to renew once more his predecessors' offer of a compromise boundary along the 49th parallel, an offer the British had rejected several times. When the British minister rudely rebuffed this proposal without even referring it to his government, Polk took a more bellicose line. Calling on Congress to give notice of the termination of joint occupancy, he asserted the American claim to the whole of the territory.

For a time war threatened, but both sides were ready for any face-saving solution along the 49th parallel. Polk allowed intimations to reach the British that if they made a proper proposal he would submit it to the Senate for advice. Such a proposal came in June 1846, and the Senate advised its acceptance. The 49° boundary already established east of the Rockies was extended west to the Pacific with a short detour down the Strait of Fuca to leave Britain the whole of Vancouver Island. (See map on page 109.)

THE MEXICAN WAR

Polk's bold Oregon game with the British was rendered more dangerous by his bellicose diplomacy in another quarter. For a time, he seemed to be courting simultaneous wars with Great Britain and with Mexico. The principal prize in the latter case would be Mexican California with its splendid

Pacific harbors. There can be little doubt that Polk was determined to secure the vast domain between the southwestern borders of the United States and the Pacific and that he deliberately provoked war when the Mexicans refused to sell it.

Having won its independence from Spain in 1821, Mexico was a proud young republic with a political system so unstable that any government compromising the national honor was sure to be driven from office. The Texas Revolution had been a severe blow to Mexican pride. Stubbornly refusing to recognize Texan independence, the Mexicans regarded the annexation of Texas by the United States as an act of aggression and had broken off diplomatic relations.

It was at this point that Polk entered the White House. One of his first acts was to order an American army to the western frontier of Texas to ward off any attack by Mexico while the formalities of annexation were being completed. He was less justified in authorizing the army to advance beyond the traditional Texan boundary at the Nueces River and in announcing his determination to enforce the unfounded Texas claim that its territory extended to the Rio Grande River. Then he sent a minister to Mexico with an offer that the United States would assume the unpaid claims of American citizens against Mexico for property losses during the Mexican Revolution in return for Mexican acceptance of the Rio Grande boundary. In addition, the envoy was to try to purchase New Mexico and California.

Since the Mexicans had not indicated any willingness to reopen regular diplomatic negotiations, it should not have been surprising that they refused to receive Polk's minister. Nevertheless Polk chose to regard this rebuff as a cause for war. He had already ordered the American army to advance to the Rio Grande, and he prepared to ask Congress for a declaration of war. The Mexicans saved him the trouble by precipitating hostilities. A Mexican force encountered an American patrol just east of the Rio Grande, and in the ensuing skirmish 16 Americans were killed or wounded. Polk got the news just in time to modify his war message. Mexico, he told Congress, "has invaded our territory and shed American blood upon the American soil." War was declared on May 13, 1846. Presidential claims of "invasion" and of the shedding of American blood on American soil were properly questioned in Congress — to little avail. Polk wanted war and a continental empire, and his conduct of relations with Mexico illustrated the almost unlimited power of the president in foreign policy and as commander-in-chief.

The Mexican War, whatever its morality, was militarily the most successful of American wars. General Zachary Taylor led the army on the Rio Grande into north central Mexico and at Buena Vista in February 1847, won a brilliant victory over a superior Mexican force commanded by General Santa Anna. Shortly thereafter, another American army under General Winfield Scott landed at Vera Cruz on the Gulf Coast and by September had occupied the enemy capital, Mexico City. Meanwhile Colonel Stephen Kearney had led another American army across the plains from Missouri, seizing Santa Fe on the upper Rio Grande and then moving on west across the mountains and deserts to establish American authority in California.

When General Scott captured Vera Cruz, President Polk sent Nicholas P. Trist, chief of the State Department, to accompany Scott's army and seize upon any opportunity for negotiating a peace that would give the United States the territory it wanted. The fall of Mexico City reduced that country to political chaos, and by the time Trist found a government stable enough to negotiate, he had infuriated President Polk by insubordinate behavior. Defying an order to return home, Trist went ahead and negotiated the Treaty of Guadelupe Hidalgo, signed in February 1848. By this treaty, Mexico recognized the Rio Grande boundary and ceded New Mexico and California, while in return the United States was to assume the claims of its citizens against Mexico and pay Mexico $15 million. Since these were the terms Polk had instructed the repudiated diplomat to secure, he signed Trist's treaty, and the Senate ratified it.

TOWARD THE FIRST SECESSION CRISIS

Despite the brilliance of its military victories and the vastness of its territorial acquisitions, the United States emerged from the Mexican War more deeply divided and distracted than ever. The enthusiastic expansionism of people like President Polk had been partly an effort to find a cause that would unite all Americans in a new burst of patriotic nationalism and furnish a vaccine against the insidiously spreading infection of sectional enmity. But the infection had already taken too firm a hold, and the remedy served to intensify rather than alleviate the disease.

The enthusiasm for expansion was most widespread in the Northwest and the Southwest and among Democrats; in the East and among Whigs, the transparently aggressive character of the Mexican War had made it unpopular with many from the beginning. The Whigs carried on a constant criticism of the administration's war policy, and northern Whigs began to denounce the war as a southern project for expanding the area of slavery. Northern voters were told, too, that a slavery-dominated Democratic party had demonstrated its indifference to the interests of the free states by reducing the tariff, cutting off appropriations for rivers and harbors, and surrendering the American claim to the whole of Oregon. The war helped to crystallize in thousands of northern minds the conviction that the area of slavery and the political power of slavery must not be allowed to expand.

In the summer of 1846, while Congress was debating a bill appropriating money for negotiations with Mexico, a Pennsylvania Democrat named David Wilmot offered an amendment declaring that slavery should be forever barred from any Mexican territories to be acquired. The Wilmot Proviso, though defeated when first introduced, infuriated southern members of Congress and provoked a struggle of such mounting violence that within three years it would bring the country to the brink of secession and civil war.

The end of the Mexican War made it indispensable to enact some legislation for government in the new territories, but no legislation could be passed without settling the status of slavery there. Northerners dominated the House of Representatives and insisted on the Wilmot Proviso while Southerners, relying on a Senate still evenly balanced between slave and free states, asserted their right to migrate with their property, including slaves, into the territory they had helped to win. President Polk urged that the Missouri Compromise line of 36°30′ be extended to the Pacific as the boundary between slave and free territory, telling Northerners that slavery could never get a foothold in the arid Southwest no matter what Congress provided. But Polk made the serious blunder of announcing that he would under no circumstances accept a second term. Having expended his patronage in getting his ambitious program through his first Congress, he was less and less able to control Democrats in Congress as his term neared its end, and the extremists, both North and South, defeated his and all other efforts to reach a compromise solution.

It was in this atmosphere that the presidential election of 1848 occurred. The free-soil issue had split both parties deeply along sectional lines. The rift was potentially deeper among the Whigs because antislavery sentiment was stronger in the northern wing of their party, but they successfully obscured their differences by again adopting the strategy of nominating a military hero. This time he was General Zachary Taylor, the hero of Buena Vista, a plain, honest old soldier who owned a plantation and slaves in Louisiana. Democratic differences were more conspicuous because Polk's no-second-term position had prompted a prolonged intraparty struggle over the nomination. At the cost of great bitterness, the Democratic convention finally nominated Senator Lewis Cass of Michigan, hated by the Van Buren-ites for his role in blocking their chieftain's nomination four years previously.

The major party nominations provoked the formation of a formidable antislavery third party. Deeply suspicious of the slaveholding Taylor, the more fervently antislavery Whigs organized a Free Soil party with the Wilmot Proviso as their platform. They were quickly joined by the "Barnburners," or Van Buren Democrats, who were just as anxious for revenge against Cass and the rival "Hunker" faction of the New York Democratic party as they were to stop the spread of slavery. The new party nominated Van Buren for president and Charles Francis Adams, Whig son of John Quincy Adams, for vice president.

Taylor's personal popularity, his nonpartisan posture, the special appeal that his slaveholding status gave him in the South, and the Barnburner secession from Cass in the North made the outcome a foregone conclusion. "Old Rough and Ready" did not have to say where he stood on the territorial question, while Cass advanced a compromise solution of great future significance but little immediate appeal to the more zealous defenders of the southern and northern positions. This compromise was the doctrine of popular sovereignty by which the settlers in the territories would be left to settle the status of slavery for themselves. Taylor won handily, while the Free Soilers garnered a substantial popular vote and elected nine representatives.

THE COMPROMISE OF 1850

By the time Taylor took office in March 1849, the discovery of gold in California had attracted a horde of unruly immigrants and created a desperate need for legislation providing government in the new territories. Meanwhile, Southerners had been further infuriated by proposals in Congress to abolish slavery and the slave trade in the District of Columbia. Calhoun was passionately exhorting Southerners to abandon the old parties and unite in a new sectional party to defend the South's rights and safety. The more radical Southerners were demanding that the South secede if the Wilmot Proviso were applied in any form to any territory, and a number of southern governors and legislatures took measures looking toward secession in such an eventuality. In this crisis, the new president, to the shock of those Southerners who had supported him because he was a slaveholder, encouraged the Californians to bypass the territorial stage, to draw up a state constitution without congressional authorization, and to apply directly for admission as a free state. Thus Taylor's first Congress met in December 1849, to find a free California waiting on its doorstep and passions running so high that members carried Bowie knives and revolvers and the House of Representatives took three weeks and 63 ballots to elect a Speaker.

The aged Henry Clay now stepped forward to rally the forces of moderation and compromise, presenting a series of proposals as an "omnibus" settlement of all the disputed questions arising from the slavery issue: (1) California was to be admitted as a free state; (2) the remainder of the Mexican cession was to be organized into two territories, Utah on the north and New Mexico on the south, leaving the status of slavery for their inhabitants to settle. The Utah territory was to provide a government for the large body of Mormons who had migrated to the shores of the Great Salt Lake in 1846 after being driven out of their settlements in Missouri and Illinois. The New Mexico territory involved an additional complication because Texas claimed that its territory extended to the upper Rio Grande, embracing Santa Fe and half of the old Spanish-Mexican province of New Mexico. Clay therefore further proposed that: (3) Texas should give up its claims to the New Mexican area in return for which the United States would assume the Texas public debt; (4) the slave trade but not slavery should be abolished in the District of Columbia; and (5) the old federal Fugitive Slave Law of 1790, the enforcement of which had been increasingly defied and impeded in the North, should be strengthened.

Southerners complained that Clay's compromise would cost the South its equal strength in the Senate while making only the single concession to the South of a stronger fugitive slave law. Formidable opposition also came from President Taylor and the bulk of the northern Whigs, who were determined that the advance of slavery should be decisively halted. Even after Taylor died in July 1850, and was succeeded by the procompromise Vice President Millard Fillmore, Clay was unable to gain a majority for his omnibus proposal. Only when the Illinois Democrat, Stephen A. Douglas, took command and broke Clay's omnibus bill into separate proposals did the various compromise measures pass.

The success of the compromise depended on the willingness of the aroused lower South to accept it. In Georgia, Mississippi, and other states, party lines broke down as Whigs and moderate Democrats joined forces to defeat the advocates of secession. The country's factions breathed sighs of relief, and the majority of politicians everywhere committed themselves to the compromise measures as a "final solution" of the slavery controversy.

In the presidential election of 1852, the Democratic nominee, Franklin Pierce of New Hampshire, won because of his allegiance to the compromise. Again the Whigs had turned to a military hero, nominating General Winfield Scott. But Whigs in the South could no longer sustain themselves as copartisans of the increasingly antislavery northern Whigs. With southern Whigs being forced into the Democratic party, the Whig party was already dying as a national entity, and Scott was its last presidential candidate.

FOR FURTHER READING

Frederick Merk has written an important work on *Manifest Destiny and Mission in American History* (1963); Ray A. Billington is the author of the best general account of *The Far Western Frontier, 1830–1860* (1956); and Henry Nash Smith's *Virgin Land* (1950) is a brilliant interpretation of the meaning of the West for the American imagination. The trade between Missouri and Santa Fe is described by a participant in Josiah Gregg's *Commerce of the Prairies* (1844); the fur trade is vividly and soundly reconstructed in James P. Ronda's *Astoria and Empire* (1990). Francis Parkman's account of his experiences along *The Oregon Trail* (1849) is a classic, while John D. Unruh's *The Plains Across* (1979) provides a scholarly examination of overland migration from 1840 to 1860. Marquis James's *The Raven* (1929) is a vivid biography of the Texas leader Sam Houston; Frederick Merk has collected essays on *The Oregon Question* (1967); Norman Graebner explores the *Empire on the Pacific* (1955); and David Alan Johnson is the author of *Founding the Far West* (1992). The political history of the 1840s is best followed through three biographies: Robert Seager, II, *And Tyler Too: A Biography of John & Julia Gardiner Tyler* (1963); the third volume of Charles M. Wiltse, *John C. Calhoun* (3 vols., 1944–1951); and Charles Sellers, *James K. Polk, Continentalist: 1843–1846* (1966). Robert W. Johannsen in *To the Halls of the Montezumas* (1985) describes the war with Mexico, and Elbert B. Smith covers *The Presidencies of Zachary Taylor and Millard Fillmore* (1988). David M. Potter's *The Impending Crisis* (1976) offers a full analysis of the developing sectional controversy of the late 1840s; Joseph G. Rayback's *Free Soil* (1970) examines the election of 1848; Chaplain Morrison's *Democratic Politics and Sectionalism* (1967) probes the Wilmot Proviso; and Holman Hamilton's *Prologue to Conflict: The Crisis and Compromise of 1850* (1964) explains the temporary resolution of the controversy.

TABLE 7. PRESIDENTIAL ELECTIONS AND MAJOR EVENTS, 1852–1861

1852	**Franklin Pierce** (Democrat) elected over Winfield Scott (Whig). Harriet Beecher Stowe publishes *Uncle Tom's Cabin*.
1854	Kansas-Nebraska Act repeals Missouri Compromise and organizes Kansas and Nebraska territories on principle of squatter sovereignty.
1856	**James Buchanan** (Democrat) elected over John C. Frémont (Republican) and Millard Fillmore (American).
1857	*Dred Scott* vs. *Sanford*. Roger B. Taney's Supreme Court declares that Congress cannot bar slavery from the territories. Buchanan fails to force the admission of Kansas to statehood under the proslavery Lecompton Constitution. Hinton Rowan Helper publishes *The Impending Crisis of the South*.
1858	Lincoln-Douglas Debates. In his contest with Abraham Lincoln for Senator from Illinois, Stephen A. Douglas argues, in his "Freeport Doctrine," that slavery cannot survive in a territory without positive supporting legislation.
1859	John Brown's raid on Harper's Ferry.
1860	Radical Southerners break up the Democratic party by withdrawing when the Charleston convention refuses to endorse their demand for a congressional slave code. **Abraham Lincoln** (Republican) elected president over Stephen A. Douglas (Northern Democrat), John C. Breckinridge (Southern Democrat), and John Bell (Constitutional Unionist).
1860–1861	Seven states of the lower South secede and organize the Confederate States of America.

14

★ ★ ★ ★ ★ ★

A House Dividing, 1843–1860

HOPING that the Compromise of 1850 had finally settled the slavery controversy, the American people again turned their energies to the march of enterprise. The 1850s were a decade of unprecedented economic growth and prosperity, the climax of the market revolution and the further development of the industrial revolution. Yet the very process of economic growth and physical expansion provoked a renewal of sectional conflict that could be resolved only by civil war.

CULMINATION OF THE MARKET REVOLUTION

The exuberance of the forces generating the market revolution had also generated boom-and-bust cycles that had periodically inhibited the country's full potential for economic growth. Not until the years between 1843 and 1857 did the developed market economy have a chance to show what it could do in an extended period without a major depression.

The results were spectacular. Between 1844 and 1854, the total value of all commodities produced rose by 69 percent, the highest gain for any decade until the 1880s. Accompanying this rise in gross production was an equivalent gain in the efficiency of production, with output per worker rising by 10 percent in the 1840s and 23 percent in the 1850s, the latter increase again to be unequaled until the 1880s. This rapid economic growth was in part a further acceleration of the market revolution in its various aspects following a slackened pace during the 1837–1843 depression.

Commercial agriculture resumed its growth at a faster rate than ever. By 1846 the formerly protectionist Northwest was exporting so much wheat to foreign markets that it turned toward free trade and provided the votes by which the tariff reductions of that year were passed. By 1850 the Northwest exceeded the Northeast in wheat production, and this was only a prelude of things to come. The advance of the agricultural frontier north into Wisconsin and west across Iowa into eastern Kansas and Nebraska, coupled with the widespread use of Cyrus McCormick's mechanical reaper, pushed north-western wheat production from some 30 million bushels in 1850 to almost 100 million bushels in 1860. Meat packing and the production of corn and hogs expanded almost as spectacularly.

Similarly in the South, the cotton crop increased by 60 percent in the 1840s and 100 percent in the 1850s. Sugar production in Louisiana rose four-fold between the mid-1830s and 1859. The increasing productivity and prof-itability of southern agriculture were reflected in the rising price of slaves. In the 1790s, a prime field hand could have been bought for $300; by 1840, the price had risen to $1,000; by 1860, it ran up to $1,500.

The impressive growth of a regionally specialized commercial agriculture was closely related to the perfection of a national system of transportation and communication that provided facilities for swift, cheap, and efficient interregional and international exchanges of goods and services. Turnpikes, canals, and steamboats had been effective enough for the earlier stages of the market revolution, but not until the 1850s was the transportation system brought to full efficiency by the creation of a great railroad network.

Although railroad construction had received a start in the 1830s, only local lines had been completed before the depression of 1837–1843 stalled further progress. As late as 1848, the country had only 6,000 miles of track. Mileage doubled in the next four years and reached 30,000 by 1860. By 1857 the country had invested a billion dollars in railroads, two thirds of that during the preceding seven years.

Particularly important was the completion in the early 1850s of five great trunk lines connecting the Atlantic ports of Boston, New York, Philadelphia, Baltimore, and Charleston with the Ohio and Mississippi valleys by way of Albany and Buffalo, Pittsburgh, Wheeling, and Atlanta and Chattanooga. From these terminals the eastern trunk lines rapidly developed new western railroads to the emerging transportation and commercial centers of Chicago, St. Louis, and Memphis. By 1855 a passenger could travel in two days from one of the Atlantic cities to Chicago or St. Louis for a fare of $20. Radiating out from the trunk lines were feeder lines that brought cheap transportation and commercial production to virtually every part of the country.

The flood of products harvested by an expanded agriculture and brought to the coast by a perfected transportation system helped push American exports from $144 million worth of commodities in 1850 to $334 million worth in 1860. Imports climbed to an even higher level, the trade deficit being bridged by exports of California gold, which rose from $5 million in 1850 to $58 million by the end of the decade. This swelling of foreign com-merce brought with it a vigorous revival of the American shipping trade.

Another element in the economic expansion was the upsurge of immigration from abroad, especially from Germany and Ireland after the potato famine created widespread destitution in 1846. Immigrants to the United States had not numbered more than 10,000 a year before 1825, but exceeded 100,000 in the mid-1840s and reached an annual level of around 400,000 in the early 1850s. Between 1844 and 1854 nearly 3 million new Americans arrived from abroad. Many of these people supplied the labor for the factories that were springing up in the East; others did the hard, dirty work in railroad and canal construction. The Germans established strong colonies in such northwestern cities as Cincinnati, St. Louis, and Milwaukee, while still other immigrants swelled the tide of agricultural migration into Wisconsin, Iowa, and beyond.

INDUSTRIAL DEVELOPMENT

The impressive economic gains of the late 1840s and the 1850s were more than a matter of growth along established lines. The rounding out of the vast and lucrative national market set the stage for the industrial revolution in the United States. A new sector of the economy was moving into the dynamic role. Earlier, the profits of the American carrying trade during the Napoleonic Wars had provided the initial impetus that jarred the economy out of its static staple-exporting phase. Then the swelling flood of commercial crops, cotton above all others, had fueled the transportation revolution and the creation of a national market economy. From the 1850s on, industry became the primary stimulant for a sustained and massive expansion of production that would create the most abundant economy that history had yet known.

At mid-century, manufacturing had spread far beyond New England. In fact, capital investments and value of industrial production in the Middle Atlantic states were nearly twice that of New England. Pennsylvania and New York led all states in manufacturing. To be sure, the nation's industrial economy remained immature and, despite rapid antebellum industrial growth in the Ohio Valley and the Chicago area, was concentrated in the East. The trans-Mississippi West, of course, was undeveloped, while the South was overwhelmingly agricultural. Farm products still accounted for the bulk of the nation's exports. Farm employment claimed nearly 60 percent of its labor force, compared to only 12 percent for manufacturing and the remaining percentage in trade and service occupations. And American consumers still depended heavily on foreign-made goods.

Yet the surge in American manufacturing activity, particularly in the 1840s and 1850s, was spectacular. During the 1850s the value of manufactured goods nearly doubled, from $1 billion to just under $2 billion; between 1842 and 1860 the output of pig iron quadrupled. In those decades the value added by American manufacturing — the difference between the value of raw materials used and the value of finished goods — soared higher than in other decades of the nineteenth century.

Cities grew in much the same fashion. In 1820 only 6 percent of all Americans lived in places having 2,500 or more people. By 1860 the percentage had more than tripled, and New York became the first city to contain a million people. The greater part of this urbanization occurred after 1840. Much of it was produced by the increased volume of international and interregional trade that funneled through the cities, creating jobs. But industrial development and new technology were also important to urban growth. The advent of the stationary steam engine as a substitute for waterpower in the 1840s freed manufacturing from riverside locations; this greatly accelerated the tendency of industry to settle in cities and thus contributed to urban growth. In 5 of the 15 largest cities in 1860, more than 10 percent of the population were engaged in manufacturing, while some of the newer and smaller cities like Newark, Lowell, and Lynn were almost wholly industrial. Thus, by any measure, a rapidly transforming economy was approaching what some economists call the takeoff stage. On the eve of the Civil War the United States remained an agricultural nation, but it trailed only England in industrial production and would soon become the world's industrial leader.

Labor conditions, however, were anything but ideal, and not for many decades would industrial workers begin to share in the vast wealth created by the industrial revolution. The steady trend away from domestic manufactures to the factory system — toward the concentration of production in ever larger industrial units — undermined the independence of the old artisan class and created a growing new working class of permanent wage earners. This shift in the status and prospects of working people gave rise in the 1820s and 1830s to a number of labor unions of skilled artisans in such crafts as printing, shoemaking, tailoring, and the building trades. The craft unions organized city federations in New York and Philadelphia; workers' parties entered local politics; and there were strikes for the 10-hour day. In 1834 a National Trades Union was formed. The mass of workers — the unskilled or semiskilled laborers who staffed the new mechanized factories — remained unorganized, however. Then, even the early craft-union movement was swept away by the Panic of 1837. As prosperity returned in the 1840s, the craft unions were reborn. Strikes became numerous and successful enough so that the 10-hour-day was standard by the mid-1850s. Again a National Trades Union was organized, and again a depression in 1857 largely wiped out skilled labor's organizational gains.

CONFLICT AGAIN

With North and South riding the greatest tide of prosperity either section had ever known, it may seem strange that the decade of the 1850s ended in intersectional strife. Indeed direct conflicts of economic interest between the sections over national legislation seemed at the lowest ebb since the Panic of 1819. Southerners were no longer frustrating the Northwest's demands for federal aid to internal improvements; between 1850 and 1860, the federal government granted 18 million acres of the public lands to aid construction of 45 railroads in 10 states. The tariff issue no longer engaged passions as northern industry continued to flourish under the low rates of 1846.

Yet the very lushness of prosperity and growth was fostering imperial visions in the two sections: in the South an expanding cotton-slavery empire, and in the North an expanding free-soil empire. As these competing expansionist impulses headed toward a collision, they were inevitably intensified by the moral dimensions of the slavery question

The South's growing insecurity over the institution of slavery was particularly dangerous. By the 1850s the North was rapidly outstripping the South in population and potential political power; Northerners were demonstrating their deepening disapproval of slavery by blocking enforcement of the stringent new Fugitive Slave Law, one of the few concessions to the South in the Compromise of 1850. These circumstances help explain the mounting stridency with which Southerners proclaimed the merits of slavery, and explain more specifically the South's hysterical reaction to two famous books published during the 1850s. The first, Harriet Beecher Stowe's novel *Uncle Tom's Cabin* (1852), was a sentimental portrayal of slavery's brutal impact on some appealingly drawn slave characters. The second, Hinton Rowan Helper's *Impending Crisis of the South* (1857), was an all too effective argument by a nonslaveholding North Carolinian that slavery was disastrous to the nonslaveholding white majority in the South. Both books were not only denounced, but violently suppressed in the South, while in the North they won wide audiences and helped harden antislavery sentiment.

Paradoxically, the South had more power in the federal government in the 1850s than it had had since Jeffersonian days. The campaign of 1852 demonstrated that the northern and southern wings of the Whig party were too far apart on the slavery question to hold together any longer, leaving the Democrats as the one great national party. Northern Democratic politicians competed against each other for promotion in the party and the federal government by going as far as they could toward satisfying southern demands and thereby winning southern support. Therefore the South came to have the dominant voice in the Democratic presidential administrations of Franklin Pierce and James Buchanan. As long as the Democrats remained a national party and the South's northern Democratic allies could win elections in a good part of the North, the South could in effect control the country and counteract the northern advantage in population and representation. But eventually the South, out of its insecurity, demanded more from its northern Democratic allies than they could grant without losing elections in the North.

What the South was demanding in the 1850s was the right for slavery to expand. This insistence grew out of complicated motives. This southern demand was in part the cotton-slavery imperialism of a prosperous and expansive social and economic system. The demand for slavery was also an effort to bolster the South's slipping proportion of representation in the federal government through the creation of additional slave states. Finally, the South was demanding that Northerners recognize the moral legitimacy of slavery by acknowledging its right to grow and thus relieve the white South from the intolerable burden of justifying and defending an unjustifiable and indefensible social system.

THE TERRITORIAL QUESTION

By the 1850s there was clearly no further room for new slave states within the territorial limits of the United States under the political arrangements that prevailed. The Missouri Compromise of 1820 barred slaves from the remaining unorganized parts of the Louisiana Purchase, the Oregon territory had been organized on free-soil principles, and geography seemed to prohibit slavery's spread over the arid wastes of the New Mexico and Utah territories.

Under these circumstances, expansionist Southerners turned their attention to the Caribbean area, and the Pierce administration attempted to purchase Cuba from Spain. This effort had the advantage of appealing on nonsectional grounds to a nationalistic "Young America" group which wanted to continue the expansionism of the 1840s. But when a trio of southern-oriented diplomats issued the Ostend Manifesto proposing that Cuba be seized if it could not be purchased, there was such an adverse reaction in the North and in Spain that the Cuba project had to be dropped. Despite this setback, many Southerners continued to agitate throughout the 1850s for expansion into the Caribbean area and to support illegal filibustering expeditions that sought to overturn weak Central American governments and pave the way for American annexations.

With the outlook for foreign expansionism dim, a small group of southern politicians began a fateful effort to push slavery into that part of the Louisiana Purchase reserved as free soil. Democratic Senator Stephen A. Douglas of Illinois was anxious to pass a bill providing territorial government for the Kansas and Nebraska country, partly to facilitate the start of a transcontinental railroad that might terminate in his home town of Chicago. Senator David R. Atchison of Missouri, representing a slaveholding constituency across the Missouri River from the area in question, had staked his political life on a promise that his constituents would be able to take their slaves into the new territory. Atchison joined with a group of powerful southern senators to insist that no territorial bill would pass unless it contained a clause repealing the Missouri Compromise prohibition of slavery. Douglas gave in to their demand, a weak President Pierce was persuaded to use all the power of the national administration to secure enough northern Democratic votes to pass the bill, and the Kansas-Nebraska Act of 1854 was the result.

Douglas argued that the act was simply an extension of the democratic "popular sovereignty" principle already applied to the New Mexico and Utah territories by the Compromise of 1850. But indignation blazed up in the

MAP 4: THE KANSAS-NEBRASKA ACT, 1854

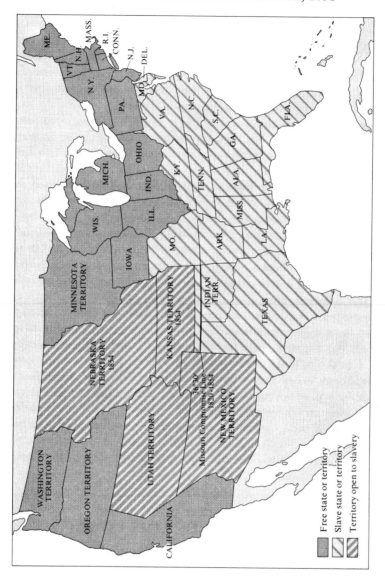

North at this cynical abrogation of a sacred compromise and at the servile northern Democrats who obeyed an "aggressive slavocracy." While only a small minority of Northerners were disposed to interfere with slavery where it already existed, far more were ready to stop its further spread. With the Kansas-Nebraska Act, cotton-slavery imperialism provocatively challenged free-soil imperialism. The immediate response was the organization of a new sectional party in the North calling itself "Republican" and vowing its opposition to the least extension of the area of slavery.

Meanwhile Kansas, the more southerly of the two new territories, was filled with violence and bloodshed as proslavery and antislavery factions contended for control of the territorial government. New England abolitionists contributed guns and funds for free-soil immigrants, while "border ruffians" from Missouri crossed the river to furnish illegal ballots and armed support to the proslavery faction. When President Pierce again yielded to southern pressure and recognized a proslavery legislature elected largely by illegal voters from Missouri, the enraged free-soilers elected their own legislature and governor. A proslavery force raided the free-soil capital, and in retaliation, a fanatical abolitionist named John Brown invaded an isolated proslavery settlement and butchered five inoffensive residents. In the sporadic violence that followed, more than 200 people were killed.

In retrospect, the demand for repeal of the Missouri Compromise appears to have been a suicidal strategy for southern interests. Southern opinion generally was not strongly in favor of such a demand, and even many of the more radical Southerners admitted that slavery would probably never be established in any of the disputed territories. What the South was really demanding was an acknowledgment of its technical right to take slaves into all territories, an acknowledgment of the legitimacy of slavery. For the sake of this technical right, southern leaders put their northern Democratic allies in an untenable position in their home constituencies and called into existence a formidable antislavery party that would soon destroy their control of the federal government.

BUCHANAN RIDES THE STORM

The new Republican party, drawing heavily from former Whigs and outraged Democrats, grew by leaps and bounds in the North. As the presidential election of 1856 approached, the Democrats were also threatened by another new party, the Americans or Know-Nothings, who appealed to anti-immigrant, anti-Catholic sentiment. To meet this double challenge, the Democratic national convention dropped the discredited Pierce and nominated the cautious, conservative, and prosouthern James Buchanan of Pennsylvania. The new American party nominated ex-President Fillmore and drew a substantial vote, especially from former Whigs in the South, but carried only one state. The major feature of the election was the strong showing of the new Republican party, which carried all but five of the free states for its candidate John C. Frémont. Only by the lavish use of money in Pennsylvania and Indiana and by the support of an almost solid South did the Democrats squeak through with a bare electoral majority.

The attempt to apply the popular sovereignty principle was deepening the chaos in Kansas and Washington. Southerners were insisting that popular sovereignty did not allow the people of a territory to bar slavery until they came to draft a constitution preparatory to admission as a state. Shortly after Buchanan's inauguration in March 1857, a southern majority on the Supreme Court upheld this southern contention in the celebrated case of Dred Scott. Chief Justice Roger B. Taney's opinion denied the slave Scott's contention that he had been made free by residence in the free territory of Iowa; Taney wrote that Congress could not bar slavery from the territories — and it was a logical inference that territorial legislatures could not either.

While northern opinion was reacting to this further evidence of southern aggression, President Buchanan was trying to remove the issue from politics by pushing Kansas into statehood. Failing to get a fair referendum on slavery in Kansas, the president unwisely succumbed to southern pressure and endorsed a proslavery state constitution drafted by a notoriously unrepresentative convention at Lecompton. At this point, Senator Douglas and a number of other northern Democrats, fighting for political survival at home, revolted against the president and blocked the admission of Kansas under the Lecompton Constitution.

At the height of the Kansas crisis in 1857, the further strain of a severe financial crisis hit the country. The Republicans capitalized on the hard times to broaden their appeal. The southern-dominated Democratic Congress had just passed the Tariff of 1857, reducing protection to the lowest level since 1812. It was easy to blame the depression on the new tariff and to win support from hard-hit manufacturers and industrial workers by promises of higher rates. At the same time, the Republicans made themselves more appealing to northwestern farmers by agitating for a homestead act giving free homesteads of 160 acres to settlers on the public lands. A wave of religious revivals following the financial crash further excited the public mind and intensified the Northerners' moral sensitivity on the slavery question.

THE ELECTION OF 1860

Under these unsettling circumstances, the slavery debate began to be dominated by the approaching presidential election of 1860. Stephen A. Douglas of Illinois was the leading aspirant for the Democratic nomination and perhaps the only Democrat who could win enough support in the North to be elected. But Douglas was in an exceedingly difficult dilemma, reflecting the dilemma of his party. In order to be nominated, he had to allay southern suspicions arising from his opposition to the Lecompton Constitution, but it was questionable whether he could allay these suspicions and win the nomination without taking a position so prosouthern that he would lose the subsequent election. And in the meantime, he had to win re-election to the Senate against the leading Illinois Republican, a shrewd Springfield lawyer named Abraham Lincoln.

In the famous series of seven debates between Douglas and Lincoln across Illinois in 1858, Douglas sought to escape his predicament by taking an ambiguous position. On the one hand, he maintained his doctrine of popular sovereignty, which would technically permit Southerners to take their slaves into the territories and deny territorial legislatures the right to bar slavery before statehood. But at the same time he assured the Illinois voters, in what came to be called the Freeport Doctrine, that slaves could never be successfully held in a territory unless the territorial legislature had passed a slave code or positive legislation for protecting and policing slave property. Douglas won the senatorial election in the Illinois legislature by a narrow margin, but his Freeport Doctrine made him even less acceptable to Southerners as a presidential nominee. Lincoln emerged from the debates as a major Republican figure in a Midwest increasingly committed to the modernizing ideas of "free soil, free labor, and free men." Affirming his own moral aversion to human bondage as "an unqualified evil" and his party's opposition to any extension of slavery, he had held his own against a formidable debater. He had also articulated the hope of many Northerners, including immigrants and disaffected Democrats, that the nation's territories remain "places for poor people to go to, and better their condition."

The South, however, was committed to slavery. Still a premodern and pre-industrial society, the southern states demanded a Union that would maintain slavery, not create freedom. Following the Lincoln-Douglas debates, southern demands reached an extreme of presumption and folly. The more radical Southerners had already begun to suspect that slavery, as Douglas claimed in the Freeport Doctrine, could not be sustained in the territories without a slave code. Now they moved beyond the claim that neither Congress nor territorial legislatures could bar slavery from the territories and began demanding that the federal government protect and guarantee slavery in the territories through enactment of a congressional slave code. Most Southerners were not insistent on this radical demand, and certainly very few Southerners thought of actually taking slaves into the territories. But as tension increased and excitement mounted, southern politicians feared to be outdone in defending their constituents' supposed interests, and the most extreme positions came to the fore. Southern insecurity had generated demands for more and more guarantees and assurances; these apparently aggressive movements of the slaveholding section had frightened the North into more determined resistance and spawned the Republican party; and this hardening resistance in the North had intensified southern insecurity and generated even greater demands.

Southern insecurity reached a peak of near hysteria in October 1859, when the violent abolitionist John Brown, of Kansas fame, led a raid on the federal arsenal at Harpers Ferry, Virginia, seizing guns and ammunition with which he planned to arm a wholesale slave rebellion. Though Brown and his followers were quickly subdued, a paroxysm of terror ran through the South, and terror quickly turned to rage when it was learned that respectable antislavery people in the North had backed the plot.

Against this background, the Democratic national convention assembled at Charleston, South Carolina, in April 1860. Radical Southerners insisted that the convention endorse their demand for a congressional slave code. When the pro-Douglas majority refused, after violent debate, the delegates from eight states of the lower South withdrew, and the convention had to adjourn. Two separate Democratic conventions then met in Baltimore, the northern-dominated one nominating Douglas and the southern-dominated one nominating John C. Breckinridge of Kentucky. Meanwhile, the Republicans, who had no support in the South, had met in Chicago to nominate Abraham Lincoln, and union-minded, old-line Whigs from the border states, calling themselves the Constitutional Union party, had put John Bell of Tennessee into the running as a fourth candidate. In effect, this four-way contest was not one election but two. Free-state voters chose between Lincoln and Douglas; in the slave states, the contest was between Bell and Breckinridge. At this critical moment, the American party system no longer operated in a nationwide context. In the realm of partisan politics, the erosion of unionism was all but complete.

Lincoln had no support *outside* the free states, but in the free states he made an almost clean sweep that was by itself enough for a majority in the electoral college (but only 39 percent of the popular vote). For the rest, Breckinridge carried most of the South handily; Bell won three border slave states; and Douglas, though running second to Lincoln in popular votes, won the electoral votes of only Missouri and half of New Jersey.

SECESSION

For years the small but steadily growing body of radical southern fire-eaters had been looking forward to this day, and they lost no time in making the most of their opportunity. South Carolina had been in a secessionist mood since the days of nullification, impatiently waiting for her stolid sister states to awaken to their danger. At last enough of the southern population was sufficiently aroused by the election of Lincoln, a "Black Republican," and South Carolina could lead the way. Hastily calling a state convention, the Palmetto State formally repealed its ratification of the federal constitution on December 20, 1860. Within six weeks, South Carolina was followed by the six Gulf States: Mississippi, Florida, Georgia, Alabama, Louisiana, and Texas.

As the border states hesitated, the waning Buchanan administration fretted in helpless impotence. The politicians at Washington scurried about seeking a formula for compromise, but the victorious Republicans would not listen to a proposal that countenanced the slightest extension of slavery, while the Southerners demanded at least a token concession on the territorial question. Meanwhile the seceded states sent delegates to Montgomery, Alabama, organized themselves as the Confederate States of America, and chose Jefferson Davis of Mississippi as their president.

CONFLICTING HISTORICAL VIEWPOINTS: NO. 6

What Caused the Civil War?

The Civil War is perhaps the best illustration of the ancient truism that the historian's view of the past is colored by his or her perception of the present. Southerners and Northerners debated the causes across regional lines. State's-rightists, nationalists, and economic determinists offered their own predictable explanations for the catastrophe's origins.

The first scholarly assessment came from the pen of James F. Rhodes, a turn-of-the-century historian with a strong nationalist persuasion. In his History of the United States *(7 vols., 1893–1906), Rhodes argued that the war was fought over the issue of slavery: "Of the American Civil War it may safely be asserted [that] there was a single cause, slavery." Almost universally accepted for two decades, Rhodes's thesis was disputed and ultimately displaced during the 1920s and 1930s. But during the period of civil rights activism following World War II, his interpretation won renewed support. In an authoritative modern reaffirmation of the slavery hypothesis, Allan Nevins concluded that "the main root of the conflict . . . was the problem of slavery with its complementary problem of race-adjustment." Nevins's magisterial* Ordeal of the Union *(4 vols., 1947–1971) also identified "minor roots," including constitutional, political, and economic factors. But the issue of slavery and the future of blacks in American society, he insisted, were fundamentally the causes of the Civil War.*

On the eve of the Great Depression, Charles and Mary Beard argued that economic conflict, not slavery, caused the war. In The Rise of American Civilization *(2 vols., 1927), the Beards viewed the conflict as one between rival forms of capitalism. According to this reform-minded husband-and-wife team, the Civil War was a "Second American Revolution" in which northern industrialists sought successfully to dominate southern agriculturists. Although Charles Beard would later abandon this interpretation, it has remained popular among radical scholars. Both William Appleman Williams's* The Contours of American History *(1961) and Barrington Moore's* Social Origins of Dictatorship and Democracy *(1966) offer variations on the Beardian theme.*

Other historians interpreted the war as an inevitable clash of regional rivals. Arthur C. Cole, for example, argued in his The Irrepressible Conflict *(1934) that the North and the South were two distinct civilizations, two separate societies drawn ineluctably into conflict by the very nature of their differences. But other scholars denied there were irreconcilable ideological, institutional, or economic differences between the sections. Indeed,*

James G. Randall (The Civil War and Reconstruction, *1937), Avery Craven* (The Repressible Conflict, *1939), and Kenneth Stampp* (And the War Came, *1950) viewed the Civil War as an avoidable and needless conflict. Writing in the eras of World War II and the Cold War, these anti-war historians blamed blundering politicians and moral fanatics for a holocaust that should never have happened.*

In one form or another, each of these major interpretations has sup- porters among the present generation of historians. For example, in The Impending Crisis *(1976), the latest and perhaps the best synthesis of this much analyzed period, David Potter returns to the theme of Rhodes and Nevins. Although not arguing the issue of inevitability, Potter agrees that the institution of slavery lay at the heart of the problem. Exploring the paradoxical relationship between an ascendant American nationalism and a growing and disruptive sectionalism, he finds no basic nor irresolvable ideological, economic, or cultural differences dividing North from South. The conflict, then, was one over values — values centering on the issue of slavery. Likewise, Kenneth Stampp has recently updated his repressible conflict interpretation in* America in 1857 *(1990). Closely examining the events of that crucial year, Stampp places much of the blame for civil war on the shoulders of President Buchanan and his "tragic miscalculations," especially his decision to support the pro-slavery minority in Kansas, which divided the Democratic party and paved the way for Republican electoral success in 1860.*

Perhaps the conflict that divided the Union more than a century ago will inevitably continue to divide the scholarly community. As Thomas J. Pressly remarked in his analysis of how Americans Interpret Their Civil War *(1954), "The further the Civil War receded into the past, the greater the strength of the emotions with which these divergent viewpoints were upheld."*

FOR FURTHER READING

For economic development in the 1840s and 1850s, the references listed at the end of Chapter 9 will continue to be useful. Marcus Lee Hansen's *The Atlantic Migration, 1607–1860* (1940) and Kerby A. Miller's *Emigrants and Exiles* (1985) are good accounts of the upsurge of immigration during these years. John Commons and others have written the standard *History of Labor in the United States* (4 vols., 1918–1935); Bruce Levine weaves together the themes of German immigration, labor conflict, and the com- ing of the Civil War in *The Spirit of 1848* (1992); and Robert May exam- ines *The Southern Dream of a Caribbean Empire* (1973). The drift toward Civil War is traced by Avery Craven, *The Growth of Southern National- ism, 1848–1861* (1953); by William J. Cooper, *The South and the Politics of Slavery* (1978); and by Michael Holt, *The Political Crisis of the 1850s* (1978). In *Origins of Southern Radicalism* (1988), Lacy K. Ford describes the secession movement in South Carolina; Michael P. Johnson does the same for Georgia in *Toward a Patriarchal Republic* (1977). Thomas Alexander has analyzed congressional voting in the 1850s as an index to *Sectional Stress and Party Strength* (1967), and Eric Foner's *Free Soil, Free Labor, Free Men* (1970) is a major study of early Republican ideology. The more illuminating biographies include David Donald, *Charles Sumner and the Coming of the Civil War* (1960); Robert Johannsen, *Stephen A. Douglas* (1973); Glyndon Van Deusen, *William Henry Seward* (1967); and Drew Gilpin Faust, *James Henry Hammond and the Old South* (1982). *The Dred Scott Case* (1978) is an account by Don Fehrenbacher, while *The Slave States in the Presidential Election of 1860* (1945) have been analyzed by Ollingen Crenshaw. Modern readers will gain much insight from those two famous books of the 1850s, Harriet Beecher Stowe's *Uncle Tom's Cabin* (1852) and Hinton Rowan Helper's *The Impending Crisis of the South: How to Meet It* (1857).

15

★ ★ ★ ★ ★ ★

The Civil War, 1861–1865

WHEN Abraham Lincoln arose to deliver his inaugural address on March 4, 1861, few people had any very clear idea of how the secession problem should be handled. Some voices in the North counseled letting the "erring sisters depart in peace." The abolitionist minority called for a holy war to free the slaves. Majority opinion in the North was increasingly convinced that the Union must somehow be preserved, but there was no clear mandate for military coercion of the seceded states. The war that finally came, like most wars, came not because anyone deliberately willed it, but out of a chain of circumstances whose result reflected only imperfectly the conscious collective will of North or South. Insofar as a guiding will affected the outcome, it was the will of Abraham Lincoln.

LINCOLN AND THE SECESSION CRISIS

The new president was known to the country only as a tall, homely, and apparently uncultivated lawyer-politician from the prairies of Illinois. He had won brief notice years earlier when his opposition to the Mexican War caused Illinois voters to repudiate him after a single term in Congress. Not until his debates with Douglas in the senatorial campaign of 1858 had he attracted national attention. Elected president by a minority of the voters, he had given little public indication of his policy in the months between the election and the inauguration. Actually he had blocked all efforts at compromise by privately opposing any arrangement that left the slightest room for the expansion of slavery. But this position could be put down to political expediency — compromise on the territorial question would have left the infant Republican party little reason for existence — and gave no clue as to what he would do when he assumed office.

Certainly Lincoln was not prepared to lead a crusade to free the slaves. He had insisted that slavery was wrong and that its expansion should be

TABLE 8.   PRESIDENTIAL ELECTIONS AND MAJOR POLITICAL EVENTS, 1860–1865

1860	**Abraham Lincoln** (Republican) elected over Stephen A. Douglas (Northern Democrat), John C. Breckinridge (Southern Democrat), and John Bell (Constitutional Unionist).
1860–1861	Seven states of the lower South secede and organize the Confederate States of America.
1861	Confederates bombard Fort Sumter, beginning the Civil War.
	Virginia, North Carolina, Tennessee, and Arkansas secede and join the Confederacy.
	Morrill Tariff. Substantial upward revision of duties, beginning a long period of high protection.
	Trent affair. Union naval officer seized two Confederate diplomats from a British vessel.
1862	Homestead Act provides free farms of 160 acres to actual settlers.
	Morrill Land Grand Act grants land to the states for agricultural and mechanical colleges.
	Pacific Railroad Act. Federal subsidies for a railroad from Omaha to California.
	Slavery abolished in the territories and the District of Columbia.
	Second Confiscation Act. Freeing escaped or captured slaves of Confederates.
1863	Lincoln's Emancipation Proclamation. Declaring free all slaves in Confederate areas.
	National Bank Act, with a supplementary act of 1864, establishes a system of banks issuing a uniform paper currency based on holdings of federal bonds.
	Turning point of the war in July, when Union forces capture Vicksburg on the Mississippi and stop Lee's invasion at Gettysburg.
	Lincoln announces his "10 percent plan" for the easy restoration of the seceded states to the Union.
1864	Lincoln vetoes the Wade-Davis bill, containing a harsher congressional plan for restoration of the seceded states to the Union.
	Abraham Lincoln (Republican) re-elected over George B. McClellan (Democrat).
1865	Lee surrenders to Grant at Appomattox Courthouse.
	Lincoln assassinated.
	The Thirteenth Amendment abolishes slavery throughout the United States.

stopped so that the country might look forward to its eventual peaceful extinction. But he had repeatedly denied any disposition, "directly or indirectly," to interfere with slavery where it already existed. Nor were his social values notably advanced. In his debates with Douglas the lanky Republican denied that he was "in favor of bringing about in any way the social and political equality of the white and black races." A "physical difference" would prevent the two races from ever living together on equal terms, he had said, and, therefore, "I, as much as any other man, am in favor of having the superior position assigned to the white race." He wanted slavery excluded from the territories so that "white men may find a home — may find some spot where they can . . . settle upon new soil and better their condition in life . . . as an outlet for *free white people everywhere.*"

The inaugural address revealed both a leader of unsuspected stature and a position around which northern opinion could rally. With an eloquence that no president since Jefferson had attained, Lincoln pleaded for preservation of the Union. "The mystic chords of memory," he said, "stretching from every battlefield and every patriot grave to every living heart and hearthstone all over this broad land, will yet swell the chorus of the Union, when again touched, as surely they will be, by the better angels of our nature." In trying to touch these chords, he reassured the South in the most positive terms that he would countenance no act against slavery in the states where it already existed.

But the address also had a vein of iron. The Union, said Lincoln, was perpetual, any violent acts against the authority of the United States were "insurrectionary or revolutionary," and these statements were to be taken "as the declared purpose of the Union that it *will* constitutionally defend and maintain itself." Though the federal government would not initiate hostilities, the president told the South, it would "hold, occupy, and possess" the federal forts and other property in the seceded states and collect the import duties there.

In retrospect, Lincoln clearly committed himself to a course that led directly to one of the bloodiest wars in history. But war was not his purpose. Eight of the 15 slave states were still in the Union. By refusing to recognize secession while at the same time declining to proceed forcibly against the secessionists, Lincoln was seeking to reinforce the manifest Unionist sentiment in the upper South. He wanted to keep the upper South from seceding, hoping that latent Unionism would eventually overcome secessionism in the seven seceded states of the lower South.

There were weaknesses in this union-saving strategy. One was that Lincoln exaggerated the strength of Unionist sentiment in the lower South. Another was the likelihood that the effort to hold the federal forts in the seceded states would lead to armed conflict. Armed conflict was the more likely because the more fiery secessionists were ready to provoke a crisis that would force the upper South to choose sides.

The issue of peace or war reached a crisis at Charleston, South Carolina. Practically all the federal forts and other property in the lower South had been taken over by the seceding states before Lincoln's inauguration. Of the few posts remaining in federal hands, the unfinished and lightly garrisoned Fort Sumter, located in the entrance to Charleston's harbor, had become the symbolic focus of the whole controversy over federal property. Sumter had sufficient supplies to hold out only six weeks, and a decision about its future could not be postponed. Lincoln finally informed the Confederate authorities that he was sending a naval expedition to reprovision Sumter. They in turn ordered their general at Charleston to demand the fort's immediate evacuation and, in case of refusal, to bombard it. The demand was made and refused, and on April 12, 1861, the Confederate shore batteries opened fire.

Lincoln responded by calling on the states for 75,000 troops. Rather than make war on their fellow Southerners, four states of the upper South — Virginia, North Carolina, Tennessee, and Arkansas — reluctantly followed the lower South out of the Union. The four slave states of Delaware, Maryland, Kentucky, and Missouri remained with the Union, though the last two had strong secessionist movements and furnished many soldiers to the Confederacy. The tables were turned on the secessionists when the strongly Unionist western section of Virginia seceded from Virginia and laid the basis for the new state of West Virginia under the aegis of the Union. Meanwhile the Confederacy acted to consolidate the adhesion of the upper southern states by moving its capital from Montgomery to Richmond, Virginia.

THE WAR BEGINS

A spirit of martial ardor swept over both sections in the spring of 1861. Northerners expected a short and easy war, while Southerners seemed oblivious to the overwhelming superiority in human and material resources against which they would have to contend. The 5.5 million free people of the 11 Confederate states faced a population of 22 million in the 23 Union states. The North had a four-to-one advantage in free males of fighting age and would muster twice as many soldiers. Even if one southern soldier was worth two Yankees — as Southerners loudly proclaimed — how were southern armies to be supplied and transported? The North had 80 percent of the country's factories and most of the coal and iron. Approximately 22,000 miles of railroad traversed the North compared to 9,000 in the South, and the North's rail network included a series of vital trunk lines between its eastern and western areas, whereas the sprawling southern regions lacked such efficient rail connections.

Not least of all, the North had Abraham Lincoln. Lincoln was never a very popular president, yet he was a consummate politician, an eloquent and inspired statesman, the symbol of an enduring Union, and an astute war leader whose military judgments were often better than those of his generals. The Confederacy, on the other hand, was less effectively led. For all his humanity, courage, and dignity, Jefferson Davis possessed neither the political nor the military gifts of his Yankee counterpart.

At the war's outset, however, the Union's advantages were not obvious. The South made a remarkable military showing, and some seasoned international observers thought it would prevail. In part, the South's initial successes were due to the strategic advantage of fighting a defensive war. The North was compelled to attack and not only to invade but to occupy the South. Southern commanders had the logistical advantage of shorter supply lines. Moreover, Jefferson Davis had at his command several outstanding generals: Albert Sidney Johnston, Joseph E. Johnston, Thomas J. ("Stonewall") Jackson, and pre-eminently Robert E. Lee. After much soul-searching, these officers had left the United States Army and had taken up arms for a new nation against the country they had once sworn to defend. Secession stripped the Union of many of its more talented officers, and Lincoln was several years in finding a truly able commander.

The Appalachian highlands, thrusting deep into the South, divided the war theater into two zones. Throughout the conflict, the greatest public attention was focused on the East, where the rival armies menaced each other's capitals, which were only 100 miles apart. The Confederate armies, magnificently led by Joseph E. Johnston and then by Robert E. Lee, repeatedly repelled Union invasions aimed at Richmond. In the first major battle of the war in July 1861, Union General Irvin McDowell's army of 30,000 was turned back by a smaller Confederate force at Bull Run in northern Virginia. Lincoln's next commander, 34-year-old General George B. McClellan, was a brilliant military administrator but not an able field commander. The cocky "Little Mack" ferried an enormous, well-trained invasion force down Chesapeake Bay and up the York River to the eastern outskirts of Richmond. But his troops were driven back by Lee and Stonewall Jackson in the series of hard fought battles that constituted the Peninsula Campaign of May–June 1862. Later that summer (August 29–30), Lee trounced another Union army led by John Pope in the second battle at Bull Run. Lee followed up this victory with an audacious advance across the Potomac River into Maryland; McClellan's army caught up with Lee's at Antietam Creek, some 50 miles northwest of Washington, in September 1862. In one of the war's crucial battles, the much larger Union army (70,000 Northerners to the 40,000 Confederates) inflicted so much damage that Lee had to withdraw to Virginia. In a single day of fighting, each side sustained some 12,000 casualties. Typically, the cautious McClellan failed to press his advantage and lost the opportunity to defeat Lee decisively.

Back on his home ground, Lee was again invincible. He defeated the blundering General Ambrose E. Burnside, McClellan's replacement, at Fredericksburg, Virginia, in December. In May 1863, Lee and Stonewall Jackson's forces repelled a Union army of more than double their numbers, led by Major General Joseph E. ("Fighting Joe") Hooker, Burnside's replacement, at Chancellorsville, Virginia. In the latter encounter, Jackson was killed accidentally by his own troops. Seeking to capitalize on the victory at Chancellorsville, Lee risked everything in a June invasion of the North, hoping to cut the east-west trunk railroads in Maryland and Pennsylvania, to imperil Washington, and to persuade the Union to make peace before the North's superiority in arms and materiel became irresistible. On July 1, 1863, Lee's 70,000 men and the 90,000 Union soldiers of George G. ("Old

Snapping Turtle") Meade, Hooker's replacement, assembled on opposing ridges outside the southern Pennsylvania town of Gettysburg. For three days during the greatest battle of the war, wave after wave of gray-clad Confederates swept against the entrenched Union position. On the hot, dry afternoon of July 3, Lee committed the costliest blunder of his career. In a last desperate charge against the center of the Union line, he sent General George Pickett with three divisions (15,000 troops) across the valley and up the Union-held Cemetery Ridge. The Confederates were cut down by withering Union fire. Casualties on both sides were staggering: the Confederates sustained more than 28,000 killed, wounded, or missing; the Union losses were slightly fewer. Repulsed at fearful cost, the South's last hope of victory gone, Lee had no recourse but retreat to Virginia.

While Lee's gamble was failing in the East, the Confederacy's military doom was being more plainly spelled out in the West. At long last Lincoln found a winning general, Ulysses S. Grant — an obscure, former junior officer in the Mexican war who had come out of retirement to join the Union cause. Using the Mississippi, Tennessee, and Cumberland rivers, which offered natural invasion routes for Union gunboats and armies, Grant drove steadily, from Cairo, Illinois, into the South. Forts Henry and Donelson, guarding the Tennessee and Cumberland rivers, fell to him in February 1862. Pressing southward on the Tennessee River, Grant inflicted a severe blow to the main Confederate army in the west during the bloody two-day battle at Shiloh (April 6–7). Both sides suffered severe losses; the outnumbered Confederates lost one-quarter of their forces, 11,000 troops compared to the 13,000 Union casualties. Also, Confederate General Albert Sidney Johnston, like many others in this era of primitive medical care, died of a minor wound. The southern troops retreated to Mississippi. Meanwhile, Union gunboats steamed up the Mississippi River from the Gulf of Mexico to take New Orleans, and others came down the Mississippi from the north to destroy a Confederate fleet at Memphis, Tennessee. The last stronghold on the river, Vicksburg, Mississippi, fell to Grant in July 1863, following a six-week siege, which exhausted Confederate forces and reduced the civilian population to eating rats and mules. With the surrender of General John C. Pemberton and 30,000 troops at Vicksburg, Grant had cut the Confederacy in two.

THE CONFEDERACY AT WAR

The burden of directing the Confederate war effort fell almost wholly on the shoulders of Jefferson Davis. Lacking able subordinates in his cabinet and in the Confederate Congress, Davis perhaps took on too much of the burden of detailed administration and sometimes made poor decisions concerning military strategy and commanding officers. But only an able and conscientious executive could have kept the Confederacy operating and its armies fighting, given the staggering difficulties that he faced.

At the beginning of the war, Davis had high hopes of aid from Europe. France's Napoleon III was openly sympathetic as were the ruling upper classes in Great Britain, and both of these countries went so far as to recognize the Confederacy's belligerent status. But Davis was counting on the economic power of the South's cotton to produce more substantial aid — full diplomatic recognition, financial assistance, and perhaps even military intervention. The South might have built up large credits for the purchase of supplies in Europe by shipping its cotton abroad. Instead, the Confederate authorities placed an embargo on cotton exports, expecting that this would force British cotton mills to close and thus bring pressure on the British government to intervene more openly on behalf of the Confederacy. Unfortunately for the Southerners, the British mills had a year's surplus of raw cotton on hand, some alternative sources of supply were available, and although some of the cotton mills eventually shut down, their unemployed workers remained sympathetic to the more democratic North and exerted their influence against any aid to the South.

The South's best chance to drive a wedge between Great Britain and the North came in November 1861 when a United States naval vessel stopped the British ship *Trent* on the high seas and took off the Confederate diplomats James M. Mason and John Slidell. But the United States promptly released Mason and Slidell, and Lincoln's skillful minister in London, Charles Francis Adams, was increasingly successful in preventing the British from aiding the Confederacy either directly or indirectly. And France refused to act without British support.

Meanwhile Lincoln had ordered the Union navy to blockade southern ports; by the time the Confederacy decided to ship cotton to Europe in exchange for supplies, this was no longer possible. Cut off from all outside goods (except a trickle brought in by swift blockade runners), the Confederacy was increasingly hard put to supply its armies with munitions or its people with the ordinary necessities of life.

As the struggle wore on and as the Confederacy's prospects expired under mounting Union industrial and military strength, the South's early optimism was replaced by growing discouragement, apathy, and disaffection. Secessionist sentiment was anything but universal in the Upper South and mountain regions. In the hill counties, the Confederate conscription law, which exempted overseers and owners of 20 or more slaves, was especially resented. Having no direct interest in slavery, some poor Southerners came to view the struggle as "a rich man's war and a poor man's fight." The disparity in materiel was also a factor. Union soldiers were adequately provisioned; sometimes encumbered federal soldiers jettisoned their unwanted articles. Often Confederate troops, on the other hand, lacked food and clothing and depended on captured Union supplies for arms. Draft evasion in the South increased following the Union victories of July 1863, and desertion became so widespread that by the end of 1863 one-third of the Confederate army was absent without leave — clearly, the morale of poorly paid Confederate soldiers was at low ebb. Desperate for manpower, the Confederacy in 1864 reached out to "the cradle and the grave," drafting men from 17 to 50 years of age; by war's end, it had resolved to draft slaves.

The South's enthusiasm for the war was probably less than wholehearted from the beginning. Its tradition of localism bred dissention. Fractious governors in some states and even Vice President Alexander Stephens resisted the inevitable centralizing policies necessary to the conduct of the war and defied the Richmond government. Raging inflation, transportation shortages, and a federal blockade brought extreme civilian privation and unrest; in 1863 bread riots broke out in several cities, including Richmond where President Davis helped restore order. The Confederacy's most serious problem, however, lay in the growing indifference of many wealthy and powerful Southerners. Never unreservedly committed to a separate southern nation, substantial portions of the planter class resented the "usurpations" of the Richmond government, particularly policies that hurt their financial interests. A growing disenchantment with the Confederate cause was thus a major factor in the South's military collapse.

LINCOLN AND THE WAR

Like Davis, Lincoln also faced troubles, for wartime dissent was not confined to the South. In the border states (slave states that remained in the Union), anti-Union sentiment was widespread, and in the non-slave North, support for the war was not universal. As civil strife dragged on unsuccessfully for the North, "Copperheads" — allegedly disloyal Democrats who were as dangerous as poisonous snakes — stepped up their demands for a negotiated settlement. Led by such spokesmen as Clement L. Vallandigham, former congressman from Ohio, and supported by Old Northwestern newspapers, these "Peace Democrats" found their greatest strength in Illinois, Indiana, and Ohio. Unlike the "War Democrats," who despite their differences with a Republican administration followed Stephen A. Douglas in supporting the war effort, the Peace Democrats opposed Lincoln's government at every turn. A diverse group, they included some southern sympathizers, but most were loyal Unionists who for varied reasons decried "King Abraham's" leadership and thought the war to be ill-advised, unnecessary, and even unconstitutional.

Much opposition centered on conscription, a novel wartime expedient that ran counter to the nation's tradition of voluntary military service. The draft law of 1863 exempted not only the unfit, but also those wealthy enough to hire a substitute or to pay $300. Since conscription fell disproportionately on the urban poor and immigrants, the law was widely resented. Riots occurred in a number of cities. The bloodiest riot took place in New York City, where for three days predominantly Irish working-class gangs vented their anger on blacks until federal troops arrived to end the looting and lynching. Not the least of Lincoln's problems was this unwillingness of whites to risk life and limb in what they viewed as a black cause.

Problems were also created by those strongly opposed to slavery. Lincoln was hounded by a group of "radical" Republicans who wanted to make the war an antislavery crusade and who advocated a punitive policy toward the South. Under the leadership of people like Senator Charles Sumner of Massachusetts and Representative Thaddeus Stevens of Pennsylvania, the Radicals gained great power in Congress. They set up a joint congressional Committee on the Conduct of the War, which constantly criticized and interfered with the president's conduct of military operations.

The split between radical Republicans and moderate or administration Republicans did not affect cooperation on common interests, and a series of major laws was passed by the wartime Congresses. The Morrill Tariff Act of 1861 marked a turn toward higher protective duties, and subsequent legislation of 1862 and 1864 pushed duties to unprecedented levels, inaugurating an era of extravagant protectionism that would last into the twentieth century. The long fight for free land culminated in the Homestead Act of 1862, granting 160 acres to any family that wished to settle on the public domain. The Morrill Land Grant Act of 1862 donated public lands to the states for support of agricultural and mechanical colleges. In the same year Congress finally authorized the long projected transcontinental railroad, granting 30 million acres and millions in federal bonds to the Union Pacific and Central Pacific railroad companies to build a line from Omaha to the Sacramento River. By an act of 1863, Congress established a national banking system, with member banks issuing a stable currency of uniform national bank notes on the basis of their holdings of federal bonds. In passing these important measures to serve the interests of northern farmers and business enterprise, the Congress was simply legislating the Republican platform since Southerners were no longer there to oppose it.

No measures aroused the controversy in the Republican party that the subject of slavery created. Anxious to mollify the loyal slave states of Delaware, Maryland, Kentucky, and Missouri, Lincoln stoutly resisted doing anything to suggest that abolition of slavery was a northern war aim. In the fall of 1861, he removed the Radicals' favorite general, John C. Frémont, from command in Missouri for declaring that the slaves of rebels were free. Meanwhile he sought unsuccessfully to interest Congress and the loyal slave states in a plan of gradual, compensated emancipation with the federal government footing the bill. His constitutional amendment would have granted states up to 37 years to abolish slavery.

The Radicals were determined to force the issue, and in 1862 pushed through Congress legislation abolishing slavery in the territories and in the District of Columbia. More important was the Second Confiscation Act of 1862, declaring forfeit the property of all persons supporting the rebellion and proclaiming escaped or captured slaves to be "forever free." By this time, Lincoln was becoming aware that an emancipation policy would be of value in helping to win the war, especially by gaining friends for the Union in Europe. Finally, on January 1, 1863, he issued his Emancipation Proclamation. This famous proclamation was not the universal measure it has often been said to be. It freed only those slaves living in rebel areas — those who were at the moment beyond the reach of Union law — and justified even this largely rhetorical gesture on the grounds of "military necessity." Only as the Union armies advanced did the freedom proclaimed by Lincoln's document become an actuality for the slaves. Not until 1865 did the Thirteenth Amendment, forbidding slavery throughout the country, become a part of the Constitution.

The Emancipation Proclamation did not allay the Radicals' suspicion of Lincoln, but they failed to block his renomination for president in 1864. In this wartime election, the Lincoln Republicans ran as the Union party, appealing to War Democrats by nominating for vice president Andrew Johnson, the Tennessee Senator who had remained loyal to the Union. The regular Democratic nomination went to General McClellan, many of whose supporters were calling for peace negotiations. The long string of Union defeats in the East has so strengthened antiwar sentiment that Lincoln might have been defeated but for some timely military successes in the West on the eve of the election.

Despite his political difficulties, the war so changed the structure of American government and society that Lincoln wielded presidential power that his predecessors could never have dreamed of. Commanding vast land and naval forces, initially without benefit of competent professional military leadership, he intruded more often into day-to-day military operations than he wanted. A civil libertarian, he nevertheless stretched executive authority in the name of national security by ordering the arrest of disloyal and disruptive citizens. Under his direction, the government tampered with private mail, closed several dissident newspapers, suspended in "extreme" cases the writ of habeas corpus (traditional safeguard against arbitrary arrest), and incarcerated without trial thousands of men for draft evasion or suspected disloyalty.

The government's role, moreover, was greatly expanded. To ensure efficient transportation and communication, the government subsidized a transcontinental railroad, built additional track, and assumed the direction of telegraph and rail lines. To finance a war that required daily expenditures of up to $2 million, Congress taxed and borrowed heavily; at war's end, the national debt was $2.6 billion. Congress created a Bureau of Internal Revenue and imposed the first income tax. It doubled the protective tariff, reformed the banking and monetary system, and fostered scientific agriculture. During the war the federal bureaucracy necessarily burgeoned, and afterward, federal expenditures never again fell to prewar levels.

TOWARD APPOMATTOX

The fall of Vicksburg to Grant and Lee's failure at Gettysburg, both in July 1863, doomed the Confederacy. And Lincoln had finally found a successful general. Before leaving the West, Grant consolidated Union control of Tennessee with a victory at Chattanooga. In the spring of 1864, Grant was made general-in-chief of all the Union armies. Now his grand strategy was a two-pronged final offensive against the South, with General William T. Sherman leading one great Union army south from Chattanooga into Georgia and with Grant himself leading another army from Washington toward Richmond.

The twin offensives were launched simultaneously in May 1864. The two Union armies of around 100,000 each pressed back Confederate armies of around 60,000. In the West, Sherman steadily pushed the Confederates south and by September won the important rail center of Atlanta. He made an audacious decision to abandon his line of supply and wage a war of destruction between Atlanta and the sea. Devastating the countryside as he went, he was in Savannah by December, and the Confederacy was further segmented. Turning north, Sherman reached Columbia, South Carolina, in February 1865 and by March was in east-central North Carolina.

By demoralizing the Confederate areas south of Virginia, Sherman greatly facilitated Grant's advance on Richmond. In the Spotsylvania Wilderness and at Spotsylvania Courthouse in May 1864, Lee inflicted heavy casualties on the invading Union troops as he had so often done in the past. But this Union general did not withdraw to lick his wounds as had all his predecessors. By flanking movements, he kept pressing south toward Richmond. At Cold Harbor, Lee again inflicted frightful losses on the Union army, but still Grant pushed inexorably south, passing just east of Richmond and crossing the James River. Lee managed to shield Richmond as Grant moved around it to the south and southwest toward Petersburg. By June, the two armies were entrenched facing each other in a long line bending from Richmond southward around the southern side of Petersburg.

Grant would not let go, and as the siege went on through the summer and fall and winter, his superiority in numbers began to tell. Remorselessly he kept extending his line to the west, and Lee's line became steadily thinner and more vulnerable. By April, Lee could extend his line no more and had to pull out of his entrenchments, abandoning Richmond and Petersburg. But by this time Grant had cut off all the roads leading south over which Lee might effect a junction with the only remaining Confederate army of any strength. On April 9, 1865, at Appomattox Courthouse, Lee bowed to the inevitable and surrendered. One month later the fleeing Jefferson Davis was captured in disguise in Georgia and imprisoned at Fortress Monroe. The Confederacy was dead — and so were some 260,000 Confederate and 360,000 Union soldiers. In blood, if not in dollars, it was the costliest war in American history.

LINCOLN AND THE SOUTH

The treatment of the vanquished South was a point of contention between Lincoln and the Radicals. Lincoln wished to bring the rebellious states back into full membership in the Union as rapidly and painlessly as possible. By the time Union forces occupied Arkansas in December 1863, the president was ready with his "10 percent plan" of reconstruction. Under this plan he proposed to extend amnesty and restore confiscated property to all Confederates who would take a simple loyalty oath, excluding only high civil and military officers of the Confederacy or its states. As soon as 10 percent of a state's 1860 electorate had taken the oath, the state could write a new constitution and rejoin the Union.

The Radicals, however, feared with considerable reason that if the southern states were reconstructed on this basis, the old ruling class would return

MAP 5: THE CIVIL WAR

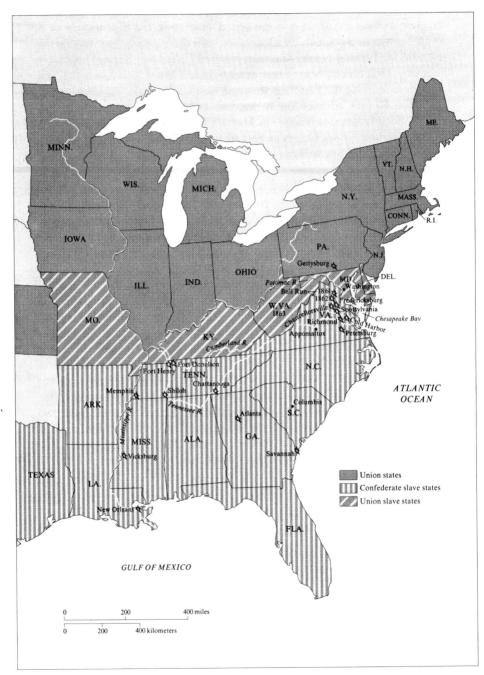

MINN.

ME.

WIS.

MICH.

VT.

N.H.

N.Y.

MASS.

IOWA

CONN.

R.I.

PA.

Gettysburg

N.J.

ILL.

IND.

OHIO

DEL.

Potomac R.

MD.

Washington

Bull Run

1861

1862

Fredericksburg

W. VA.

1863

Chancellorsville

Spotsylvania

MO.

VA.

Richmond

Old Harbor

Chesapeake Bay

Appomattox

Petersburg

K.Y.

Cumberland R.

Fort Donelson

Fort Henry

TENN.

N.C.

Chattanooga

ATLANTIC

Memphis

Shiloh

OCEAN

ARK.

Tennessee R.

Columbia

Mississippi R.

Atlanta

S.C.

MISS.

ALA.

GA.

TEXAS

Vicksburg

Savannah

LA.

New Orleans

	Union states
	Confederate slave states
	Union slave states

FLA.

GULF OF MEXICO

0   200   400 miles

0   200   400 kilometers

to power and the freed blacks would be little better off than they had been under slavery. Anxious for a thorough reconstruction of southern society, they insisted that black men be given the ballot and that the old rebel leadership be effectively excluded from political life. As a counter to Lincoln's plan they secured the passage in 1864 of the Wade-Davis bill. This measure required a majority, rather than 10 percent, of the 1860 voters to take a loyalty oath before reconstruction could begin and further insisted on disfranchisement of ex-Confederate leaders.

Lincoln allowed the Wade-Davis bill to die by pocket veto, but the Radicals had one tactical advantage. A state would not be fully restored to the Union until its representatives were seated in Congress, and the Radical-controlled Congress had full power over the admission of members. The Radicals used this power to deny admission to the first southern representatives who appeared under Lincoln's 10 percent plan. In March 1865, as the war drew to a close, the Radicals gave a further indication of their objectives by creating the Freedmen's Bureau to assist the ex-slaves in adjusting to freedom and to protect their rights.

The sharpening struggle between Lincoln and the Radicals was suddenly cut short on Good Friday, April 14, 1865, five days after Lee's surrender at Appomattox. As Lincoln sat in a box at Ford's Theater in Washington, John Wilkes Booth, an actor and Confederate sympathizer, fired a fatal bullet into the president's head, crying "*Sic semper tyrannis!* The South is avenged!"

A grieving nation suddenly discovered a tragic hero. To Lincoln's strength, humility, eloquence, and magnanimity was added the quality of martyrdom. He had presided over the bloodiest war in the American experience, preserving the Union as the land of liberty and last best hope of humanity. Hesitantly and grudgingly, but in the end unmistakably, he had also made the war a struggle to enlarge the sphere of American liberty. Yet the Emancipation Proclamation and the Thirteenth Amendment were only a beginning. It was Lincoln's Radical critics who saw most clearly that the task of completing emancipation still lay ahead, and even his great talents could hardly have been equal to this Herculean task. Perhaps it was a timely martyrdom that translated Abraham Lincoln — a man groping toward an ideal only dimly perceptible in his society and age — into the Great Emancipator. For a century and more to come, Lincoln, the symbol, would remind his fellow Americans that the egalitarian dream was still unfulfilled.

FOR FURTHER READING

The best one-volume history of the Civil War is James M. McPherson's *Battle Cry of Freedom* (1988), but Allan Nevins's classic *Ordeal of the Union* (4 vols., 1947–1971) is still important. Divergent interpretations of the North's reaction to secession are presented by David M. Potter in *Lincoln and His Party in the Secession Crisis* (1942) and by Kenneth M. Stampp in *And the War Came* (1950). The northern conduct of the war can be followed through the biographies of Lincoln. One-volume studies include *With*

Malice Toward None (1977) by Stephen B. Oates, *The Presidency of Abraham Lincoln* (1994) by Philip S. Paludan, and *Lincoln* (1995) by David Herbert Donald. For greater detail, see the chronologically successive volumes by James G. Randall (completed by Richard N. Current) on *Lincoln the President* (4 vols., 1945–1955). LaWanda Cox analyzes *Lincoln and Black Freedom* (1981). Special aspects of the North during the war are treated in George Fredrickson's *The Inner Civil War* (1965), Phillip S. Paludan's *A People's Contest* (1988), and Iver Bernstein's *The New York City Draft Riots* (1990). The blacks' role in the struggle is analyzed in Joseph T. Glatthaar's *Forged in Battle* (1990), Dudley Cornish's *The Sable Arm* (1956), and Benjamin Quarles's *The Negro in the Civil War* (1953). Emancipation and its legacy are explored in Eric Foner's *Nothing But Freedom* (1983) and Clarence L. Mohr's *On the Threshold of Freedom* (1986). Emory Thomas surveys *The Confederate Nation* (1979), while both Richard E. Beringer, et al., in *Why the South Lost the Civil War* (1986), and Paul D. Escott, in *After Secession* (1978), explore the weaknesses of Confederate nationalism. The Confederacy's *King Cotton Diplomacy* (1966) is the subject of Frank L. Owsley, while D. P. Crook's *The North, the South, and the Powers* (1974) examines the maneuverings of both sides. The military history of the war from the viewpoint of the northern armies may be followed in the vivid volumes by Bruce Catton: *Mr. Lincoln's Army* (1951), *Glory Road* (1952), and *A Stillness at Appomattox* (1954). A more detailed and professional evaluation of the northern military effort through 1863, with greater attention to the western campaigns, is Kenneth P. Williams's *Lincoln Finds a General: A Military Study of the Civil War* (5 vols., 1949–1959). Herman Hattaway and Archer Jones offer a general military survey in *How the North Won* (1983). The fighting as viewed from the southern side is best followed in the distinguished study by Douglas Southall Freeman, *R. E. Lee: A Biography* (4 vols., 1934–1935). Thomas L. Connelly, in *The Marble Man* (1977), critically examines the life and legend of Robert E. Lee. Alfred M. Josephy, Jr., reports on *The Civil War in the American West* (1991). John F. Marszalek details the life of *Sherman* (1993), and Charles Royster looks at the Civil War careers of both Sherman and Stonewall Jackson in *The Destructive War* (1991). Bell Wiley has described *The Plain People of the Confederacy* (1943) and the common soldiers of the South in *The Life of Johnny Reb* (1943); Reid Mitchell explores the everyday lives of northern soldiers in *The Vacant Chair* (1993); Catherine Clinton and Nina Silber have collected essays on women and the war in *Divided Houses* (1992); and George C. Rable's *Civil Wars* (1989) looks at white women in the South during the war. Of the multitude of personal accounts of contemporaries, three very different ones may be singled out as having special interest: the *Personal Memoirs* (2 vols., 1885–1886) of General Grant; *A Diary from Dixie* (1905) by Mary Boykin Chestnut; and *The Diary of Edmund Ruffin* (3 vols., 1972–1989), edited by William K. Scarborough.

The Civil War and Reconstruction

President Lincoln issued the Proclamation of Emancipation in 1863 before the end of hostilities. This lithograph of the proclamation made in 1865 by J. Mayer & Co. shows "before and after" scenes of a slavery sale and free blacks. (*Library of Congress*)

Lincoln, as Commander-in-Chief, is shown with General George B. McClellan and a group of officers at the headquarters of the Army of the Potomac. Photograph by Matthew Brady. (*Library of Congress*)

Union troops — the
96th Pennsylvania
Infantry — at Camp
Northumberland
near Washington.
Photograph by
Matthew Brady.
(*Library of
Congress*)

With the aggressive leadership of Generals Grant and Sherman, Union victories wrought destruction on southern cities and countryside. The ruins of Richmond, Virginia, on the James River, were photographed by Matthew Brady. (*Library of Congress*)

Confederate troops often lacked uniforms and other supplies, as this photograph of an army camp reveals. The Union army was generally better equipped. *(Library of Congress)*

Often unsuccessful in its early encounters with Confederate forces, the Union Army sustained many deaths and casualties. In June 1862, Matthew Brady photographed the wounded at a Union field hospital at Savage Station, Virginia. *(Library of Congress)*

Blacks fought on both sides of the conflict. This black gun crew participated in the battle of Nashville. (*Chicago Historical Society*)

FROM THE PLANTATION TO THE SENATE.

During Reconstruction, blacks were elected to the U.S. Congress. This poster shows, from left to right: Senator Hiram R. Revels, Representative Benjamin S. Turner, the Reverend Richard Allen, Frederick Douglass, Representatives Josiah T. Walls and Joseph H. Rainy, and the writer William Wells Brown. (*Library of Congress*)

Black sharecroppers
in the South often
found conditions
after Reconstruction
little better than
slavery. Victims of
white discrimination
and the crop lien
system, they lived in
poverty and too often
in virtual peonage.
(*Brown Brothers*)

16

★ ★ ★ ★ ★ ★

Reconstructing the Union, 1865–1890

IN THE GENERATION after the Civil War, economic expansion absorbed most of the nation's energies. The people's attention, however, centered at first on the Reconstruction of the Union and the new order in the defeated South. They faced difficult questions involving the rights of the freed slaves.

THE PROBLEM

The problems of Reconstruction were numerous. The most obvious and easiest problem was the physical rebuilding of shelled cities and ruined railroads. Harder to reconstruct was the defeated section's economic life. The South's industry was at a standstill; much of its farming land was lying idle. Its labor system was destroyed, investment capital was lacking, the savings of many people were wiped out by the collapse of Confederate currency and bonds. Beneath every other problem lay that of a new relationship between the South's two races. All that was clear about the country's 4,500,000 blacks was that none of them remained a slave. Some 286,000 were Union soldiers; a few were settled on confiscated plantations in the sea islands off the Carolinas; and many were simply wandering, drifting from Union army camps to southern cities with great hopes and no means of support. Nearly everybody assumed that they were to continue to work on the land. A few radicals had suggested that they would become landowners, and the sea islands experiment raised some hopes. White Southerners assumed that blacks would work as laborers for white landowners.

By 1865 three southern states were already reconstructed under the easy terms offered by President Lincoln, which demanded only that 10 percent of the citizens take an oath of future loyalty and recognize that slavery was ended. Once this was done, elections were held for both state governments and federal Congress. But Congress refused to admit these delegates.

To settle this difficulty, Americans turned to the Constitution. What was the status of a sovereign state that had seceded and been forced to return to the Union? Was it still a state or was it, as Thaddeus Stevens insisted, merely a conquered province? Who would decide: Congress or the president? The president was commander-in-chief of the armed forces and had the power to pardon. But Congress had the right to admit new states, to make rules for territories, and to judge the qualifications of its own members. Long before Lincoln's death, the executive and congressional branches of government had been at loggerheads over these issues. In this unprecedented situation, the Constitution offered few unambiguous answers to these questions.

More important in the long run than the constitutional question was the state of mind of three main groups: the ex-slaves, the defeated white Southerners, and the victorious Northerners. Though able black leaders soon appeared, most of the ex-slaves were not only illiterate but inexperienced, both in participating in politics and in dealing with such economic institutions as wages and rent. Many pathetic stories are told about the strange hopes and fears of these displaced people. Yet the basic desires of the freed blacks were clear. What they wanted was real freedom, and the signs of that freedom were the right to move around the country, access to education, and ownership of land.

Right after the war, according to northern travelers in the South, shock rather than bitterness was the most common state of mind among southern whites. With their institutions destroyed, what was to become of them? Most pressing of all, without slavery, how was the cotton going to be picked and planted? At first, many looked northward for their answers.

Northern whites comprised the third and largest group, which was by no means a united body. Nearly half were Democrats. Only a few Democrats had been willing to accept the breakup of the Union, but many had sharply criticized the conduct of the war and had opposed emancipation. The sole purpose of the fighting, the party's leaders had insisted, should have been the restoration of "the Union as it was." In the 1864 elections, the Democrats had lost some ground, yet they still mustered a formidable 45 percent of the votes. Not even the Republicans were sure of what they wanted. The group called "Radicals" agreed that Lincoln had been too weak, too lenient on the South, but they agreed on little else. Republicans were also divided on such matters as the tariff and finance, and few had thought through the future status of the blacks.

Two paradoxes made constructive action inordinately difficult. First, slavery had been abolished and the ex-slaves armed by a nation that believed overwhelmingly in the inherent inferiority of the black race. Even among the abolitionists, only a few had accepted blacks as intellectual and political equals.

Second, during Reconstruction the government had to undertake a program of drastic, even revolutionary measures. Yet nearly all nineteenth-century Americans had been taught that government action should be sharply limited. This had been said by Jefferson, Jackson, and Lincoln. Schools and colleges taught as gospel truth the maxims of *laissez-faire* political economy, that is, minimum governmental interference in the economy.

The choice faced by the North, in its simplest terms, was the choice offered to every victor: occupation or conciliation. Most Northerners preferred the latter, but they wanted conciliation on northern terms: the South must recognize its errors and govern itself — according to northern ideas.

Yet to whom in the South could government be confided? To the ex-rebels who were, many Northerners believed, still rebels at heart? To the ex-slaves whom most Northerners regarded as members of an inferior race? Even if they were given the vote, the freedmen, inexperienced in politics and a minority in all but two states, could hardly govern alone. They would have to have the support either of a substantial number of southern whites or of sufficient occupying forces. With or without black suffrage, the same choice existed: conciliation or occupation.

PRESIDENTIAL RECONSTRUCTION

The first alternative, conciliation, was attempted under the authority of Presidents Lincoln and Johnson and is often referred to as Presidential Reconstruction. It is hard to tell how Lincoln's "10 percent plan" might have worked if it had been continued. This plan had already been sharply challenged by Congress, and Lincoln himself had said that it was only one of many possible approaches. The Wade-Davis bill, the most extreme congressional substitute, had been left unsigned by Lincoln.

Like Lincoln, President Andrew Johnson embodied the log-cabin tradition of humble origins. He was a tailor by trade and learned to read only as an adult. A resident of eastern Tennessee where slaves were few, and a former Jacksonian Democrat, he had been an outspoken opponent of secession and a lifelong enemy of the southern planter class. Yet he was not committed to either rights of blacks or the Republican party. Though honest and able, Johnson lacked Lincoln's gifts of patience and political realism. Soon the very Republicans who had hailed his remarks about the infamy of treason and the punishment of traitors found him to be too soft on the former Confederates and too eager to forget and forgive.

Like his predecessor, Johnson offered amnesty to those who would sign an oath of allegiance. Exceptions included important Confederate officials and Confederates who owned more than $20,000 worth of property, seemingly the leaders of the Old South. Those who took the oath were to vote for constitutional conventions for each state, which were, in turn, to repeal the ordinances of secession, to abolish slavery, and to repudiate Confederate war debts. The state thus reconstructed could then elect a new government and send representatives to Washington. By the end of 1865, all the states had actually passed through either the Lincoln or the Johnson version of this process, and in conservative and southern eyes, Reconstruction was over. Southern government was functioning, and the people, black and white, were returning to work.

Much in the new order was deeply disturbing to northern opinion. Some reconstituted states elected prominent Confederates to state and federal office. Most enacted special "Black Codes" to regulate the conduct of freed blacks. To former slaveholders, such rules seemed natural and necessary; to freed blacks and many Northerners, the rules looked much like the slave codes of the antebellum period. In some states, blacks were not allowed to assemble, to intermarry with whites, to possess alcohol or firearms, or to pursue a skilled trade. In others, the labor of petty offenders could be sold at auction; in some, black children could be apprenticed to white men without the consent of indigent parents. Most codes provided for strictly enforced compulsory labor contracts, and for the binding out (forced apprenticing) of unemployed blacks declared vagrant. In South Carolina, the code spelled out the intent of such contracts: blacks were to engage only in agricultural labor or in domestic service. In Mississippi, blacks could work, but not own, agricultural land. Even some white Southerners found these measures to be unduly provocative of Yankee sensibilities.

In 1865–1866, northern opinion was further affronted by outbreaks of racial violence in the South. Responsibility for race riots was of course disputed, but the victims nearly always turned out to be blacks or pro-black whites. To Radical Republicans, it seemed that life was not safe in the South for those who supported a change in southern society, and this change the Radicals were determined to bring about. To some this was a moral duty; to others, a political necessity.

In the spring of 1866, Congress extended the life of the Freedmen's Bureau, a wartime organization designed to supervise and aid the ex-slaves, and passed a Civil Rights Act prohibiting many kinds of discriminatory legislation. Congress also refused to admit the representatives of the new southern state governments, among them former Confederate officials: the vice president, six cabinet officers, four generals, and numerous other high-ranking civilian and military leaders of the secessionist government.

Johnson could not expect to carry forward his policy without regard for such formidable congressional opposition. Yet the imprudent Johnson, like other presidents in other battles with Congress, seemed to grow steadily less flexible and more defiant. He blamed southern race riots on the Radicals, minimized southern denial of black rights, and pardoned thousands of southern leaders. In the spring of 1866, he vetoed both the Freedmen's Bureau bill and the Civil Rights Act, arguing that such measures were unconstitutional and that blacks were not ready for full citizenship. When the Fourteenth Amendment was proposed to guarantee blacks equality before the law, he condemned it on similar grounds.

By this time, Johnson had gained the support of Democrats and solidified the Republican party against him. In the fall, he toured the country and violently denounced his opponents as traitors, particularly Thaddeus Stevens and Charles Sumner. In the November congressional election, Johnson was repudiated at the polls. The Republicans won two-thirds of both Houses, and the Radical leadership moved into key positions of power. The pendulum of power had swung to the congressional side; a new phase of Reconstruction was at hand.

CONGRESSIONAL RECONSTRUCTION

During congressional, or Radical Reconstruction, the alternative to conciliation, military occupation, was finally given a trial. The purpose behind this move was still reform; the South was to be occupied only until her society could be altered and a new electorate formed. This meant attempting something like social revolution, and it was clear that in this revolution blacks must play a major part.

The Freedmen's Bureau and Civil Rights bills, both repassed over the president's veto, established that the former slaves were to be protected by the federal government during a transitional stage. They were not, however, to be given land; in this property-loving age only a few suggested such an extreme measure, and local experiments in this direction (including one in Mississippi on land owned by Jefferson Davis) were abandoned. Ultimately, the failure to attempt some form of land redistribution and provide some measure of economic security for former slaves assured their continued dependence on their former masters.

Federal protection for blacks already implied a change in the relationship between the federal government and the states, and this change was spelled out in the Fourteenth Amendment submitted to Congress in June 1866. The first section of this amendment provided that no state should infringe any citizen's "privileges or immunities," nor "deprive any person of life, liberty or property, without due process of law," nor deny to any person "the equal protection of the laws." Thus individuals were guaranteed by the *Union* against oppression by the *states*. (The Bill of Rights already protected individual liberties from the federal government.)

The second section of the amendment edged toward black suffrage. It provided that if a state denied the vote of any of its male citizens, its representation should be reduced accordingly. The third and fourth sections barred leading Confederates from Congress or federal office and forbade states to repudiate the federal or recognize the rebel debt. Obviously this all-important amendment could not be ratified by three-fourths of the states without some southern support. As President Johnson urged southern states not to ratify, Congress moved on to still more drastic reconstruction action.

The First Reconstruction Act, passed in March 1867, divided the South into five military districts, wiping out the existing state governments. Under military supervision, each state was to elect a constitutional convention. Delegates to these conventions would be chosen by vote of the whole male population, including the freed blacks and excluding leading Confederates.

Each constitution was to be ratified by a majority of the state's new electorate and approved by Congress. When the new state had ratified the Fourteenth Amendment, its representatives might be admitted to Congress. This act was clarified and tightened by further legislation, and in 1870 Radical Reconstruction was completed by the ratification of the Fifteenth Amendment, once and for all forbidding suffrage discrimination on the basis of "race, color, or previous condition of servitude."

All these actions were taken against the firm opposition of the president and in the face of the nearly certain disapproval of the Supreme Court. To safeguard Radical Reconstruction, Congress made the most drastic attempt in American history to establish the dominance of a single branch of government. To disarm the court, Congress simply withdrew certain kinds of cases from Supreme Court jurisdiction, and the court prudently refrained from challenging this action. Johnson, however, could be rendered powerless only by impeachment and conviction for "treason, bribery, or other high crimes or misdemeanors." Failing after much effort to find serious evidence of "crimes," Congress saw its best chance for impeachment in the Tenure of Office Act passed in 1867. This act, of dubious constitutionality, forbade the removal of cabinet officers without congressional sanction. Johnson challenged it by trying to remove Secretary of War Edwin Stanton, an appointee of Lincoln. In the spring of 1868, the House of Representatives impeached the president in a long, confused, and shaky set of charges. Anger ran so high that his accusers failed by only one vote to secure the two-thirds of the Senate votes necessary for conviction.

RADICAL RECONSTRUCTION IN ACTION

How did the Radical program actually work in the South? To this crucial question, historians have developed two opposite answers. A generation ago, most accounts said that Radical Reconstruction had been a dreadful mistake. According to this traditional view, southern state governments, dominated by ignorant blacks, self-seeking carpetbaggers, and despicable southern "scalawags" (that is, collaborationists) had imposed a reign of terror, extravagance, and corruption. Finally the South, supported by a revival of moderate opinion in the North, had risen in revolt and thrown off the yoke. The very name given to those who overthrew Reconstruction, *redeemers*, speaks to the conclusions of this perspective.

More recently this version has been challenged by an opposite one. According to this second, neo-Radical view, Radical Reconstruction was a long overdue attempt to bring justice and progress to the South. It was sustained in the South not only by federal forces but by determined black support. Its defeat was brought about by brutal terrorism and northern betrayal.

The truth about this abortive social revolution is various and complex. It is clear that some Radical governments were indeed both extravagant and blatantly corrupt. Yet the redeemer governments that followed were not notable for political or fiscal probity, and both extravagance and corruption were common in both the North and South. Moreover, the Radical governments scored some accomplishments, bringing to the South broader suffrage for whites as well as blacks, relief for the poor, and the beginnings of free, popular education. Taxes did go up (though not to northern levels), but tax monies were put to valid social uses.

Could Radical Reconstruction have effected a permanent change in southern institutions and customs? Successful Reconstruction would have demanded either prolonged northern occupation, repeated federal intervention, or some degree of cooperation between southern whites and blacks. For the first two alternatives, Northerners proved to have no enduring appetite. The third — white-black cooperation — seemed initially more promising. Many southern whites did make an effort to accept the new situation, though many did not. Contrary to legend, some scalawags were well intentioned, just as many carpetbaggers were honest and many black leaders were well informed and moderate. But any permanent alliance among these elements faced great difficulties. The cooperating southern whites were willing to accept black voting only under white leadership; the blacks demanded political equality. Predictably, the necessary coalition failed.

Conservative whites quickly regained power. With this shift in power, violence against blacks and their political allies continued to escalate; at first determined to suppress the Ku Klux Klan and other secret terrorist organizations, Congress grew weary of the attempt. In one state after another, with differing degrees of fraudulent and forcible action, conservative southern whites achieved victory at the polls. In 1877 when President Hayes withdrew the last federal troops, the cycle was complete: the South was "redeemed" and restored to native white rule. At first, the new "lily-white" governments, mostly led by the prewar planter class, allowed blacks some token participation in politics. Then in the 1890s, governments claiming to represent poor whites came to power. Denouncing the alleged political "fusion" of aristocrats and blacks, these governments effectively nullifed the Fifteenth Amendment (universal manhood suffrage) and drove southern blacks out of politics. These acts were accomplished partly by violence and intimidation and partly by the discriminatory application of such legal sophistries as the grandfather clause, the literacy test, and the poll tax. Faced with the most flagrant violations of federal law, the federal government and northern public opinion looked the other way. White Northerners, including some former abolitionists, came to value national harmony more than equal rights.

SOCIAL RECONSTRUCTION

Since blacks never received the "40 acres and a mule" for which they had longed in 1865, they had to work for white landowners. As money to pay them was lacking, the only possible solution was some form of tenantry. The result was the sharecrop and the crop-lien systems. Throughout the South, sharecroppers, both white and black, received their seed, tools, and staple necessities from landlords to whom they turned over a third or a half of their produce. Most, and often all, of the remaining produce went to pay long-standing debts accumulated by the tenants at country stores or plantation commissaries with high monopoly prices and exorbitant rates of interest. The system was not slavery, and it got the crops planted and harvested. Yet the black farmer — forever in debt and unable to move, without education or political privileges, subject to white courts and terrorism — could hardly be called free. Indeed, recent research suggests that the shadow of slavery still darkened southern race relations as *peonage* (the use of laborers bound in servitude because of debt) was fairly widespread. To make matters worse, planter-class paternalism was supplanted by an increasingly virulent race hatred among whites who feared their inability to control their former slaves.

In the 1880s, the white-ruled South put on a spectacular drive for industry. Heavy inducements were offered to attract capital, and much was accomplished in developing steel, lumbering, tobacco, and, especially, textile industries. However, by the turn of the century, the region had barely held its own; the South's percentage of the nation's industry was about that of 1860. Even this, in a rapidly expanding economy, was a considerable achievement. But the price was heavy. In southern mill towns, disease and child labor were endemic. Most industry profits were flowing out of the section. Until World War II, the South remained both poor and overwhelmingly agrarian.

Perhaps the saddest chapter in all American history is the general acceptance in the North of the failure of so much effort. Thirty years after the war, most people took for granted a southern system that included not only disfranchisement, economic dependence, and rigid social segregation of blacks, but also recurrent violence. In 1892 and 1893, for example, more than 150 blacks were lynched each year; they were often sadistically tortured, and virtually always the crimes went unpunished. If Reconstruction was a tragedy, it was because it heightened interregional tensions without either lessening racial hatred or securing a place in the national mainstream for the former slaves.

How could the people who had defied the Fugitive Slave Act, fought the war, and voted for Radical Reconstruction accept this situation? First, it was easy to emphasize the seamy side of Radical Reconstruction, the greed and corruption with which the process was sometimes executed. Next, most white Northerners shared the white southern assessment of black worth. White supremacist assumptions were reinforced by turn-of-the-century American imperialism. If the "little brown" Filipino was a lesser breed of man in need of the firm, guiding hand of a superior white American nation, should not the Afro-American be left to the direction of his southern white betters? Moreover, the conventional wisdom of the age argued that stateways could not change folkways, that government was powerless to change customs or alter social mores. Thus a failure of northern resolve partly explains the failure of Reconstruction. The courts, Congress, the White House, and a popular majority all came, in time, to accept the view that white Southerners knew best how to handle the race problem. It also seems likely that failure was built into the system itself. Federalism, whatever its

TABLE 9. EVENTS OF RECONSTRUCTION, 1863–1877

Date	General tendency	National events	State events
1863	**Presidential Reconstruction**	Lincoln Plan announced.	Governments set up in Louisiana, Arkansas.
1864		Wade-Davis Plan pocket-vetoed by Lincoln.	
1865		Lee surrenders. Lincoln shot. Johnson Plan announced.	Governments partly functioning in Virginia, Tennessee.
1866		Freedman's Bureau bill and Civil Rights bill vetoed. Fourteenth Amendment submitted to states. Congressional elections: Radical gains.	All remaining states reorganized under Johnson Plan. Tennessee readmitted.
1867	**Height of Radical Reconstruction**	Reconstruction Acts. Tenure of Office Act.	Military Rule in effect.
1868		Impeachment of Johnson. Fourteenth Amendment in effect. Grant elected.	North Carolina, South Carolina, Florida, Alabama, Louisiana, Arkansas readmitted under Radical governments.
1869	**Conflict**	Fifteenth Amendment in effect. First Enforcement Act.	Conservative government restored in Tennessee. Virginia readmitted under moderate government.
1870		Congressional elections: Republican majorities reduced.	Moderate government restored in North Carolina. Mississippi, Texas, Georgia readmitted under radical government.
1871		Second and third Enforcement Acts.	Conservative government restored in Georgia.
1872		Grant re-elected.	
1873			
1874	**Restoration of White Rule**	Congressional elections: Democrats gain control of House.	Conservative government restored in Arkansas, Alabama, Texas.
1875		Civil Rights Act (declared invalid 1883).	Conservative government restored in Mississippi.
1876		Hayes-Tilden disputed election.	Federal troops removed from Louisiana, South Carolina.
1877			Conservative government restored in Florida, South Carolina, Louisiana.

other advantages, proved to be an imperfect instrument for the protection of black rights. As the experience of the post–World War II civil rights struggles suggests, the Fourteenth and Fifteenth Amendments were often unenforceable in the face of adamant white opposition. The traditions of federalism, which required wide-ranging deference to local, state, and regional customs, seemed to deny effective enforcement of a colorblind Constitution. In the last analysis, the left wing of the Republican party, for all its apparent radicalism, accepted prevailing constitutional conservatism. The Radicals created a formal structure of racial equality — and in the process no doubt promised much more than most northern whites would willingly see the nation deliver — but they did not challenge a federal system that permitted intransigent southern whites to sabotage congressional intent. Still "old republican" in their fear of the centralized national power necessary to reconstruct the South, the Radicals returned to the old federal balance of national and state power, a position sustained by the Supreme Court in a series of cases beginning in the 1870s.

In the Slaughterhouse Cases (1873) the court found that the Fourteenth Amendment conferred no new privileges or immunities that would protect blacks from state power. In the Civil Rights Cases (1883), it decided that the Fourteenth Amendment did not prevent *individuals*, as opposed to states, from practicing discrimination. In *Plessy* vs. *Ferguson* (1896), the court held that "separate but equal" accommodations for blacks in trains (and by implication in restaurants, schools, hotels, and the like) did not violate their rights. Few inquired very carefully into whether accommodations were indeed equal.

If blacks found the promises of Reconstruction largely empty, the period had a brighter side for whites. A great Civil War had been settled on remarkably magnanimous terms, without the postwar blood-letting, executions, confiscations, and mass incarcerations that have characterized internecine struggles in other times and places. As the two sides inched toward reconciliation, it was all too easy to forget that Afro-America was paying most of the bill for the intersectional accord.

The upshot, then, of the greatest struggle in American history seemed to be a tragic failure. Yet the story had not ended. Blacks had gained a few rights and a great many hopes. And in neither the North nor the South was the national conscience really at ease.

CONFLICTING HISTORICAL VIEWPOINTS: NO. 7

Was Reconstruction a Tragic Era?

Until the 1930s, historians generally agreed that Reconstruction was a period characterized by sordid motives and human depravity. It was the "Age of Hate," "The Blackout of Honest Government," "The Dreadful Decade," and "The Tragic Era." In 1939, however, Francis Butler Simkins, a distinguished southern scholar, urged his fellow historians to adopt "a more critical, creative, and tolerant attitude" toward the period. In a notable essay

(Journal of Southern History, *1939*), *Simkins suggested that the traditional interpretation of Reconstruction was rooted in "the conviction that the Negro belongs to an innately inferior race."*

Until Simkins's time, most white students of Reconstruction did in fact approach their work with decidedly racist views. In the first serious history of the era, James Ford Rhodes's enormously influential History of the United States from the Compromise of 1850 *(7 vols., 1839–1906), blacks were described as "the most inferior race." Similarly, in John W. Burgess's* Reconstruction and the Constitution *(1902), blacks were characterized as inherently inferior beings incapable of "subjecting passion to reason." Although Rhodes and Burgess were sharply critical of the motives and actions of congressional radicals, the traditional interpretation of Reconstruction is best identified with the work of William A. Dunning. A Columbia University scholar and the author of* Reconstruction, Political and Economic *(1907), Dunning and his many students uncovered a wealth of factual information about the period. But their work was seriously marred by their pro-southern and anti-black biases. They portrayed the postbellum scene in darkly tragic hues of unrelieved brutality, scandal, corruption, and licentiousness. According to the Dunningites, Reconstruction was not only unnecessary but harshly cruel to the prostrate South and ruthlessly exploitive of the ignorant ex-slaves.*

Black scholars — most notably W. E. B. Du Bois, author of Black Reconstruction *(1935) — vigorously disputed Dunning School conclusions. But in an age of virtually unchallenged white supremacy, few Caucasians thought to question simplistic characterizations of vindictive radicals, venal carpetbaggers, reprobate scalawags, and barbarous blacks. A shift in the climate of racial opinion, however, ushered in a new era of Reconstruction historiography. Reflecting a growing national sensitivity to civil rights, historians since the 1930s have turned Dunning's conclusions inside out. First in a series of monographs and biographies, then later in such sweeping syntheses as John Hope Franklin's* Reconstruction After the Civil War *(1961), Kenneth Stampp's* The Era of Reconstruction *(1965), and Eric Foner's* Reconstruction *(1988), revisionists discarded racial stereotypes and viewed the postbellum period in a generally favorable light. According to Franklin and Stampp, traditional studies grossly exaggerated not only the extent of corruption, fraud, and black rule, but even the length of radical control. Both Franklin and Stampp emphasized that Reconstruction was a tragic era only in that it failed to ensure blacks economic, political, and social equality. Foner's recent survey pays particular attention to the role played by blacks in shaping Reconstruction; he also stresses that although many issues raised during the era were not resolved for decades or remain unresolved today, the bold experiments launched during Reconstruction ultimately represented a revolutionary beginning to America's unfinished effort to integrate the former slaves fully into American life.*

FOR FURTHER READING

Leon Litwack's *Been in the Storm So Long* (1980) lyrically describes the transition from slavery to freedom. Dan Carter's *When the War Was Over* (1985) and Michael Perman's *Reunion Without Compromise* (1973) analyze presidential Reconstruction. Eric L. McKitrick in *Andrew Johnson and Reconstruction* (1965) offers a view of Lincoln's successor. Janet Herman's *Pursuit of a Dream* (1981) and Willie Lee Rose's *Rehearsal for Reconstruction* (1964) examine land redistribution experiments that failed. William Gillette traces the *Retreat from Reconstruction* (1979); Allen Trelease explores the *White Terror* (1979) of the Reconstruction Ku Klux Klan; and Michael Perman explains *The Road to Redemption* (1984). Among numerous state studies, the best are Thomas Holt's *Black Over White* (1977), Joel Williamson's *After Slavery* (1965), and V. L. Wharton's *The Negro in Mississippi, 1865–1890* (1947). James L. Roark's *Masters Without Slaves* (1977) examines planter life and thought during war and Reconstruction, and Lawrence N. Powell in *New Masters* (1980) studies Northerners who became southern planters during or after the war. C. Vann Woodward's justly celebrated trilogy (*Reunion and Reaction* [1951], *Origins of the New South* [1951], and *The Strange Career of Jim Crow* [1955]); Paul Gaston's *New South Creed* (1970); and Ed Ayers's *The Promise of the New South* (1992) are valuable for understanding the South during the post-Reconstruction period. Stephan DeCanio in *Agriculture in the Postbellum South* (1974) and Robert Ransom and Richard Sutch in *One Kind of Freedom* (1977) offer strikingly different conclusions about the nature of the southern economy. Neil McMillen explores the *Dark Journey* (1989) of black Mississippians during the Jim Crow era.

17

★ ★ ★ ★ ★ ★

The Triumph of American Industry, 1865–1893

LIKE A VAST and bloody wound, the Civil War seems to divide nineteenth-century American history into two parts. Yet America's industrial expansion, the most important development of the postwar years, was under way before the war and continued during it. This immense process would have taken place if slavery or secession had never been heard of and still would have transformed world history. American industrial growth was not unique: England had gone through a similar transformation earlier, Germany experienced an industrial transformation about the same time as the United States, and such transformations were taking place before the end of the century in Japan and other countries. But American industrialization was larger in scale than that of any other country and perhaps transformed the national culture more profoundly. The American tendency to overstate the nation's economic miracles should be checked at the outset, however, by the realization that the United States trailed other industrial nations in important respects. By 1900 its impressive gross national product (GNP) may have made it "the prime industrial power of the planet." But its product per capita — the per capita value of its industrial production, which is a more valid measure of individual welfare than the GNP — was exceeded by Germany, France, and Sweden.

"THE SECOND AMERICAN REVOLUTION"

Many historians have credited America's industrial surge specifically to the Civil War. In their influential *The Rise of American Civilization* (1927) Charles and Mary Beard, for example, argued that the war was in reality a Second American Revolution, a social and economic conflict in which the nation's once-dominant agricultural interests were deliberately driven from their places of power and privilege by the expanding industrial forces of the North and East. In their view, war production, the system of wartime finance, and such wartime business achievements as the high protective tariff, banking and currency stabilization, and the construction of a transcontinental railroad were instrumental in the growth of an industrialized economy. Indeed, even Reconstruction, in the Beards' interpretation, was designed largely by industrial interests to keep the agricultural South away from the corridors of power while their program was perfected and entrenched.

More recent research has cast doubt on the thesis of the Second American Revolution. Industrialists and business people were by no means united on the issues of the Civil War or Reconstruction. Nor were they in accord on the economic programs presumably executed for their private interests under cover of a great national tragedy. In the eyes of most Americans, including industrialists, the war and its aftermath were political, not economic, struggles. The triumph of industry was not a planned and masterful capture of the government by powerful insiders.

Recent scholarship, moreover, has also challenged the economic importance of the war. According to one index, *the value added by manufacturing* — the difference between the value of raw materials before and after manufacturing — the century's largest percentage gains took place in prewar decades, most notably in the 1840s and 1850s. Though the war created certain demands: shoes, blankets, weapons, and woolen cloth for uniforms, many scholars argue that these necessities diverted productive resources and that the rate of technological improvement slowed during the crisis. Indeed, one of America's great economic advantages in the nineteenth century was that *except* in the 1860s economic growth did not have to be shaped for military ends.

It remains true, however, that industry did receive unprecedented governmental support during the war, reached new production heights in wartime, and continued this rise, with few interruptions, for the rest of the century. Though industrialization and the modern factory system antedated the Civil War, the year 1860 (if not the war itself) represents a turning point in American economic life. The antebellum period produced no giant conglomerations of wealth and influence to compare with the great postwar railroad, manufacturing, and banking empires. Even in the 1850s, the largest industrial operations were relatively small-scale and possessed few big-business characteristics, such as huge capital requirements, high fixed costs, separation of ownership and control, diversity and multiplicity of function, geographically scattered operations, and political and economic might. Thus, the "Lords of Creation," as Frederick Lewis Allen aptly called them — the Carnegies, Dukes, Hills, Morgans, Rockefellers, Swifts, and Vanderbilts — and the astonishing riches and power they amassed belong to the half century after 1860, the Age of Enterprise.

PRECONDITIONS OF GROWTH

In many areas outside of politics, postwar conditions were even more favorable to industrial expansion than those that had brought about the 1850s boom. The production demands of the transportation revolution were creating a foundation for America's heavy industry. The railroad lines were the nation's pioneer big businesses, its first large-scale companies. The railroad promoters led the way to business consolidation, to the accumulation of vast pools of capital, and to the corporate form of business organization. Railroad enterprises seemed to nurture the nation's economy; they consumed the lion's share of its finished and natural products, its coal, iron, steel, and timber. Railroads changed American life by linking raw materials to processing centers and agricultural produce to urban consumers, by standardizing time and work habits, by connecting the far-flung points of the national market, and by speeding the development and population of the West.

In addition, the railroads' need for governmental largesse, particularly in the inhospitable reaches of the trans-Mississippi region, helped create a sympathetic climate for business development. Because railroads were generally recognized as the key to economic growth and therefore often as essentially public projects, they were given substantial public support. Though private investors, primarily British, provided much of the construction costs, state and federal interest-free loans and outright gifts of land were lavish. Land grants approached 200 million acres, roughly an area the size of Belgium, the United Kingdom, and Spain combined. This generosity and such innovations as steel rails, a standard gauge, automatic and uniform coupling devices, and air brakes assured phenomenal growth. By 1900 the United States accounted for one-third of the world's railroad tracks, some 200,000 miles of steel rails that included five east-west transcontinental lines.

Preceding and accompanying the transportation revolution was a revolution in agriculture, which was characterized by mechanization, dramatic increases in production, and a vast expansion of cultivated land. The wheat crop illustrates this revolution. On the prairies of Illinois and Indiana, in the new and booming spring wheat belt of Minnesota and North Dakota, in the great valley of California, and in good years even on the dry plains of Montana, new varieties of wheat produced ever-bigger crops. By 1896 one farmer, equipped with such mechanized marvels as the harvester, twine binder, and steam thresher, could reap more wheat than 18 men six decades before had reaped. Transformed into flour in the new American rolling mills, this crop became the mainstay of industrial populations at home and abroad.

The story was much the same for other basic food commodities: geographical expansion, advancing mechanization, and development of widening markets. After 1870 these and parallel developments in Russia, Canada, Argentina, and elsewhere glutted the world market. Farm prices fell, farm problems proliferated, and agricultural distress became a major political and economic headache. But to those interested primarily in increased industrial production, more and cheaper food was an unalloyed blessing.

America's natural resources turned out to be even more plentiful than anybody had suspected. Deposits of coal and iron, the main essentials for heavy industry, were found within transportable range in many places from the Appalachians to the Great Lakes. The center of copper production moved from Michigan to Montana and Arizona. Like the minerals, the timber of Wisconsin and the far Northwest seemed inexhaustible. The problem was not to save resources, but to multiply methods of using them ever faster.

Americans also seemed to possess a large share of inventive talent. Though much of the nation's industrial progress came on borrowed European technology, some crucial improvements in basic industry, such as the Bessemer and open-hearth processes of steel production, were of combined European and American origin. Perhaps because of the needs of a continent-sized democracy, Americans excelled in the field of communication and business machines. They produced the telephone, the typewriter, the stock-market ticker tape, the linotype, the cash register, and the adding machine. Urban needs brought further American adaptations of worldwide scientific development. In the 1870s electricity was introduced as a source of light and power; by the 1890s electric street railways, incandescent light, and the phonograph had become common fixtures of urban life. The public was inclined to credit this "American ingenuity" to the romantic figure of the lone inventor — to the likes of Thomas Alva Edison, one of the most popular men of his time. Remarkable as Edison's achievements were, industrial capitalism was sustained not by the occasional dramatic inventive breakthrough but by the steady increments of technological improvements from anonymous scientists and engineers, the new university-trained technologists of the machine age.

Another precondition to growth was people. They were needed to operate the factories and to swell the markets, and they came. In the half century after 1870, 26 million immigrants arrived from Europe and Asia, and 20 million of them stayed. Between 1870 and 1900, the population of the United States grew from nearly 40 million to some 76 million, swelled by the immigrants. They were not always welcome. Many Americans, particularly those of "old-immigrant" (Anglo-Saxon) stock, looked askance at these often ragged and seemingly ignorant peasants. Organized labor feared and resented the tide of cheap and docile immigrant workers. But the demands of industry prevailed. Except for Orientals who were excluded early, the cries of alarmed nativists went unheeded until the passage of restrictive and pointedly discriminatory immigration legislation during and following World War I. (See Chapter 20.)

The immigrant influx affected the occupational and social progress of the native population unevenly. It is ironic that old-stock whites, usually the group most resentful of "New Immigrants," often discovered that these new workers pushed them out of menial labor jobs into clerical and white-collar positions. On the other hand, the relatively small number of blacks in the industrial centers found that increased European immigration limited their own occupational opportunities, because white foreigners, even those who could speak no English, were more acceptable to both industry and white labor than native-born Afro-Americans. The immigrants themselves generally lacked career mobility. Rarely organized in labor unions and often stigmatized by differences of language, custom, and religion, they supplied industry's demand for a cheap and stable work force.

Like people, capital flowed westward across the Atlantic. At the turn of the century, about a third of all American railroad securities was owned by

Europeans, who were mostly British. Much capital investment came, however, from Americans. Between 1869 and 1898, some 13 percent of the national income went into industrial expansion. This high figure reflects, in part, profitable and competitive innovation; in part, it reflects the ability of the period's industrial capitalists, the most constructive of whom used their money to expand their enterprises rather than to live lavishly. The great capital investment certainly reflects the rise of the modern investment banking houses; centered on Wall Street in New York City, they marketed industrial securities and ultimately promoted consolidation in a once-competitive economy.

THE CONSOLIDATION MOVEMENT

Nearly all conditions in the United States seemed to favor large-scale enterprise. Demand at first seemed inexhaustible. New urban populations needed consumer goods, while expanding agriculture, transportation, and industry itself needed machines. In some industries, particularly steel and oil, technology became so expensive that only very large units could meet the staggering fixed costs of production. Mounting competition caused prices to decline during the last half of the century, putting a premium on economic efficiency and large-scale production. Depressions squeezed out weak competitors, underlining the disadvantages of cutthroat competition and pointing to the desirability of merging rival operations into single units. The direction throughout the period was toward monopoly, although in most cases the process stopped short at *oligopoly,* a term economists use to describe control of a market by relatively few sellers. Theoretically, competition may have been the life of trade, but in the free enterprise jungle, consolidation was a surer way to profit.

In the consolidation movement, as in other areas, the railroads led. The industry was immersed in the ruinous competition of rate wars because it had expanded more rapidly than the demand for rail services, and it was desperate to meet its high costs. Seeking order and profits in what they saw as a destructive and chaotic marketplace, some railroad barons tried cooperation. Initially reaching gentlemen's agreements and then entering into written pooling agreements, they formed cartels or loose associations to limit competition and to share profits. Voluntary measures without standing in court, these devices were generally short-lived. Moreover, they amounted to price fixing, and such collusion raised eyebrows, if not legal questions. Thus the railroads became early targets of public indignation, political scrutiny, and finally government regulation. In time the agreement and the pool gave way to more formal combinations in railroading and in other industries.

Bigness could take several forms. A large firm might expand or *integrate horizontally,* attempting to monopolize a single product by buying out competitors. Or a diverse empire might *vertically integrate* by tying together many related but not identical enterprises at several levels of production and distribution. John D. Rockefeller and his associates built the first trust in 1882, when the stockholders of the nation's largest refineries abandoned a loosely structured cartel arrangement and exchanged their voting shares for certificates of the Standard Oil Trust. In the process, the management of some 90 percent of the industry's refining capacity was transferred to a single board of trustees. Having consolidated horizontally, Standard Oil then moved vertically, from crude oil wells to barrel factories to pipelines — all the way to the markets at home and abroad. Until its dissolution under the Sherman Anti-Trust Act in 1911, Standard Oil dominated the industry in the United States and much of the world.

Other prime examples of horizontal and vertical consolidations include Gustavus Swift's meat-processing empire and Andrew Carnegie's iron and steel operations. Building a huge integrated organization that encompassed stockyards, slaughterhouses, refrigerated railroad cars, and marketing operations, Swift left other packers, Armour and Morris among them, with no choice but imitation. By 1890 the meat-packing industry was dominated by a handful of firms. Carnegie likewise moved from raw supply to marketing. After honing his business skills in railroading, he opened a Pennsylvania steelworks in 1873 and eventually controlled ore and coal fields, Great Lakes carriers and railroads, coke ovens, pig iron and steel converting plants, and rolling mills. Although he never monopolized his industry, he did command annual earnings of $25 million and control 25 percent of the nation's steel. In 1901 Carnegie sold his massive operations to the master consolidator and finance capitalist J. P. Morgan. Morgan made the Carnegie Company (along with his own Federal Steel Company) the centerpiece of the United States Steel Corporation, which became the first billion-dollar corporation and the controller of at least 60 percent of the American steel business.

The consolidation process in steel, oil, meatpacking, and railroads was repeated in many other industries: tobacco, cottonseed oil, sugar, explosives, whiskey, nonferrous metals, flour, sewing machines, and rubber and electrical goods. In finance, too, the process occurred. The House of Morgan and its closest rival, Kuhn, Loeb, and Company, overshadowed all investment banking houses. They controlled much of the nation's capital and credit supply, and played midwives at the birth of many industrial giants.

In some areas, competition survived, among them labor-intensive, low-technology industries like furniture, food, and clothing. Relatively modest production costs encouraged the development of new firms in these industries. In other areas, market forces were restored. This happened in the low-technology salt industry: the monopoly power of the National Salt Company was broken after 1900 by the re-entry of rival sellers.

In the more technologically advanced industries where economies of scale (cheaper per unit production of large factories) were critical, the consolidators generally had their way. Whether by trusts, holding companies, or the creation of huge corporations, industrial consolidation grew rapidly in the United States. From 1888 to 1905, 328 giant combinations or consolidated businesses (representing 40 percent, or $7 billion, of the nation's manufacturing capital) were formed; half of them possessed monopoly power in their industries.

Born of changing technology and the quest for market dominance, the consolidation movement marked the end of highly competitive capitalism and the beginning of "price leadership." Explicit price-fixing was rarely necessary in the new order. Wary of federal anti-trust proceedings and comfortable with profits assured by tacitly accepted "standard" prices, oligopolistic industries competed in areas other than price: advertising, design variation, or bureaucratic efficiency. Small businesses failed by the thousands, and the social costs of this narrow concentration of economic power were incalculable.

The consumer did not invariably lose under consolidation. Large enterprises could often deliver goods more cheaply than smaller ones. Some industries that were typified by extraordinarily high fixed costs were "natural" monopolies. Until its recent court-ordered divestiture, American Telephone and Telegraph was an obvious example. Checked by state and federal regulatory agencies, this giant holding company (owner of Bell Telephone and Western Electric) managed consistently handsome profits and yet provided the most efficient and very likely the cheapest mass communication system in the world.

THE ACHIEVEMENT AND
ITS CONSEQUENCES

There was reason for widespread public admiration of the industrial accomplishment. Before the end of the century, industrial growth had built factories from Michigan to Georgia, had drawn workers for them from the farms and villages of the world, had linked factories to mines, forests, and ports, and as a result had made the United States one of Earth's great producers of wealth.

The most spectacular accomplishment may have been the American railroads, by 1900 the largest and finest system in the world. But there was also steel, a luxury product at midcentury that became the mainstay of the industrial age, the stuff of rails, oil drilling equipment, steam turbines, ships, and skyscrapers. By 1900 the United States produced as much steel as its two closest competitors (England and Germany) combined. Oil, a once-worthless by-product of the salt industry, became almost overnight the chief illuminant and lubricant of the machine age. By 1900, Americans produced and used more oil than any other people.

The benefits of large-scale industrial development were not uniformly distributed. Though much of the wealth created by industry was plowed back into the productive process, a great deal of it made life easier, more efficient, and pleasanter for some workers including the expanding clerical class. By the 1890s, the rising popularity of sports, the sharp increase in the numbers of high school students, the flood of magazines and popular novels, and even the bicycle craze testified to the presence of a substantial, growing, and relatively leisured middle class. Industrial workers (see Chapter 20) fared less well, and the national economy was marked by gross disparities in wealth. In the three decades after 1865, however, real wages may have risen by as much as half, due to stable hourly rates and falling living costs.

The expansiveness of industrialization also invaded the nation's cities, "the supreme achievement of the new industrialism." By 1900, 40 percent of the American people lived in urban places having a population of 2,500 or more, compared to only 15 percent in 1850. The trend was not universal, for the South and the western mountain and plains states were hardly touched by urbanization. Though more people earned their living on farms than in factories as late as 1900, cities in the regions of the Great Lakes, the Pacific Coast, and the East burgeoned as rural Europeans and Americans made their way to the nation's industrial and business centers. Much of this astonishing growth came in the 1880s, when the populations of more than 100 cities doubled. By 1890 there were 26 cities with more than 100,000 people, and a decade later, six of those cities had populations of over 1 million.

The city was both an irresistible magnet and a profound disappointment. It promised economic opportunity and amenities like the incandescent light, the telephone, indoor plumbing, and the trolley. But too often the newcomers exchanged one form of drudgery and poverty for another. Haphazardly built, the late nineteenth-century American city suffered from growth that was unplanned and unregulated. The poor were packed into barracks-like tenements; provisions for recreation, sanitation, fire and police protection, education, and water supply were inadequate for the multiplying population.

To the confident promoters of the new order, urban blight, not unlike poverty itself, was the inevitable by-product of human progress. They believed the benefits of headlong industrialization and urbanization far outweighed their costs. Yet in nineteenth-century America, as elsewhere in the industrial world, costs were largely met by those who could least afford them. In a shocking portrait of the other half of the urban-industrial world, immigrant-journalist Jacob Riis portrayed the victims of economic progress: the sallow, joyless factory child, the shoemaker displaced by mechanization, the uprooted and often despised immigrant, the seasonally and cyclically unemployed worker. These submerged Americans knew that the moral, social, and psychological costs of industrialization were as tangible as its rewards.

The nation was generally of two minds about the new industrialism: it applauded the material promise of a mature economy, and it feared the darker implications of concentrated power and wealth. Given the American devotion to property rights, the political influence of business, and the conservatism of the American polity, regulation appeared to be the most acceptable answer to monopoly power. State regulatory commissions and federal regulatory agencies, such as the Interstate Commerce Commission (1887), the Federal Trade Commission (1913), and the Federal Communication Commission (1934), were appointed. Regulatory agencies were designed to protect the unorganized buying public from highly organized sellers, and sometimes they did. Yet government regulators have not been noticeably hostile to private profits, and the business community, despite its initial fears, recognized the benefits accruing from the stability of a regulated market.

Perhaps because industrial consolidation threatened to narrow the channels of economic opportunity, Americans clung to their traditional notions of upward mobility. The 119 popular novels of Horatio Alger, expressions of post–Civil War American materialism and optimism, underscored the faith in unlimited opportunities awaiting the virtuous and industrious. The rags-to-riches theme was an axiom of the Age of Enterprise, and was reiterated in speeches, sermons, textbooks, newspapers, and literature. Skeptics had only to look at Andrew Carnegie, that former bobbin boy of immigrant, working-class stock, or to the humble origins of E. H. Harriman, who rose from railroad office boy to master of the Union Pacific Railroad. Despite these individual success stories, the captains of industry typically were not poor immigrant or farm boys who made good. Nearly all were native-born, and the majority emerged from advantaged circumstances. The literature on the period also is ambivalent about the new industrialism. The nineteenth-century poet Walt Whitman lamented "the depravity of the business classes" of his time. His judgment was widely shared by historians. In the best known critique, written during the Great Depression, Matthew Josephson likened the industrialists to "robber barons," the rapacious predators of medieval Europe who cheated, swindled, and robbed without compunction. Later scholars, however, have often been less interested in the industrialists' moral character than in analysis of the structure and nature of the industrial achievement. Influenced, no doubt, by the politically conservative climate of Cold War America, these historians characterized the "industrial states-men" as innovative, venturesome risk-takers who brought order to a chaotic industrial scene and economic progress to the nation.

In a sense, both views of the nineteenth-century industrialists are right, and in fact they address different issues. The best among these bold and colorful moguls were constructive builders who left behind not only baronial palaces and immense fortunes but legacies of achievement and of long-range benefit to a developing industrial nation. But they could be contemptuous of the public welfare. Their attitude is suggested by John D. Rockefeller's declaration: "God gave me my money." The disregard for legal canon and popular concerns is plain in the remarks attributed to railroad baron Cornelius Vanderbilt ("What do I care about the law? Hain't I got the power?") and to his son, William ("The public be damned!"). At their worst, the industrialists were corporate scavengers, as lawless, exploitative, and avaricious as any medieval knight gone bad.

Thus, the Age of Enterprise is viewed with ambivalence: the deeds of these new Lords of Creation inspired confidence in some quarters and dismay in others, and their machines churned out both abundance and poverty. But there is no uncertainty about the outcome: the revolution was irreversible. A new and increasingly centralized order had arrived, sweeping away landmarks, destroying traditional patterns, and raising but not answering difficult questions.

FOR FURTHER READING

Daniel Boorstin's *The Americans: The Democratic Experience* (1973) is a good point of departure for studying economic development. Perhaps the best brief account of *The Rise of Big Business* (1972) is by Glenn Porter. It should be supplemented by more detailed accounts: Edward Chase Kirkland's *Industry Comes of Age* (1961); Alan Trachtenberg's *The Incorporation of America* (1982); and Olivier Zunz's *Making America Corporate* (1990). Comparing Matthew Josephson's *The Robber Barons* (1934) or Gabriel Kolko's *Railroads and Regulation* (1975) with Alfred Chandler's *The Visible Hand* (1977) would be beneficial. Valuable biographies from the period include Harold Livesay's *Andrew Carnegie and the Rise of Big Business* (1975), Joseph Walls's *Andrew Carnegie* (1970), Allan Nevins's admiring *John D. Rockefeller* (1953), David Freeman Hawke's *John D.* (1980), and Frederick Lewis Allen's *The Great Pierpont Morgan* (1949). Histories of selected subjects include John N. Ingham's *Making Iron and Steel* (1991), Lee Benson's *Merchants, Farmers, and Railroads* (1955), and Donald J. Pisani's *From the Family Farm to Agribusiness* (1984).

18

★ ★ ★ ★ ★ ★ ★

The Last West, 1860–1890

WHILE the United States was struggling with the tragic heritage of an old region, it was also confronting the problems of a new one. Between 1860 and 1880, half the present area of the country was occupied and exploited. By 1860, settlers were fast filling up the eastern parts of Kansas and Nebraska. San Francisco and Sacramento were bustling towns, and farming was well established in the Willamette Valley of Oregon. Between these two distant borders — the Pacific settlements and the states just west of the Mississippi — lay a vast region of plains and mountains barely penetrated by European civilization.

Two things make this last and greatest West different from all earlier frontier regions. First, far more than ever before, this West was the frontier of an urban and industrial country. Second, its geography made it much less hospitable to settlers than any earlier American frontier.

PLAINS AND MOUNTAINS

From Jamestown to the Mississippi River, though the conditions of frontier life might have been hard, there had normally been enough rainfall for farming. Long accustomed to forest, pioneers of the last generation had encountered from northeastern Illinois to eastern Kansas rich prairies covered with tall grass and had learned to overcome their suspicion of treeless land. This was a lesson they were going to have to unlearn a little farther west.

Beyond the prairies lay the Great Plains, which begin at an invisible line of semiaridity that runs a wavering course, more or less close to the 98th meridian, from eastern North Dakota to the Texas Panhandle. Some of the area west of this line, particularly in its northeastern parts, could be profitably farmed by those who knew how. Westward toward the Rockies, however, the Plains grow steadily higher, drier, and less fertile. In 1860 nothing grew there but the short native grass, and aside from the soldiers who

227

TABLE 10. WESTERN HISTORY, 1860–1895

Year	Mining rushes	Indian wars	Miscellaneous events	States (in capitals) and territories
1858			Butterfield-Overland Express (transcontinental stage route).	
1859	Nevada (gold and silver). Colorado (gold).		Pony Express.	1859 OREGON
1860	1860–1866 Idaho (gold).			
1861			Pacific Telegraph.	1861 KANSAS, Colorado, Nevada, Dakota
1862	Arizona (gold). 1862–1864 Montana (gold).	1862 Massacre of whites, Minnesota.	Homestead Act.	
1863				1863 Arizona, Idaho
1864		1864 Arapaho-Cheyenne War Massacre of Indians, Sand Creek, Colorado.		1864 NEVADA, Montana
1865		1865–1867 War with Western Sioux.		
1866			Long Drive to Sedalia, Missouri.	
1867	Wyoming (gold).	1867 Indian Peace Commission.		1867 NEBRASKA
1868		1868 War on Southern Plains.	Union Pacific Railroad completed.	1868 Wyoming
1869				
1871		1871 War in Texas Panhandle.		

Year	Mining rushes	Indian wars	Miscellaneous events	States (in capitals) and territories
1873	Deeper portion of Comstock Lode, Nevada (richest strike ever).		Timber Culture Act.	
1874		1874 Red River War.		
1876	Black Hills, Dakota (gold).	1875–1876 War in Black Hills.	Barbed wire patented.	1876 COLORADO.
1877	Leadville, Colorado (silver, lead).	1877 Nez Percé uprising, Idaho.	Desert Land Act.	
1878			Timber and Stone Act.	
1879	Tombstone, Arizona (silver).			
1882	Butte, Montana (copper).		1882–1883 Santa Fe, Southern Pacific, and Northern Pacific routes completed.	
1885		1885 Capture of Geronimo and end of Apache War.	1885–1886 Disastrous winters, end of range cattle industry.	
1887		1887 Dawes Act.	Drought and western farm crisis.	
1889		1889–1890 Ghost Dance, Battle of Wounded Knee.	First Oklahoma rush.	1889 NORTH DAKOTA, SOUTH DAKOTA, MONTANA, WASHINGTON
1890				1890 WYOMING, IDAHO
1893			Great Northern Railroad completed.	

guarded the wagon trails at a few forts, it remained in the possession of its ancient inhabitants. These included the jackrabbit, antelope, coyote, and buffalo (all biologically adapted to live in arid country), along with the Plains Indians, who were culturally adapted to live on the buffalo.

Beyond the Plains lay the Rockies, rich in minerals and long penetrated by fur trappers, and beyond them the intermountain plateaus, made up mostly of sage brush desert, jagged mountain ranges, and, in the Southwest, true desert dotted with cactus and mesquite. Some of the land in this forbidding province could be irrigated and used, as had been demonstrated by Spaniards on the Mexican borderlands and Mormons near the Great Salt Lake. Beyond these plateaus lay the Pacific mountain chains: first the Sierra Nevada and the Cascades and then the Coast Ranges, with rich valleys between.

The whole region had been given the bad name of the Great American Desert. Only the strongest motives could draw settlers into it. These motives were the same as those that had first drawn Europeans across the Atlantic: religious freedom (in the case of the Mormons), adventure, independence from one's neighbors, and most common of all, desire for land and gold.

THE MINERS

Between 1859 and 1864, gold rushes occurred at scattered points in what later became the states of Nevada, Colorado, Idaho, Montana, and Arizona. One more major rush, to the Black Hills of South Dakota, took place in 1876. In each case, the boom went through nearly identical stages. First, as the fever spread following word of a promising strike, hundreds, perhaps several thousand restless opportunists converged on the spot; they included greenhorn prospectors, veterans of other mining booms, and such camp followers as merchants, prostitutes, gamblers, and more ordinary bandits. The rough-and-ready gold town itself seemed to appear overnight, a jumble of ramshackle rooming houses, shops, and whiskey mills. Women were rare, commonly outnumbered by men by three to one. Although the lawlessness of the West has probably been exaggerated, justice was often informal. An association of miners arbitrated claim disputes, and a rough semblance of law and order was maintained by citizens' vigilance committees. More settled communities appointed sheriffs, who were themselves not always models of civic probity.

When the easy pickings available through placer (surface) mining gave out, mining towns often became ghost towns. Sometimes a second metal was found and a second rush occurred, as in the cases of Colorado silver or Montana copper. Occasionally, as in Nevada in 1873, deeper digging uncovered a major lode and another bonanza. Often, after the raw surface metal was gone, organized exploitation with expensive machinery and deeper drilling produced richer results. Meanwhile, the impecunious "sour doughs," the original pick-and-basin miners, found work with the new mining companies or moved on to the next likely wilderness in the United States, Canada, Alaska, or beyond.

This haphazard but intense exploration of mineral resources doubled the world's gold supply, with important results for American political history. Silver production also increased sharply and created in a few western states a special economic interest that provided political power for more than half a century. In many cases, towns created to serve the needs of miners found other means of livelihood and survived when the mines closed. These new populations, scattered throughout the West, raised new problems, particularly those of transportation and protection against Indians.

TRANSPORTATION

The earlier Oregon migrants and California gold seekers traveled either around Cape Horn, across the Isthmus of Panama, or over the American plains. Beginning in the late 1850s, stage lines (notably Wells, Fargo, and Company) and wagon trains reached across the country. At the end of the 1850s, the enterprising firm of Russell, Majors, and Waddell developed the short-lived but spectacular pony express, which transported letters (initially at five dollars per half-ounce) from Independence, Missouri, to San Francisco in 10 days of fast relay riding. In 1861 this system was displaced by a coast-to-coast telegraph line.

Meantime, the secession of the South had settled the old arguments about the route for a railway, and in 1862 work was started under heavy government subsidy. The Central Pacific climbed painfully east through the Sierra from Sacramento, while the Union Pacific drove west along the wagon train route from Omaha via Cheyenne to South Pass. In 1869, while the nation celebrated, top-hatted dignitaries met at Promontory, Utah, to watch the driving (and retrieval) of the golden spike linking the two roads. For the next decade and a half, mostly a time of depression, the Union Pacific–Central Pacific remained the only coast-to-coast route. Then in the prosperous early 1880s, three more lines were completed: the Southern Pacific and the Santa Fe systems through the Southwest, and the Northern Pacific from St. Paul to Portland, Oregon. In 1893, a fourth road, the Great Northern, connected St. Paul and Seattle by a route still farther north. This last railroad, unlike its competitors, was developed without government subsidy by the public-spirited James J. Hill, chiefly by promoting development of the surrounding region.

THE INDIAN TRAGEDY

Penetration of the plains and mountains by miners, migrants, and stage coaches had made Indian troubles inevitable. The long and bloody struggle for the last West is one of the least pleasant stories in American history. A peaceful solution of this conflict between an aggressive, expanding nineteenth-century civilization and a nomadic, stone-age culture dependent on vast hunting spaces was probably not possible. Yet, mistakes made a hard problem worse. Part of the fault lay with divided councils, civilian administrators squabbling with soldiers, soldiers disagreeing among themselves, and settlers arguing with eastern humanitarians. Part of the long tragedy arose from inevitable anger over traditional Indian methods of war. Yet no Indian atrocity was more grisly than such white actions as the Sand Creek massacre of 1864, when several hundred men, women, and children of a tribe trying to surrender were exterminated and their bodies mutilated by a detachment of U.S. troops.

Many Native Americans, from the Utes of the Great Basin and the Nez Percés of Idaho to the Modocs of northern California, fought the whites at one time or another. But the most serious opponents of frontier advance were the Sioux of the Northern Plains and the Apache of the Southwest. Divided into small, efficient war bands led by such resourceful leaders as Red Cloud and Crazy Horse, the Sioux proved remarkably adept at high-speed, mounted warfare. On their swift ponies, they were expert with the short bow and later with rifles, and they provided their white enemies with little more target than a heel and a hand. The Apaches, who had been fighting Mexicans for years, were equally dangerous and still more elusive in their own country of desert and rocky canyon.

The long struggle with the Plains Indians began with a Sioux massacre of whites in Minnesota in 1862. Fierce fighting with Sioux and many other tribes continued through the Civil War years and sporadically in the 1870s. The last serious Sioux war broke out in 1876 when the Dakota gold rush penetrated the Black Hills, recently guaranteed to the Indians. But as late as 1890, a messianic ghost dance ritual on the Northern Sioux reservation led to an uprising and one last tragic slaughter at Wounded Knee, South Dakota. Long before this, the Plains Indian's way of life had been destroyed with the slaughter of the buffalo. These animals, once among the most numerous in the world, were almost exterminated in the decade after 1870 by railroad hunters, sport shooters, and professionals catering to the eastern demand for hides. Meantime the Apache wars in the Southwest dragged on until Geronimo, the last important chief, was captured in 1885.

Since the Monroe administration, the government's official policy had been to move the Indians beyond the reach of the white frontier. Once not only Oklahoma but the whole plains area had been talked about as permanent Indian country. Inevitably, reservations had become smaller and more crowded with the advance of the settlers, and forced Indian resettlement had to be supplemented with doles of beef, staples, and clothing.

In time, foolish and cruel government policies toward native Americans produced protest campaigns, all of them well-intentioned and some helpful. As the Indian menace ebbed, idealistic eastern sympathizers, many of them members of the Philadelphia-based Indian Rights Association, argued that a policy amounting to conquest, pauperization, and in some cases virtual genocide, was intolerable. Helen Hunt Jackson, an Easterner living in the West, became the most effective critic of federal Indian policy. Her best-selling books, *A Century of Dishonor* (1881) and *Ramona* (1884), dramatized the Native American's plight and stirred the nation's conscience. The Indian, most reformers believed, should be extended the benefits of white civilization and assimilated into the dominant culture, rather than maintained in primitive tribal condition. This proposal sat well with nineteenth-century ethnocentrism and also with the wish of land-hungry whites for reservation land. After a number of minor reforms, the Dawes Act of 1887 reversed Indian policy. Tribal authority and ownership of land was gradually to be extinguished, and reservation land was to be parceled out to individual Indians, each head of family receiving 160 acres. Such allotments were to be held in trust pending complete ownership after 25 years. Indians living in nontribal fashion were to become citizens. Land not so parceled out could be sold by the government to individual settlers with the proceeds of the sale going toward Indian education.

This well-intentioned statute proved disastrous to the Indians. Most of the reservation land, particularly the most desirable, went to white settlers. Tribal authority was destroyed and individual Indians were often victimized by white neighbors. Some received allotments too soon; others were deprived of incentive by the waiting period. In 1934 this misguided policy was reversed by the Indian Reorganization Act, which attempted to protect what remained of tribal life.

THE OPEN RANGE

Before the Indians and buffaloes had quite vanished, the plains began to be occupied by cattle, the advance guard of the expanding American economy. The range cattle industry, so much the staple of legend that the reality is hard to see, was actually a boom-and-bust episode typical of the period's economic history.

Longhorn cattle were developed in Texas, and from Hispanic sources there, the Anglo-American (and sometimes Afro-American) cowboy got his distinctive dress, his high-backed saddle, and some of his colorful vocabulary. Forage was free on the unoccupied grassland, and the buffalo was no longer abundant enough to compete for the grass. A market for cattle was provided when railroads reached Kansas in the 1860s. Thereafter, huge herds of 2,000 to 3,000 steers were driven 1,500 miles across the Texas plains to the cow towns of Sedalia, Missouri, and Abilene and Dodge City, Kansas. The drive north from Texas at about 15 miles a day was a dangerous, lonely, and difficult business beset by Indians, angry homesteaders, diseases, drought, and stampedes. From these towns, cattle went by rail to the packing centers of Chicago and Kansas City for slaughter, and then by refrigerated railroad car to the industrial markets of the East. Some 10 million cattle were driven across the plains in the two decades after 1866.

Texas longhorns were tough, wiry beasts, and it soon proved more profitable to drive them still farther and fatten them up en route through the open grasslands of western Kansas and Nebraska, the Dakotas, Wyoming, and even Montana. For a while, free grass, cheap cattle, and rising demand brought about boom conditions. Romance attracted such eastern dudes as Theodore Roosevelt, who had his fling as a rancher in South Dakota; 30 percent dividends attracted English syndicates. Soon, inevitably, even the vast plains became overcrowded. As in the mining camps, competition was regulated by semilegal codes. Cattle rancher associations divided up the government-owned unfenced range, regulated the annual roundup when new calves were separated and branded, and dealt summarily with rustlers.

By the early 1880s, two new enemies of the cattle industry appeared. The first of these was the prairie farmer advancing hopefully onto the dry plains and fencing the land. The second enemy was sheep. The sheep industry had spread from the New Mexico plateaus via the Colorado parks and Utah tablelands to the western plains. According to cattle owners, sheep cropped the range too closely, destroyed turf with their hooves, and drove away the cattle, which were superior and had arrived first.

The end of the open-range cattle industry and thus of the classical age of the American cowboy came with the disastrous blizzards of 1885–86 and 1886–87 when millions of cattle froze and starved. From this point on, successful ranchers abandoned traditional ways, enclosed the range, scientifically improved their herds, and put the once-independent "saddle tramp" to mending fences and growing fodder. The legendary cowboy, however, would be reincarnated, first in the fiction of writers like Zane Grey, then in motion pictures, and finally on television.

THE FARMERS

In the 30 years after the Civil War, more land was settled than in the whole of American history before that time. This great movement of population belonged only in part to the history of the Great Plains. Much of the new population completed the job of settling the fertile prairies. However, once the farmers solidly occupied eastern Kansas, Nebraska, and the Dakotas up to the line of semiaridity, they inevitably spilled over it into the plains. Some tried their luck as far west as Wyoming and Montana. In many ways, the experience of these western settlers was like that of prairie farmers in the past generation. In other ways, both the new environment and the changing national economy made this last chapter of frontier farming different.

This was the first migration of farmers to take place since that great farmer victory, the passage of the Homestead Act of 1862. Under this law any head of family who lived on and cultivated his claim for five years could get title to 160 acres free. This amount of land seemed generous to legislators familiar with conditions farther east, but on the Great Plains, where farming cost more and was more risky, it was not enough to make a profitable venture. Later legislation made some attempt to adapt to western realities. The Timber Culture Act of 1873 allowed a homesteader another 160 acres if the homesteader planted at least a quarter of it in trees. The Desert Land Act of 1877, lobbied through by cattle ranchers, allowed a prospective irrigator of dry lands to buy 640 acres for 25 cents an acre down. These irrigators would get title in three years on payment of the balance, provided they could prove they had irrigated a portion of the land. The Timber and Stone Act permitted the purchase of western lands not suitable for farming but valuable — sometimes very valuable — for timber or stone at the absurdly low price of $2.50 an acre.

All these laws, like many earlier American land laws, played into the hands of speculators; many of the laws invited fraud. Cattle, lumber, and land companies used their employees as false homesteaders and hired new immigrants for the same purpose. The country was too big for careful government scrutiny, so all but a small part of the land settled by farmers in this period was acquired, contrary to congressional intent, not from the federal government but from speculators and other intermediaries. Some land was acquired from land companies and some from western states that had received land under the Morrill Act for the purpose of promoting education.

The biggest of all the land sellers, however, were the railroads. The first transcontinentals and some other railroads had received enormous grants along their rights of way. Their main interest was not in revenue from direct sale of this land but in building the population in the areas they served. Thus railroads offered favorable terms, free inspection trips, agricultural information and demonstrations, credit, and even prize bulls. They also advertised. In their promotions, the Great Plains seemed to be a new Canaan. Railroad agents together with state immigration bureaus and steamship-line employees attracted newcomers by flooding Europe with leaflets about the low prices, bountiful yields, and easy profits of western farming. In 1882, the peak year for this kind of migration, 105,000 Scandinavians and 250,000 Germans crossed the ocean, many heading for agricultural life in the Midwest and beyond.

As farmers moved farther west, they confronted new problems: frequent tornadoes, prairie fires, swarming grasshoppers, torrid summer heat and searing winds, and killer blizzards and subzero winter temperatures. Where there were no trees, farmers spent their first winters in dugouts or sod houses. For heat they burned animal chips (dried buffalo or cattle dung), corncobs, or hay. Fencing presented a problem until the invention of barbed wire in 1874. To make wells, the settlers had to dig down hundreds of feet in the drier areas. To save what surface moisture there was, they learned to plow deeply and to harrow the surface to make a dust mulch. Finally, the farmers needed machines to harvest crops quickly in a region where the weather could change rapidly and ruin a season's work.

For fencing, for expensive well-drilling machinery and windmills to pump the water, for steel or chilled-iron plows to break the heavy prairie sod, for harvesters, threshers, and binders, as well as for the land itself, farmers needed credit. In the good harvest years of the early 1880s, credit was plentiful at high interest rates. In the Red River Valley of Dakota and the San Joaquin Valley of California, wheat ranches of scores of thousands of acres gave an early foretaste of industrialized agriculture. Elsewhere in the new areas, a more modest prosperity prevailed. Farmers built better houses; farming towns paved their streets and improved their schools. The price of land skyrocketed.

To many, it seemed that the Great American Desert (as the relatively arid West was often called) had at last been conquered. Advances had been made in techniques of "dry farming" and in the use of new varieties of drought- and cold-resistant wheat. Farmers, of course, hoped that good times would continue indefinitely. Cooperative experts frequently testified that the climate of the plains was changing and that tree planting, irrigation, and even the building of railroads and telegraphs somehow brought more rain. In fact, the Great Plains were nearing the end of a cycle of relative humidity. In 1887 the first of a series of rainless summers withered the crops in the fields. When credit also quickly dried up, the boom collapsed. Many who had moved beyond the line of semiaridity hastened eastward in despair. Half the population of western Kansas disappeared in four years; whole towns were deserted. The American farmer was learning that nature could fix the limits of agriculture.

THE HERITAGE OF THE FRONTIER

In 1893, historian Frederick Jackson Turner said that a period in American history had closed in 1890 with the end of the frontier. Until its passing, the frontier had molded American character and institutions. It had also, Turner and his followers believed, served as a safety valve for urban discontents. Without the frontier, the Wisconsin historian argued, this would be a very different country.

Much of this "frontier thesis" has been disputed. More government land was disposed of in the decade after 1890 than in the decade before. "Free land," moreover, had always been something of a delusion, for much had gone to speculators rather than directly to small farmers. And city workers without training, equipment, savings, or credit experienced special difficulties when they tried to "go west." In fact, since the Civil War at least, most people seeking to escape poverty had moved in the opposite direction, from the farm to the city.

Yet it was true, as Turner said, that the 1890 census for the first time found no continuous border beyond which the country was unsettled. It was true also that a great many people in the 1890s *felt* that a period was ending with the filling up of the West and that American problems in the future would be different and perhaps more difficult. While few historians agree with Turner that American individualism, egalitarianism, and nationalism come entirely from the ever-retreating West, few would deny that the American temperament owes something to both the reality and the legend of the frontier.

One obvious legacy of the West, and of this last West in particular, was a habit of violence. From vigilantes, frontier sheriffs, and cattle rancher associations, the West drew a tradition of rough justice. From mining camps and cowtowns and end-of-track railroad settlements came the western custom of roughhouse. And in the twentieth century, violence sometimes hung on in still less attractive forms such as the bloody labor wars of Colorado, which also had their class dimensions, and the persistently high homicide rates of some western states. Perhaps violence was inseparable from some of the more attractive traits of the frontier legend — the devotion to individual freedom and equality thought of as western.

In politics, the West has shown certain consistent traits. Sometimes the western liking for innovation has made easterners think it radical. Four far-western states pioneered in women's suffrage. The Initiative and Referendum came from the West and so did that last extreme of egalitarianism, the popular recall of judicial decisions. Yet the West has given the nation such vigorous conservatives as Senator Barry Goldwater and Presidents Richard Nixon and Ronald Reagan. Sometimes western radicalism and western conservatism are inextricably blended in the same people. What Westerners have in common, perhaps, is a fierce devotion to individual independence, a contempt for tradition, a willingness to try something new, and a delight above all in defying whatever mysterious forces are currently meant by the term "the East."

FOR FURTHER READING

Ray A. Billington and Martin Ridge's *Westward Expansion* (1982) is a usable general Turnerian history of the West, while Richard White's *"It's Your Misfortune and None of My Own"* (1991) and Patricia Limerick's *The Legacy of Conquest* (1987) offer examinations of the region that incorporate the insights of the new western history. Walter P. Webb's *The Great Plains* (1931) is a fascinating and controversial interpretation of the region by a devoted native. Rodman Paul's *Mining Frontiers of the Far West, 1848–1880* (1974) and Mark Wyman's *Hard-rock Epic* (1979) are the most scholarly overviews of the subject, but they do not supplant Mark Twain's *Roughing It* (1872). J. D. W. Guice in *The Rocky Mountain Bench* (1972) comments on the quality of frontier justice. Discussions of Indian-white conflict include Robert F. Berkhofer, Jr.'s *The White Man's Indian* (1978); Robert M. Utley's *The Indian Frontier of the American West, 1846–1890* (1984); Francis Paul Prucha's *American Indian Policy in Crisis* (1976); Angie Debo's *A History of the Indians in the United States* (1970); and Dee Brown's *Bury My Heart at Wounded Knee* (1971). Both Robert M. Utley's *Cavalier in Buckskin* (1988) and Evan S. Connell's *Son of the Morning Star* (1984) detail the life of the controversial George A. Custer. Robert A. Dykstra looks at *The Cattle Towns* (1968). Studies by David Dary, *Cowboy Culture* (1981), and Philip Durham and Everett L. Jones, *The Negro Cowboys* (1965), examine aspects of the much fabled western drover. The problems of the plains farmer are authoritatively discussed by Fred A. Shannon in *The Farmer's Last Frontier* (1945) and effectively portrayed in the works of Hamlin Garland, especially *Main Travelled Roads* (1891).

The role of women in resettling the West is examined in Sandra L. Myres, *Westering Women and the Frontier Experience* (1982), and Peggy Pascoe, *Relations of Rescue* (1990). Roy M. Robbins in *Our Landed Heritage* (1942) surveys public land policy, and Robert V. Hine explores *Community on the American Frontier* (1980). Henry Nash Smith's *Virgin Land: The American West as Symbol and Myth* (1950) is an important and highly sophisticated interpretation of the effect of the West on American thought and emotion.

MAP 6:   THE AMERICAN WEST, 1860–1890

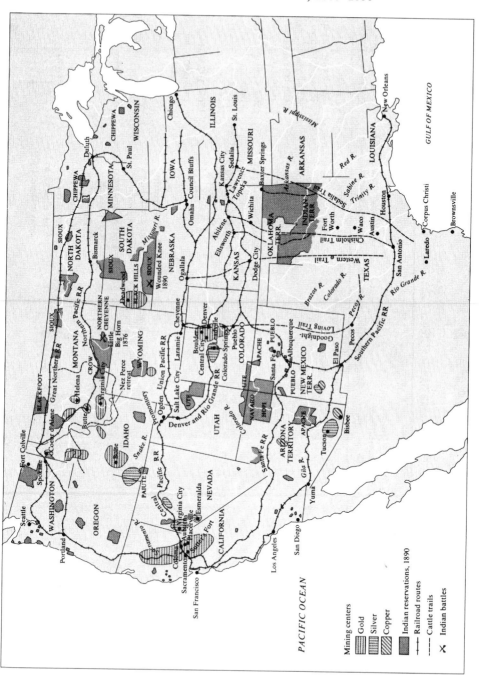

Mining centers
Gold
Silver
Copper
Indian reservations, 1890
Railroad routes
Cattle trails
X   Indian battles

TABLE 11. AMERICAN POLITICS, 1868–1896

Year	President	Presidential vote (in thousands) R	D	Control of House of Representatives R	D	Other	Major tariff legislation	Financial and other important legislation	Business conditions
1867							Reduction narrowly beaten.		To 1869 Moderate prosperity for agriculture. Moderate depression for industry.
1868	Grant *R*	3,013	2,707	*149*	63				
1869								Resolution to pay bonds in coin.	1869 Collapse of farm prices.
1870				*134*	104	5	Slight reductions.	Bonds refunded at lower rates.	
1871									1869–1873 Moderate prosperity for industry.
1872	Grant *R*	3,597	2,843	*194*	92	14	10 percent off protected articles. Coffee, tea, free.	Most remaining internal taxes repealed.	
1873								End of silver coinage. Greenback expansion vetoed.	1873 Panic.
1874				109	*169*	14			
1875							10 percent cut restored.	Resumption Act (greenbacks to be convertible 1879).	Depression

Year	President						Tariff	Legislation	Economic events
1876	Hayes *R*	4,037	4,284	140	153	14		Bland-Allison Act. Resumption (greenbacks convertible).	1879 Recovery.
1878				130	149				
1879									Prosperity
1880	Garfield *R*	4,453	4,414	147	135	11			
1882				118	199	10		Pendleton Act.	
1883							"Mongrel Tariff."		Panic and depression. 1885 Partial recovery.
1884	Cleveland *D*	4,850	4,880	140	183	2			
1885									
1886				152	169	4			
1887							Cleveland Tariff Message.	Interstate Commerce Act.	1887 Collapse of farm prices. Uneven prosperity
1888	Harrison *R*	5,447	5,538	166	159		Mills bill (reduction) passes House.		
1889								Omnibus bill (4 western states).	
1890				88	235	9	McKinley Tariff (increase).	Sherman Anti-Trust Act and Sherman Silver Purchase Act.	Minor panic.
1892	Cleveland *D*	5,183	5,555	127	218	11			
1893								Repeal of Sherman Silver Purchase Act.	1893 Major panic.
1894				244	105	7	Wilson-Gorman Tariff (slight reduction).		
1895									
1896	McKinley *R*	7,102	6,493	204	113	40			Depression

19

★ ★ ★ ★ ★ ★

The Political Parade,
1868–1892

THE POLITICS of the generation after the Civil War is generally considered to be one of the least important and most sordid topics in American history. During this period, the American people were concentrating on industrial development. Politics, it is said, became a meaningless sideshow in which second-rate politicians made pompous speeches while special interests maneuvered for advantage behind the scenes. This picture has much truth in it, but it is not complete. Much was at stake politically, though the campaign slogans did not always reflect the real issues.

THE STAKES OF THE GAME

Political affairs were, for instance, deeply affected by the period's three depressions: the major one of 1873–1879, the minor one of the mid-1880s, and the collapse initiated by the panic of 1893. These depressions and related events, such as the fall of farm prices in 1869 and 1887, greatly influenced people's political behavior. They did not, however, produce effective governmental action. Only in the depression of the mid-1890s did demands for relief and remedy absorb political argument briefly, and even then the call for action was temporarily rejected. Throughout the period after 1868, depressions affected people mainly by motivating them to vote for the party out of power. They also influenced people's attitudes toward the two big economic arguments of the period, those over the tariff and over the currency.

According to the period's dominant economic theory, it was not part of the government's duty to interfere with the business cycle. Distress would always be remedied in the long run by the action of the invisible, all-powerful laws of political economy. The government's role in the economic sphere was simple: (1) it should raise enough money for its own modest wants by equitable means; (2) it should provide a sound currency; and (3) perhaps (there was disagreement on this point) it should seek to advance the national products in the international market. But the Civil War had thrown these traditional economic functions way out of kilter. In its great need, the government had raised huge sums by any means available. It had placed internal taxes on everything in sight, from coal and iron to billiard tables. It had, for the first time, taxed incomes. Partly to make up for these taxes, it had increased the moderate prewar protective tariff. It had issued $450 million worth of fiat money, or greenbacks not backed by gold, and floated immense loans. Most people agreed that the problem was to get rid of these burdens and go back to the simple old ways. These actions proved harder than they sounded.

Removing the income tax and other internal taxes was easy enough to do, and this was largely accomplished by 1872. It seemed obvious that the tariff came next. Many people thought that the high wartime rates constituted unfair favors to special interests and placed a heavy burden on consumers. At first, most politicians took it for granted that the rates must go down. Somehow, though, tariff reduction bills that passed one house tended to be amended piecemeal in the other house and again in conference committee until they were no longer reduction bills.

Part of the difficulty lay in the nature of Congress, in which each member represented certain constituents and, consequently, very often a geographical and economic special interest. Each commodity was likely to have its own powerful advocate. It soon developed that the easiest way to compromise between two conflicting interests, such as raw wool and woolen textiles or raw sugar and refined sugar, was to do some kind of favor for each. Thus, despite many attempts, wartime rates were never substantially and permanently lowered. By 1890 the Republican party and a minority of the Democrats were openly committed to raising protection still higher, though the opposition continued to be both sizable and fervent. Certainly this issue was a real one; the rates on steel rails or woolens mattered a great deal to some people and the price of sugar to others.

A problem that accompanied the high tariff — and one unknown to modern readers — was the treasury surplus. Governmental functions were so comparatively simple that increased revenues could not easily be spent. Consequently too much of the limited supply of money accumulated in the treasury. One way to handle this problem was suggested by Grover Cleveland in 1888: lower the protective tariff. Other suggestions, however, proved more politically appealing. One could, for instance, lower the nonprotective tariff rates on articles like coffee, tea, or sugar that were not made in this country. This was done in 1872 and again in 1890. It had the advantage of reducing the income of the government only and not of private interests. And money could always be spent on veterans' pensions, river and harbor improvements, and subsidies to silver miners, railroad builders, and other powerful groups.

The other main economic argument arising from Civil War finance centered upon inflation. Right after the war, businesses were deeply divided on this matter and so were the still prosperous farmers. Gradually, however, as farm prices sank in the 1870s and then again in the late 1880s and 1890s, farm opinion turned toward inflation. At the same time, bankers, eastern editors, and some businesses became more and more convinced that tampering with the value of money was dishonest and invited disaster. Many economists today would agree that the country's money supply during the whole period was insufficient and inflexible. Certainly many who lived in that era believed this because of their own bitter experiences.

Three main methods of encouraging inflation attracted widespread support. The first was the suggestion, sometimes called the Ohio Idea and incorporated in the Democratic platform in 1868, that the government bonds be paid in the fluctuating greenback currency instead of in gold. Congress turned down this suggestion decidedly in 1869, resolving to pay bondholders in "coin or its equivalent." It proved possible, however, to refund the bonds at lower than original rates of interest.

The next method of encouraging inflation centered upon the greenbacks, toward which there were different attitudes. One group said that more of the "money of the people" should be issued to relieve financial tightness. Another said that the existing greenbacks should be retired as fast as possible. A third, the group that won the argument, said that existing greenbacks should remain in circulation but no more should be issued. In 1875, Congress resolved that $300 million in greenbacks should be left in circulation, but that on January 1, 1879, greenbacks should be made redeemable in gold. Despite a rise, during the depression of the late 1870s, of angry demands for more greenbacks, this policy was carried out on time. In the good times of the early 1880s, agitation against this accomplished fact gradually declined.

The third inflationary proposal to get a big following was the demand for "free" coinage of silver. Traditionally, gold and silver had been the basis of American money, and since 1834 the official ratio between the value of the two metals had been sixteen to one. Since this undervalued silver in terms of world prices, people had hoarded the silver dollars, which gradually disappeared. In 1873, the coinage of silver was quietly ended, an act later known to farmers and other debtors as the "crime of 1873." In the 1880s, however, the huge silver strikes of the Far West greatly increased the supply of silver. If the silver dollar were to be coined at the old ratio, it would be the cheaper, and therefore the dominant coin. This would expand the currency and also help the silver-mining interests, strategically located in underpopulated western states and therefore disproportionately strong in the Senate.

The gold standard, the money of imperial Britain and of international bankers, was blamed for all the farmer's troubles. Pressure to go back to free coinage of silver at sixteen to one became almost irresistible, and twice Congress was forced to make a half-hearted concession to the silver forces. In 1878 the Bland-Allison Act directed the Treasury to purchase $2–4 million worth of silver bullion a month at market prices and to coin it into dollars. In 1890 the Sherman Silver Purchase Act required the purchase of the whole output of the silver mines and the issuance thereon of treasury notes. However, by action of the Secretary of the Treasury, these notes, like the silver dollars coined under the previous legislation, remained convertible into gold on demand; thus the gold standard was still intact.

Aside from the tariff and money, the main recurrent issue was political reform. From the late 1870s on, it became painfully clear that the government did not, as standard theory said it should, stay out of economic competition. Its favors in terms of tariffs and tax remissions and subsidies were bought by influence and even money. Some members of the well-established eastern middle class became deeply aroused on moral grounds. Perhaps they were alarmed also by the power of the new rich, who did not share their own traditions of public service. In any case, these essentially conservative reformers, Republican by normal allegiance but independent by conviction, became a surprisingly powerful influence. As parties were evenly balanced, professional politicians might hate the reforming Mugwumps but could not ignore them.

The chief proposal of these reformers was the development of a federal civil service. This would end bribery and corruption, take the power of appointment away from unscrupulous politicians, and perhaps create a class of devoted, impartial public servants like those said to exist in England and Germany.

"Snivel service," as the indignant professional politicians called the movement, never achieved its ideal of completely just, impartial administration. It did, however, make it harder to get away with outright fraud and theft. Some of the most powerful politicians of the day were kept out of the presidency because their records were not pure enough to satisfy the reform element. And after many frustrations, the civil service movement did finally secure, in 1883, the passage of the Pendleton Act. Under this, certain federal offices were filled by competitive examination, rather than by the cruder forms of patronage that exchanged government jobs for political support. Since that time, presidents have frequently added to the number of offices under civil service, especially when the opposing party has been about to come to power. The increase of federal employees has, however, prevented reform from destroying traditional political methods.

Tariff, money, and civil service reform were the most important of the obvious political issues, and, underlying these, business depressions played a big part in politics. On the surface, however, campaigns were fought over whatever false issue lent itself best to emotional slogans, torchlight parades, and bitter hatreds more or less forgotten between elections. The first of these false issues, sadly enough, was Reconstruction — a real and tragic problem subordinated to the political battle. While people lost interest in the fate of southern blacks, Republican politicians "waved the bloody shirt," blaming their opponents for all the horrors of war. Conversely, Southerners and Democrats dwelt on the alleged horrors of black rule.

After attacks on rebels, blacks, and carpetbaggers began to pall, there were always Catholics, immigrants, and foreigners in general to be assailed. One big section of the population could be counted on to respond to fear of the Pope, and another always cheered an attack on Great Britain. Finally, the war records, drinking habits, appearance, and marital life of leading candidates could be raised as political issues.

THE RULES AND THE PLAYERS

The character of post–Civil War politics can partly be explained by two political facts: the overwhelming power of Congress and the remarkably even division between the two great parties. In Reconstruction, Congress effectively broke the power of the executive branch. Real power in the period after 1870 was centered in the Senate, which was so business-oriented and so flush with wealthy members that it became known as the Millionaires' Club. Powerful and arrogant, some leading senators — Rhode Island's Nelson W. Aldrich and Ohio's Mark Hanna among them — created nearly unbeatable personal political machines in their home states. Appointed at their behest, both state and federal officeholders could be assessed for campaign contributions. When this was theoretically outlawed by the 1883 Pendleton Act, local business interests could still be heavily tapped. Thus the "right kind" of governors and members of Congress would be elected, and subservient legislatures would send the real rulers of their states back again and again to the Senate. With the presidency weakened, there was no powerful advocate for general national needs, and politics took such forms as *spoilsmanship* (the distribution and seeking of patronage) and *logrolling* (the trading of political favors).

The Civil War and Reconstruction demoralized the Democratic party but by no means destroyed it. Though the Republicans held the presidency during all but Grover Cleveland's two terms, 1884–1888 and 1892–1896, the Democrats won a popular plurality more often and controlled the House of Representatives more than half the time. National elections frequently depended on a few thousand well-distributed votes.

Since no single interest group commanded a majority, each party had to appeal to many elements. The Republicans could count on the Union veterans and the blacks, when and where they could vote. Those business people who favored the high protective tariff voted Republican and so, usually, did believers in the gold standard (though many western Republicans were inflationists). In good times, midwestern farmers could be counted on for Republican votes. To a large group of respectable middle-class Protestants, it was unthinkable to vote Democratic. The clergyman who said in the abusive campaign of 1884 that the Democrats were the party of "Rum, Romanism, and Rebellion" went too far and may have helped Cleveland more than the Republican candidate, James G. Blaine of Maine. But he voiced a stereotype that many took for granted.

After Reconstruction, the Democrats started with the Solid South. Most immigrants in the coastal cities, neglected by Anglo-Saxon Republicans and helped by efficient Democratic bosses, were also safely Democratic. Western farmers and much of labor tended to vote Democratic when times were bad. Thus the Democrats were potentially a party of moderate protest, of agitation for low tariffs, and of cheap money. Yet in the East and Midwest as well as the South, some party leaders were ultrarespectable lawyers and business executives. This kind of conservative Democrat (Cleveland was a prime example) might favor foreign trade and a lower tariff, but oppose any other kind of change as vigorously as the staunchest Republican.

Each party was thus divided. The Republicans had three factions. The Stalwarts, led by Senator Roscoe Conkling of New York, were all-out believers in party regularity and the bloody shirt. They even favored a third presidential term for Grant in 1880. At the opposite pole were the liberal or independent Republicans, the Mugwumps, who joined civil service reformer Carl Schurz in deserting their party for Cleveland in 1884. Between these extremes were the Half-Breeds led by the "Plumed Knight," Senator James G. Blaine; they were much like the Stalwarts, but less blatantly partisan. Rivalry between these factions was such that in 1884 when Senator Conkling was asked whether he would support the party's candidate, Senator Blaine, he replied, "No, thank you, I don't engage in criminal practice." In the Democratic party, the factions included Bourbons (reactionaries) and near radicals, supporters of the corrupt New York City machine (Tammany Hall), and reformers.

With such party divisions, it is not surprising that the two parties tended to select colorless, compromise presidential candidates and to write meaningless platforms. Because the parties needed to play down divisive issues, it was necessary to play up personalities, scandals, and party regularity. In crucial states in tightly contested campaigns, bribery and violence were not rare.

The system seemed to work in spite of itself. The nation's industry expanded; its presidents and some other politicians were honest and often reasonably competent. Party discipline, growing stronger through the period, accomplished the government's business and usually kept the most divisive issues out of politics. Interest groups were able to influence government but seldom dominated it altogether. Stable rather than innovative, the political order of the Gilded Age served business better than popular interests. Yet in relatively peaceful and prosperous times the political system seemed to satisfy Americans. When widespread popular discontent raised its head in the 1890s, political habits necessarily, if reluctantly, changed.

THE GRANT ERA

When Ulysses S. Grant was elected in 1868, many people expected a dignified, masterly administration in the Washington tradition. Naturally, the chief national hero of the Civil War was flattered by politicians and big business. Equally naturally, Grant, who before the war had had little interest in politics and no experience of success, enjoyed the flattery. Originally inclined toward a lenient Reconstruction policy, he was skillfully maneuvered by the Radicals into their camp. His appointments dismayed his admirers.

Though he chose real leaders like Hamilton Fish, the New York aristocrat who became Secretary of State, the appointees also included routine politicians, incompetents, seedy relatives of the Grants, military men out of jobs, and crooks. Grant's personal integrity made his muddling political naiveté all the more tragic.

In financial matters Grant was moderately conservative, vetoing a measure to increase the greenbacks but battling the Supreme Court to defend the validity of those in circulation. Secretary Fish handled foreign affairs with surprising effectiveness. In 1871 the difficult issues arising out of England's wartime friendliness to the Confederacy were sensibly settled by arbitration. To placate reformers, the Civil Service Commission was set up, but it was not allowed initially to interfere with the serious matter of patronage.

By 1872 the reformers were tired of Radical Reconstruction, irritated by the failure of tariff reduction, and disgusted by the administration's moral laxity. Determined to block Grant's re-election and "turn the rascals out," they held a separate Liberal Republican convention and nominated for the presidency the vain and thin-skinned veteran reformer and editor Horace Greeley of the *New York Tribune*. Hoping to make a "new departure" and end the constant attacks on their patriotism, the Democrats nominated Greeley also. Greeley, a former Whig, Republican, abolitionist, and relic of the antebellum past, was an odd Democratic candidate. Vulnerable to ridicule as a utopian for his many causes (including vegetarianism, spiritualism, and Fourierism) he was disastrously beaten.

With Grant re-elected and reformers momentarily discredited, the way seemed clear for Stalwart domination. However, the Democrats captured the House of Representatives in the depression year of 1874 and used their victory to investigate the Republican administration. A sinister pattern was revealed in department after department: the purchase of political favors for money. This corruption, known as "Grantism," tarred great causes like the building of the Union Pacific. Corruption honeycombed the Indian Service, the Freedmen's Bureau, and the collection of internal revenue; it touched ambassadors, cabinet members, and even the president's private secretary. In the face of investigation, the hero of Appomattox realized that something was the matter and apologized on the grounds of his own political inexperience.

THE DISPUTED ELECTION

In 1876, Republican regimes remained in power in only three southern states. With the South back on the Democratic side and many Northerners hostile to the administration, it seemed likely that the Democrats would return to power. To prevent this unthinkable disaster, the Republicans nominated the honest and able, though rather uninspiring, Rutherford B. Hayes of Ohio. The Democrats also bid for the reformers by nominating Samuel J.

Tilden, who as governor of New York had destroyed the grafting Boss Tweed ring in New York City.

Tilden won a sizable popular plurality, capturing New York and several other northern states in addition to the South. It seemed clear that he had won the election. The Republicans, however, claimed the votes of the three southern states still under carpetbagger rule: Florida, South Carolina, and Louisiana. In each of these states, the Democrats had intimidated blacks, and both parties had been guilty of other dubious practices. After a long and bitter dispute, the conflicting returns from these states were referred to an electoral commission; acting on strictly party lines, it gave the election to Hayes by one vote.

Certain Republicans had approached certain Democrats in advance to make sure this result would be accepted. The Compromise of 1877, as this has been called, somewhat resembles the prewar compromises. Like them, it was made by conservatives for the purpose of preventing trouble. Southern Democratic leaders were assured that, if they accepted Hayes's election, he would remove the troops from the remaining southern states and that the South would receive its share of railroad subsidies and similar federal favors. Conservative southern Democrats, many of them former Whigs who believed in supporting industry, had no love for the agrarian Democrats of the Northwest. The Republican conservatives, on the other hand, hoped to build up their party in the southern states. This hope did not mature, however, and by the next election, the bloody shirt was again waving in the breeze. One result of the compromise stood: the North was through intervening on behalf of the southern black. Once again, conservative white Southerners controlled the South, and the stage was set for the disfranchisement and segregation of the former slaves.

THE PRESIDENTIAL SEESAW

Hayes made a serious effort to reform the federal bureaucracy, an effort that involved him in a bitter fight with the Stalwarts of his party. But that did not go far enough to please the reformers. A financial conservative, he stood firm against inflation. A believer in the principle of a single presidential term, Hayes made too many enemies to be renominated even if he had changed his mind. After a stalemate between the Stalwart backers of a third term for Grant and the partisans of James G. Blaine, the oratorically gifted but somewhat tarnished "Plumed Knight" of the Half-Breeds, the nomination went to the moderately reform-minded James A. Garfield of Ohio. To placate the defeated Stalwarts, the Republicans gave the second place on the ticket to Chester A. Arthur of the New York Custom House, a perfect representative of machine politics. Garfield won a close election against General Winfield Scott Hancock and, like his predecessor, began struggling with the Stalwarts over patronage. On July 2, 1881, this promising president was shot by a psychotic office-seeker, who cried out, "I am a Stalwart and

Arthur is President now." After lingering in pain for several weeks, Garfield died on September 19 — a martyr, many thought, to the spoils system.

To the surprise of most public-spirited citizens and to the dismay of some friends, the handsome, genial Arthur made an honest and able executive. Turning against his old cronies, he fought against corruption in the post office and machine politics in his own bailiwick. He backed the Pendleton Act, the first real civil service law, and even attempted to put through a thorough revision of the tariff. In this he failed, and the so-called Mongrel Tariff of 1883 was amended out of all reform meaning.

In 1884 the Half-Breeds finally pushed through the nomination of their hero, Blaine. The Democrats nominated Grover Cleveland, the stout and solid governor of New York, who had a reputation for honesty and independence. In a campaign that reached a peak of scandal-mongering on both sides, Cleveland won.

To the horror of many Republicans, a Democrat was in power — the first since 1860. No disaster ensued, however. Cleveland dealt effectively with the most obvious and immediate problems facing the government. One of these was the rising treasury surplus. Instead of dissipating this surplus through continually bigger pensions for veterans, a move that he courageously opposed, Cleveland insisted on tariff reduction. In 1887, using the most forthright language employed by any president since the war, he attacked the high tariff as the creator of oppressive monopolies and managed to push a tariff reform bill through the House of Representatives, though not through the Senate.

The protective tariff, therefore, was the one national issue that played a big part in the campaign of 1888. The Republicans nominated the cold and correct Benjamin Harrison of Indiana, grandson of Old Tippecanoe. Since it was clear what was at stake, they were able to go farther than usual in "frying the fat," that is, wringing campaign contributions out of protected industries. Despite these and less savory tactics, Cleveland won a popular plurality; however, Harrison secured a majority of the electoral votes.

For some reason, the Harrison administration took this doubtful mandate as a green light for an extreme program along Stalwart lines. With liberal pension acts and rich pork-barrel appropriations for rivers and harbors, post offices, and the like, the new Congress launched a successful assault on the surplus in the old-fashioned manner. The administration leaders gave their cordial support to the complex and ultraprotectionist McKinley Tariff of 1890. To put this across, it was necessary to make several accommodating gestures toward the western critics of the administration. For the first time, the tariff offered protection to farm products as well as to manufactures. The administration supported both the Sherman Silver Purchase Act and anti-monopoly legislation. The admission of six western states and an unsuccessful attempt to give Congress power to control southern elections completed the strategy of the administration high command.

In 1890 the Republicans were repudiated overwhelmingly in Congress, and in 1892, Cleveland was vindicated by re-election. Despite the reappearance, however, of his corpulent and familiar figure, there were signs that the conventional pattern of politics was changing. In the heavily Democratic Congress there were several members of a new third party calling itself the People's party and demanding a whole list of radical reforms. Shortly after Cleveland's inauguration, a severe financial panic alarmed businessmen. This was only the beginning; the second Cleveland administration was to face a host of new problems at home and abroad. Or, more accurately, it would encounter old problems that could no longer be ignored.

FOR FURTHER READING

Any serious study of the period should include James Bryce's classic *The American Commonwealth*, (2 vols., 1888). Matthew Josephson's *The Politicos* (1938) is dated but still fascinating. Two good but very different overviews of the period are John A. Garraty's *The New Commonwealth* (1968) and Nell I. Painter's *Standing at Armageddon* (1987). Richard L. McCormick's *The Party Period and Public Policy* (1986) is a useful collection of essays on nineteenth-century politics. Morton Keller's *Affairs of State* (1977) places post–Civil War political battles in a broad context, and Paula Baker's *The Moral Framework of Public Life* (1991) offers a gendered interpretation of Gilded Age politics. Michael E. McGerr explores *The Decline of Popular Politics* (1986) in the late nineteenth and early twentieth centuries. Robert Marcus describes the *Grand Old Party* (1971); J. Rogers Hollingsworth's *Whirligig of Politics* (1963) looks at the democracy from Cleveland to Bryan; and Daniel Rothman's *Politics and Power* (1966) studies the Senate closely. Irwin Unger in *The Greenback Era* (1964) relates financial controversy to political ideological divisions; Ari Hoogenboom in *Outlawing the Spoils* (1961) examines civil service reform; and John Sproat in *"The Best Men"* (1968) investigates the reform efforts of the Mugwumps. For the Grant administration, see William S. McFeely's *Grant* (1981). Other biographies of note include Justus D. Doenecke's *The Presidencies of James A. Garfield and Chester A. Arthur* (1981) and Ari Hoogenboom's *Rutherford B. Hayes* (1992). The disputed Hayes-Tilden election is interpreted by C. Vann Woodward in *Reunion and Reaction* (1951), and Mark W. Summers in *Railroads, Reconstruction and the Gospel of Prosperity* (1989) examines how the failure of Republican economic promises for the South ultimately doomed the southern Republican party.

20

★ ★ ★ ★ ★ ★

The Ripening of Protest, 1870–1896

IN THE 1890s, sharp criticism of industrial and urban conditions roiled the calm political waters of the United States. Once confident that serious unrest was impossible in America, conservatives became alarmed by strident social criticism and class resentments and began to talk of a revolutionary menace. Though dissent was widespread and originated in part from radicals, the mass of the discontented generally sought redress through reform rather than revolution. Much discord could be traced to the painful adjustments required of a nation that, as Richard Hofstadter wrote, "was born in the country, but has moved to the city."

One important challenge to the new socio-economic order was the force of tradition and the reluctance of native-born farm people and foreign-born peasants to accept the rule of clock and machine. Though industrial capitalism ultimately brought a rising standard of living, abundant goods and services, and wider opportunities, initially its long-range benefits were not appreciated by workers and farmers, who had experienced its uncertain, boom-bust cycles. Those who endorsed industrial capitalism were also committed to traditional values, demanding the loyalty and dedication of workers under radically altered circumstances. And these unfolding ideological struggles of the Gilded Age colored the nation's political arguments for much of the twentieth century.

DEFENDERS OF LAISSEZ FAIRE

Many educated people of the nineteenth century believed, in the tradition of competitive individualism, that human affairs were ruled by immutable natural law. According to the central law of political economy, the general good was best served by the unrestrained pursuit of individual self-interest.

If such competition caused social suffering, this was an unfortunate but necessary spur to greater effort. Rewards went to those who earned them through hard work and right living, whereas poverty was almost always a punishment for vice and sloth. People believed it to be foolish and immoral for the state or any private organization to intervene in economic affairs. As formal economic theory, this argument is known as classical economics.

Late in the nineteenth century, classical economic theory was attacked by a new generation of reform-minded scholars associated with the American Economic Association (AEA). Until then, however, laissez faire was not only the test of economic orthodoxy, but as the first president of the AEA observed, "It was used to decide whether a man were an economist at all." Laissez-faire economists in the United States borrowed heavily from Adam Smith (*Wealth of Nations*, 1776). Like Smith's disciples on both sides of the Atlantic, they taught that economic competition unchecked by the state assured human progress. Laissez faire, as one Harvard professor explained, means " 'things run themselves' . . . which means, of course, that God regulates them by his general laws, which always, in the long run, work to good."

Leading ministers also argued that laissez faire was the law of both science and God. The Reverend Henry Ward Beecher of Brooklyn's Plymouth Church (whose annual salary was over $20,000) took an extreme view when he said that any sober, nonsmoking laborer could feed a family of six on a dollar a day: "Water costs nothing; and a man who cannot live on bread is not fit to live." Some Protestant churchmen, influenced by the Calvinist ethic of individual achievement and responsibility, justified unbridled competition on ethical and religious grounds; they found no conflict between God and Mammon and were confident that, as the Episcopal Bishop of Massachusetts said, "Godliness is in league with riches." Commanded by the tenets of this "gospel of wealth" to be their brothers' keepers, the rich did have an obligation to the poor. But the yawning disparities in worldly goods between the industrialists and their workers were the proper concerns, in Andrew Carnegie's words, of "the man of wealth . . . the mere trustee and agent of his poorer brethren," and not of the state.

The Protestant establishment also took to the social applications of Darwinian science. Initially troubled by the theory of evolution, toward the end of the 1800s the nation's prominent churchmen discovered its "providential purposes" and, as readily as others of their social class, accepted Social Darwinism. According to the English philosopher Herbert Spencer and his American disciple William Graham Sumner of Yale University, the unimpeded struggle for existence was the means by which the human race had reached its present high development; social action or state regulation of any kind would disrupt the natural design, encourage the unfit, fetter the strong, and thereby slow progress. In the "survival of the fittest," Spencer's adaptation of Darwinian natural selection, apologists for the status quo found scientific confirmation of the values of competitive individualism.

Taught by political economists and preached by the clergy, the doctrines of laissez faire and Social Darwinism were also invoked by jurists. During the 1880s and 1890s, the Supreme Court gradually worked out an interpretation of the Fourteenth Amendment that made it, too, a bastion of business. To protect the former slaves, the amendment prohibited states from depriving "any person of life, liberty, or property, without due process of law." The court, however, interpreted the amendment to mean that no state could deprive any corporation of liberty or property. "Liberty" was read as liberty of contract, and "person" could mean corporation. "Without due process" covered any sort of unreasonable regulation of, say, hours of labor or railway rates. What was reasonable depended on the tenets of laissez-faire capitalism. By such logic, the court employed federal law (the Sherman Anti-Trust Act) to limit labor strikes but not to limit the growth of big business.

The conservative Supreme Court Justices, like most other defenders of laissez faire, seemed oblivious to the fact that the doctrine of competitive individualism, however useful as an ideology for the propertied class, was out of date in an age of large-scale enterprise. The dominant economic tendency of the industrial revolution, as Chapter 17 illustrates, was away from competition toward monopoly.

REVIVAL OF REFORM

Not all Americans were agreed with Social Darwinism, though up to the 1890s, classical economics and Darwinian individualism were in the ascendant. But the growing inequities caused by the industrial revolution stirred reformers to challenge the social and economic utility of unrestricted competition.

Some evils of the period, like recurrent corruption in government and fraud in business, raised no new moral problems; these were recognizable evils requiring punishment. Under the new economic order, however, the line between legitimate action and wrong-doing was less clearly drawn. Bribery was wrong, but were investment tips to helpful public officials and special prices for favored insiders wrong, or merely questionable?

Monopoly was a closely related problem. From the early days of the Republic, Americans had feared concentrated power. Increasingly, the nation's industrial experience suggested that giant concerns threatened opportunity, perhaps competitive individualism itself. Railroads drew the first fire. By the mid-1880s, when the Supreme Court began to overturn state regulatory laws, demand for national railroad legislation became overwhelming. In 1887 the Interstate Commerce Act forbade certain unfair practices, required that rates be published and "reasonable," and set up a commission to investigate abuses and to appeal to the courts for redress.

In 1890, mounting demand for general antimonopoly legislation was met by the Sherman Anti-Trust Act, which nominally prohibited all contracts, combinations (monopolies), or conspiracies that restrained interstate or foreign trade. Like the Interstate Commerce Act, this measure was not enforced for many years. Both acts presented an interesting paradox: government intrusion in the name of laissez faire by regulating to preserve free competition.

Another major area for reform was the exploding American cities. The process of suburbanization enabled by new forms of public transit tended to insulate the advantaged classes from the problems of innercity life. Yet even those who believed the poor deserved to be poor could not ignore the social impact of rapid, unregulated industrial and urban growth. Though not new on the urban scene, the slums with their crime, disease, overcrowding, decaying housing, poverty, and unemployment had expanded and their conditions had rapidly worsened.

Among the first to show concern for the urban poor was a new breed of Protestant clergy, who could not square the cramped ethics of laissez faire with the Golden Rule. This Social Gospel movement owed much to the example of the Salvation Army (the so-called slum angels imported from England in the 1870s) and to clerical concern with the erosion of metropolitan church attendance. Advised by the conservative Protestant clergy to accept their lot, the alienated working class stayed away from organized religion in droves. In contrast, Washington Gladden and other reform-minded ministers urged their parishioners to apply the law of love to labor relations and to the relief of poverty. Christian socialist clergy, notably Baptist Walter Rauschenbusch, went beyond these injunctions to advocate a radical restructuring of society. The Social Gospel movement's mainstream, however, saw no inherent conflict between capitalism and Christianity and sought to make social conditions better by applying their religious beliefs to their actions.

Somewhat more readily than Protestants, the Roman Catholic Church — with its large following among working-class immigrants — also linked religion to reform. Scarcely touched by the Calvinist alliance between business and faith and certainly influenced in 1891 by Pope Leo XIII *(Rerum Novarum)*, the Roman Catholic Church in America officially favored "the equality of rich and poor" and recognized "the employers' moral obligation to pay fair wages." At about the same time, Reform Judaism moved that wing of the Jewish faith in much the same direction.

Until the late nineteenth century, relief to the poor had been administered through individual handouts or crowded and inadequate poorhouses. Proponents of laissez faire endeavored to deny charity to the "undeserving poor" and to severely limit it to the "deserving poor" lest their characters be spoiled. By 1890, however, distinctions between the deserving and undeserving poor were fading due to shocking descriptions of slum life, such as Jacob Riis's *How the Other Half Lives*, and to the development of the social work movement. About 100 settlement houses, all modeled after London's Toynbee Hall, were formed as "neighbors to the poor." Jane Addams's Hull House in Chicago and Lillian Wald's Henry Street Settlement in New York are outstanding examples of settlement houses, which provided health, education, welfare, and recreation services in congested tenement districts.

Thus, their consciousness raised, many Americans found it impossible to accept the theories of laissez faire. Among the most radical were Daniel De Leon of the faction-ridden Socialist Labor party and the less doctrinaire Eugene V. Debs of the Socialist Party of America, who were Marxist. Others, including Edward Bellamy, author of the enormously popular *Looking Backward* (1888), sought to supplant competition and private ownership with a utopian socialist order of cooperation and collectivism. Henry George, perhaps the most influential American social theorist of the period, targeted land monopoly for extinction. The author of the best-selling *Progress and Poverty* (1879), George traced all social evil to private gain from increased land values. A confiscatory *single tax* on that "unearned increment," he believed, could reduce the contrast between "the House of Have and the House of Want." George's assault on laissez faire helped lead to a more critical appraisal of the nation's social problems.

Less radical than George were many academic theorists, including such social reformers as Lester Frank Ward and Richard T. Ely. They accepted the broader contours of the free enterprise system, but denied that unrestrained competition assured either equity or progress. A pioneer sociologist, Ward challenged Social Darwinist assumptions about the social development of the human animal with a reform Darwinism that preferred cooperation to conflict, rational choice to natural selection, purposeful intelligence to blind struggle. Although he did not deny the validity of evolutionary theory, Ward argued in *Dynamic Sociology* (1883) and *Applied Sociology* (1906) that human beings, by virtue of thought and will and through social planning and positive social action, could direct the process of nature and alter their environment in beneficial ways. The "New School" economist Richard T. Ely, one of an emerging group of European-educated American critics of laissez-faire capitalism also embraced the state as an instrument for social progress. An unabashed meliorist, Ely never doubted that human beings, through government, could correct the worst ills of an urban and industrial society.

A dark side to the attack on laissez faire involved immigrants. In the best tradition of the free market, the United States was open to all who sought liberty and opportunity. During the 100 years after 1820, some 38 million immigrants came — 5,250,000 of them in the 1880s alone. Old-stock Americans were alarmed by the influx of Asians during the middle of the century and, after 1870, of Italians, Greeks, Russians, Poles, and other southern and eastern Europeans. Most of these people were Roman or Orthodox Catholics, and some were Jews. The new immigrants became the objects of fear and prejudice in a hitherto largely Anglo-Saxon and Protestant nation. These prejudices found expression in the Nordicism of Madison Grant, author of *The Passing of the Great Race* (1916). Added to an ugly mix of anti-Semitism, anti-Catholicism, nativism, and xenophobia were the concerns of organized labor, which was always less hospitable than management to the seemingly endless stream of job-hungry newcomers. Often destitute, not speaking English, and disoriented by the swift transition from their villages to the unsavory environment of city slums, the immigrants seemed to resist Americanization. In many cities they organized their own communities and cultural societies, maintained their native languages, religious customs, and newspapers, and clung to Old World customs. Some foreign born, moreover, became mainstays of urban political machines, trading votes for badly needed assistance from corrupt city bosses. To many middle-class Americans, then, sections of New York, Chicago, and San Francisco were as alien as Naples, Prague, and Shanghai.

Whether demand for immigration restriction came from reformers, conservatives, or both, the result was a series of government actions. In 1882, Congress excluded Chinese, a group especially resented by organized labor. In the same year, convicts, paupers, and criminals were banned, and this list was later amended to include anarchists and other "undesirables." In 1885, the importation of contract labor was forbidden. In 1907 by executive agreement, the Japanese were effectively excluded. A decade later, over Woodrow Wilson's veto, Congress imposed literacy requirements for immigrants. Then, during 1921–1927, Congress passed laws limiting immigration according to nationality quotas designed to restrict Latins and Slavs.

LABOR MOVEMENT

An effective workers' response to industrialism, despite the hardships they endured, developed more slowly in the United States than in most other industrialized nations. Earnings did increase between 1860 and 1890 by about half, largely because of falling food prices, but wages were exceedingly low. Unskilled workers earned $1.00 to $1.50 a day, enough to live on but not enough to tide them over illness, accident, and unemployment, nor to provide for old age. By 1900 the average work week was 60 hours long, and the average worker earned $400 to $500 annually, less than the minimum ($600) required for a "subsistence-plus" standard of living. In addition to low pay, workers faced unhealthy and unsafe conditions in mines and factories, which had high mortality and accident rates. Some workers lost jobs due to technological advances, while many more were cyclically unemployed.

Would-be labor organizers experienced great difficulties. Management was generally hostile to workers' organizations, and in fact organized itself (the General Managers' Association and the National Association of Manufacturers) to keep labor from doing the same. Large sections of the press and the public shared this antiunion sentiment, and government could nearly always be counted on to side with owners against their employees. Frequent economic depressions, industrial spies, and "goon squads" made pro-union sentiment dangerous. Workers were aware that thousands of the unemployed and the new immigrants eagerly waited to replace those fired and blacklisted for union activity. Finally, a heterogeneous work force, composed of many nationalities, lacked the working-class solidarity that effective labor organization seems to require.

The first post–Civil War unions attacked these problems with prewar idealism. The National Labor Union (NLU) and the Knights of Labor, for example, were broadly reformist, industrial unions that sought to unite all segments of the work force (agricultural and industrial, skilled and unskilled) and to supplant the wage system with worker-owned "producer cooperatives." The NLU survived only until the depression of the 1870s. The Knights flourished briefly in the late 1870s and early 1880s and had 750,000 members at peak strength, but like the NLU, its energies were scattered. In 1886 at a labor rally in Chicago's Haymarket Square, a bomb killed and injured police; the Knights were unjustly associated with the incident in the public mind. The union lost members and perished in the depression of the 1890s. Its major competitor and successor was the American Federation of Labor (AFL).

Samuel Gompers, who founded the AFL in the 1880s, was a tough-minded cigar maker who had absorbed the craft tradition of his trade. He blamed the Knight's defeat on loose organization, naive idealism, and political involvement, and thus organized the AFL along craft rather than industry-wide lines. Gompers called for "pure and simple unionism," by which he meant the pursuit of such issues as higher wages, shorter hours, and union protection, including if possible the *closed shop* (one that employed only union members). To reach these goals, Gompers avoided politics and employed such traditional tools as the strike and the boycott. His organization had no quarrel with the existing capitalist system, and Gompers (although once sympathetic to socialism) attempted to deny socialists influential positions within the AFL. Under his leadership the AFL stood apart from radical organizations like the Molly Maguires and, somewhat later, the Industrial Workers of the World. These two organizations represented some of the most oppressed workers and were targets of industrial and government suppression. In the essentially conservative American labor movement, they did not enjoy the appeal that the pragmatic AFL did.

By adapting to existing conditions rather than fighting them, the AFL survived in the hostile world of the nineteenth century. It weathered the depression of the 1890s and by 1900 had half a million members and a limited measure of public recognition. It proved unable, however, to organize the large groups of immigrant workers in heavy industry. Many members of the labor movement, including a strong minority within the AFL itself, wanted to change the organization's nature — to add political activity to trade union methods, to abandon craft for industrial unions, and, above all, to "organize the unorganized." In the disturbed mid-1890s, this opposition got so strong that Gompers lost the leadership of the AFL for a year.

The mainstream of the American labor movement did not evince the anticapitalist rhetoric and radical ideology of some of its European counterparts, but this did not mean that nineteenth-century workers were contented or that no industrial strife existed. History of the period bristles with accounts of violent labor-management struggles — the most violent, thought the young Winston Churchill at the turn of the century, of any western industrial nation. In the two decades after 1880 there were some 23,000 strikes involving more than 6.5 million workers. Sometimes, as in the railroad strikes of 1877 or the Pullman Strike of 1894, the turmoil spanned much of the continent. In other cases, as in the Chicago Haymarket riot or in the steel strike at Carnegie's Homestead, Pennsylvania, plant in 1892, the violence was localized. Whatever their scope, some encounters were marked by pitched gunfire-and-dynamite battles between workers and industrial guards. In the great interstate railroad convulsion of 1877 workers fought militia in Baltimore, Buffalo, Chicago, Pittsburgh, and San Francisco until order was restored by federal troops. More than 100 workers were killed in some two weeks of turmoil that paralyzed rail traffic from West Virginia to California. Incredibly, only 3 Pinkerton strikebreakers and 10 workers died in an exchange of rifle and cannon fire at Homestead 15 years later, but some 8,000 state militia were used to crush the strike of some 4,000 steel workers. In these and in the great majority of the period's work stoppages, the workers' grievances were legitimate and their objectives were limited. But management routinely portrayed all strikes as revolutionary activity, and government (local, state, and federal) usually intervened at management's request.

Although strikes generally centered on such bread-and-butter issues as wages and hours, much of the period's unrest can also be traced to worker resentment of a modernizing economy. Industrialization required cultural as well as economic adjustments. Many people entered the factories with the pre-industrial work habits of farmers and artisans. Both native- and foreign-born "prefactory" peoples rarely shared the industrialists' notions of time and labor, and resisted adopting the work ethic so highly prized by cost-conscious managers. Accustomed to the irregular rhythms of agriculture, the farm folk often resented the rapid pace and rigid discipline of clock, steam, and electricity. The craftsmen watched in alarm as their status declined and their skills were rendered obsolete by machine production. Few welcomed the repetitive specialization of labor required by the factory system. Except for such examples as the Knights of St. Crispin, which struggled futilely to prevent the mechanization of boot and shoemaking in the 1870s and the scattered acts of machine-smashing during the 1877 railroad strike, however, organized expressions of worker hostility to modernization were rare. Yet the conflict between old ways and new expectations accounts for much of the popular malaise of the Gilded Age and is part of the social costs of economic progress.

THE FARMERS AND POPULISM

Farmers also suffered from the effects of modernity. Although their problems in the three decades after 1865 were varied and complicated, the most pressing were international in scope. Almost without realizing it, once largely self-sufficient American farmers had become commercialized growers, who raised specialized cash crops for a wildly fluctuating international market. They competed not just with other American farmers but with farmers in Canada, Argentina, Russia, India, Australia, and New Zealand. The origins of this process can be traced to the staple-exporting economy of the colonial period (see Chapter 9). The process speeded up with the emergence of a national market economy in the early Republic and matured in the post–Civil War age of steam and electricity. The farmers' world was transformed by the revolutions in communication and transportation, which came with the intercontinental steamships, transcontinental railroads, and transoceanic cables that shrank the globe and forged an integrated international market.

In such a market — where vast new crop lands had opened and productivity had increased with the application of machines and science — supply quickly outstripped demand, and the price of farm commodities fell. Saddled with the high fixed costs of land and machinery, farmers responded by growing ever larger crops, further aggravating their problems. They sold the products they raised in a free market, but had to buy the manufactured goods they needed from a tariff–protected market. The consequences for the farmers were chronic indebtedness and acute distress.

Although the uncertainties of modern agriculture were often international in origin, farmers generally blamed conditions closer to home. Agriculturalists believed that the money supply was inadequate and inflexible and that retiring greenbacks, decreasing the number of banknotes in circulation, and above all taking silver out of the currency had been mistakes. Also, they blamed exploitative intermediaries: the railroads and grain elevators with their high rates, the bankers with their usurious interest, and the tariff–protected farm implement combines with their monopoly prices.

These ills were compounded in two regions by local conditions. The over-expanded wheat farmers of the plains were hit by devastating droughts, and in 1887 an especially sharp price fall toppled their inflated credit structure. Southern farmers found that the sharecrop and crop-lien systems, which had evolved during the postwar shortage of capital, served neither the landlords nor their tenants well. The region suffered, moreover, from an oppressive racial climate that subordinated all issues to that of white supremacy. Occasionally and in only a few southern states did agrarian radicals, spokesmen for white dirt-farmers, make common cause with black farmers against railroads and landlords. Discontented poor whites were apt to blame their troubles on their black neighbors and to classify their enemies as "nigger lovers."

Though independent and, in many ways, conservative, farmers of all sections were not reluctant to organize or to ask the government to help relieve their distress. Their demands took two forms: inflation to bring their prices up, and regulation to bring their costs down. Toward these ends they turned, in succession, to the Patrons of Husbandry (the Grange), the Greenback-Labor party, the Farmers' Alliance Movement, and the Peoples' (or Populist) party. Of these, the two parties were avowedly political. The other two, the Grange movement and the Alliances, *officially* eschewed politics in favor of social and educational functions and such activities as cooperative grain elevators, marketing associations, and general stores. Both, however, were effective political pressure groups and influenced state legislatures. Reaching peak strength in 1874 with more than one million members, mostly in the South and Midwest, the Grange gave its name to state laws regulating railroads and grain elevators; many of these Granger laws were invalidated by the Supreme Court in the 1880s. The Alliances, really three distinct networks (the Northwestern, the Southern, and the Colored Alliances), flourished in the 1880s with a combined membership of four to five million. These organizations advocated reforms like free coinage of silver, a federal income tax, direct election of senators, and regulation or nationalization of transportation and communication companies. In 1890, Alliance candidates ran so well in the gubernatorial, legislative, and congressional races of southern and plains states that the movement formed the Peoples' party two years later.

The first Populist platform, drawn up at the party's initial national convention in Omaha in 1892, summarized, in angry and dramatic language, most of the discontent of the period. It called for inflation by using legal tender notes, silver, and other methods. Railroad land grants were to be recovered, and aliens were to be forbidden land ownership. Railroads and telephone and telegraph industries were to be nationalized. In an effort to attract labor support, the platform called for the eight-hour day, immigration restriction, and the abolition of Pinkerton industrial detectives. Miscellaneous radical sentiment was cultivated by denunciation of land monopoly, demand for the income tax, and a general statement that the powers of government should be extended as much as was necessary to secure the end of injustice and poverty. Finally, expressing the deep confidence in increased democracy of most American radicalism, the platform praised the *initiative* (a petition by which voters propose a law) and the *referendum* (the submission of a law to popular vote) and called for direct election of senators. Running on this platform, General James B. Weaver, the first Populist candidate for the presidency, received a million votes.

Stirred by this promising first effort, some hopeful radicals believed that the Populist movement was going to sweep to power, uniting all the diverse kinds of discontent, upsetting the two-party system as the Republicans had in 1856–1860, and driving out the monopolists and "gold bugs" (advocates of a single monetary standard: gold).

CLEVELAND'S LAST STAND

Despite the Populist showing, their goals had no currency with the winning Democratic candidate, Grover Cleveland. The 1892 election brought to the presidency a conservative representative of the eastern and hard-money wing of the Democratic party. When the Panic of '93 swept banks and railroads into bankruptcy and depression set in and unemployment soared, he doggedly opposed not only the high tariff but inflation. At every cost, he believed, demagogues and meddlers must be restrained while the immutable law of supply and demand effected recovery.

Cleveland's immediate problem was an inadequate supply of gold to meet current treasury obligations. The prohibitive rates of the McKinley Tariff had cut federal income, while expenditures had been increased during the previous administration by political appropriations for internal improvements, pensions, and especially payments for silver under the Sherman Silver Purchase Act. Cleveland succeeded in repealing the act. To cut federal spending further, he vetoed pensions and other pork-barrel legislation; to replenish gold reserves, his administration sold government bonds for gold and borrowed from the Morgan banking syndicate. These actions met the crisis of a continuing gold drain, but they alienated many Democrats. As a result, Cleveland lost congressional support for effective tariff reform and later lost control of his party.

In the congressional elections of 1894, the Republican opposition swept Congress and the Populists increased their popular vote by 40 percent. That year the Pullman strike, the most serious of the period, began after the financially pinched company fired one-third of its workers and slashed wages by 30 to 40 percent. Pullman workers then flocked to join Eugene V. Debs's American Railway Union, and the strike spread west beyond Chicago. With turmoil threatening to tie up essential transportation, a federal judge (under authority of the Sherman Anti-Trust Act) ordered Debs to end it. That order failed, so Cleveland ill-advisedly sent in federal troops on the request of the union-busting railroad General Managers' Association. Debs went to jail; when he emerged, he was a socialist.

The Pullman strike aroused fears of widespread social disorder in a time of severe depression. Conservatives were alarmed again when an "army" of the unemployed marched on Washington under the leadership of ex-Greenbacker Jacob Coxey and others. Neither large nor revolutionary, the object of these groups was to dramatize the plight of the jobless and to demand federal works programs. While trying to address a rally near the Capitol, Coxey was arrested for walking on the grass. His army, only about 500 men, women and children, peacefully melted away.

Although Cleveland remained confident that his laissez-faire policies would cure the nation's economic problems, a challenge to the status quo far more formidable than Coxey's would soon emerge from his own party.

THE BATTLE OF '96

Republican presidential candidate William McKinley was a former congressman and governor from Ohio. Nominated on a hard-money, protectionist platform, McKinley was best known for the high tariff that bore his name. Behind him stood Senator Marcus Alonzo Hanna, an Ohio industrialist and talented Republican party kingpin. To run opposite McKinley, the Democrats offered 36-year-old William Jennings Bryan. At their national convention, the former Nebraska congressman, a political spellbinder who backed the free coinage of silver, had swept Democrats off their feet by his "cross-of-gold" speech.

For the first time since 1860, the parties were clearly divided on a single issue. To the silver forces, Bryan was a knight in armor riding to do battle for the little man. His credentials as the "great commoner" were so impeccable that he ran as the presidential nominee of the Populists and the National Silver Republicans as well as the Democrats. To conservative gold-bugs, on the other hand, he was an anarchist, an atheist, and a wild-eyed "Demo-Pop." No radical, he was thoroughly traditional in religion and morality and reflected the aspirations of millions of Westerners and Southerners who felt alienated by an industrial order. When the votes were counted, however, McKinley had won handily.

Among the possible explanations for Bryan's defeat are the rise in farm prices and Republican pressure tactics reportedly used on factory workers. Another plausible reason is that in 1896 the forces of discontent were either not strong enough or not united enough to prevail against a skillful and well-financed opposition. Conservatives thought McKinley's victory ended the threat to the status quo and gave a green light for prosperity. This impression deepened when good times returned soon after the election. Discoveries in South Africa and Alaska increased the supply of gold and thus of dollars. European crop failures and rising industrial production helped to raise the farmer's prices. For the next several decades, many farmers would enjoy a golden age, and the disadvantaged seemed to have no taste for crusades.

In the South, similarly, normality of a sort returned. In North Carolina at the height of the Populist excitement, some blacks had achieved political office. Now the frustrated agrarian radicals nearly all returned to militant segregationism, a position many of them had never left. For another two generations, Southerners stood united in defense of white supremacy.

Critics of the status quo, however, had not lost all. In the fashion of American third parties, the Populists did not win the presidency, but most of their programs eventually won the favor of one or both major parties. Moreover, a small minority of determined radicals emerged from the Pullman strike and other defeats of the 1890s to provide articulate criticism of American society in the next generation. The Socialist party, formed in 1901, became something close to a coalition of American radicals under the leadership of Eugene V. Debs.

Few of the middle-class reformers who had been aroused by late-nineteenth-century problems returned to a belief in laissez faire. Though they did not agree on any overall social analysis or program, they continued to press for particular governmental actions to redress grievances. Thus the 1890s laid down the lines on which conservatives, liberals, and radicals would argue for the next half-century. In domestic controversy and, as we shall see, in foreign policy the second Cleveland administration marked both an end and a beginning.

CONFLICTING HISTORICAL VIEWPOINTS: NO. 8

Was Populism Constructive?

Until after World War II, historians were generally sympathetic to Populism. Openly critical of the values and excesses of a business civilization, such early scholars as Solon Buck (The Agrarian Crusade, *1920) and John D. Hicks* (The Populist Revolt, *1931) saw much to admire in the Populist critique of an industrializing America. In his enormously influential synthesis, Hicks portrayed the Populists as constructive liberal reformers in the tradition of Jefferson and Jackson. Although their programs failed and white, urban-rural, farmer-labor coalition of democratic reform," Goodwyn their movement disintegrated, Hicks concluded that they not only focused the nation's attention on many of its gravest problems but offered an agenda for twentieth-century reform.*

Hicks's classic study remains the best point at which to begin a serious study of Populism, but during the 1950s, numerous revisionists questioned its interpretation. Disturbed by wartime fascism abroad and postwar Mc-Carthyism at home, these scholars probed the darker side of Populism. Unlike Hicks, they fastened on its anti-social and negative, rather than its constructive and positive, features. In Populism they discovered the antecedents of much that was distasteful and evil in American society. In an essay in The Radical Right *(Daniel Bell, ed., 1963), Peter Vierick, for example, found in Populism "a mania of xenophobia, Jew-baiting, intellectual-baiting, and thought-controlling lynch-spirit"; Victor Ferkiss uncovered "Populist Influences on American Fascism" (Western Political Quarterly, June 1957). The behavioral scientists were generally the most critical, but it was the historian Richard Hofstadter who offered the most persuasive revision of the Hicks thesis. In his Pulitzer Prize–winning* Age of Reform *(1955), this distinguished scholar acknowledged "much that is good and usable in our Populist past." Yet he noted much more that was retrograde and sinister. He faulted the benighted Populists for their chimerical remedies and romantic longings for a "lost agrarian Eden" as well as for their nativism, anti-Semitism, and paranoia — irrational obsessions that he believed foreshadowed twentieth-century authoritarianism.*

At its best, as in Hofstadter's work, revisionism presented a subtle and suggestive argument that enriched our knowledge of agrarian unrest. More often, however, Populism's critics were neither temperate nor convincing. Yet, while their conclusions said more about their fears for the present than about their understanding of the past, they did provoke a reexamination of the nature of Populism. In the 1960s, a decade of reawakened interest in radical causes, a body of widely varying studies emerged to rehabilitate the Populist image in scholarly literature. Among the first of these was C. Vann Woodward's "The Populist Heritage and the Intellectual" (American Scholar, 1959), a moderate and judicious essay that praised the southern Populists for their noble but abortive experiment in racial accommodation. Similarly, Walter Nugent's The Tolerant Populists *(1963) celebrated broad-minded Kansas agrarian reformers, and Norman Pollack's* The Populist Response to Industrial America *(1962) portrayed humane and radical midwestern farmers who sought realistic solutions to the evils of industrialism. Robert F. Durden's* The Climax of Populism *(1965) denied that Populists were radical, but he absolved them of retrogressive and nativist tendencies; Michael Rogin's* The Intellectuals and McCarthy *(1967) used statistical methods to prove that Populism was not the ancestor of McCarthyism.*

The most sweeping account of Populist virtue came with the publication of Lawrence Goodwyn's Democratic Promise: The Populist Moment in America *(1976). Uncommonly passionate, this influential study has replaced Hicks's* Populist Revolt *as the standard history in the field. Praising the noble, unsuccessful effort of the Populists to build a "multisectional, black-*

viewed their movement as a valid alternative to both socialism and capitalism. Growing out of the Farmers' Alliance movement, the Populists were the architects of a "culture of generosity," the hopeful builders of a cooperative commonwealth, and the "last American reformers with authentic cultural credentials to solicit mass support for the idea of achieving the democratic organization of an industrialized society." In the last two decades, Goodwyn's Populists have come under attack from a number of critics, who note that Populism took different forms in various parts of the country and who believe Goodwyn overemphasized the radicalizing nature of the Alliance cooperative movement. Nevertheless, no new comprehensive synthesis on the order of Hicks, Hofstadter, or Goodwyn has yet emerged.

FOR FURTHER READING

Daniel Walker Howe's *Victorian America* (1976) is an important anthology of the period's social thought. Charles H. Hopkins examines *The Rise of the Social Gospel in American Protestantism* (1967), and Susan Curtis's *A Consuming Faith* (1991) surveys the lives of fifteen leading social gospel advocates. Irvin G. Wyllie in *The Self-Made Man in America* (1954) examines the impact of change on social thought and myth. The starting place for city problems is *The Rise of the City* (1933) by Arthur M. Schlesinger, Sr.; Raymond Mohl's *The New City* (1985) is a more recent synthesis that incorporates the scholarship of the new urban historians; and William Cronon's *Nature's Metropolis* (1991) is an intriguing study of urban growth in Chicago. John Bodnar in *The Transplanted* (1985) and Alan M. Kraut in *The Huddled Masses* (1982) convey the immigrant's point of view, while Susan Glenn in *Daughters of the Shtetl* (1990) focuses specifically on the experiences of female immigrants. John Higham in *Strangers in the Land* (1955) and David H. Bennett in *The Party of Fear* (1989) analyze native hostility to immigrants; both Robert C. Bannister in *Social Darwinism* (1988) and Richard Hofstadter in *Social Darwinism in American Thought* (1944) consider the impact of evolution on the Gilded Age. Good introductions to the labor movement include Herbert Gutman's *Work, Culture and Society in Industrializing America* (1976), David Montgomery's *The Fall of the House of Labor* (1987), Bruce Laurie's *Artisans into Workers* (1989), and Melvyn Dubofsky's *The State and Labor in Modern America* (1994). For the perspective of a radical labor spokeswoman, see the memoir of anarchist Emma Goldman, *Living My Life* (1931). Additional examinations of the farmers' revolt can be found in Bruce Palmer, *"Man Over Money"* (1980); Steven Hahn, *The Roots of Southern Populism* (1983); and Robert McMath, *American Populism* (1993). Among the many fine autobiographies, see especially those of Jane Addams, Samuel Gompers, and William Allen White. Among innumerable biographies: C. Vann Woodward, *Tom Watson* (1938); Clifford H. Scott, *Lester Frank Ward* (1976); Paolo E. Coletta, *William Jennings Bryan* (3 vols., 1964–1971); and Nick Salvatore, *Eugene V. Debs* (1982). Robert H. Wiebe's *The Search for Order, 1877–1920* (1967) is a penetrating analysis, useful for this chapter and the three following.

MAP 7: AMERICAN OVERSEAS EXPANSION TO 1917

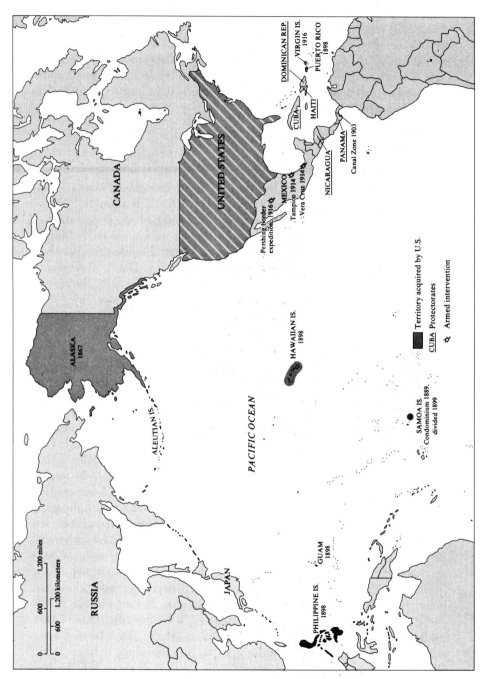

VIRGIN IS. 1916

DOMINICAN REP.

PUERTO RICO 1898

CUBA

HAITI

PANAMA
Canal Zone 1903

NICARAGUA

MEXICO
Tampico 1914
Vera Cruz 1914

Pershing border
expedition, 1916

UNITED STATES

CANADA

ALASKA
1867

ALEUTIAN IS.

HAWAIIAN IS.
1898

PACIFIC OCEAN

SAMOA IS.
Condominium 1889,
divided 1899

Territory acquired by U.S.

CUBA Protectorates

☆ Armed intervention

GUAM
1898

PHILIPPINE IS.
1898

JAPAN

RUSSIA

1,200 miles

1,200 kilometers

600

600

0

0

21

★ ★ ★ ★ ★ ★

Imperial America, 1898–1914

FROM THE PEACE of Ghent in 1814 until almost the end of the nineteenth century, the United States remained aloof from international power politics. It was able to do so because of a fortunate combination of circumstances: the European balance of power, British control of the high seas, and growing American *potential* for armed resistance. Very few nineteenth-century Americans realized the transitory nature of this combination. Most believed that American freedom from foreign danger was permanent and "natural." The United States, Americans believed, was the greatest nation on earth. Following the advice of the founders, the Republic chose to demonstrate this greatness only by peaceful growth.

Once colonial expansion was completed, public interest in foreign affairs, where it existed at all, concentrated on four traditional concerns. The first was a great sympathy for republican and constitutional institutions and a belief that the world was moving toward free government. Second, the public felt that the United States had a special interest in the Western Hemisphere since the Monroe Doctrine and should increasingly claim dominance in the Caribbean. Third, Americans had a special, and highly ambivalent, relationship with England. This led to frequent clashes over such issues as the boundaries of New World British possessions, American sympathy for Canadian rebellion, use of the Newfoundland fishing grounds, and British interest in Central America. These clashes often led to violent denunciation from both sides, but all were settled peaceably, usually by British concessions made partly in the interest of commerce. The fourth concern was the desire to expand foreign trade, especially in the Far East. Partly the unrealized dream of a commercial minority, this concern led to the establishment of relations with Japan, China, and Korea, the acquisition of a few tiny Pacific islands, and the development of a protectorate in Hawaii.

THE END OF ISOLATION

Historians have often seen the Spanish-American War of 1898 as a watershed, a clear departure from the past, the point of American emergence into world politics. Yet the extent of change can be exaggerated. All four traditional concerns mentioned above were involved in the crisis of the 1890s. There was no sudden increase of American might; since industrialization, the United States had been a potential great power. Nor did 1898 mark a sudden, permanent shift in popular interest. After a flurry of argument over imperialism, most Americans resumed, in the early twentieth century, their habitual concentration on home affairs. However, 1898 did mark something of a change in American commitments. From this point on, both the United States and the European powers assumed that America had some interest in world crises ranging from North Africa to the Far East.

Many reasons have been given for this change. The most obvious suggestion embodies the traditional economic interpretation of imperialism: the American economy had reached maturity and therefore America, like other advanced industrial countries, needed new raw materials and foreign markets. Some historians, arguing that the growing economy still absorbed most of the nation's productive energies, would deny substantial connection between American expansion abroad and internal American economic development. The connection, however, was frequently made by turn-of-the-century farmers and business people who, particularly after the depression of 1893, saw a relationship between domestic prosperity and foreign markets. Although most business leaders, like most citizens, were probably anticolonialists, there was nonetheless a highly articulate and influential group of business leaders who believed that industrial overproduction and recurrent panics required secure overseas markets and sources of natural supply. Similarly, western farmers, who were themselves business people and under pressure from mounting surpluses, frequently were among the expansionists who looked to outside markets for relief. Although American foreign policy was not driven by the single engine of materialism, economic considerations played a leading role in the tragicomedy of American expansion.

Other explanations for the departures in foreign policy include the revival and restatement of "manifest destiny" in the form of Anglo-Saxonism — the idea that the racially superior "Anglo-Teutonic" American nation had a civilizing mission beyond its New World continent. In an age when many native whites confidently claimed superiority over blacks and new immigrants, whites believed that the world's savage, heathen masses would benefit from the extension of white civilization. Often racism of this kind was linked to the pseudoscience of Social Darwinism; strong races, it was alleged, needed warlike competition to maintain their virility.

Divine obligation was another factor in foreign policy changes. Evangelical Protestants — particularly denominations with foreign missions — promoted an imperialism of righteousness in which Americans would lead, not merely by remote example but by their physical presence among the unredeemed races. The most influential exponent of this doctrine was the Reverend Josiah Strong, author of the best-selling *Our Country* (1885); he urged the United States, with its Anglo-Saxon "genius for colonizing," to spread the blessings of Protestantism and democracy "down upon Mexico . . . Central and South America, out upon the islands of the sea, over upon Africa and beyond." Strong reminded his readers of the practical implications of America's overseas presence: the civilizing process creates "more and higher wants," and "commerce follows the missionary."

For equally practical, though military reasons, Strong's grandiose vision was also shared by the nation's naval lobby and especially by Captain Alfred T. Mahan, president of the Naval War College and student of seapower's influence on history. A modern agricultural and industrial nation, Mahan reasoned, needed overseas markets for its surpluses, and exploitation of overseas markets required an efficient merchant marine and the protection of a strong navy, both of which, in turn, meant acquiring overseas harbors and coaling stations. Thus, a great nation must be expansionist.

Expansion in general and an enlarged navy in particular were strongly advocated by the nation's "foreign policy elite," a group of able and highly placed men, most of whom had upper-class eastern backgrounds. An early representative was William H. Seward, the secretary of state (1861–1869) who added Alaska and Midway Island to the national domain and who spoke as early as 1850 of "the empire of the seas" as the only true empire. At the turn of the century, the elite's brightest and most articulate members included: Senator Henry Cabot Lodge of Massachusetts, member of the Senate Foreign Relations Committee; Theodore Roosevelt, McKinley's assistant secretary of the navy; and Elihu Root, a future secretary of war. Roosevelt was perhaps the most aggressively imperialist and belligerent, but his attitudes were not unrepresentative of his time and class. A historian of American naval and Indian fighting as well as a politician, Roosevelt believed that war — any "righteous" war — would unite the country, divert it from "sordid" issues, and promote manly virtues in its youth.

American expansionism must also be viewed in the wider context of the balance of power and a second great era of European imperialism. Many of the major European nations, driven by much the same forces that were driving Americans to expand, were already vying for territory and influence in the world's underdeveloped regions. These examples whetted the American appetite for empire. Having carved up Africa, the European powers began looking toward two remaining areas: the Near East occupied by the weak Ottoman Empire, and the Far East occupied by the still weaker empire of China. Each empire was thought to be too rich a plum to fall to any single European power, however, so the western nations agreed to support the independence of both empires, while staking out their own spheres of economic influence and uneasily eyeing each other.

A final reason for change in U.S. foreign policy was the fact that established patterns of influence were in flux. Since the German victory over France in 1871, the continent had been dominated by a recently unified Germany and its allies, while the seas were controlled by Great Britain. In the 1890s, the situation grew more fluid. Germany, under its ambitious young ruler Wilhelm II, challenged Britain with a program of naval construction. Britain, sensitive to threats to her sprawling empire, began to cast about for allies. In the Far East, a new power, Japan, was challenging traditional Russian interests in Korea and Manchuria. Inevitably, the new-found interest of the United States in world affairs drew the attention of the other nations.

All these forces are reflected in the developments of 1898. First the United States became involved in an avoidable, if minor, conflict for a seemingly traditional reason: political liberty in the Western Hemisphere. Then the war shifted to the Far East, where the American dream of commerce with the Orient was reawakened. Backed by a rising chorus of imperialist arguments, the nation became involved in great power politics.

FORERUNNERS OF EXPANSION

Some political leaders and many influential opinion shapers showed an early interest first in the Caribbean and then in the Pacific area. Secretary of State Seward had acquired the first noncontiguous territories for the nation, but he had failed in his post–Civil War dream of annexing Caribbean bases. President Grant also had expansionist aspirations toward the Dominican Republic. In the 1880s, struggling against the high tide of popular isolationism, Secretary of State James G. Blaine (1881, 1889–1892) sought unsuccessfully again for Caribbean footholds and wrangled with Britain over rights to build a canal across the Isthmus of Panama. His successor, Frederick Freylinghuysen, negotiated a canal treaty with Nicaragua in 1884 that died in the Senate. Back as Secretary of State in 1889, Blaine broached the idea of Pan-Americanism: Western Hemispheric unity under U.S. leadership. The Pan American Conference of 1889 was ineffectual, however, and Pan-Americanism itself was damaged by Blaine's high-handed efforts to mediate South American disputes. Hemispheric unity was also impaired in 1891 when the United States seemed to threaten war with Chile over a waterfront riot involving American sailors.

The most important overseas ventures in this period took place in the Pacific. American interest in the distant and primitive Samoan archipelago was primarily naval, and a clash with Germany led, in 1889, to the establishment of a joint Anglo-German-American protectorate in Samoa. U.S. involvement in the Hawaiian Islands was more significant. Since the beginning of the 1800s the islands had been visited by American traders, whalers, and missionaries. Their descendants had become prosperous sugar planters who held the power in the islands' picturesque native monarchy. From 1842 on, the United States repeatedly asserted its claim to Hawaiian trade; in the 1880s Secretary Blaine warned potential rivals that the islands were "essentially part of the American system." Under an earlier treaty (1875), Hawaiian sugar entered the rich American market duty free, and in 1887 the United States was granted exclusive rights to Pearl Harbor. Political absorption came after 1893 when the white minority — its sugar economy jeopardized by new tariff arrangements and its influence threatened by the Hawaiian nationalism of a new native monarch — toppled popular Queen Liliuokalani. The revolution was encouraged by the American ambassador and was assisted by American troops. Although this planters' republic was immediately recognized by the United States, efforts to gain formal annexation were frustrated by anti-imperialists (some of whom feared to absorb a racially mixed territory) until 1898.

Although the delay in Hawaii's annexation may be largely attributed to the anti-colonialist sensibilities of President Cleveland, even he had no reluctance in asserting American hegemony in the Caribbean. For some time the British had tried to redraw a disputed boundary between British Guiana and Venezuela; in 1895, when Britain rejected American pressure to arbitrate, Secretary of State Richard Olney warned that the United States was "practically sovereign in this hemisphere." Anglophobes called for war, and for once the Cleveland administration was almost popular. Preoccupied with a colonial crisis in South Africa and concerned about its lack of allies, Britain submitted to arbitration. While the episode did not indicate that the United States was in fact sovereign in the whole hemisphere, it did suggest that American power in the Caribbean might soon equal its interest there.

The most pressing challenge to American control of the Caribbean was in Cuba. A remnant of Spain's once-great New World empire, Cuba was chronically rebellious, yet no Spanish government could afford to let it go. Following a bloody and failed insurrection ending in 1878, Cuba enjoyed comparative prosperity, sustained by the American sugar market and enhanced by the McKinley Tariff of 1890, which made sugar duty-free. Then in 1894, when the sugar duty was restored by the Wilson-Gorman Tariff, Cuba faced a depression, and another insurrection set in. The insecure Spanish talked of eventual concessions but embarked on brutal repression of the Cubans. Spanish atrocities and Cuban suffering, exaggerated but not unfounded, were deplored in the sensationalist American newspapers of Joseph Pulitzer and William Randolph Hearst. Patriotic groups, labor organizations, reformers, and members of Congress demanded American intervention. President Cleveland resisted pressure for war and urged Spain to grant Cuba autonomy.

"THE SPLENDID LITTLE WAR"

Inaugurated in 1897, President McKinley represented a more expansionist party and was himself an advocate for a strong navy. Nevertheless, he was devoted to peace on religious grounds. His government appeared to be progressing toward obtaining major Spanish concessions in Cuba when two accidents killed all chance for peace. First, the de Lome letter fell into the hands of the American press; this unflattering characterization of McKinley was written by the Spanish minister in Washington. Second and far more important was the loss of the *U.S.S. Maine* in February 1898. Sent to Cuba on a "courtesy visit," the American naval vessel was blown up at anchor in Havana Harbor, and 260 men were killed.

Although prominent political and business leaders urged calm, "yellow journalists" and other hawks called for war. McKinley temporized, hoping to preserve the peace, while jingoists in his own party likened his backbone to "a chocolate eclair." The Spanish to avoid war recalled de Lome, expressed sympathy for the dead, and denied (with truth, it seems almost certain) responsibility for the marine disaster. On American demand, Spain abandoned its concentration camps for Cuban civilians and with reluctance and delay agreed to request an armistice with the rebellious Cubans, but not to submit to American mediation.

But the pressure for war against Spain was too great in the United States. Alarmed by the swelling martial spirit, reluctant to divide the country, and afraid that Congress might declare war against his will, McKinley on April 11 requested authority to use arms to restore order in Cuba. A formal declaration of war came two weeks later. Although some thought it folly to fight for a territory that would not be annexed, anti-imperialists in Congress pushed through the "Teller Resolution" binding the United States not to take over the island.

War with Spain, it seemed, offered something to everyone. Many business people, although initially not eager for a war for Cuban independence, now agreed with farmers and agro-industrialists like meatpackers and flour millers that Spain had been an obstacle to developing a flourishing export market. Expansionists saw the war as an opportunity for new territory. Humanitarians and evangelicals hoped that the banishment of the Catholic oppressor would bring opportunities of another sort.

Most Americans, however much they saw opportunities in Cuba, knew little about Spain's larger colony in the Far East, the Philippine Islands, where another colonial rebellion was under way. Theodore Roosevelt, as assistant secretary of the navy, was aware of these Pacific islands and had directed Commodore George Dewey to assemble the United States Asiatic Squadron at Hong Kong and to prepare, in the event of war over Cuba, to attack the Spanish fleet in Manila Bay. Roosevelt's purpose — whether it was American rule of the Philippines or obtaining a new coaling station — is subject to debate. On May 1, however, Dewey issued his celebrated order: "You may fire when ready, Gridley." The Spanish fleet of 10 ships was destroyed, without any American lives lost. This victory delighted press and public, and one newspaper called it "the greatest naval engagement of modern times." Dewey had no force to occupy Manila; troops arrived months later, and with the support of the Filipino leader Emilio Aguinaldo, they took the city the day after the war ended. Native insurgents and Spaniards were left to dispute posession of the rest of the archipelago.

Meantime, in the Caribbean the war proceeded far less favorably at first. American coastal cities panicked at mythical reports of Spanish raids, and mobilization was inefficient. Confusion marred the encampment of American forces in Florida and their embarkation for Cuba. Fortunately for the United States, Spanish equipment, tactics, and morale were in worse shape.

With the Spanish fleet cornered in Santiago Bay, in mid-June the Americans landed an invasion force of 17,000 troops. Among them were four regiments of black soldiers whom awed Spaniards called "Smoked Yankees"; also present were two other units: "Teddy's Terrors," the horseless regiment of Ivy League polo players, cowboys, and western badmen who made up Roosevelt's fabled Rough Riders; and the soldiers led by "Fighting Joe" Wheeler, the aging, former Confederate officer who reportedly cried, "We've got the damn Yankees on the run!" A number of small but bloody engagements during the approach to Santiago gave Americans, including Colonel Roosevelt, a chance to prove their courage under fire. On July 3 the decrepit Spanish fleet sailed bravely out of the harbor to meet certain destruction by American naval gunfire, and on July 17 Santiago surrendered, leaving the United States in control of eastern Cuba. In early August, General Nelson A. Miles completed a nearly bloodless conquest of Spain's Puerto Rico, and the fighting ended.

Even so, the United States was not in an easy position. American forces occupied only one end of Cuba and one city in the Philippines. Dressed in blue winter uniforms, equipped with obsolete Springfield rifles, and fed on hardtack and repulsive canned meat (called by the press "embalmed beef"), American forces in Cuba were ridden with dysentery and malaria and threatened with yellow fever. Lieutenant Colonel Roosevelt, among others, was demanding their recall. At home in the Florida camps, because of disgraceful neglect of sanitation, disease was spreading. Many more lives were lost by disease than by enemy action; of the 5,462 American dead, only 379 died in combat.

Fortunately for the United States, Spain, without a navy and even more poorly prepared than the Americans, had no hope of continuing hostilities. On August 12, 1898, scarcely four months after war began, an armistice was signed. Secretary Hay pronounced it "a splendid little war." Colonel Roosevelt later allegedly declared, "It wasn't much of a war, but it was the best war we had."

PEACE AND EMPIRE

As armistice terms, the United States insisted that Spain withdraw from Cuba and cede to the United States Puerto Rico, an island in the Ladrones (Guam), and the city and harbor of Manila. The fate of the rest of the Philippines (more than 7,000 large and small islands with about eight million people) was decided during the peace conference. At first reluctant to annex much distant territory, McKinley feared another upsurge of public opinion like that which had swept the country into war. Eventually he convinced himself that it was the duty of the United States to "uplift and civilize" the entire Philippines. Reluctantly, Spain agreed to cede them in exchange for $20 million.

In the Senate, the treaty faced serious opposition from the anti-imperialists. This diverse coalition included most northern Democrats and the familiar minority of eastern, reform-minded Republicans. It brought together such contrasting individuals as Bryan, Cleveland, Andrew Carnegie, Samuel Gompers, and Mark Twain. Libertarians argued passionately that empire over subject peoples would violate the Declaration of Independence and the Monroe Doctrine. Others pointed out that the Constitution provided no way of governing territories never destined to become states. Racists insisted that Filipinos were unassimilable, and strategists argued, more persuasively, that a Far Eastern possession would endanger American security.

On the other side, the treaty's proponents argued that the flag, once planted overseas, should not be pulled down, that annexation represented the will of God, and that it was America's duty to Christianize the Philippines (which were actually one of the principal outposts of Christianity in the Far East). The strong interest of Japan and Germany in the spoils of the Spanish Empire furnished another argument for annexation. Germany eventually picked up the Caroline Islands and all the Ladrones (Marianas) except Guam. The business community, in its concern for the expansion and protection of foreign trade, favored retention of the Philippines. Annexationists also pointed to strategic considerations: both Hawaii and the Philippines would be useful to the United States in resisting European encroachment on China.

Reluctantly the conservative Senate leadership agreed to go along with the president. Yet the opposing sides remained fairly even. The treaty would not have passed had not Bryan, as head of the Democratic party, decided to support the treaty and fight the issue of annexation in the coming election.

In their 1900 convention, the Democrats declared that anti-imperialism was the "paramount issue"; the Republicans accepted the challenge. Theodore Roosevelt, one of the war's principal heroes, campaigned as McKinley's running mate. It cannot be proved that McKinley's solid victory constituted an endorsement of annexation, however. Many voted once more for the gold standard, the high tariff, and prosperity.

Perhaps the strongest real reason for retaining the Philippines was the lack of a clear alternative. It was obviously out of the question to suppress the revolt and return the islands to Spain, and nobody wanted to hand them to Germany or Japan. Disunited and in places uncivilized, the islands seemed unable to sustain independence without at least the protection of the United States. Yet many continued to feel that annexation was a mistake, both moral and strategic.

The imperialist tide carried with it not only the Philippines, Puerto Rico, and Guam, but also Hawaii and Samoa. Increased American concern with the Far East in general, together with a competing Japanese interest in the Hawaiian Islands and Hawaii's commercial and military usefulness, furnished decisive arguments for their annexation in 1898. In 1899, the Samoan protectorate was ended and the islands were divided between Germany and the United States.

Meanwhile in Cuba, which the United States had sworn not to annex,

American forces, performing a heroic job of cleaning up yellow fever, quarreled with their Cuban allies. In 1902, the Americans withdrew, but not before the Platt Amendment was incorporated into the Cuban-American treaty and the Cuban constitution, making Cuba a virtual American protectorate. This measure granted the United States both the right to intervene in Cuban affairs to insure continued Cuban independence and stability (and it did intervene in 1906 and several times thereafter), and an American naval station (Guantánamo) on the island. The much-resented Platt Amendment was abrogated during the 1930s, leaving Cuba politically, but not economically, independent of the United States.

America's imperial experience started tragically. Aguinaldo's Filipino insurgents, bitter at not receiving the national independence that they thought had been promised, proclaimed a Philippine Republic and turned their guerrilla tactics against the United States. In the ensuing war, which lasted until 1902 (and broke out occasionally until 1906), about 5,000 Americans, 20,000 guerrillas, and 200,000 Filipino civilians died in combat or from disease. Having promised to bring these Asians "the good-will, the protection, and the richest blessings of a liberating rather than a conquering nation," the United States grossly underestimated Filipino desires for independence and paid both moral and material costs of empire. Although both sides committed atrocities, humanitarians recognized that American counterinsurgents employed the same savage measures that Spain had used in Cuba. As if to complete the mockery of the nation's ideals, the Supreme Court in the so-called Insular Cases ruled that the Constitution did not follow the flag and that its safeguards (including protection against internal tariffs) need not be fully applied to "unincorporated territories."

Despite these ironies, the colonial record of the United States was relatively good, and its imperialism was more economic than political. Throughout its dependencies, American investments and exports mounted sharply, and despite the ruling of the Insular Cases, substantial free trade was established; good work in education, sanitation, and civil authority was undertaken. Movement toward popular government began with the establishment of a legislature in Puerto Rico in 1900, and the Puerto Ricans were given American citizenship in 1917. In 1901, civil goverment replaced military rule in the Philippines, which received an elective assembly in 1907. The Filipinos were slated for eventual independence (which came following World War II) and were, therefore, not granted citizenship.

POWER POLITICS

The American venture into empire fulfilled neither the worst fears of the anti-imperialists nor the grandest expectations of the imperialists. Yet its effects on foreign policy were profound. American hegemony in the Caribbean was underlined, and Britain, long the chief rival, acknowledged it. In the second Hay-Pauncefote Treaty of 1901, England acceded to American demands for exclusive control of the proposed Isthmian canal, abrogating her own treaty rights to equality in this venture. Conditioned in part by a developing German-British rivalry, Anglo-American accord flourished. British support during the Spanish-American War, British agreement on the common goals of stability and the status quo in the Caribbean and the Far East, and a common cultural and (some believed) racial heritage pleased many Americans. In the twentieth century, the great rapprochement was completed. As the great powers chose sides for the next war, it seemed logical that the United States would favor the Atlantic, rather than the Central European, powers.

The developing friendship between the United States and Britain proved useful in the Far East, where the American foothold was tenuous. Annexation of the Philippines greatly increased the United States' stake in world trade and global politics, a fact underscored by Asian developments at the close of the century. Since 1895, China, the "Sick Man of Asia," had been forced by Japan and the European colonial powers to surrender spheres of exclusive economic interest. Expressing concern for the "territorial integrity" of the disintegrating empire, Secretary of State John Hay dispatched the first of his Open Door notes. In identical messages to the six leading imperial rivals (Austria, England, France, Germany, Japan, and Russia), Hay asked for a guarantee of commercial equality for all nations within their spheres. The idea sat well with the British (its original authors), but the Russians refused and the others equivocated. Nonetheless, the audacious Hay announced that the powers had agreed to leave open the door to the China trade.

In 1900, Chinese resentment of foreign exploitation overflowed in the so-called Boxer Rebellion. In nationalistic rage against the "foreign devils," members of the secret Boxer society besieged the international legations in Beijing (Peking). The United States joined Japan and the European powers in suppressing this uprising. Hay, fearing that the disorders invited further dismemberment of the Celestial Kingdom, demanded "equal and impartial" trade arrangements for all nations throughout all of China.

The Open Door was more a reaffirmation of traditional American opposition to international trade barriers than it was a new policy. Although successive generations of Americans would interpret U.S. opposition to partition of China as a act of friendship, it was also aimed at protecting an Oriental market for American goods. Explicitly stating a long-standing principle, the Open Door notes became pillars of American diplomacy.

The new century brought a new president but no substantial change in foreign policy. Upon McKinley's assassination in 1901, Theodore Roosevelt became chief executive. Roosevelt was an expansionist who believed that peace and stability required the firm but benevolent supervision of the enlightened great powers. More knowledgeable and interested in foreign affairs than his immediate predecessors, he understood the relationship between power and policy. Yet in contradiction to his much-quoted adage, he often did not speak softly and his stick was sometimes not big enough.

A friend of John Hay and an apostle of what many called the "large policy," the Rough Rider dabbled in the troubled waters of the far Pacific with the enthusiasm that was his trademark. Suspicious of Russian designs on China and eager to maintain the balance of power in Asia, he supported "tiny Japan" in the Russo-Japanese War, fought over rival interests in Korea and Manchuria from 1904 to 1905. After a series of Japanese victories, he mediated the Peace of Portsmouth, which unfortunately satisfied neither belligerent. Try as he did thereafter, he found no effective way to cement Japanese-American relations nor to offset Japan's rising power. In the Taft-Katsura Agreement (1905), he won Japanese recognition of the American place in the Philippines by conceding Japanese suzerainty over Korea. When Japan protested the segregation of Oriental school children in San Francisco, he arranged an international compromise that ended the segregation (but not other forms of discrimination) and restricted Japanese immigration under a "gentlemen's agreement" (1907). So that this conciliatory gesture would not be seen as weakness, he dispatched the navy's Great White Fleet on a "practice cruise" around the world. Although the long-range effect of this ploy was probably an East-West naval arms race, it may also have produced the Root-Takahira Agreement (1908), in which the United States and Japan agreed to respect the "integrity of China" and the status quo in the Pacific. This agreement acknowledged Japan's dominance in Manchuria, and seemed to guarantee the safety of the Philippines. It had little effect, however, on the continuing slide of United States–Japanese relations.

BAD NEIGHBOR POLICY

In the Western Hemisphere, Roosevelt wielded policy with greater confidence. He viewed Latin America as a semi-barbaric American dependency in need of Anglo-Saxon guidance. Under his leadership, U.S. dominance of the Central American and Caribbean areas was all but completed. His most important initiative was getting an isthmian canal constructed. The Senate chose the Panamanian route over the Nicaraguan partly to appease powerful investors in the French Panama Canal Company. Panama was a Colombian province, however, and the Republic of Colombia refused the American terms. Never one to permit the "interest of collective civilization" to be blocked by "Dagoes," Roosevelt considered seizure, but decided on subtler tactics. With tacit American support, agents of the French company prompted restive Panamanians to declare their independence and to negotiate a canal-zone treaty favorable to the United States. The revolution succeeded only through Roosevelt's connivance and the timely intercession of the American navy; the affair represented a dark chapter in bad neighbor politics, and gave credibility to Latin cries of "Yankee imperialism." Later Colombia was compensated, and in 1914, the Panama Canal was opened on equal terms to all nations.

On two earlier occasions, the president had intervened when Venezuela and the Dominican Republic were threatened by foreign creditors for their bad debts. These experiences convinced him, however, that if the United

States wished to prevent European intrusions in the Western Hemisphere, it must police the "wretched republics" itself. This Roosevelt Corollary claimed for the United States, a "civilized nation," the right of intervention to prevent "chronic wrongdoing." The policy distorted the spirit of the Monroe Doctrine, and offered fresh evidence of an old determination to make the Caribbean an American lake. Although under the later administrations of Herbert Hoover and Franklin Roosevelt the United States did modify its policies and eventually repudiate the right of unilateral intervention, it intervened in the internal affairs of at least six hemispheric countries from 1900 to 1920.

Under William Howard Taft, Roosevelt's successor, American interventionism took a decidedly economic turn, while later under Woodrow Wilson, it assumed the form of a "missionary imperialism" in which the president asserted the American right to enlighten and uplift, by force if necessary. To the nation's southern neighbors, both variants seemed familiar. Far more than his predecessor, Taft believed in using American foreign investment as an instrument of policy. Skeptics called this "dollar diplomacy," but the Republican chief executive argued that furthering private ventures led to peace and prosperity for the recipient nations. But in the Caribbean, dollar diplomacy involved the United States in unpopular military ventures, while in the Far East, it led to a startling departure from realism. Roosevelt had recognized the limits of American power in Asia; Taft and his Secretary of State Philander Knox, on the other hand, tried to force American participation in Chinese railway development and to pry open the door to the Japanese sphere in Manchuria. Neither effort succeeded.

The liberal, idealistic Wilson administration repudiated the diplomacy of both Roosevelt's big stick and Taft's dollars. President Wilson promised a new diplomacy based not on American self-interest but on the highest humanitarian ideals. Some have found in his high moral purpose the standard for American international policy; others saw in it a naive misunderstanding of the nature of humanity and nations. Harbingers of the promised Wilsonian departure included: the appointment of William Jennings Bryan as secretary of state, perhaps the first pacifist to serve as foreign minister to a great power; the negotiation of a Senate-aborted treaty of compensation and apology for Colombia; the negotiation of some 30 unilateral "cooling-off treaties" designed to render war obsolete; and the appointment of a governor-general to prepare the Philippines for self-government.

Wilson, for all his sincere anticolonialism, was capable of expediency. He believed that capitalism marched hand in hand with democracy and that the spread of both was in the interest of all. He also agreed with Theodore Roosevelt that the autonomy of Latin American nations was conditional on the needs of American national security (particularly the Panama Canal) and on the orderly processes of just government. When the occasion required (as it seemed to occur more often under Wilson than under Roosevelt or Taft), he promoted stability and American ideals in Latin America with the U.S. Marines. He intervened in Cuba, established American protectorates in Haiti and the Dominican Republic, and supported a dictatorship in Nicaragua.

The most egregious conflict between principle and practice came during the Mexican Revolution, when he carried the United States to the brink of war in order to teach troubled Mexico "to elect good men."

Wilson's Mexican policies were apparently shaped more by his idealism and support for the liberal, democratic revolution initially led by Francisco Madero, than by the $2 billion in American investments in Mexico. Yet, though Wilson resisted the all-out war demanded by Rooseveltian nationalists and the business interests, he eventually emerged as the enemy of the revolution he had hoped to assist. The affair began in 1913 when, contrary to long-standing American precedent, Wilson withheld U.S. recognition from the government of General Victoriano Huerta, Madero's assassin, on the grounds that it had come to power undemocratically. Persuading the British to withdraw recognition, Wilson supplied arms to Huerta's major rival, Venustiano Carranza, and found a pretext to block a German munitions shipment to Huerta by seizing the Mexican port of Vera Cruz. Huerta abdicated in favor of Carranza.

Wilson then found the new provisional regime too radical and ill-disposed to American guidance, so he shifted his support from Carranza to Francisco "Pancho" Villa. Wilson thought that the picturesque border bandit was a broadly popular social reformer. Upon realizing his mistake, Wilson moved toward friendlier relations with Carranza, so Villa, desperate to provoke American intervention, raided a New Mexican town. Wilson sent a punitive expedition of 11,000 troops some 300 miles into Mexico. The elusive Villa escaped and the American troops were withdrawn, but not before they had clashed with Carranza forces. In the end, increasingly preoccupied with the war in Europe, Wilson formally recognized Carranza in March 1917.

That Carranza fulfilled many of the ideals of Mexico's revolution cannot be credited to Wilson. Despite promising a moral diplomacy, Wilson had intervened more high-handedly in the affairs of Latin America than either Roosevelt or Taft. However well intentioned, his spiritual imperialism left a heritage of inter-American mistrust.

CONFLICTING HISTORICAL VIEWPOINTS: NO. 9

Why Imperialism in 1898?

In 1968, at the very summit of the national debate over American interests in Southeast Asia, the historian Walter LaFeber wrote (Texas Quarterly, Winter 1968): *"The line from the conquest of the Philippines in 1898 to the attempted pacification of Vietnam . . . is not straight, but it is quite traceable." This interpretation of the events of 1898 was timely, but it was not new. Well before LaFeber's birth, Charles Beard had also concluded that America's turn-of-the-century imperialism was no accident but the result of "the present economic system."*

While others, notably Samuel Bemis (Diplomatic History of the United States, 1936), *viewed the Asian adventure of the 1890s as "The Great Aber-*

ration," unplanned and unrepeated, Beard (The Rise of American Civilization, *1927;* The Idea of National Interest, *1934) dismissed any "fortuitous aspects" in the events ending with the annexation of the Philippines. The road to empire, he believed, was paved with economic interest, and the Americans who followed it to Manila were unabashed commercial expansionists. To the dean of the "Old Left" historians, American imperialism, the natural culmination of "over a century of commercial development," owed little "to fate, the accidents of history, the current of events, destiny, and the gifts of the gods." In this judgment LaFeber, perhaps the most gifted of the New Left scholars, agreed. His* New Empire: American Expansion, 1860–1898 *(1963) emphasized "the economic forces that resulted in commercial and landed expansion," and his 1968 essay concluded that "the Spanish-American conflict can no longer be viewed as only a 'splendid little war.' It was a war to preserve the American system."*

The economic interpretation, although the oldest and most durable, has many critics. The most influential of these, Julius Pratt, author of The Expansionists of 1898 *(1936), after painstaking examination of the commercial press, asserted that "an overwhelming preponderance of the vocal business interests of the country strongly desired peace." Conceding that the business community wanted an expanded overseas trade, he contended nonetheless that most of them became imperialists only after the Spanish-American War began. To Pratt and many others, the Spanish-American War, although spurred by a yellow press and a martial temper, was a war to liberate Cuba. To be sure, it brought imperial opportunities that were welcomed by the business community — but these were windfalls.*

The question, of course, remains: Why imperialism? By reading these works and those listed below, the student may perhaps formulate his or her own answer.

FOR FURTHER READING

Charles S. Campbell's *Transformation of American Foreign Relations* (1976) is an admirable synthesis of scholarly work on the period from 1865 to 1900. An excellent account of the emergence of the United States into power politics is Ernest R. May's *Imperial Democracy* (1961), but see also Walter LaFeber's studies mentioned above; William Appleman Williams's revisionist classic, *The Tragedy of American Diplomacy* (1972); Robert Beisner's *From the Old Diplomacy to the New* (1986); Paul Kennedy's *The Rise and Fall of the Great Powers* (1988); and David Healy's *U.S. Expansionism* (1970). Robert Beisner in *Twelve Against Empire* (1968), E. B. Tompkins in *Anti-Imperialism in the United States* (1970), and C. Roland Marchand in *The American Peace Movement and Social Reform* (1972) focus on the opponents of expansion. Useful biographies include Howard Wayne Morgan's *William McKinley and His America* (1963) and Kenton J. Clymer's *John Hay* (1975). Both Graham A. Comas's *An Army for Empire* (1971) and Philip S. Foner's *The Spanish-Cuban-American War and the Birth of*

American Imperialism (2 vols., 1972) are useful studies of the Spanish-American War. Marilyn Blatt Young in *The Rhetoric of Empire* (1968) and Michael H. Hunt in *The Making of a Special Relationship* (1983) explore U.S. China policy; James C. Thomson, Jr., Peter W. Stanley, and John C. Perry look at American relations with China, Japan, and the Philippines in *Sentimental Imperialists* (1981). W. B. Gatewood, Jr.'s *Black Americans and the White Man's Burden* (1975) considers the black response to American imperialism; Robert W. Rydell's *All the World's a Fair* (1984) taps an unlikely source to reveal the nationalist and racist views of Americans in the late nineteenth and early twentieth centuries. Roosevelt's foreign policy is examined by Howard K. Beale in *Theodore Roosevelt and the Rise of America to World Power* (1956). The history of the interoceanic waterway is told by David McCullough in *Path Between the Seas* (1977) and by Walter LaFeber in *The Panama Canal* (1978). Dana Munro's subject is *Intervention and Dollar Diplomacy in the Caribbean* (1964); Walter LaFeber investigates United States–Central American relations in *Inevitable Revolutions* (1983). Gordon Levin offers a study of *Woodrow Wilson and World Politics* (1968), and Wilson's career, diplomatic and political, is meticulously detailed in the multi-volume work of Arthur Link, *Woodrow Wilson* (1947–1965).

TABLE 12. THE PROGRESSIVE ERA, 1898–1916

Year	President	Domestic events	Foreign policy: Europe, Asia	Foreign policy: Latin America
1898			Spanish-American War. Open Door Policy.	
1900	**McKinley** *R* (September 6, 1901, assassinated)	Gold Standard Act.	Boxer Rebellion.	
1901		Newlands Reclamation Act.		Platt Amendment.
1902		Elkins Act.		Venezuela Incident.
1903		Coal strike settled. Panic of 1903.		Panama Affair.
1904	**Roosevelt** *R*	Northern Securities case.		"Roosevelt Corollary."
1905			Russo-Japanese War and Peace of Portsmouth.	
1906		Hepburn Act. Pure Food and Drug Act.	Algeciras Conference on Morocco.	
1907		Panic.	"Gentlemen's Agreement" on Japanese immigration.	

Year	President	Domestic events	Foreign policy: Europe, Asia	Foreign policy: Latin America
1908	Taft *R*	Conservation conference.	Root-Takahira Agreement.	
1909		Payne-Aldrich Tariff.		
1910		Mann-Elkins Act.		Mexican Revolution.
1911		"Rule of Reason" decisions.	Chinese Railway Consortium.	
1912	Wilson *D*			
1913		Underwood Tariff. Federal Reserve Act.		"Watchful Waiting" in Mexico.
1914		Federal Trade Commission Act. Clayton Anti-Trust Act.	**August** War in Europe.	Tampico and Vera Cruz incidents.
1915			**May** *Lusitania* sunk. **May** United States threat and German concession on submarine warfare.	
1916	Wilson *D*	Federal Farm Loan Act. Adamson Act.		Mexican border warfare.

22

★　★　★　★　★　★

The Progressive Era,
1901–1917

THE NEW sense of power abroad that marked the turn of the century was accompanied by a new nationalism and a quest for order at home. No one embraced these related matters — imperialism and progressivism — more readily than the irrepressible Theodore Roosevelt.

Young and dynamic, Vice President Roosevelt became president when William McKinley was killed by an assassin in September 1901. Although this tragic incident is often taken as the beginning of a new period of adjustment and reform, the Progressive era was not born of one violent act. Its sources lay deep in the economic, social, and moral history of the country.

A series of reform initiatives rather than a single reform movement, progressivism was animated by varied, confusing, and sometimes contradictory impulses: efficiency and social justice, scientific management and fair play, and professional reorganization and moral regeneration. Complex, diffuse, pluralistic, the meaning of the movement and the characteristics of its adherents defy easy analysis and historical consensus. For all its ambiguities, the aggregate of causes known as progressivism can be understood as an essentially urban, middle-class response to social and economic change and a search for order and equity in a rapidly changing age. As Thomas Alva Edison confided to Henry Ford, there was reason to believe that sweeping demographic and technological changes had thrown the nation "out of gear." Not content, in the inventor's words, "to run a new civilization in old ways," the progressives set out to "make the world over."

THE MATURE ECONOMY

By 1900 the American economy was relatively mature. It was no longer necessary to concentrate all resources and efforts on the expansion of productive capacity. Production continued to increase fairly rapidly in the new century, but not at the fantastic rate of the previous period.

Progressivism owed some of its nature, if not its existence, to the fact that the period 1901–1914 was one of relatively stable prosperity. There was no prolonged depression like those of the 1870s and 1890s, and there were only two brief financial panics (1903 and 1907). The farmer, that perennial step-child of the American economy, entered a rare period of relative content-ment. Of course, many farmers were continually having a hard struggle, and some farm evils like tenancy were still increasing. But average farm income, for a change, was moving upward. This was partly due to the demand by city populations at home and abroad, which were increasing faster than farm produce. By 1900 only 35 percent of Americans lived on farms.

For some of the new urban population, crowded into slums and immigrant ghettos, things were less than cheerful. Real wages for industrial labor rose more slowly than in earlier decades. Never were social contrasts more ex-treme, from the multimillionaire with a Fifth Avenue palace and a 50-room Newport cottage, to the tubercular child working in a cotton mill or the garment worker in the tenement sweatshop. America led the world in the number of industrial accidents. Thus it is only with careful qualification that the Progressive era can be called a time of contentment. It was more a pe-riod of hope, especially for the politically articulate middle class.

Business consolidation reached a peak at about the turn of the century. During the Progressive era, the largest firms retained but did not increase their share of the nation's industry. However, this was enough to make big business the main target of progressive criticism. Its defenders argued that not all consequences of bigness were bad; for instance, there was more money for such advances as electrification and research laboratories. Public relations and advertising received much attention from progressives and so did the new scientific management of Frederick W. Taylor. Taylor, originally an engineer, urged that each movement of each worker be made as efficient as possible through close study, minute division of function, and rigorous supervision. Working toward similar objectives with less theory, Henry Ford began production of his Model T in 1909; by 1914 he was producing a quarter of a million cars a year, all black.

One aspect of business consolidation that received a great deal of pro-gressive attention was the tendency toward banker control. Only a dozen great investment houses, led by J. P. Morgan's, could float the securities necessary for the period's gigantic mergers, like that of U.S. Steel in 1901. These private bankers, controlling insurance and trust companies as well as industries and railroads, could draw on a large part of the national savings as well as on their foreign connections. Proponents of stability, he and his allies tried to end what they called cutthroat competition, to prevent risky investment, and to rescue sick industries before their financial collapse. In return, they exacted not only high fees but control. Through seats on the governing boards of railroads, steel companies, and many other corpora-tions, they could enforce their own ideas of sound operation on American business. Sometimes the bankers were unimaginative and unenterprising (they were very reluctant, for instance, to back automobile manufacturers). They did not worry much about working conditions in the industries they controlled. And as the period's two panics testify, they did not always achieve the stability at which they aimed.

THE PROGRESSIVE MIND

The main complaint of the progressives was directed against what they regarded as immoral and irresponsible power, personified by Morgan and the mighty, invisible "Money Trust." Antimonopoly feelings were as old as the Republic. Most of the remaining progressive ideology continued the previous period's ambiguous social concerns, concerns that reflected both an acceptance of the need to organize and modernize and at the same time a yearning to return to the less complex world of farms, small towns, and moral individualism. Settlement workers were still coping with urban poverty; social gospel ministers continued to reinterpret Christianity in terms of temporal human needs, and social scientists were still challenging the basis of nineteenth-century individualism. But the discontent of the early twentieth century had a new tone, set by an optimistic, though not complacent, middle class. Leaders of progressivism were fairly prosperous professionals or members of the business community, usually in their early forties, often Anglo-Saxon and Protestant; they were motivated by moral indignation and personal ambition.

Although historians generally agree that progressives were moderates who sought political and socio-economic amelioration, not revolutionary change, the age had its radicals. In the century's first decade, one congressman and many local officials representing the Socialist party were elected. In 1912, Socialist presidential candidate Eugene V. Debs garnered 6 percent of the popular vote. Radical intellectuals, including writers Randolph Bourne, Upton Sinclair, and Jack London, confidently looked forward to the nation's socialist future. On the far left were the syndicalist Industrial Workers of the World (IWW), organized in 1905 and led by William D. (Big Bill) Haywood and the legendary Mother Jones. The IWW offered a mix of interracialism, industrial unionism, and Marxian class conflict to workers unserved by, or dissatisfied with the conservative trade unionism of the AFL.

For most progressives, however, the pressing questions were not humanitarian but moral and political. Their primary aim was not the eradication of poverty or class disparities, but the creation of a rational, stable, and efficient political and social order. First, progressives wanted to end corruption, to throw out the crooks and to return power to "good citizens" like themselves. Their urban reforms were more notable for their efficiency and centralization than for their responsiveness to constituent pressures. Second, progressives wanted to control big business, not in the interest of socialism or of social leveling, but in the interest of a more humane and rational free enterprise system. Some of them, including the followers of jurist Louis Brandeis, wanted to break up large corporations and return to a more competitive age. Others, Theodore Roosevelt among them, concluded that

trusts were not inherently evil and, properly regulated in a partnership between government and business, might provide socially useful economies of
scale.

Because they found American life fundamentally good, progressives
wanted to preserve its promise for the future. Rejecting nineteenth-century
determinism, they believed that science, government, and the public morality were all changing, and changing for the better. Although most subscribed to moral absolutes, they generally saw no other immutable laws.
Following philosopher William James, they were usually pragmatists; they
rendered judgments on the basis of concrete experiences or consequences,
rather than according to general metaphysical principles. In educational theory, John Dewey and his fellow instrumentalists insisted that children
should be taught to solve problems arising in their environment, rather than
to learn the wisdom of the past. The law and the Constitution were reinter-
preted as guides to action, rather than as changeless codes of universal and
literal application. At the height of the Progressive era, people talked not
only of the New Freedom of Woodrow Wilson and the New Nationalism of
Theodore Roosevelt, but also of the new literature, the new psychology, the
new woman, and less frequently the "new negro."

Optimism gave these middle-class reformers much of their confidence and
courage; it also blinded them to some intractable contemporary problems
concerning minorities. A few reformers — among them Oswald Villard, Lillian Wald, Jane Addams, and Clarence Darrow — agitated for Afro-American rights and joined the black militant W. E. B. Du Bois in organizing the
National Association for the Advancement of Colored People (NAACP) in
1909. But progressivism was largely for whites only, and most adherents
shared the nearly universal belief that blacks were inherently inferior and
socially unassimilable. The movement's moral blind spot is shown in the
career of Governor (and later Senator) James K. Vardaman of Mississippi. A
fire-eating white supremacist who rose to power by agitating the racial fears
of his poor white constituents, Vardaman was nevertheless a champion of
the red-neck and the first Mississippi governor to qualify as a democratic
reformer. His racism, of course, was cruder and more blatant than that of
most other reform governors of his age. But his racial values differed from
those of his more genteel counterparts more often in degree than in kind.

A similar attitude of indifference verging on hostility was applied to the
new immigrants who crowded the cities after 1880. Although appalled by
urban slum conditions, otherwise humane and tolerant reformers rarely
challenged nativism. Indeed, some of them led campaigns aimed at restricting southern and eastern European immigration.

THE PROGRESSIVE ACCOMPLISHMENT

Exposure of corruption fueled the reform movement. A vogue for sensational
accounts of corruption and monopoly began with books like Henry Dema-
rest Lloyd's attack on Standard Oil (*Wealth against Commonwealth*, 1894).

The new fashion was taken up by sensational newspapers like those of Hearst and by a new crop of popular, cheap, ably edited magazines led by *McClure's*. Muckrakers, as Roosevelt called the new journalists, attacked big business, the unions, the churches, the press itself, state and city government, and finally the U.S. Senate. While many people read the muckrakers for sheer excitement, some were stirred to action.

Some of the most important progressive crusades started outside politics in such fields as charity organization, education reform, or juvenile courts (concern for the young was characteristic). Sooner or later, however, most concrete accomplishments had to be registered in political action.

The first progressive political offensive was directed against the most obvious target: America's swollen cities, where grafting utilities and protected vice were all too obvious. City reform got under way in the 1890s, and in the first decade of the century many cities moved from boss rule to reform. Some moved back soon enough, but often the cycle left a heritage of public waterworks, public or highly regulated street railways, tenement laws, and playgrounds.

Still more was accomplished in the states, perhaps the most important laboratories of reform. In 1900, Robert M. La Follette, one of the most militant and uncompromising progressive leaders, became governor of Wisconsin. Working closely with experts from the state university, he made Wisconsin a "laboratory of democracy." Reformers won control of one state after another in the Middle West and then in the far West, East, and South. Typical state reforms featured devices intended to keep the bosses and the railroads out of power and the people — or at least the respectable middle class — in control. The direct primary, preferential popular election of U.S. senators (still officially chosen by legislatures), and woman's suffrage fostered this aim.

FEMINISM AND REFORM

Women, too, benefitted from the reform impulses of the age. Although many progressive leaders, Presidents Roosevelt and Wilson among them, were reluctant and belated supporters of woman suffrage, the political aspirations of American women could no longer be denied. By 1896 the four western states of Wyoming, Utah, Colorado, and Idaho had granted women the vote. But no further gains were made until suffragists in Washington and California won referendums in 1910 and 1911. Despairing of success through state-by-state action, the "woman movement" (as it was then often called) swung its considerable energies behind the "Anthony Amendment" to enfranchise all adult women at a single stroke. The movement's modern origins dated from 1848, but not until the National American Woman Suffrage Association (NAWSA) was formed from two rival organizations in 1890 was there significant unity of action. Led first by Elizabeth Cady Stanton and Susan B. Anthony and after 1900 by Carrie Chapman Catt and Anna Howard Shaw, NAWSA focused on federal legislation. Essentially middle-class and moderate, the association sometimes cooperated and sometimes clashed with such radical feminists as Alice Paul and Lucy Burns of the Congressional Union (later called the Woman's party). In 1914, the cause won the official support of the conservative and influential General Federation of Women's Clubs. In the end, suffragists of all persuasions won. The Nineteenth Amendment cleared Congress during 1919 and was ratified and became law in August 1920 in time for the presidential election of that year.

Having won the battle for suffrage, many women believed that the war for women's rights was over. In fact, it was scarcely begun. The concerns of working-class women, for example, centered more often on the conditions of life and labor than on the ballot. Suffrage meant less to these denizens of the textile and garment sweatshops than to the middle-class women who dominated the women's movement. Moreover, the most advanced women's rights advocates, the social feminists, recognized that the franchise brought few real social changes and that the list of women's grievances remained painfully long. Women were still hemmed in by male notions of "true womanhood"; the woman's "sphere," not unlike the black's "place" remained one of subordination. Like Charlotte Perkins Gilman (*Women and Economics,* 1898), social feminists advocated the emancipation of women from smothering gentility and enforced domesticity. Like her they favored a comprehensive redefinition of women's status in society and the elimination of gender-related impediments to economic opportunity. Progress in these areas, however, came very slowly and major breakthroughs would come only in the 1960s and 1970s.

By 1910 one-fifth of the American work force was female and one fifth of all adult women (7.8 million) worked outside the home. The great majority worked as domestic servants or as unskilled factory labor, particularly in textile and garment sweatshops. Black women were nearly always confined to such menial work as agricultural day laborers, laundresses, cooks, and servants. A growing number of white women did find work as stenographers, typists, and bookkeepers, but these clerical positions — like those of school teaching and nursing — were already defined as "woman's work" and pay was accordingly very low. Only a few entered the professions of law, medicine, or higher education. By 1920 a "lady lawyer" was a great rarity and only 5 percent of the nation's medical school graduates were women. In sum, the domestic stereotype still prevailed; even educated women were generally expected to forgo careers for the "natural" female duties of housewifery and child rearing.

Nonetheless, there were modest advances. By 1900 the great majority of high school graduates were female. Traditional sexual barriers to higher education continued to erode and by 1920 most colleges and universities in the United States were coeducational. Divorce became increasingly common, particularly in urban areas. The double standard of sexual and social behavior, though still very much in force, was slowly giving way. The "revolution in morals and manners" commonly identified with the 1920s was rooted in the social ferment of the Progressive era.

Most important, many middle-class women assumed leadership roles in progressive crusades for social justice. In the field of social work and urban reform, Jane Addams and Florence Kelley, both of Chicago's Hull House, and Lillian Wald of New York City's Henry Street Settlement House, were preeminent. Ida Tarbell, among the most notable investigative journalists of her time, exposed the monopolistic practices of Standard Oil. Mary White Ovington championed civil rights for blacks. And both Emma Goldman and Margaret Sanger defied public convention and the medical profession to pioneer in the field of birth-control education. These and countless other women agitated not only for the Nineteenth Amendment but for such progressive causes as industrial safety standards, consumer protection, judicial and penal reform, child and female labor laws, kindergartens, and temperance. Indeed much of the behind-the-scenes research and lobbying that sustained local, state, and federal reform legislation was performed by women.

THE PROGRESSIVE HERO

Theodore Roosevelt's inauguration brought to the presidency, for the first time since Jackson, a popular hero, and Roosevelt was the first president since Lincoln to stretch the powers of his office. On the surface he was ever the irrepressible Teddy — noisy, impulsive, even violent, given to dramatic self-promotion and a boyish affinity for the strenuous life. Most of his impulsiveness, however, came either early or late in his career or was confined to minor issues. His major domestic decisions as president were usually shrewd compromises that served his administration and his nation well. An aristocrat by birth, a public servant by inclination, he brought to the office political experience, a keen mind, and broad learning. Even without McKinley's untimely demise, he would likely have become president.

Roosevelt was a master of timing. When McKinley died, Republican leader Mark Hanna cried, "That wild man . . . that damned cowboy is President." But Roosevelt quickly reassured conservative business and financial interests, which dominated his party, that he would continue McKinley's policies and cabinet. At the same time, he put out a trial balloon by denouncing the trusts and moved further in that direction when public response was favorable. In 1904, he easily defeated a conservative Democrat, Judge Alton B. Parker, for re-election. President in his own right and conscious of the progressive tide throughout the country, he moved further toward reform objectives. Then in 1907, when the financial panic seemed to demand caution, he followed the suggestions of J. P. Morgan. Finally, in 1908–1909, about to leave office, he called for a host of drastic reform measures. This accomplished nothing immediately but left a program that his successors could not ignore.

The domestic accomplishments of his administration are important, but his dramatization of domestic reform issues and his demonstration of the possibilities of the presidency had greater effect. Roosevelt assumed office as "His Accidency" and as heir to a tradition of congressional ascendancy dating from Andrew Johnson's impeachment; thus, he was inaugurated president of a republic that expected little from its chief executives. With the exception of Cleveland, his predecessors since Lincoln were mediocre, colorless men, and political power had rested with congressional leaders like Hanna and state party bosses like Thomas Platt of New York. Alternatingly bold and cautious, he reveled in the exercise of political power. Under his leadership and that of Wilson, the initiative returned to the White House and the president assumed primary responsibility for shaping public opinion and the congressional will.

During his first years in office, Roosevelt won recognition as a proponent of labor and an opponent of trusts. In both cases his reputation was unduly inflated. During the bitter anthracite coal strike of 1902–1903, he broke precedent and refused to send troops to the coal fields to restore order. Angered by the intransigence of the operators and impressed by the legitimacy of the miners' demands, he persuaded both sides to submit to arbitration. Improved hours and wages (but no union recognition) resulted — a milestone in labor history. But he never again intervened on labor's behalf. His fame as trustbuster can be traced to his first message to Congress, in which he urged creation of a Department of Commerce and Labor, including a bureau of corporations, to keep tabs on interstate commercial and industrial abuses. His administration successfully challenged the legality of Northern Securities, a massive railroad holding company, and went on to begin similar proceedings against the so-called Beef Trust, Standard Oil, American Tobacco, and several dozen other corporate behemoths. But Taft busted more trusts than Roosevelt, who believed that, properly regulated, these inevitable aggregations of power and wealth could serve the public interest.

His role in the development of the federal regulatory state was modest. In 1903 he signed the Elkins Act, supported by the railroads themselves, and in 1906 the Hepburn Act. These measures outlawed the rebate and gave the feeble Interstate Commerce Commission additional supervisory authority over railroads, including the power to set aside existing schedules and determine reasonable rates pending court review; they represented compromises between the demands of reformers and those of stand-pat conservatives. Additional consumer protection came in 1906 with the federal Pure Food and Drug Act and the Meat Inspection Act. Roosevelt initiated neither measure, but supported them once convinced of their need. His most systematic regulatory contribution came in the areas of conservation and wilderness preservation. A celebrated outdoorsman and champion of the national interest, Roosevelt won public acceptance for comprehensive land-use planning and scientific conservation. Over opposition of ranchers, miners, timber companies, and other interests accustomed to private use of public resources, he set aside millions of acres of public land as permanent wildlife refuges, mineral and water-power reserves, and national forests and parks.

Having promised not to seek re-election in 1908, Roosevelt arranged the nomination of his friend, Secretary of War William Howard Taft, who handily defeated two-time loser William Jennings Bryan. Roosevelt, who went on an African safari, left undone two of the nation's most pressing tasks: tariff reform and banking regulation.

TAFT AND THE INSURGENTS

A former judge, governor of the Philippines, presidential troubleshooter, and cabinet officer, Taft was an intelligent administrator, well qualified for the office. Yet his presidency was marked by failure and the disruption of his party. Critics caricatured him as a fat and lazy reactionary; his problems lay not in his weight (nearly 350 pounds) but in his inexperience in elected office and in his limited conception of the presidency. His devotion to Roosevelt's policies was genuine and he worked hard for programs in which he believed. But his cramped view of presidential prerogatives and preference for the ordered gentility of conservatives over the "yelping and snorting" of reformers poorly served the progressive cause.

Perhaps no Republican coming to power in 1909 could have succeeded. Since the Panic of 1907, times had been less prosperous and increasingly impatient progressives demanded attention to unsolved problems: trusts, taxes, and tariffs. Roosevelt had adroitly sidestepped these issues. But even his magic could only have deferred the developing conflict between Republican reformers (called insurgents) and the Republican old guard. Stand-pat conservatives still controlled party machinery, but aggressive, ambitious Republican progressives, mostly from the Midwest, were increasing their congressional power with each election.

Blaming the rising cost of living on the high Dingley Tariff (1897), reformers easily pushed a modest downward tariff revision through the House of Representatives. In the Senate, however, the protectionists won out, and the resulting compromise bill was anything but a triumph for reform. To the dismay of progressives in both parties, Taft signed the Payne-Aldrich Tariff and called it the best ever passed by Congress. The insurgents also felt betrayed by other Taft actions. Although he favored the reform effort to end Speaker Joseph G. Cannon's absolute control of the all-important House Rules Committee, he sided publicly with the reactionary "Uncle Joe," lest the old guard frustrate his administration's programs. Taft again alienated the reformers when he exonerated Richard A. Ballinger, his controversial development-minded Secretary of the Interior, of charges that he not only had opened to private sale previously closed public lands and waterpower sites, but also had fraudulently assigned federal coal reserves to commercial interests. Taft also fired Ballinger's implacable accuser, Chief Forester Gifford Pinchot, Roosevelt's friend and fellow champion of the national interest. At this point (although Ballinger was later replaced with an arch-conservationist) the breach was irreparable between the president and the insurgents who saw him as a reactionary and a traitor to the Roosevelt heritage.

Appearance is not necessarily reality, however. Despite his political ineptitude, Taft was a committed conservationist, and his record of progressive accomplishment compared favorably to Roosevelt's. He actively supported the Sixteenth Amendment (income tax), and he worked for other important measures: the Mann-Elkins Act (1910) strengthening the Interstate Commerce Commission, the Postal Savings and Parcel Post acts, and the establishment of a federal Bureau of Mines and a Children's Bureau. Taft was a more literal interpreter of the Sherman Act than Roosevelt and instigated twice as many antitrust proceedings as the trustbuster.

REPUBLICANS AND PROGRESSIVES, 1910–1912

Divisions within the Republican party widened further during the off-year elections of 1910, when the administration threw its powers, including patronage, against its own party's progressive wing. The insurgents, in turn, denounced dollar diplomacy, tariff betrayal, and conservation setbacks, and sometimes supported progressive Democrats. The Republicans suffered an electoral drubbing and the old guard was repudiated. In the congressional races, the Democrats won control of the House, and a coalition of Democrats and insurgent Republicans seized the Senate. Taft's problems, of course, grew worse; his renomination seemed in doubt.

Roosevelt's role in the coming Republican debacle of 1912 was conditioned by his personal ambition, his appetite for controversy, and his personal sympathies for the insurgent cause. While abroad, he had been kept apprised of the developing confrontation by both sides. Following his famous "New Nationalism" speech in Osawatomie, Kansas (August 1910), the long-rumored rift between Roosevelt and his old friend Taft broke into the open. Subsequent Roosevelt addresses were watered down for the consumption of eastern conservatives, but in Kansas progressives had been electrified and the old guard alarmed by his call for an extension of government regulatory authority and the subordination of private interests to the public welfare. Taft lashed out unmistakably at "political emotionalists" and "neurotics," and Roosevelt soon characterized Taft as a reactionary "fat head." In 1912, Roosevelt, urged on by seven progressive Republican governors, announced that his hat was in the presidential ring. Meanwhile, a second challenge to Taft came from the Progressive Republican League, established by the insurgents in 1911; initially La Follette was its favorite, but when the Wisconsin senator faltered, the insurgents enthusiastically switched their support to Roosevelt.

Waging a vigorous campaign for the Republican nomination, Roosevelt defeated Taft in those states that had adopted the new direct primary system. But Taft controlled party and convention machinery and enough delegates to ensure his own renomination. The Roosevelt following withdrew from the GOP, formed its own organization, and promptly nominated its hero by acclamation. The Bull Moose party's platform contained a long list of reforms: legislation prohibiting child labor and establishing minimum wages for women and social insurance; the initiative, referendum, and recall; direct election of senators; preferential presidential primaries; and woman suffrage. Its foreign policy planks, though favoring international peace, were distinctly Rooseveltian and nationalistic.

More than a group of Roosevelt worshippers, the Progressive party of 1912 was an attempt to adapt traditional American individualism to new conditions and to combine old and new ideas. Its uneasy mix of practicality and moral uplift was to find echoes in the New Deal.

Roosevelt's venture turned out badly for his supporters and himself. It deepened the Republican split, for a time handing over the party to the old guard and thus paving the way for the conservative new era of the 1920s. The defeat destroyed Roosevelt's important role in American politics, and it retarded the job of adapting traditional liberalism to twentieth-century realities. The split assured a Democratic victory.

WILSON AND THE PRESIDENCY

Woodrow Wilson had a varied and largely academic career before he became the Democratic presidential candidate in 1912. The son of a Presbyterian minister and a Virginian, Wilson was trained both as a lawyer and a political scientist. A scholar and university lecturer, he became president of Princeton University; in 1910 after a quarrel with university regents, he left and was nominated for the governorship of New Jersey at the age of 53. A Jeffersonian devoted to individual liberty and state rights, he had opposed the Populists, organized labor, and the social service state. Influential Democrats had identified him as a possible savior of the party from "Bryanism."

To the dismay of corrupt New Jersey party leaders, Wilson would not be a figurehead, and gradually emerged as a progressive. He pushed a comprehensive program of reform through the state legislature, including a direct primary law, utilities' regulation, a corrupt practices act, and a workmen's compensation law. A presidential hopeful by this time, he conciliated Bryan and other progressives, while retaining the support of some conservative elements in the party. To many Democrats, delighted by Republican discord, he appeared to be a unity candidate, likely to heal the long-standing rift between Democratic factions: Bryan's rural, southern and western, reform-minded group and Cleveland's urban, Eastern, business-minded contingent.

During the ensuing campaign, one of the liveliest in American history, Socialist Eugene V. Debs and Taft were quickly overshadowed by the contest between the New Freedom of Woodrow Wilson and the New Nationalism of Theodore Roosevelt. Wilson's campaign speeches were as progressive as Roosevelt's but strikingly different in style and content. Though both were bookish, strong-willed, and moralistic, the barrel-chested and toothy Roosevelt was warm, gregarious, and enthusiastic, while the lean and eloquent Wilson tended to be cool, aloof, and detached. The public made Roosevelt the most popular living American and fondly called him Teddy and TR. Wilson, on the other hand, inspired respect, not popular affection; he exuded dedication, high-mindedness, and at times self-righteousness. Where Roosevelt called for a federal regulatory state powerful enough to control inevitable, and in many ways beneficial business corporations, Wilson argued the need for destroying monopolies and returning to a decentralized, competitive economy. Neither was a proponent of laissez faire, but

Wilson was the most suspicious of the power of big government. While Roosevelt advocated a broad program of social justice and political reform, Wilson insisted that the restoration of business competition would minimize the need for government paternalism. No candidate commanded a majority of the popular vote, but Wilson placed first with 42 percent. Roosevelt garnered more votes than any third-party candidate in history, running well ahead of Taft, but he was buried by Wilson's electoral-college landslide.

Many doubted that a former college professor with little practical political experience could hold together the coalition of immigrants, white Southerners, Bryanites, and eastern commercial interests that made up the Democratic party. Nor did Wilson's personality always inspire confidence. Often inflexible, rarely torn by self-doubt, he sometimes viewed complex issues in terms of dogmatic absolutes. Yet he brought superb gifts to the presidency. Wilson proved to be a principled statesman, a sensitive interpreter of the public will, and a skillful, tough-minded, and forceful politician who brought progressivism to full flower.

As president, Wilson's first concerns were the tariff and banking. With the help of progressives of both parties, the Democratic president guided through Congress the Underwood Tariff, reducing the rates to about pre–Civil War levels; the tariff bill also included a moderate income tax to offset the loss of revenue. His banking reform was the most sweeping in U.S. history.

The Federal Reserve Act of 1913 steered a middle course between the advocates and the enemies of a central bank and between the proponents of either public or private control. The Federal Reserve System divided the country into 12 districts, each with a Federal Reserve Bank owned by member banks and governed by a mixed public-private board. Acting as agents of member banks, Reserve Banks were empowered to pool resources in times of financial crisis and to issue a new and elastic currency, the Federal Reserve note (the paper money used to the present day). The entire system was supervised by a presidentially appointed board, which could regulate the money supply and interest rates as the economy seemed to require. Although the act was generally hailed by progressives and condemned by bankers, it was a shrewd compromise between the public and the private interest — regionally decentralized, privately owned, and publicly controlled.

The third major accomplishment of Wilson's first years was new trust legislation. The Federal Trade Commission Act established a presidentially appointed board with power to investigate corporate practice and issue cease-and-desist orders (subject to judicial review) against unfair methods of competition. The next law, the Clayton Anti-Trust Act, prohibited specific practices, including discriminatory prices leading to monopoly, and interlocking directorates; it also exempted labor organizations from its anti-trust provisions. For a time at least, business leaders consulted the government before attempting further consolidation.

With these major enactments, Wilson announced that his reform program was completed. Following the business panic of 1914, he seemed unduly conciliatory of conservative opinion; he appointed bankers to the Federal Reserve Board, refused support for either women's suffrage or child labor legislation, opposed federal loans for farmers, and sanctioned racially segregated facilities in federal departments. To go beyond the limited reforms of the New Freedom, he told unsatisfied reformers, would violate state rights, and undermine individualism.

In 1916, however, he moved left. Finding his own initial program too limited and also recognizing the need to win progressive votes, he supported and signed in an election year the measures he had earlier opposed: an act providing long-term rural credits, a child-labor law (later held unconstitutional), an interstate highway construction program, a federal aid to vocational education law, and an act establishing an eight-hour day for railroad workers — thus embracing much of Roosevelt's New Nationalism. In the national election, however, he faced a unified Republican party with Roosevelt back in the GOP fold. Although he defeated Republican reform governor and later Chief Supreme Court Justice Charles Evans Hughes, he was again denied a popular majority, with 49.4 percent of the vote.

THE MEANING OF PROGRESSIVISM

The Progressive era left a mixed record of failure and achievement. It had not produced, or tried to produce, a new social system. It had made only the barest beginning toward the redistribution of wealth or the control of private accumulations of power. While ultraconservatives lamented the end of free enterprise, the million or so Americans who wanted to move toward socialism were impatient with progressive caution. Despite the efforts of southern white progressives, the South still lagged far behind the rest of the country in health and wealth. The deepest rooted American form of inequality was almost untouched, North or South. In the face of massive discrimination, many blacks accepted the program of Booker T. Washington, who counseled the temporary acceptance of social discrimination and the adoption of modest economic goals. A few black intellectuals, led by W. E. B. Du Bois, joined a few progressive whites to form the NAACP. But the crusade for racial justice attracted little support, and civil rights for blacks would not become a tenet of American liberalism until World War II.

Some progressive accomplishments proved impermanent. It was plain to close observers, even before 1917, that the reform fervor was declining and the opposition gathering strength. Soon, in wartime, much of the progressive program was to take on a different meaning, and in the postwar decade many progressive enactments were emasculated or abandoned. During the 1920s, a period of conservative Republican ascendancy, the regulatory agencies fell into the hands of the interests they were meant to control. Conservative state and federal courts qualified and in many cases struck down progressive legislation designed to protect workers and consumers. Some measures, including those designed to reform city politics and initiative and referendum, failed to achieve the desired results of greater citizen participation and more responsible government.

But all progressive effort was not in vain. Big business, neither destroyed nor much weakened, was never again as defiant of public opinion as it had been. Immensely valuable national resources had been saved for the future. New paths for possible later government action were made possible by the income tax and other measures. Outside the arena of politics, dedicated reformers left countless playgrounds, schools, clinics, and parks. In architecture, poetry, social science, and psychology, innovation had characterized the Progressive era.

More important than any concrete accomplishment of the progressive movement was its general reassertion of the will to adapt. Like other countries, America had been confronted by the huge problems of industrial civilization. Faced with this challenge, the country had not failed to find resources of courage and vitality. More than anyone realized, these resources were to prove indispensable in the coming decades.

CONFLICTING HISTORICAL VIEWPOINTS: NO. 10

Who Were the Progressives?

Few phenomena of American history are more controversial than the Progressive movement. For more than six decades, scholars have offered conflicting answers to such questions as: Why did the movement begin and end when it did? What were its major objectives? Was its impact on the national experience salutary or otherwise? What was its relationship to other reform movements before and since? On these topics there is so little agreement among historians that Peter Filene has written "An Obituary for the 'Progressive Movement'" (American Quarterly, *Spring 1970), arguing that the very concept should be abandoned as a figment of the scholarly imagination.*

The nature of this continuing historiographical debate is perhaps best suggested by conflicting assessments of the social origins of the reformers. In his analysis of The Progressive Movement *(1915), Parke De Witt, the first scholar to study progressivism, accepted the interpretation offered by the reformers themselves. Like them, he viewed their movement as an uncompromising onslaught against big business. The period, he concluded, was one of conflict between "the people" and "the interests." Essentially the same idea pervaded the two most famous historical studies written during the 1920s. Vernon L. Parrington's* Main Currents in American Thought *(3 vols., 1927–1930) and Charles and Mary Beard's* The Rise of American Civilization *(1927) viewed progressivism as the lineal descendant of a reform tradition that stretched back in American history to the age of Jefferson and Jackson. Pitting the masses against business moguls and crooked politicians, the movement was the twentieth-century phase of the age-old struggle between democracy and aristocracy, equality and privilege. The Progressives, then, were the people themselves, rank-and-file, democrats with a small* d, *who waged the battle for reform in defense of their national birthright.*

Writing from within the progressive frame of reference, such scholars as De Witt, Parrington, and Beard were, in effect, involved participants whose sympathetic and simplistic analysis of progressivism was not shared by historians of later generations. The events of the 1920s and 1930s offered new historical vantage points from which to view the movement. To those who lived through the political reaction of "normalcy" and the economic crisis of the Great Depression, progressivism generally seemed less idealistic and much less effective than earlier scholars assumed. As early as 1932, John Chamberlain, a young Marxist, studied the era closely and then bade Farewell to Reform. *The progressives, he concluded, were nostalgic conservatives seeking to restore a simpler past, not liberal reformers responding to the challenges of industrialism and urbanism. Although Harold U. Faulkner could still celebrate progressivism as* The Quest for Social Justice *(1931), most scholars from Chamberlain's time forward shared his doubts about the nature of the movement.*

Thus both George Mowry's The California Progressives *(1951) and Richard Hofstadter's* The Age of Reform *(1955) portrayed the era as one in which the urban middle class sought to restore its position of leadership. The Progressives were not selfless crusaders for popular democracy, these scholars affirmed, but bourgeois victims of status anxiety. Drawn from the old and established professional elite (lawyers, educators, ministers, editors), whose standards of morality and order had been offended by political bosses and a flood of new immigrants, and whose influence had been eclipsed by a new class of industrial and financial plutocrats, the Progressives struggled to restore traditional standards of probity and to regain their lost power and deference.*

In a vein somewhat different from Mowry and Hofstadter, Samuel P. Hays in The Response to Industrialism, 1885–1914 *(1957) and Robert Wiebe in* Businessmen and Reform *(1962) cast additional doubts on the traditional view that progressivism was basically a people's crusade against big business. In fact, both argued that special interests often favored meaningful reforms that the people opposed. In their view, the Progressives were neither disinterested do-gooders nor disquieted bourgeois but realistic conservatives, a new class of bureaucratic-minded professionals who sought to bring order and efficiency to a chaotic and wasteful society.* The Search for Order, 1877–1920 *(1967), Wiebe's second book and the most systematic expression of this organizational interpretation, suggested that in their quest for stability and system, the new middle-class Progressives often found ready allies in big corporate managers.*

Richard L. McCormick in From Realignment to Reform *(1981) has recently suggested a variation of this organizational thesis more concerned with uncovering why reform occurred when it did than pinpointing who exactly the reformers were. McCormick found that special-interest groups* arose in New York State during the Progressive period as a result of the rapid changes wrought by industrialization and urbanization. As American citizens came to recognize how business interests often corrupted party politics in an industrial society, and as their attacks on party politicians increased, the party system declined in importance, only to be replaced by special-interest groups, many dominated by businessmen or bureaucratic professionals. Thus, in McCormick's view, progressivism developed because of a political transformation necessitated by modernization and in a direction unintended by those originally critical of existing political arrangements.

Other scholars also abandoned the attempt to trace the social origins of reform to the middle class or to any specific social group. J. Joseph Huthmacher (Mississippi Valley Historical Review, 1962) and Michael Paul Rogin and John L. Shover (Political Change in California, 1970) emphasized working-class (particularly Catholic and immigrant) support for progressive programs. David P. Thelen in The New Citizenship (1972) went further to argue the futility of attributing social movements to particular social groups. Noting that Wisconsin Progressives, not unlike their conservative critics, drew their ranks from farmers, workers, professionals, and business people, he emphasized issues more than classes, and concluded that "no particular manner of man became a progressive."

Since World War II, then, historians have redefined the sources of progressivism and its relationship to the business community. Although delineating the conservative tendencies inherent in the progressive mind, most scholars still accept the traditional equation of progressivism with reform. New Left historians, however, have denied even that. Gabriel Kolko, for example, has described the movement as The Triumph of Conservatism (1963). In his view, the Progressives were not reformers at all, and the chief characteristic of the era was not orderly change in the public interest but complete control by business interests. Clearly, Kolko's is a minority view, but his total inversion of the traditional interpretation serves as a reminder that history is art, not science.

FOR FURTHER READING

Overviews of the period include the books by Samuel P. Hays, Richard Hofstadter, and Robert Wiebe mentioned in the essay above, but see also John Milton Cooper's The Pivotal Decades, 1890–1920 (1990) and John Chambers's The Tyranny of Change (1992). Among several studies of the Rough Rider are John M. Blum's The Republican Roosevelt (1954) and Lewis L. Gould's The Presidency of Theodore Roosevelt (1991). Paolo Coletta's The Presidency of William Howard Taft (1973) is a sympathetic portrait. Of the immense literature on Wilson, the most valuable biography is Arthur Link's multi-volume study; Link summarizes Wilson's first administration in Woodrow Wilson and the Progressive Era (1954). Kendrick A. Clements's

The Presidency of Woodrow Wilson (1992) is a brief biography, and John Milton Cooper's *The Warrior and the Priest* (1983) is a striking double biography of Roosevelt and Wilson. There are good accounts of other important figures of the age; see, for example, Allen Davis's *American Heroine: The Life and Legacy of Jane Addams* (1973), Ellen Chesler's *Woman of Valor: Margaret Sanger and the Birth Control Movement in America* (1992), William Holmes's *The White Chief: James K. Vardaman* (1970), Robert Westbrook's *John Dewey and American Democracy* (1991), David Levering Lewis's *W. E. B. Du Bois* (1993), Kathryn Kish Sklar's *Florence Kelley and the Nation's Work* (1995), Louis R. Harlan's *Booker T. Washington* (2 vols., 1972–1983), and David Thelen's brief *Robert M. La Follette and the Insurgent Spirit* (1976). Among the many valuable autobiographies, see especially William Allen White's (1946). Books on the urban scene include Harold L. Platt's *The Electric City* (1991), Zane Miller's *Boss Cox's Cincinnati* (1968), and Bradley Rice's *Progressive Cities* (1977). Statewide studies include Lewis L. Gould's *Progressives and Prohibitionists* (1973), on Texas; and John F. Reynolds's *Testing Democracy* (1988), on New Jersey. There are uncounted histories of particular reform topics. Among these are Sheila Rothman, *Woman's Proper Place* (1978), Aileen Kraditor, *The Ideas of the Woman Suffrage Movement* (1965), Marjorie Spruill Wheeler, *New Women of the New South* (1993), and Alice Kessler-Harris, *Out to Work* (1982), on feminism; Louis Filler, *The Muckrakers* (1976), on the new journalism; Theda Skocpol, *Protecting Soldiers and Mothers* (1992), on the origins of the welfare state; J. Morgan Kousser, *The Shaping of Southern Politics* (1974), on suffrage reform; and George Wright, *Life Behind a Veil* (1985), Temple Kirby, *Darkness at the Dawning* (1972), and John Dittmer, *Black Georgia in the Progressive Era* (1977), on blacks. Socialism's story is told, in part, by Mary Jo Buhle's *Women and American Socialism* (1981) and Melvyn Dubofsky's *We Shall Be All* (1969). Intellectual histories of the period include James T. Kloppenberg's *Uncertain Victory* (1986), Morton White's *Social Thought in America* (1957), and David Noble's *The Progressive Mind* (1981). Alan Dawley's *Struggles for Justice* (1991) is a good survey of progressivism and the topics covered in the following three chapters.

23

★ ★ ★ ★ ★ ★

The Era of the First Overseas War, 1914–1920

THE WAR that began in August 1914 brought to an end a century of relative peace, apparent democratic progress, and European domination of the world. It helped bring about the first Communist revolution. For the United States it ushered in a period of economic world power and political isolation. It brought far greater steps toward governmental direction of the economy than most progressives had dreamed of. All this drastic innovation produced intense emotional confusion: Americans moved in a rapid zigzag from neutrality to crusading excitement to disillusion and revulsion. President Wilson's progressive idealism and moralism seemed to connect the nation at peace to the nation at war.

THE WAR AND AMERICA

In 1914, most Americans found it hard to understand why all Europe went to war over the murder by a Serb of the heir to the throne of Austria-Hungary. Actually, the European great powers, all heavily armed, had long been engaged in a struggle for empire and prestige. They were organized in two huge, approximately equal alliances, each fearful of the other. One consisted of the two Central European empires of Germany and Austria-Hungary (with the doubtful adherence of Italy); the other consisted of Britain, France, and Russia. When Austria-Hungary, afraid of the disintegration of its multinational empire, demanded severe punishment of Serbia, Germany backed its ally's demands. Russia felt it necessary to assist Serbia, and France was linked to Russia. When Germany invaded France through Belgium (whose neutrality had been internationally guaranteed), England came somewhat reluctantly into the war. Later the Central Powers were joined by Turkey and Bulgaria; the Western Allies by Italy, Japan, Greece, Rumania, and other countries.

TABLE 13. THE WAR AND THE TWENTIES, 1914–1929

Year	President	Political events	Economic conditions	Foreign policy	Miscellaneous
1914			1914 Depression.		
1915			1915–1916 Recovery: war orders.		1915 Movie, "Birth of a Nation."
1916	Wilson *D*				
1917			**April** War declared.		
1918		1917–1918 War prosperity. Republicans win Senate.		**January** Fourteen Points. **November** Armistice.	
1919		**September** Wilson's collapse. Volstead Act.	1919 Inflationary boom strikes.	**June** Versailles Treaty signed.	Red Scare. First regular radio station. Sinclair Lewis, *Main Street.*
1920	Harding *R*	Prohibition and women's suffrage in effect. Palmer's raids.	Deflation and recession.	**March** Treaty finally defeated in Senate.	19th Amendment.
1921		Immigration quotas established.	1921 Depression.	1921–1922 Washington Conference.	Sacco and Vanzetti trial.
1922		Fordney-McCumber Tariff. Progressive gains in Congress.	Recovery.		
1923	**August** Death of Harding. **Coolidge** becomes president.	1923–1924 Exposure of "Harding Scandals."	Prosperity		

Year	President	Political events	Economic conditions	Foreign policy	Miscellaneous
1924	Coolidge *R*	La Follette Third Party Movement. National Origins Act — immigration quotas.		Dawes Plan for Germany.	
1925					Scopes Trial. Klan membership peaks. Theodore Dreiser, *American Tragedy;* F. Scott Fitzgerald, *Great Gatsby.*
1926					
1927		Coolidge vetoes McNary-Haugen farm bill.	1927 Decline in construction and auto industries.	U.S.–Mexican differences compromised.	Lindbergh flight. Marcus Garvey deported.
1928	Hoover *R*			United States renounces right of intervention in Latin America under "Roosevelt Corollary."	
1929			**September–October** Wall Street crash.	Young Plan for Germany.	Ernest Hemingway, *Farewell to Arms;* William Faulkner, *The Sound and the Fury.*

When war broke out, most Americans, believing themselves secure and immune, thought that their country could and should stay out of it. Many quoted, or misquoted, the country's founders on the subject of foreign entanglements. Progressives often associated war with reaction, and socialists thought of it as a product of dying capitalism. To ensure American neutrality, Jane Addams, Lillian Wald, and other social reformers joined the American Union Against Militarism, and feminist Carrie Chapman Catt organized the Women's Peace party. Both Andrew Carnegie and Henry Ford subsidized the peace movement; Ford sent a "peace ship" to Europe in 1915 to promote an early armistice. Some intellectuals and many idealists on both sides of the Atlantic, having convinced themselves that humankind had outgrown its need for the cruder forms of international violence, expressed shock that civilized, twentieth-century nations would resort to war.

President Wilson advocated a scrupulous neutrality, partly because he saw no compelling American interests at stake and partly because he recognized that the ethnically diverse American nation was not united on whether to intervene. Most of the eastern, Anglo-Saxon elite, including many editors and journalists, rated British law and literature highly and identified their own values with those of Western European civilization. Large groups remembered the Marquis de Lafayette, holding a traditional sympathy for France, and felt outrage over the invasion of neutral Belgium. Some influential individuals argued, on less lofty grounds, that American safety depended on British control of the seas. For two decades the United States had moved toward rapprochement with Britain; a British defeat, these Anglophiles believed, would threaten Wilsonian designs for an open world of free commerce and national self-determination.

Though Allied war propaganda fell on many friendly ears, a sizable portion of Americans favored the Central Powers. Most Irish-Americans and many Midwesterners continued to associate Britain with empire, aristocracy, and oligarchy. Some progressives identified Great Britain as the center of the hated international Money Trust, and reformers often thought of Germany as the birthplace of government-sponsored social meliorism. To the well-organized and articulate German-American minority, the Fatherland was an innocent victim of Allied encirclement.

More obvious than in Jefferson's day, neutrality was made difficult by economic and strategic considerations. In 1914 the country was entering a depression, and war orders promised economic recovery. From the beginning, America took the traditional position that all belligerents were free to buy war materiel wherever they chose. Because of British naval power, only the Allies could buy desperately needed American goods. Originally inclined to insist on cash sales, Wilson and his first Secretary of State Bryan early withdrew their opposition to loans and bank credits. By 1915, American industry was booming, and American prosperity was bound up in Allied success. A German victory, an embargo on munitions, a prohibition of loans, or a sudden peace would have meant financial crisis.

Undoubtedly this economic involvement influenced some American opinion. Yet business, and particularly big business, was by no means dominant in the formation of American foreign policy. Some progressives were against whatever business leaders supported. And the president, who bore the responsibility for foreign-policy decisions, had demonstrated in the Mexican crisis a deep hostility to "selfish interests." While Wilson loved British culture and disliked German militarism, he was determined to maintain peace. He was also determined, as always, to defend America's national honor and its power. Both were essential to the overriding goal: the promotion of worldwide democratic progress. The president's most influential advisers, including his close friend Colonel Edward House, were strongly and openly pro-British. Like the president, they believed that the two Atlantic nations were "bound together by common principle and purpose."

Thus the forces affecting American policy were fairly evenly balanced. Most Americans wanted to stay out, and most hoped for Allied victory. Neither economic interest nor Allied sympathy was strong enough to counter the traditional dislike of becoming involved in Europe's troubles. Perplexed by conflicting emotions, many Americans responded most to surging nationalism. Only a direct challenge to American rights and feelings could tip the balance toward war. This challenge arose out of a familiar problem: neutral rights at sea.

Once again, as in the time of Napoleon, a great land power and a great sea power were fighting an all-out war. Each preferred to remain on good terms with America, the world's most powerful neutral. Neither, in the long run, could afford to give up any weapon necessary to victory. The British, as expected, used their navy to blockade Germany and to deny it essential supplies. The Germans countered, attempting to cut off British trade with a new weapon, the submarine or U-boat.

Enormously effective, the submarine was also vulnerable and ethically, and (in terms of international law) perhaps legally questionable. Under the conventions of war, a warship was required to warn an enemy merchant vessel and to remove passengers and crew before sinking her. If, however, a U-boat did surface to warn its victim, it could be destroyed by an armed merchant ship. In at least one famous case, a German submarine that had surfaced for this purpose was sunk by a British decoy ship, disguised as an American merchant vessel. Thus the Germans, throughout the war, faced a difficult choice. They could not use their only effective sea weapon in the only effective manner without killing civilians. Yet killing civilians, in 1914, was regarded by the West as illegal and brutal. Submarine warfare, which might bring Germany victory, could at the same time add to Germany's enemies and thereby bring defeat.

In dealing with blockade and counterblockade, the Wilson administration had three possible choices, each with its advocates. The first was strict neutrality, favored by Secretary Bryan, many congressional Democrats, and much midwestern opinion. Of the many methods proposed to implement such a policy, the most plausible was to prohibit American citizens from traveling on armed ships and thus to prevent the most dangerous kind of incidents. Under this plan, protests against both German and British blockade excesses would be filed for postwar negotiation. This policy, or any policy of abandoning or diminishing American neutral rights, was rejected by Wilson on grounds of national honor.

The opposite extreme would have been to intervene early on the Allied side. This would not only have ended the dilemma about neutral rights, it would have shortened the war and given America a more decisive voice in the peace. This action was advocated by Theodore Roosevelt, which hardly recommended it to Wilson. Such a choice was completely contrary to tradition and would have divided the country disastrously.

The third choice, and one that attracted Wilson from time to time, was American mediation, either to moderate the war or to end it. With Europe immersed in the carnage of total war, the president accepted personal and national moral responsibility to try to restore peace. Mediation efforts took two forms. The first was an effort to induce Britain to modify her blockade or cease from arming merchant vessels in return for German abandonment or modification of submarine warfare. The second was the attempt to persuade both belligerents to state negotiable war aims.

Both kinds of effort at mediation, sporadically pursued and probably illusory, had clearly failed by 1916. Neither side was willing to abandon weapons it considered essential, and neither would abandon the prospect of victory. As the bloodshed mounted, so did fear and hatred, until compromise became impossible.

To force peace, America would have had to threaten both sides with losing the war. To cut off munitions to Britain might result in German victory. To intervene on the Allies' side would require a heavily armed America with a united public opinion. Thus, effective mediation was made impossible by the whole nature of the American political system. Thus the policy adopted was, and perhaps had to be, a constantly shifting compromise among the three alternatives: neutrality, intervention, and mediation.

FROM NEUTRALITY TO WAR
IN FOUR ACTS

The first stage of American policy, from the outbreak of war to February 1915, was characterized by benevolent neutrality toward England. After the shocking invasion of Belgium, the Germans gave little direct offense to America, while the British blockade became increasingly rigid. In it, most commodities were gradually considered to be war contraband, neutral ships were stopped at sea and taken to port for search, and trade with other neutrals who might transship to Germany was severely rationed. Yet American protests were moderate in tone, British concessions were considerable, and, most important, no American was killed. The United States even accepted without much ill feeling the British proclamation of a mined war zone in the North Sea, where few American ships went.

The second stage, running from February 1915 until May 1916, was dominated by German submarine warfare. In February, Germany proclaimed a submarine war zone around the British Isles, cutting the main Atlantic sea lanes. From this point on, the U.S. administration refused to accept the legality of submarine warfare and announced that Germany would be held to "strict accountability" for American losses.

On May 7, 1915, the oceanliner *Lusitania*, unarmed but carrying some war cargo, was sunk off the Irish coast. Of the 1,198 passengers drowned, 128 were Americans. In a series of very strong notes, Wilson demanded that Germany accept responsibility for these losses and abandon its methods of submarine war. After repeated warnings, partial or temporary German concessions, and further sinkings, Wilson in March 1916 made it clear that a continuation of unrestricted submarine warfare would mean a break in German-American relations. Although Roosevelt had objected in the past to Wilson's "weasel words," the implication of war was unmistakable. Germany somewhat grudgingly promised that henceforth her raiders would warn before sinking. This seemed a major American victory. The nation was, however, practically committed to go to war if and when Germany changed her mind. To give some meaning to his implied threats of force, Wilson gave his backing in late 1915 to a preparedness program, including increased army and navy appropriations and heavy new taxes.

The third stage, from May 1916 to February 1917, brought somewhat less tense relations with Germany, increased irritation against England, and the peak of Wilson's efforts for a negotiated peace. In this period Britain, hard pressed in war and confident of American tolerance, stepped up her enforcement of the blockade. American mail was searched, and American firms believed to have dealt with Germany were blacklisted and barred from British trade. Wilson found these actions almost intolerable, and Congress made gestures of retaliation.

In November, Wilson narrowly won re-election, following a campaign in which he was attacked by isolationists who thought him a war monger and by internationalists who agreed with Roosevelt that he was "yellow." Wilson partisans pointed to his success in keeping America out of war, as well as to his increased domestic progressivism. Once elected, the president made his most ambitious mediation effort, a public request to both sides for a statement of war aims. When this effort failed and it became clear that neither side was interested in compromise, Wilson became increasingly disillusioned with the Allied cause. On January 22, 1917, in an eloquent speech, he declared that the world's only hope lay in a "Peace without Victory" for either side.

The fourth and final phase started a week later when Germany, in a desperate bid for victory, announced the resumption of unrestricted submarine warfare. Wilson had no alternative but to break relations, yet he still refused to ask for war. On March 1, the administration released to the press an intercepted German note, the so-called Zimmerman telegram, which proposed, in the event of war with the United States, an alliance with Mexico to recover lost territories. Meanwhile Wilson, despite a filibuster by Robert La Follette and other antiwar progressives, started arming American ships. Only at the beginning of April, after a series of new sinkings, did Wilson seek a congressional declaration of war. Among the few dissenting votes was that of Representative Jeannette Rankin of Montana, the first woman to serve in Congress. Averring that "peace is a woman's job," she voted no, and in 1941 repeated the act by opposing U.S. intervention in World War II.

AMERICA AT WAR: PATRIOTISM AND DISCONTENT

Though many Americans had expected limited, almost painless participation in the war, Allied exhaustion made limitation impossible. On the brink of starvation, Germany was still sinking British ships faster than they could be built; England, virtually drained of its young manhood, was beset with civilian and military labor shortages; the French army was demoralized and mutinous; and Russia, having suffered staggering casualties, was convulsed by revolution.

The first Russian Revolution in March 1917 had caused America to welcome Russia as a constitutional state and possible ally in the war against Prussian autocracy. In November, however, Lenin and the Bolsheviks overthrew the moderate Kerensky government. In March 1918 the Bolsheviks signed a treaty with Germany, surrendering large territories and releasing German troops for the Western Front. Germany began a series of major offensives that penetrated deeply into Allied-held territory and threatened to defeat the war-weary Allies before the Americans could arrive on the scene.

Faced with this crisis, the United States built a massive conscript army; by November 1918, 2,000,000 Yanks had safely been convoyed to France. American naval forces greatly reduced the German submarine menace. The American Expeditionary Force, initially distributed among Allied armies and later united under General John J. Pershing, played a decisive part in the bloody operations from mid-April to November 1918. In the first major American engagement, doughboys of the Second Division stopped a German advance at Château-Thierry, and then in June 1918 drove the enemy out of Belleau Woods. During July in the Second Battle of the Marne, one of the war's turning points, American troops helped halt another German drive against Paris. In the great Allied counteroffensive, the Meuse-Argonne engagement in September and October, General Pershing's forces cut German supply lines and drove the enemy back toward its frontier. By November, the war was over.

To support American military operations, the administration experimented with a planned economy in which the production, distribution, and consumption of American goods was regimented as never before. Money for huge loans to the Allies, as well as for America's war effort, was raised by a fairly democratic system of war finance. About one-third of the total was raised by taxes, compared to about one-fifth in the Civil War. For this purpose, incomes and corporate profits were taxed at unheard-of rates. In 1918, incomes of over $1 million were assessed a total tax of 77 percent. (In 1913, a top rate of 7 percent had seemed high.) Federal war bonds were sold to

65 million customers in four great drives. Even so, the war was financed partly by inflation and mostly through expansion of bank credit by action of the new Federal Reserve System.

After fumbling with various regulatory devices in the first war winter, Congress in the spring of 1918 gave the president almost dictatorial powers over the war economy. Under his control, 500 war agencies policed the productive effort. The War Industries Board allocated raw materials, determined priorities, and standardized products. The War Trade Board supervised foreign commerce. The War Labor Board opposed strikes and lockouts, but also promoted union recognition, the eight-hour day, and uniform wages. The Food Administration under Herbert Hoover guaranteed the purchase of, and set the prices for major farm commodities, thereby using powers granted by Congress (Lever Act) to increase food production. The Fuel Board and the Shipping Administration similarly increased production in their spheres. Railroads, telegraph, and telephones were taken over and efficiently managed by the Railway Administration.

Despite blunders and confusion, the United States achieved a fairly efficient, regulated economy — a form of state capitalism — that reached full-capacity production just as the war ended. Some advanced progressives prophesied that these gains for centralization would never be lost; most citizens, however, accepted the new system as the wartime expedient that it was, and supported it largely for patriotic reasons. Business flourished, as it always does in times of war. Corporate profits, buoyed by cost-plus federal contracts, increased at least threefold between 1914 and 1919. Yet business people objected to wartime taxes, resented labor's modest gains, and in general carped about governmental regimentation. Farmers, though faring well, resented the fixing of price ceilings and noted that price floors had never been set in a depression.

The labor shortage, exacerbated by male military enlistments and declining immigration, created unprecedented opportunities for minorities and women. Blacks, welcome only in the most menial industrial jobs up to this time, found their labor in high demand. Between 1916 and 1918, nearly 500,000 Afro-Americans left the South for wartime jobs in northern cities. Thousands of Mexican-Americans left the Southwest and moved in the same direction, but many more Hispanics, their numbers increased by relaxed immigration laws, found employment as agricultural workers in California and neighboring states. Although woman's place was still thought to be in the home, perhaps a million women out of a female workforce of eight million held jobs in war industries, and many others performed useful war-related volunteer work.

Thus, despite minor discontentments, governmental direction of the war economy marked a momentous step in a generally continuing direction. There was no return to laissez faire. After the war, the government was to act as a partner to business, and later, under Franklin Roosevelt's New Deal, wartime precedents were invoked to meet a national depression.

Like the president's war powers, radical steps were taken to manage public opinion, with frightening consequences. Despite evident popular enthusiasm, the government was concerned about national unity. The Committee on Public Information, administered by the progressive journalist George Creel, blanketed the country with some 75 million pamphlets and uncounted speeches about "Why We Are Fighting" and "The Meaning of America." The Post Office barred antiwar publications from the mails. The Espionage (1917) and Sedition (1918) acts cracked down on "spies" and "traitors" by forbidding abusive words and contemptuous deeds about, or against the U.S. flag, government, Constitution, uniform, or military. About 1,500 persons, including Eugene Debs, Emma Goldman, and most other leading socialists, were imprisoned for sedition, often on dubious charges, and a number of presumably undesirable aliens were deported. States and private vigilance organizations, such as the Boy Spies of America and the American Anti-Anarchy Association, committed even greater excesses. Self-appointed patriots declared open season on disloyalty, nonconformity, and "heresy" or radicalism. The German language, German-American actors, and German music were banished from schools, the stage, and concerts, respectively. Religious pacifists and other "slackers" were humiliated, physically abused, and in some cases lynched. Rigid censorship and political repression were imposed on educational institutions, the press, and the movie industry. Some mobilization of opinion may have been necessary, but official abuses of civil liberties during the Wilson administration were extreme in a democracy, and substantially worse than during either the Civil War or World War II. As the postwar Red Scare of 1919 would demonstrate, patriotism was more easily aroused than controlled (see Chapter 24).

Yet, for all the repression and hysteria, the American people knew little of the horrors of war. Few civilians knew or understood the remote and hideous world of the Western Front, a world of barbed wire and rat-infested trenches, of appalling butchery and rotting corpses, crowded field hospitals, poison gas, shrapnel, and shell shock. At war's end, Americans proudly noted that their arms and troops had tipped the balance in the Allies' favor. But the price paid in American lives was relatively small; in an intense six months of fighting, the United States sustained about 100,000 combat-related deaths, about half in battle and half due to disease. By contrast, in four years the Russian combat dead numbered 1,700,000; the Germans, 1,600,000; the French, 1,400,000; and the British, 900,000 — 20,000 of them in a single day. All told, about 10 million people died in the bloodiest and most costly war in history.

THE FAILURE OF A WILSONIAN PEACE

Wilson became the worldwide prophet of a democratic peace, a singular spokesman for moral ideas in a world at war. In substantial measure, he had advocated intervention to give the Americans a decisive role in shaping a just and lasting postwar agreement between the warring countries. On January 8, 1918, ten months before the armistice, Wilson outlined to Congress his famous Fourteen Points, the terms for peace.

The first five points were general liberal formulae: open treaty making, freedom of the seas, removal of trade barriers, arms reduction, and impartial adjustment of colonial claims in the interest of the natives. Most of the remaining points were concerned with the readjustment of boundaries in the interest of the Wilsonian principle of national self-determination even for small nations. The final point, the most important to Wilson, provided for an association of nations to maintain the peace. A number of the Fourteen Points were contrary to provisions in the secret treaties already negotiated among the Allies. Wilson knew of these treaties but ignored them, doubtless believing that he could force the Allies to abandon them.

Its military situation hopeless, Germany asked Wilson on October 6 for an armistice based on his announced program. Despite Allied objections, the Fourteen Points were accepted as the basis for peace, but not without several specific reservations. On November 11, military authorities finished negotiating a truce that disarmed Germany and made further resistance impossible.

In January 1919 at Paris, the victorious Allies started negotiating among themselves the peace terms to be imposed on Germany. Accompanied by an undistinguished peace delegation and a large corps of experts, Wilson left for Paris. Frantic ovations throughout Europe apparently convinced him that it was his mission alone to force a generous peace on the world. His bargaining power was limited by several factors, however. First, despite his misguided and narrowly partisan appeal for a Democratic Congress, the voters elected Republican majorities to both the Senate and the House in 1918. Thus, even as he attempted to check Allied ambitions, his leadership was apparently repudiated at home. Then, having negotiated a preliminary peace document with the provision for a League of Nations, he came back to Washington to find more than a third of the Senate opposed to the League convenant as then drafted. Returning to Paris, he had to face the Allied leaders with his authority further weakened. Another limiting factor was the fact that Allied leaders, bound by the secret treaties between them, were determined to secure their nations from further attack and to make Germany pay for the long struggle.

Despite a courageous fight, Wilson had to make many concessions from his original plan. To Italy he had to concede sizable German-speaking border areas. Japan secured not only Germany's island colonies (which were to play a crucial part in World War II), but also, against Chinese opposition, German interests in the Shantung Peninsula. To France, who desired the dismemberment of Germany, Wilson had to concede very severe terms regarding the defeated nation. Germany was stripped of colonies and merchant marine, disarmed, and forced to surrender border areas. Perhaps more important, Germany was required to admit its guilt for the war as a basis for reparations, whose sum would be fixed later by the Allies. With hindsight it is easy to see the inadequacies of the Versailles settlement. Too harsh to effect a reconciliation between conquered and conquering nations, it also failed to restore an Anglo-French world hegemony. Japan was thwarted, China chaotic, the colonial world restive, and all nonwhites irritated by the failure of a clause affirming racial equality.

In addition, Bolshevik Russia was proclaiming world revolution, and communist revolutions seemed to threaten both Asia and Central Europe. Hoping to smash Bolshevism before it could spread, Allied forces with American participation invaded Russian territory during her years of upheaval and civil war. Wilson also joined an Allied economic blockade and withheld American diplomatic recognition from the new Soviet state. These and other Allied anti-communist gestures figured importantly in Soviet alienation from the West and contributed to tensions leading 25 years later to the Cold War.

To Wilson, exhausted and implacable, all the faults of the Versailles settlement were compensated for by the gains for self-determination and above all by the establishment of the League of Nations. It would, he hoped, supervise the administration of former German colonies by their new masters under the mandate system. It would secure the reduction of armaments, preserve the independence and integrity of all nations, mediate disputes, and even use force against those resorting to war. For this great ideal, Wilson came home to fight an uncompromising moral battle for the covenant of the League.

At first, the treaty's chances looked good. Wilson's prestige was still great, and the idea of a League of Nations had long attracted American support. But the treaty aroused many kinds of opposition. Among its enemies were the disappointed minorities of German, Italian, and Irish descent, isolationists who feared that the League would involve America in European affairs, liberals who objected to the compromises of democratic principle, and a less easily identifiable, but large group of Americans reacting against wartime enthusiasm and sacrifice.

The Senate, where the treaty's struggle centered, was divided into three groups: loyal Wilsonian Democrats in favor of the treaty and the League; a group of about a dozen senators, including La Follette, Borah, and Johnson of California, who were "Irreconcilables," all-out foes of both issues; and "Reservationists," who were inclined to accept the treaty with certain changes defining and restricting the authority of the League.

In the long struggle, opposition to the treaty was marshaled by Henry Cabot Lodge, an enemy of Wilson and a master tactician. In order to attract the crucial Reservationists, Lodge proposed not rejection but alteration of the treaty. The changes were carefully calculated to sound plausible but to be unacceptable to Wilson. Lodge knew his opponent. Wilson forbade Democrats to accept the reservations, thus making impossible the two-thirds majority necessary for passage of the treaty. Without reservations, the treaty was opposed by Irreconcilables and Reservationists; with reservations, it was opposed by Irreconcilables and loyal Democrats.

Refusing to accept defeat, Wilson embarked on a nationwide speaking tour. The people, he said, must not allow the Senate to "break the heart of the world" by rejecting the treaty. Prematurely aged and emotionally exhausted, Wilson broke down in the midst of his tour and had to be taken back to Washington. There he suffered a severe stroke and was partly incapacitated for the rest of his presidency. Sick, isolated, but grimly determined, he continued to forbid his followers to compromise. Wilson's loyal followers rejected the reservations, and the treaty failed to get ratification.

Once more Wilson appealed to the final authority, the American people, announcing in the spring of 1920 that the coming presidential election would constitute a "solemn referendum" on the treaty. In the campaign, the Democratic candidate, Governor James M. Cox of Ohio, supported the treaty and the League. The Republican candidate, Senator Warren G. Harding of the same state, opposed it only ambiguously, and some of his supporters favored it equally vaguely.

Harding won by the most sweeping majority since Monroe. It is impossible to prove that the election constituted a real referendum on foreign policy. It was certainly affected by many domestic issues, including the breakdown of Wilson and, to a considerable extent, of his administration. In another sense, however, the election of 1920 was a major decision; the campaign, the press, and the results indicated that the American people wanted a president as little like Woodrow Wilson as possible, and this is what they got.

CONFLICTING HISTORICAL VIEWPOINTS: NO. 11

Why Did America Enter World War I?

Contemporary accounts of U.S. intervention in World War I were generally favorable to Wilsonian policies. The war was a noble and necessary war, many firsthand observers agreed, and Americans could take pride and satisfaction in their role in it. Reinforcing this initial view were two semi-autobiographical publications: Burton Hendrick, ed., The Life and Letters of Walter H. Page *(3 vols., 1922–1926), and Charles Seymour,* The Intimate Papers of Colonel House *(4 vols., 1926–1928). Both House and Page had helped shape American policy, and neither questioned the wisdom of U.S. intervention.*

*A revisionist interpretation, however, was not long in developing. Disillusioned by the failures of Wilson's peace and threatened by the gathering clouds of war in Europe and Asia, many Americans in the 1920s and 1930s traced the nation's involvement not to idealism or self-interest but to folly, sentimentalism, and greed. Scholarly advocates of this view included Harry E. Barnes (*Genesis of the World War, *1926), C. Hartley Grattan (*Why We Fought, *1929), and Charles C. Tansill (*America Goes to War, *1938), all of whom argued that Wilson's policies were neither wise, necessary, nor beneficial to the United States. In their accounts, U.S. intervention was attributed to the pernicious influences of misguided Wilsonian Anglophiles, skillful British propagandists, and grasping American munitions makers and international bankers.*

Although the revisionist view was in many ways an accurate reflection of popular, or at least congressional, sentiment during the postwar and De-

*pression years, it has not been widely accepted by historians. A more sat-
isfactory argument was offered by Charles Seymour, whose* American
Diplomacy During World War I *(1934) has been called "the first historian's
history of intervention." Treating American involvement as a historical problem rather than as a moral issue, this Yale professor asserted that Wilson,
although pro-Allies, struggled valiantly to remain neutral. Anticipating later
interpretations such as Arthur Link's* Wilson the Diplomatist *(1957) and
Ernest May's* The World War and American Isolation *(1959), Seymour concluded that Wilson had little choice but to lead the nation into war. In the
final analysis, he believed, the German submarine was the cause of American intervention. In close agreement, Link and May have stressed the
tragedy of Wilson's dilemma and the limited range of his alternatives. While
they, too, endeavored to avoid judgment, their studies stress the essential
correctness of presidential policy.*

*Also critical of revisionism were such "realist" historians as George Ken-
nan (*American Diplomacy, *1950) and Robert Osgood (*Idealism and Self-
Interest in America's Foreign Policy, *1953), who argued that in 1917 the
United States entered the right war for the wrong reasons. Having experienced World War II, realists doubted that the United States could have avoided
World War I. Their primary complaint, then, was not that Wilson carried
the nation into war, but that he did so in the name of morality and legality, not national security and self-interest.*

*Radical historians, on the other hand, denied that American intervention
could be attributed to altruism and idealism. In their view, the war was
waged not to make the world safe for democracy but to make the world's
markets safe for American economic expansion. Although perhaps best argued in William Appleman Williams's* The Tragedy of American Diplomacy
*(1962), a subtle and challenging variation on this theme is presented in N.
Gordon Levin's* Woodrow Wilson and World Politics *(1968). According to
this scholar, it was Wilson's aim to build "a new rational international-
capitalist order, safe from war and revolution and open to [American] commercial and moral expansion."*

FOR FURTHER READING

In addition to the studies mentioned above, students interested in the diplomacy of American interventionism should consult Ross Gregory's *The Origins of American Intervention in the First World War* (1971) and Patrick
Devlin's *Too Proud to Fight* (1974). Also of interest to the conduct of the
war are Robert H. Ferrell's *Woodrow Wilson and the First World War*
(1985) and Ellis Hawley's *The Great War and the Search for a Modern
Order* (1979). The social and economic history of the home front are described in David Kennedy's *Over Here* (1980), Barry D. Karl's *The Uneasy
State* (1983), Maurine Greenwald's *Women, War, and Work* (1980), and
Florette Henri's *Black Migration* (1975). The wartime state of civil liberties is described by Zechariah Chafee in *Free Speech in the United States*

(1941); by Paul Murphy in *World War I and the Origin of Civil Liberties* (1979); by William Preston in *Aliens and Dissenters* (1966); and by Emma Goldman in *Living My Life* (1931). The misuse of history by wartime historians is the subject of Carol S. Gruber's *Mars and Minerva* (1975) and G. T. Blakey's *Historians on the Home Front* (1971). Studies of Wilson and the peace include Ralph Stone, *The Irreconcilables* (1970); Lloyd Ambrosius, *Woodrow Wilson and the American Diplomatic Tradition* (1987); and Lloyd C. Gardner, *Safe for Democracy* (1984). The beginnings of Soviet-American relations are described in William Appleman Williams's *American-Russian Relations* (1952) and in Peter G. Filene's *Americans and the Soviet Experiment* (1967).

24

★ ★ ★ ★ ★ ★

The Twenties: Prosperity and Social Change

AMERICANS today view the postwar decade in at least three ways. It was the Jazz Age, the Roaring Twenties, and the romantic heyday of flappers and flivvers. It was also the period of Coolidge prosperity, conservative retrenchment, and isolation. Finally, it was the period of the "lost generation," of Ernest Hemingway, F. Scott Fitzgerald, and T. S. Eliot — an era marked by literary rebellion and experimentation.

Even at the time, different kinds of people saw America from differing angles. Entrepreneurs and farmers, Freudians and fundamentalists, all were reacting at varying rates and ways to a changing social and economic order. Some changes, like industrialization and urbanization, had been going on for a long time and were accelerating. Others, like the importation of challenging new ideas (among them psychoanalysis and relativity), had begun before the war. Still other changes directly resulted from the war, which was itself a traumatic break with national tradition.

Some Americans accepted change passively, if not willingly; others clung tenaciously to tradition and fought every departure from old ways. Other Americans, among them notably Henry Ford, accepted innovation in areas like technology and transportation, but fought it in areas like manners and morals. Even for the most conservative, however, tradition seemed hard to define, let alone restore.

This period of flux was cushioned by relatively good times. For many Americans, though clearly not all, the Twenties were years of peace and prosperity — the last to occur for a long time.

POSTWAR ADJUSTMENTS, 1918–1920

Ironically, high-minded Woodrow Wilson, not vacuous Warren G. Harding, ushered in the spiritually cramped postwar reaction and disillusionment. Wilson more than any evangel of the resurgent Old Guard set the tone of the "New Era."

The immediate aftermath of the war was anything but placid. The fight over the treaty was only the first round of a frustrating struggle to liquidate the war and, less consciously, the idealism that led to America's involvement in it. In 1919, advanced progressives and labor leaders were talking about planned and masterful nationwide reconstruction and some were predicting the nationalization of basic industries. Actually, nothing was further from popular demand or administration intent. From the armistice on, government contracts were canceled, employees dismissed, and regulatory powers abandoned. Soldiers were rapidly discharged with only minimum provisions for re-employment.

Congress abandoned regulation and reform less rapidly than the administration. Immediately after the war, two progressive causes reached nationwide victory. The Eighteenth (prohibition) Amendment, pushed hard by the Methodist Church and the Anti-Saloon League, was passed through a combination of moral zeal, desire to conserve resources, and dislike of German-American brewers. In October 1919, the Volstead Act was passed over Wilson's veto and ended forever (most of its friends and enemies thought) the manufacture, sale, transportation, and possession of intoxicating beverages. In the same year, the Nineteenth Amendment made women's suffrage a nationwide reality.

In dismantling controls, the postwar Congress had a mixed record. The railroads, returned to private hands by the administration, were placed under stringent regulation by the Esch-Cummins Act of 1920. This law's purpose, however, was partly to promote, rather than to prevent, consolidation into fewer systems. From then on, the railroad industry, threatened with truck and bus competition and overbuilt in places, was treated more like an invalid than like a tyrannical giant. The government-built merchant marine was returned to private interests, and here too subsidy was needed more than control. In the vital area of water power, Congress established in 1920 a new regulatory agency, the Federal Power Commission, to license development and operation.

For the most part, however, the wartime-directed economy was dismantled without planning and without disaster. In the spring of 1919, after a very brief postwar slump, business began to pick up. At the time, the upturn was credited to unsatisfied consumer demand, but economists today credit government spending, temporarily continued in the form of loans to the Allies and European relief operations. Rapidly, recovery turned into speculative boom, as wholesale prices rose by about 30 percent.

Instead of Imperial Germany, the main public enemy in 1919 seemed to be the high cost of living. Salaried people on fixed incomes were badly pinched by runaway inflation. Labor was restive, fearful that its wartime gains might be lost and threatened by increasingly anti-union employers. Four million workers, more than ever before, went on strike for higher wages, shorter hours, and better conditions. Though these were traditional union objectives, conservatives in most cases portrayed work stoppages as revolutionary acts inspired by Bolsheviks. This portrayal was successful particularly in the Seattle general strike, the United Mine Workers' strike, the bitter and bloody steel strike, and the Boston police strike. Public opinion, local and state governments, and the Wilson administration sided strongly with management, and the unions generally lost these battles.

Along the nation's troubled racial front, there was also violence and disorder. Beginning with the savage East St. Louis riot of 1917 and climaxing with a violent eruption in Chicago during the Red Summer of 1919 (so called because of the bloodshed), American cities began a painfully uneasy adjustment to the growing presence of new waves of black migrants. Pushed out of the South by discrimination and violence and drawn to northern industrial centers by wartime employment and the promise of a better life, blacks by the thousands came to occupy the blighted slums of Buffalo, Chicago, Cleveland, Detroit, New York, and other cities. In time, these black newcomers found somewhat better economic, political, and educational opportunities. But during the war and its aftermath, their presence was bitterly resented by whites who feared social equality and job competition. There were at least 26 urban race conflicts during the Red Summer, and in Chicago alone a chain of white violence, black counterviolence, and official repression left 23 blacks dead and thousands more homeless. Outraged by these bloody encounters — and the 83 lynchings of 1919 — the NAACP and allied organizations launched a campaign that resulted in 1921 in the first antilynching bill ever passed by the House of Representatives. In the Senate, however, a southern filibuster prevented its enactment. During the postwar decade, lynch mobs killed at least 330 Americans, nearly all of them southern blacks.

Many white citizens blamed racial unrest, strikes, the high cost of living, and foreign crises on one simple cause: radical conspiracy. The Third International, calling from Moscow for world revolution, was echoed by the two new American communist organizations: the Communist Labor party (cofounded by John Reed) and the Communist party (composed largely of aliens). Although the parties could legitimately claim no more than 50,000–70,000 members, their very presence alarmed many Americans. Public opinion was also aroused by a few unexplained bombings believed to be of anarchist origin. Many conservative citizens feared — and a few ardent radicals hoped — that revolution was at hand.

In January 1920, politically ambitious Attorney General A. Mitchell Palmer ordered a series of raids on alleged foreign radical organizations. Using intelligence dossiers compiled by J. Edgar Hoover, director of the new Bureau of Investigation, Palmer's agents summarily arrested more than 4,000 people in 33 cities; some 250 alien radicals, including Emma Goldman, were deported to the USSR aboard the "Soviet Ark." Little evidence of dangerous revolutionary activity was uncovered, but many zealous individuals, organizations, and governmental units turned their hostility from Germans to radicals. Eager to win congressional support for a peacetime sedition act, Palmer even warned that revolutionaries planned to overthrow the United States government on May Day of 1920. The New York legislature expelled five duly-elected Socialist representatives; some communities required school teachers to take loyalty oaths; several states made it illegal to fly the red flag of Bolshevism. In 1921, two philosophical anarchists, the hapless Nicola Sacco and Bartolomeo Vanzetti, were arrested for a robbery and murder on evidence that seemed to rest on public hostility toward alien radicals. Despite impassioned agitation for their release, they were finally executed in 1927. Half a century later, they were posthumously pardoned.

Well before this execution, in fact before the end of 1920, the Red Scare began to ebb. Though Palmer's excesses were widely ridiculed, the public's fear of the alien, the dissenter, and the nonconformist continued to manifest itself in race riots and lynchings, in anti-Semitic whisperings, in crusades against alarming ideas, and in suspicion of foreigners. All these tendencies play a part in the growth of the Ku Klux Klan, a secret organization founded in 1915 in imitation of its Reconstruction namesake. Stronger in the West and Midwest than the South — and with surprising strength in some larger cities and in New England — the Klan was militantly anti-Catholic, anti-Semitic, antiforeign, antiliberal, and antimodern. At its peak in the early 1920s, thousands participated in "One Hundred Percent Americanism" parades, perhaps 5 million enrolled in the Klan (and bought hoods and bedsheet robes), and at least two states came under its political control. Only in the mid-1920s, when most kinds of hysteria gave way to complacency, did the Klan lose strength.

In 1919–1920, many Americans came to associate Wilsonian idealism with frustrated hopes and divisive emotions, with the unsolved problems of Europe, with war propaganda and foreign entanglements, and with the high cost of living and the Red Menace. Even the most devoted Wilsonians had to admit a shattering contrast between the vigorous leader of 1913 or the inspired prophet of 1917 and the sick, stubborn, old man of 1919, presiding over an administration zealous in hounding radicals but helpless in dealing with social or economic problems. Unsurprisingly, the country turned with relief toward a completely opposite type of leadership.

INDEPENDENT INTERNATIONALISM

Warren G. Harding was a small-town editor, a regular McKinley and Taft Republican, and a handsome, genial man with a modest intellectual endowment and undemanding moral standards. Conceivably, he was a more forceful and able president than the bumbling misfit that several generations of historians have portrayed him to be. But even his most sympathetic biographer concedes that his term of office was scarred by gross mismanagement. To his credit, he announced a plan to staff his administration with his party's "best minds." A few of these were secured, including Charles Evans Hughes as the new secretary of state, Henry C. Wallace as secretary of agriculture, and Herbert Hoover as secretary of commerce. In too many cases, however, the administration was staffed with presidential cronies. A major center of power was the notorious "little house on K Street," where members of the "Ohio Gang" exchanged male jokes, played poker, and drank prohibited whiskey. Harding's heterogeneous group of the talented and the tawdry made decisions of great importance, most of them highly popular in their time. Indeed, a nation that had seemed reluctant to embrace such exceptionally able chief executives as Lincoln and Wilson gave its heart to the good-natured and second-rate Harding.

In his campaign, Harding, whose oratory rarely rose above platitudes, avoided defining his foreign policy. Much of the Republican party was bitterly isolationist, but an important faction including ex-President Taft insisted that a new administration work out a less offensive substitute for the League of Nations. Whatever the election really meant (and clearly it was no "solemn referendum" on the League), Harding drew from it the conclusion that American entry into the League was a dead issue. U.S. membership in the World Court, which Harding and his Republican successors favored, was blocked by conservatives in the press and Senate.

Despite strong isolationist sentiment, total disengagement from world affairs proved impossible. The United States pursued what has been called an independent internationalism. As the world's greatest manufacturing, exporting, and creditor nation, it could hardly return to its traditional isolationism, and American policies during the 1920s vigorously promoted the nation's overseas trading advantages. American exports more than doubled during the decade; American investors, encouraged by both the State Department and favorable tax laws, penetrated foreign markets as never before. Private American capital sustained the new German Republic, propped up congenial governments throughout Latin America, and helped the relatively moderate banking and industrial regime in Japan. Americans vied with the British and French for Near Eastern oil areas, and developed copper interests in Chile. Because all these ventures were done in the name of profit rather than politics and, above all, because military force was invoked only in minor instances in the Caribbean, the Republican administrations of this decade could appease isolationists with pious references to the founders' anti-entanglement doctrines.

In the Far East, the original home of the Open Door Policy and the traditional center of Republican foreign interest, Secretary Hughes and other key Harding international advisers endeavored to stabilize the balance of power. During the war, Japan had taken steps to dominate China and to gain military hegemony in East Asia. Traditional American commitments to the trading and territorial integrity of China still ran well beyond America's military power. Attempting to limit naval armaments and to promote Far Eastern stability, the Harding administration sponsored the multinational Washington Conference of 1921. Participating nations included Great Britain, France, Italy, the Netherlands, Portugal, Belgium, China, and Japan. Here the United States entered into a series of interlocking multilateral treaties that limited the construction of capital ships, partially rolled back Japanese territorial expansion, terminated the embarrassing Anglo-Japanese Alliance, recognized the Pacific status quo, and reaffirmed the Open Door. In return for these concessions (many from the Japanese), the United States surrendered the possibility of naval superiority and agreed not to fortify its posses-

ing policies. Prewar progressivism, with its underdog sympathies and anti–big-business sentiments, lived on in the hearts of millions of teachers, preachers, social workers, unionists, and others. In the new postwar circumstances, however, both high morale and unity seemed hard for progressives to attain.

In 1922, the most promising of a series of progressive coalitions took shape in the form of the Conference for Progressive Political Action (CPPA), a federation of farm organizations, discontented labor groups, moderate Socialists, and assorted Bull Moosers and other progressives. In the congressional elections of 1922, the CPPA scored some startling successes. Harding Republicans lost many seats to both the Democrats and the progressive Republicans.

In the Sixty-Eighth Congress, Senate investigations disclosed a series of scandals equaled only in the Grant administration. Harding cronies in the Veterans Bureau, the Departments of Justice and Interior, and other agencies had dispensed favors for financial inducements. The worst revelation was that government oil lands (held for naval needs) at Teapot Dome, Wyoming, and Elk Hills, California, had been secretly transferred to private speculators. Betrayed by his appointees, Harding complained that the presidency was "a hell of a job." "I have no trouble with my enemies," he confided to a journalist. "But my friends, my God damned friends."

Harding fell ill while returning from an Alaskan junket; on August 2, 1923, he died of a stroke in San Francisco. His office was assumed by Vice President Calvin Coolidge, the "High Priest of Stability" and the perfect incarnation of conventional Republican morality. In all fairness, this taciturn Vermonter (the most cruelly caricatured of presidents) was not entirely the political cipher of the "Silent Cal" joke. He was, in fact, conventional and uninspiring. His most memorable expression seems almost self-mocking: "The business of America is business." Much in his public career was virtuous, and he brought to the presidency more knowledge of domestic and foreign affairs than he has been credited with.

During 1922–1924, many people thought that the Harding scandals and the progressive gains foreshadowed a political upheaval. The CPPA backed the redoubtable "Fighting Bob" La Follette as a "Progressive" presidential candidate. The La Follette platform had an oddly dissonant reform ring for 1924: antimonopoly, public ownership of railroads, conservation, farm relief, and curbing of the Supreme Court. The Wisconsin Senator, whose antiwar record was now an asset in his own region, looked formidable enough to unnerve conservatives. The Republicans, renominating Coolidge on a status quo and laissez-faire platform, denounced La Follette and his "radical" following. Meanwhile the Democrats, deeply divided on such issues as the Klan and Prohibition, finally settled on an unpromising conservative candidate, John W. Davis. In the election, La Follette carried nearly 17 percent of the popular vote and ran ahead of Davis in many western states, but Coolidge won in a landslide. A business-oriented public voted for more of the same.

THE NEW ERA

For the rest of the decade, American prosperity took center stage. The basis for the good times was an increase in productivity based on advances in technology, mass production, and scientific management. Industrial output and foreign investments soared; worker productivity in manufacturing rose by one-half. New industries abounded, including automobiles, commercial aviation, and chemicals. The most spectacular advances came in the production of electric power and light and such durable consumer goods as refrigerators, vacuum sweepers, and washing machines, and in the construction of suburban houses and urban skyscrapers. By 1925, Ford's "Tin Lizzy" cost $260, well within the reach of many families; by 1929, one American in five had an automobile. Radios, household appliances, and prepared foods became standard fixtures of the "good" American life.

Changing patterns of consumption, stimulated by the new mass-advertising industry and assisted by credit and installment-plan purchasing, seemed to render obsolete the Puritan virtues of hard work, self-denial, and saving. As a workweek of five and one-half days became increasingly common for industrial workers, leisure and the pursuit of amusement became possible for great numbers of people. With extra time on its hands and money in its pockets, the public turned its attention to a new pantheon: movie stars, athletes, and heroes like Charles Lindbergh, the Lone Eagle, whose solo flight across the Atlantic in 1927 made him the most popular American. Close in popularity were the sports heroes: baseball's Herman "Babe" Ruth, boxing's Jack (the "Manassa Mauler") Dempsey, and collegiate football's Harold "Red" Grange, (the "Galloping Ghost"). In an increasingly collectivized, motorized, and standardized mass society, the triumphs of these individuals — including that of Gertrude Ederle, the first woman and the first American to swim the English Channel — captured newspaper headlines and the popular imagination. The nation's appetite for fantasy was fed by the cinematic exploits of dashing Rudolph Valentino, sultry Clara Bow (the "it" girl), and Theda Bara (the "vamp").

The screen and the sports arena were not the sole amusements for postwar Americans. Some turned to jazz, the unique, black musical idiom. Perfected by such Afro-American band leaders and instrumentalists as Joe "King" Oliver and Louis Armstrong, jazz was popularized by such white band leaders as Ted Lewis and Paul Whiteman. Other middle-class pastimes included golf, tennis, and the frivolities that gave the "Era of Wonderful Nonsense" its name — six-day bicycle races, marathon dancing, the Charleston, mahjongg, and flagpole-sitting. Collegians, it was said, not only strutted the latest dances in bellbottoms and sleeveless dresses, but swallowed goldfish! A "revolution" in sexual morality, apparently more widely discussed than exercised, seemed to herald the death of Victorian prudery. Some historians, as the Viewpoint essay argues, have made too much of these popular diversions to the neglect of an emerging machine and business civilization, but this decade of evanescent prosperity was notably an age in which urban Americans in growing numbers learned to play.

The postwar boom brought with it a new ideology as well as fads. American business, according to its enthusiasts, had accomplished the dreams of past radicals without coercion or class struggle. Poverty and war were both overcome, and cutthroat competition had been replaced by economic cooperation and social service. The new business leaders, it was said, were committed to high wages and deeply interested in employee welfare. Some firms introduced paid vacations, recreation halls, group insurance, and old-age pensions. Thus, in a new era of enlightened "welfare capitalism" and uncritical popular support for business, there was no further use for labor unions or radicalism.

THE CRITICS OF THE 1920s

The benefits of the new affluence were not universally shared, nor was there a universally sanguine view of the benefits of cultural change. The farmers' depression began at the beginning of the decade, and business failures were widespread. Real wages for industrial workers rose, but not in proportion either to productivity or profits. Economic statistics for the period are unreliable, but some economists place the unemployment rate at 10–13 percent; 50 percent of the people, by one estimate, lived below the poverty line. In 1929 the average factory worker made less than $1,500 annually; the combined income of the richest 0.1 percent equalled that of the poorest 42 percent. Although the middle and upper classes were thriving, large numbers of Americans — coal and textile workers, southern dirt farmers, seasonal laborers, unorganized workers, the elderly, single women, most blacks and Hispanics — were experiencing hard times.

Later developments would demonstrate that the prosperity of the New Era was as unsound as it was uneven. Business consolidation, after a brief pause in the trust-busting years, flourished again and often led to dangerous practices. Prices were more often administered than competitive. Insider groups sometimes built crazy pyramids of holding companies. In the late 1920s, too much money went to outright speculation in land or stocks, and not enough into genuinely productive investments. Chain stores crowded out local retailers of food, merchandise, and pharmaceuticals. Most serious was the distribution of income that put little purchasing power in the paychecks of average consumers.

Important minorities also refused to join in the chorus of complacency. Surviving congressional progressives, led by Senator George Norris of Nebraska, prevented the administration from turning over to private interests the government-built nitrate plants on the Tennessee River. (In turn, Coolidge and his successor were able to block Norris's own plan for a government-run Tennessee dam and power system.) Prodded by the Farm Bloc, Congress passed ambitious farm relief laws. Of these, the most discussed was the McNary-Haugen bill, vetoed in 1927. This was a complex scheme providing for government purchase and sale abroad of surplus farm commodities.

Other important dissenters expressed themselves outside the political arena. Many people, often those living in isolated and provincial areas, resented modern ways, machines, and large cities. Uneasy in an increasingly complex and uncertain world, these Americans clung to the conventions of a simpler past, their identity and moral values rooted in family, church, and community. The Klan, the Red Scare, the immigration restriction movement, Prohibition, and even the evangelism of Sister Aimee Semple McPherson and Billy Sunday reflected the discontent of those who recoiled from the apparent secularism, materialism, and hedonism of an urban age. The most dramatic expression of this clash of cultures was the Fundamentalist crusade that seemed to pit the Bible against Darwinian science. Sixty years after the publication of Charles Darwin's *On the Origin of Species*, a number of southern Bible-belt states proscribed the teaching of evolutionary theory in the public schools. In 1925, when the American Civil Liberties Union challenged the first of these laws in the famous Scopes trial in Tennessee, no less a figure than William Jennings Bryan appeared to champion the "Old Time Religion."

Equally hostile to the dominant tendencies of the age were the literary insurgents and other intellectual critics of the culture of materialism. Although the Lost Generation had its roots in an exuberant prewar rebellion against moral and esthetic conventions, its members became more deeply alienated in the Twenties. Repelled by postwar intolerance and by what they thought to be the vulgar materialism and spiritual emptiness, many American intellectuals expressed their worries about its culture in lectures and in print. Some fled to more congenial environs — to the sophistication of Paris, the primitivism of Mexico, or New York's Greenwich Village. Whether in exile or at home, the nation's literary avant-garde experimented with new expressive forms and assailed the "organized stupidity" of the American "boobosie."

The most perceptive of the discontented recognized that more was at stake than any set of national mores. Old questions, put in new forms, were raising doubts about human nature itself. Americans were confronting problems common to all people but particularly distressing to those who inherited a tradition of individual freedom. To some popular behaviorist psychologists, the human person was a bundle of predictable and controllable responses to physical stimuli. To Freudians, human beings were ruled by emotional drives far below the level of consciousness. Neither view seemed to offer much hope to those who cared most for individual freedom. Squarely confronting these and other intellectual challenges, some Americans produced excellent and profoundly serious novels or poems. Others laid the foundation for a deeper and richer criticism of contemporary civilization than had yet been possible.

Afro-Americans, perhaps more than any other group, indulged in this spirit of national self-criticism and personal re-evaluation, and explored the failures of American society. The black literati of the Harlem Renaissance shared the discontented white intellectuals' distaste for bourgeois values and joined their insurrection against traditional literary forms. But the alienation of the black artists seemed more firmly rooted in the day-to-day realities of American life. In a rich outpouring of poems and novels, they celebrated the emergence of a "New Negro" — race-proud and militant, impatient with white injustice, determined to fight for basic human dignity. Joined by a confident new generation of black musicians, dancers, painters, and actors, they struggled to work out a new attitude toward blackness and the cultural heritage of their African past. In a parallel development, the inarticulate black denizens of the nation's industrial slums found a symbol of race pride in the exotic figure of Marcus Garvey and his Universal Negro Improvement Association. Unlike either Booker T. Washington or W. E. B. Du Bois, Garvey stirred the imagination of the impoverished black masses. His back-to-Africa movement, like his dream of an African empire, died in embryo. But his immense popularity (estimates of his following range from one to four million) exposed the depths of Afro-American despair.

The discontent of some intellectuals and the dissatisfaction of much of its black minority were not widely shared by other segments of the population. Indeed, traditional Lost Generation accounts have doubtless exaggerated the degree and the depth of alienation and dissaffection among even the most discerning and sensitive elements of society. Everybody was not happy or rich in the mid-1920s, but prosperity was still a substantial fact, and those who were the most satisfied were also the most influential. More people than ever before moved to the suburbs, drove to the beach, or dreamed of a summer in Europe. Prosperity could be measured not only in baseball gate receipts but in such substantial terms as houses, schools, and hospitals. What civilization, complacent citizens could legitimately ask, had ever done so much for so many?

Ignoring his critics, President Coolidge continued to issue his laconic and reassuring statements, take his afternoon naps, continue his predecessor's probusiness policies, and remain generally popular. The federal government persisted in trimming its costs, and Secretary Mellon assured the continued support of business.

In foreign affairs, success seemed equally conclusive. In Europe, the mid-1920s were an era of apparent economic stabilization, of Franco-German rapprochement, and of increased prestige for the League of Nations. Despite congressional suspicion, the administration was able to develop a habit of unofficial cooperation with the League for many purposes. In Mexico, where conflict between the forces of social revolution and American business interests dragged on, the Coolidge administration managed to compromise serious differences over subsoil oil rights. Americans also believed that they could attain lasting international peace. Barred by Congress from toying with collective security, the Coolidge administration made further but generally unsuccessful efforts to negotiate disarmament in 1927, an effort carried on by Hoover with somewhat more success in 1930. In August 1928, largely through American efforts, 15 nations signed the Kellogg-Briand Pact renouncing war as an instrument of national policy.

HOOVER AND SMITH

In 1928 the two major presidential candidates presented a colorful contrast, though in retrospect their platforms did not. Both were essentially pro-business moderates, and except for Prohibition, their views were similar. Alfred E. Smith, the Democrat, did have a more progressive record in civil liberties and labor. The candidates, however, seemed to embody the post-war cultural conflicts that divided rural and urban, native and alien, provincial and cosmopolitan, traditional and modern. Hoover, his roots in a small Iowa town, came from old-immigrant stock and was a Protestant (Quaker) and a "dry." Smith was a New Yorker, an Irish-Catholic, and a "wet"; he had Jewish advisers and ties to Tammany Hall. Without question the campaign was sullied by intolerance and bigotry, particularly anti-Catholicism. But the Republicans had prosperity on their side, and in the end the election turned on economic issues, not on Smith's religion. Herbert Hoover, architect of the New Era, promised four more years of the good life, and that was enough for many voters.

The larger significance of the election is open to question. Some historians have attributed future Democratic triumphs to Al Smith's success with urban voters. Others, however, argue that Franklin D. Roosevelt's election and the new Democratic coalition are explained by the Depression, not by Smith's impressive showing in the cities.

Whatever the election's meaning for the future, the new Hoover administration seemed to promise increased efficiency and broader humanitarianism within the framework of the Harding-Coolidge policies. Yet Hoover, the ablest of the three postwar presidents, encountered disaster at home and menace abroad. Whether one looked at the peaceful and prosperous 1920s with nostalgia or distaste, the era would soon seem a strange interlude in the tragic and turbulent history of the twentieth century.

CONFLICTING HISTORICAL VIEWPOINTS: NO. 12

Were the Twenties Roaring and Reactionary?

Few decades in American history have suffered more superficial analysis than the 1920s. In popular thought and in all too many serious works of history, the years between the armistice and the crash have been described — after a contemporary newspaper advertisement for a motion picture — as years of "beautiful jazz babies, champagne baths, midnight revels, [and] petting parties in the purple dawn." Most studies of the postwar decade, like the talkies, are animated by stock characters typecast as "flaming youth," "discontented intellectuals," or "self-complacent Babbits."

This conception of the 1920s as the Jazz Age of a Lost Generation was the work of many hands. But its chief architect was the self-styled "retrospective journalist" Frederick Lewis Allen, whose Only Yesterday (1931) *is probably the most readable and widely read account of the decade. In Allen's view, it was a unique segment of American life with an atmosphere*

*and style of its own. Isolated somehow from its past and curiously uncon-
nected to its future, the decade was a frivolous interlude in which a nation, on the rebound from Wilsonian idealism, plunged into "a revolution
of manners and morals."*

*Allen's portrait, however impressionistic and superficial, profoundly in-
fluenced a generation of historians who viewed the period as an unfortunate interregnum between progressivism and the New Deal. The two best
overviews of the period, William E. Leuchtenburg's lively social history*
(The Perils of Prosperity, 1958) *and John D. Hicks's political, economic,
and diplomatic survey* (Republican Ascendancy, 1960), *emphasize the decade's
more frivolous and retrograde impulses.*

*In the late 1950s, however, more subtle and complex images of the 1920s
began to emerge. Growing numbers of scholars became skeptical about conventional emphasis on the spectacular, the bizarre, and the unique. Upon
close examination, many found continuity as well as change in the postwar
decade. Parting the curtain of speakeasies, marathon dances, and raccoon
coats, they perceived what Arthur Link has called "the exciting new frontier of American historical writing." A good example of this new view is
Roderick Nash's* The Nervous Generation (1970), *which did much to mute
the roar in the Roaring Twenties. A survey of formal thought and popular
culture, this study pointedly deemphasized the degenerate bohemian and
the flagpole sitter and argued that the period was notable for neither disillusioned cynicism nor happy revelry.*

*Similarly, recent political and diplomatic histories no longer teem with
one-dimensional political Philistines and resolute isolationists. Arthur Link*
(American Historical Review, *July 1959) and Clark Chambers* (Seedtime
of Reform, 1963), *for example, revealed powerful reform currents at work
in a decade once presumed to be conservative. Robert K. Murray* (The
Harding Era, 1969), *Donald McCoy* (Calvin Coolidge, 1967), *and David
Burner* (Herbert Hoover, 1978), *among others, have offered provocative
new studies of these Republican presidents that help dispel familiar, oversimple notions and that differ sharply in important particulars from earlier and markedly less sympathetic biographies. And foreign relations spe-
cialists, notably William Appleman Williams, have challenged "The Legend
of Isolationism in the 1920s"* (Science and Society, *Winter 1954).*

*Thus, in the past few decades, historical perceptions of the 1920s have
been altered. Although many areas of disagreement remain, there is broad
scholarly discontent with Jazz Age stereotypes. However enjoyable and en-
chanting, the traditional, breezy survey à la Allen lacked the depth and com-
plexity historians now bring to their analyses of the 1919–1929 decennium.*

FOR FURTHER READING

The works mentioned above by Allen and Hicks, however flawed in emphasis, remain useful introductions to the period. William Leuchtenburg's
recently revised *The Perils of Prosperity* (1993) is perhaps the most useful
general survey of the 1920s.

Economic history is excellently summarized by George Soule in *Prosperity Decade* (1947), while Roland Marchand explains the rise of a new and important part of economic life in *Advertising the American Dream* (1985). Irving Bernstein's *The Lean Years* (1960) is a revealing history of labor from 1921 to 1933. Lewis E. Ellis illuminates *Republican Foreign Policy* (1968), and Robert Murray examines the *Red Scare* (1955). Kenneth Jackson surveys *The Ku Klux Klan in the City* (1967), while Kathleen M. Blee looks at *Women of the Klan* (1991). Ray Ginger's *Six Days or Forever* (1958) analyzes the Scopes trial. Garvey's career is the subject of E. David Cronon's *Black Moses* (1974) and Judith Stein's *The World of Marcus Garvey* (1986); Nathan Huggins has surveyed the *Harlem Renaissance* (1971). An influential contemporary sample of American society is Robert and Helen Lynd's *Middletown* (1929). President Hoover's Research Committee on Social Trends summarizes a great mass of interesting material in *Recent Social Trends* (2 vols., 1933). Norman H. Clark's *Deliver Us from Evil* (1976) is a provocative interpretation of the "noble experiment." Warren J. Belasco in *Americans on the Road* (1979) examines the rise of American "automobility." For literary history, the best source is contemporary writing, and the best introduction is Alfred Kazin's *On Native Grounds* (1942).

The Great Depression and the New Deal

The Great Depression in 1929 began with the stock market crash in October 1929. This photograph of Wall Street in New York City shows the milling crowds outside the stock exchange in that fateful month. *(Brown Brothers)*

Full recovery from the Depression did not come until mobilization for World War II created jobs. Many banks that closed their doors in the early Depression years did not reopen; this one in Haverhill, Iowa, photographed in 1939, is an example. *(Library of Congress)*

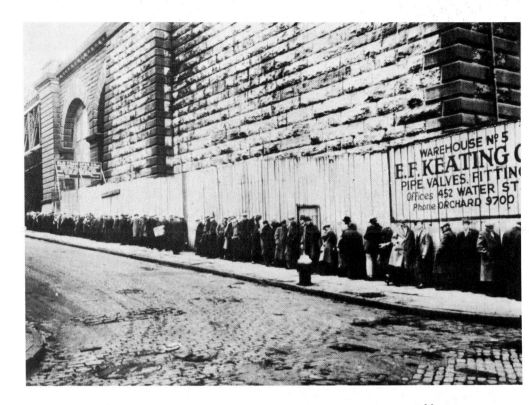

The election of the optimistic Franklin D. Roosevelt ended over a decade of Republican political ascendancy. This cover of the *New Yorker,* with its portrayal of a gloomy Hoover and a victorious Roosevelt on their way to the inaugural in 1933, was never published. Apparently it was considered inappropriate after there was an attempt to assassinate Roosevelt. *(Franklin D. Roosevelt Library)*

Jobless Americans haunted the cities, looking for work and seeking food doled out by private and public agencies. Photographed during the early 1930s, the long bread line near the Brooklyn Bridge in New York City shows graphically the impact of the Depression. *(Library of Congress)*

Union strength grew during the Depression, and New Deal legislation fostered workers' rights. CIO strikers are shown picketing a New York City radio station in December 1937. (*Library of Congress*)

The Depression extended through the 1930s, despite government intervention. Millions of workers were still unemployed, and many Americans lived in extreme poverty. This family in the sawmill town of Gibbs City, Michigan, was photographed in 1937. (*Library of Congress*)

The New Deal and its proliferation of government agencies received mixed reviews. Cartoonist Clifford Berryman in 1934 drew a skeptical view of these alphabetical remedies. (*Library of Congress*)

The effects of the Depression hit not only industrial workers and farmers but also white-collar workers. Many middle-class men found employment as manual laborers in federal projects. WPA workers here are shown excavating a trench in a New York City Park. *(Brown Brothers)*

Threshing Wheat shows a midwestern farm in the 1930s painted by Thomas Hart Benton. Shown also on the cover of *Volume II: Since the Civil War* of this text, the painting dramatizes the farm environment. *(1939, tempera on panel, 26 × 42 in., unframed. Permanent Collection, The Sheldon Swope Art Gallery, Terre Haute, Indiana)*

25

★ ★ ★ ★ ★ ★

Depression and New Deal, 1929–1938

IN THE SUMMER of 1929, while stock prices rose beyond all relation to earnings or dividends, most industrial and financial experts predicted nothing but permanent prosperity. Signs of trouble, including a general decline in consumer spending and particularly sharp reductions in the production and sale of housing and automobiles, went unnoticed. In September the market hesitated nervously, and then in late October a devastating series of crashes canceled 40 percent of the paper values of common stocks.

Despite the continuing optimism of government and business leaders, the crash of 1929 was not a mere correction of inflated values. Like the panics of 1873 and 1893, it turned into a severe and prolonged depression. In the years from 1929 to 1933, as stock prices fell ever lower and confidence evaporated, manufacturing production was halved and building nearly stopped. Banks and businesses failed; farm income, already low, was cut in half; worst of all, unemployment grew steadily. By 1932, at least one in every four Americans were jobless. Prosperity, and with it the spirit of the New Era, had disappeared.

The impact of the Great Depression on those who lived through it is hard to exaggerate. At the lowest economic level, the unemployed faced the threat of starvation when charities, cities, and states ran out of relief funds. Apple selling and bread lines became common sights; shanty towns sprang up on the edge of cities; men and women were sometimes seen pawing through restaurant garbage. At the opposite end of the scale, some respected financiers were caught misusing investors' funds; only a few killed themselves or fled to Europe. Both bankers and big businessmen rapidly lost public prestige. In the large, previously contented middle class, people unused to disaster lost savings, houses, jobs, and hope. Even those who suffered no personal privation found it hard to dispel fear. Anyone might be the next victim of a disaster that nobody understood.

Why did catastrophe paralyze the richest and most productive country in the world? At the time, many blamed the more obvious weak spots in the economy: the loose and ill-coordinated banking structure and the irresponsible financial manipulation that had piled one holding company on another. Later, New Dealers insisted that Republican policies had crippled foreign trade, encouraged inequality and concentration, fostered the boom, and then clung doggedly to financial conservatism after the crash. On the other hand, President Hoover was always to believe that the Depression was almost beaten when the election of a Democrat destroyed business confidence. In the long run, many historians have concluded that the causes were the unsoundness and inadequacy of the previous decade's prosperity. In the 1920s, prosperity depended as never before on mass consumption, but inequality in the distribution of profits and a too rigid price structure limited consumption. By 1929, demand for automobiles and some other products was apparently about filled. Attractive outlets seemed to be lacking for large-scale investment. In other words, the prosperity of part of one country in a poor world could not continue. The New Era picture of liberal and enlightened American capitalism, while not totally false, was not true enough.

HOOVER AND THE DEPRESSION

On entering office in 1929, President Hoover found himself confronted by two familiar problems of the Twenties: farm relief and the tariff. Each of these grew more difficult with the Depression. Like Coolidge, Hoover fought off farm bloc proposals that seemed to involve subsidy and price fixing. In their place, Hoover secured the passage of a complex measure establishing a Federal Farm Board empowered to promote such time-honored remedies as cooperative marketing. By 1930 the Stabilization Corporations also created by this law were buying and storing surplus wheat and cotton. Already the government was up to its neck in nondisposable surpluses, and prices were still going down.

As part of his farm program, Hoover proposed another old panacea — tariffs — on agricultural products. This led Congress to further demands for industrial protection and the enactment of the Smoot-Hawley Tariff, signed by Hoover despite the protest of more than 1,000 economists. The high rates of this measure ended all prospects of reviving foreign trade.

In his anti-Depression measures, President Hoover, the elected representative of New Era know-how, broke sharply with the past. When Secretary Mellon recommended that the government allow prices and wages to fall until recovery set in according to traditional laissez-faire formulae, Hoover decided that such a drastic purge might kill the delicate patient. His first action, following New Era doctrine rather than nineteenth-century economic theory, was to call conferences of business leaders in which employers were urged to maintain wages and production. When this proved ineffective, Hoover used available government machinery to cut taxes, liberalize credit, and prop farm prices.

By 1930 the administration turned to more drastic remedies. In that year, however, the long-brewing revolt against the Republicans was brought to a boil by the Depression, and Hoover lost the support of Congress. Many administration measures failed, but the president managed to secure large public works appropriations and measures to refinance home mortgages and further stimulate credit. A new agency, the Reconstruction Finance Corporation, lent large sums to banks, railroads, and businesses and also eventually to states, cities, and agricultural credit corporations. To stem international financial disaster, Hoover called successfully in 1931 for a one-year moratorium on German reparations and Allied debt payments.

Thus, in a major break with the past, the Hoover administration assumed governmental responsibility for fighting an economic crisis. Yet the Hoover measures, sweeping and large-scale as some seemed by the standards of the 1920s, were not adequate to the dimensions of the crisis. Moreover, the president flatly refused to meet two widespread demands. First, he opposed currency inflation. Second, he fought all direct, federal unemployment-relief measures. Either of these actions, he sincerely believed, would have grave effects on American tradition and character.

As the plight of the unemployed became desperate, Hoover was wrongly perceived as heartless by the public. By 1932, dejection, apathy, and bad luck seemed to have destroyed the administration's earlier vigor. In that year, a "Bonus Army" of unemployed servicemen assembled in Washington to demand immediate cash payoff of 20-year insurance policies provided for World War veterans by legislation in 1924. Panicking at a minor threat to order, the administration directed the U.S. Army to destroy the veterans' camp with tanks and tear gas. This episode helped to make Hoover, a sensitive man, the worst-hated president since Cleveland. Although not without personal warmth and humor in his private life, the public Hoover too often appeared to be a dour and dogmatic technocrat, aloof, uncompassionate, more troubled by falling corporate profits than by soaring unemployment.

Having forecast during the campaign "the day when poverty would be banished from the nation," his name quickly became the byword of personal misfortune and mass suffering. In a matter of months, his reputation collapsed, and the "great humanitarian" of 1928 became the scapegoat of the nation's worst economic disaster. His re-election was obviously unlikely.

Whether through political inexperience or through personality limitations, the hapless president lost the confidence of the nation and never managed to project the jaunty, crowd-winning confidence or the style of easy leadership that endeared his Democratic successor to a generation of Depression-weary voters. Democratic Governor Franklin D. Roosevelt of New York was little known to most of the public. A Hudson River aristocrat from the Democratic branch of his family, he had been influenced by his cousin Theodore as well as by Wilson, whom he had served as assistant secretary of the navy. After a losing campaign for the vice presidency in 1920, Roosevelt had been crippled by poliomyelitis. Though he never again walked unassisted, he recovered his physical strength and resumed his political career. In 1924 and 1928 he supported the presidential campaigns of

Al Smith, and kept his own name before the party's leaders. In 1928, bucking a Republican trend, he was elected governor of New York, where he tackled depression problems with great energy. Although sometimes dismissed during the presidential campaign as an unknown quantity with no particular ideas of his own, Roosevelt's years in Albany had nevertheless been uncommonly fruitful. As governor of the nation's most populous state, he was a champion of social welfare and reform legislation, which included the first state relief agency, social security and labor measures, public works programs, and regional planning. His gubernatorial years had also demonstrated that he was a master of radio, a skilled manipulator of public opinion with a resonant voice and a winning manner.

The trait that the public immediately saw in the Democratic Roosevelt was a gay, unflappable confidence — a welcome opposite to Hoover's dogged gloom. To Roosevelt's critics, his cheerful nonchalance, his willingness to experiment, his tolerance of contradictions, and his impatience with theory meant superficiality and arrogance. To his admirers, however, his flexibility seemed to reflect a bedrock of courage and a genuine humanitarian and religious concern for the underdog. Either way, FDR's energy, his zest for life and leadership, and most of all his infectious optimism were welcomed by a dispirited people.

Nominated by adroit maneuvers in a close Democratic convention, FDR pledged "bold, persistent experimentation" and "a new deal for the American people." Beyond these pledges, his campaign stances were vague and sometimes contradictory. He called for public power development and other progressive reforms, but the Democratic platform promised a 25 percent cut in spending and a balanced budget. Hoover, meanwhile, asked the people to sustain his own battle with the Depression and grimly predicted disaster if his opponent won. The result was hardly in doubt; the Roosevelt landslide approximately equaled the Hoover victory of 1928.

During the interregnum before the new administration could take over in March 1933, Hoover tried hard to persuade the president-elect to commit himself to a balanced budget, maintenance of the gold standard, and other central Republican policies. Roosevelt committed himself to nothing and was blamed by Republicans for a further economic downturn. In February, the Governor of Michigan announced a bank holiday to prevent financial collapse, and other states followed suit. By inauguration day, all banks were shut, and some cities turned to issuing temporary currency. In the Midwest, farmers resorted to old methods of semiviolent protest against a hopeless situation; milk trucks were overturned and mortgage sales forcibly halted. Unemployed vagrants, many of them boys, were roaming the country. As never before, the stage was set for masterful presidential action.

THE FIRST NEW DEAL

In his arresting inaugural, Roosevelt promised that he would, if necessary, ask for powers to fight the Depression equal to those given presidents in wartime. America's resources were adequate for the task ahead; the only thing it had to fear was "fear itself." Resounding with confidence and vigor, the speech committed the administration to no single course. For a while, nearly all Americans, from bankers to tenant farmers and unemployed, counted on Roosevelt to give them their demands. The New Deal, taking various forms through the next years, is best understood as a continuing experimental response to these demands. Behind each measure demanded by the president lay group pressures, party needs, presidential advisers, and congressional blocs. To understand the New Deal fully, one would have to understand two profound mysteries: American society and Franklin D. Roosevelt.

In the spring of 1933, Congress passed a series of administration measures with unheard-of speed. Roosevelt later summarized his objectives as "Relief, Recovery, and Reform," and this First New Deal can be described in terms of these Three Rs.

Relief for the country's most urgent needs started with legislation to open and sustain the sounder banks, leaving the weaker ones shut. Direct federal help for the unemployed began with the Civilian Conservation Corps (the CCC), which set young men to work on reforestation and other conservation projects. Larger unemployment relief programs included federal grants to states and plans for vast public works. Relief for home and farm owners was the main purpose of further legislation to refinance mortgages.

Recovery of the economy called forth the most spectacular measures of the First New Deal, measures that demonstrated its lack of consistent economic theory. Approaches to recovery included the Economy Act, which reflected the traditional belief that government spending somehow caused economic decline; the Trade Agreements Act, which gave the president power to negotiate low-tariff agreements in order to revive foreign trade; and even the Beer and Wine Revenue Act, which legalized one promising industry. (By year's end the Twenty-first Amendment swept away Prohibition completely.) The most important recovery programs of the First New Deal, however, relied on two main methods: first, raising prices by restricting output and controlling competition; and second, inflating the dollar, now irresistibly demanded by western Democrats.

During the campaign, Roosevelt and some of his advisers had declared that the expansion of the American economy, like that of the frontier, was finished. In the future, better distribution and planned production would replace violent competition. This theory owed something to Herbert Croly and the Bull Moose movement and something to Herbert Hoover and the trade associations of the 1920s. The ambitious National Industrial Recovery Act (NIRA) gave industry the legal right to agree on binding codes of common practice. These codes would, it was hoped, end sharp practices, unfair treatment of labor, and unjust, below-cost cuts in prices. How much they would permit prices to *rise* was never clearly settled. To make such agreements possible, the antitrust laws were suspended. To compensate for this favor to industry, workers were promised in the famous Section 7A of the NIRA the right "to organize and bargain collectively through representatives of their own choosing . . . free from the interference, restraint, or coercion of employers. . . ."

Reflecting a somewhat similar purpose, the Agricultural Adjustment Act (AAA) of 1933 sought primarily to raise farm prices by many complex methods. Its most striking feature was a system of subsidies to be given farmers who agreed to decrease production. Such payments were to be financed by taxes on the industries that processed agricultural products.

Inflation, the other principal recovery device, was provided for in an amendment to the AAA, sponsored by Senator Elmer Thomas of Oklahoma, who remembered Bryan's crusade against gold. The Thomas Amendment gave the president power to inflate the currency in many ways. Moving reluctantly at first, Roosevelt took the dollar off gold, sanctioned special measures to support the price of silver, and eventually stabilized the currency at about 60 percent of its former value.

Reform — that is, deliberate effort to render the social system more just or humane and preclude future depressions — could be seen in the new programs to regulate stock exchanges and investment banking, in the labor clause of the NIRA, and, most clearly of all, in the Tennessee Valley Authority (TVA). This daring project, bringing to fruition the long frustrated dreams of Senator Norris and other progressives, was designed to remodel a whole river system by building a series of dams. Among its objectives were cheap power and fertilizer, flood control, soil and forest conservation, the improvement of inland waterways, and new recreational areas. Reform and recovery were both objectives of the National Housing Act of 1934, which provided insurance of loans to promote repair and modernization of homes, farms, and small plants.

NEW DEMANDS AND A SECOND NEW DEAL, 1934–1936

Through these and other laws, the First New Deal seemed to have scored a qualified success. Its first actions brought a sharp rise in production and prices. Then the rate of recovery slowed, and people realized that the Depression had not disappeared. The elections of 1934, increasing the already large Democratic majorities, showed clearly that a majority approved the administration's efforts. But more was needed; the First New Deal had brought to light a whole series of new demands.

Farmers had benefited from price rises but were still distressed. Some of them had been disturbed by the destruction of crops and animals undertaken as an emergency measure in time of surplus. Then in 1934, the worst drought in the nation's history threatened to change surplus to shortage. Thousands of tenants and sharecroppers were driven from the land and left destitute. In part caused by the drought, this hardship also seemed in part to be caused by the AAA, which encouraged landlords to mechanize and cut acreage. So far, it seemed to many angry small farmers, the New Deal farm program had most helped the richest.

The unemployed demanded faster relief than was provided by the cautious handling of public works. Organized labor, which had reached a low point in 1933, took new courage from Section 7A with its guarantees of freedom to organize. But as new millions rushed into the ill-prepared unions, problems arose. Employers, many of them still hostile to "outside" organizations, thought that Section 7A had authorized them to form more or less docile company unions. Workers insisted that only national organizations could be effective. The National Labor Board, formed by the president to arbitrate multiplying controversies, lacked both authority and consistent policy.

Business and industry, at first eager for New Deal help and willing to promise drastic reform, had become restless with partial recovery. Despite gains made through NIRA codes, many business leaders resented excessive government interference in the details of their operations. Some hoped to exclude the government altogether and to make the program into one of simple business self-regulation on the Hoover pattern. On the other hand, progressives were charging that big business already dominated the codes and gouged consumers. Worried liberals, looking both at NIRA and AAA, doubted whether raising prices and cutting production were the best answers to widespread scarcity.

Thus the administration, which had tried to please everybody, found itself attacked from right and left. Conservatives looked back with nostalgia at the probusiness policies of the Republican years or lamented the end of laissez-faire and traditional individualism. Just below the surface of some fervent complaints ran an undercurrent of fear that the balance of power in the country was shifting away from those who ought to be in charge, in the direction of the shiftless, the irresponsible, and the foreign born. Not a few outraged citizens concluded, with no foundation in fact, that the whole New Deal was a socialist conspiracy against free enterprise, sound money, and American tradition.

At the other extreme, the tiny Communist party of the United States had made some progress. It was aided in 1935 by a sharp change in the international communist line. Instead of denouncing all non-communist efforts at reform as insipid and useless, communists were now to call for a "United Front" and to make every effort to work with "progressives" and "anti-Fascists." During the period from 1935 to 1939, while this line endured, the communist movement achieved some influence among American intellectuals and among some elements of labor. More important than actual communist gains, which remained numerically small, was the conviction, or half-conviction, fairly widespread among intellectuals, that capitalism could not recover.

Still more important in practical politics was the rapid spread of economic panaceas. Most of these appealed, as in the past, to disgruntled rural and small town people, and most involved a combination of currency tinkering and old-fashioned anti–big-business rhetoric. Among them were the Townsend Plan for liberal old-age pensions; the inflationary suggestions of Father Coughlin, the radio priest who denounced international bankers in speeches having anti-Semitic overtones; the sweeping production-for-use plan of Upton Sinclair in California; and the glittering, enticing "Every Man a King" proposal of Huey P. Long, a talented, ruthless spokesman of the dispossessed, who became governor and near-dictator of Louisiana. All these plans, however illusory, gained their strength from two undeniable truths. First, the richest country in the world had too many poor people. Second, the New Deal had not yet produced a convincing remedy.

Disappointed by the bitter response of the wealthy (his own class) and concerned by these threats from the left, the president backed a new set of measures. This Second New Deal, often seen as more liberal than the first, was not aimed at systematic alteration of the economic or social system. Indeed, one important group of the new young advisers who prepared it were under the influence of Louis D. Brandeis, who had helped to prepare Woodrow Wilson's "New Freedom" program and had imbued his followers with a dislike of bigness and a fervent belief in competition and diversity. The Second New Deal contained no measures aimed at economic planning or direct regulation of business on the NIRA scale, and none whose objectives were as sweeping as those of the TVA. Its main object, like that of its predecessor, was to get the economy going and to correct in the process some obvious injustices. Some measures had the further, highly traditional purpose of breaking up concentrations of power.

The new measures were sometimes proclaimed in combative tones. Often they were carried through with hard-boiled political efficiency. Obviously, some of them reflected the demands of newly articulate groups. It is not surprising that members of the business community, remembering the placid 1920s, were both resentful and alarmed. To many young people and to believers in social experiment, on the other hand, the Second New Deal brought a time of excitement, when almost any goal seemed possible and almost any method worth a try.

In the sphere of unemployment relief, the administration committed itself to the conservative principle of providing work rather than welfare. A special agency, the National Youth Administration, provided jobs for unemployed youths and assisted students to stay in college. The Second New Deal's principal relief agency was the gigantic Works Progress Administration (WPA) led by former social worker Harry Hopkins, a devoted, self-sacrificing, and sometimes imperious New Dealer. The army of WPA workers built roads, schools, parks, and countless other projects. In addition to construction work, the WPA offered different kinds of employment for actors, painters, musicians, and writers. Astounded conservatives and delighted liberals found the government sponsoring symphony concerts, excellent guidebooks, colossal murals of varying quality, and theatrical productions — some of the last were experimental, and others left-wing.

Existing farm programs were supplemented by efforts to help the poorest, most neglected farmers. The Resettlement Administration tried to move families from submarginal land, and the Rural Electrification Administration brought power lines to areas not served by private utilities.

In the Social Security Act, the United States, entering the field much later than other leading industrial countries, laid the foundations for a system of old-age, unemployment, and disability insurance financed largely by employer and employee contributions. The Revenue Act of 1935, though whittled down in Congress, sharply increased taxes on high incomes, corporations, and estates. The Banking Act of 1935 increased the power of the Federal Reserve Board to buy and sell government securities in the open market for stabilization purposes, and the Public Utility Holding Company Act restricted the practice of piling one company on another in the fashion popular in the late 1920s.

Finally, as the new labor problems became more and more pressing, the president, in 1935, gave his backing to a bill long advocated by Senator Robert F. Wagner of New York. The Wagner Act outlawed employer coercion and support of company unions. Henceforth an employer was required to bargain with the union chosen by a majority of his employees in government-supervised, secret-ballot elections.

Sweeping changes in the size and shape of organized labor were partly a cause and partly an effect of new government policies. Since NIRA days, organizers had turned their attention to the long-unorganized millions in such great industries as steel, automobiles, rubber, and textiles. Inevitably, swelling numbers and this change of direction strained the traditional craft organization of the American Federation of Labor (AFL). Led by John L. Lewis, the colorful and domineering head of the United Mine Workers, a group of rebels formed within the AFL a Committee for Industrial Organization. This group, expelled in November 1935, became in 1938 the independent Congress of Industrial Organizations (CIO).

In a series of hard-fought, sometimes bloody, strikes, the CIO attacked the long-defended bastions of American heavy industry. This time the outcome of labor warfare was a sweeping union victory. Beginning with the surrender of U.S. Steel and General Motors in 1937, America's most powerful corporations were to make agreements with CIO unions. By that year, organized labor had already grown from a Depression low of under 3 million members to more than 7 million, and it was still growing fast.

Not only the size but the nature of the American labor movement was changed. Most of it, unlike the labor movements of other industrial countries, continued to accept the capitalist system of production. (An important faction of the CIO, later to be expelled, was under communist influence.) But American labor by the mid-1930s was far more deeply committed to political action to further its social objectives than it had been before.

In 1936 the Republicans, sharply denouncing the New Deal, nominated Alfred M. Landon, the moderately liberal governor of Kansas, to oppose Roosevelt. In a victory that surpassed all but Harding's, Roosevelt got more than 60 percent of the popular vote and carried all states but Maine and Vermont. In this election, the Democrats were supported for the first time by an emerging, powerful, but unstable coalition consisting of labor, most farmers, recent immigrants, blacks, and the South; the Republicans had the support of most people in business. Though this pattern was to vary from election to election with changing circumstances, it would affect American politics for several decades.

DEADLOCK AND A THIRD NEW DEAL, 1937–1938

Despite the resounding election victory in 1936, the New Deal in 1937 and 1938 ran into a series of partial defeats. The first was in its conflict with the Supreme Court; seven of the court's nine members were Republican appointees, four of these unyielding conservatives. In its sessions of 1935 and 1936, the court threatened to dismantle the New Deal, overturning such measures as the NIRA and the AAA. According to a majority of the justices, Congress had unconstitutionally delegated detailed legislative power to administrative agencies and had gravely misinterpreted the taxing power, the interstate commerce clause, and other intentions of the Constitution's framers.

To the president and many advisers, the majority opinions appeared not only unduly narrow but menacing to the whole structure of New Deal reforms. Both the Wagner Labor Relations and the Social Security acts seemed doomed. Determined to make the court more responsive to the popular will, but fearing that a constitutional amendment would take too long, Roosevelt proposed, in February 1937, judiciary reorganization legislation. Under its authority, the court's conservative composition could be altered by the appointment of up to six additional judges, one for each justice over the age of 70. Some people — including Democrats in Congress — were shocked by Roosevelt's "court-packing plan," and many resented his disingenuous plea for greater judicial "efficiency." While argument raged, the court itself shifted unexpectedly to a pro–New Deal tack. A number of important statutes, though similar to those nullified earlier, were suddenly sustained by the court, and one laissez-faire justice retired. As one wag said, this "switch in time saves nine," for it made court reform less pressing. Roosevelt's bill was defeated, but he later claimed, with some justification, that though he had lost the battle, he had won the war. He did eventually appoint eight Supreme Court Justices (including Hugo Black, William Douglas, and Felix Frankfurter), and the Roosevelt court built a distinguished, liberal record in the areas of civil liberties, civil rights, and labor law. The bill, however, was probably FDR's greatest political mistake, for it damaged Democratic unity and impaired his leverage in Congress.

Presidential prestige was further injured by the onset of a new economic recession. In the summer of 1936, production, profits, and wages (though not employment) edged toward the levels of 1929. Apparently this was partly because of large government spending for New Deal purposes and for payment of the veterans' bonus (finally provided by Congress over Roosevelt's veto in 1936). The president, worried about deficits and mounting debt, acted to tighten credit and cut the budget, particularly WPA funds. In the fall, a sudden collapse seemed to bring back conditions of 1932. Farm prices headed down again, unemployment grew, and some critics concluded that the administration had failed to find a solution for the Depression.

Whether this was true or not, the New Deal proved in 1937–1938 that it had not lost its energy. Expenditures were sharply increased for relief, public works, and, under the Wagner-Steagall bill, for public housing. Whereas earlier governmental expenditures had usually been defended only as humanitarian necessities, now spending was advocated partly as a means of inducing recovery. This reflected the increasing influence among economists, in and out of the administration, of the theories of the English economist J. M. Keynes. Keynes argued impressively that in time of depression, deficit spending by government was necessary in order to induce recovery and "prime the pump" of private investment.

Partly to further recovery by breaking up price fixing (a direct reversal of the First New Deal's objective), antitrust prosecutions were vigorously increased. A new Farm Security Administration tried hard to help the tenant farmers and migratory workers, who were still America's most poverty-stricken people. A new AAA sought to raise all farm income by many devices, including new measures for crop restriction and government loans on stored surplus crops. Finally, the Fair Labor Standards Act of June 1938, made possible by the Supreme Court's new attitude, established modest minimum wages and maximum hours for most employees and killed that old and tough enemy of American progressives, child labor. Some innovations of this last New Deal, including compensatory spending and wage regulation, proved to be among the most permanent and substantial changes brought about in the whole period.

THE MEANING OF THE NEW DEAL

The 1938 congressional elections ended the New Deal period. Not only did conservative Republicans gain sharply in the West, but conservative Democrats in the South beat off Roosevelt's daring attempt to defeat them and thereby turn the Democratic party into a clear-cut New Deal organization. Though Roosevelt remained popular and existing New Deal measures remained in effect, further concerted or rapid reform action was impossible. For the next quarter-century, the same conservative coalition was normally to control Congress.

Why did the New Deal lose momentum in 1938? The most obvious reason is that foreign crisis began to draw the country's attention away from domestic reform. But many have blamed the slowdown partly on the program's own shortcomings — particularly its shifting approach to economic problems, its effort to combine incompatible groups of supporters, and its dependence on Roosevelt's personal leadership. Conservatives and radicals heatedly disagree as to whether the New Deal attempted too much or too little. Whatever the reasons for the New Deal's decline, this much is certain: there were still 10 million unemployed persons in 1938. Not until the United

TABLE 14. THE NEW DEAL, 1932–1938

	Labor	Agriculture	Business and industrial recovery	Relief	Reform	Miscellaneous
1932			Reconstruction Finance Corporation established.	Relief and Construction Act. Federal Home Loan Bank Act.		Bonus March. Election of **Roosevelt**.
1933	Section 7A of NIRA. 13 million unemployed.	Agricultural Adjustment Act. Farm Credit Act.	Thomas Amendment to AAA (inflation). Emergency Banking Act. Economy Act. Beer and Wine Revenue Act. Banking Act of 1933 (guaranteed deposits). National Industrial Recovery Act.	Civilian Conservation Corps. Federal Emergency Relief Act. Home Owners Loan Act. Public Works Administration. Civil Works Administration.	Tennessee Valley Authority. Federal Securities Act.	Twenty-First Amendment (Repeal of Prohibition).
1934		Cotton Control Act. Federal Farm Bankruptcy Act.	Gold Reserve Act. Silver Purchase Act. Trade Agreement Act (reciprocal trade treaties).	Civil Works Emergency Relief Act.	Securities Exchange Act. National Housing Act.	Johnson Act.

343

	Labor	Agriculture	Business and industrial recovery	Relief	Reform	Miscellaneous
1935	National Labor Relations (Wagner) Act.	Resettlement Administration. Relief Electrification Administration.		Works Progress Administration and National Youth Administration.	Banking Act of 1935. Social Security Act. Public Utility Holding Company Act. Revenue Act (wealth tax).	First Neutrality Act.
1936		Soil Conservation and Domestic Allotment Act.				Neutrality Act extended. Soldier's Bonus. **Roosevelt** re-elected.
1937		Farm Security Administration. 7.5 million unemployed.		Business recession begins.	Court Reorganization Bill (not passed). Wagner-Steagall Housing Act.	Neutrality Act revised. Depression (fall).
1938	Fair Labor Standards Act.	Agriculture Adjustment Act of 1938. 10.4 million unemployed.				Billion dollar naval expansion. Republican gains in Congress.

States mobilized for World War II would it emerge from the Depression. Though the Roosevelt administration did not fully solve the problems of modern industrial society, it was not alone. No other nation completely succeeded, and several, including Germany and Italy, abandoned their liberties in the process of trying.

In retrospect, though Republicans and conservative Democrats still decry Roosevelt's "radical innovations," the New Deal seems notable for its essential conservatism. The administration clearly had no quarrel with the wage system, wealth and profits, or private property. Roosevelt addressed the worst American crisis since the Civil War, as he said, from the perspective merely of "a Christian and a democrat." Under the New Deal dispensation, the harsher edges of the nation's political and economic system were softened. If democratic capitalism was not precisely saved, it was surely revitalized. While much of the world was turning to collectivism either of the extreme right or extreme left, Roosevelt steered a middle course. Without upheaval, without even major constitutional change, the government under his leadership ameliorated the effects of the Depression and assumed major responsibilities not just for the welfare of business but for the general public's welfare. The significance of the New Deal years is to be found not in the success or failure of particular policies or programs, but in a revival of creativity, confidence, and hope — qualities sorely needed in the decades ahead.

CONFLICTING HISTORICAL VIEWPOINTS: NO. 13

How New Was the New Deal?

To many conservative observers, the New Deal was a destructive experiment in socialism. Al Smith angrily denounced the "Brain-Trusters" as Marxists in Jeffersonian clothing, and Herbert Hoover shuddered when he contemplated the horrors of "New Deal collectivism." Yet, with the exception of Edgar Robinson — whose deprecatory The Roosevelt Leadership *(1955) is read largely for its novelty — this contemporary judgment has found no support among historians. Whatever else it was, scholars generally agreed, the New Deal was not socialism. Richard Hofstadter (Age of Reform, 1955) called it the "New Departure" and Carl Degler (Out of Our Past, 1959) termed it the "Third American Revolution." They both agreed that the New Deal departed in fundamental ways from the American reform tradition, but neither viewed it as particularly radical or dangerous. The New Deal was something of a break with the past, these liberal scholars argued, but it was also an essentially constructive and healthy response to the challenge of the Great Depression.*

The argument for benign discontinuity was widely, although not universally, accepted. Many distinguished historians, including Arthur Link, Henry Steele Commager, and Eric Goldman, believed that Roosevelt's programs evolved naturally from traditional American reform impulses. In Rendezvous with Destiny *(1952), Goldman discovered the New Deal's antecedents in the ideas and policies of Theodore Roosevelt, Woodrow Wilson, and even Herbert Hoover. The roots of the New Deal, he concluded, were firmly fixed in the soil of traditional American values.*

Although once heatedly debated, the revolution-evolution controversy is no longer an issue dividing the scholarly community. In recent years, historians have worried less about the origins of the New Deal and more about its effectiveness. Liberal sympathizers, most notably Arthur M. Schlesinger, Jr., have cast the Roosevelt administration in a most favorable light. Sharply contrasting New Deal dynamism with the static "Old Order," Schlesinger's brilliant Age of Roosevelt *(3 vols., 1957–1960) portrayed FDR as a commonsense democrat who spurned "dogmatic absolutes" and sought a middle way between the extremes of "chaos and tyranny," laissez-faire and collectivism. Other liberal scholars, including James MacGregor Burns* (Roosevelt: The Lion and the Fox, *1956) and William E. Leuchtenburg* (Franklin D. Roosevelt and the New Deal, *1963), were less laudatory. Although generally favorable, Leuchtenburg focused on the limited effects of New Deal recovery and reform measures; Burns, though not without sympathy for Roosevelt, faulted the Democratic president for failing to embrace Keynesian economics and to recast his party as the party of reform.*

In the 1960s, radical scholars offered vastly more damning analyses. Such New Left scholars as Howard Zinn (ed., New Deal Thought, *1966) and Barton J. Bernstein* (ed., Towards a New Past, *1967) attempted to expose the poverty of the New Deal imagination and the essential conservatism of its leadership. In their view, Roosevelt was the creature of corporate capitalism; he failed to solve the problems of the Depression, and he made no effort to create an equitable society.*

Most historians of the last two decades have moved away from debating whether the New Deal was a good or bad development and toward trying to explain why it took the form it did. Scholars such as Barry Karl (The Uneasy State, *1985) and Alan Brinkley* (The End of Reform, *1995) have focused on the political and ideological constraints that Roosevelt and other New Dealers faced as they fashioned the reforms of the 1930s.*

FOR FURTHER READING

President Hoover's revealing *Memoirs* (3 vols., 1951–1952) describe his own administration well and comment without admiration on the policies of his successor. Arthur M. Schlesinger, Jr., in *The Crisis of the Old Order* (1957) provides an unflattering portrait of Republican leadership from a liberal Democratic point of view. The more sympathetic studies of Joan Hoff Wilson (*Herbert Hoover*, 1975) and David Burner (*Herbert Hoover*, 1978) reflect the revisionist consensus on the first Depression president. The 1929 debacle and the Depression are illuminated by John Kenneth Galbraith in *The Great Crash* (1972), Michael A. Bernstein in *The Great Depression*

346 A Synopsis of American History

(1987), and John A. Garraty in *The Great Depression* (1987). *The Bonus March* (1971) is analyzed by Roger Daniels.

The Roosevelt literature is exceptionally full. Patrick J. Maney provides a useful, brief biography of FDR in *The Roosevelt Presence* (1992). It should be supplemented with the more comprehensive studies by Burns, Leuchtenburg, and Schlesinger mentioned above and by Frank Freidel's *Franklin D. Roosevelt* (1991). Some of the most interesting and contradictory works are those by FDR's contemporaries. Compare, for example, Frances Perkins's *The Roosevelt I Knew* (1948) and Raymond Moley's *After Seven Years* (1939). Studs Terkel's *Hard Times* (1970) contains many personal accounts of the 1930s. Of an enormous literature on American Marxism in the 1930s, one of the most readable and understanding accounts is Murray Kempton's *Part of Our Time* (1955). In *Making a New Deal* (1990), Lizabeth Cohen details how industrial workers built a New Deal from the bottom up, while Irving Bernstein's *The Turbulent Years* (1970) provides a useful institutional history of the labor movement in the 1930s. Roger Biles considers *The South and the New Deal* (1994); Harvard Sitkoff describes *A New Deal for Blacks* (1978); Abraham Hoffman analyzes the world of the *Unwanted Mexican Americans in the Great Depression* (1974); Alan Brinkley details Huey Long and Father Coughlin's *Voices of Protest* (1982); Winifred Wandersee assesses the impact of the Depression on women in *Women's Work and Family Values* (1981); and Susan Ware covers the contributions of female New Dealers in *Beyond Suffrage* (1981). Aspects of the era's intellectual history are detailed by Charles C. Alexander in *Nationalism in American Thought, 1930–1945* (1969) and by Richard H. Pells in *Radical Visions and American Dreams* (1973).

26

★ ★ ★ ★ ★ ★

The Reversal of Foreign Policy, 1931–1941

DURING MOST of the 1930s, American attention was centered on domestic problems. Yet foreign events, occurring in the same period, were to affect the United States even more profoundly than the New Deal. The fragile international order established at Versailles and propped by prosperity broke down. Aggressive military states threatened to dominate Europe and Asia. To meet this challenge, America moved from relative disarmament to colossal military power, and American opinion swung from an extreme of isolationism to unprecedented acceptance of worldwide commitment. This commitment was to prove permanent, and under its stress American tradition and society were to be profoundly altered.

THE BREAKDOWN OF ORDER, 1931–1933

When Hoover took office, he intended to carry on, with only slight revision, the foreign policies of the New Era. More internationalist in outlook than Coolidge, he carried much further the policy begun under Coolidge of substituting conciliation for intervention in Latin America. Cautiously, the Hoover administration moved closer to cooperation with the League of Nations. In any efforts to preserve world peace, however, he was determined to stick to noncoercive political or economic methods. At the London Conference of 1930, the administration worked hard, with some success, to reduce further naval armament according to the pattern set by the Washington Conference of 1921. This was the last victory for disarmament. The effort to limit land armies at Geneva in 1932–1933 resulted in complete failure. By that time, the very idea of arms limitation was rejected by several powerful states.

The Versailles order in Europe had always been unstable. With American power withdrawn, France and England confronted fascist Italy, the Soviet

Union, and defeated, unstable Germany. If these discontented powers were to be united and armed, their strength could outweigh that of the defenders of the status quo.

In the late 1920s, the Central European order was upheld to some extent by American investment. In 1931, partly because of the withdrawal of American funds, a major Austrian bank failed, and panic threatened to spread to Germany. To prevent further collapse, Hoover suggested a one-year suspension of payments of both German war reparations and Allied debts to the United States. After a damaging delay caused by French suspicions, this "Hoover moratorium" was accepted. Frightened by the growing power of the aggressive Hitler movement in Germany, the Western Allies finally, in 1932, agreed to cancel almost all reparations — but they were too late to save the German Republic. The United States refused to cancel war debts in a parallel manner. While most countries paid the first installments due after the end of the moratorium, these were, in most cases, the last payments made.

In 1931, Britain, the home of laissez-faire economics, found it necessary to abandon the gold standard for a managed currency, and many other countries promptly followed suit. Hoping to restore currency stability, the United States helped plan a World Economic Conference that would give first priority to stabilizing the international monetary exchange rate.

The most dramatic collapse of international order occurred in the Far East. Since the Washington Conference, Japan had been ruled by conservative cabinets, and American-Japanese relations had been relatively good. The Japanese military leaders, however, were becoming increasingly angry at arms limitation and civilian control. Since Theodore Roosevelt's Treaty of Portsmouth, Japan had possessed railroad and port rights in Manchuria, where many Japanese saw an opportunity to acquire raw materials and living space. In 1931, taking advantage of incidents in Manchuria produced by rising Chinese nationalism, the Japanese army embarked on a program of conquest in this vast, nominally Chinese region. This action, carried out apparently against the will of the civilian government in Tokyo, violated not only the League Covenant but also the Republican party's security structure, consisting of the Washington Nine-Power Treaty and the Kellogg Peace Pact. The Open Door and Chinese integrity, moreover, were part of Republican tradition.

Thus Hoover had to act, but once more American commitments in the Far East outran American power. Furthermore, the deepest beliefs of the Quaker president ruled out either military reprisal or cooperation with the League in economic sanctions. In addition, England, whose collaboration would have been necessary for effective action, had no wish to provoke Japanese threats to its own huge Asian holdings. Resorting to purely moral force, Secretary of State Henry L. Stimson announced that the United States would not recognize any situation brought about by force in violation of the Open Door or Chinese integrity. After much hesitation, the League took a somewhat similar stand, advising its members not to recognize the Japanese puppet state of Manchukuo. Neither the so-called Stimson Non-

Recognition Doctrine nor world disapproval deterred Japan in Manchuria, although Japan did withdraw from a brief military occupation of Shanghai undertaken in 1932 in retaliation for a Chinese boycott. At the same time, despite Hoover's abhorrence of coercive international action, the United States had become further involved in the defense of the crumbling international order.

THE NEW DEAL AND THE WORLD, 1933–1937

In the first years of the New Deal, American isolationism reached its peak. To the disillusion of the 1920s was added the new disillusion of the Depression. A host of plays, movies, and novels depicted the horrors of war, and in 1935 a Senate investigation seemed to show that munition makers caused most wars for the sake of sordid profits. Many Americans believed that European propagandists had made a sucker of the United States in 1917 and were trying to do it again. At the same time, former American allies were defaulting on their obligations and finding it difficult to sustain their own League of Nations. (Throughout the decade, European appeasement and American isolationism were called on to justify each other.)

Traditional suspicion of Europe was only one of a number of components, all powerful and some mutually contradictory, of the isolationist frame of mind. Many young people were deeply affected by pacifism, and some liberals wanted to concentrate on building a good society at home. On the other hand, conservatives were suspicious of foreign threats to American tradition. Many Midwesterners and most Irish-Americans maintained their historic suspicion of British imperialism.

As Japanese expansion slowed down to assimilate its gains, American-Japanese relations seemed to improve. And though nearly all Americans disliked the brutal Hitler regime that took power in Germany in 1933, few proposed to do anything about it.

In the early years of the New Deal, Roosevelt failed to challenge the dominant isolationist creed, though as a follower of his cousin Theodore and Wilson, he could hardly accept it. He was primarily concerned with getting his program of national economic reform through Congress and into action, and he badly needed the support of midwestern isolationist progressives. Therefore, he refrained from opposing such measures as the Johnson Act of 1934, which forbade loans to nations in default.

In cooperation with some isolationists or continentalists, Roosevelt supported a modest program of naval building and continued the program of improving relations with Latin America. The nonintervention policy was restated and backed in practice by abandonment of the direct right of intervention in Panama and Cuba. But when the nationalist and moderately radical government of Ramon Grau San Martin came to power in Cuba in 1933, Washington, thinking that government "too radical," withheld recognition and encouraged its overthrow by an army sergeant, Fulgencio Batista, in

1934. Batista remained the strong man of Cuba until overthrown in 1959 by Fidel Castro. In 1938 the expropriation of all foreign-owned petroleum company properties by Mexico was accepted, after much bitter opposition by the oil magnates, and compensation agreed upon. At the Inter-American Conference in 1936, intervention by one state in the affairs of another was condemned, and mutual consultation provided for in case of threats to the peace of the hemisphere. This Good Neighbor Policy, though it by no means ended all Latin American suspicion of the United States, was to produce good results in wartime when most Latin American countries were to be first friendly neutrals and then allies.

In economic matters, the main drive of the early New Deal was nationalistic. In order to save his own program of raising prices through currency inflation, Roosevelt abruptly reversed his early approval of exchange stabilization and, in so doing, broke up the World Economic Conference in London. On the other hand, Cordell Hull, the new secretary of state, had a deep southern-Democratic belief in lower tariffs, and Roosevelt succeeded in getting congressional backing for the Hull program. From 1934 on, the administration negotiated mutual tariff reductions through reciprocal trade treaties. Hope for a revival of international trade was also involved in Roosevelt's decision in 1933 to recognize Soviet Russia. This action, long prevented by ideological hostility, was supported by political realists and business leaders who prophesied (mistakenly) a major expansion of Russian-American trade.

American isolationist policies were little changed by the new challenges to world order that occurred in the mid-1930s. In 1935, Mussolini's Italy invaded Ethiopia, and in the same year Adolf Hitler felt strong enough to remilitarize Germany in defiance of the Versailles Treaty. In the next year, German troops marched into the Rhineland where the same treaty prohibited their presence. In July 1936, Francisco Franco opened a Fascist rebellion against the republican government of Spain, and in 1936–1937 the Berlin-Rome-Tokyo Axis united the major dissatisfied, essentially aggressive states. All these actions were dealt with ineffectually by the Western European powers. In the Ethiopian affair, the League invoked only half-hearted sanctions, England condoned German rearmament in a naval treaty, and western countries, through a policy of nonintervention, denied munitions to the Spanish government. Turning increasingly to the left, that government got some aid from Russia, while the Spanish rebels were more effectively supported by Germany and Italy.

American policy toward these crises was dominated by a determination to keep out of war rather than to keep war from occurring. The neutrality legislation of 1935–1937 was designed to prevent the particular kinds of mistakes that were believed to have drawn America into World War I. The first neutrality law, passed in 1935, forbade arms shipments to all belligerents, rejecting an administration wish to discriminate between aggressor and victim. In the Ethiopian crisis, this was supplemented by a "moral embargo" on oil, the commodity most needed by Mussolini. American refusal to take stronger action gave an excuse for the League to refuse an outright oil embargo. The second neutrality law (1936) forbade loans to belligerents. In 1937 a congressional resolution, requested by the president, extended the application of the neutrality system from international war to the Civil War in Spain; thus, American arms were shut off from the Loyalist government, which helped to ensure Franco's success. Finally, the neutrality law of 1937 made the existing prohibitions permanent and, in addition, forbade American travel on belligerent ships. It also gave the president power, for two years, to list commodities other than munitions that belligerents would be required to pay for and transport in their own ships (the cash-and-carry provision). Thus the United States had reversed the policies of Woodrow Wilson. Neutral rights were waived in order to stay out of war. It seemed clear to the aggressive nations that they had little to fear from American counteraction, as long as America itself was not attacked.

DEEPENING CRISIS AND CAUTIOUS CHANGE IN POLICY, 1937–1939

Once more, a shift in American policy was brought on by events in Asia, not Europe. Japan, which had continued to press from Manchuria into North China until 1933, made a truce in that year. In 1937, fighting broke out again near the Beijing-Tientsin railway for which Japan had certain treaty privileges. Since the ensuing war, though full-scale, was undeclared, the American neutrality legislation was not automatically applied. Partly in order not to cut off arms to China, and partly to keep some anti-Japanese action in reserve, Roosevelt refrained from invoking the neutrality laws, and America shipped some war materials to each belligerent. However, in October 1937, Roosevelt expressed his feelings about Japanese action with new vigor. Referring to a "spreading epidemic of world lawlessness," he suggested that aggressors be "quarantined."

Alarmed isolationist reaction made it plain to the president that he had moved beyond public opinion. The United States joined in the League of Nations' condemnation of Japanese action but opposed sanctions. In December, when Japanese planes sank the American gunboat *Panay* on the Chiang Jiang Zangbo (Yangtze River) in China, apologies were accepted without much excitement. Once more, world disapproval without action failed to deter Japan, and its forces proceeded to bomb and occupy the principal Chinese cities. By 1938, it had set up a puppet government in China and committed itself fatefully to the establishment of a New Order in East Asia.

Lacking a clear European policy, the United States played only a minor role in the major European events of this period, periodically and fruitlessly appealing for moderation and conciliation. In 1938, Hitler absorbed Austria and began threatening Czechoslovakia. This led to the Munich Agreement among Britain, France, Italy, and Germany, which forced Czechoslovakia to surrender certain strategic frontier districts inhabited by German-speaking people. This settlement was brutally nullified in March 1939 when Hitler took over the rest of Czechoslovakia. During the same spring, Italy invaded

Albania, while Hitler seized the Lithuanian town of Memel and unmistakably began threatening Poland. This time, however, Britain and France promised to aid the prospective victim, and it became evident that major war was imminent.

Roosevelt, who shared this opinion, believed also that Britain and France could win with American material help. He therefore called for a cautious and moderate program of rearmament, mainly on the basis of continental naval and air defense. He also asked Congress to repeal the arms embargo to make it possible for belligerents to buy American munitions on a cash-and-carry basis. Though most press opinion favored this action, it was defeated by isolationists in Congress. This was to be their last major victory.

In the summer of 1939, while Britain and France were making a half-hearted effort to make a defensive alliance with Russia, Stalin instead suddenly concluded pacts of trade and nonaggression with Hitler. This apparently left Germany free to attack Poland without becoming involved in a major two-front war, and on September 1, Hitler's troops crossed the Polish frontier. France and England, this time, declared war as they had promised. Poland, destined to be the most tragic victim of World War II, was quickly overrun. As German troops advanced through western Poland, Russian troops occupied the eastern part of the country.

With war a reality, Roosevelt was able (in November 1939) to prevail on Congress to repeal the arms embargo and place shipments of both munitions and other commodities on a cash-and-carry basis. Once more, as in 1914, the Western Allies were free to come and get American arms, provided that they could pay cash and provide shipping. This seemed enough to assure western victory without further American commitment. Most observers predicted that the major belligerents would settle into a long stalemate, confronting each other across "impregnable" French Maginot and German Siegfried lines.

CATASTROPHE AND THE END OF NEUTRALITY, 1940–1941

In the spring of 1940, the stalemate war came to a sudden end as the Germans conquered first Denmark and Norway and then the Low Countries. In a lightning assault from Belgium, mobile German units poured into France and in a month had crushed and demoralized the French army, supposed by many to be the world's strongest. It seemed impossible to resist the new German combination of parachutists, dive-bombers, and tanks. On June 22, France surrendered. The Germans occupied half the country, leaving the collaborationist government at Vichy in charge of the rest.

Thinking he had won his war, Hitler hoped that England would make a compromise peace. Instead, though isolated and almost without land armament, the British replaced ineffective Neville Chamberlain with Winston Churchill as prime minister. He announced his determination not only to resist but ultimately to destroy the Nazi regime. In the air battle of Britain, though British cities were heavily bombed, the Royal Air Force defeated the German effort to clear the way for invasion. It began to seem possible once more that American support might sustain England, and many Americans wanted to do this at all costs. Others, however, insisted that the most important objective still was to keep America out of war.

In the ensuing foreign policy argument, one of the most important in American history, both sides were made up of diverse elements. On the anti-interventionist side with the traditional midwestern isolationists were: Anglophobes, including many Irish-Americans; people who thought Britain's cause hopeless; pacifists; young people who had heard with horror about the intolerance and hate generated by World War I; middle-aged people who had shared the postwar disillusionment; progressive reformers reluctant to give up domestic objectives; and some, but not by any means all, of those who disliked Roosevelt because of his domestic policies. This diverse coalition was supported by the small group influenced by the Communist party, which had supported collective security until 1939 and was to support war after 1941, but which was isolationist during the two years of the German-Soviet alliance. Those who favored drastic action in support of Britain included, as in 1914, many influential Americans conscious of deep ties to British culture. These were joined by those who were outraged by atrocity stories, this time true, about Nazi barbarism. Most important, perhaps, were the increasing numbers who felt that American security would be seriously threatened by Nazi control of the Atlantic.

Most Americans, probably, were neither isolationists nor outright interventionists. Most wanted to help Britain and also to stay out of the war. The decisive question was which of these last objectives was the more important. Before the fall of France, opinion polls seemed to show that most Americans wanted first of all to keep out of war. After it, the majority gradually shifted; most concluded that British survival came first. This decision, however, was neither universal nor clear-cut, and the administration did not help to clarify the choice.

Insofar as one can understand Roosevelt's policy, he appeared by no means neutral in his sympathies and clearly wanted to contribute as much material aid as possible to Britain. This policy, he said, would keep America out of war. At first, he doubtless believed that this *would* be so, and until very late he hoped that it *might* be the case. Always conscious of the dangers of hostile public reaction, and once more desperately anxious to put over his program, he continued to say that America would stay out of war when he must have known that this was no longer certain. Whether a franker policy would have had better results, either at the time or in the long run, will long be debated.

The steps taken by the administration and approved by a majority of Congress and public opinion, were drastic enough. In May, Roosevelt called for increased defense appropriations and for airplane production of 50,000 a year. At Charlottesville, Virginia, on June 10, he promised continued material help to "opponents of force." In September, by executive agreements, he traded 50 over-age destroyers, desperately needed by Britain, for defense bases in British Western Hemisphere possessions. In the same month, Congress adopted the first peacetime conscription law in American history.

In the fall of 1940, foreign policy argument was channeled into an election campaign. Because of the national emergency, the Democrats broke the anti–third-term tradition to renominate Roosevelt. His opponent Wendell Willkie, though a utility company president who had fought TVA, was a representative of the liberal wing of the Republican party. Accepting much of the New Deal, Willkie attacked mismanagement and bureaucracy. Since Willkie accepted the necessity of aiding Britain and since both candidates promised that America would stay out of actual foreign war, there was little difference on foreign policy. In the closest victory of his presidential career, Roosevelt got 55 percent of the popular vote.

Once more in office, Roosevelt asked for and got a still more binding commitment to British victory. In March, Congress passed the lend-lease bill, giving the president authority to transfer equipment, rather than money, directly to nations whose defense was vital to that of the United States. In response to urgent appeals from the beleaguered British, munitions were furnished in enormous quantity. In the spring of 1941, British and American staff officers discussed common strategy in the event of American belligerency. In August, Roosevelt and Churchill, meeting at sea, committed themselves to the liberal principles of the Atlantic Charter, promising a free and warless world "after the final destruction of the Nazi tyranny."

Committed to Hitler's defeat, America could not allow its shipments of munitions to be destroyed by the increasingly powerful German submarine offensive. In the summer of 1941, the United States entered into undeclared naval warfare with Germany. American ships reported submarine sightings to the British. American troops occupied Greenland and Iceland, and American ships began convoying British and American shipping to Iceland, halfway across the Atlantic. Sinkings occurred, and in September, Roosevelt denounced German "piracy" and ordered American naval vessels to "shoot on sight."

Meanwhile, the war in Europe had profoundly changed. Unable to knock Britain out of the war before American deliveries became effective, Hitler decided to secure his continental flank. Germany already controlled Hungary, Rumania, and Bulgaria, and in April 1941, its armies conquered Yugoslavia and Greece. Germany's moves toward the East intensified Hitler's growing difficulties with his quasi-ally, Stalin. In June 1941 the Germans invaded the Soviet Union, penetrating so deeply that it looked for some months as if they would win another major victory. Promptly both Churchill and Roosevelt announced that any enemy of Hitler was a friend of theirs, and lend-lease aid to Russia began. While Russian participation stimulated anti-interventionism in some quarters, it reduced it in others. For the first time, it seemed, a coalition existed that could actually destroy the Nazis, and the United States was a member of it in all but actual land fighting.

For some time, Roosevelt had concluded that official American participation in war would be desirable, and a majority of the public had decided, according to the polls, that war would be preferable to British defeat. Hitler, however, was by no means eager to provoke further American intervention and add another great power to his already formidable list of opponents. Once more, the crucial development came from the other side of the world.

WAR WITH JAPAN

In the Far East also, the Hitler breakthrough of 1940 precipitated great changes. To Japan, it seemed to offer a last chance to consolidate her new East Asian order and thereby to end the costly and indecisive "China incident." By moving southward toward the colonies of occupied France and Holland and hard-pressed Britain, Japan could secure needed supplies of oil, rubber, and tin.

So far, Roosevelt, concentrating on the European danger and not eager for involvement on another front, had continued the rather ambiguous U.S. policy toward Japan with one important change. In July 1939 the United States threatened future economic measures by giving a six-months' notice of the abrogation of her 1911 commercial treaty with Japan. In July 1940, sensing that a Japanese forward movement was at hand, the president prohibited the export of some kinds of oil and scrap metal. Later measures tightened this embargo and increased the pressure on Japan to find alternate sources.

In September 1940 the Japanese, with Hitler's diplomatic assistance, forced the Vichy government to concede ports and bases in the northern part of French Indochina. In that same month, Germany, Italy, and Japan signed the Tripartite Pact, forming the Axis alliance and obliging each to help the other in case of attack by any power not now at war. Since a special article excluded Russia, this could mean only the United States.

There were still, however, powerful Japanese who hoped to achieve Japan's goals without war with America. Through much of 1941, the attitudes of both countries were set forth in a series of negotiations. Japan was willing, at most, to refrain from armed aggression in Southeast Asia and even to "interpret" in America's favor the promises of the Tripartite Pact. But to pay for peace in the Far East, even in the event of war with Germany, the United States would have had to restore Japanese-American trade, help Japan to obtain oil supplies from the Netherlands East Indies, and recognize (or at least cease to obstruct) her new order in China. The United States was unwilling to accept these terms and offered instead to restore trade and help Japan gain some of its economic goals provided it gave up its military objectives both in Southeast Asia and China. Once more, the American commitment to the Open Door and Chinese integrity assumed enormous importance.

In July 1941, following Germany's invasion of the USSR, Japanese forces moved into southern Indochina and headed for Malaya and the Dutch East Indies. Roosevelt promptly responded by freezing all Japanese funds in the United States. In August, still hopeful of keeping the United States neutral, Prince Konoye, the Japanese premier, requested a "Pacific Conference"

with Roosevelt. Though Konoye suggested the possibility of further important concessions, Roosevelt refused to meet unless there was some preliminary agreement on basic issues. In October, the Konoye government fell,
and the new Tojo government prepared for war.

Well before the complex Washington discussions of November 1941, the
positions of each side had been made clear, and the two positions had proved
incompatible. The American government considered trying to gain time by
presenting proposals for a temporary Pacific truce, but decided against this.
Knowing that an attack was at hand, the Americans restated for the record
their earlier position. On December 7, 1941, Japanese planes attacked and
severely crippled the American fleet at Pearl Harbor, in the Hawaiian Islands. The next day, Congress declared war, and three days later Germany
and Italy declared war on the United States.

Later, Roosevelt was much criticized, first for not pursuing further the
effort for peace with Japan and second for not preventing the Pearl Harbor
disaster. It was even argued (though never convincingly) that his real objective was to force Japan to attack the United States and thereby to get America into war with Hitler. A compromise with Japanese ambition, short of
surrendering old American commitments and betraying American allies,
would probably have been difficult to achieve. It is arguable, however, that
a Roosevelt-Konoye meeting might have gained time and, less plausibly,
that it might have strengthened the opponents of Japanese militarism. As
for the second charge, it seems that by late November 1941 the American
government had decided that war was inevitable and that further stalling
would be of no use. Roosevelt knew before December 7 that a Japanese
movement was actually under way, and warnings were sent to American
Pacific bases to that effect. Apparently because an attack was expected farther west, the warnings to Pearl Harbor were insufficiently frequent and
emphatic, and defensive action was neglected. Thus a small cloud remained
over the official version of the Pearl Harbor incident. At the time, however,
the Japanese "sneak attack" united the American people for war as nothing
else could have.

FOR FURTHER READING

An able study of *American Diplomacy in the Great Depression* (1957) is
offered by Robert H. Ferrell. Lloyd C. Gardner examines *Economic As-
pects of New Deal Diplomacy* (1964). The most formidable attacks on the
Roosevelt foreign policy are Charles A. Beard's *President Roosevelt and the
Coming of the War* (1948) and Charles C. Tansill's *Back Door to War* (1952).
Wayne S. Cole in *Charles A. Lindbergh and the Battle Against American
Intervention in World War II* (1974) and Thomas C. Kennedy in *Charles
A. Beard and American Foreign Policy* (1975) examine the work of two
prestigious opponents of American interventionism. William L. Langer and
S. Everett Gleason's *The Challenge to Isolation, 1937–1940* (1952) and *The
Undeclared War, 1940–1941* (1953) are well-documented and informative

studies, generally favorable to U.S. policy. Other notable accounts include David Reynolds's *The Creation of the Anglo-American Alliance, 1937–1941* (1981), Robert Dallek's *Franklin D. Roosevelt and American Foreign Policy, 1932–1945* (1981), Robert A. Divine's *The Illusion of Neutrality* (1962), Arnold Offner's *American Appeasement: United States Foreign Policy and Germany* (1969), and Roberta Wohlstetter's *Pearl Harbor: Warning and Decision* (1962). American relations with Japan are assessed by Herbert Feis in *The Road to Pearl Harbor* (1950), and Gordon W. Prange offers an exhaustive account of the surprise attack in *Pearl Harbor* (1986). In *Prelude to Downfall* (1967), Saul Friedlander surveys American relations with Nazi Germany on the eve of war.

27

★ ★ ★ ★ ★ ★

War for the World, 1941–1945

FROM DEFEAT TO VICTORY, 1941–1944

Through the winter and spring of 1941–1942, the United States confronted its most serious challenge since 1861. One headline after another reported successful Japanese invasions: Malaya, Guam, Wake, Hong Kong, Singapore, the Dutch East Indies, Burma, and the Western Aleutians. On May 6, 1942, the last organized American forces in the Philippines surrendered at Corregidor. The New Order in Greater East Asia was almost a fact. Any counteroffensive against Japan, it seemed, would have to conquer concentric rings of islands scattered over vast ocean areas.

Hitler, meanwhile, held firmly the productive power of Western Europe. His first invasion of the Soviet Union was turned back in the winter of 1941–1942 after reaching the outskirts of Moscow. His second, beginning in June 1942, reached deep into the Caucasus Mountains and entered Stalingrad on the Volga River. Britain was threatened with the collapse of her Atlantic supply line. Sinkings mounted after American entry, many of them occurring within sight of American coastal cities. The worst fears of western leaders were that the Soviet Union would collapse and Britain starve long before American power became really effective.

Already Anglo-American staff conferences had decided that the main Allied offensive must be directed against Germany, the more formidable enemy, while a holding action was carried on in the Pacific. But any offensive seemed a long way away, and even a holding action was not immediately apparent.

By summer and fall of 1942, more hopeful news began to appear. Japanese naval power, checked at the Coral Sea in May, was ended as an offensive threat at Midway in June. In August, American troops began a grim and

TABLE 15. WORLD WAR II, 1939–1945

	Diplomatic	Pacific theater	European theater	Home front
1939 — Outbreak	**March 14** Germany annexes Czechoslovakia. **March 31** Anglo-French pledge to Poland. **August 23** German-Russian Pact.		**September 1** Germany invades Poland. **October 14** Soviet Union invades Finland.	**November 4** Neutrality Act of 1939 (cash and carry).
1940 — Disaster	**September 3** United States–British "Destroyer Deal." **September 27** Japan-Germany-Italy Tripartite Pact.	**September 22** Japan gets bases in French Indochina.	**April 9** Germany invades Norway, Denmark. **May 10** Germany invades Benelux. **June 22** German-French armistice. **August–September** Battle of Britain.	**September 16** Selective Service. **November 5** Roosevelt defeats Willkie.
1941 — Intervention	**July 26** United States freezes Japanese funds. **August 14** "Atlantic Charter" statement by Roosevelt and Churchill. **November** United States–Japanese Washington negotiations.	**July 24** Japan occupies French Indochina. **December 7** Pearl Harbor.	**April** Germany invades Greece, Yugoslavia. **April–May** United States extends protective action in Atlantic. **June 22** Germany invades Soviet Union.	**March 11** Lend-Lease Act. **June** Fair Employment Practices Committee. **November 17** Neutrality Acts repealed. **December 8** Declaration of War.

(Continued on page 360)

TABLE 15. WORLD WAR II continued

	Diplomatic	Pacific theater	European theater	Home front
1942 — Low point	**May** Molotov in Washington. **June** Churchill in Washington. **August** Moscow Conference (Stalin, Churchill, Harriman).	**February 15** Singapore surrenders. **May 6** Corregidor surrenders. **May 7–8** Coral Sea. **June 3–6** Midway. **August–February** Guadalcanal.	**January–June** German offensive in North Africa. **Summer** German offensive in Soviet Union. **September–February** Stalingrad. **November 4** El Alamein. **November 8** U.S. landings in North Africa.	**1942–1945** 6 million women enter labor force. **January 30** Office of Price Administration established. **February–March** Japanese-American "relocation." **November** Republican gains in Congress. **December 2** First self-sustaining nuclear reaction (Chicago).
1943 — Allied unity	**January 14–24** Casablanca Conference (Roosevelt, Churchill). **August 11–24** Quebec Conference (Roosevelt, Churchill). **November 22–26** Cairo Conference (Roosevelt, Churchill, Jiang [Chiang]). **November 28–December 1** Teheran Conference (Roosevelt, Churchill, Stalin).	**Throughout year** Allied gains in South Pacific (Solomons, New Guinea). **November 21** United States invades Gilberts (Tarawa) (start of central Pacific offensive).	**January–May** Allied victory in North Africa. **July–December** Russian offensive. **July 10** Sicily invaded. **September 9** Italy invaded (Salerno).	**November 5** Senate resolution for international organization. **Summer** Urban race riots.

1944 — Victory in sight

July 1–22 UN Monetary and Financial Conference (Bretton Woods).
August 21–October 7 Dumbarton Oaks Conference (plans UN).
October 9–18 Second Quebec Conference.

January 31 Marshalls invaded.
June 18 Marianas invaded.
October 23–25 Philippine Sea.
November 24 Beginning of air attack on Toyko.

June 6 Normandy invaded.
July 25 St. Lô breakthrough.
September 12 United States enters Germany.
December "Battle of the Bulge" (German counteroffensive).

United States reaches twice Axis war production
G.I. Bill of Rights.
November 7 Roosevelt defeats Dewey.

1945 — The Atomic Age

Februrary 4–11 Yalta Conference.
April 23–June 26 San Francisco UN Conference.
July 17–August 2 Potsdam Conference (July 26, ultimatum to Japan).
September 2 Japan surrenders.

February Manila recaptured.
February–March Iwo Jima.
April–June Okinawa.
August 6 Hiroshima.
August 9 Nagasaki.
August 14 V-J Day.

March 7 Rhine crossed.
April 25 United States and Soviet forces meet on Elbe.
May 8 V-E Day.

April 12 Roosevelt dies; Truman takes office.
July 16 First atomic bomb exploded, Alamogordo, New Mexico.

bloody offensive in the Solomon Islands. In October, the British stopped the German drive toward Suez at El Alamein; the next month, American forces landed in North Africa and began fighting German troops. In the gigantic battle of Stalingrad, in many ways the turning point of the Second World War, the Russians, while sustaining incredible losses, captured a German army and began the reconquest of the vast territories they had lost.

In 1943, the Allies passed decisively to the offensive. After hard fighting, German forces were cleared from Africa, and in the summer and fall Anglo-American forces invaded Sicily and Italy. Though Mussolini fell from power and Italy surrendered, the Italian dictator escaped, and bitter German resistance formed in central Italy. In the Pacific War, the island-hopping strategy provided the means of American victory. Sea and air power made it possible to isolate and bypass Japanese garrisons; it would not be necessary to reconquer the vast Japanese holdings one by one. Bitter fighting brought control of the Solomons, and in November the battle of Tarawa began the Central Pacific campaign.

By this time, the technique of amphibious warfare was so highly developed that it became possible to land on any hostile shore with sufficient preparation, provided one was willing to accept immense casualties. The crucial difficulty was maintaining a beachhead after landing. This was borne out in June 1944 in the long-awaited landing in Normandy. This attack on the heavily defended French coast, the greatest amphibious operation in history, was seriously endangered by bad weather and stubborn resistance. By the end of July, however, a breakthrough at St. Lô ended the Normandy campaign and opened the campaign of France. American tank units were able to sweep around the defenders as German forces had in 1940. By November most of France and Belgium had been liberated by Anglo-American forces, but in December a fierce counterattack surprised Americans in the Ardennes Forest.

On the eastern front in 1944, the Russians entered Poland, Yugoslavia, Hungary, and even East Prussia. In the Pacific the island-hopping campaign continued through the Marshalls, Marianas, and Carolines. In November, bombers from the Marianas began devastating raids on the Japanese home islands. In the Philippines, American re-entry brought on the greatest naval battle in history at Leyte Gulf, where the remaining power of the Japanese navy was broken. By the end of the year, though much fighting remained in Europe and on the Pacific, victory and the problems of victory were in sight.

THE HOME FRONT

Perhaps the greatest single factor in this victory was American production of ships, tanks, planes, and the infinitely varied tools of modern war. In 1941, only a halting buildup of war production had begun, and shipments to Britain had depleted American supplies. Once more, organizing a democratic capitalist nation for war purposes proved difficult. Despite bureaucratic battles, bottlenecks, and waste, however, the task was handled with imagination and astonishing scale. By 1943, the vast American industrial complex was oriented to the war effort, and by 1944 America was producing twice the total war output of the Axis powers.

This achievement came, moreover, without the extreme measures of coercion urged by experts. There was no single production czar and no draft of labor. Incentives worked better than compulsion. Industrialists received very high rewards in depreciation allowances and government war-plant construction, though corporation profits and high individual incomes were heavily taxed. Business, and especially big business, played a major part in planning; it accepted a partnership with the government as it had in World War I and had not in the New Deal period. Labor, too, cooperated in the war effort. Strikes, much deplored in the press, were few. Labor kept the gains of the New Deal, including a 40-hour week with time and half for overtime. Wages rose rapidly, and unions expanded from 10 million to nearly 15 million members.

War brought prosperity and with it fundamental social change. The mechanism of economic growth, true to Keynesian theory, was government spending on an unprecedented scale. In 1936, the biggest New Deal spending year, a comparatively modest federal outlay of $8 billion had caused much alarm. In 1945, when federal expenditures reached $98 billion, unemployment practically vanished, and the country seemed to reach new levels of production and prosperity. As war industry redistributed the population, the Pacific Coast gained wealth and power. High wages and farm prices, together with war taxes, produced a greater measure of economic equality than ever before.

In a full employment economy, blacks were accepted in jobs previously closed to them. Pressed by A. Phillip Randolph and the March on Washington Movement, Roosevelt created the Fair Employment Practices Commission in a partially successful effort to ensure equal employment opportunities. The military, however, remained rigidly segregated. The one million black men and women in uniform were generally assigned to menial tasks, and (with such signal exceptions as Brigadier General Benjamin O. Davis) Afro-Americans were rarely accepted as officers. Racial ill-will was manifested in riots on military bases, and in bloody riots in 1943 in Harlem, Los Angeles, Mobile, Newark, and other cities. The war brought both black militance and black gains; black leaders promoted the "Double V," victory at home as well as abroad. Many historians now regard these years as the seedtime of the postwar civil rights revolution.

Women, too, entered the war economy in unprecedented numbers, many as clerical workers and many more, in the fashion of Rosie the Riveter, as factory hands. Black women left domestic service for higher paying industrial jobs. Married women with children left home and nursery to join the war effort. Although wartime labor shortages temporarily undercut traditional notions of "woman's place," women war workers were paid less than men, and most were expected to retire "when the boys come home."

Many changes accelerated or begun during the war proved to be permanent. Neither wages, prices, employment, government expenditures, nor taxes were to return to prewar levels. Control of inflation, as well as prevention of depression, became federal responsibilities. In addition to the economy, government became deeply involved in race relations, public information, and the promotion of scientific endeavor. Minorities and women would never again be content with prewar patterns of exclusion and discrimination. Perhaps most fateful of all, the size, political influence, and economic importance of the armed forces in the United States had been enormously and permanently expanded, although few Americans suspected this and that demilitarization would not come with peace.

In politics, the war brought a superficial unity. Since the United States had been attacked, overt opposition to the war was negligible. Startling worldwide commitments seemed to be accepted; and it appeared that isolationism had died at Pearl Harbor. The government under Roosevelt and Attorney General Francis Biddle engaged in few of the Wilson administration's excesses during World War I. Allied to the Soviets, Americans felt less threatened by radicals. German-Americans, Italian-Americans, and even fascist sympathizers generally enjoyed the protection of the Constitution. One national group, however, presents a staggering exception to such tolerance: 117,000 Americans of Japanese ancestry, two-thirds of them citizens of the United States, were interned at the start of hostilities. Responding to white racism and military pressure, the administration moved Japanese-Americans from their West Coast homes — first to temporary, barbed-wire concentration camps and then to isolated "relocation centers" in the interior. Most Japanese-Americans were resettled in the East or Midwest before war's end and some eventually received financial recompense, but an ugly precedent had been set.

If there was less overt opposition and less hysteria than in World War I, there was also less idealistic enthusiasm. The Four Freedoms (freedom from hunger, fear, injustice, and oppression), Henry A. Wallace's glowing picture of a "Century of the Common Man," Wendell Willkie's commitment to "One World" were highly effective in liberal circles. None of these, however, came as close to producing a nationwide response as Wilson's appeal to "make the world safe for democracy." For many Americans, this was less a crusade than (as Roosevelt called it) a "War for Survival."

American opinion, deeply divided in 1941 over both the New Deal and Roosevelt's interventionist foreign policy, was not magically reunited in wartime. But division had to manifest itself in indirect ways — in hostility to the Europe-first policy, resentment of price control, exaggeration of strikes, and (despite much countereffort) criticism of the Allies. Some liberals attacked the government for its tactical compromises with Vichy or alleged tenderness toward the British Empire. A larger group remained deeply suspicious of collaboration with the Soviet Union, and a still larger faction was determined to prevent the postwar survival of the New Deal.

In 1942 the Republicans sharply increased their strength in Congress. In 1944, Roosevelt, like Lincoln, won a wartime election, this time against the rather ineffective opposition of Thomas E. Dewey. In the same year, many arch isolationists lost their seats in Congress. Thus Franklin Roosevelt, again like Lincoln, retained the decision-making power of a wartime president. But for this he paid a price. It was necessary — or so he decided — to postpone discussion not only of important unsettled domestic controversies, but also of some of the thorniest unresolved international problems. The only goal on which all could agree was military victory.

THE GREAT ALLIANCE

In international relations, America did not follow precedents set during World War I. Then the United States had been gingerly cobelligerent; now it was a full-fledged ally, bound to refuse a separate peace. America led in efforts to form a second international organization, and this time public opinion and even the Senate seemed heartily to back the proposal for a new United Nations.

President Roosevelt placed his hopes both for victory and postwar stability on the "Four Policemen": Britain, China, the Soviet Union, and the United States. But only with Britain was full cooperation possible. Similar national traditions, plus the mutual admiration of Roosevelt and Churchill, helped make the Anglo-American war effort the most successful international operation in history. But, despite this closeness, major differences appeared.

The Americans were used to thinking of war in terms of an all-out drive for victory followed by a return to peace and normality. The British had some experience of victory's delusions and costs. Many American leaders were suspicious of British efforts to cling to empire. Above all, Roosevelt and Churchill differed in the later stages of the war over Soviet relations.

In 1942, American political and military leaders demanded an immediate cross-channel invasion of Europe, partly to prevent collapse of the eastern front in the Soviet Union. Churchill accepted the necessity of such an operation in the future, but thought it impossible without further buildup and fought hard for diversionary operations in southern Europe. After 1943, his reasons were partly political: western penetration of the Balkans and Central Europe would prevent Russian domination of these areas. This argument was settled by compromise. To Stalin's chagrin, the Normandy invasion was put off until 1944, while the North African and Italian campaigns represented a partial concession to Churchill's views. A Balkan front was never opened.

Roosevelt's program for making China a great power was a failure because it was based on an illusion. He backed Jiang Jieshi's (Chiang Kai-shek's) Nationalist government, which shared control of the huge country with a well-entrenched Communist movement led by Mao Zedong (Mao Tse-tung). Each side fought the other as well as Japan. Exhausted by the long war, the oppressive Nationalist regime was further weakened by corruption. Neither General Joseph Stilwell nor anybody else could bring about a major Chinese contribution to victory. Yet at Cairo in November 1943, Roosevelt, Churchill, and Jiang agreed that after the war China would get back Manchuria as well as Formosa and the Pescadores. The first of these pledges was largely nullified by the Yalta Agreement, and the second became the source of long-term trouble. No amount of Anglo-American wishing could make a divided China a stable ally.

By far the most difficult relationship was, of course, with the Soviet Union. America began this wartime association with a recent past of deep hostility toward that nation. During the period of the Russo-German Pact, American opinion had been outraged by Soviet moves into eastern Poland and Rumania; by the absorption of the three small Baltic states — Latvia, Lithuania, and Estonia; and, above all, by the Winter War with Finland, which had refused to surrender certain border districts considered by the USSR necessary to its defense. With the German-Soviet break, however, both Roosevelt and Churchill immediately recognized the crucial importance of Russian contributions to the war. To help keep Germany occupied in the east, America sent the Soviet Union lend-lease aid amounting to $11 billion. Temperamentally optimistic and used to thinking in terms of only one opponent at a time, many Americans managed to convince themselves that the USSR had fundamentally changed. Many presumed that the two countries would remain friendly after the war, and that this accord would be the mainstay of world peace. This opinion, many historians once believed, was shared by Roosevelt and his principal advisers, liberal and conservative, civilian and military. Recent research, however, suggests that the administration was less than optimistic about postwar Soviet-American relations.

Through 1943, some success was achieved in shaping common military objectives. Good feeling reached its height in late November 1943, when Roosevelt, Stalin, and Churchill met at Teheran, Iran. There the coming offensive against Hitler was roughly coordinated. It was agreed that German military power must be permanently eliminated, perhaps by division of the country. In Yugoslavia, Allied aid was to go only to Tito, the communist leader of one branch of the underground. Both the eastern and western frontiers of Poland were to be shifted radically to the west. From here on, as Soviet armies penetrated Eastern and Central Europe, postwar control of this area became the principal subject of inter-Allied argument. While fully aware that the USSR's losses entitled it to some security and realistic about its unquestioned power in the area, Churchill wanted to bargain sharply with Stalin. He was willing, for instance, to concede Soviet predominance in Rumania and Bulgaria in return for British predominance in Greece and equality in Yugoslavia and Hungary. Poland presented a harder problem. Russian forces had set up a government in Poland independent of the exile government in London; the latter had contributed large fighting forces to the Allied side, and on its behalf Britain had gone to war. Churchill was willing to put pressure on the London Poles to accept the realities of Soviet power, but he was not willing to recognize the unqualified sovereignty of the Soviet-supported Polish government. He wanted to use Allied bargaining power, including troop dispositions, to secure as favorable a Polish settlement as possible.

Roosevelt was unwilling to concur completely in Churchill's policy of firmness. He too was concerned about Polish freedom and could not ignore the

MAP 8:   THE EUROPEAN WAR

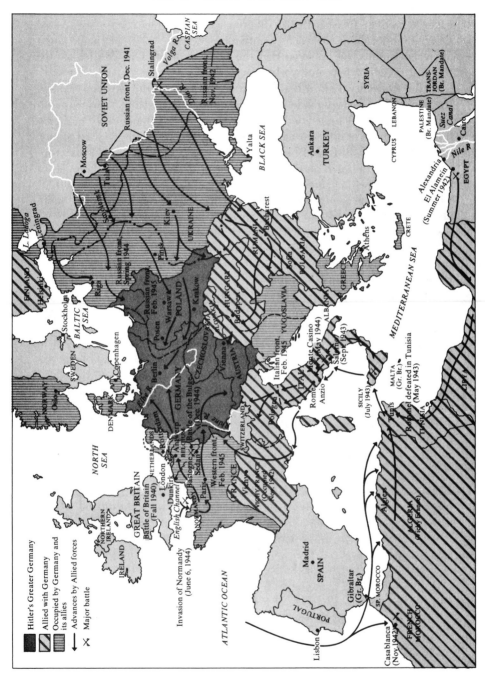

strong feelings of Polish-Americans, but he was aware also of America's historic dislike of power politics. Confident of his own diplomatic skills, he was eager to mediate Russian-British differences and willing to defer inter-Allied disagreements about sovereignty until after the war. While not naive about Soviet ambitions, he believed that the survival of the Grand Alliance was the best hope of a peaceful world.

At the February 1945 Allied conference in Yalta in the Russian Crimea, the approach of victory made postwar planning unavoidable. Germany's ultimate fate was left undecided, but the Allies agreed temporarily to divide it into four zones of military occupation by the Big Three (the United States, Britain, and the USSR) and France. Germany was to be assessed heavy reparations, but a decision on the amount was postponed. Poland's boundaries were settled: Russia gained rights to large territories in Eastern Poland for which Poland was compensated with German territories to its west. Stalin also reluctantly agreed to a more representative interim Polish government and to free Polish elections. Elsewhere in liberated Eastern Europe, the Soviets accepted the principle of "broadly representative governments." In the Far East, Churchill and Roosevelt recognized the Soviet puppet state of Outer Mongolia (nominally Chinese), and ceded to Russia the Asian territories lost to the Japanese in 1904–1905. In return, Stalin not only pledged to enter the war against Japan, but to sign a treaty of friendship with Jiang's regime rather than with Mao's.

At Yalta, the Big Three also agreed to meet in the United States to form a United Nations Organization. Some of its structure had already been determined at a conference in Dumbarton Oaks in Washington. Of the world organization's two most important organs, the Assembly and the Security Council, the latter was to act by unanimity. Its effectiveness, all understood, would require close collaboration, for neither the United States nor the USSR would surrender the power of veto.

Later, during the Cold War, the Yalta Agreement was bitterly attacked by American conservatives as a betrayal of China and a sellout to Stalinism in Eastern Europe. Some alleged treason; many came to believe that Roosevelt was too sick to be competent. In fact, though not well, the president was able to bargain realistically. The agreement represented a series of tradeoffs, more or less mutually unsatisfactory, and it was probably as favorable as time and circumstance permitted. Because they were uncertain of the effectiveness of the untested atomic bomb and expected fanatical resistance to invasion of the Japanese home islands, Roosevelt and his military advisers were more than eager to have Soviet forces participate in the final stage of the Pacific war, for which enormous numbers of casualties had been projected. Moreover Russian troops were already occupying much of Eastern Europe, including Poland, and the treaty represented not so much a concession to Stalin as a recognition of postwar realities. Given the context, even the vague agreement on free elections seems reasonable, if not wholly realistic. Roosevelt recognized that the American people were not prepared to impose their will in areas occupied by Soviet arms. Most important, the president had won Soviet approval for a United Nations, an American conception that would be organized and headquartered on American soil. The great powers emerged from Yalta with their alliance intact. In retrospect, FDR's judgment seems valid. The agreement was, he said, "the best I can do."

When Roosevelt returned from his long journey, exhausted but optimistic, most Americans gratefully accepted his statements that a future of democracy and peace had been assured. In the months ahead, Soviet actions in some parts of Eastern Europe made it clear that free elections and broad representation meant different things to the Soviets than they did to Western Allies. Having been attacked so often from the west, the USSR was not likely to allow governments hostile to it to exist in states along its western border. In some of these countries, notably Poland and Rumania, it was equally doubtful that governments that would be democratically chosen could be friendly to the Soviets. When American commanders discussed with German agents in Switzerland possible surrender terms for German forces in Italy, Stalin suspected the United States of plotting to deny the USSR a role in the peace negotiations. Depressed by increasing friction, Roosevelt came to doubt the future he had planned. Before these doubts could lead to action, however, he died of a cerebral hemorrhage on April 12, 1945. America mourned his passing, and people on both sides of the Atlantic recognized that the world had lost one of its most gifted statesmen.

FROM YALTA TO HIROSHIMA

The victory of 1945 was clouded by Allied dissent and darkened by cruelty and destruction. In the spring of that year, however, this was not apparent to the American people, and even the president's death failed to spoil the news of success on every front. In Europe, the German counteroffensive had been stopped at Bastogne, Belgium, before the end of 1944. By March 1945, American forces had crossed the Rhine. In early April, when American troops reached the Elbe River, General Dwight D. Eisenhower decided on military grounds not to push forward toward Berlin, but first to make sure of the Southern Alpine redoubt where it was believed that the Nazis might make a last stand. This decision, communicated to Stalin, was protested by Churchill. It was, however, upheld by Harry S Truman, the new president, on the basis of prior agreements among the Allies on zones of occupation. A little later, Eisenhower refused to press toward Prague, Czechoslovakia, and the Russians occupied both Central European capitals. On May 1, while Soviet troops were entering Berlin, Hitler killed himself, and three days later Germany surrendered to England, the Soviet Union, and the United States.

As American forces drew closer to the Japanese home islands, they continued to meet fierce resistance. No Pacific battles were harder fought than Iwo Jima in February or Okinawa in May. Off the latter island, as in the Philippines, Japan made use of a strange and effective weapon, the suicide plane. Hundreds of kamikaze pilots dove deliberately at American ships.

This and other fanatical behavior convinced most Americans that they were in for a desperate fight in Japan itself.

Actually, Japan's resistance was almost at an end. American submarines had cut off necessary supplies, and since November, American bombers had inflicted terrible destruction. In June, the Japanese war cabinet fell, and a new government began unsuccessfully to seek Soviet mediation.

President Truman and Winston Churchill, meeting at Postsdam, demanded on July 26 that Japan surrender. If Japan did, they promised, the Japanese would neither be destroyed nor enslaved; if it did not, it would meet "utter destruction." Since Truman had received word of the first explosion of an atomic bomb, he was in a position to carry out this threat. It had long been decided that the new weapon would be used against the enemy for maximum effect, rather than being dropped first on uninhabited territory as a warning. Some of the president's advisers believed that use of the new weapon would greatly increase the power of the United States in the postwar settlement, particularly in relations with the Soviet Union. On August 6, an atomic bomb was dropped on the city of Hiroshima. On August 8, the USSR hurriedly entered the war in advance of the agreed time. The next day, another atomic bomb hit Nagasaki, and on August 14, Japan agreed to the Postsdam terms. A formal surrender was signed aboard the *Missouri* in Tokyo Bay on September 2, 1945.

Even in the euphoria of victory celebrations, some Americans could not avoid asking themselves how it happened that their country, with its deeply humanitarian traditions, had been the first to use history's most terrible weapon. The Hiroshima bomb killed 80,000 people and injured many more, some of whom died horribly in the ensuing weeks and months. Yet in 1915, the United States had been genuinely outraged by the death of 1,198 civilians on the *Lusitania*. Throughout the 1930s, and as recently as 1939, Americans had denounced aerial bombing of civilian populations.

The advent of the atomic bomb typified several tendencies, good and bad, that ran through the history of the war. The bomb was, in the first place, a typical result of the American civilian war effort. It depended on a bold decision based on immensely complex science and engineering and was conceived by scientists from many countries, some of them refugees. Thus, the atomic bomb was a product of a liberal society associated with some of the best American traditions.

At the same time, the bomb's use in war was the climax of a period of mounting inhumanity for which all major nations bore some responsibility. The worst atrocity of the period was the systematic German annihilation of 6 million Jews. In places, Russian treatment of political and national minorities was almost as bad. Bombing of cities was carried out by Axis nations from Shanghai in 1932 to Rotterdam in 1940. Destruction of German cities was carried to new lengths by Britain and America in 1943–1944, when 300,000 civilians were killed. The American fire bombings of Japan — including the incendiary bombing of Tokyo in March 1945, the most destructive air raid in history — killed about 330,000. Thus the atomic bomb could be viewed as just another weapon and the annihilation of Hiroshima and

371

MAP 9: THE PACIFIC WAR

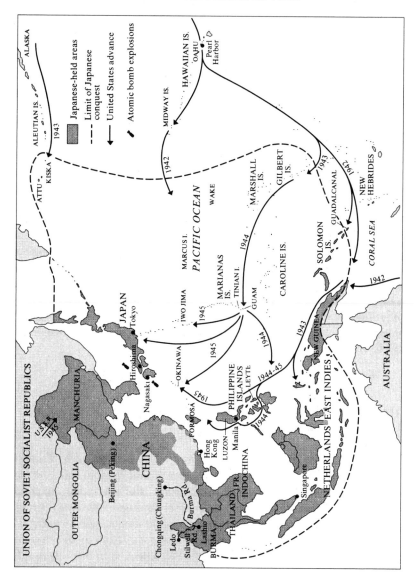

Nagasaki could be taken for granted by callous people. More sensitive individuals could still defend the action as a means of shortening the war and thus reducing both Japanese and American losses in the long run.

Postwar examination by American experts seemed to indicate that Japanese resistance had been almost over before Hiroshima. (Somewhat similarly, precision bombing of industries and transport turned out to have been far more decisive than city destruction in Germany.) But whatever the military or other judgments on the use of the atomic bomb in 1945, its existence became henceforth a major and incalculably frightening fact.

Thus the United States came to the end of a period of great and revolutionary achievement. From a policy of isolation, it had emerged to a stance of worldwide involvement. It had helped to build a great alliance, and through this and its productive and military achievements, the United States had helped destroy in Nazi Germany one of the worst regimes in history. All this had been accomplished without the destruction of either economic or political liberty at home.

The price for these great achievements started with a million American casualties, but that was only a beginning. Millions of people in Europe and Asia were starving in their ruins. Hate and fear were rampant as never before in modern history. Another totalitarian state, the Soviet Union, had been brought to immense worldwide power. The peaceful, democratic world promised by Roosevelt, and by Wilson before him, was soon to seem nowhere in sight.

CONFLICTING HISTORICAL VIEWPOINTS: NO. 14

Why Was the Atom Bomb Used on Japan?

Soon after the destruction of Hiroshima and Nagasaki, President Truman's mother commented: "I'm glad Harry decided to end the war. He's no slow person. He gets where he's going in short order." But where was he going? More particularly, was the decision to level the Japanese cities purely a military one, or did it have political and diplomatic dimensions as well? Was the use of the "ultimate weapon" designed to defeat Tokyo or to intimidate Moscow? In short, did the Cold War with the Soviet Union begin before the hot one with Japan ended?

For several decades these questions have stirred scholarly debate. In Truman's own Memoirs (Vol. 1, 1955) and in the writings of his Secretary of War, Henry L. Stimson (Harper's Magazine, February 1947), the decision to bomb the island nation was described purely in humanitarian and military terms. In Stimson's words, the nuclear devices were used "in order to end the war in the shortest possible time and to avoid the enormous losses of human life which otherwise confronted us." Some scholars, however, questioned the candor of the president and his secretary. Among the earliest to do so was P. M. S. Blackett, a British physicist whose Fear, War, and the Bomb (1948) asserted that "the dropping of the atomic bomb was not so much the last military act of the second world war as the first major operation of the cold diplomatic war with Russia."

Blackett's conclusion won support from Gar Alperovitz, a Harvard scholar and one-time State Department employee who sharply criticized the Truman administration's Atomic Diplomacy *(1965). Drawing heavily upon Stimson's own diaries, he addressed the question of "the influence of the bomb on certain questions of diplomacy." Admittedly, the reverse question — "the influence of diplomacy upon the decision to use the bomb" — could not be answered from available sources. Yet he found evidence that "strongly suggests" — and he so implied in much of his book — that the weapon was used chiefly to demonstrate American power and thereby to make the USSR more manageable in Central and Eastern Europe.*

The critics of Truman's "atomic diplomacy" have critics of their own. Michael Amrine, author of The Great Decision *(1959) and other studies of American atomic policy, condemned Alperovitz as a "cold-blooded cousin of . . . Dr. Strangelove" and charged that his thesis was based on unsubstantiated and highly convoluted conjecture. The distinguished diplomatic historian Herbert Feis agreed with Amrine. In his own study,* The Atomic Bomb and the End of World War II *(1966), a revision of an earlier work entitled* Japan Subdued *(1961), Feis concluded that Secretaries Stimson and Byrnes were aware that the A-bomb might not only "subdue the Japanese" but also "monitor Russian behavior." He warned, however, that this awareness should not be "distorted" into accusations of "atomic blackmail," saying "the impelling reason for the decision to use [the bomb] was military."*

Martin Sherwin provided a balanced addition to the controversy in A World Destroyed *(1975), a thoughtful analysis of the complex interactions of science, policy, and diplomacy. Although placing himself closer to Alperovitz than to Feis, Sherwin disputed the revisionist thesis that the bomb was used primarily, if not exclusively, to impress the Soviets. The American nuclear arsenal was created solely to win the war, he argued, and Truman used it to that end. But Sherwin also believed that both Roosevelt and Truman intended to wage atomic diplomacy against the Soviets. Discovering an unsuspected degree of continuity in American wartime and postwar policies, he contended that Roosevelt, perhaps not less than Truman, shared Churchill's deep suspicions of Stalin's intentions. Together the wartime president and prime minister secretly plotted to retain exclusive control of atomic energy as insurance against postwar Soviet ambitions. The Anglo-American partnership died with Roosevelt, but his successor continued shortsighted wartime nuclear policies that, in Sherwin's view, contributed to the origins of the Cold War. While scholars continue to debate many of the particulars of why America decided to use the atomic bomb in Japan, most now accept Sherwin's conclusion that the bomb was used primarily as a military weapon and secondarily as a diplomatic tool.*

The recent controversy over an exhibit at the Smithsonian Institution's Air and Space Museum, however, indicates that even the moderate revisionist ideas of Sherwin have not been accepted by much of the American public. Outraged by scholarly suggestions that America's motive for using

374

the atomic weapon on Japan might have been anything other than military necessity, veterans' groups and congressional leaders lodged protests about the content of a planned exhibit on the Enola Gay *(the plane that delivered the atomic weapon to Japan), eventually forcing the museum to ban revisionist ideas from the exhibit.*

FOR FURTHER READING

William L. O'Neill offers a useful survey of America at home and abroad during World War II in *A Democracy at War* (1993). For military and diplomatic history, probably the single most valuable work is Churchill's monumental though not infallible *The Second World War* (6 vols., 1948–1953). American involvement is traced by Charles B. MacDonald in *The Mighty Endeavor* (1986) and by A. Russell Buchanan in *The United States and World War II* (2 vols., 1964). Geoffrey Perret's *There's a War to Be Won* (1991) is a readable narrative of military activities in all theaters, while Ronald H. Spector focuses on the American war against Japan in *Eagle Against the Sun* (1985). Robert A. Divine's *Roosevelt and World War II* (1969) is brief and sympathetic, while James MacGregor Burns's *Roosevelt: The Soldier of Freedom* (1970) is more detailed and critical. Richard Polenberg in *War and Society* (1972), John Morton Blum in *V Was for Victory* (1976), and Neil A. Wynn in *The Afro-American and the Second World War* (1976) contribute to an understanding of the home front. Doris Kearns Goodwin, in her prize-winning *No Ordinary Time* (1994), weaves a dual biography of Franklin and Eleanor Roosevelt with the story of the American home front during the war. The tragic tale of Japanese-American internment is told by Roger Daniels in *Concentration Camps, North America* (1981) and by Peter H. Irons in *Justice at War* (1983). Lawrence S. Wittner examines the peace movement during and after the war in *Rebels Against War* (1984). One of the most thorough accounts of inter-Allied negotiations is Herbert Feis's *Churchill, Roosevelt, Stalin* (1967). Gaddis Smith has provided a valuable but brief examination of *American Diplomacy During the Second World War* (1985). Chester Wilmot in *The Struggle for Europe* (1952) gives a stimulating and intelligent English criticism of American strategy and diplomacy. Diane Shaver Clemens in *Yalta* (1970) offers a revisionist view. Developing East-West tensions are explored in John Gaddis's *The United States and the Origins of the Cold War* (1972), in Daniel Yergin's *Shattered Peace* (1977), and in Lloyd C. Gardner's *Spheres of Influence* (1993). Among important memoirs are those of Secretaries of State Cordell Hull, Edward R. Stettinius, and James F. Byrnes; of Admiral William D. Leahy; and of Generals Dwight D. Eisenhower and Omar Bradley.

28

★ ★ ★ ★ ★ ★

The Perils of Peace, 1946–1961

ALTHOUGH the origins of the East-West tension known as the Cold War date back to the time of the Bolshevik Revolution, Russo-American antipathy took an ominous turn in the aftermath of World War II. At best, the Grand Alliance of the United States, Britain, and the USSR had been a marriage of convenience. Faced by a common enemy, the Big Three worked in relative harmony for the war's duration. As victory approached, however, it became clear that Allied unity was fragile.

In July 1945, following the German surrender, Truman, Stalin, and Churchill (soon to be replaced by Clement Attlee as Britain's prime minister) met in Potsdam, Germany. They issued an ultimatum to Japan and they agreed on demilitarizing Germany, along with prosecuting Nazi war criminals. But they could agree on little else. Unable to reach accord on the future of Germany and Eastern Europe, they reaffirmed the Yalta agreements and postponed decisions for future conferences of their foreign ministers. The American president left the conference, his first meeting with Stalin, convinced that the Soviets "were planning world conquest." He was cheered by news of the successful atomic bomb tests because the bomb would hasten the defeat of Japan and because "I'll have a hammer on those boys [the Soviets]." Even as the Axis collapsed, the wartime partners were becoming postwar antagonists.

NEITHER PEACE NOR WAR

When Roosevelt died, Truman told reporters, "The moon, the stars and all the planets fell on me." Indeed, the world in which he was unexpectedly asked to play a leading role was turbulent and perilous. The only nation to

MAP 10:   THE COLD WAR UP TO 1960

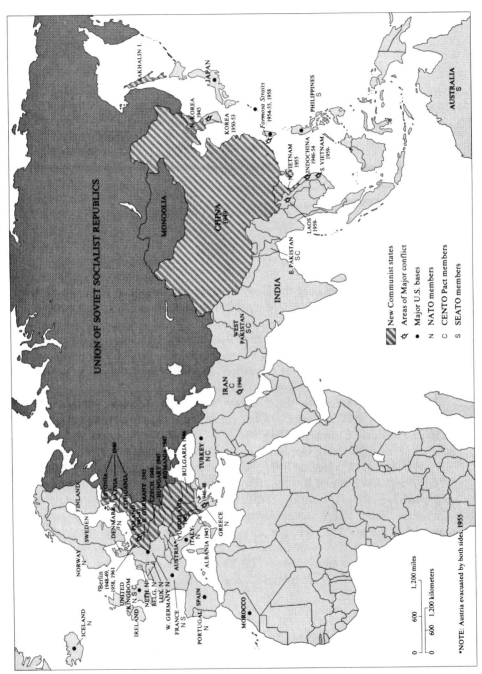

emerge from the war with its military and economic strength enhanced, the United States was the sole remaining global power. Western Europe, once a center of world power, was physically shattered; its economies were prostrate. England's might and wealth, like its once great empire, were greatly diminished. France, an occupied country during the war, groped haltingly toward national reunification. Germany was literally torn asunder, a divided and disputed battleground between East and West. In the Far East, both the old colonial order and Japan's New Order were on the brink of destruction. Restive colonial peoples in the Orient, the Middle East, and Africa were astir with nationalist strivings. All the world seemed in flux.

Although ill-prepared, Truman mastered his job quickly and proved to be an uncommonly knowledgeable, hardworking, and resolute chief executive. Faced from the outset with awesome and dangerous decisions, he made all of them with courage and some with intelligence. From first to last, he was primarily concerned with the developing Russo-American power struggle. As international tension mounted over time, the rivalry assumed global dimensions.

For the moment, East-West rivalry centered on Eastern and Central Europe, where American hopes for a democratic and capitalist world order collided with Soviet security needs. The advantage in that region, of course, lay with the Soviets. Because of the war offensives, Russian troops already occupied these areas and could impose Soviet-oriented governments on the states liberated from Nazi control.

Given the clash of ideologies and national interests, given the dangerous vacuum created by the collapse of the Axis nations, conflict between the two surviving world powers was perhaps unavoidable. Both were operating in an unstable climate of fear and suspicion, and were entrapped by their own inflexible perceptions and simplistic rhetoric. But neither side understood the sources of the other's anxieties. All too quickly, the United States and the USSR abandoned diplomacy for bombast and confrontation.

Conscious to the point of paranoia that its European approaches were vulnerable and determined never again to be invaded from the west, the USSR would settle for nothing less than a buffer of Soviet-directed nations on its borders. Unwilling to brook serious opposition within its newly claimed sphere of influence, the Soviet Union imposed its harshest policies on Poland and Rumania, where its interests were most crucial and anti-Russian sympathies nearly universal. Somewhat more subtly, coalition governments in Hungary, Bulgaria, and Albania were also subverted; in 1948, democratic Czechoslovakia fell to a Soviet-inspired *coup d'état*. Except for neutral Finland (which ceded territory and paid reparations to the Soviets) and Marshal Josep Broz Tito's independent Marxist state, Yugoslavia, all of Eastern Europe was under direct Soviet control. In the Middle East, the Soviets only honored a wartime agreement to withdraw from Iran on the oil-rich Persian Gulf due to western prodding. Stalin also pressed hapless Turkey for a toehold on the strategic Black Sea straits.

Although the reasons for the tightening Soviet grip on Baltic, Central and Eastern European, and Balkan states have been interpreted in various ways,

TABLE 16. THE TRUMAN YEARS, 1945–1952

Year	Domestic	The atom	Europe	Asia
1945	April 12 Death of F.D.R. Truman becomes president. November Coal strike.	Baruch Plan rejected. McMahon Act (AEC).	July 17–August 2 Potsdam Conference. August 21 End of lend-lease. November 20–October 1 Nuremburg trial.	August 14 Sino-Soviet Treaty. December Beginning of Marshall mission to China.
1946	June–November End of price controls. November 5 Republicans capture both Houses.		November 4–December 12 Foreign ministers complete treaties with German allies (ratified 1947).	January–April Iran incident.
1947	March 22 Truman loyalty program. June 23 Taft-Hartley Act. July 26 National Security Act.		March 12 Truman Doctrine (aid to Greece and Turkey). June 5 Marshall Plan announced. November–December London Conference (Britain, Russia, United States) breaks up over German question.	January End of Marshall mission to China.
1948	June Selective Service revised. November 2 Truman defeats Dewey.		February Communist coup, Czechoslovakia. June Yugoslav-Russian break. June 24 Berlin blockade begins.	May 15 Israel independent, recognized by United States.

Year	Domestic	The atom	Europe	Asia
1949	October 14 Smith Act convictions.	First Russian atomic explosion.	April 4 North Atlantic Treaty. May Russians agree to end Berlin blockade.	January 20 "Point Four" announced. Chinese Nationalists defeated. December 8 Jiang to Formosa.
1950	January 21 Hiss convicted. February 9 McCarthy attacks State Department. September 23 McCarran Act. November 7 Republican election gains. December Hoover attacks Truman foreign policy.	United States starts work on hydrogen bomb.		January Acheson "defense perimeter" speech. June 25 North Korean attack. November 26 Chinese attack in Korea.
1951	1951–1952 Corruption disclosures, foreign policy and communism argument.		April Eisenhower Headquarters in Paris opens.	April 11 MacArthur recalled. July 10 Korean Peace talks open. September 8 Japanese Peace Treaty.
1952	April 8 Truman seizes steel mills. June 30 McCarran-Walter (Immigration) Act. November 4 Eisenhower defeats Stevenson.	British atomic explosion. United States hydrogen explosion.	August 2 West German peace Contract (occupation ends).	

many scholars believe that Stalin's policies were defensive in character, though provocative and brutal. Mindful of Allied military intervention in Russia following World War I and fearful of a resurgent Germany and continued "capitalist encirclement," Stalin violated his Yalta agreements. But his postwar aims were limited and conditioned not by Marxist doctrines but by traditional Russian national security considerations. His ambition was not world conquest but the establishment of a Soviet sphere of influence, one to offset the admittedly more benign American spheres in Western Europe and Latin America.

Timely Western concessions to Stalin's minimum-security demands, some now argue, could have moderated Soviet behavior and eased East-West tensions. This view of Soviet motives for expansion and possible alternative Western responses differs sharply from the traditional historical interpretation. This traditional or "orthodox" argument posits (see Viewpoint No. 15) that America reluctantly but valiantly responded to the challenge of Soviet expansion. Clearly the revisionist view runs counter to what President Truman and his closest advisers thought to be the lesson of the Munich agreement with Hitler. The Western democracies, they noted, had attempted and failed to appease the aggressive designs of one dictator in 1938. They would not now try to appease another; they would not, as Truman said, continue to "baby" Stalin. The administration feared that having "sovietized" Eastern Europe and ruthlessly consolidated his personal power within the USSR, the insatiable Soviet dictator now sought westward extension of communist control. Still reeling from the war, Western European economies were faltering, and Communist parties were active and strong in France and Italy. By 1947 the administration had concluded that only a "get tough" American policy could stem the rising "Red tide."

CONTAINMENT

To counter this perceived danger from the East, America had only limited options. Churchill's proposal for a frank division of Europe into spheres of influence had been rejected out of hand by Roosevelt. In Truman's cabinet, only Secretary of Commerce Henry Wallace favored a relatively "free hand" for the Soviets in Eastern Europe, and he was soon fired by a president who was out of patience with "parlor pinks" and "crackpots." Liberal hopes for resolving international disagreements through the United Nations were frustrated at every turn by Great Power suspicions and by the veto provision that severely limited the international body's coercive authority. Stalin's refusal in 1946 to cooperate in the Baruch Plan — which provided for the abandonment of the American nuclear monopoly *after* the world's atomic energy was brought under international control — was particularly disappointing. (Stalin proposed that American stockpiles be destroyed *first*.) "Hardliners," on the other hand, hoped to use American power to challenge Soviet gains and to push toward the traditional American goals of democracy and the Open Door everywhere. Toward this end, economic leverage was clumsily applied in 1945 when the United States abruptly terminated Soviet lend-lease (including shipments already at sea) and conveniently misplaced a Soviet loan request. If these gestures were intended to make the USSR more tractable, they backfired. Some wanted to use the U.S. atomic advantage to roll back the communist threat. But the Soviets could not be easily intimidated, and a "preventive" war was not only morally repugnant to Americans, but was politically impossible in an open, democratic society. In the end, the logical and perhaps only practical response was containment.

Although this policy was in formation since 1945, it was not formally articulated until the publication of George F. Kennan's "Mr. X Paper" in 1947. In this unsigned article, Kennan wrote: "The main element of any U.S. policy toward the Soviet Union must be that of a long-term, patient but firm and vigilant containment of Russian expansive tendencies." The unspoken concession was American acceptance of Soviet control in Eastern Europe as an accomplished fact. But there the line was drawn. There should be no bluster, no threats, Kennan believed, but only "the adroit and vigilant application of counter-force" wherever further Soviet extensions threatened.

The first major application of counterforce came with the Truman Doctrine, announced in March 1947. Responding to Soviet pressures on Turkey for joint control of the key Bosporus waterway and to communist guerrilla attacks on the conservative British protectorate of Greece, Truman persuaded Congress to approve a $400 million program of military and economic assistance for those two beleaguered nations. The intention, the president explained, was to "support free peoples who are resisting attempted subjugation by armed minorities or by outside pressures." The withdrawal of Yugoslav assistance to the Greek leftists, together with American military aid, allowed the Greek government to defeat the insurgency and to end the civil war. Having committed itself to counterrevolutionary policies, the United States found itself, as it would repeatedly in the years ahead, supporting an undemocratic and unpopular regime merely because it was anticommunist.

In June 1947 the Truman administration proposed a more general program of European economic recovery. In a speech at Harvard, General George Marshall, then secretary of state, offered to assist the recovery of *all* European nations. The USSR denied its satellites this opportunity, and few Americans believed that the United States would in fact provide aid for communist nations. But Western European countries promptly presented a united recovery plan. After considerable debate, and some conservative opposition, Congress established the European Cooperation Administration; by 1952, when the aid program ended, nearly $13 billion had been appropriated for its purposes. This "Marshall Plan" or, as it was officially called, European Recovery Plan (ERP), was the greatest success of American postwar policy. It laid the basis for the startling European recovery and unprecedented European unity of the 1950s. It also served American strategic and economic interests by strengthening Western European capitalism and enlarging the American export market. Because ERP provided credits rather than cash — and thus assured that aid dollars would be spent in the United

States — it promoted one of the greatest peacetime economic booms in U.S. history. Similarly, in 1949, the administration proposed Point Four, a technical aid program designed to undermine the appeal of communism by extending the benefits of American scientific and industrial progress to underdeveloped nations, and particularly to Latin America. Again, American economic self-interest was linked to the crusade against communism.

Stalin responded to these initiatives by tightening his grip on Eastern Europe. Midway through the congressional debate on the Marshall Plan, a communist coup d'état brought Czechoslovakia into the Soviet orbit. Denouncing the European economic recovery program as American imperialism, Soviet leaders organized the Warsaw Alliance of satellite nations and the Cominform (Communist Information Bureau) to ensure orthodoxy throughout their sphere. The most threatening Soviet countermove, however, came in Germany, a vital East-West pressure point. Reacting to American efforts to promote the economic stability and political unification of Trizonia, the three western zones, Stalin boycotted the Four Power Control Commission and closed all surface access to Berlin (located 100 miles inside the Soviet sector).

The most severe test of American resolve so far, the Berlin blockade threatened with starvation the city's western garrisons and West Berlin's 2 million pro-Western inhabitants. The object of the blockade was to force the Western Allies out of Berlin and/or to frustrate Western plans for a united West Germany. No doubt the Soviets feared a resurgent, anti-communist Germany. The Berlin blockade, many Truman advisers believed, left the United States with but two unattractive alternatives: capitulation or force. In the spirit of the containment policy, however, Truman chose instead an around-the-clock airlift of American supplies into the beleaguered city. After 324 days and nearly 300,000 flights of cargo totalling 2.5 million tons, the Soviets lifted the blockade. Armed confrontation had been avoided, but the division of Germany was complete. In September 1949 the (West) German Federal Republic was proclaimed at Bonn, and in the following month the (East) German Democratic Republic was created, having as its capital East Berlin.

Alarmed by the fall of Czechoslovakia and the Berlin blockade and encouraged by economic recovery, Western Europe moved toward unity and asked for American defense commitments. In April 1949 the United States broke with its historic distaste for binding alliances and joined the North Atlantic Treaty Organization (NATO), a 20-year pact proposed by Truman to link the United States, Canada, Great Britain, France, and eight other Atlantic nations (and later Greece, Turkey, and West Germany) in mutual defense. Under the NATO agreement, an attack on one would be interpreted as an attack on all. The Soviet Union protested this "violation" of the United Nations' spirit and, not without justification, again cried "encirclement."

The creation of NATO in 1949 represented a militarizing of containment, a process that only gradually developed in the early Cold War years. Under popular and congressional pressures for rapid demobilization following World War II, the administration reduced both the army (from 8.3 million troops in 1945 to 593,000 in 1950) and the navy (from 3.4 million to 382,000). Truman maintained low defense budgets through 1949, resisting the military's request for drastic defense increases following the Berlin blockade. The president also denied a defense establishment request for military control of the atomic weapons' stockpile. The stockpile itself remained small — 11 bombs, all of the "fat-man" type used on Hiroshima — until tests in 1948 allowed for the production of more advanced bombs. Although the National Security Act (1947) was designed to unify the military establishment (as well as to create the National Security Council and the Central Intelligence Agency), genuine unification did not occur, and the president remained skeptical of the conflicting demands of the armed services for budget increases.

Only in the crisis year of 1949, with the "fall" of China and the detonation of a Soviet atomic device in August, did Truman move quickly. First he increased the atomic weapons' stockpile, and second and more important, he authorized the development of a hydrogen bomb. This decision to build a bomb one thousand times more powerful than the "fat-man" was opposed on moral grounds by some of the nation's top scientists, and George Kennan and Albert Einstein warned that "general annihilation beckons." But Truman, pressured by the Joint Chiefs of Staff and convinced that the Soviets were developing their own H-bomb, made the decision without public discussion or congressional authorization. As the nuclear arms race rapidly developed, a joint committee of the Departments of State and Defense prepared NSC-68, a policy statement that would militarize and globalize containment. NSC-68 proposed that the defense budget be tripled and that the United States should no longer distinguish between national security and global security. Truman approved the plan in the fall of 1950 as the Cold War turned hot in Korea.

RED SHADOW OVER ASIA

The singular American postwar success story in Asia was Japan's occupation by the U.S. armed forces and its reconstruction. American power was not seriously contested by the USSR. General Douglas MacArthur issued his orders through Emperor Hirohito and received a surprising measure of cooperation from the Japanese. Japanese industry and U.S. funds helped MacArthur carry through a political and economic program that helped remake the Pacific nation along more democratic and nonmilitaristic lines.

Elsewhere, Asian problems defied American solutions. At war's end, two groups vied for control of China: the Nationalists of Jiang Jieshi (Chiang Kaishek) and the Communists of Mao Zedong (Mao Tse-tung). The Nationalists enjoyed the recognition of most nations, including the Soviet Union. Not eager for a strong and united China, and no doubt finding Mao too independent, the Russians in this case honored their Yalta agreements. The United States briefly encouraged a coalition government; when that collapsed in the face of renewed civil war, Truman resumed American support (totalling $3 billion) for Jiang. In the end, Jiang lost the struggle through lack of popular support and ineptness; in 1949, the Nationalist Chinese remnant followed him in flight to the island of Formosa (Taiwan), and Mao was victorious. The red flag now flew over the whole Eurasian mainland, from the Baltic to the Yellow Sea.

The political fallout from Mao's victory in China severely damaged both Truman's leadership and congressional foreign policy bipartisanship. Although time would demonstrate that the Sino-Soviet powers were uneasy ideological bedfellows — that communism was not the international monolith many Westerners thought it to be — most Americans were alarmed by the prospect of a mainland Communist China. Neo-isolationists and Asia-firsters — like archconservative Republican Senator William Knowland of California, but also Democrats like Representative John F. Kennedy — blamed the Truman administration for the "betrayal" of Jiang and the "fall" of China. Senator Joseph R. McCarthy spoke darkly of the treason of "egg-sucking liberals." Some saw partisan advantage in the administration's apparent failures. Other observers recognized that in 1948 and 1949 the United States had neither the troops nor the will for the massive intervention that would be required to save the Nationalists. In retrospect, it is arguable that by rebuffing Mao's several early diplomatic overtures and then by not recognizing his mainland government, the United States lost (as it did in North Vietnam's Ho Chi Minh) a chance to nurture an "Asian Tito" — a popular nationalist leader, a communist, but one who was independent of Moscow. In 1950, Mao signed an accord with Stalin.

The next Asian crisis came in Korea, where postwar zones of Russian and American military occupation had solidified into hostile northern and southern political entities. Following Japan's defeat, the United States supported Korean reunification under UN supervision; the Soviets blocked the attempt. Both sides withdrew their occupying forces by 1948. Although Korea (and Formosa) was excluded when Secretary of State Dean Acheson defined American strategic interests in the Pacific in January 1950, Syngman Rhee's Republic of (South) Korea received both military and economic aid from the United States. Little noticed at the time, Acheson's omission stood out boldly on June 25 when Kim Il-sung's North Korean troops suddenly invaded South Korea.

The origins of the Korean War remain obscure. Many historians now argue that North Korea acted on its own without either the encouragement or the knowledge of the Soviets. American leaders at the time thought otherwise. Assuming that Moscow was behind the invasion, Truman ordered supplies to South Korea and the U.S. Seventh Fleet into the straits between China and Formosa. Because the USSR happened to be boycotting the United Nations and was not there to exercise its veto, President Truman obtained from the UN Security Council a demand for North Korean withdrawal and an appeal for member nations to aid in South Korea's resistance. With no other authorization, he became the first (but not the last) American commander-in-chief to wage a foreign war without congressional consent. Within a week of the invasion he unilaterally sent in U.S. air, sea, and ground forces. Although the counterattack was waged as a UN international police action and 15 other nations sent in small contingents, General Douglas MacArthur was in supreme command, and 90 percent of his forces were either American or South Korean.

At the outset, MacArthur boasted that given a free hand by Washington, he could end the war with "one arm tied behind my back." Later he promised to have the troops home first by Thanksgiving and then by Christmas. Instead, UN forces were initially hurled back by the invaders. But MacArthur, who acted under a mandate from the UN General Assembly for a "unified and democratic Korea," recouped skillfully and drove the North Koreans across the 38th parallel and pushed northward toward the Chinese boundary at the Yalu River. Begun as a limited intervention to repel the invaders, the Korean War became a crusade to destroy the communist regime in the North. Chairman Mao, President Nehru of India, and others warned that an expanded war to unify Korea risked Chinese intervention. General MacArthur assured the president that even in that unlikely eventuality, American might could prevail. In October, the North Korean capital at Pyongyang was captured. In November, as American aircraft bombed bridges on the Korean-Chinese border, MacArthur's troops were poised for final victory, only to be surprised by the direct entry of China into the war and a massive Chinese counteroffensive; they were flung southward once again. By December, 1950, the communists again controlled the North.

Chagrined by these reverses and convinced that the primary communist threat now lay in Asia, MacArthur demanded permission to carry the war into China. Truman himself thought briefly of using the atomic bomb. But fear of a protracted land war in China and possible Soviet intervention prevailed. MacArthur's request was denied. The general, defying tradition and the Constitution, announced that there was "no substitute for victory" and repeatedly appealed the commander-in-chief's decision to the press and people. He was removed from his post in April 1951 for insubordination.

Scholars generally agree that the president acted wisely, both in limiting the war to Korea and in relieving his gifted but headstrong general of command. Such military advisers as General George Marshall, then secretary of defense, and General Omar Bradley, chairman of the Joint Chiefs of Staff, suggested that the recall of MacArthur was overdue. It was nevertheless a politically costly decision that precipitated an angry public and congressional debate. Never popular, the president was burned in effigy, and his popularity ratings slumped further. Republican leaders talked of impeachment. Senator Joseph McCarthy and Representative Richard M. Nixon raised the specters of appeasement and possible treason. Trial "MacArthur-for-President" balloons were sent up, but the controversy slowly died and the general faded from public view.

The Korean stalemate, however, dragged on and the administration successfully pressed its case for rearmament under NSC-68. In 1950–1951, only partly for Korean purposes, the military budget was quadrupled, and the number of armed forces was increased to 3,500,000. In Europe, where recovery was well advanced, American aid shifted from an economic to a mil-

itary emphasis. NATO built a combined force with General Dwight D. Eisenhower in command. Seemingly on every front the administration
continued to search for anti-communist military advantages. First, the Allies
formed a European Defense Community, but France refused (for the moment) to permit independent West German rearmament. Also, treaties were
signed with Japan that permitted American forces to remain in Japan and
that lifted economic and rearmament restrictions on that nation (which, remarkably, refused to rearm). Finally, the United States entered mutual defense pacts with the Philippines, Australia, and New Zealand.

The hot war in Korea and especially the Truman-MacArthur controversy
revealed an American dissatisfaction with containment as a foreign policy
strategy. Preferring tidier solutions to international problems, the American
people longed for decisive victory, a quick and total resolution of postwar
tensions. The North Korean invasion had been repulsed without provoking
World War III. But 25,000 American soldiers had died in the first year of
fighting, and an end to the war was not in sight. Nor had the larger struggle
against a perceived communist menace produced satisfactory results. What
began as a regional problem in Eastern Europe had become a crisis of global
proportions. Instead of guarding a limited defense perimeter, the United
States seemed committed to resisting communist encroachments in the most
remote and difficult theaters. China was "lost," Europe was apparently divided permanently, and the German problem continued to defy solution.
Postwar rearmament brought its accompaniment of conscription, inflation
(comparatively moderate by more recent standards), and high taxes. Spy
exposés in the United States, Canada, and Great Britain suggested that Soviet agents had penetrated the highest levels of the Allies' governments.
Both the USSR and the United States were developing bombs vastly more
powerful than those dropped on Hiroshima and Nagasaki. Unsurprisingly,
national confidence was shaken, and many Americans were profoundly
disquieted.

FOREIGN POLICY DEBATE AND
RED SCARE II

Popular unrest first took the form of a public debate over foreign policy —
similar in some ways to the debates of 1898–1900, 1914–1917, and 1939–
1941, but less reasoned than any of them. Extremists, usually of the opposition party, suspected conspiracy in such Roosevelt-Truman domestic and
foreign policies as the New Deal, Pearl Harbor, the alliance with the USSR,
the Yalta "sell-out," the "theft" of atomic secrets, the "betrayal" of China,
the no-win stalemate in Korea, and the deposing of MacArthur. Less hysterical critics argued, as former President Hoover did in 1950, that it was a
mistake for America to make any commitments on the continents of Europe
or Asia. Republican Senator Robert Taft promoted greater reliance on air
power, less on ground troops. Many urged that timid or uncooperative allies
be disregarded and that the United States impose its own peace on a trou-

bled world. Demoralized liberals, on the other hand, faulted the administration for propping up reactionary regimes and relying too much on military, rather than economic, anti-communist measures. A number of Americans, then, found truth in the Republican campaign slogan: "To err is Truman."

The president's critics offered more vitriol than they did feasible alternatives. Increasingly the argument centered on one issue: communists in government. Although this great postwar fear and the witch hunt it engendered became known as McCarthyism, the junior senator from Wisconsin did not create it; he merely proved to be the most successful exploiter of pervasive public anxieties. Dread of domestic subversion, although subsiding after the post–World War I Red Scare, had sporadically troubled the American political scene since 1917. Anti-Roosevelt conservatives gravitated easily to the issue of subversion. From its formation in 1938 the House Un-American Activities Committee (HUAC) had devoted most of its energies to imaginative exposures of "communist influence" on New Deal agencies and programs. The Smith Act of 1940 was passed to limit free speech and assembly of radicals and other "subversives." Following the sensational exposure of apparent Soviet wartime spying within the Canadian government, Truman instituted a "loyalty program" (1947) and, somewhat later, evoked the Smith Act to prosecute American communists for conspiracy. His intention, in large part, was to deprive Republicans of the communists-in-government issue; perhaps he also sought public support for his anti-Soviet foreign policies by overdramatizing the menace within. By 1951, some 2,500 alleged security risks (including suspected alcoholics and homosexuals) were dismissed from federal employment without due process. Despite attempted safeguards, the probe led to widespread abuse and uneasiness. In time, it also seemed to legitimize a wider and infinitely more destructive anti-communist crusade.

Though deplored by civil libertarians, these measures neither departisanized the internal security question nor allayed popular alarm. In 1947, HUAC began searching for communists among Hollywood screen writers and directors. The next year, self-confessed former Soviet agent Whittaker Chambers identified Alger Hiss, once a middling State Department employee who had accompanied Roosevelt to Yalta, as a communist and Russian spy. Hiss denied the allegation, and liberals generally rallied to his defense. Truman referred to HUAC proceedings against the former New Dealer as a "red herring" designed to divert public attention from Republican failings. But Chambers's charges (relentlessly pursued by Representative Richard Nixon, who took personal charge of the investigation) proved hard to refute. Recent research seems to implicate Hiss in at least low-level espionage activities. In January 1950, he was tried and convicted of perjury in his denial of Chambers's charges (the statute of limitations on espionage having run out). The next month, Truman ordered the production of the hydrogen bomb, and the British revealed that nuclear scientist Klaus Fuchs had spied for the Russians at the U.S. Los Alamos atomic-bomb project. Fuchs's confession led investigators to Julius and Ethel Rosenberg; these two Americans were arrested some months later (and convicted and electrocuted in 1953) as his accomplices. These espionage cases set the stage for Senator Joe McCarthy.

McCarthy began his crusade in February 1950 with the claim that he had a list of 205 communists known to Secretary Acheson who were employed by the State Department. The administration vehemently denied the charge, and a Senate Foreign Relations subcommittee found it to be "a fraud and a hoax." Amid rising public furor, McCarthy twice changed the number of State Department "reds" (to 57 and 81) and never produced his list. But he brashly (and without foundation) named other communist "agents," "dupes," and "traitors," including General Marshall and Secretary Acheson. The entire Democratic party, he averred, was stained with "historic betrayal." Having played midwife at the birth of a second Red scare, Truman now found his party and administration to be the object of its attack.

Some responsible conservatives in both parties initially objected to this mudslinging. But McCarthyism was good politics, and the Senator quickly won financial support from the extreme anti-communists of the radical right. At first offended by McCarthy's "recklessness," Senator Robert A. Taft, "Mr. Republican" himself, began to encourage attacks on liberals and Democrats. "If one case doesn't work," he advised his Wisconsin colleague, "then bring up another." During the congressional elections of 1950, several McCarthy critics were defeated. Other politicians employed his tactics, notably California Congressman Nixon in his Senate race against the allegedly "pink lady," liberal Democrat Helen Gahagan Douglas.

As in the anti-German hysteria of World War I, states, cities, and private organizations took up the crusade. Self-appointed patriots purged libraries and in some cases burned books. Teachers and government employees were required to sign loyalty oaths. The broadcasting and motion picture industries black listed allegedly subversive writers and actors. Adrift in a sea of character assassination and guilt by association, the nation seemed prepared to sacrifice individual freedom, decency, and common sense for internal security. A two-thirds majority in the House and Senate overrode Truman's veto and enacted the McCarran Internal Security Act (1950), which among other drastic measures provided that *suspected* subversives could be interned, without trial, by presidential order in time of "international security emergency." Although Truman denounced the McCarran Act as "a long step toward totalitarianism," his administration, as the law required, selected sites for the construction of what even the most strident congressional Red-baiters called "concentration camps." Congress did not fund camp construction, and the bill was repealed some two decades later.

During McCarthy's reign of slur and innuendo, few people or institutions of power openly opposed him. Although opinion polls suggest that his mass support has been overestimated, he was widely thought to be the most powerful figure in Washington and politically invincible. Conservatives and even such Republican moderates as Eisenhower (elected president in 1952), who loathed his methods, found the senator too useful to repudiate. Liberals and Democrats, stung by conservative charges of "fellow traveling" and eager to protect their own anti-communist credentials, generally remained silent. Except for major metropolitan newspapers, the nation's press was broadly sympathetic. The Senate, true to its tradition of noninterference, ignored McCarthy's excesses as long as possible. Only when the senator overreached himself, and began to smear "communist sympathizers" in the Protestant clergy, army, Eisenhower administration, and Senate was he finally called to task. In 1954, during the Army-McCarthy television hearings, the senator's swaggering manners and unethical methods shocked the nation. Soon thereafter, the Senate condemned him for conduct unbecoming a senator. Ignored by his colleagues and by the press, he quickly lapsed into obscurity and died in 1957.

Having run its course, the second Red scare faded with McCarthy. Later in the decade, the Supreme Court, presided over by Earl Warren, a liberal Republican, delivered a number of decisions that restricted the scope of congressional committees and in other ways reaffirmed the importance of traditional individual freedoms. At the polls, the congressional elections of 1954 demonstrated that the Red issue had lost its potency, and in 1956 it was hardly used. In the prosperity and complacency of the middle Eisenhower years, hysteria died down more quickly than it might have under more vigorous counterattack. Yet the costs of tolerating McCarthyism were high. An ugly image had been presented to the world, sections of the government service had been demoralized, and some important issues of foreign policy seemed to have been placed beyond the range of effective discussion. As McCarthyism waned, a shrill minority on the Far Right added Eisenhower and Warren to their list of worldwide conspirators.

MASSIVE RETALIATION AND THE NEW LOOK

In the election of 1952, both presidential candidates (Democrat Adlai E. Stevenson and Republican Dwight David Eisenhower) were political moderates who shared Truman's perceptions of the origins and nature of the Cold War. Of the two, "Ike," the grandfatherly war hero, was the popular favorite. The articulate and witty Stevenson, on the other hand, was often dismissed as an intellectual. His major handicap, however, was voter discontent with Truman. The political opposition portrayed Truman as an incompetent president, surrounded by traitors and crooks, committed to a hopeless war. The election of Stevenson, the Republicans alleged, would bring more of the same: "Korea, Communism, and Corruption." Republican vice presidential candidate Nixon called Stevenson "Adlai the appeaser," and McCarthy impuned his patriotism with sly references to "Alger Stevenson." Eisenhower, for the most part, stayed above the unseemly fray, while his running mate led the assault on the Democrats. In October, General Eisenhower promised that if elected he would fly to Korea to end the war. That and his attractively bland and reassuring manner helped to produce a Republican landslide.

TABLE 17. THE EISENHOWER ADMINISTRATION, 1952–1960

Year	Domestic	Space and the atom	Europe	Asia, Latin America, and Africa
1952	**November** Eisenhower elected.	**November 1** Eniwetok hydrogen explosion (United States).		**December** Eisenhower visits Korea.
1953	**1953–1954** McCarthyism. Recession.	**August 20** Russian H-bomb.	**March 5** Stalin's death. **June** Riots in East Berlin.	**July 27** Korean armistice.
1954	**April–June** Army-McCarthy hearings. **May 17** Supreme Court outlaws school segregation. **November** Democrats capture Congress.	**March 1** Bikini H-bomb (United States).	**August 30** France rejects EDC.	**May–June** Guatemala Crisis. **July 21** Geneva Agreement. **September 8** SEATO Pact.
1955	**July 11** Dixon-Yates contract cancelled.		**May 15** Austrian Peace Treaty. **July 18–23** Geneva meeting (Eisenhower, Bulganin).	

Year	Domestic	Space and the atom	Europe	Asia, Latin America, and Africa
1956	**November** Eisenhower elected with Democratic Congress.	Stevenson proposes H-bomb ban.	**February** Khrushchev denounces Stalin crimes. **October–November** Hungarian insurrection.	**October** Suez Crisis.
1957	Recession. **September 24** Troops to Little Rock. Civil Rights Act.	**May 15** British H-bomb. **October 4** Sputnik.	**March 28** European Common Market.	**January 5** "Eisenhower Doctrine" in Middle East.
1958	**November** Democratic gains in Congress.	**January 31** United States satellite. **March 31** Russia suspends tests (United States follows).		**May** Lebanon Crisis.
1959	**July** Steel strike.	**September 13** Soviet "Lunik" hits moon.	**September** Khrushchev visits United States.	**February 16** Castro premier of Cuba.
1960	Recession. **November** Kennedy elected.	**February 11** French atomic explosion. **July 20** Polaris sub launches missile.	**May** U2 incident. **November** West Berlin threatened.	**June** Tokyo riots. **June 30** Congo independent; civil war. **August** Laos Crisis.

During most of Eisenhower's presidency, his principal foreign policy adviser was Secretary of State John Foster Dulles, a man of formidable experience, energy, and consistency. A committed cold warrior, Dulles seemed to view American-Soviet rivalry in starkly simple terms of good and evil. Though possessed of a shrewd and sometimes subtle mind, his inflexible anti-communism and his bellicose rhetoric were not well suited for diplomacy. During the presidential campaign, he called for the "liberation" of Soviet satellite countries and promised to "unleash Jiang" and to "roll back" the Iron Curtain; as secretary of state, he alarmed many Americans and their allies by boasting that the administration had gone to the brink of war three times in pursuit of peace. Yet Dulles enjoyed the president's confidence. He may have played the role of pugnacious international stalking horse for a president who generally shared his world view, but not his confrontational style of leadership.

Having promised peace, economy, and a "dynamic" alternative to the "negative, futile, and immoral policy of 'containment,' " Eisenhower and Dulles proclaimed a bold new solution to international problems. Instead of reacting to every communist challenge with expensive but limited and indecisive counterpressure, Dulles said, the United States would assume the initiative and resort to "massive retaliation" at times and places of its own choosing. Expenditures and conventional forces would be cut back, and nuclear weapons would be further developed and air-strike capabilities expanded. The development of a powerful nuclear deterrent force — and a well advertised willingness to use it — would make further communist challenge, even Soviet aggression by proxy, unthinkable. Corollaries of this "new look" in defense were more emphasis on anti-Soviet defense pacts and the development of additional air bases from Spain to Iran. NATO armies in Europe would also be equipped with tactical atomic weapons.

The Eisenhower strategy drew heavy criticism abroad and at home. Some thought it inappropriate in light of a new Soviet emphasis on peaceful coexistence following the death of Stalin in March 1953 and the subsequent rise of the more conciliatory Nikita Khrushchev. Critics noted that however ideologically satisfying, the proposed Republican alternative to containment was absurd and technologically obsolete — a transparent bluff that would only tie American hands in the face of Soviet adventurism. Would the United States, they asked, risk a nuclear exchange over a single, limited aggressive act? Under Khrushchev the Soviets shifted from Stalin's steamroller techniques to subtler forms of East-West competition in underdeveloped countries. Would the United States counter Soviet attempts to exploit revolutionary nationalism in the former colonies of the Third World with possible international holocaust? A new balance of terror, moreover, suggested that the United States lacked the nuclear supremacy on which massive retaliation was premised.

In 1953, the Soviet Union tested its first hydrogen bomb only months after the Americans had exploded theirs. Further evidence of advanced Soviet weapons technology came in 1957 with the launching of Sputnik, the world's first space satellite.

CONTAINMENT REPUBLICAN STYLE

In reality, the Republican administration departed from the foreign policy of its Democratic predecessor only in its rhetoric. Faced with complex and perilous international situations and eager to mollify the conservatives who had harried the "no win" strategy of Truman and Acheson, the administration talked change and practiced continuity. Anti-Soviet, nationalist uprisings in East Berlin (1953) and Hungary (1956), for example, were encouraged by American promises of support. But when these challenges to Soviet hegemony were brutally crushed, the administration protested through the United Nations, but prudently attempted neither "liberation," "roll back," nor "massive retaliation." Similarly, Eisenhower permitted Dulles briefly to "unleash" Jiang in 1953 and ordered the Seventh Fleet (then patrolling the Straits of Formosa) to refrain from preventing a Nationalist attack on the People's Republic. Nationalist commando raids subsequently harrassed the mainland, and the Communists responded (in 1955 and 1958) with artillery bombardments of Jiang's garrisons on the off-shore islands of Quemoy and Matsu. Jiang could not invade in force without American support, and Eisenhower, after consulting allies, would not risk a second major Asian war.

Even before his inauguration, Eisenhower went to Korea; Dulles later threatened to end the war with atomic weapons. That threat and pressure from Khrushchev may have moved the North Koreans to resume negotiations. The armistice of July 1953 brought a troubled peace on essentially the same terms as Truman had sought. After the expenditure of more than 33,000 American lives and some $50 billion dollars, American policy makers had no realistic choice but to redivide the Korean peninsula at roughly the old boundary, with the United States committed to assist and defend South Korea.

Elsewhere in the Far East (see Chapter 30), the administration addressed a crisis in Indochina with much the same mixture of bellicosity and restraint and again decided to contain, rather than roll back, a perceived communist menace. After the 1954 defeat of French colonialism by communist-led Vietminh (Indochinese nationalists), the administration took part in the partition of Indochina and the division of Vietnam, and committed the United States to supporting an anti-communist but undemocratic regime in the South. The United States also organized an "Asian NATO," the Southeast Asia Treaty Organization (SEATO), which pledged signatory nations (Great Britain, France, Australia, New Zealand, Pakistan, the Philippines, Thailand, and the United States) to construe an attack on one as an attack on all. A special protocol extended the treaty to cover the Indochinese nations of Laos, Cambodia, and South Vietnam. In the Far East, as in Europe, the "new look" looked much like the old.

In the Middle East, Eisenhower's policies were influenced by sometimes contradictory concerns. One was the region's immensely important oil resources, long defended by Britain and coveted by the USSR. To protect growing American economic interests in the region and to offset Soviet influence, the administration looked to the Arabs, who as Moslems seemed to be logical foes of communism. That objective, however, was enormously complicated by another American objective, the survival of Israel. Most of Israel's neighbors, particularly the displaced Palestinians, resented the Israelis as interlopers and denied the right of the Jewish state to exist.

The magnitude of the problem is suggested by the administration's relationship with Gamal Abdel Nasser, an independent Arab nationalist. Frustrated by the Egyptian leader's profession of neutrality in the Cold War, Eisenhower and Dulles first attempted to win his support with the promise of aid for the construction of the Aswan High Dam, and then withdrew the offer when he turned to the Soviet bloc for arms. Nasser promptly seized the Anglo-French Suez Canal, allegedly to finance the dam. When the French, British, and Israelis invaded Egypt, the Soviet Union threatened to send "volunteers"; Eisenhower persuaded the invaders to withdraw. The incident strained U.S. relations with its allies and greatly damaged Western prestige in the Middle East. Nasser moved closer to the Soviets, who financed his dam. Alarmed by this turn of events, the administration augmented the anti-Soviet Baghdad Pact or Central Treaty Organization (CENTO) of 1954 with the Eisenhower Doctrine, which pledged American aid to Middle Eastern nations threatened by communist aggression. Under it, the United States intervened in Jordan and Lebanon in 1957 and 1958 to counter Nasser's influence.

In the Western Hemisphere and elsewhere among developing nations, the Republicans fared little better. During Truman's administration, there had been such promising developments as the Rio Pact in 1947 (a collective security treaty signed by all American nations) and the formation of the Organization of American States (OAS) in 1948, (the most encouraging symbol of inter-American unity). Latin America remained, however, a place of social misery, political instability, and anti-Yankee sentiment when the Republican administration took office. Clearly secondary to Europe in U.S. concerns, the region was not included in the Marshall Plan. Not unlike most of the Third World, its people worried more about encroaching want than communist advances.

The Eisenhower administration's meddling in Guatemala served only to underscore U.S. preference for compliant, reactionary regimes, rather than for social progress under revolutionary movements. Prodded by the American-owned United Fruit Company, Dulles terminated U.S. aid to that nation's leftist but constitutional government. The hard-pressed Guatemalans turned to the Soviet Union for financial support. Its darkest suspicions apparently confirmed, the administration used Central Intelligence Agency (CIA) agents to promote a right-wing coup in 1954 and immediately recognized the repressive new military government. Widely applauded in the United States but condemned by NATO allies, this ill-advised intervention seemed all too familiar to Third World countries, where American talk of democracy and morality often met with skepticism. In 1953, the CIA had also subverted a popularly elected but uncompliant government in Iran. American support (sometimes administered through the CIA) propped up numerous right-wing dictatorships, notably in Cuba, the Dominican Republic, Nicaragua, and Portugal. In 1958, Americans were shocked to discover the intensity of anti-Yankee sentiment in Latin America when Vice President Nixon's good will tour was cut short by violent demonstrations in Venezuela.

COEXISTENCE

Amid these uncertainties and setbacks there was one bright spot: the on-again, off-again thaw in the Cold War. Encouraged by Khrushchev's softer line at home and abroad, his support for a negotiated settlement in Korea, and his willingness to accept a reunified, independent Austria (1955), Eisenhower (over Dulles's opposition) met the Soviet leader in Geneva. No substantive agreements were reached, on either the unification of Germany or the arms race. But the fragile "Spirit of Geneva" seemed briefly promising, and the two sides exchanged delegations of ballerinas, farmers, and other goodwill ambassadors. In 1958, following unsuccessful efforts to negotiate a nuclear test-ban treaty, the two powers (under immense international pressure) temporarily suspended atmospheric testing. The following year (after Dulles's death), Eisenhower invited Khrushchev to tour America and discuss Soviet plans to terminate further Western access to Berlin. Again nothing was settled, but Khrushchev delayed on Berlin and the strained cordiality known as the "Spirit of Camp David" offered cause for hope. Then another summit conference and a presidential tour of the Soviet Union were aborted in 1960 when an American spy plane was downed deep inside Soviet territory.

At best, Eisenhower left a mixed legacy. For reasons largely beyond American control, the nation's relative power in the world had declined. The Soviets had achieved nuclear parity; developing nations chafed under Great Power dominance; and Europeans, particularly the French, grew less dependent on the United States and more critical of NATO. Administration support for repressive governments in Latin America and U.S. opposition to revolutionary nationalist movements everywhere undermined the nation's prestige and cast doubt on its claim to leadership of the "free world." Despite a temporary thaw in East-West relations, the administration did not fully exploit the opportunities for long-term accord with the USSR in the post-Stalinist era. Yet the administration's deeds were generally more restrained than its rhetoric. Under Eisenhower the nation enjoyed eight years without direct involvement in war. Ike should also be remembered for his interest in arms reduction and his somber admonition about the dangers posed by the military-industrial complex.

CONFLICTING HISTORICAL VIEWPOINTS: NO. 15

Who Started the Cold War?

For more than forty years, the governments of the Soviet Union and the United States offered remarkably similar explanations for the origins of the

Cold War. Each side characterized the conflict as a morality play in which the other was cast as the villain. Both presumed to act in the name of the world's "peace-loving" peoples, and each portrayed the other as an imperialist power bent on global conquest.

Articulated initially by top officials in the Truman administration, including George F. Kennan (Foreign Affairs Quarterly, *July 1947*), *head of the State Department Policy Planning Staff, the official American interpretation of Cold War origins was not seriously questioned by most historians in the United States until the 1960s. Although scholarly accounts were often less hysterical than those by journalists and other popular writers, historians generally agreed that the Soviet Union's aggressive designs threatened the stability of the postwar world. Indeed, one of the most methodical and authoritative apologists for American diplomacy was Herbert Feis, a State Department adviser-turned-historian. In a series of books* (Between War and Peace, *1960;* The Atomic Bomb and the End of World War II, *1966;* Churchill, Roosevelt, Stalin, *1967; and* From Trust to Terror, *1970), Feis argued that in its Cold War policies the United States was merely responding to a Soviet challenge. Fomenting revolution and seeking conquest, the Soviet state, he believed, shattered the Grand Alliance, violated its Yalta agreements, and forced a reluctant and war-weary United States to assume the leadership of a threatened free world.*

Although the orthodox view dominated popular and scholarly writing throughout the 1950s, there were from the beginning of the Cold War a few precocious dissenters who raised disturbing questions about American policy. Years before popular disenchantment with the war in Vietnam found reflection in a multitude of revisionist attacks on American postwar policy, the philosopher-journalist Walter Lippmann (The Cold War, *1947), questioned the rationale for containment. And such "realist" historians as Hans Morgenthau* (In Defense of the National Interest, *1951) and William Mc-Neill* (America, Britain, and Russia, *1953) offered early challenges to assumptions of exclusive Russian guilt. But the first systematic revision of the traditional view was probably William Appleman Williams's* American-Russian Relations, 1871–1947 *(1952). In this volume and in such later works as* The Tragedy of American Diplomacy *(1959) and* The Contours of American History *(1961), Williams attributed the onset of the Cold War to the dollar diplomacy of the United States. Linking American foreign policy to the "needs" of American capitalism, he viewed containment as the latest manifestation of a traditional American diplomacy of economic expansionism dating at least from the days of the Open Door. American counterrevolutionary activities, then, were designed not to contain communist aggression but to promote commercial penetration of Eastern Europe.*

Williams's thesis was documented and extended by a number of New Left scholars. In The Politics of War *(1968) and* The Roots of American Foreign Policy *(1969), Gabriel Kolko, for example, offered an unrestrained indictment of American policy. Although typical of much New Left scholarship on the period, Kolko's work was more extreme than studies by such thoughtful radicals as Walter LaFeber and Lloyd Gardner. In his balanced*

America, Russia, and the Cold War *(1967), LaFeber surveyed the entire era and concluded that both powers must share the blame for the war of nerves. In* Architects of Illusion *(1970), Gardner was also highly critical of American policy shapers, but he too conceded that "neither side could fully control events, or even freely respond to them in many instances."*

The critics of revisionism are numerous, and most historians reject the economic determinism of the New Left. But recent scholars have also shown little willingness to defend the simple pieties of the orthodox interpretation. Thus, in The United States and the Origins of the Cold War *(1972) and* Strategies of Containment *(1982), among the most persuasive post-revisionist studies, John L. Gaddis concluded that "leaders of both super-powers sought peace" and that "neither side can bear sole responsibility for the onset of the Cold War." Likewise, Melvyn Leffler, who focuses primarily on American policymakers in* A Preponderance of Power *(1992), has argued in a similar nonaccusatory tone that although American officials sometimes made mistakes, on the whole they responded "prudently" as they developed national security policies in response to valid concerns and questions about potential Soviet ambitions in a complex postwar world.*

Post-revisionists have clearly established that the question of who started the Cold War is more complex than either orthodox or revisionist scholars ever admitted and that both the United States and the former Soviet Union played critical roles in the onset of the conflict. But with the end of East-West tensions and the opening of Soviet archives, the question of Cold War origins will undoubtedly continue to be debated.

FOR FURTHER READING

In addition to the studies above, aspects of the early years of the Cold War are covered in the following: Robert A. Pollard's *Economic Security and the Origins of the Cold War* (1985), Daniel Yergin's *Shattered Peace* (1977), Bruce R. Kuniholm's *The Origins of the Cold War in the Near East* (1986), and Michael Hogan's *The Marshall Plan* (1987). Michael Schaller looks at *The United States and China in the Twentieth Century* (1990); Bruce Cumings explains *The Origins of the Korean War* (2 vols., 1981–1990); Burton Ira Kaufman surveys *The Korean War* (1986); and Robert A. Divine presents essays on *Eisenhower and the Cold War* (1981). The memoirs of both Truman and Eisenhower are useful, and those by Kennan and Acheson are indispensable. Biographies of the key players in formulating American Cold War policy include Walter Isaacson and Evan Thomas's *The Wise Men: Six Friends and the World They Made: Acheson, Bohlen, Harriman, Kennan, Lovett, McCloy* (1986), and Wilson D. Miscamble's *George F. Kennan and the Making of American Policy* (1992). Robert Griffith in *The Politics of Fear* (1987), Richard Fried in *Nightmare in Red* (1990), and Stephen J. Whitfield in *The Culture of the Cold War* (1991) consider aspects of the McCarthy phenomenon. Allen Weinstein in *Perjury* (1978) offers an account of the celebrated Hiss-Chambers case.

29

★ ★ ★ ★ ★ ★

People of Plenty, 1946–1961

THE RETURN of full employment during World War II did not cure the "depression psychosis" of a people grown accustomed to hard times. Remembering the soup kitchens and breadlines, and the idle farms and darkened factories of the 1930s, Americans entered the postwar period with mixed emotions. They welcomed an end to the blood letting, but feared that wartime boom would become peacetime want. In 1939, the last prewar year, there were still 9.5 million persons unemployed; in 1945, Americans doubted that a demobilized economy could absorb 10 million war workers plus the 12 million men and women who had been in the armed forces.

This fear of unemployment proved groundless. The high employment war years were followed by the longest sustained period of peacetime prosperity in history. The gross national product (GNP, the sum value of all goods and services produced), which had reached $100 billion in 1929 and fallen to $70 billion during the Depression, soared by 1948 to $174 billion (using the same dollar value), and was still climbing. Farm income fell after 1947, but industrial wages rose and so did labor's share of total national income. Although the cult of motherhood and domesticity was intensified by the postwar baby boom, women — and particularly married women — continued the wartime employment trend, taking jobs in the expanding postwar economy in substantial numbers. By 1950, one in four American wives worked outside the home; by 1960, 31.6 million women (40 percent of the total) were gainfully employed, up from 16.8 million in 1946. Businesses, big and small, flourished. Veterans, under the "G.I. Bill of Rights," flocked to colleges in unprecedented numbers. In the warm glow of economic expansion, the doubts and anxieties of the Depression generation gradually evaporated.

RESURGENT PROSPERITY

Inflation, not depression, proved to be the most pressing economic problem. Their earnings fattened by high wages, their savings accounts bulging by a half-decade of full employment, consumers weary of wartime privations gave into their pent-up desire for things. Supplies, however, were limited in the early reconversion period; shortages quickly developed in nearly everything: houses, automobiles, clothes, shoes, sugar, butter, refrigerators, beefsteak, and small appliances. As wartime price controls were relaxed, the overall cost of living rose 70 percent between 1946 and 1950. Though vexing, the problem was short-lived. During the next twenty years, few Americans worried much about inflation. The economic picture was generally so excellent that even the minor recessions of 1949, 1952, 1957, and 1961 caused little anxiety. Swept along by enormous government expenditures in the Cold War arms race, by swollen military spending during the Korean and Vietnam conflicts, and by the unflagging consumption of a burgeoning population, the American economy slackened only when it was overtaken early in the 1970s by a crisis of "stagflation" that brought ominously high levels of both inflation and unemployment.

During the period from World War II through the Vietnam War, the GNP quadrupled. Although expanding more slowly than that of some industrializing nations, the American GNP, in absolute terms, outperformed all others. Some older industries, including coal and textiles, declined, but others, notably steel, grew steadily. Still others — housing, automobiles, and aircraft — expanded spectacularly, and the new "glamour industries" — chemicals (including plastic and synthetic goods), electrical appliances, and electronics (radios, tape recorders, phonographs, and television) — grew at rates that astonished even optimistic investors. Perhaps most gratifying of all, disposable per-capita income more than doubled, and the average wage earner benefited more fully from the industrial system than at any other time in the national experience.

The new prosperity was not universal. Agriculture, which claimed an increasingly smaller share of the labor force (8.5 percent in 1960), continued to be a problem sector. Technological and scientific innovations contributed to the overproduction of staple crops, which forced prices down and small growers out. The trend from family farms to agribusiness seemed irreversible. Elsewhere in the economy, disparities in income and wealth remained about as great as in the 1920s. By the late 1950s, the richest 5 percent received more income than the poorest 40 percent. In any given year, depending on economic fluctuations, one-fourth to one-third of the population lived below the government's poverty line. More than half of the elderly, nearly 20 percent of the whites, and more than half of the nonwhites were officially classified as poor. Ill-fed and ill-housed, generally born into deprivation, the poor were tucked out of view in urban slums and *barrios* or in migrant camps and rural hovels. Although carefully documented in the 1960s, this "culture of poverty" was easily overlooked amid the otherwise impressive prosperity of the complacent fifties.

In their celebration of a triumphant capitalism, Americans also overlooked a new wave of business concentration that surpassed the consolidation movements of the McKinley and Coolidge eras. Despite federal anti-trust legislation dating to the 1890s, large-scale enterprise dominated nearly every area of the economy. By 1960, some 600 businesses (0.5 percent of the total) controlled more than half of all corporate income in the United States. The most conspicuous example was the once-competitive automobile industry; smaller manufacturers went out of business during the 1950s, leaving the domestic market to General Motors, Ford, Chrysler, and the much smaller American Motors. The postwar merger movement, moreover, took new forms, such as the conglomerate and the multinational, in which business ownership transcended not only related enterprises but national boundaries.

BABY BOOM AND SUBURBIA

A primary symbol of postwar affluence was population growth. Depression couples, with their shrunken expectations, married late and normally limited family size to two children. The birth rate fell to 6.5 per thousand in 1933, and averaged only 18 per thousand for the entire decade of the thirties. Beginning with a crop of "furlough babies" during World War II and increasing during the "nesting" phase of the postwar period, the rise in birth rate mounted to 25.8 per thousand in 1947, and remained at 25 or above every year from 1951 to 1957.

The baby boom was both a cause and an effect of the economic boom. A cyclical phenomenon, population growth brought increased demands for goods and services, which created more jobs, which heightened prosperity, which stimulated population growth. Viewing this self-sustaining process, demographers and other experts (perhaps some who had earlier projected a long-term population decline) worried that the nation would soon have standing room only. In the 1960s, however, domestic environmental and economic concerns and a global population explosion fostered an appreciable reduction in American population growth. In the prosperous fifties, however, an increasing birth rate combined with a declining death rate to give the United States a rate of increase roughly equal to India's.

Among the first concerns of the growing American family was a better place to live. During the 1930s the national housing standard deteriorated badly. New construction all but stopped, as hard-pressed families pooled their resources in single dwellings. A dozen occupants in a one-bedroom apartment were not unusual in many cities. The return of good times brought increased demand for shelter; the federal government and private developers tried to meet this demand by the construction of large-scale urban, suburban, and all too few public housing developments. During the 1950s, new housing expanded faster than new households, at a rate of more than one million dwellings a year. By 1960, at least half of all existing dwellings had been built since World War II. The federal role in this suburban growth was particularly great. Through the grace of the Federal Housing

Administration (FHA), the Veterans' Housing Administration (VHA), and income tax deductions on mortgage interest payments, a majority of Americans for the first time in the twentieth century owned their own homes. Federal highway programs, chiefly for the construction of an interstate system, also accelerated the movement from city to suburb.

Often the postwar homemakers found themselves in standardized tracts, with row upon row of nearly identical "ticky-tacky" houses on small, treeless lots. Frequently, these were mushroom communities built almost overnight by fast-buck speculators, without planning or government oversight. They appeared on the outskirts of cities and along the new freeways. Occasionally, as with the Levittowns on Long Island and in Pennsylvania, the builders and merchandisers of low-cost, mass-produced developments created not merely "bedroom towns" but self-contained settlements complete with churches, recreational facilities, and shopping centers.

Although often physically and socially more differentiated than their detractors alleged, these postwar projects were widely described as indistinguishable "warrens for the middle class." They were said to be homogenous centers of stultifying "togetherness," of harried commuting fathers and child-centered, mother-dominated homes, of credit-poor consumers anxiously accumulating gadgets and conveniences to "keep up with the Joneses." In time, much of suburbia was to be swallowed by the almost uninterrupted metropolitan sprawl that linked Boston to Washington (Boswash) or San Francisco to San Jose (San-San). However much they yearned for the bucolic life of small town and country, these Metro-Americans were destined to live in megalopolis, amid eight-lane highways, parking lots, rapid transit systems, and town-house complexes.

But if life beyond the city limits was not universally appealing, it nevertheless had its attractions. Encouraged by relatively low-cost housing and improved transportation — but also by city congestion and social disorganization — roughly as many people moved from the urban core to the suburbs in the 1950s as came from Europe in the peak years of immigration. By 1970, suburbia claimed more people than either the central cities or rural areas and small towns. Those left behind were generally poor, elderly, and nonwhite. As the white middle-class pursued its dreams in suburbia, the central cities increasingly became the preserve of minorities: blacks, Hispanics, and American Indians.

CONSUMERISM, "THE AMERICAN WAY OF LIFE"

The expanding population and housing market were matched by unparalled growth in the market for consumer goods. All but insatiable in its appetite for things, the postwar consumer society was sustained by constantly rising wages, easy flowing credit, and intensive advertising. Confident that higher future earnings would make repayment possible, if not painless, Americans borrowed as never before. Between 1945 and 1952, consumer credit increased by 800 percent. The nation's advertising budget soared, from $3 billion in 1945 to $12 billion in 1960. Bombarded by increasingly sophisticated sales campaigns in the print and broadcast media, Americans turned desire into need and indulged themselves in a welter of objects.

The stuff of nearly everyone's dreams was the automobile, the great American status symbol, the means of social as well as spatial mobility. During the 1950s, an average of nearly seven million new cars and trucks were sold every year. Although doomed to short life through planned obsolesence, the automobile was a luxury liner of gaudy convenience, comfort, and conspicuous consumption. Sporting "futuristic" styling and tail fins in the fifties and somewhat sleeker, though even larger, lines in the sixties, it often came equipped with an endless array of frills: stereo radios, tinted glass, air conditioning, and electrically powered windows, brakes, and steering. The ripple effect of the industry sustained a vast number of consumer services and enterprises, from motels and drive-in restaurants to filling stations and highway construction.

The television set was, if anything, more ubiquitous. Developed in the late twenties but still a rarity in 1945, television rapidly became the dominant medium of mass entertainment and advertising in the United States. By 1952, two-thirds of all families owned one; a decade later, at the close of television's "golden age," hardly any did not. In the 1970s, color TV, once the ultimate symbol of working-class success, became so commonplace that families without one felt deprived.

The social and cultural consequences of the national obsession with the tube remain little explored. Radio and film lost their central place in the entertainment field, but both responded creatively and survived in altered forms. Mass-circulation magazines, including *Look*, *Collier's*, and *Life*, eventually folded. Social dancing to the "big band" sound never recovered. Consumer response to the TV dinner suggested that family table talk was similarly doomed; social commentators worried that the art of conversation would be lost to the artfulness of Milton Berle and "Gun Smoke." By the mid-1950s, educators noticed that the baby-boom children, the first generation to grow up with television, were more preoccupied with the vapid fare of video than with the printed word. Optimists spoke of the salutary "homogenizing tendencies" of a medium that permitted all Americans, regardless of race, class, or region, to share the same visual and aural experiences; one scholar concluded that "the television set has democratized experience." Others feared that "high culture" would be swept away in the tidal wave of enthusiasm for home entertainment tailored for a mass audience.

Patterns of consumption varied to meet the lifestyles of the consumers, but the array and volume of goods met all tastes. In the fifties, home freezers and high-fidelity stereophonographs were accorded the status of "necessities." By the end of that decade, the houses and garages of suburbia were littered with sporting goods, power tools, tape recorders, automatic dishwashers, barbecues, boats, electric toothbrushes, can-openers, hair-dryers, and nail-groomers. Special markets were developed for particular consumer groups: anglers, amateur photographers, pet lovers, scuba divers, and backpackers. The teen-age market, once nonexistent, rapidly became a multi-billion-dollar business, specializing in records, cosmetics, surfboards, junk food, soft drinks, clothes, 3-D movies, and motorcycles.

New institutions catered to the demands of the consumer culture: supermarkets, shopping malls, and credit cards, to name a few. In the 1950s, the large retail food store became the envy of the world: a spacious, glistening shrine to American abundance where shoppers pushed overladen, stainless steel carts among rows of well-displayed and hygienically packaged cartons, cans, and frozen foods. The great shopping malls that spread in the 1960s contained even more goods. In these sprawling indoor emporia of shops, stalls, and stores, consumers could dine in a cafeteria or a pizza stand, buy a mink stole or a hula-hoop, play pinball, purchase a paperback book or a bayberry-scented candle — and in some cases ride an elephant or go skating. If the piped Muzak annoyed some, there was comfort in the air-conditioned and plant-laden atmosphere and in the knowledge that the credit card was rapidly making cash obsolete.

A PACKAGED SOCIETY

To most Americans the consumer culture was the supreme achievement of the world's most vigorous economy. Vice President Nixon, in his famous "kitchen debate" (1959) with Khrushchev, could think of no more effective rebuttal to the claim of communist superiority than the dazzling array of household appliances available in the United States. More skeptical observers, on the other hand, decried the ethic of accumulation and lamented the development of an "abundance psychology."

Books of social criticism, freed from the Depression-era preoccupation with hard times, analyzed *The Crack in the Picture Window* (1956) and *The Split Level Trap* (1960). The postwar American male was described as *The Organization Man* (1956) or *The Man in the Gray Flannel Suit* (1956) who was lost in the *Lonely Crowd* (1950) where "belongingness," the "organization ethic," and "other-directedness" were more highly prized than traditional values of thrift, individualism, and self-reliance. Members of the new white-collar class, it was said, were the victims of "status anxiety," and were manipulated and dehumanized by corporate greed. Suburban schools produced a standardized product, better trained in "life adjustment" and "peer orientation" than in the three *R*s. According to its critics, this was a "packaged society," an "air-conditioned nightmare," in which art, sex, politics, religion, and even the sentiment of Mother's Day were merchandised in a mass market.

In the 1960s, the social commentary grew shriller as the children of the middle class became disenchanted with the war in Vietnam and the supermarket society. Drawing in part on the experience of the nonconformist "beat generation" of the fifties — and the poetry and novels of Lawrence Ferlinghetti, Allen Ginsberg, and Jack Kerouac — the "counter culture" rejected the values, if not always the benefits, of the consumer culture. More recently, double-digit inflation, a slower growth rate, depleting energy supplies, and despoiled natural resources have cast other shadows across our affluent society and have forced Americans for the first time since the Great Depression to face diminishing expectations.

During the fifties, however, the detracters of American society were not listened to. For the moment, though turmoil, confusion, and national self-doubt lay just ahead, the People of Plenty took their material well-being for granted. Repeatedly assured that never in any nation had so many so much, they assured themselves that the good life lay within the grasp of every American who deserved it. It seems unsurprising, then, that the politics of the period was not notably committed to social causes.

THE POLITICS OF ABUNDANCE: HARRY AND IKE

Harry S Truman, the first postwar president, like his successors, lived in the shadow of FDR. Chosen to his own astonishment as Roosevelt's running mate in 1944, he became chief executive by happenstance — Roosevelt's death. Lacking the New Dealer's elegant manner and patrician good looks, Truman was friendly, earthy, unmistakably middle-class. He had only a high school diploma; his brief career as a Kansas City clothier ended in bankruptcy. Except for his wartime role as chairman of a Senate investigating committee, his two terms in that body were distinguished only by his loyalty to the New Deal. But he was much more than the embodiment of the common man. Though never popular during his years in office, many historians now describe him as the most underrated chief executive, and some rank him as a "near-great" president.

In domestic affairs, Truman was committed to social justice and shared abundance. Beginning in September 1945, he proposed the long list of reforms later called the "Fair Deal": a full employment program; increased minimum wages and broader Social Security; public housing and slum clearance; additional TVA-like regional development projects; federal aid to education and health protection; federal control of atomic energy; and an end to racial discrimination in voting and employment.

Except for early action on the employment and atomic energy bills, the Seventy-Ninth Congress was uncooperative. The conservative coalition of southern Democrats and northern Republicans, who gave his foreign policy initiatives bipartisan support, blocked his domestic programs at nearly every turn. In 1946 — amid the chaos of reconversion and mounting public dissatisfaction with rising prices and strikes — the Republicans gained control of both House and Senate. The new Eightieth Congress, the first Republican Congress since the Hoover administration, quickly cut government spending and taxes. The controversial Taft-Hartley Act, passed over Truman's veto, indicated a conservative swing in labor policy, but it proved not to be the union-busting measure that management wanted. It authorized anti-strike injunctions, outlawed the *closed shop* (which forbade the hiring of nonunion workers), and permitted so-called right-to-work laws prohibiting the *union shop* (which required new workers to join the union).

As the election of 1948 approached, Truman's prospects seemed bleak. Conservatives of both parties opposed his domestic programs. Liberals faulted his handling of the 1946 railroad and coal-mining strikes and longed for the magic of FDR. The New Deal coalition and the Democratic party itself seemed to be falling apart. The left wing threatened to follow Henry A. Wallace, who favored more progress at home and more conciliation abroad. A strong civil rights plank in the platform brought the secession of many conservative Southerners, who supported the "Dixiecrat" movement of Governor J. Strom Thurmond of South Carolina. The confident Republicans, once more fighting their right wing, renominated Governor Thomas E. Dewey of New York.

The situation was actually more favorable to Truman than it seemed. The people were not yet deeply divided about foreign policy, and some had resented Republican efforts to frustrate reform and curb labor. The two Democratic secessions proved advantageous. Wallace's well-intentioned protest movement, compromised and thus doomed to insignificance by its Communist supporters, drew antiradical fire away from Truman. Thurmond carried only four Deep South states, and his candidacy helped keep northern blacks in the Democratic camp. The old New Deal coalition held, giving Truman an upset victory. The Democrats regained control of Congress.

Jubilantly, a newly confident president called once more for the enactment of the Fair Deal, to which he added a new farm program, additional civil rights measures, and repeal of the Taft-Hartley Act. Again, though Democrats nominally controlled the Congress, the conservative coalition held fast. Congress cooperated by extending some existing programs. Social Security was expanded, the minimum wage was increased, and new public housing units were funded. But there were no new departures — no new TVAs; no new farm program, no prepaid national medical plan, nor federal aid to education; no revision of labor legislation; and no break-throughs in civil rights law. Under his own authority as commander-in-chief, the president ordered the armed forces to begin desegregating; he also appointed blacks to important offices, intervened in federal court cases on behalf of black litigants, and strengthened the Civil Rights Section of the Department of Justice.

Beyond these achievements, however, Truman's domestic record is unimpressive. Called to lead in a period of economic abundance and international crisis, his first priority was always foreign policy. Inheriting the political stalemate of Roosevelt's last peacetime years, but not the sense of national emergency that gave the New Deal its broad support, Truman's domestic legislative struggles were waged against uneven odds. But he kept the reform tradition intact and before the national conscience. Future generations and future Congresses would be kinder to the man and more receptive to his programs than were his contemporaries.

In the presidential campaign of 1952, the Republicans made much of the "mess in Washington" (an allusion to minor scandals involving Truman's subordinates) and of "creeping socialism" (a reference to New Deal programs, particularly TVA). The party chose the moderate General Dwight David Eisenhower, not the conservative idol Robert A. Taft. Eisenhower called himself a "modern Republican" and a "dynamic conservative," by which he meant that he was "conservative when it comes to money and liberal when it comes to human beings." That ambiguous distinction, like much of the new president's syntax, baffled many observers. But it was a fair description of the character and style of an affable general-in-politics who preferred consensus to conflict and who was more frequently opposed by his party's right wing than by the Democrats.

More comfortable at presiding than leading, ill at ease with governmental solutions to national problems, he left his successors a back-log of unresolved social problems. If Ike mounted no new crusades, he also sounded no retreat from the reform tradition. He was immensely popular and well suited to the conservative national mood. Some historians argue that his executive talents have been underestimated, and many believe that, despite his failure to build a Republican majority, the general was not the political innocent he appeared to be. He was, as Vice President Nixon observed, "far more complex and devious . . . than most people realized."

Initially, the Republican administration offered a businessman's government. The president, whose reverence for business leaders bordered on awe, conceded that Senator Taft was "twice as liberal" as he on social welfare issues. The cabinet was dominated by wealthy corporate executives — "eight millionaires and a plumber" — who hastily dismantled Korean wartime controls and paid lip-service to the gospel of small government, balanced budgets, and free enterprise. Administration efforts to win business confidence included tax concessions, increased "partnership" of government and private enterprise in public power and atomic energy development, and support for state, rather than federal, control of tideland oil resources.

Midway through the first term, however, Eisenhower's economic and social policies shifted from right to center. The Treasury Department modified its conservative, anti-inflation measures to fight a recession in 1954, and recovery came swiftly. The Republican Congress, moreover, proved somewhat receptive to familiar kinds of reform. There were modest extensions of Social Security and public housing, and a Department of Health, Education, and Welfare (HEW), initially a Truman proposal, was created. The return to Democratic control of Congress after the 1954 elections brought little change to this moderate course. Such controversial programs as health insurance or federal support of education were regularly defeated or heavily amended. Secretary of Agriculture Ezra Taft Benson's efforts to revise Democratic farm policies resulted in lower price supports. But declining farm income and heavy pressure from farm organizations prompted the administration to support many New Dealish measures, including a "Soil Bank" scheme to reduce agricultural acreage.

Government spending, so long denounced as the road to socialism, was cut back only moderately after the Korean War. It remained higher than the 1950 post–World War II low of $45 billion and, by 1957, was to reach a new peacetime high of $82 billion — more than half directed to defense expenditures. Government decisions continued to affect every part of the economy. Eisenhower successfully blocked federal construction of a dam and hydroelectric plant in Hell's Canyon, Idaho. But his efforts to curb federal power production in the Memphis area by favoring a private utility group over TVA were frustrated by revelations of excess profits and conflict of interest. Also, Eisenhower's effort to remove federal controls on natural gas production ended in failure. When HEW Secretary Oveta Culp Hobby opposed the free distribution of polio vaccine as "back door" socialism, public indignation forced her resignation. Neither budgetary considerations nor fear of "statism" deterred presidential support for such massive federal works projects as the St. Lawrence Seaway (jointly undertaken with Canada) and the Interstate Highway System (the largest road-building program in history).

The most important social advance of the period, that made by Afro-Americans, was a product of judicial activism and black initiative, not administration action. At mid-century, blacks were still generally subject to enforced segregation in the South, and throughout the nation they were far behind whites in jobs, income, housing, education, and health. In 1954 — in *Brown vs. Board of Education,* a case brought by the NAACP — the Supreme Court reversed its 1896 "separate but [nominally] equal" doctrine, and ordered the desegregation of public schools. In 1955–1956, blacks in Montgomery, Alabama, led by young Martin Luther King, Jr., launched a successful boycott to end segregation in that city's buses. Similar nonviolent, direct-action campaigns by black and white civil rights activists eventually brought additional progress in voting, public accommodations, and housing. But change came slowly. The *Brown* decision (which was soon extended to all public institutions) and the emerging civil rights movement provoked fierce opposition in the South, particularly in the lower tier of states, where massive resistance campaigns were led by white supremacist Citizens' Councils.

Although he cautiously acknowledged the desegregation order as the law of the land, Eisenhower refused otherwise to lend his considerable moral authority to the crusade against racism. But in 1957, when Arkansas Governor Orval Faubus attempted to obstruct the court-ordered desegregation of a Little Rock high school, the president used federal troops to enforce the decree. He also signed the first Civil Rights Acts (1957 and 1960) passed by Congress since Reconstruction. In civil rights, as in other areas of human welfare, Eisenhower provided little executive support.

The diffidence of Eisenhower's leadership led some to dismiss him as "the bland leading the bland." But Eisenhower was the most effective Republican campaigner since Warren G. Harding; despite a heart attack in 1955, he was re-elected in 1956 by a landslide. Whatever his deficiencies, Eisenhower gave the great majority of Americans the kind of presidency they wanted. Eight years of "modern Republicanism" did not solve the nation's critical domestic and foreign problems; however, peace was preserved, general abundance (despite brief recessions) was maintained, and a once-corrosive political atmosphere was tempered.

In the presidential campaign of 1960, Eisenhower gave his nominal blessings to Vice President Nixon, and then stood by unenthusiastically while the new Republican standard bearer ran on the administration's record. The Democratic challenger, John F. Kennedy, a Roman Catholic, was then only 42 years old; he exuded confidence and vigor and promised to "get America moving again." Kennedy's victory was by the narrowest of margins, and its meaning was not readily apparent. Popular suspicions about Kennedy's great wealth and religion were offset by his personal charm and political skill. But Nixon's strong showing suggested that the nation was not ready for bold new directions. The Democrats retained control of Congress, but Republicans and conservatives of both parties registered gains. Although the presidential guard had changed, there was no mandate for the bold new programs Kennedy's campaign had promised. In time, of course, the election of 1960 would emerge as a point of transition from the politics of tranquility to the politics of reform. At the moment, however, one thing was certain: the people still liked Ike.

FOR FURTHER READING

Among the more thoughtful overviews of the postwar years are William Chafe's *The Unfinished Journey* (1995), William Leuchtenburg's *A Troubled Feast* (1979), and James T. Patterson's *Grand Expectations* (1996). The social and intellectual impact of American affluence is treated in David Potter's *People of Plenty* (1954), but the books mentioned in the text should also be consulted. J. Ronald Oakley's *God's Country* (1986) describes America in the 1950s; Kenneth Jackson provides a wide-ranging, historical examination of suburbanization in *The Crabgrass Frontier* (1985); Elaine Tyler May surveys white middle-class families during the fifties in *Homeward Bound* (1988); and Erik Barnouw looks at the evolution of television in *Tube of Plenty* (1990). Aspects of the period's economic history are delineated in Herman Miller's *Rich Man, Poor Man* (1964), John Kenneth Galbraith's *The Affluent Society* (1958), and Michael Harrington's *The Other America* (1962). Richard Kluger's *Simple Justice* (1975) is a history of the *Brown* decisions, while Taylor Branch's *Parting the Waters* (1989) details the first decade of the civil rights movement. Numan Bartley in *The Rise of Massive Resistance* (1969) and Neil McMillen in *The Citizens' Council* (1971) chronicle southern reactions to desegregation. Of the many books on the Truman administration, see especially Robert H. Ferrell's *Harry S. Truman* (1994), David McCullough's *Truman* (1992), Robert Donovan's *Conflict and Crisis* (1977) and *The Tumultuous Years* (1982), and Michael J. Lacey, ed., *The Truman Presidency* (1989). Useful studies of Eisenhower's presidency include Stephen Ambrose's *Eisenhower: The President* (1983), Charles Alexander's *Holding the Line* (1975), and Fred Greenstein's *The Hidden-Hand Presidency* (1982). Gary Reichard's *The Reaffirmation of Republicanism* (1979) examines the 83rd Congress.

30

★ ★ ★ ★ ★ ★

Promise and Frustration, the 1960s

THE EARLY 1960s were notably optimistic years. Riding a wave of unprecendented affluence, the people looked confidently toward the fulfillment of the American dream. A new president, young and vigorous John F. Kennedy, was the self-proclaimed tribune of "a new generation," who had pledged to lead the nation out of drift and conformity. Bold federal initiatives against poverty and discrimination promised ready solutions to the most nagging American social ills. Abroad, the power and prestige of the United States remained immense. New divisions within the communist bloc carried assurances of diminished Soviet influence and the relaxation of East-West tensions.

By 1968, however, Americans were plagued by multiple domestic and international crises. The twin goals of social and economic justice seemed as illusive as ever. Politically and culturally polarized, deeply mired in an unpopular war it could not win, the nation was awash with discontent. Some observers worried that America had lost its social cohesion and was coming apart.

IN SEARCH OF THE NEW FRONTIER

John Fitzgerald Kennedy inspired public adoration more common to entertainers than to politicians. He was blessed with keen intelligence, an urbane and elegant style, and a self-deprecating sense of humor. Virtually alone among post–World War II presidents, his popularity seemed to increase with each month that passed. His public esteem, however, won him little congressional support. At the time of his assassination, less than one third of his legislative program had been enacted. Inevitably, his brief, tragic presidency raised expectations that could not be realized.

TABLE 18. THE KENNEDY-JOHNSON YEARS, 1961–1968

Year	Black revolution	Other domestic events	Vietnam War	Other foreign events
1961	Freedom Riders.	**January Kennedy** inaugurated.	**December** Kennedy pledges help to South Vietnam.	**April** Bay of Pigs. **August** Berlin wall.
1962	**October** Troops to Oxford, Mississippi.	**April** Steel price dispute. **November** Election; slight Republican gains.		**October** Cuban missile crisis.
1963	**April–May** Birmingham incidents. **August** March on Washington.	*Feminine Mystique* published. **September** Tax cut passed. **November 22** Kennedy assassinated.	**November** Fall of Diem.	**August** Above-ground test-ban treaty signed.
1964	**January** Poll tax amendment. **June 3** Civil rights workers murdered in Mississippi. **July** Civil Rights Act.	**August** Economic Opportunity Act. **November** Johnson wins election.	**August** Tonkin Gulf incident.	**October** Chinese atomic bomb.
1965	**August** Voting Rights Act. Watts riots.	**July** Medicare enacted.	**February** "Operation Rolling Thunder" begins. **June** U.S. troops in combat.	**April** U.S. troops to Dominican Republic.
1966	**January** Robert C. Weaver, first black cabinet member. Black Power movement. National Organization for Women formed.	**November** Election; Republican gains.	**February** Bombing of Hanoi, Haiphong.	**July** France withdraws from NATO command organization.
1967	**June** Thurgood Marshall appointed to Supreme Court. **July** Riots in Newark, Detroit.		**January** U.S. offensive. **September** Elections in South Vietnam.	**June** Israeli-Arab War.
1968	**April 4** Martin Luther King assassinated. **April 10** Civil Rights Bill passed.	**June 5** Robert Kennedy shot. **November** Nixon elected president.	**February** Tet offensive. **May** Paris peace talks. **November 1** Bombing of North Vietnam ended.	**August** Soviet invasion of Czechoslovakia.

The first challenge to the Kennedy promise — "to get the country moving again" — was a sluggish economy. Having inherited a lagging growth rate, 6 percent unemployment, and a staggering balance-of-trade deficit, the new administration encouraged economic expansion through increased civilian and military spending. To hold down inflation, the president issued wage-price guidelines and "jawboned" steel companies into rescinding a price hike.

Although Congress responded favorably to the administration's defense and space research-and-development programs, it turned down most social welfare proposals. Kennedy's stop-gap bills for investment tax-credits, employee retraining, public housing, and increased minimum wage and Social Security benefits were enacted. Congress also passed the landmark Trade Expansion Act (1962), which stimulated foreign trade through reciprocal tariff agreements. But the president's Area Redevelopment Act (1961), designed to aid chronically depressed areas, was so amended that most of the funding went for highway construction — more beneficial to business interests than to the poor. Conservatives blocked Kennedy's requests for nearly everything else: programs to assist unemployed youth and migrant workers, a new Department of Urban Affairs, expanded unemployment insurance benefits, Medicare for the aged, federal aid to education, and a tax cut designed to increase consumer spending.

Despite these setbacks to New Frontier reforms, the economy improved dramatically. Between 1960 and 1964, both the GNP and total federal expenditures (much of the latter for defense) increased by nearly 25 percent. The annual inflation rate (1 to 2 percent) was minimal, but the unemployment rate never fell below 5 percent.

In confronting the country's worst social problem, the unequal status of blacks, Kennedy was again sharply limited by the dominant congressional coalition of Southern Democrats and generally conservative Republicans. Defeated in several legislative battles and afraid of tying up all domestic and foreign action in a filibuster, the administration relied mainly on executive action. Blacks were increasingly appointed to office, pressure against discrimination was applied through government purchasing policies, and after some hesitation a presidential order forbade discrimination in federally financed housing. Robert F. Kennedy, the president's brother, was appointed Attorney General by the president, and vigorously attacked the problem of black voting rights in the South.

As in the 1950s, the most important advances for blacks were made through the increasingly militant, though nonviolent civil rights movement. Strongly supported by college students, clergy, and other white sympathizers from the North, the movement was opposed in the South by threats and mounting violence. By the end of 1962, the efforts of "freedom riders," supported by the Attorney General in the face of violent white resistance, achieved the end of segregation in transportation. In October 1962, federal troops were sent to Oxford, Mississippi, when mob violence and the resistance of the governor threatened to bar a black, James Meredith, from the state university. The threat of similar action prevailed the following year in Alabama, and university desegregation was under way in all states.

The year 1963 saw the peak of the peaceful victories of the civil rights movement and the beginning of a new stage. Violent resistance sharply increased; in Birmingham, Alabama, police dogs were used against marchers, and four black girls were killed in a church bombing; in Jackson, Mississippi, Medgar Evers, an NAACP field secretary, was killed from ambush outside his home. Throughout the lower South, unpunished acts of white violence against the persons and property of blacks rose sharply. In June, the president proclaimed a state of moral crisis in the nation and committed the government more fully than at any time since Reconstruction to the achievement of equality. A new civil rights bill attacking discrimination in public accommodations was introduced in Congress as a major administration objective. In August, the nation seemed profoundly impressed by a peaceful march of a quarter of million people in Washington, under the leadership of Martin Luther King, Jr.

Superficially, it seemed that great progress was being made peacefully on this crucial front, and opportunities undoubtedly increased for many blacks, especially those with skills and education. Yet the economic gaps between most blacks and most whites were not lessened, the city ghettoes remained almost unaffected, and there were signs that some blacks were losing their patience with moderate leadership. It was also clear that a large and determined white minority was ready to oppose any real social equality for the black population.

KENNEDY AND THE WORLD

Perhaps the most important development of the 1960s was a deterioration of the opposing pacts formed by the United States and the Soviet Union with their respective allies in the early Cold War period. In 1960, as the Sino-Soviet split widened, the USSR withdrew technicians from China, and during the rest of the decade hostility between the two great communist nations escalated. From time to time, Soviet satellites in Eastern Europe increased their efforts for autonomy, and in the Soviet Union itself, intellectuals fought for freedom of expression. Though neither Communist party dictatorship in the USSR nor Soviet control of Eastern Europe was seriously threatened, Soviet freedom of action was more limited than at any time since World War II. The situation had obvious advantages for American policy. It also meant, however, that Russian leaders felt the need of some major success, either peaceful or military, to consolidate their leadership in a divided communist world.

The Western alliances put together under Truman and Eisenhower were no more secure than the Soviet's. Like his predecessors, Kennedy tried to promote European economic and military unification. With a stronger trans-Atlantic partnership in mind, he persuaded Congress to adopt the reciprocal trade law of 1962 that permitted tariff reductions of up to 50 percent with

European Common Market nations. France, under General Charles de Gaulle, insisted on maintaining an independent and highly nationalistic stance. In January 1963, De Gaulle blocked England's effort to enter the European Common Market. Insisting on a separate French nuclear force, he resisted European military unification and refused to join in efforts for nuclear disarmament. England, generally loyal to its special relationship with the United States despite many disagreements, became increasingly less able to play the role of Great Power, especially in the Far East. Japan, America's principal ally in that region, continued under U.S. protection to prosper without rearming. Without solid alliances, a stable balance of power, or a powerful international defense pact, Kennedy dealt with each crisis as it arose according to the means available.

In military terms, the means increased. Robert McNamara, the talented secretary of defense, successfully imposed modern administrative techniques and Kennedy policies on the massive military establishment. Whatever remained of Dulles's reliance on massive retaliation was scrapped in favor of a balanced development of nuclear, conventional, and guerrilla capabilities. The mistaken impression of Soviet military superiority, fostered by Kennedy's campaign emphasis on a nonexistent missile gap, gave way to a clear American lead in most areas of armament. Between 1960 and 1967, the number of American Inter-Continental Ballistic Missiles (ICBMs) quintupled; in McNamara's judgment the nation had "more than we require." Rocket development was further demonstrated by successes in putting astronauts into space. In the various theaters of foreign policy, both America's increased might and its inability to solve every international problem became clear.

Far more than its predecessors, the Kennedy administration turned its attention to the problems of the impoverished and unstable Third World. The Peace Corps was formed and recruited young Americans for service in regions that needed their efforts. With less success, the president tried to persuade Congress to provide massive aid for struggling, underdeveloped economies. A special effort to promote unity, economic development, and nonrevolutionary social change in Latin America was given the name of the "Alliance for Progress." Though only the barest beginning was made in the social and economic goals of the alliance, goodwill was increased. Willingness to tolerate diversity and neutrality led to some other successes, especially in relations with African states. A Chinese attack on Indian borders in 1962 led India to turn a friendlier face toward America.

One of America's closest neighbors, Cuba, remained on unfriendly terms. When Cuban guerrilla forces led by Fidel Castro ousted a pro-U.S. but reactionary dictator in 1959, many Americans welcomed the arrival of an apparently more democratic leader. But sympathy gave way to suspicion as the Cuban Revolution turned leftward. Within the administration, Vice President Nixon, convinced that Castro was a communist, advocated U.S. military intervention to topple him. President Eisenhower secretly authorized the CIA to train an invasion force of anti-Castro Cuban exiles. In April 1961, with some misgivings (and without an attempt to negotiate U.S.–Cuban differences), the new Democratic president approved this ill-advised act of American adventurism. Misled about the extent of support likely in Cuba, the administration provided logistical assistance but refused decisive military help. The resulting humiliating defeat at the Bay of Pigs increased Kennedy's suspicion of military adventure and expert military advice.

The truculent side of Khrushchev's changeable policy was shown at the West's most vulnerable point, Berlin. In a meeting with Kennedy in Vienna in June 1961, Khrushchev refused to give up his threat to negotiate a treaty with East Germany that would have the effect of ending the occupation rights of the Western Allies. Kennedy let it be known that the defense of Berlin was an American commitment even to the extent of nuclear war. To emphasize the point, the president increased draft quotas, asked Congress for additional military spending, and outlined a civil defense program including the construction of nuclear fallout shelters. The crisis climaxed in August 1961, when the East German government closed the border to the city's western sector and began the construction of a concrete-and-barbed-wire wall between East Germany and West Berlin. Because it stopped the flow of East Germans to the West, this barrier made the presence of a Western enclave within the communist world more tolerable to the Soviets. The Berlin tension gradually subsided, but the wall remained as a ghastly reminder of East-West division.

A more serious conflict with the Soviets developed in Cuba in 1962, where the Cold War seemed perilously close to turning hot. In August, American reconnaisance planes reported that the Soviet Union, contrary to repeated and specific assurances, was building in Cuba sites for short-range missiles (220 miles) capable of striking the southernmost reaches of the United States with nuclear warheads. Soviet and Cuban intentions are subject to debate. Kennedy linked this challenge to the Berlin crisis and interpreted it as an extension of Soviet nuclear capabilities. But his response was also colored by political considerations. Because he had been humiliated by the Bay of Pigs fiasco, and because the installations were made known on the eve of a congressional election, he felt compelled to act decisively. Some historians believe that he overreacted, that the missiles were defensive and designed to deter further U.S. intervention; in their view, continued American efforts to destabilize Castro's regime — including a plot with organized crime figures to have the Cuban leader assassinated — raised legitimate Cuban security concerns.

In a series of tense meetings, Kennedy and his advisers debated various responses ranging from pacific to belligerent. Kennedy chose neither extreme. On the one hand, the administration was unwilling to propose, under pressure, the reciprocal withdrawal of Soviet missiles from Cuba and American missiles from Italy and Turkey. (The latter bases, rated obsolete, were soon quietly withdrawn; missile-carrying submarines were regarded as less vulnerable.) On the other hand, Kennedy also rejected an immediate though limited airstrike recommended by his military advisers and others. Instead, he announced that he had ordered American warships to stop and search vessels coming to Cuba that might contain offensive weapons. In case this

MAP 11: THE UNITED STATES, THE CARIBBEAN, AND CUBA

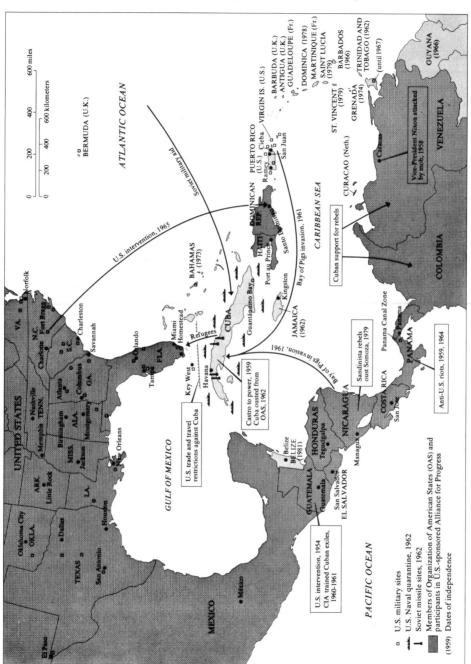

proved insufficient, he ordered military concentrations preparatory to possible invasion of the island, which might mean a direct clash with Russian personnel at missile bases. Again, the president rejected the idea of a face-to-face negotiated settlement.

To Khrushchev, Kennedy publicly pledged not to invade Cuba if the installations were removed. The Soviet leader, who had earlier promised that the missiles would fly in Cuba's defense, accepted Kennedy's terms, and a dozen Soviet vessels turned back before encountering the American blockade. "We're eyeball to eyeball," Secretary of State Dean Rusk observed, "and I think the other fellow just blinked." For the moment, it seemed that American boldness and Russian prudence had produced not only a victory for Kennedy but a chance for peace. Shrewdly refraining from any tendency to gloat over its success, the administration stressed the mutual advantages of the Soviet-American disengagement. It had been the single most dangerous moment since World War II. It proved to be Khrushchev's Bay of Pigs and Kennedy's most politically popular hour.

Although the crisis ultimately spurred a Soviet effort to close the missile gap — this gap real and in the American favor — East-West tension lessened. A "hot-line" was installed between Washington and Moscow and arms-reduction talks were resumed. In 1958, as part of the last rapprochement, both powers had suspended nuclear testing pending disarmament negotiations. In the fall of 1961, during the last great Berlin crisis, the Soviets resumed testing, exploding the largest bombs yet. The United States quickly followed suit. In 1963, however, a complex and determined American diplomatic effort produced a treaty banning atmospheric, but not underground, tests. Ratified by the Senate despite conservative fears, this treaty was signed by the USSR, the United States, Britain, and many other countries, but not by France or China. Further gestures toward détente were promised, and in October the United States agreed to a large sale of wheat to the Soviet Union.

JFK IN VIETNAM

Kennedy's important though limited foreign policy successes were unfortunately not to be duplicated in Vietnam. Once a remote and peripheral concern of the United States, Vietnam rapidly became the scene of the nation's longest (1950–1975) and most unpopular war. During World War II, Ho Chi Minh's nationalist Viet Minh forces cooperated with the United States in the common struggle against the Japanese. In 1945, Ho modeled his country's Declaration of Independence after the American document, and thereafter repeatedly expressed his good will for the government and people of the United States. Roosevelt had affirmed that the United States would not assist in the re-establishment of colonial rule in Southeast Asia, but Truman refused Ho's appeals for military and economic assistance in the Vietnamese War of national liberation from the French (1945–1954). The reasons are numerous and complex, but the most important include: American eagerness to strengthen ties with its European Cold War partner and American reluctance to make common cause with Ho, founder of the Vietnamese Communist party. In 1950, following the "fall" of China and the invasion of South Korea, fear of further Communist gains in Asia (particularly in Japan and the Philippines) prompted Truman to recognize the French puppet regime. By 1954, American taxpayers were underwriting nearly 80 percent of the cost of France's colonial war.

In 1954, Eisenhower considered but finally refused unilateral American military intervention to save the collapsing French. Yet he, too, misunderstood the nationalist character of Ho's revolution. Reading East-West conflict into an indigenous and fundamentally anticolonial struggle, he described a non-communist Vietnam as vital to American security. Following Ho's victory over the French, American economic and military aid was shifted to the anticommunist but increasingly repressive dictatorship of Ngo Dinh Diem in Saigon. The CIA began secret "counter-insurgency" activities in North Vietnam. In 1956, the administration blocked the national elections mandated by the Geneva Conference to reunify Vietnam because, as Eisenhower later noted, "possibly 80 percent of the population would have voted for the Communist Ho Chi Minh."

Until 1960, Diem's enemies in the South received only sporadic assistance from Hanoi. In that year, insurgents with the support of Ho's government organized the National Liberation Front, political arm of the Vietcong (South Vietnamese Communists). Unwilling to permit a Communist victory, and convinced that Vietnam was "the keystone to the arch, the finger in the dike" of the Asian Cold War, Kennedy picked up where Eisenhower left off. Responding to the intensifying civil war in the South, he secretly increased the American military presence. By late 1963, U.S. aircraft were flying reconnaisance and support missions for South Vietnamese troops, and the nearly 17,000 U.S. "advisers" were unmistakably engaged in combat.

Increased American support, however, brought only frustration. Despite repeated Pentagon assurances that overwhelmingly favorable "kill ratios" and "body counts" assured a non-communist victory, the United States was not winning when Kennedy was assassinated on November 22, 1963. By that date, the unpopular Diem had been assassinated by his own generals. His government gave way to a succession of others, none more successful or popular. Subsequently, as the increasingly unpopular war ground on, the slain American president's aides argued that if Kennedy had lived to be re-elected, the United States would have been spared much of the agony of the escalated war under Lyndon Johnson. That contention is unprovable.

THE GREAT SOCIETY

The contrast between the elegant, rational, slightly aloof, and handsome Kennedy and his successor, Lyndon Baines Johnson, was great. Tense, ambitious, hard-driving, gregarious, and earthy, Johnson had risen to wealth and political power through the hard school of Texas politics. His enemies considered him unscrupulous and coarse. In the opening days of his admin- istration, however, most Americans were reassured by his emphasis on fa- miliar programs of domestic reform. Modeling his approach on that of Frank- lin Roosevelt and concentrating on domestic affairs — particularly on the problems of poverty — Johnson called his program the Great Society and made clear his intent to build a new and workable consensus, the first since New Deal days. While courting business and Congress, the new president hoped to retain the support of liberals and intellectuals. The administration's brightest hope was that the first wholly southern president since the Civil War would reconcile the South to the advancement of blacks. Committing himself to this cause more eloquently than to any other, Johnson succeeded in pushing through in 1964 Kennedy's Civil Rights bill, which included fur- ther support for blacks in voting rights, education, job opportunities, and public accommodations. A further massive tax reduction gave rise to record economic advance. The Economic Opportunity Act spelled out Kennedy's proposal for a "War on Poverty" in terms of job training, grants to cities, and other measures. As the election of 1964 approached, Johnson gave the impression of masterful success.

Conservative Republicans, restive since New Deal days with moderate candidates of the Eisenhower variety, nominated Senator Barry Goldwater of Arizona. Their convention had a highly organized anti-liberal fervor, which alarmed many moderate Republicans. Goldwater, a personally attrac- tive if unduly forthright man, urged upon farmers an end to agricultural programs, proposed the sale of the TVA in Tennessee, and criticized Social Security to the elderly. In the campaign, he played into Democratic hands, permitting Johnson to portray him as a "trigger-happy" reactionary whose election would imperil the reform tradition and world peace. Even his cam- paign slogan — "In Your Heart, You Know He's Right" — backfired. In an obvious reference to the presidential hand on the nuclear button, Democrats retorted: "In Your Heart, You Know He Might." While the challenger de- nounced big government, labor unions, rising crime, and declining morals, Johnson promised a reassuring combination of moderate reform at home and restrained but steadfast resistance to aggression abroad. In the balloting, Johnson won all but six states and the biggest popular landslide (61 percent) since 1936.

With the increased Democratic majorities in Congress, the power of the conservative Republican-Southern Democrat coalition was broken for the first time since 1938. Demonstrating his practical political skill and experi- ence, Johnson pushed through the "Congress of Fulfillment" a coordinated reform program. Laws passed in 1965 and 1966 centered on many concerns, old and new. Black equality was promoted by the Voting Rights Act, easily the most effective civil rights measure ever enacted. Johnson also appointed the first black cabinet member and the first black Supreme Court Justice, Thurgood Marshall. Kennedy's Medicare program of health insurance for the aged and Medicaid for the poor were approved, breaking a long taboo against federal support of medical care. Traditional sectarian opposition to federal aid to education was overcome, and the president, who was largely self-educated, took special pride in such measures as the Elementary and Secondary Education Act and the Higher Education Act. The complex problem of urban poverty was addressed through such innovations as rent subsidies (the Housing Act) and the Demonstration Cities program. Finally, Johnson also won congressional support for highway safety and anti-pollution programs and for two additional cabinet-level departments, Transportation and Housing and Urban Development. Not unjustly, the president claimed the most spectacular legislative record since Franklin Roosevelt's "hundred days" in 1933.

THE AGONY OF POWER

Despite domestic achievements, by the middle of the decade the United States, potentially a great society, was clearly a divided and confused one. In both foreign and domestic affairs, the Johnson administration inherited the unsolved problems and shifting balances of the last decades. In both spheres, old policies were pushed to new lengths. In both, increased commitments seemed, by 1965 or 1966, to bring increased frustration.

The disintegration of the international alliances continued to offer a strange mixture of menace and opportunity. By 1966, De Gaulle had announced France's withdrawal from the NATO military organization. China, at last a nuclear power but torn by domestic turmoil, was denouncing Russian revisionism as bitterly as it attacked American imperialism. Though the suddenly deposed Khrushchev was replaced by Leonid Brezhnev in October 1964, the United States and the USSR continued their rapprochement gingerly. Johnson was able, in the wake of Kennedy's test-ban treaty, to win congressional support for a consular treaty (establishing additional consulates in both the United States and the USSR). There was also a Soviet-American understanding not to place nuclear warheads into orbit, and additional cultural exchanges were arranged. In 1968 the two powers also signed a nonproliferation treaty, which was designed to prevent the further spread of nuclear weapons.

To both Great Powers, the restless and impoverished Third World seemed to present impossible problems. The Alliance for Progress failed to solve Latin America's economic or political problems, and in one instance the president reverted to older methods. In the Dominican Republic, where the liberal government was overthrown by a military coup in 1963, a revolt against the new military regime threatened civil war in 1965. Stating reasons ranging from protection of American lives to preventing a triumph of Castroism, Johnson sent 22,000 troops to the island. Fortunately a compromise among contending factions eventually produced a regime with some claim to legitimacy. Yet the Johnson action was widely denounced as a throwback to Theodore Roosevelt's gunboat diplomacy.

The problems of power were most tragically illustrated, however, in the interminable struggle in Vietnam. When Johnson took office, the prospect for an American solution could not have been bleaker. Diem's death was followed by a long period of political instability in the South; the National Liberation Front (NLF) had grown increasingly formidable, and the Viet Cong controlled nearly half of South Vietnam; North Vietnamese involvement in the struggle against the Saigon regime was mounting. In effect, the president had but two choices: escalation in pursuit of a military victory, or a negotiated compromise with Hanoi for a coalition government in Saigon. Although he campaigned as the peace candidate and promised not to send Americans to fight "Asian wars," Johnson found negotiation unacceptable and ultimately moved to "Americanize" the war against "international communism" in Indochina.

Determined to win the war, but wary of congressional interference and public criticism, the president moved cautiously until the controversial Tonkin Gulf incident. In August 1964, a U.S. destroyer cruising in the gulf in an area of recent South Vietnamese naval action, was attacked — once inside North Vietnamese territorial waters and, according to disputed evidence, a second time in international waters — by North Vietnamese PT boats. Ordering retaliatory action against enemy torpedo-boat bases, the administration requested and got from Congress (which knew nothing of American air raids against the North) blanket authorization for whatever further military action might prove necessary to repel attacks on American forces. The measures also authorized American assistance to Southeast Asian states that requested it. During the presidential campaign, Johnson emphasized the limited character of the reprisals; in the fall of 1964, he resisted pressure for U.S. bombing raids against the North. His critics soon charged, however, that the Senate had been duped into granting the "functional equivalent" of a declaration of war. The Tonkin resolution — whatever the circumstances of its passage and whatever Johnson's reason for introducing it — later provided crucial justification for the escalation of American involvement.

In February 1965, an attack on an American barracks in Pleiku became the pretext for systematic air raids on North Vietnam. "We seek no wider war," Johnson affirmed. But the new aerial offensive against the North, "Operation Rolling Thunder," shifted from transport to factories and fuel dumps and included buildings in the center of large cities. The raids were defended less in terms of specific reprisals and more as part of an effort to stop troop infiltration into the South or to force North Vietnam to negotiate by showing that victory was impossible. Partly in support of the intensified air offensive, American ground forces were massively increased. By 1968, more than one-half million U.S. troops were engaged in an effort to search for guerrillas and to destroy them throughout the country.

By 1967, it was clear that this massive military presence was not succeeding in its objectives. The American buildup was more than matched by increased enemy activity. Rolling Thunder had little effect on North Vietnamese supply lines, and infiltration of Northern troops increased. Repeated and complex suggestions of negotiations failed to promise solutions acceptable to the Johnson administration. The weak South Vietnamese government remained corrupt and unpopular, and the desertion of its troops was a continuing embarrassment. U.S. attempts to secure parts of the country for the promotion of agrarian reform were failing. Amid the mounting carnage of American "pacification" efforts and search-and-destroy missions — and particularly after the bloody My Lai massacre (March 1968) of unarmed peasants by an American unit — the administration's characterization of the war as a struggle between tyranny and freedom grew less credible.

At home, as the casualties increased (25,000 Americans had died in Vietnam by 1968) and the end seemed no nearer, the war was denounced more widely and more intensely than any American war since 1865. Opponents included powerful senators, much of the press, large sections of the liberal clergy, and a large number of fervent and articulate young people. On the left of the antiwar movement, some critics insisted that the Vietnam War was part of a long pattern of American aggression, that the administration had no intention of negotiating and desired permanent bases, and that the outcome would be war with China and possibly Russia. Other critics believed the war impossible to win, and incompatible either with the needs of domestic policy or the effort of worldwide stability. Still others were appalled by the very heavy bombing of both halves of Vietnam (by 1968, America had dropped a greater tonnage of bombs on Vietnam than had been dropped on Europe and Asia together in World War II), by the use of napalm and fragmentation bombs, by the forcible relocation of villages, and by the chemical destruction of crops and forests. The minimum demands of the growing antiwar movement were the end of bombing in the North, recognition that the NLF must play a part in the government of the South, and the scaling down of operations. Defenders of the administration, while insisting that they were willing to negotiate and denying any intention of carrying the war to the North, insisted that South Vietnam must be defended. They insisted that communist success in Vietnam would mean the spread of communist power through Southeast Asia, the collapse of American efforts everywhere to prevent the expansion of communism, especially through Chinese-style guerrilla wars, and immediately, bloody reprisals against government supporters in South Vietnam. The president argued that the failure to defeat Hanoi threatened the security of Hawaii and even San Francisco.

THE BLACK REVOLUTION

By 1967, the unsuccessful war in Vietnam was obviously only one of a number of pressing and divisive problems facing the United States. The most serious was the disaffection of the black minority. While both civil rights progress and violent resistance to it continued in the South, a series of cataclysmic events turned the nation's attention to the northern black ghettoes. In August 1965, a riot in Watts, a black section of Los Angeles, resulted in 34 deaths and 30 hours of looting and arson. For the next three years, scenes of burning buildings, helmeted troops, and even tanks moving down city streets became almost commonplace on American television screens. The worst disturbances took place in Newark (23 killed) and Detroit (43 killed) in July of 1967, but few major cities escaped violence altogether. In 1967 alone, there were 41 major disturbances.

A final wave of urban rioting followed the murder on April 4, 1968, of Martin Luther King, Jr., by a white man in Memphis, Tennessee. The leading black advocate of nonviolence, Dr. King better than any other American had articulated black aspiration and appealed to the nation's moral conscience. His death triggered a great outpouring of grief and riots in 125 cities.

The inflammatory rhetoric associated with black militance was scarcely less disquieting than the disorders themselves. Though most Afro-Americans, as opinion polls revealed, still believed in integration and longed for racial reconciliation, a growing minority subscribed to Black Power, not so much a doctrine as a cry of rage that could mean anything from bloc-voting and separate economic development to outright separatism. By 1966, "white liberal" had joined "Uncle Tom" as a term of black militant abuse. Strident cries of "Burn, Baby, Burn," "Off the Pigs," and "Kill Whitey" suggested that innercity blacks had come, in James Baldwin's words, "to hate the hater."

The civil rights movement, which had grown younger, blacker, and less patient with the pace of change, was torn by factional and racial strife. In 1966, both the Student Nonviolent Coordinating Committee (SNCC) and the Congress of Racial Equality (CORE) officially abandoned their philosophical traditions of biracialism and nonviolence. Such Marxist-oriented revolutionary movements as the paramilitary Black Panther party and the nationalist Republic of New Africa advocated the territorial separation of black from white. The themes of black chauvinism and retaliatory violence, once preached primarily by the Nation of Islam (Black Muslims), seemed increasingly attractive to young innercity blacks.

Whites feared that these developments portended race war. Conservatives cried that the "Negro Revolution" threatened to tear the nation apart, and many liberals were afraid that black activists, frustrated in their efforts to reform the American system, sought its destruction. Yet no important ghetto disturbances occurred after 1968, and despite militant rhetoric, those before that date had few revolutionary implications. Opinion polls confirmed that the great majority of black Americans wanted nothing more radical than a share of the good life. The principal victims of the convulsive long hot summers of the 1960s had been blacks themselves; destroyed property nearly always lay within the ghetto, and the dead and injured were mostly black. According to the National Advisory Commission on Civil Disorders report in February 1968, the riots were spontaneous upheavals, chiefly caused by white racism and the "explosive mixture" it fostered: police brutality, slum housing, poverty and welfare dependency, job discrimination and unemployment, and blighted opportunity. To counter the threat of a completely and permanently divided society, the commission recommended a sweeping program for additional jobs, education, housing, and "income supplementation."

The problem was more easily identified than solved. Many whites demanded not additional reforms but repression. Instead of a new commitment to equality, the white community in many cities increased its armament. The principal urban response seemed to be more sophisticated riot-control training for police. President Johnson, preoccupied by Vietnam and wary of a white backlash, ignored most of the Advisory Commission's recommendations and pressed only for the open housing law that he had been advocating since 1966. This measure, which became the Civil Rights Act of 1968, banned discrimination in the sale of some 80 percent of housing. It also imposed stringent penalities for incitement to riot.

Meanwhile, the momentum of reform had slowed. Disenchanted reformers noted that the War on Poverty had done more for landlords and construction companies than for the children of depressed rural areas or ghettoes. Many antipoverty programs had been hastily devised, oversold, and underfunded. Although much had been done to soften the burdens of the poor, the elderly, and the blacks, the nation's social problems seemed as intractable as ever. And President Johnson, having squandered his great consensus of 1964 on the nation's most unpopular war, found his domestic programs in neglect and his leadership in ruins by 1968.

OTHER PROTESTS

A parallel and in some ways remarkably similar social problem, sexual discrimination, was also thrust upon the national conscience in the 1960s. In 1963, a presidential commission reported widespread discrimination against women workers, who comprised more than a third of the nation's labor force. That same year, Betty Friedan's *The Feminine Mystique* forcefully attacked the socialization process whereby woman's role was defined exclusively as wife and mother. Neither publication attracted immediate widespread public attention, yet both were symptoms of the awakening of feminism from a slumber of four decades. Having won the vote, the women's movement, after nearly a century of vitality, had collapsed during the 1920s. It was reborn, however, amid the passions of the 1960s. Constituting 51 percent of the population, women were not a minority. But many feminists came to identify with other oppressed groups. Stirred by student protests and the civil rights and antiwar movements, women activists again addressed the problems of their sex. Although the resulting feminist resurgence seemed to take the nation by surprise, the grievances expressed were all too apparent. The Nineteenth Amendment had enfranchised women but it had not redefined their role in home and society. Nor had it opened the way to educational and employment equality. In the four decades since the suffrage amendment was ratified, women's position relative to men had in fact deteriorated in important areas. A smaller percentage of the nation's college students, both graduate and undergraduate, were women in 1960 than in 1920 or 1930. Well-intentioned but often arbitrary "protective legislation" denied them access to some desirable occupations; they had only limited access to managerial and executive positions; and they were generally denied equal pay for equal work.

To attack these injustices Friedan and several other women formed in 1966 the National Organization for Woman (NOW), a worthy successor to Susan B. Anthony's and Carrie Chapman Catt's NAWSA. NOW, which proved attractive primarily to middle-class white professional and business women, represented the moderate wing of the Women's Liberation movement. Often identified as the "feminist's NAACP," it waged a dignified program of public education and lobbied for more equitable state and local legislation. But younger activists, often those associated with the New Left, were generally critical of NOW and formed their own radical groups. Among these small and often factious units, the most notable was probably WITCH (at first Women's International Terrorist Conspiracy from Hell, but later sometimes called Women Infuriated at Taking Care of Hoodlums or Women Inspired to Commit Herstory), a tiny but shrill, loosely knit "nonorganization" that employed street theater to dramatize sexual injustice.

Whatever their persuasions, the new feminists, like their sisters a half-century earlier, faced the ridicule and hostility of tradition-minded men and women who either argued that woman's place was defined by biology or that sexual equality would destroy the institutions of marriage and family. There was some triumph as well as much abuse. At the most abstract level, sexual bigotry was not routed, but it retreated a little as women in growing numbers became sensitive to sexual issues. More particularly, governments, both state and federal, began to respond to this new sensitivity. Title VII of the 1964 Civil Rights Act forbade both sexual and racial job discrimination; HEW sponsored "affirmative action" programs for women as well as minorities; Congress enacted in 1972 an Equal Rights Amendment to the Constitution, which was not ratified by all the states; the Supreme Court in 1973 issued a remarkably liberal abortion ruling. To be sure, sexism, like racism, possessed subtleties that seemed to defy government solution. But the status of women had indisputably improved during the first decade of women's liberation.

A very different kind of protest in this age of change and unrest was that of the self-conscious youth culture. In 1964, a number of northern university students had gone to Mississippi as "summer soldiers" in the civil rights movement. The violence they encountered undermined their respect for authority, and the success of nonviolent methods suggested new kinds of power. Radicalized by the experience and disenchanted with the "sandbox politics" of student government, some students were prepared to oppose an "impersonal," "authoritarian," and "irrelevant" academic order.

The first major confrontation between collegiate rebels and administrators came in 1964 at the University of California at Berkeley, where the Free Speech Movement challenged campus restrictions on student political activity. Largely successful in securing its immediate objectives in Berkeley, the movement spread as a shrill but comparatively small minority of the nation's college students turned to social agitation and identified with such New Left organizations as Students for a Democratic Society (SDS), formed in 1962. Objectives varied from campus to campus, ranging from student participation in matters of governance and curriculum, to increased minority representation in student bodies and faculty, to the dissociation of universities from the military-industrial complex. Toward the end of the decade, as U.S. involvement in Southeast Asia escalated and student draft deferments were ended, grievances concentrated on the war that many college youths thought was an extension of a racist, imperialist, and militarized nation.

In some cases, student energies were benignly channeled into off-campus experiments, such as "free universities" or to the antiwar "teach-ins," which brought students and professors into extended discussions about the war. In others, explosive confrontations occurred between youths and the police. Campus ROTC and administration buildings became targets of student sit-ins and even arson. In 1968, after the murder of Dr. King, a strike led by the SDS forced temporary closure of Columbia University. The next year, gun-wielding black youths intimidated Cornell University administrators into concessions. Following the American invasion of Cambodia in 1970, student protest erupted on hundreds of campuses; in Ohio and Mississippi, authorities opened fire on campus demonstrators, killing a total of six and wounding more than a dozen others.

The youth movement also had a less overtly political side, one that led not to confrontation with authority but to withdrawal into personal experience. Many adults failed to distinguish between the radical activists of the New Left and the hippies, or flower children — and some youths experimented with both forms of rebellion. Both groups inhabited what came to be called the counterculture; both shared an affinity for casual sex, hallucinogenic drugs (most commonly "acid" or LSD), rock and roll, long hair, and pseudo-proletarian dress. But the true "freaks," as hippies called themselves, chose to "drop out" rather than to agitate. Drawing on the experience of post–World War I bohemians on both sides of the Atlantic and, more particularly, on that of the "beat generation" of the 1950s, the flower children rejected bourgeois values and the traditions of Western thought. Preferring emotion to reason, oriental mysticism to science, community to individualism, and self-fulfillment ("doing one's thing") to material success, they pursued an alternative life style in rural communes or urban "crash pads."

At the time, much was made of a generation gap between young and old. Many adults worried that the baby-boom cohort (then in late adolescence and early adulthood) had run amuck. In truth, however, the 1960s were notable for continuity as well as change, and many of the nation's young people were about as straight as their parents. Opinion polls revealed that the youth movement was a movement of *some* youth. Typically, the cultural and political rebels of the "tumultuous' sixties" were the children of well-educated, white, middle-class parents and attended the more cosmopolitan and prestigious universities. Noncollege white youths, often resentful of their more affluent counterparts, frequently had little sympathy for black liberation, the peace movement, woman's rights, or public disorder. Even on the most politicized campuses, the student left was a distinct, if voluble, minority. In time, some cultural affectations and drugs of the youth revolution would become adopted widely, and not merely among the young. More fundamentally, the counterculture had a lasting impact on American attitudes toward such important matters as sex, marriage, work, leisure, career, and war. But the tumult of the sixties and the pervasiveness of youthful radicalism have been exaggerated.

THE WARREN COURT

More fundamental and perhaps more controversial challenges to the status quo came from an unexpected and usually conservative source, the Supreme Court. Under the leadership of Earl Warren (1953–1969), perhaps the most influential chief justice since John Marshall, the court became a major agency of social change in the 1950s and 1960s. Although not widely heralded as a legal scholar, Warren was a compassionate and practical jurist who presided during an era of wide-ranging judicial activism that delighted liberals and enraged conservatives.

Following the famous 1954 decision in *Brown* vs. *Board of Education*, the Warren Court extended its concerns with fairness, justice, and equal protection for all citizens in a series of landmark decisions. In the 1957 cases of *Yates* vs. *United States* and *Watkins* vs. *United States*, the court softened the excesses of post-McCarthy anti-communism. In the *Yates* decision, the court hobbled the repressive Smith Act (1940) and extended First Amendment guarantees of free speech to communists and other subversives by distinguishing between "advocacy . . . as mere abstract doctrine" and "advocacy which incites to illegal action." In *Watkins* the court curbed the much-abused investigatory powers of the House Un-American Activities Committee.

The court also pressed forward on school desegregation. In 1964 it declared that the time for "all deliberate speed" had passed; in 1969 it ordered recalcitrant white southern school administrators to begin desegregation "at once." In other cases the justices abolished segregation in public recreation, public transportation, and private business; they sanctioned the sit-in demonstrations of young blacks, arguing that state enforcement of trespass laws violated the Fourteenth Amendment. The court's liberal majority also used the "equal protection" clause of the same amendment to protect urban voters from rural overrepresentation. In a series of cases beginning with *Baker* vs. *Carr* (1962), the court ordered congressional and legislative reapportionment on the basis of "one man, one vote."

The judicial ideal of fairness was also apparent in a series of decisions (*Gideon* vs. *Wainwright*, 1963; *Escobedo* vs. *Illinois*, 1964; *Miranda* vs. *Arizona*, 1966) that reformed legal procedure by extending federal guarantees to criminal justice proceedings at the local and state levels. In the name of free speech, the court overturned laws against pornography and prohibited prayer and Bible reading in the public schools.

Although widely hailed by civil libertarians and social activists, these and other rulings provoked angry public dissent. Many worried that the court was "coddling" criminals; others feared that its rulings encouraged subversion and atheism. Extremists, led by the right-wing John Birch Society, demanded the impeachment of Earl Warren. In 1968, presidential candidate Richard M. Nixon campaigned on the promise to remake the court by appointing "strict constructionist" judges.

THE GREAT SOCIETY IN RETREAT

By 1968, Johnson's Great Society, like the equalitarian doctrine of the Warren Court, had collided with mounting popular anxiety and conservatism. Indeed, the Johnson administration was seemingly beleaguered on every front. At home, the disenchantment of the young was augmented by the rising frustration of the extreme right wing and of the substantial, but amorphous, group later identified by Richard Nixon and other conservatives as the "Silent Majority" (see Chapter 31). Outraged by student protest and black militance and confused by a rising chorus of complaints from such previously quiescent groups as Indians, homosexuals, welfare recipients, migrant workers, and women, these anxious "Middle Americans," particularly working-class whites, feared social and moral upheaval. Self-reliant, family-oriented, conventionally religious, and patriotic, they angrily responded to this new age of protest and permissiveness with demands for political change and "law and order."

Abroad, American problems seemed worse. In February 1968, the Viet Cong launched the Tet offensive that produced heavy fighting and widespread destruction in thirty South Vietnamese cities, including Saigon. Although the invaders suffered heavy losses and were driven back, the intense fighting completed the destruction of some friendly villages and forced the Americans to abandon much of the "pacified" countryside. The surprise attacks also dealt a staggering blow to Johnson's political prospects and to American expectations of military victory. Recognizing that four years of intensified commitment had not even secured the capital from invasion, Americans in growing numbers questioned administration policy, and the president himself denied Pentagon requests for more American ground troops. The peace movement gained new recruits.

Elsewhere in the world, Soviet-American relations remained tense. The eruption of war between Israel and the Soviet-backed Arabs threatened to produce a Great Power confrontation in June 1967. A smashing Israeli victory prevented immediate disaster, but American powerlessness in this crisis seemed to demonstrate the dangers of overcommitment in Vietnam. In January 1968 the U.S. spy ship *Pueblo* was captured by North Koreans off the Korean coast. By responding with negotiations rather than armed counteraction, the administration avoided further military engagement in the Far East, but not humiliation. Again, in the following August, the administration could do nothing but stand by while Soviet tanks crushed a budding movement toward political and intellectual freedom in Czechoslovakia.

Meanwhile, the leadership crisis deepened. Despite Johnson's reputation for political wizardry, his popularity polls declined sporadically from a high of 80 percent to a disastrous 35 percent in the fall of 1968. In 1966, Democratic election losses had reinstated the conservative Republican-Southern Democrat coalition in power in Congress. The new realities were shown by drastic cuts in foreign aid and in funds for such administration social programs as Medicare and open housing. By the time of the 1968 presidential campaign, presidential appointments (including that of a new Chief Justice) were being rejected and even the treaty for stopping the spread of nuclear weapons was stalled in the Senate.

Thus, as a new presidential election approached, the Johnson landslide of 1964 seemed distant indeed. By 1968, consensus had become division; even the spectacular Johnson prosperity seemed threatened by a sharp upturn in prices and a declining economic growth. In March, sensing the futility of his own candidacy and challenged from within the Democratic party by Senators Robert F. Kennedy and Eugene McCarthy (both of them "peace candidates"), the president ended the bombing of North Vietnam, urged a negotiated settlement, and declared he would not seek re-election. This apparent victory for the party's antiwar forces, however, was offset by the assassination of Robert Kennedy in June. McCarthy attracted many of Kennedy's supporters and arrived at the convention as the favorite among Democratic voters. But the delegates, after voting down a peace plank, nominated Vice President Hubert Humphrey, a veteran liberal, who despite private doubts about the war had loyally supported administration policies. In the streets outside the convention, angry and frustrated antiwar demonstrators, a few of whom hoped to disrupt the proceedings within, were clubbed by police while the world watched on television. The popular reaction reflected the growing polarization of American society: many citizens were shocked and outraged at police violence against the young, but many others applauded police containment of unruly dissidents. The bloody melee seemed all the more unseemly in contrast to the well-managed Republican convention. Amid apparent order and restraint, the convention nominated Richard Nixon and his obscure running mate, Spiro T. Agnew, a conservative favorite of the party's increasingly vital southern wing.

During the campaign, both Humphrey and Nixon stressed "law and order" and supported the negotiations then proceeding unproductively in Paris with the North Vietnamese. Humphrey belatedly tried to dissociate himself from Johnson's war policies. Nixon spoke vaguely of a secret plan to end the fighting. Faced with seemingly unattractive alternatives, many mainstream voters picked the least objectionable major party candidate. But a substantial number refused to support either. The articulate, but impotent, left wing either boycotted the election or cast protest ballots for symbolic radical candidates; the disaffected right, far more formidable, turned to American Independent party candidate George C. Wallace, an Alabama segregationist who developed remarkable support among blue-collar workers and noncollege youths.

The balloting was unusually close. Humphrey, struggling vainly to hold the crumbling Democratic coalition, commanded the Eastern cities and the minorities, especially blacks. But he lost the upper South and the election

to Nixon, who swept the traditionally Republican strongholds of the Middle
and Far West. Despite the shattering of the Johnson consensus of 1964 and
an apparent shift to the right, there was little cause for jubilation in the GOP.
By election day, early predictions of an easy Republican triumph had eroded
to a hairline victory. Nixon's share (43.4 percent) of the total popular vote
was smaller than that of any president since Wilson. For the first time since
Zachary Taylor in 1848, a newly elected president faced an opposition Congress. Indisputably, a nation divided by war and tormented by fear of violence and race had repudiated the party in power. But the incoming administration faced seemingly insurmountable domestic and foreign problems
without a popular mandate and without congressional support.

FOR FURTHER READING

William L. O'Neill's *Coming Apart* (1971) is a splendid "informal" history
of the 1960s; Allen Matusow's *The Unraveling of America* (1984) is an important analysis of liberalism and its failures during the 1960s; and Charles
Morris's *A Time of Passion* (1984) is a valuable survey of the 1960s and
1970s. Two first-rate but unabashedly supportive books by members of
Kennedy's staff are Arthur M. Schlesinger, Jr.'s *A Thousand Days* (1965)
and Theodore Sorensen's *Kennedy* (1965). The best scholarly accounts of
the Kennedy presidency are James Giglio's *The Presidency of John F.
Kennedy* (1991), David Burner's *John F. Kennedy and a New Generation*
(1988), and Herbert Parmet's *JFK* (1983). Kennedy's assassination is detailed in Gerald L. Posner, *Case Closed* (1993). Paul Conkin's *Big Daddy
from the Pedernales* (1986) is a valuable study of Johnson's entire political
career. Robert Caro's *The Path to Power* (1982) and *Means of Ascent* (1991)
offer a detailed and highly critical account of Johnson's early years to 1948,
while Robert A. Dallek's *Lone Star Rising* (1991) is a much more sympathetic account of Johnson's life to 1960. Johnson guardedly speaks for himself in *The Vantage Point* (1971), and Doris Kearns in *Lyndon Johnson and
the American Dream* (1976) provides a psychobiography. *The Great Society Reader* (Marvin E. Gettleman and David Mermelstein, eds., 1967) is
highly partisan and should be supplemented by narrower monographs such
as James T. Patterson's *America's Struggle Against Poverty* (1995). The judicial activism of the Supreme Court is assessed by G. Edward White in
Earl Warren (1982) and by David M. O'Brien in *Storm Center* (1993),
while Victor Navasky has dissected *Kennedy Justice* (1971). Harvard Sitkoff
surveys *The Struggle for Black Equality, 1954–1992* (1993); Hugh Davis
Graham explains national politics during *The Civil Rights Era* (1990); Malcolm X has written a moving *Autobiography* (1966); and John H. Bracey,
August Meier, and Elliott M. Rudwick analyze *Black Nationalism in America* (1970). Studies of other disaffected groups include William H. Chafe's
Women and Equality (1977); Sara M. Evans's *Personal Politics: The Roots
of Women's Liberation in the Civil Rights Movement and the New Left*
(1979); Stephen Cornell's *The Return of the Native* (1988); Alvin Josephy's

Red Power (1972); John D'Emilio's *Sexual Politics, Sexual Communities: The Making of a Homosexual Minority in the United States, 1940–1970* (1983); and Carlos Munoz, Jr.'s *Youth, Identity, and Power: The Chicano Movement* (1989). David Garrow's *Liberty and Sexuality* (1994) explains the background to the abortion debate. Richard Maxwell Brown's *Strain of Violence* (1975) contributes to an understanding of an unhappy American tradition. Kirkpatrick Sale sympathetically analyzes *SDS* (1973), while Jim Miller is more critical of the organization in *"Democracy Is in the Streets"* (1987). Todd Gitlin offers a vivid history of the New Left and the counterculture in *The Sixties* (1989). Several Cold War crises are presented by Michael R. Beschloss in *The Crisis Years: Kennedy and Khrushchev, 1960–1963* (1991). Raymond L. Garthoff offers *Reflections on the Cuban Missile Crisis* (1989), as does Robert F. Kennedy in *Thirteen Days* (1969). Important studies of the war in Southeast Asia include Frances Fitzgerald's *Fire in the Lake* (1972), George Herring's *America's Longest War* (1986), Marilyn B. Young's *The Vietnam Wars* (1991), Ronald Spector's *After Tet* (1993), Stanley Karnow's *Vietnam* (1991), Neil Sheehan's *A Bright Shining Lie* (1988), and Neil Sheehan, et al., *The Pentagon Papers* (1971).

TABLE 19.   SOUTHEAST ASIA, 1969–1975

1968	**November Richard M. Nixon** elected president.
1969	**Spring** Secret U.S. bombing of Cambodia begins.
	April Peak U.S. troop strength in Vietnam.
	August Phased troop withdrawal begins.
	October Vietnam mobilization demonstration.
	November Nixon announces "Vietnamization" policy.
1970	**April** U.S. and ARVN forces invade Cambodia.
	May Campus disorders; Kent State killings; "hard hat" rally in support of war.
1971	**January–March** United States supports ARVN "incursion" into Laos.
	June Pentagon Papers leaked to press.
1972	**Spring** Haiphong Harbor mined; Hanoi bombed.
	October Kissinger announces that "peace is at hand."
	November Nixon re-elected.
	December "Christmas Bombing" of North Vietnam.
1973	**January** Paris accords end U.S. involvement in Vietnam.
	March Last U.S. combat troops leave Vietnam.
	August Bombing of Cambodia halted.
1974	Nixon resigns; **Gerald R. Ford** becomes president.
1975	**March–April** Congress denies further military aid.
	April Khmer Rouge take Phnom-Penh; Vietcong seize Saigon.
	May *Mayaguez* incident.

31

★ ★ ★ ★ ★ ★

Crises of Confidence, 1970–1980

OF DECADES (IMMEDIATELY) PAST

In a memorable inaugural address, John F. Kennedy had challenged Americans to "ask not what your country can do for you — ask what you can do for your country." A dozen years later, in an apparent evocation of that challenge, Richard M. Nixon at his own second inauguration in January 1973 urged Americans to "ask — not just what will government do for me, but what can I do for myself." However similar, the phrases carried very different meanings. The differences reflected the contrasting personal styles and (rather less starkly contrasting) social philosophies of these two chief executives, and marked the decade of change and turmoil that had intervened. But the two inaugural admonitions may also suggest, in ways unintended by either president, the differing tempers of the decades upon which they left their marks.

The 1960s are likely to be recorded in the book of popular thought as a time when American public figures were assassinated with alarming frequency; when campus ROTC buildings and inner-city ghettos went up in smoke; when disruptive racial confrontations and violent student demonstrations overshadowed all other issues of national concern; when the "love generation," the unkempt children of the middle class, withdrew to a workless counterculture of sex, drugs, and rock and roll. But the 1960s were not merely years of rebellion and dissent. The Age of Protest was also a period of social concern and moral commitment, during which the United States addressed some of its more pressing social ills. To be sure, the millennial aspirations of the decade's social planners and political activists now seem naive. Too often the problems they addressed defied solution. Civil rights legislation and affirmative action programs did not, and perhaps could not,

MAP 12:   SOUTHEAST ASIA AND THE VIETNAM WAR

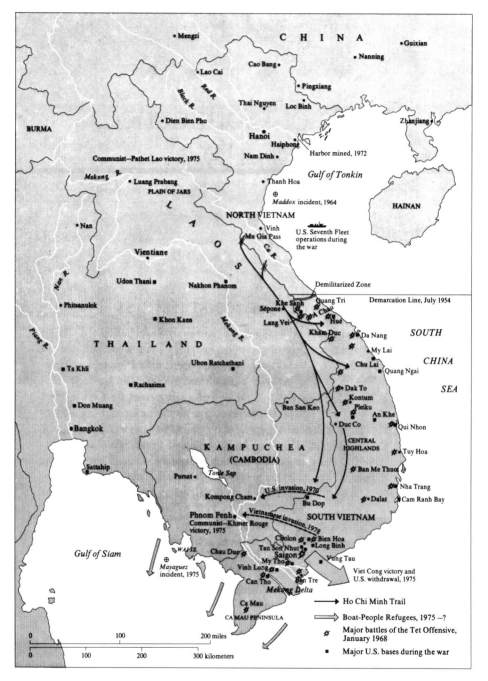

CHINA

- Mengzi
- Guixian
- Nanning
- Lao Cai
- Cao Bang
- Pingxiang
- Thai Nguyen   Loc Binh
- Dien Bien Phu
- Zhanjiang

BURMA

Black R.   Red R.

Hanoi
Haiphong
Nam Dinh
Harbor mined, 1972

Communist–Pathet Lao victory, 1975

Mekong R.   • Luang Prabang
PLAIN OF JARS

• Thanh Hoa

Gulf of Tonkin

HAINAN

Nan R.

• Nan

Vinh
Mu Gia Pass
NORTH VIETNAM

Maddox incident, 1964

L A O S

U.S. Seventh Fleet
operations during
the war

Vientiane

Udon Thani ■   Nakhon Phanom

Demilitarized Zone

Nan R.

• Phitsanulok

Khe Sanh   Quang Tri   Demarcation Line, July 1954
Sépone •   A Chau
Lang Vei   Hue

• Khon Kaen

Mekong R.

Kham Duc   • Da Nang

T H A I L A N D

SOUTH

• My Lai

Chu Lai
Quang Ngai

CHINA

■ Ta Khli

Ubon Ratchathani

SEA

• Dak To
Kontum
Pleiku
An Khe

■ Rachasima

Ban San Keo

■ Don Muang

• Duc Co   Qui Nhon

■ Bangkok

CENTRAL
HIGHLANDS   • Tuy Hoa

K A M P U C H E A
(CAMBODIA)

• Ban Me Thuot

Ping R.

Sattahip

Tonle Sap
Pursat •

Nha Trang

U.S. invasion, 1970

Bu Dop   • Dalat   Cam Ranh Bay

Kompong Cham •

Phnom Penh •
Communist–Khmer Rouge
victory, 1975

Vietnamese invasion, 1978   SOUTH VIETNAM

Cholon   Bien Hoa
Tan Son Nhut   Long Binh
Saigon

Gulf of Siam

WATS.   Chau Doc
My Tho

Vung Tau

Mayaguez
incident, 1975

Vinh Long
Can Tho   Ben Tre

Viet Cong victory and
U.S. withdrawal, 1975

Mekong Delta

Ca Mau
CA MAU PENINSULA

0	100	200 miles
0	100 200	300 kilometers

→ Ho Chi Minh Trail

⇨ Boat-People Refugees, 1975 –?

✿ Major battles of the Tet Offensive,
January 1968

■ Major U.S. bases during the war

produce a color- and gender-blind society. The War on Poverty proved to be much less than "unconditional" and the dizzying welter of agencies and programs it enlisted did not, as Lyndon Johnson hoped, "throttle want" in an otherwise affluent society. Although organizations as disparate as the National Organization for Women, the National Farm Workers' Association, and the American Indian Movement articulated minority grievances, women, Chicanos, and Indians along with blacks found that the benefits of American justice and opportunity remained unequally distributed. The failures of the 1960s, however, have been unduly emphasized. Although the "sensibility of the sixties" may have faded, the decade stands as one of the great ages of American reform, a time of achievements in such areas as school desegregation, women's and minority rights, education, environmental and consumer protection, health and welfare. Nor should it be forgotten that because of the social activism of the passionate visionaries of the 1960s, the burdens of class, race, and sex are less oppressive today than ever before.

In the 1970s, however, retrenchment — not reform — was the watchword. The faltering of the liberal Democratic coalition brought Nixon and Gerald Ford to the office held by Kennedy and Johnson. Although neither was an inflexible ideologue, these conservative Republican chief executives, like the "Middle Americans" they presumed to represent, had little taste for social experimentation. Whatever else it would be called, the period following Nixon's inauguration in January 1969 would not be known as a season of reform.

The peace movement also collapsed in the 1970s. Despite the widespread popular outrage occasioned by the American invasions of Cambodia (1970) and Laos (1971), the antiwar movement lost its momentum when Nixon ended the draft and began phased troop withdrawals. More than half a million American soldiers were brought home from South Vietnam between the elections of 1968 and 1972. In the spring of 1970 student demonstrators on 448 campuses were either on strike or had closed down their institutions. Several years later, as the war ended and the Selective Service System gave way to an all-volunteer army, the focus of student concern was more often the grade-point average than international peace.

The student left, including the Students for a Democratic Society (SDS) and its offshoot, the Youth International Party (Yippie), also abruptly disappeared with the war that had done so much to nourish it. Its leaders, the youthful rebels who set out to destroy "the establishment" in the 1960s, sometimes tried to join it in the 1970s. "Last year, Jerry Rubin came here and told us to pull this rotten system up by the roots," one puzzled undergraduate at the University of Rochester reported in 1971. "This year, he came here and told us to register to vote in the primary." Older if not always wiser, some radical youth leaders of the 1960s turned from the politics of confrontation to what Yippie spokesman Rubin called the "inner revolution of the '70s." Rubin himself experimented with "a smorgasbord course in New Consciousness," which included seemingly everything from Gestalt therapy, bioenergetics, and est to jogging, health foods, yoga, and acupuncture. Following this exhausting therapeutic regimen, he wrote a new book, *Growing (Up) at Thirty-Seven* (1976), and became a Wall Street securities analyst. His Yippie colleague, Abbie Hoffman, author of the 1968 publication *Revolution for the Hell of It*, went underground for a time to avoid imprisonment on drug charges and then dropped out of politics. Tom Hayden, founder of the SDS and always a thoughtful New Left activist, ran unsuccessfully for the U.S. Senate but was later elected to the California state assembly; his codefendant in the "Chicago Eight" conspiracy trial, Panther party leader Bobby Seal, tried and failed to be elected mayor of Oakland, California. Others turned to Oriental mysticism, among them Hayden's former SDS associate, Rennie Davis, who bought a Mercedes and became the disciple of teenage guru Maharaj Ji. Still others joined former Panther official Eldridge Cleaver, former Nixon hatchet man Charles Colson, and President James Earl Carter as born-again Christians. Of course, a great many "old revolutionaries" of the 1960s remained true to their radical ideals. But American youth in the 1970s was more committed to individual development than to social reform.

The decade of the 1970s had its popular movements, of course, but even protest often assumed conservative forms. Singer Anita Bryant led a crusade against civil rights for homosexuals. Resentful whites, convinced that the minority-rights campaign had gone too far, challenged affirmative action on grounds of "reverse discrimination." Many applauded when the Supreme Court's ambiguous *Bakke* ruling (1978) restricted the use of quotas to achieve racial balance in college-admissions programs. In 1978, conservative Republican Howard Jarvis won voter support for California's Proposition 13, which slashed property taxes by 57 percent, severely limited state social services, and launched a nationwide tax revolt. A "Right-to-Life" coalition of Roman Catholics, evangelical Protestants, and other conservatives sought an anti-abortion amendment; opponents of the welfare state endeavored to make federal budget deficits unconstitutional; and a militant and well-financed gun lobby, led by the National Rifle Association, worked to offset public support for handgun control.

The conservatism of the decade also slowed the advance of the women's rights movement. Despite such achievements as Title VII of the Civil Rights Act of 1964, which forbade sexual discrimination in the workplace, and the Equal Credit Opportunity Act (1974), which promised equal access to bank loans and credit cards, the disadvantages of womanhood remained all too numerous. In the decade after 1970, the percentage of women entering the labor market was at a substantially higher rate than that of men. By 1980, 42 percent of all American workers were female; more than half of all married women and 90 percent of female college graduates worked outside the home. In one of the most important social and economic developments of the century, the two-career family had become the American norm. But women, like blacks and Hispanics, were heavily concentrated in poorly paid, entry-level jobs. Although an increasing number found management positions in government and industry, many more continued to work in clerical, secretarial, and other "sexually segregated" occupations. In 1980, the median wage for women was 60 percent of that for men. Added to changing family patterns and a sharply rising divorce rate, these wage disparities were particularly onerous. During the 1970s single-parent households increased by nearly 80 percent, and most of them were headed by women. The persistence of gender-related wage and occupational discrimination ensured that a great many of these new American families were poor.

Another and not unrelated problem was the development of an antifeminist backlash, much of it inspired by tradition-minded women. Organizations of conservative women — Fascinating Womanhood and Total Woman — emerged late in the decade to challenge the objectives of the women's liberation movement. Styling themselves "pro-family" and "anti-libber," they opposed the Equal Rights Amendment (ERA) — first introduced in Congress in 1923 — on the questionable grounds that it would foster unisex restrooms, conscription of women, and homosexuality. Effectively countering the pro-ERA feminist lobby led by the National Organization for Women, the right-wing Republican activist Phyllis Schlafly organized a national "Stop ERA" movement, which blocked this endeavor to outlaw economic or social discrimination based on sex.

In 1979, many of these "anti's" — anti-feminist, anti-busing, anti-gay, anti-abortion, anti-intellectual, anti-communist — united under the banner of the Moral Majority, a fervid band of "New Right Christians" dedicated to Americanism and a more righteous political order. Led by Jerry Falwell, a radio-TV evangelist, the Moral Majority plunged into a series of right-wing causes, issued morality ratings for elected officials, and worked to defeat liberal Democrats in Congress. Although its political influence may be overrated, the organization played an important role in the conservative election victories of 1980 and counted among its supporters such influential politicians as Ronald Reagan and Senator Jesse Helms, the North Carolina fundamentalist who once spoke for the segregationist Citizens' Councils.

Such were the crusades of the seventies. To one degree or another, all were legitimate expressions of the concerns of broad categories of a diverse body politic. But collectively they seemed to reflect the cramped spirit of an age that was less hopeful, less expansive, and less generous than the one before.

THE "ME DECADE" — THE AGE OF NO CONFIDENCE

The apparently divergent contours of the 1960s and 1970s could also be charted in ways that transcended the merely political. As noted elsewhere in this volume, the historian's tendency to periodize, to make the past intelligible to the present by organizing it into manageable blocks of time, has its hazards. History, it seems worth repeating, is an all but seamless fabric; its developments are notable more often for continuity than for change. At close range, what appears distinctive in human conduct and institutions more often than not loses its particularity when viewed from a longer perspective. Still, the temptation to find peculiar meaning in current events is irresistible.

The 1970s were not half over before self-styled "new journalist" Tom Wolfe labeled it the "Me Decade." Wolfe, who won an enthusiastic readership with such "pop analyses" of the 1960s scene as his *Pump House Gang* (1968) and the *The Electric Kool-Aid Acid Test* (1968), found in the 1970s a new "alchemical dream" that promised not to make base metals into gold but to remake oneself. The spirit of the 1970s, he averred, was most clearly seen in the "Me movements," in est, Arica, and Scientology; in encounter sessions, assertiveness training, Oriental meditation groups, and charismatic Christianity; in the new national passion for "changing one's personality — remaking, remodeling, elevating, and polishing one's very self . . . (Me!)"

In a lighter vein, political humorist Russell Baker, the Peter Finley Dunne of his generation, deplored "the growing public absorption in the hedonism of public pleasure and private consumption — the hunt for the ideal restaurant, the perfect head of lettuce, the totally satisfying relationship." Articles in *Esquire, New Yorker,* and *Harper's* diagnosed the narcissistic preoccupation of the 1970s. In *The Culture of Narcissism* (1978), the most fully developed cultural analysis of the politically quiescent and socially passive 1970s, the historian Christopher Lasch similarly argued that "Americans have retreated to purely personal preoccupations." After the political turmoil and social dissidence of the recent past, "people have convinced themselves," Lasch observed, "that what matters is psychic self-improvement: getting in touch with their feelings, eating health foods, taking lessons in ballet or belly dancing, immersing themselves in the wisdom of the East, jogging, learning how to 'relate,' overcoming the 'fear of pleasure.' " In the judgment of some contemporary observers, Americans of the 1970s had turned from the War on Poverty and the peace movement, from political passion and social commitment, to join Jerry Rubin in a "journey into myself," to self-discovery, psychic growth and intimate encounters — to what Lasch called "strategies of narcissistic survival."

Inevitably, commentators found it easier to describe than to explain the apparently different sensibilities of the two decades immediately past. Few doubted, however, the importance of demography. The youth culture of the 1960s was, by all accounts, a by-product of the postwar baby boom. For reasons not yet satisfactorily explained, the period immediately following World War II was one of unprecedented population growth in the United States. Between 1948 and 1953 the number of births rose by nearly 50 percent. By the mid-1950s the boom crested. By 1960, again for reasons not fully understood, the total number of births began to drop sharply. By the mid-1970s the "population bomb" was defused and the nation approached what demographers called ZPG (zero population growth).

But the baby-boom generation was not so easily dispensed with. A disproportionate bulge in the nation's population curve, it passed through the 14- to 24-year-old age category in the 1960s. (In 1960 the center of population gravity in the United States was the 35 to 40 age group; by 1965, the center had shifted to age 17.) In a less demanding age, in one less vexed by issues of race and war, the social impact of this extraordinary cohort might have been very different. But the postwar generation reached late adolescence and early adulthood at a critical moment in American history, and it gave that decade of youthful rebellion its special character. By the 1970s, a decade of falling birth rates had pushed the center of population gravity upward. By 1980, 11 percent of the population was over 65 (compared to 4 percent in 1900). Inexorably, the youth of the 1960s reached the dread age of 30. Population dynamics do not in themselves determine social behavior, but they can help define shifting styles in the recent past. One of the counterculture's most talked-about books was Charles Reich's *The Greening of America;* in 1970 when that publication appeared, the rebellious youth culture, harbinger of what Reich hoped would be "Consciousness III," was already subsiding. In the decade that followed, America was not so much greening as graying.

The character of the "Me Decade" was also linked to what the historian Henry Steele Commager called the "Age of No Confidence." Lasch's subtitle — "American Life in an Age of Diminishing Expectations" — suggested, and other social analysts generally agreed, that the culture of narcissism, the new ethic of self-preservation, reflected the erosion of the optimism of the 1950s and 1960s. In 1941, Henry Luce, publisher of *Time, Life,* and *Fortune,* proclaimed the advent of the "American Century," an age in which "the most powerful and vital nation" would go unchallenged in a world it would dominate "for such purposes" and by "such means" as it alone saw fit. In fact, throughout the nearly four centuries of their New World experience, Americans had shared the exuberant faith of Puritan leader John Winthrop that theirs was a "Citty Upon a Hill" with "the eies of all people Uppon us." With Thomas Jefferson, they believed that they were the chosen people of a "New Israel." This sense of American exceptionalism, which suggested that the nation stood somehow apart from the tawdry stream of human history, survived and was embellished by the Second World War. Among the world's great nations, the United States alone had emerged from the most terrible of wars not only unscathed but with its wealth and power enhanced.

But the American Century lasted only a generation. As the 1960s ended, traditional presumptions of American omnicompetence and omnipotence were in tatters. Heretofore confident of their nation's role as both global police officer and moral preceptor, Americans now faced defeat in Vietnam and declining influence around the world. Never doubting the strength of the "almighty dollar" or the seemingly perpetual expansion of their gross national product, they soon were flooded by economic ills — unchecked inflation, economic stagnation, declining productivity rates, staggering trade deficits, and a sharply devalued dollar. Following the Arab oil boycott of 1973 came a creeping awareness that the United States was dangerously dependent on uncertain, rapidly depleting, and ruinously expensive foreign energy supplies. As the energy crisis of the 1970s unfolded, the American people — who with roughly 6 percent of the world's people produced about one-third of its goods and consumed more than one-third of its petroleum — slowly and imperfectly came to understand what the impending exhaustion of nonrenewable natural resources could mean to an industrial society and its economy.

The unsettling news of the 1970s, then, was that the United States, too, lived in a world of limits — limited world influence, limited economic growth, limited natural resources, and limited expectations for a better future. At least since the Enlightenment, the spirit of Western humanity has been elevated by faith in progress, the assumption that human society was, if not perfectable, at least infinitely meliorable. Despite the evidence to the contrary, Western democracies in general and the American nation in particular enjoyed a sense of limitless possibilities. In the last century that optimism was repeatedly tested by thinkers from Charles Darwin to Oswald Spengler. More concretely, the horrors of two world wars, the spread of totalitarianism, the Nazi holocaust, the threat of nuclear destruction, the contagion of world lawlessness and terrorism — all suggested that whatever its state of grace, humanity's course was not inevitably upward.

In the face of such dangers and uncertainties, the sanguine Western spirit sagged noticeably. Even the Americans, those seemingly incurable optimists, began to feel this malaise in the 1970s and 1980s. With the end of the American Century at hand, with the American Dream of unlimited abundance subject to doubt, the American people began uneasily to discard comfortable myths about their own virtue and uniqueness.

By definition, contemporary historical writing is shortsighted. The instant analyses of our times will be challenged by those who enjoy greater perspective. Future writers may well find unsuspected social purpose in the "Me" age. Very likely the configurations of the "Culture of Narcissism" and the "Age of No Confidence" will seem overdrawn. For the moment, Thomas Jefferson's "chosen people," the 226 million inhabitants of the "Citty Upon a Hill," appeared to be engaged in the disquieting task of joining the human race.

NIXON AND THE (FIRST) NEW FEDERALISM

Of the four men who served as presidents since 1969, Richard Milhous Nixon alone seemed to have both national and international political expertise. A veteran of both houses of Congress, vice president for two terms and well versed in American politics, and a widely traveled student of foreign affairs, he brought experience and intellect to the White House Oval Office. Doubts about his political methods and personal character, however, haunted his presidency. Reserved and formal, he was one of the most isolated presidents in American history. He was defensive and suspicious of the news media and rarely held press conferences. Intense, hardworking, but uncomfortable in the public eye, he maintained a low executive profile and spent much of his time at Camp David, the presidential retreat, or at his private estates in California and Florida. Nixon chose conservative and reasonably competent cabinet officers but, with the exception of Attorney General John Mitchell, generally denied them access to the Oval Office. Although he delegated power and responsibility freely, he did so, not to the cabinet but to intensely loyal subordinates led by presidential assistants H. Robert Haldeman and John D. Ehrlichman. Called the "Disneyland Mafia" and "The Germans," even by White House staffers, these men had few contacts with the parties or Congress and had little experience in public affairs. Jealously protective of Nixon's time and energies, they erected a "Berlin Wall" that was rarely penetrated even by cabinet members, top Republican officials, or congressional leaders. The president preferred to operate, as one of his speech writers noted, in a "soundproof, shockproof bubble."

Before assuming office, Nixon revealed that foreign affairs would be his principal concern: "I've always thought this country could run itself domestically without a president." True to his word, he gave international issues, particularly the Vietnam War, priority throughout his first term. But one domestic legacy of the Johnson administration, a runaway economy, required much presidential attention. Having promised the nation both "guns and butter," Johnson had refused to seek a tax increase to finance the rapidly escalating Southeast Asian war. By 1968 the result was a raging inflation that threatened not only the dollar's value, but the nation's role as a Great Power and the U.S. quality of life.

Nixon's free-market response to this crisis proved inadequate. By tightening the money supply (through higher interest rates) and balancing the budget, the Republican president hoped to curb inflation without economic controls or even wage-price guidelines. The ineffectual result was called "Nixonomics." Economists coined a new term, *stagflation,* to describe the disastrous combination of sharply rising living costs and recession. Under strong public pressure, the administration reversed itself in August 1971. Now proclaiming himself a Keynesian (after liberal British economist John Maynard Keynes), Nixon briefly froze prices and wages, adopted budgetary deficits (the largest in peacetime history), and then pursued a fitful course of "schizoid economics" — moving from stringent controls to voluntary restraints, to a second price freeze and renewed controls.

Although a temporary respite from stagflation in 1972 deprived the Democrats of an election issue, economic problems reached crisis proportions early in Nixon's second term. By mid-1973, as the president imposed his second price freeze in 15 months and prepared to reinstitute stringent price controls, corporate profits and wages were soaring, the stock market was in a prolonged slump, and consumer costs, especially for food, were spiraling at a rate unequaled since the early post–World War II period. By that date, the administration had already twice devalued the dollar in a desperate attempt to offset mounting trade deficits by improving the competitive position of American goods in foreign markets. In large part, the administration's erratic economic policies were rooted in the president's own stalwart Republicanism. Despite his use of economic activism, he remained to the end a devoted free marketeer.

That same traditional conservatism also placed him at odds with the liberal social programs of his Democratic predessors. Again, there was confusion at first and much inconsistency in word and deed. Convinced that many Great Society programs were unwise and unworkable, Nion proposed to decentralize authority and emphasize local solutions to local problems. But acting upon the advice of Daniel Patrick Moynihan, his urban affairs adviser, he delayed immediate action. A "neoconservative" (ex-liberal) Democrat who had served in the administrations of both Kennedy and Johnson, Moynihan persuaded Nixon that wholesale dismantlement of the Great Society programs would further divide a nation torn by an unpopular war, a rising crime rate, and domestic unrest. To nearly everyone's astonishment, bills authorizing extension of antipoverty programs — including such conservative targets as Job Corps and Model Cities — won presidential support and were enacted by Congress. In August 1969, Nixon shocked his party's right-wing by advocating a Family Assistance Payments (FAP) plan to provide every American family with a guaranteed annual income of at least $1,600. Although the administration's policies often enraged environmentalists, Nixon also created the Environmental Protection Agency in 1970 and signed (though he had not supported) the Clean Air Act, Water Quality Improvement Act, and the Resource Recovery Act. In January 1971 the president proclaimed a "New American Revolution . . . as profound, as far-reaching, as exciting as that first revolution 200 years ago." The watchword of his administration, Nixon said, was reform.

Whatever his watchword, the president's personal instincts and political philosophy favored retrenchment and consolidation, not innovation and reform. Having drifted uncertainly in its first two years, the administration moved resolutely toward the "New Federalism" and the conservative policies and programs that would "reverse the flow of power and resources from the states and communities to Washington." In October 1972, under heavy pressure from the administration, Congress enacted a "revenue sharing" measure to return to local government over a five-year period $30.2 billion in federal monies. Revenue sharing was not a windfall, however, as the nation's hard-pressed city officials readily understood. The administration's first-term domestic energies had been largely devoted to beating back appropriation bills for social programs. When that failed, Nixon used his veto (19 times during the Ninety-Second Congress alone); when his vetoes were overridden, he simply (and unconstitutionally) "impounded" or refused to spend congressionally authorized funds. In his budget proposals for fiscal 1974, the frugal Republican chief executive slashed previously budgeted federal grants for social services and community development. The crisis of the cities, he said, had passed.

The Nixon administration's conservatism, although emerging slowly in legislative areas, was immediately apparent in areas outside the control of a Democratic Congress. Fulfilling a campaign promise to appoint a no-nonsense attorney general, Nixon named John Mitchell, his campaign manager and former law partner. Gruff and taciturn, Mitchell served — until his resignation to manage Nixon's re-election campaign in 1972 — as the stern symbol of a law-and-order administration. With one eye fixed on the crime rate and another on the mood of the electorate (particularly Wallace's 13 percent), he sponsored a controversial "no-knock" crime law for predominantly black Washington, D.C., advocated preventive detention and stop-and-frisk laws, claimed an unrestricted government right to eavesdrop electronically on suspected "security risks," and dealt harshly with antiwar demonstrators and other political dissidents.

Fear of crime was but one facet of a pervasive national malaise that had emerged gradually in the late 1960s as the nation's most salient political issue. However troubled by the stalemate in Vietnam, the American people seemed more deeply disturbed by such domestic ills as drug abuse, racial disorder, and violent protest. Identified originally as the Wallace "backlash" but later more accurately described as the "Social Issue," this widespread dysphoria portended, some analysts believed, a fundamental national political realignment. Indeed, White House strategists viewed the Social Issue as the cement for a majority Republican coalition of the unyoung, the unpoor, and the unblack. In the first test of that strategy, the midterm elections of 1970, the results were inconclusive. However much they disliked "scroungy student dissenters," "pusillanimous pussyfooters," and the "effete corps of impudent snobs," the voters themselves seemed as concerned with runaway inflation as with the Social Issue. The Democrats retained control of Congress.

In the administration's design for a new Republican coalition, the conservative white voters of the South were of central importance. Increasingly disenchanted by the liberal, pro-black policies of the national Democratic party, white Southerners admired Nixon more than any recent president. He did not sweep the region in 1968, but he dominated the upper South and, without Wallace in the running, could easily have carried every southern state except Texas. To an administration that took pride in playing political hard ball, it seemed only logical to absorb the Wallace vote by openly courting the troubled white South.

This "southern strategy," of course, ran counter to Afro-American aspirations. Despite the race chauvinism of youthful black militants and a growing black emphasis on separate economic and cultural development, the great majority of Afro-Americans still hoped for assimilation in a colorblind society. Black fears, aroused by Nixon's attacks on forced integration and busing, were not allayed by his pre-inaugural promise to do "more for the Negro" than any other president. Few were surprised when he reversed his predecessors' policy of executive engagement in the civil rights struggle. In 1969, for the first time since World War II, the Justice Department intervened on behalf of white defendants in school desegregation cases. Attorney General Mitchell relaxed government equal rights compliance standards and shifted the burden of civil rights enforcement to the courts. Though the administration exploited and even nurtured the white backlash, the civil rights achievements of the past seemed secure. Over Nixon's opposition, the Democratic Congress extended the Voting Rights Act of 1965. In 1969 the Supreme Court refused to delay school desegregation in Mississippi; in 1972 it ruled in favor of busing to achieve racially balanced classrooms. The South, despite the southern strategy, became the nation's most desegregated region, and segregated northern inner-city schools came under judicial attack. Nixon's campaign promise to promote "black capitalism" proved empty, but he supported the extension of the Civil Rights Commission, opposed federal tax-exemptions for all-white academies, and advocated labor union desegregation. Ironically, then, the Nixon record on civil rights, though modest, was better than either the president or his critics would admit.

In his judicial appointments, Nixon broke with the policies of his immediate predecessors. Harshly critical of liberal judicial activism, the Republican president sought to remake the Supreme Court in his own conservative image. Although he failed in two attempts to appoint conservative Southerners with segregationist records to the Supreme Court, he filled four court vacancies with judicial conservatives. Joined by one and sometimes two of the other five justices, the Nixon appointees (perhaps only one of whom was a genuine "strict constructionist") were expected to reverse nearly two decades of Warren Court liberal activism. Once again, however, there was more continuity than seemed apparent. The decisions of the reconstituted court neither expanded nor eroded basic civil liberties and rights. Contrary to White House wishes, it ruled in favor of abortion and against state aid to parochial education. Its principal departures from early Supreme Court rulings came in a tougher attitude toward criminals and pornography. But not until the mid-1980s would the Court move sharply rightward.

TOWARD A GENERATION OF PEACE

The caution and ambivalence that so often marked Nixon's domestic policies found no parallel in his bold handling of international affairs. Promising a "full generation of peace" through negotiation, not confrontation, he moved quickly to normalize relations with the Peoples' Republic of China and the Soviet Union. In both cases, détente was complicated by the president's reputation as an intractable cold warrior. A vigorous Red-hunter during his congressional career, he had often found his political opponents "soft" on communism. Though initially viewed by Kremlin leaders as the most belligerent in a long line of anti-communist presidents, he proved more flexible than any of his post–World War II predecessors in his dealings with communist nations. Placing ideology aside, he pursued a policy of realism based on the ancient maxim that nations have no permanent friends or enemies, only permanent interests. In this exercise in *Realpolitik*, Nixon was assisted by Henry Kissinger, a former Harvard professor, who served as director of the National Security Council, and was perhaps the most remarkable foreign policy adviser ever to serve the White House. Kissinger did not formally become head of the Department of State until 1973, but he was the nation's chief diplomat throughout the first term.

The most spectacular examples of the new realism in American diplomacy came in 1972. In February, while a nation of television viewers watched via satellite, the president journeyed to Beijing (Peking) to lay the groundwork for a resumption of Chinese-American relations. Although denied recognition by the United States and its Western allies since the triumph of Mao Zedong in 1949, mainland China was a major power armed with nuclear weapons and populated by one-fifth of the world's people. In 1971 the Peoples' Republic was admitted to the United Nations with American support, and, over ineffectual American opposition, Jiang's Nationalist regime was ousted. In a second internationally televised summit meeting, Nixon became the first president since Franklin Roosevelt to set foot on Soviet soil when he conferred in Moscow in May 1972 with Soviet party leader Leonid Brezhnev. A year later, a second Nixon-Brezhnev meeting occurred in Washington amid rising hopes of a permanent thaw in the Cold War. Seasoned diplomatic observers cautioned that other summits had been followed by deteriorating relations, and ultraconservatives, Vice President Agnew among them, were alarmed by the open camaraderie between the nation's chief executive and the leaders of its postwar adversaries. But the president declared that 1972 had been a year of unparalleled "achievement for peace," and most Americans believed him.

The summits were followed by substantive agreements. As Nixon's second term began, China and the United States had not exchanged formal diplomatic recognition, but relations between the two nations were vastly improved and a cultural and economic exchange was begun. The first phase of the Strategic Arms Limitations Talks (SALT) with the Soviets placed short-term (five years) ceilings on offensive nuclear weapons, including ICBMs (intercontinental ballistic missiles) and submarine-based missiles, and limited each country to two ABM (antiballistic missile) sites. These were significant agreements although they were weakened by the failure to control the number of warheads each missile could carry. The new technology of MIRVed warheads (multiple independently targetable re-entry vehicles) allowed the escalation of the arms race to continue. The United States and the Soviet Union also signed cooperative agreements on trade, cancer research, and space exploration, and began negotiating a "Mutual and Balanced Force Reduction" for Europe.

Soviet-American rapprochement, however, was tenuous. Divergent East-West interests in the Middle East and Africa threatened renewed tension. In the first major test of détente, the Yom Kippur war of 1973, revenge-minded Egyptians attacked Israel to recover territories lost in 1967. The Russians aided the Egyptians and the Americans supplied the Israelis, but a larger international crisis was avoided when the big powers forced a cease fire. No long-range solution resulted, however, and the strategic location and oil riches of the Middle East made it a likely setting for continued East-West rivalry.

Soviet interests also posed a threat to American ambitions for an independent but pro-Western black Africa. The collapse of Portuguese colonialism in Angola and Mozambique and black restiveness under minority white rule in Rhodesia and South Africa piqued the interests of both major powers. These and other international developments suggested that to Nixon and

Kissinger, local issues in Asia, Africa, and the Middle East held little importance by themselves. Rather, superpower relationships were the administration's passion.

In 1972 the administration's most pressing problems remained in Vietnam. Elected on a campaign pledge to end the war and win the peace by a
"secret plan," Nixon sought an early conclusion to the fighting through negotiations in Paris with the North Vietnamese. When these talks, underway
since the autumn of 1968, proved unproductive, the president shifted to a
policy of "Vietnamization." Designed to "de-Americanize" the war by trans-
ferring American combat responsibility in Vietnam to South Vietnamese
(ARVN) soldiers, the policy reversed a decade of accelerating troop strength
by gradually withdrawing American forces. Although the success of Vietnamization and the future of the wobbly Saigon regime remained in doubt, troop
withdrawals continued throughout the first term. From a peak strength of
550,000 in April 1969, the number of American soldiers fell to 27,000 in
early 1973; American annual combat deaths dropped from a 1968 high of
14,592 to only 300 in 1972.

As American involvement in Vietnam declined, the war was carried to
other theaters in Southeast Asia. In secret missions unknown to even
congressional leaders and the Secretary of the Air Force, American aircraft
bombed communist "sanctuaries" inside Cambodia throughout most of 1969
and well into the spring of 1970. On April 30, 1970, U.S. and ARVN soldiers
invaded Cambodia; the following winter ARVN troops with American air
support moved into Laos. Although defended by the administration as vital
to American withdrawal, these limited but much criticized "incursions" provoked domestic disorders. In May, on campuses across the country, students
picketed and struck, and at riot-torn Kent State University, four of them
were killed by Ohio national guardsmen. The bloodletting at Kent, soon
followed by a similar though unrelated tragedy at all-black Jackson State
College in Mississippi, brought a sense of renewed urgency to the peace
movement. But a substantial majority of the voters remained steadfast in
support of the president who promised to shorten the war by widening it.

In the end, it was negotiation, not Vietnamization, that brought American
troops home. Although Kissinger returned from Paris in October 1972 to
announce that "peace is at hand," the war carnage continued for three
months. During the Christmas season, when it appeared that negotiations
had stalled, the president dispatched B-52s to rain bombs in unprecedented
tonnage on Hanoi and Haiphong. At last, however, late in January 1973, the
longest war in U.S. history ended. The Paris Accords, signed by the United
States, North and South Vietnam, and the National Liberation Front, provided for a supervised cease-fire, complete American withdrawal, and a pris-
oner exchange. While the nation celebrated "peace with honor," the U.S.
air war over Cambodia continued. Not until mid-August 1973, after Congress terminated funds for all military operations in Southeast Asia, did
Nixon end the bombing sorties against the enemies of Lon Nol's corrupt
military regime in Phnom Penh, the Cambodian capital. With Congress and
the public unwilling to continue to support the ineffective Indochinese anti-

communist governments, Nixon's successor, Gerald Ford, proved incapable of delivering promised military support to Cambodia and South Vietnam. In April 1975, Cambodia fell to Khmer Rouge troops. Later that month, the South Vietnamese regime also surrendered to communist insurgents. Following a hasty evacuation of American personnel and Vietnamese children from Saigon, the long American nightmare in Southeast Asia ended. The toll had been awesome: 56,000 American combat dead; uncounted hundreds of thousands of Asian casualties; and some $350 billion in direct American war costs and veteran benefits.

"WHITE HOUSE HORRORS"

The administration's foreign policy successes offset early Republican fears of a one-term Nixon presidency. The president's popularity had slumped markedly following the midterm elections of 1970. Early in 1971, opinion pollsters revealed, he trailed Senator Edmund S. Muskie of Maine in public esteem. Popular enthusiasm for Nixon's peace initiatives abroad and favorable developments at home, however, soon brought renewed hopes. During the early months of 1972, the good news from Beijing and Moscow was matched by a dramatic, though temporary, economic upswing that brought new jobs and stabilized prices. Soon thereafter, Muskie's bid for the Democratic nomination was crippled by a feeble showing in the hotly contested Democratic primaries; in May, Wallace's threat to Nixon's southern support was eliminated when the Alabamian was critically wounded in an assassination attempt. Then in July an army of enthusiastic and idealistic amateurs capitalized on recent Democratic convention reforms and nominated Senator George McGovern. A liberal South Dakotan, McGovern rallied supporters through his issues of immediate peace in Vietnam, reduced military spending, and sweeping tax and welfare reforms. He was branded by Republicans and conservative Democrats as the candidate of "amnesty, acid, and abortion." His efforts to brand the Nixon administration as the "most corrupt in American history" proved ineffectual. On election day, he led the Democrats to their worst defeat in half a century.

Only half the eligible voters (some 55 percent) turned out, but Nixon won an electoral (521 to 17) and popular (60.7 percent) vote landslide. Except for Lyndon Johnson's triumph of 1964, no president had ever polled a larger popular majority; except for Franklin Roosevelt's record-shattering sweep of 1936, no president had ever won more electoral votes. Still, Nixon's was a personal rather than a party victory; ticket-splitting voters returned solid Democratic majorities to both houses of Congress.

But if the mandate of 1972 was unclear, Richard Nixon's second-term intentions were not. Having built a structure of peace through détente abroad, he turned to restructuring the nation's domestic priorities; he diffused federal responsibilities for local problems and decreased federal spending for "visionary" and "unworkable" social services. By eliminating such programs as Model Cities, Job Corps, Community Action, and Neighborhood Youth, the goverment could hope not only to ease mounting inflationary and tax pressures, Nixon said, but to free additional monies for revenue-sharing grants to hard-pressed cities and states.

This "New Federalism" proved no more appealing to the 93rd Congress than it had to the 92nd. Lawmakers from both parties were angered by apparent executive usurpations of legislative prerogatives. In the tradition of strong chief executives, Nixon, despite his self-styled strict constructionism, had governed in the grand manner. Without either the advice or consent of Congress, he had initiated the invasion of Cambodia and Laos, the mining of Haiphong Harbor, and the resumption of saturation bombing of Hanoi. He had invoked executive privilege to shield White House policy makers from congressional inquiry and had impounded funds slated by Congress for programs that he opposed. Although precedents for such extraordinary assertions of presidential authority were numerous, aroused congressional leaders began urging redress of an imbalance of power. At stake, many believed, was the governmental doctrine of checks and balances itself.

The overriding issue of Nixon's second term, however, was the abuse, not the accretion, of executive power. During the presidential campaign of 1972, two Nixon campaign aides were arrested for their roles in a conspiracy to burglarize and plant illegal wire taps in Democratic National Committee headquarters in Washington's Watergate Building. Although Democrats cried "political espionage," the White House denied executive involvement, and Nixon dismissed the incident as a "third-rate burglary attempt." Vice President Spiro T. Agnew — who would resign when it became known that he had accepted bribes from contractors — even suggested that the Democrats had burgled their own National Committee.

The voters, for the most part, showed little interest, and in November the unseemly affair was buried in the Nixon victory landslide. Or so it seemed until early in 1973, when congressional investigators, aided by a courageous federal judge and a vigorous press, began exposing White House crimes and scandals that shocked the nation and raised profoundly disturbing questions about Nixon's fitness for leadership. Almost daily throughout the spring and summer, evidence of official misconduct and lawlessness mounted. By autumn, most of what Attorney General Mitchell later called the "White House horrors" were fully in view. Nixon's popularity collapsed, and for the first time in more than a century, there was serious talk in Congress of the impeachment of a president.

At the heart of the Nixon scandals lay, of course, the Watergate break-in and subsequent efforts by highly placed administration officials to limit the investigation and conceal or destroy evidence. But there were also allegations that the White House, or its Committee for the Re-Election of the President, engaged in: (1) unethical and illegal campaign practices ranging from "dirty tricks" against Democratic hopefuls to the extortion of illegal contributions from corporations and interest groups desiring government favors; (2) efforts to politicize such nominally independent and traditionally nonpartisan government agencies as the Federal Bureau of Investigation (FBI) and the Internal Revenue Service; and (3) illegal and wide-ranging domestic security and intelligence gathering operations. Additionally, there were charges that Nixon's income and property taxes were not in order, that his estates in California and Florida were acquired under questionable circumstances, and that federal funds (totaling nearly $10 million) spent on improvements for these private dwellings often had little to do with presidential security. Quite apart from the scandal, allegations of constitutional abuses included the misuse of impoundment and executive privileges; the secret and unauthorized air war against Cambodia; and the continued conduct of the war in Southeast Asia after the repeal of the Gulf of Tonkin Resolution. To some of Nixon's harshest critics, these too were impeachable offenses.

Initially the White House tried to ignore the uproar; then it issued a series of general denials of executive wrongdoing. But each presidential statement raised more questions than it answered. At first Nixon refused even to permit his aides to testify before the Select Senate Committee on Presidential Campaign Activities. Under mounting congressional pressure, he reversed this position but refused investigators access to secret White House tape recordings of selected presidential conversations and telephone calls. When these recordings were subpoenaed by the Justice Department's independent special prosecutor, the president fought compliance through two federal courts, promising obedience only to a "definitive" ruling of the Supreme Court. After months of negotiation and litigation, Nixon agreed to turn over the disputed material — but not before he had fired the special prosecutor and forced the resignation of the Attorney General and Deputy Attorney General, and not before Congress moved toward his impeachment. To the nation's astonishment, however, the surrendered tapes did not contain conversations presumed by investigators to be most relevant to the inquiry. The president's lawyers attributed these critical gaps in the evidence to equipment failure and secretarial error. Evidence rapidly accumulated, however, to prove the obvious: Nixon, though apparently not implicated in the burglary itself, was engaged in a conspiracy to obstruct justice by concealing evidence.

In July 1974 a unanimous Supreme Court, acting upon a second special prosecutor's request, ordered the White House to surrender other recordings of 64 key presidential conversations. Following the release of this incriminating material, the House Judiciary Committee voted to recommend three articles of impeachment to the House of Representatives. Charged with obstruction of justice, abuse of power, and contempt for constitutional procedures on a scale without parallel in American history, Nixon resigned on August 9 rather than face impeachment. Still denying criminal action, he acknowledged that the loss of public confidence rendered him incapable of leadership. Returned to private life, the first American chief executive to resign in disgrace continued to assert that he had been victimized by the zeal of his friends and the malice of his enemies. Nixon was later pardoned by his successor, but 25 administration officials, including his attorney general and two top White House assistants, were sent to prison. Four Nixon cabinet officers were named in criminal cases.

FORD'S INTERLUDE

And thus Gerald Ford became the thirty-eighth president. In every respect, his ascent was as incredible as Nixon's fall. A veteran congressman from Michigan and former House minority leader whose highest political ambition was to be speaker, Ford had been nominated vice president after Spiro Agnew's resignation from that office in 1973. Ford became the first vice president to assume office under the procedures outlined in the Twenty-Fifth Amendment and the first nonelected president. He had, as he said, "received the vote of no one."

Decent, open, and gregarious, Ford restored some measure of public confidence in the integrity of the presidency. But he failed to provide convincing leadership, and a broad segment of the press and public wondered openly if he was qualified to be president. His imprudent decision to pardon Nixon, without an admission of guilt from the former president or a full disclosure of his misdeeds, stirred controversy and reopened the wounds of Watergate. Some critics who remembered Ford's earlier efforts to derail the congressional Watergate investigation and his later promise not to pardon Nixon, cried "corrupt bargain." Others believed that unconditional immunity from prosecution for Nixon should be accompanied by equal presidential compassion for Vietnam-era draft evaders. Ford provided a program of conditional amnesty, however, that required two years of alternate government service for the youthful dissenters.

The conclusion of the Watergate tragedy brought to the fore long-neglected international and domestic problems. Despite administration predictions and a temporary upturn of the business cycle in 1972, the United States in 1974 suffered its worst recession in four decades. A "stagflated" economy of high unemployment and high inflation was further aggravated by a continuing petroleum shortage that promised soaring energy costs and greater dependence on uncertain foreign supply. There were scandals in the FBI and CIA (Central Intelligence Agency), ranging from revelations of burglary and illegal surveillance to foreign coups d'état and assassination plots. Abroad, there were crises seemingly without number: a continuing and volatile Arab-Israeli standoff, ominous Soviet ambitions in the Middle East and sub-Saharan Africa, the final collapse of America's Southeast Asian allies, a Marxist-oriented revolution in Portugal, a transfer of power in post-Franco Spain, near-anarchy and the growth of communist strength in Italy, and the diminishing influence and growing isolation of the United States in the UN General Assembly.

In responding to these disquieting problems, Ford rarely veered from Nixon's course. More conservative and less flexible than Nixon, he vetoed more legislation in one year than Herbert Hoover did in four. More solicitous toward corporations than to civil rights, he pursued traditional Republican monetary and fiscal policies, warned against overly stringent controls on either intelligence agencies or private enterprise, and continued to support both the principle of détente and unprecedented peacetime defense spending. In matters of style and personality, Ford differed markedly from

Nixon, but his policies and programs were very nearly the same. He was, most Americans seemed to believe, a likeable mediocrity.

During Senate confirmation hearings in 1974, then Vice President–designate Ford disavowed any ambition to be president. Upon Nixon's resignation, however, Ford succeeded to that office, and though few thought his chances good, he sought election in 1976. Even White House officials viewed him as an underdog. Personally popular but not widely hailed for his executive talents, Ford seemed to lack the traditional advantages of incumbency. He had served half of Nixon's second term, but he had not developed a national or even a statewide constituency. Michigan's Fifth District contained the largest electorate he had ever faced at one time. His early campaign organization was remarkably inept; the candidate himself seemed curiously "unpresidential" in his electioneering.

When compared to his party's weaknesses, Ford's difficulties appeared minor. Although the Republican party had won four of the past seven presidential elections, it had dominated Congress only twice since 1932. A minority party since the Great Depression, it could now claim the allegiance of only 22 percent of the electorate. Only 19 of the nation's 50 state governors were Republicans. In control of the White House since 1969, the party had delivered peace but not prosperity nor economic stability. Its claim to be the law-and-order party had been mocked by the misdeeds of a Republican president, his vice president, and two attorneys general. Republican unity was threatened, moreover, by the party's increasingly influential right wing. Led by former Governor Ronald Reagan of California, the arch-conservatives demonstrated surprising strength in the primaries and dictated a platform that repudiated many of Ford's policies and very nearly blocked his nomination.

In the opposition camp, a profusion of candidates (variously labeled as conservatives, hawks, liberals, populists, and progressives) entered the hotly contested Democratic primaries, while former nominees George McGovern and Hubert H. Humphrey stood by expectantly. No obvious favorite emerged, but voter indifference eliminated a dozen competitors by convention time, leaving a single practical choice: Jimmy Carter, a retired naval officer, engineer, peanut farmer, and former governor of Georgia.

After a colorless campaign, the voters' alternatives seemed to lie between one candidate who could not shake his reputation as a political "bumbler" and another who made much of the fact that he was not a politician at all. The lackluster election produced a lower voter turnout than any recent presidential race. Carter carried the South and enough large midwestern and eastern states to win electoral (294) and popular (51 percent) majorities. In congressional and gubernatorial races, the electorate again clearly preferred Democratic candidates.

OUTSIDER IN WASHINGTON

President James Earl Carter, Jr., preferred to be called Jimmy. A self-proclaimed "outsider" in Washington, his governmental experience was limited to one term each as state senator and governor of Georgia. In a nation disenchanted with the "imperial presidency," Carter's inexperience was at first a political asset. In the presidential campaign he shrewdly capitalized on Watergate. From the Oval Office he urged Americans to "trust me" and cultivated an image of righteous candor: "I'll never lie to you." In the spirit of Jefferson, that other gentleman farmer from the South, he took pains to demonstrate that he, too, had the common touch. The pomp and ceremony so characteristic of Nixon's presidency were ostentatiously abandoned. Following inaugural ceremonies at the Capitol, he refused the presidential limousine and walked down Pennsylvania Avenue to the White House hand-in-hand with the First Lady. In his first televised address, a "fireside chat," he appeared in a cardigan and open-collared shirt. He wore denims and polo shirts at congressional picnics, briefly banished the musical flourishes of "Hail to the Chief" at official functions, and conferred frequently with the press. He attended town meetings in out-of-the-way places and stayed overnight in the homes of ordinary Americans. He even sent his eight-year-old daughter to an inner-city public school. In time, as the memory of Watergate receded, such self-conscious symbolism came to seem gratuitous. Gradually, a less accessible, less informal chief executive emerged, sometimes to the strains of "Hail to the Chief." This least pretentious of all recent presidents, however, must be credited for his effort to strip the presidency of its more imperial forms.

However engaging his personal style, Carter's popular support was small. During his second year in office, his approval rating fell to 40 percent. By 1979 it plummeted to 26 percent, marking him as less popular than Nixon at his lowest point. Aside from the self-evident fact that Carter, like Ford, inspired little popular confidence, there was no single explanation for his rapid descent from public favor. Some thought him to be the victim of his own demystification of the presidency; some said he was a weak swimmer out of his depth. Others thought him the legatee of the peoples' mistrust of Johnson and Nixon; a few believed that he came to be president at a time when the nation's problems were insoluble, when its bloated bureaucracy and its unruly political insitutions were unmanageable.

By all accounts, Carter was an earnest, intelligent, hardworking president who lacked neither courage nor character. To provide the practical experience he and his staff so obviously lacked, he appointed several old Washington hands, including such members of the foreign policy establishment as Secretary of State Cyrus Vance and Secretary of Defense Harold Brown, and such seasoned bureaucrats as Health, Education, and Welfare Secretary Joseph Califano and Energy Secretary James Schlesinger. However, his tangible achievements were few. He did appoint more women and blacks to high office than any other president, and he managed to trim a costly congressional pork barrel for dam and water projects and to win support for new Departments of Education and Energy. But his detailed and technically sound proposals for long overdue tax, welfare, and civil service reforms, his bill to create a consumer protection agency, and his hospital-cost containment measure got nowhere. His energy bill, the centerpiece of his domestic program, encountered withering fire from the oil and gas lobby. By shifting the measure's emphasis from conservation to development and from consumer compensation to investment incentives, Congress satisfied the demands of powerful private interests, but it passed a bill that was anything but the "moral equivalent of war" promised by a frustrated president. In its final form, the energy bill provided appreciable reductions in neither of the two most critical areas: domestic consumption and foreign dependence.

In other areas of the economy the administration's record was worse — the worst, it was said, since Herbert Hoover. During the campaign, Carter identified recession as the nation's foremost domestic problem. In his term an assortment of ills identified with a troubled economy continued unabated: unemployment (particularly for black teenagers but also for nonwhites generally); declining investment, savings, and productivity levels; stagnated or declining after-tax earnings; and mounting trade deficits. But it was high and variable inflation — which in early 1980 threatened to reach an annual rate of 20 percent — that proved to be the curse of the 1970s and Carter's greatest political liability. Spurred by sharply rising food, fuel, housing, and transportation costs, consumer prices doubled between 1967 and 1978. Between 1973 and 1978, the cost of automobiles jumped 72 percent and new homes 67 percent; in 1979 gasoline prices rose 60 percent.

Carter's approach to the crisis of double-digit inflation was hesitant, belated, and fully as conservative as his Republican predecessors. Convinced that mandatory "wage and price controls have never worked in peacetime," he did not find a workable alternative. In 1978 he proposed voluntary guidelines (7 percent) and created a Council on Wage and Price Stability to monitor the results. This was not strong medicine and the patient got worse. The Consumer Price Index rose 13.3 percent in 1979; early the following year both inflation and interest rates topped 18 percent. In March 1980, midway into the presidential primaries, Carter proposed to balance the budget through drastic spending cuts and imposed a modest federal gasoline consumption tax and new restraints on consumer credit. Such halfway measures promised no immediate relief. Short of fundamental structural changes in the economy, many economists believed a deep recession to be the most effective way to slow the rising wage-price spiral.

CARTER AND HUMAN RIGHTS

In foreign affairs the Georgia president often proceeded more imaginatively. From the outset he indicated that his administration would be less devoted to traditional balance-of-power geopolitics than to human rights. Practical considerations, however, often undercut this policy. Despite a decade-long thaw in the Cold War, conflicting Soviet-American interests in Africa, Asia, the Middle East, and Latin America often seemed to dictate continued U.S. support for repressive anti-communist regimes. Thus, following the Soviet invasion of Afghanistan in December 1979, Carter offered military aid to, and alliance with Pakistan dictator Mohammad Zia ul-Haq. Similarly, the administration's support for Russian "prisoners of conscience" sometimes clashed with the president's wish to promote détente and a Soviet-American arms reduction agreement. Despite the unattractive trade-offs apparently required by world politics, Carter more than any other chief executive since Franklin Roosevelt tried to practice the human rights doctrine that the nation preached.

Other foreign policy successes included an act of singularly bold and personal diplomacy. Carter brought together Egypt's President Anwar Sadat and Israel's Prime Minister Menachem Begin for direct negotiations that resulted in the historic Camp David accords. Although hopes for a full resolution of the Middle East crisis were not realized, Carter's initiative marked the first real break-through in Arab-Israeli relations since the October War of 1973. He also completed the normalization of relations with the People's Republic of China, and over the opposition of Ronald Reagan and other conservatives, he negotiated the gradual return of the Panama Canal to Panamanian authority.

Administration efforts to win early confirmation of the SALT II agreement were less successful. The SALT process, begun by Nixon and Kissinger in the heyday of détente, was a confusing issue to the average American who had little understanding of modern nuclear defense systems. Generally favored by a people who wanted peace, the process was nonetheless complicated by a pervasive American mistrust of the Soviet Union and by a growing fear that the United States was no longer militarily superior to its principal Cold War adversary. Some arms experts opposed SALT II on the grounds that its limits were too high and that it would accelerate rather than slow the race for strategic advantage. But others argued that the Carter administration had been outbargained by the sharp traders of the Kremlin. On balance, the treaty seemed to promise some measure of arms stability at a time when the Soviets had the edge in ICBMs and submarine missles and the United States had a substantial lead in long-range strategic bombers and nuclear warheads.

Arguments of comparative advantage, however, quickly became moot. Troubled from the outset by Soviet interests in the affairs of such third-world nations as Ethiopia, South Yemen, and Angola — and in late 1979, by the discovery of a Soviet combat brigade in Cuba — the SALT II treaty ratification process was derailed by the Soviet occupation of its hapless Islamic neighbor to the South, Afghanistan. To be sure, the Afghans, through a succession of pro-Soviet governments, had been closely allied to the USSR for a decade or more. But this was the first Soviet military action since World War II outside the Warsaw Pact countries. Given the political and religious turmoil then sweeping much of the Islamic crescent, given the proximity of the oil fields in Iran, given traditional Russian designs on the warm waters of the Persian Gulf, the Carter administration could not have ignored this latest example of Soviet aggression. With Cold War fevers rising, the administration indefinitely delayed consideration of SALT II. The president also announced an American boycott of the 1980 Summer Olympics in Moscow and an embargo of American grain and high technology exports to the USSR.

The seizure of U.S. diplomatic personnel by fanatically anti-American militants in Teheran roused the nation's martial spirit. Once praised by Carter as an "island of stability," the oil-rich kingdom of Iran, with its repressive and staunchly pro-American Shah, was toppled by religious and cultural fundamentalists bent on the creation of an Islamic republic. In November 1979, with the apparent support of the revolution's elderly spiritual leader, the austere and (to Westerners) inscrutable Ayatollah Ruhollah Khomeini, youthful militants stormed the American Embassy taking some 65 hostages and demanding the return of the Shah then temporarily in exile in the United States.

The administration's response to this violation of international conventions was restrained. Dismissing immediate military action as counterproductive, it applied economic and international pressure, but did not at first sever diplomatic relations. In time the embassy's black and women employees were released. Despite the censure of a nearly unanimous world community, the constructive intervention of the United Nations and the World Court, and the urgings of duly constituted but impotent secular officials of Iran, the militants and their patron, the aging Ayatollah, refused further compromise and kept more than 50 Americans in captivity. Having apparently exhausted all practical remedies, the president risked a military rescue mission in May 1980 that ended before it began with death for eight American commandos, due to equipment failure. After this aborted mission, the United States remained a frustrated giant. For Jimmy Carter, who had often questioned the Cold War expedient that brought American aid to counter-revolutionary regimes no matter how autocratic, the situation was surely ironical. In an American election year, in a Near Eastern theocracy halfway round the world, sentiment raged against the "American devils" who had propped up the Shah, trained SAVAK, his dread secret police, and supplied the arms he sometimes turned on his own people. To be sure, Carter had stood by the Shah after it was clear that most Iranians did not. But it was a cruel fate that forced this champion of human rights to reap the bitter harvest of a policy he had so eloquently disavowed. To ensure maximum political damage to the president, the Iranians released the hostages on Ronald Reagan's inauguration day, 14 months after their capture.

As Carter began his re-election campaign, he seemed destined to be the first elected president since Hoover to be denied a second term. Having promised the moon in 1976, he had to run on his own uninspiring record in 1980. Republican, independent, and Democratic voters dismissed him as ineffectual. Members of his own party launched a "Dump Carter" movement. Nevertheless, he denied the challenge of his Democratic rivals, among them California Governor Jerry Brown and Massachusetts Senator Edward M. Kennedy. Among the Republicans, seasoned campaign watchers believed that such relative moderates as Senator Howard Baker of Tennessee and former CIA Director George Bush of Connecticut were more "electable" than the aging (69-years-old), rigidly conservative frontrunner, Ronald Reagan. But the attractive Californian was the favorite of party stalwarts and easily won a first-ballot nomination. Progressive Republican Congressman John Anderson of Illinois defected to become a third-party candidate.

Scarcely half of the electorate voted; among those who did, 51 percent preferred Reagan. The Democrats retained control of the House, but the Republicans for the first time since 1952 seized the Senate. Among the Democratic casualties were several leading Senate liberals — including George McGovern — targeted for defeat by Protestant fundamentalists and other "New Right" political action groups. Analysts generally agreed that Reagan had benefited heavily from the issues of inflation and hostages in Iran and an election-eve debate with Carter. Also, the voting pendulum seemed to be moving to the right, as a declining birthrate and longer life expectancies produced an older electorate and major population shifts increased clout to the politically conservative Sun-Belt states of the South and West. A genuine mandate is a rarity in American politics, and only time would tell if the election of 1980, like that of 1936, marked a major partisan realignment. Liberals, finding comfort in the low voter turnout, noted that only one in four adult Americans voted for Reagan in 1980, but the new president could legitimately claim a landslide. He was elected, he seemed to believe, to roll back the Soviet threat and dismantle the welfare state.

CONFLICTING HISTORICAL VIEWPOINTS: NO. 16

Is the Presidency Too Powerful?

Soon after the ratification of the Constitution, Thomas Jefferson advised his friend and protégé James Madison that "the tyranny of the legislature is really the danger most to be feared and will continue to be so for many years to come. The tyranny of the executive power will come in its turn, but at a more distant period." Some two centuries later, following the extraordinary assertions of presidential power by Lyndon Johnson and Richard Nixon, a growing number of scholars believed that Jefferson's "more distant period" was at hand. In recent decades, they argued, the presidency had been unduly exalted; presidents had grown too aloof, too arrogant, too neglectful of congressional prerogatives. In this view, the system of constitutional checks and balances devised by the founders no longer effectively restrained executive authority. In the words of one political scientist, the man in the Oval Office had been elevated from "Servant to Sun King."

The Vietnam War and the Watergate scandals were the most flagrant and frequently cited examples of a runaway presidency. Yet most scholars agreed that Lyndon Johnson's wholesale escalation of the undeclared war in Southeast Asia, Nixon's secret bombing of Cambodia, or even John Mitchell's "White House horrors" were not so much aberrations as a culmination of the twentieth-century tendency toward presidential aggrandizement. The roots of the activist presidency could be traced to the bold examples of such assertive chief executives as Andrew Jackson and Abraham Lincoln — and more recently to Theodore Roosevelt and Woodrow Wilson, the first of the so-called "modern presidents." But closer in time and in importance was the growth of presidential power since the New Deal. In a period of almost uninterrupted crises, stretching from the Depression of the 1930s to the threat of nuclear destruction in the 1960s, executive authority in such critical areas as the economy and foreign policy had expanded enormously.

Until the intrusions of Vietnam and Watergate, scholars generally agreed that these developments were both inevitable and constitutional. In an increasingly complex and threatening world, they concluded, the nation's welfare and security required a strong president. The legislative process was properly deliberative and inherently slow. Only the president enjoyed the capacity for centralized leadership; only he possessed the control of information and communication demanded by a modern nation in a troubled world. This view, noted the political scientist Thomas E. Cronin (Congressional Record, *October 5, 1956), became "textbook orthodoxy." It was forcefully advocated by such eminent students of American government as Clinton Rossiter* (The American Presidency, *1956), Lewis W. Koenig* (The Chief Executive, *1964), and James MacGregor Burns* (Presidential Government, *1965). Perhaps the most influential spokesman for executive domination was Richard E. Neustadt, whose* Presidential Power *(1960) characterized the president as the "Great Initiator" of both domestic and foreign policy and the "Final Arbiter" in matters of war. The standard in its field for nearly a decade, this popular book has been called "a latter-day version of Machiavelli's* Prince," *a primer for chief executives who would maximize their power.*

Amid the disillusionments of war and scandal, however, this expansive view fell rapidly into scholarly disfavor. Even without the example of Watergate, Neustadt (Alliance Politics, *1970) became more cautious in his claims for presidential power. Alarmed by the president's seemingly unchecked capacity to wage war, some writers called the office a "Frankenstein monster"; an increasing number expressed fear that the ship of state had listed dangerously to its presidential side. Almost overnight a new scholarly consensus emerged; even many former aggrandizers became critics of executive authority. Among the most provocative of these was the historian Arthur M. Schlesinger, Jr., whose widely read* Imperial Presidency *(1973) elegantly lamented the development in the office of the American president of "the most absolute monarch (with the possible exception of Mao Zedong of China) among the great powers of the world." Although in earlier works Schlesinger had, by his own admission, contributed to the "rise of the presidential mystique," he now argued for a return to a "properly balanced" system of executive restraint and legislative responsibility.*

And so the pendulum swings. Taken together, these sharply diverging schools of presidential analysis — the one dominant in the 1960s, the other emerging full-blown in the 1970s — provide as neat an example of the importance of perspective to the interpretive process as the student is likely to find. With the Nixon excesses so near to mind, scholars who once lauded Theodore Roosevelt for his sweeping theory of executive "stewardship," or faulted Dwight Eisenhower for his unseemly "Whiggery," fell under the spell of the two-centuries-old mandate for separated powers. Similarly, in the aftermath of Vietnam, historians and political scientists who once praised

Franklin Roosevelt and Harry Truman for their bold foreign policy initiatives became critical of executive usurpations in the areas of war and treaty-making. Whither revisionism? Only time can tell. But president watchers seem momentarily confused about executive power. During the apparent paralysis of the later Carter years, many wondered if American institutions, and particularly the presidency, could effectively address late-twentieth-century problems. During the American buildup in Central America during the 1980s, others worried that presidential initiative might once again involve the country in a war neither Congress nor the public wanted.

FOR FURTHER READING

In addition to books mentioned in the text, other suggestive and widely varying points of departure for understanding the 1970s include M. Rossman's *New Age Blues* (1979), Tom Wolfe's *Mauve Cloves & Madmen, Clutter & Vine* (1976), and Jim Hougan's *Decadence* (1975).

A valuable survey of the decade is Peter Carroll's *It Seemed Like Nothing Happened* (1982). A multitude of books cover the Nixon era. Stephen Ambrose's *Nixon* (3 vols., 1987–1992) is a detailed political narrative. Joan Hoff in *Nixon Reconsidered* (1994), Garry Wills in *Nixon Agonistes* (1979), and Fawn Brodie in *Richard Nixon* (1980) all examine the man, his personality, and his politics. Nixon tells his own story in *RN* (1978). Stanley Kutler ably details *The Wars of Watergate* (1990), and Kevin Phillips suggestively analyzes Nixon's election strategy in *The Emerging Republican Majority* (1969). Accounts of the Nixon-Kissinger foreign policy include Kissinger's important autobiography, *White House Years* (1979); Walter Isaacson, *Kissinger* (1992); Raymond Garthoff, *Détente and Confrontation* (1985); and William Shawcross, *Sideshow: Kissinger, Nixon and the Destruction of Cambodia* (1987). A. James Reichley looks at federal policy during the Nixon and Ford administrations in *Conservatives in an Age of Change* (1981); Anthony Lukas in *Common Ground* (1986) examines the school integration/busing crisis in Boston; and Lawrence M. Friedman's *Crime and Punishment in American History* (1993) places the recent fear of crime in historical perspective.

In the post-Nixon era, John R. Greene examines *The Presidency of Gerald R. Ford* (1995); James M. Cannon in *Time and Chance* (1994) provides a valuable account of Ford's presidential tenure; and Ford offers his own description of his brief presidency in *A Time to Heal* (1980). For the Carter years, Haynes Johnson's *In the Absence of Power* (1980) explains the failure of Carter's attempt to play the role of political outsider; Erwin C. Hargrove focuses on *Jimmy Carter as President* (1988); and Gaddis Smith's *Morality, Reason, and Power* (1986) considers American diplomacy under Carter. Memoirs by notable insiders include Rosalyn Carter's *First Lady from Plains* (1984) and Zbigniew Brzezinski's *Power and Principle* (1983).

32

★ ★ ★ ★ ★ ★

The Reagan Revolution:
The 1980s

PERHAPS MORE than any other American president, Ronald Wilson Reagan presents a paradox. A divorced former movie star, he entered the White House as a symbol of traditional values and the critic of a permissive society. A sincere admirer of Franklin Roosevelt, Reagan as a Republican presidential candidate draped himself in FDR's mantle even as he carried the banner of the resurgent anti–New Deal right. By his own admission he had been "a near hemophilic liberal" during his acting days. After World War II he both helped form California's branch of the liberal Americans for Democratic Action and served as an FBI informant on subversive elements in the movie industry. During the 1950s, while touring the nation as a representative of General Electric, he moved sharply to the right; in 1964 he emerged from the Goldwater debacle as the most effective spokesman of the New Right. After two successful terms as governor of California and repeated bids for the presidency, he captured his party's nomination in 1980 and was elected as the fortieth president in a popular and electoral vote landslide.

Reagan was an uncommonly popular chief executive, notable for his easygoing temperament and his passionate ideological commitments, his unbending principles and his many compromises. He presided over eight years of often bitter partisan wrangling and growing divisions of class and race in America. The success of his presidency must await the judgment of time, but the record of his leadership in foreign and domestic affairs seems fraught with contradiction. A doctrinaire and strident anti-communist whose budget-busting defense spending brought new military competition with the USSR, he developed frank and friendly relations with Soviet leader Mikhail Gorbachev and left a legacy of arms agreements and improving relations with Moscow which promised a new era of peace. An advocate of a tough stand against international terrorism, he pledged publicly never to negotiate with hostage-takers even as his aides arranged the secret transfer of arms to Iran for the release of American hostages held by pro-Iranian terrorists in Lebanon. A self-proclaimed champion of a balanced budget, economic growth, and frugal government, he left his successor a staggering list of economic woes: a deficit of unprecedented size and an ever-widening trade imbalance, unacceptably high levels of unemployment and poverty, a declining industrial base and waning competitiveness in foreign markets, and a public confidence shaken by scandals in defense procurement, public housing, insider stock-market trading, and the savings and loan industry. Not the least of the ironies of Reagan's leadership was the transmutation, during two terms of fiscal mismanagement, of a president who was inaugurated as the scourge of "tax-and-spend Democrats" into one who would be remembered in retirement as a "borrow-and-spend Republican." Among the most popular presidents ever to serve the nation, his public approval ratings plummeted after he left the White House; the year after his retirement, the public rated him below former President Jimmy Carter.

THE FEEL-GOOD PRESIDENCY

Reagan charmed the press and public with his undisguised pleasure in being president and his confident, amiable, self-deprecating style. Any apprehensions about his age were soon dissolved by his demonstrated courage and fast recovery from an assassination attempt during his first months in office. Although his political experience was limited to the California governorship, he quickly proved himself to be a formidable shaper of public opinion and a skillful legislative tactician with impressive support on both sides of the congressional aisle. A seasoned radio and television performer, his masterful public appearances won him a reputation as "the great communicator." Critics noted, however, that he preferred set speeches to press conferences, that he was most effective when delivering well-rehearsed lines, that his strong-willed wife routinely prompted his answers to reporters, and that his administrative aides stage-managed his nearly every move. Frequently ill informed, his extemporaneous remarks often required clarification by White House staffers. A key adviser actually compared his own job with that of a man following an elephant with a shovel.

Some doubted that Reagan possessed the qualities of mind and expertise required by the office. Even presidential aides conceded that he took little interest in complex issues, was neither reflective nor curious, and thought "anecdotally" rather than "analytically." At the end of his first term, the *New Republic* pondered the delicate "ignoramus issue" and reported widespread concerns among political observers that "Reagan is the most ignorant President anyone can recall." After his retirement, scholars participating in a nationwide poll of professional historians ranked him "below average" among all presidents; 90 percent of historians surveyed believed that he lacked the intelligence required for the presidency. During his tenure, however, these doubts were not widely shared by the voters, who found Reagan — even when they did not share his uncompromising ideology — the most likable president in two decades. Having learned to mistrust both LBJ and Nixon, having never given Gerald Ford their respect or Jimmy Carter their heart, the voters admired Reagan as they had no other president since Dwight Eisenhower.

Much of Reagan's political magic could be traced to his uncomplicated vision of the American destiny and his ability to make the electorate feel good about itself. A buoyant man who preached the simple verities of God, family, and the free market, he brought to Washington a sense of purpose which contrasted sharply with the disconsolate drift of the post-Vietnam, post-Watergate period. Where Carter had spoken of a national malaise — "a crisis of confidence . . . that is threatening the very fabric of America" — Reagan exuded a refreshing, infectious optimism. In an age of diminishing expectations, Reagan perceived a "rebirth of confidence and hope and progress." His appeal lay not in his mastery of national or international issues but in his confident evocation of an "era of renewal," of unbounded growth and unrivaled American power. To those who were troubled by a new "era of limits" and relative national decline, he declared that it was "morning in America." "America is back," he said; its "best days" were yet to come.

In 1984 he was enthusiastically renominated by the most conservative Republican convention in modern times. After a campaign that turned more on personalities than on issues, Reagan and George Bush easily defeated the liberal Democratic nominee Walter Mondale, winning the popular vote and forty-nine of the fifty states. Despite a much discussed "gender gap" — and the presence on the Democratic ticket of New York Congresswoman Geraldine Ferraro, the first major-party female vice-presidential candidate — the Reagan coalition included a majority of women (57 percent) as well as substantial numbers of self-styled "Reagan Democrats," a category which included blue-collar workers and all ethnics save Jews and blacks. Whatever its policy limitations, the administration's message of pride, power, and patriotism played well in America.

THE NEW FEDERALISM REDUX

U.S. domestic maladies, Reagan never doubted, were attributable to the disease of "big, never-mind-the-cost government." To promote recovery he borrowed Nixon's slogan, the New Federalism, and prescribed massive doses of laissez faire and what came to be known as "supply-side econom-ics," a conservative economic doctrine which promised fiscal integrity through tax reductions. Although the Republicans spoke of a new begin-ning and many praised the administration's "bold departure" in domestic economic policy, Reagan's New Federalism of the 1980s recalled Calvin

Coolidge's New Era of the 1920s. Supply-side policy, as the administration's budget director conceded, found its most direct antecedent in the "trickle-down" policies of Andrew Mellon. In practice, if not precisely in theory, supply-siders believed that the administration could reduce taxes, increase military spending, and balance the budget, all at the same time. Tax cuts that favored business and the wealthy, the Reaganites reasoned, would promote prosperity and increase federal revenues by unshackling American creativity and encouraging capital investment. Deregulation would stimulate productivity by freeing both labor and capital from federal meddling. The elimination of social programs for all but the "truly deserving needy" would rid the nation of "welfare queens" and other "cheats," foster a more self-reliant citizenry, and bring government receipts and expenditures into balance for the first time since 1969. Together, the president predicted, these initiatives would provide full employment without inflation, frugal government without social distress, military strength without economic pain.

Dubbed "Reaganomics" by the press — and dismissed during the 1980 primary campaign as "voodoo economics" by George Bush — the administration's proposals received mixed reviews. Conservatives, sharing the president's extreme distaste for progressive taxes, social services, and intrusive government, were enthusiastic. Consumer advocates and environmentalists, on the other hand, feared a decline in the quality of American life; and liberals (themselves an endangered species) protested that the Reagan revolution portended a new age of opulence for the rich and austerity for the poor. Other critics, including many Wall Street analysts, doubted that free-market Republicanism could defy the laws of fiscal arithmetic by balancing the budget of a government committed to buying more arms with less revenue. The most cynical observers feared what David Stockman, Reagan's budget director, later confirmed: in the short term, Reaganites hoped to use expected revenue shortfalls to bludgeon down social spending levels. For a time, the supply-siders and the free marketeers had their way.

During 1981 the Reagan taxation and spending measures moved through the conservative 97th Congress with a speed that invited comparison with the legislative triumphs of Franklin Roosevelt and Lyndon Johnson. In the largest tax reduction in history, income taxes were reduced across the board by 25 percent over a three-year period; military outlays were sharply increased; expenditures were slashed for welfare payments, food stamps, student aid, urban transit, cancer research, health programs, school lunches, job training, housing assistance, and other social purposes. Public service employment designed to create work for the ablebodied unemployed was ended outright. Inevitably, the deepest cuts fell on the poor and the politically inarticulate; the most powerful interest groups generally managed to protect their entitlements. Despite Reaganite homilies about the dangers of dependence on government handouts, subsidies for tobacco growers and dairy farmers escaped the axe altogether. The administration sponsored Payment in Kind, a per-acre farm subsidy of most benefit to the biggest producers. Measured as a percentage of the total budget, federal allocations during the Reagan years fell in every area except defense, Social Security, agriculture, and interest on the national debt.

In related developments, the president quickly ended all price controls on gasoline and crude oil and then proposed to reverse a century-long trend toward ever more intrusive federal regulation by reducing regulatory budgets, by eliminating or diluting government regulatory standards, and by appointing anti-regulators to environmental, consumer-protection, and other regulatory agencies. Opponents of collective bargaining and government supervision of broadcasting were named to the National Labor Relations Board and the Federal Communications Commission; the Civil Rights Commission was packed with conservatives opposed to such remedies for discrimination as affirmative-action programs, court-ordered busing, and legal services for the poor; the Occupational Safety and Health Administration was assigned a director who had been repeatedly cited in the 1970s as a violator of OSHA's own standards. Anne Gorsuch Burford, an anti-environmentalist and one of the few women appointed to high office by the Reagan administration, became director of the Environmental Protection Agency. The Department of the Interior was assigned to James Watt, an anti-conservation activist and biblical literalist who advocated private development of the public domain and who once disparaged resource preservation as unnecessary in a world he thought would soon end with the Second Coming of Jesus Christ.

There were conservative setbacks as well as successes. During Reagan's first two years, Republicans controlled the Senate outright and, in alliance with conservative southern Democrats (so-called Boll Weevils), effectively controlled a nominally Democratic House. But in 1982 and again in 1984, administration support in the House slipped considerably; in 1986 and again in 1988 the voters sent Democratic majorities to both House and Senate. Although Reagan Republicans generally dominated tax policy and the relative distribution of military and social spending, the political realignment portended by the election of 1980 did not occur. While the administration presided over what might be called a policy realignment, it nevertheless found that neither the Congress nor the electorate wanted a complete repeal of the federal regulatory and social service state.

Many domestic programs were cut back and some were eliminated, but the reduction of social spending was less than either the administration or its critics claimed. The president's efforts to dismantle the new departments of Education and Energy were soon abandoned in the face of widespread opposition. Medicaid was trimmed, but Reagan failed to win congressional approval for reduced Medicare or Social Security benefits. The administration's heavy-handed deregulators — particularly in the EPA and Interior — provoked a backlash that forced the resignations of Watt and Burford, brought new vitality to the environmental movement, and renewed public support for consumer- and worker-safety regulations.

Conservative single-issue crusaders, moreover, felt betrayed by presidential neglect of New Right social policy. Reagan was applauded by many as the most "pro-gun" president; social conservatives and newly politicized evangelicals admired his stand against the Equal Rights Amendment and his support for tax credits for all-white private academies and for the teaching of "creationism" in the schools. But the Moral Majority and other ultra-conservatives were ultimately embittered by what they thought to be his halfhearted support for school prayer, anti-abortion, and anti-busing amendments. The president, some said, tried to propitiate the New Right primarily with New Right rhetoric.

When Reagan appointed Sandra Day O'Connor to the Supreme Court in 1981, the Moral Majority expressed outrage, alleging that the first woman justice, however conservative, was "soft" on abortion (as well as a symbol of advancing feminism). The Reagan constituency was generally pleased when, upon the retirement of Warren Burger in 1986, the president elevated Justice William H. Rehnquist to chief justice and appointed another judicial conservative, Antonin Scalia, to the High Court. The following year, however, brought disappointment to the conservatives and embarrassment to the administration: Robert Bork, Reagan's eccentric, controversial nominee for a third Supreme Court vacancy and a favorite of both the religious and political right, was rejected by the Senate; after a subsequent nominee admitted having used marijuana and withdrew his candidacy, the president settled on Anthony Kennedy, a more centrist justice who was quickly confirmed. Although Reagan could claim considerable success in refashioning the federal judiciary in his own conservative image, the Bork rejection remained a symbol of Reagan's inability to right every liberal wrong.

The results of Reagan economic programs were also dismaying. Inflation declined to the lowest level since 1967 (to 4 percent by 1984) in response to the tight-money "monetarist" policies pursued by the Federal Reserve Board, to stabilizing world oil and food prices, and to labor's declining bargaining power. But the American unemployment rate soon approached 11 percent (the highest since 1940). By 1982, with bankruptcies and interest rates soaring, factory utilization, grain prices, and export rates falling, and the stock and bond markets in disarray, the nation plunged into the deepest recession since the 1930s. The resulting revenue shortfall pushed annual deficits and the cumulative national debt to new and alarming heights. Faced with these fiscal problems, the president repeated his commitment to a balanced budget and attempted to use the deficit to force larger reductions in social spending. But he also vowed to continue his fiscal policies of low taxes and high military expenditures. Very likely, it was just this Keynesian expedient of deficit spending (with money borrowed largely from West European and Japanese creditors) that brought economic revival by 1984, just in time to spur Reagan's reelection bid.

In his second term the recovery continued, and administration spokesmen boasted of the "Reagan boom." But others noted that the nation's prosperity was unevenly distributed and its vital economic signs wildly erratic. The inflation rate remained low and for a time so too did joblessness. Prodded by the White House, Congress enacted a second major tax reduction in 1986, one that ended many deductions and loopholes and brought further relief to the richest Americans and some to the poorest. The stock market soared through the summer of 1987, reaching a historic high late in August only to fall faster and farther on "Black Monday," October 19, 1987, than on any other day in history. The plunge was not followed by recession, and the market soon recovered; but investors worried that mounting deficits and trade imbalances imperiled the nation's long-term economic health. Such fiscal reforms as the Congress and the White House could agree upon — including the Gramm-Rudman Act of 1985 (which mandated a balanced budget through across-the-board spending cuts) and monetary decisions designed to encourage American exports — proved ineffectual.

Eight years of radical experimentation with Reaganomics had brought modest economic growth at fearsome costs. Fueled by a massive defense buildup paid for with borrowed money, the "Reagan boom" had been unevenly distributed. By decade's end, amid a looming banking crisis and with some economists predicting a deep and protracted recession, the prosperity of the 1980s seemed largely illusory. As nearly everyone admitted, the rich had grown richer and the poor poorer. The number of homeless and hungry became a source of national shame; the gap between black and white incomes widened; poverty was disproportionately visited on women and children in inner cities. Despite the rampant consumerism and apparent contentment of the middle class, many American families lost ground and a backlog of economic problems mounted.

During the decade of the 1980s, Congressional Budget Office data reveal, middle-bracket wage earners experienced marginal gains; earnings of the bottom 30 percent actually shrank; those paid to the highest 10 percent increased by 41 percent; while the richest Americans, the top 1 percent, enjoyed an average increase of 87 percent (all in constant dollars). In the same period the nation's educational crisis deepened and its economic infrastructure (bridges, highways, railroads, etc.) continued to decay. In a business climate seemingly characterized by the fast-buck celebrity tycoon, the insider stock deal, and the hostile corporate takeover, the U.S. experienced a dizzying spiral of business mergers and the lowest rate of investment in business plant and equipment since World War II; at the same time the indebtedness of its industries mounted and both the efficiency and quality of its manufacturing declined. Personal savings remained low throughout the 1980s, and consumers were awash (proportionally) in nearly as much red ink as the government.

And red ink was the bottom line of Reaganomics: Carter's last annual deficit was $79 billion; Reagan's averaged $184 billion annually over eight years, peaking in 1985 at $236 billion. By 1989 the nation's accumulated debt stood at $2.6 trillion, several times greater than that accumulated by all previous presidents combined. In a nation suffering from mounting "innumeracy" (numerical illiteracy), a trillion of anything was beyond the ken of most citizens. Yet even without a degree in higher math, it was plain for anyone to see that the Reagan Revolution had not delivered on its promise of fiscal responsibility.

REAGAN'S FOREIGN POLICY

President Reagan's foreign policy was implacably conservative and un-abashedly nationalistic. Reviving the rhetoric of the early Cold War period, he identified the Soviet Union as "the evil empire" ready "to commit any crime, to lie, to cheat" in pursuit of its "goal of world revolution." The U.S., he believed, had learned too much from the Vietnam War (which, at any rate, he thought to be a "noble cause") and too little from the appeasement of Hitler at Munich. Despite sharply rising defense appropriations during the Carter years, Reagan charged that the nation had "starved" its military and permitted the USSR to gain a "definite margin" of nuclear superiority. Falling to "Number Two in military power" during the 1970s, the U.S. risked "nuclear blackmail." Détente, Reagan said, was a delusion; SALT I and II merely impeded the free world's struggle against a Soviet "global offensive."

Moderates in both parties deplored Reagan's strident anti-Sovietism. Three former presidents and most military authorities disputed his assessment of relative Soviet-American might; and George Kennan, architect of American containment, dismissed the president's fire-breathing rhetoric and pugnacious style of diplomacy as "childish," "unworthy" of the responsible head of a great nation. But the commander-in-chief inspired patriotic pride in the electorate and once again generally had his way with Congress. Matching his hard line with military hardware, he launched the most costly peacetime rearmament in American history — securing from Congress, as events proved, more money than could be wisely spent. With military appropriations increasing as much as 12 percent annually, the administration projected a $1.6 trillion defense budget for 1984–1988 ($2.3 trillion over eight years), much of it for a new generation of nuclear weapons designed to close what Reagan called the American "window of vulnerability" to Soviet missiles.

Since the 1960s the nation's defense establishment had sought security in a stable world order with a policy of essential military parity between the superpowers. The intent of the Reagan administration's huge defense expenditures was, as its spokesmen often said, to "negotiate from strength"; the goal was not "strategic sufficiency" but a new era of unchallenged American primacy. At their most reckless, Reaganites also talked of developing a "preemptive" nuclear strike capability and of winning a nuclear war, an implausible faith which was bolstered after 1983 by the Strategic Defense Initiative project. Popularly called "Star Wars," the costly SDI posited the use of sophisticated American technology to construct a space-based nuclear shield capable of destroying all incoming missiles with laser beams. Critics, including many scientists, dismissed the idea as prohibitively expensive and technically problematic. The Soviets, openly worrying that the device might give the United States a first-strike option, warned that its deployment would impede future arms talks by destablizing the world order. The president, apparently never doubting its feasibility, saw in this project to militarize the heavens both a nuclear survival strategy and a "bargaining chip" in future arms discussions with the USSR. Congress funded preliminary SDI research, though not at the level requested by the White House. The project was a source of deep controversy at home and abroad for years.

Reagan's hard line was mirrored by increasing Soviet bellicosity as both sides pronounced an end to détente. The American grain embargo was lifted (a campaign pledge to farmers), but prospects for additional arms limitation agreements dimmed when the administration announced that further negotiations must be linked to Soviet "good behavior." SALT II, withdrawn from Senate consideration by Carter after the Soviet invasion of Afghanistan in 1979, was discarded in 1981. Citing recent missile implacements in the western USSR, the president also announced plans to deploy additional intermediate-range Pershing and cruise missiles (under NATO auspices) in Western Europe in 1983.

Under mounting pressure from world opinion, both sides expressed renewed interest in nuclear reductions. Yet Reagan's "zero-option" proposal for a nuclear-free Europe was ignored by the USSR in 1981 (as the U.S. surely expected); and when the Strategic Arms Reduction Talks (START) opened at Geneva in 1982, neither adversary appeared ready to negotiate on terms acceptable to the other. Although great-power relations continued to deteriorate, a crisis in Eastern Europe passed without major East-West incident when the Soviet-dominated Polish government crushed a liberal movement (led by the trade union Solidarity) with martial law rather than risk a Soviet invasion. Again, in September 1983, tension mounted when the USSR inexplicably (and without official remorse) shot down a Korean commercial airliner which had wandered off course into Russian air space. This incident sparked a new round of recriminations and fed universal fear of nuclear exchange by accident or miscalculation. In late 1983, following the SDI proposal and American missile deployment in NATO countries, the Soviets terminated further arms discussion in Geneva and in 1984 boycotted the summer Olympics in Los Angeles. Upon the death of Soviet party leader Leonid Brezhnev in late 1982, additional dangers seemed to flow from a prolonged succession crisis which went unresolved until March 1985, when Mikhail Gorbachev became party chairman.

The threat of major war was particularly acute in the Third World. Distinguishing between regimes that were merely "authoritarian" (or right wing) and those that were "totalitarian" (Marxist), the administration disavowed Carter's human rights policy and returned to one of alliance with anti-communist governments, however repressive. The Reagan Doctrine — pledging to roll back Soviet influence and encourage the evolution of democracy in the developing world — pursued its brand of "quiet diplomacy" with the white supremacist regime in South Africa and with dictatorships in South America, Pakistan, and the Philippines. Results were mixed.

The administration did help to displace the corrupt tyrant Ferdinand Marcos in the Philippines in 1986. Its relations with General Manuel Noriega of Panama, however, brought only embarrassment after it was revealed in 1987 that the Central American strong man was, among other things, a drug runner. Reagan's overtures to Pretoria, moreover, were frustrated when he failed to block a congressional ban on American trade with and investments in South Africa.

The most controversial application of the Reagan Doctrine came in Central America, where the U.S. military presence was markedly increased to prevent "more Cubas." Although many observers traced Central American stife to poverty, oppression, class resentment, and economic instability, the Reagan administration found its origins in Soviet-backed subversion. Only U.S. military resolve, the president argued, could stop the Red tide before it seeped across the Rio Grande. In October 1983 American forces easily invaded the tiny Caribbean nation of Grenada and toppled its Marxist government. Critics faulted this exercise in gunboat diplomacy, but the American people were overwhelmingly supportive. (Under cover of this wave of popularity, the administration extricated itself from a potential disaster in chaotic Lebanon, but not before terrorists had killed 241 U.S. marines assigned to a peacekeeping mission which few Americans understood.) In other regional conflicts, the administration supported a ruling military junta threatened by leftist guerrillas in El Salvador and secretly trained and equipped right-wing insurgents to overthrow the left-wing government of Nicaragua. Neither intervention sat well with Congress or the public, and neither conflict yielded to U.S. military solution.

Of the two, however, the Salvadoran civil war proved to be the most politically manageable for the administration. With U.S. support, moderate and ineffectual José Napoleón Duarte was elected president of poverty-stricken El Salvador in 1984; though his regime proved unable either to reform itself or control fanatical right-wing "death squads" associated with its own oppressive army, the White House continued to certify Salvadoran progress toward human rights, the guerrilla movement (FMLN) continued its bloody insurrection, and American military aid continued to flow ($900 million during the 1980s).

Reagan's Nicaraguan policy was more controversial, perhaps because it supported an insurgency against a government recognized by the United States and most certainly because many feared it might make Central America the American Southeast Asia of the 1980s. In 1979 a popular uprising led by the Sandinista movement toppled the corrupt, authoritarian Samoza dynasty in Nicaragua. Hoping to nurture a fledgling democracy, President Carter briefly provided and then terminated economic support, charging in early 1981 that the radical Sandinistas under the leadership of Daniel Ortega had betrayed their own revolution. In 1982 the new Republican administration, convinced that Ortega was a Soviet puppet and Nicaragua a fallen domino, began a secret, "proxy war" against the Sandinista government. During the next two years it conducted intimidating military exercises in adjacent countries, covertly provided arms, logistical support, and military training for Nicaraguan exile forces known as Contras, and allowed the CIA to mine Nicaraguan harbors and even to encourage the assassination of Sandinista officials. When CIA excesses were exposed, Congress moved to limit and then, in October 1984 with the Boland amendment, to terminate all military assistance to the Contras.

The congressional will notwithstanding, Reaganites refused to abandon the ten thousand "freedom fighters" (Contras) or accept the first of what the president warned could be "a string of anti-American, Soviet-style dictatorships" in Central America. Exploiting Reagan's enormous popularity and communications skills, the White House began a media blitz which in mid-1986, by the narrowest of margins, resulted in congressional re authorization of Contra aid. Meanwhile, however, the administration continued extralegally to finance the right-wing irregulars through funds solicited from private sources at home and abroad. In mid-1985 the president's National Security Council (led by Vice Admiral John Poindexter and his aide, Lieutenant Colonel Oliver North) concocted a scheme designed to end the funding crisis and at the same time serve American interests in the Middle East.

Exposed in late 1986 and 1987, the operation linked Iran to Nicaragua in a tangle of poor judgment and questionable legality which outraged even many of Reagan's most ardent supporters. Called by critics "Iranamok" and "Contragate," the tawdry Iran-Contra affair derived from a complicated and constitutionally dubious arrangement wherein White House operatives, most notably Colonel North, managed the sale of arms to putatively moderate elements within the Khomeini government of Iran. In exchange they received help in freeing several American hostages held by terrorists in Lebanon and substantial amounts of money. Millions of dollars were then transferred to the Contras to pay for a war that Congress had (during the period of the Boland amendment, from October 1984 to September 1985) refused to fund.

North quickly shredded much of the incriminating evidence of these transactions. The president, often appearing confused and ill informed, denied that arms had been traded for hostages and insisted that he knew nothing of the rogue operation, including the unlawful resupply of the Contras. The extent of his personal knowledge, if any, was never established. Investigations by Congress and a blue ribbon panel led by former Senator John Tower (the Tower Commission), however, suggested what few Americans seemed to doubt: White House officials at the highest levels, including perhaps the president, either knew or deliberately chose not to know what any president certainly should have known about an arms-for-hostages, cash-for-Contras deal. Was an unelected lieutenant colonel, skeptics asked, conducting American foreign policy? The scandal seemed the more shocking because the law ending American military aid for the Nicaraguan guerrillas had been signed by Reagan; he had also solemnly and repeatedly vowed never to negotiate with terrorists, and he had even ordered the bombing of Libyan cities in retaliation for Muammar Qaddafi's support of terrorism against Americans.

In any event, when the first measure of peace and pluralism came to Nicaragua, it came from sources outside the United States. Following Contragate, under the so-called Arias plan (named after Costa Rican President Oscar Arias Sanchez), the five presidents of Central America arranged a cease-fire between Sandinistas and Contras. Reagan initially dismissed this plan as "fatally flawed" (as he had the Contradora peace plan of 1983), but under popular and congressional pressure the administration had little choice but to go along. In early 1990, Violeta Chamorro, wife of Nicaragua's most celebrated anti-Somozista, defeated Ortega to become president of the wartorn nation. Who won Nicaragua? Both the supporters and the opponents of the Reagan doctrine claimed victory, of course. Either way, the victors found Nicaragua ravaged by a decade of death and conflict.

Contragate was less damaging to the presidency than Watergate, yet it called into question Reagan's candor and good judgment; it raised new doubts about his age, his competence, and his passive leadership; it all but shattered public confidence in his stewardship; and it further eroded such comity as still remained between the executive and legislative branches of government. The administration's critics noted, moreover, that Contragate was not alone, that it was a major breach of trust in the larger pattern of obsessive secrecy, executive mismanagement, questionable behavior, and disdain for the law. Calling it Reagan's "sleaze factor," Democrats often pointed to a rising pile of soiled White House linen, including a series of resignations and prosecutions of top presidential aides, cabinet officers, and former administration officials charged with accepting bribes, "sweetheart" loans, and stock transactions; influence peddling; conflict of interest, and other violations of the Ethics in Government Act. The Pentagon was also periodically embarrassed by allegations of gross irregularities and widescale corruption in military procurement practices.

(In other ethical lapses unrelated to the White House — but directly bearing on the Reagan coalition — elements of the religious right fell out among themselves and became mired in public shame. In 1987, Jim Bakker, popular star with his wife Tammy Faye of the new "televangelism" so central to the conservative evangelical political movement, fell from grace in a sex and money scandal. Soon thereafter Jimmy Swaggart, another powerful figure in conservative causes and Christian broadcasting, admitted to dalliances with a New Orleans prostitute. Later that same year, a deeply mortified Jerry Falwell, leader of the once pivotal Moral Majority, announced that he was retiring from the worldly business of politics.)

None of these scandals stuck to the political skin of the "Teflon presidency" as did Contragate. Reagan's summits with Soviet leader Gorbachev (1987–1988) and a major arms agreement signed in 1988 helped to redeem the later years of his presidency.

In Mikhail Gorbachev, Ronald Reagan found a world leader as charismatic and, among the people of the United States and Western Europe at least, fully as popular as himself. Named general secretary in 1985, Gorbachev quickly proved himself to be the most dynamic and innovative Soviet leader since Lenin. In every way a striking contrast to the stolid, remote cold warrior Lenoid Brezhnev, he came to power amid a rapidly deepening Soviet political and economic crisis not fully perceived in the West. Promising a new day for the USSR, he declared his intention to bring to his people *glasnost* (political "openness"), *perestroika* (economic "restructuring"), and *novo myshleniye* (geopolitical "new thinking"). He quickly eased tensions with China and made improved U.S.-Soviet relations his highest priority.

Initially Gorbachev seemed far readier for East-West accord than Reagan. In 1985 he declared a unilateral Soviet moratorium on nuclear testing and suggested a mutual moratorium on intermediate nuclear forces (INFs, where the Soviets were clearly superior); in 1986 he offered serious compromises on strategic arms reduction, agreeing to reduce Soviet ICBMs if the U.S. would not deploy SDI; in 1988 he pressured Vietnam to leave Cambodia and Cuba to pull out of Angola. That same year he withdrew Soviet troops from Afghanistan and later disavowed Soviet intervention there. His motives were widely debated in the West. Few European or American policymakers believed that he sought for the USSR a Western-style liberal democracy; no doubt he needed respite from a ruinous arms race in order to rebuild his politically and economically bankrupt country. But his repeated and often surprising diplomatic initiatives (not a few of them opposed by hard-liners in his own government and military) stirred a world longing for peace. After a period of apparent puzzled reluctance, the Reagan administration, beset with domestic troubles of its own, turned down its Cold War rhetoric and responded constructively.

Reagan and Gorbachev met in Geneva (1985), Iceland (1986), Washington (1987), and Moscow (1988). Early progress on arms reductions was limited by disagreement over SDI. Yet even this obstacle collapsed before Soviet flexibility, and the two superpowers agreed, in the historic INF treaty of 1988, to eliminate all intermediate-range missiles from Europe. The treaty left in place perhaps 95 percent of the world's nuclear arsenal, including the more threatening strategic (i.e., long-range) nuclear missiles. Yet it was probably the most important Soviet-American treaty ever, and it was evidence that détente, after an interlude of nearly a decade, was again on track. If, as one veteran diplomat had said, Washington in the earlier Reagan years had "shivered in the icy winds of Cold War," Reagan had now surely found his place in history as co-proponent of a new and promising period of thaw.

AFTER THE REVOLUTION

In the later months of the Reagan presidency, as both major parties focused on the 1988 presidential election, commentators of widely varying perspectives observed that the Republican grip on the White House had been strengthened by Reagan's bold summitry and by the disarmament break-through, but threatened by an array of nagging problems. Eight years of Reaganism had left Americans feeling generally better about themselves. After a succession of failed or unpopular chief executives, Reagan's message of pride and patriotism restored national self-confidence. Not a "quick study," never one to linger over complicated briefing papers or to consult extensively with experts on affairs of state, Reagan preferred to leave the daily routine of executive leadership to trusted aides. Yet Reagan was also an unrivaled master of the ceremonial side of presidential leadership; by force of personality and popularity he made a revitalized executive branch once again the center for the formation of public opinion and national policy. By the end of his second term, his ability to govern had been compromised by his "lame duck" status but also by Contragate and by deepening public doubts about the integrity of some of his political "handlers," his "management style," and his attention span. Yet some observers believed — had the 22nd Amendment permitted — that Reagan could again win a majority of the voters. Delighted that it never had to challenge him again, the political opposition made it an article of faith that Reagan's policies were never as appealing as Reagan himself.

Fiscal and economic problems often dominated the public dialogue after 1986. "Supply-side economics" retained a coterie of true believers. But tax cuts for the affluent had produced unprecedented budget deficits rather than sustained economic growth, and many Americans by 1988 were worried about such matters as the soaring national debt, the "buy-up" of American business by Japanese and other foreign capital, and a housing market at once depressed and yet beyond the reach of many young families. Experts pointed to additional worries ranging from the long-term consequences of an extraordinary upward redistribution of income, wealth, and privilege during the 1980s, to the "structural unemployment" that stranded growing numbers of inner-city workers in a post-industrial (i.e., service and high-technology) economy, to the nation's overdependence on foreign energy sources and the declining American capacity to dominate a global market.

While the public never seemed to hold the president personally account-able, the Reagan Revolution also brought disillusionment and a sense that the commonweal had been too often sacrificed to private interests. Deregulation had left a harmful environmental legacy, and Reaganite neglect may actually have strengthened the clean-air-and-water lobby; although the magnitude of scandal and crisis in the nation's financial institutions was not yet known in 1988, few Americans thought that business could be trusted to regulate itself.

Racial and cultural division had, by all accounts, deepened in the 1980s. Many blacks, Hispanics, Native Americans, and feminists deeply resented Reagan policies they thought to be inimical to their rights. Working- and middle-class whites, not a few of them "Reagan Democrats," still seethed with resentment toward such liberal social remedies as affirmative action and busing. There was no consensus on how (or even whether) to address a long list of unresolved social ills and unmet human needs: increasing crime, overcrowded jails, and a staggering incarceration rate; declining health-care and educational standards; the "feminization of poverty" and such concerns of working women as maternity leave, day care, and "comparable worth" wages; AIDS (acquired immune deficiency syndrome); illegal immi-gration and multilingualism; drug abuse, welfare dependence, homeless-ness, alienated youth, and other pathologies disproportionately visited upon nonwhite inner-cities but by no means confined to them. By nearly any measure, the body politic remained conservative. Yet by 1988, liberals and moderates dared to believe, the electorate had learned from the Reagan dispensation that the costs of long-term federal social negligence were unacceptably high. Some analysts saw an increasing recognition by 1988 that the ideology of the marketplace was not in itself a panacea and that social harmony in an increasingly multiracial, multicultural, and poly-glot society required more than affirmations of traditional morality and patriotism.

Democrats, more confident than at any time since 1976, declared that the "fairness issue" would defeat the "party of wealth" and Reaganism. Republicans found cause for optimism in the peace-and-prosperity issue, in the Democratic party's propensity for self-destruction, and in the absence of any clear Democratic front-runner. Privately, however, GOP strategists worried about the future of the Reagan coalition. Reagan's political genius, as one commentator expressed it, was his ability "to bridge divisions between the country club and the fundamentalist church, be-tween the executives of the Fortune 500 and the membership of the National Rifle Association." With the genial California ideologue in retire-ment, the question seemed to be: whither the uneasy alliance of Republi-can regulars, movement conservatives, and "Reagan Democrats," of "baby boomers," Old Right establishment conservatives, and New Right cultural and religious conservatives?

FOR FURTHER READING

Useful overviews of the Reagan years can be found in Alonzo Hamby, *Lib-eralism and Its Challengers: From FDR to Bush* (1992), and William Chafe, *The Unfinished Journey: America Since World War II* (1995). Among sev-eral studies of Reagan's leadership and administration, see William Grei-der, *Who Will Tell the People: The Betrayal of American Democracy* (1992); Haynes Johnson, *Sleepwalking Through History* (1991); C. Brant Short, *Ronald Reagan and the Public Lands* (1989); Lou Cannon, *President Rea-gan* (1991); Michael Rogin, *Ronald Reagan: The Movie* (1987); Kevin Phillips, *The Politics of Rich and Poor* (1990); Larry Berman, ed., *Looking Back at the Reagan Presidency* (1990); and Garry Wills, *Reagan's America: Inno-cents at Home* (1987). Kiss-and-tell insider accounts are fairly numerous; see especially Michael Deaver, *Behind the Scenes* (1987); Alexander Haig, *Caveat* (1984); Peggy Noonan, *What I Saw at the Revolution* (1986); and

Donald T. Regan, *For the Record* (1988). Students should also consult Reagan's own autobiographies: *Where's the Rest of Me?* (1965) and *Ronald Reagan* (1992). The conservative critique of the welfare state is captured in Charles Murray, *Losing Ground: American Social Policy, 1950–1980* (1984). Theodore Draper's *A Very Thin Line* (1991) explains the Iran-Contra affair. The rise of the New Right is examined in J. David Hoeveler, Jr., *Watch on the Right* (1991); William C. Berman, *America's Right Turn* (1994); and David H. Bennett, *The Party of Fear* (1995).

Relevant studies of diplomacy, disarmament, and the international scene during the Reagan years include Paul Kennedy, *The Rise and Fall of the Great Powers* (1988); Walter LaFeber, *Inevitable Revolutions* (1984); Strobe Talbott, *The Russians and Reagan* (1984); William G. Hyland, *Mortal Rivals: Superpower Relations from Nixon to Reagan* (1987); Thomas H. Carothers, *In the Name of Democracy: United States Policy Toward Latin America in the Reagan Years* (1991); and Bob Woodward, *Veil: The Secret Wars of the CIA* (1987).

33

★ ★ ★ ★ ★ ★

A New Domestic and World Order, 1988–1996

RONALD REAGAN'S SUCCESSORS, Republican George Bush and Democrat William Jefferson Clinton, encountered a rapidly changing domestic and world order. At home, Presidents Bush and Clinton inherited a depleted treasury and faced a populace riven by growing class and racial tensions and increasingly convinced the federal government could do little good. The huge federal deficits rolled up by Reagan during his eight years in office forced Bush to renounce his pledge to conservatives to avoid raising taxes and led Clinton to make the reduction of the budget shortfall, rather than new expensive initiatives, a centerpiece of his domestic agenda. While both presidents followed perhaps the most sensible course fiscally, they suffered politically at the hands of an American public that embraced the idea (though not generally the reality) of a more limited federal government. Confronted with the apparent corruption of American political life — highlighted initially by Watergate and then reinforced by innumerable public scandals that followed in the next two decades — and bombarded by Republican rhetoric and policies that attacked the federal government, growing numbers of Americans perceived government as their worst enemy. Abroad, the end of the Cold War in 1989 meant that foreign policy could no longer be guided by the simple application of anticommunism, which had dictated America's relations with the world since the 1940s. As the only military superpower in a post-Soviet world, the United States confronted questions about how, when, and why to use its military might.

THE BUSH SUCCESSION

The 1988 election elevated Vice President George Bush to the presidency but was not a referendum on the legacy of the Reagan Revolution or on any other substantive matter. True to recent form, the campaign featured carefully packaged candidates insulated from meaningful exchanges by "photo opportunities," media "sound bites," negative advertising, and stylized TV encounters which only the least cynical still called "debates." After extended intraparty skirmishing, the Democrats narrowed their field from a pack of seven uninspiring hopefuls ("seven dwarfs") to two favorites: Michael Dukakis, the son of Greek immigrants and governor of Massachusetts; and Jesse Jackson, a former associate of Martin Luther King and the first formidable black presidential candidate in American history.

In the end it was Bush and Dukakis. Although Dukakis and his running mate, Senator Lloyd Bentsen of Texas, had an early edge in the polls, Bush managed to portray the ineffectual Democratic candidate as a passionless, out-of-touch liberal technocrat who opposed the mandatory recitation by schoolchildren of the Pledge of Allegiance but not high crime or high taxes. Putting Dukakis on the defensive from the outset, Bush sought to placate all factions of his party and secure an electoral majority by promising not to raise taxes ("read my lips"), to usher in a "kinder, gentler America" (presumably one less partisan than Reagan's), and to address the nation's unresolved social problems, not through government initiatives but by encouraging a renewed sense of noblesse oblige ("a thousand points of light"). He shocked even many of the party faithful when he chose young, inexperienced, and inarticulate Senator J. Danforth Quayle III of Indiana as his vice-presidential candidate. He seemed to betray his own patrician good taste and moderate instincts with negative campaigning that reached new depths in the manipulation of patriotic and racial symbols. And he won, carrying 54 percent of the voters and forty states, but neither the House nor the Senate. Scarcely half the electorate voted.

While Ronald Reagan stood comfortably on the far right margins of American politics, George Herbert Walker Bush seemed to prefer the middle of the road. The first patrician president since FDR, Bush was born to an aristocratic, public-spirited Connecticut family and educated in the tradition of the nation's elite (Andover and Yale). He fought with distinction in World War II and then moved to Texas where he acquired a modest fortune in the postwar oil boom and became active in a fledgling Republican party. A Yankee blueblood and heir to a tradition of moderate Eastern establishment Republicanism, Bush was always something of an outsider in conservative, once solidly Democratic Texas. He managed to win two terms in the House of Representatives, but he was twice denied election to the Senate (1964 and 1970) and was never fully at ease in the rough-and-tumble world of Texas politics.

He was, however, a political pragmatist who struggled to maintain ties with both wings of the GOP and who demonstrated a capacity to shift with the political winds from far right to center and back again. In 1964, despite a reputation for moderation on social issues, he affirmed that he was a Goldwater Republican and opposed both the Nuclear Test Ban Treaty and the Civil Rights Act. Later he adopted a more centrist stance, urging his party to eschew the "scared and reactionary" politics of "extremists" in favor of a "sensitive and dynamic" conservatism. In 1980, after serving Presidents Nixon and Ford in an impressive number of high appointive positions (among them ambassador to the United Nations, envoy to Beijing, and director of the CIA), he presented himself in the Republican primaries as a moderate alternative to Ronald Reagan and a harsh critic of supply-side economics. Once named to Reagan's ticket, however, Bush again moved sharply to the right, and as vice president he so submerged himself in administration policy that one snide conservative critic called him "Reagan's lap dog." By 1988, having won the tentative acceptance of the Republican right, he ran for president as Reagan's heir, delicately distancing himself from Contragate and divisive issues in Central America, but otherwise promising continuity with a still-popular conservative administration.

If flexibility is the coin of politics, Bush's success was dearly bought. His ideological pragmatism — combined with a reputation for indecision and with occasional lapses of public manner and speech that critics called "wimpish" and "fatuous" — raised questions about his sincerity and resolve. Popular doubts about his "toughness" were apparently eased by his no-holds-barred style of electioneering and, later, by his pugnacious style of diplomacy. Right-wing Republicans, however, never found him to be a fully credible conservative, and Democrats often said he had no "center," that his eagerness to be all things to all Republican factions betrayed a fundamental lack of conviction.

REAGAN'S THIRD TERM?

After his inauguration as the forty-first president, Bush quickly abandoned the inflammatory, win-at-any-price style of his campaign. To a nation grown weary of bitter partisanship, his "kinder, gentler" mainstream-Republican manner was widely welcomed. Critics of Reaganite social neglect momentarily hoped that an ideologically erratic but fundamentally practical president would find opportunity in a greatly diminished Soviet threat to address a mounting backlog of domestic problems. It was soon apparent, however, that Bush had few domestic priorities and that his policies at home would differ little from Reagan's. Inhibited by federal indebtedness soon to exceed $3 trillion, by Democratic control of Congress, and by the president's fear of his own party's right wing, the administration pursued the politics of symbol and gesture. It paid occasional lip service to issues dear to both sides of the political spectrum, but generally practiced a politically safe stewardship of the status quo. "We inherited a situation that was basically A-O.K.," a top administration aide reported. "People were happy with the status quo. . . . With a few changes here and there the G.O.P. could rule forever."

As a campaigner, Bush had promised to "build a better America," to be both "the education president" and "the environmental president." His domestic initiatives, however, were few. He signed a long overdue law to protect the rights of the handicapped. He supported a popular clean-air act

— a measure long favored by congressional Democrats and the first such legislation since 1977 — but he declined to lead in such areas of environmental concern as energy conservation, global warming, and deforestation. He continued the Reagan administration's policy of aggressive business deregulation, which often weakened environmental guidelines, and which culminated with expensive federal outlays to cover losses incurred by the savings and loan industry in speculative ventures following deregulation. Two bipartisan bailout measures for the failed industry totaled $130 billion, though experts agreed that the eventual cost to taxpayers would be even higher, somewhere in the range of $300 to $500 billion. Unable to persuade Congress that a controversial capital gains tax cut would offset revenue losses through economic growth, he then broke a solemn and oft-repeated "no new taxes" pledge by endorsing a five-year deficit reduction agreement which included substantial tax increases. When conservative Republicans expressed outrage, Bush blamed the Democrats for making him do it and pledged never to do it again. He endorsed vital national education goals but advocated reduced federal educational spending; he appointed a "drug czar," declared that a war on drugs was his highest priority, and quickly allowed a succession of international issues to crowd that campaign from public view.

On social issues, Bush did sign the Civil Rights Act of 1991, but he forbade colleges to use public funds for minority scholarships and vetoed an equal-employment measure, calling it a "mandatory quotas bill." Perhaps to mollify single-issue social conservatives, he advocated a constitutional amendment to outlaw flag burning, supported a bill to expand the number of federal crimes subject to the death penalty, and opposed affirmative action, most gun-control laws, abortion, and virtually all new social spending. Yet Washington observers generally agreed that the president was even less ready than Reagan to invest his personal political capital heavily in New Right causes.

Bush did, however, continue Reagan's attempt to establish the New Right social agenda by building a conservative majority on the Supreme Court, replacing retiring liberals William Brennan and Thurgood Marshall with conservative justices. One of these appointments, Clarence Thomas, represented a cynical attempt to put forward a barely qualified black conservative whom liberals would be loath to attack because of his race. But at the confirmation hearings gender, not race, became the most volatile issue. A black law professor, Anita Hill, who had previously worked with Thomas at the Equal Employment Opportunity Commission, graphically charged her former employer with sexual harassment. By the 1990s women routinely worked outside the home in every conceivable occupation but still faced discrimination in areas such as hiring, promotion, and pay, as well as sexual harassment from male co-workers and employers. While women had made substantial progress since the 1960s, the public hearings on Anita Hill's allegations focused the nation's attention on the numerous obstacles women continued to encounter in the workplace. And the reaction of Bush, most of the all-male Senate Judiciary Committee, and many other Americans, who seemed unable even to comprehend Hill's accusations, demonstrated that serious hurdles still existed to ending gender bias in this area of American life. In the end, the judiciary committee and the full Senate backed Thomas, especially after he claimed the hearings were "a high-tech lynching for uppity blacks." As the Supreme Court became more conservative, it sanctioned a number of state restrictions on a woman's access to abortion and began to roll back the array of rights claimed for accused criminals by the Warren Court.

Ultimately Bush's domestic advisers seemed intent on his reelection and little else. Asked early in 1991 what remained on the administration's domestic agenda, the president's combative, conservative chief of staff, John Sununu, replied, "Not that much." "We may end up with not that much legislation being passed," he said, "but people will understand much more [about] the difference between Republicans and Democrats, and why we need a Republican Congress." As dean of Washington correspondents David Broder noted, the administration's first home-front concern was to "cultivate the Republican conservative base and sharpen the differences with the Democrats." In sum, while painful budget and tax choices were deferred, it was politics as usual in a government torn by divisions between the party of Congress and the party of the White House.

A NEW WORLD ORDER

1989 will be remembered as the year of miracles, the year of the reverse dominoes, of hitherto unimaginable change: from Stettin on the Baltic to Trieste on the Adriatic, an iron curtain rose across the continent of Europe. In scarcely more than twelve months, from late 1989 through 1990, a Europe torn in two in the tense aftermath of World War II was made substantially whole again. In these pivotal months the Cold War ended; the larger Soviet empire, and with it the Warsaw Pact, crumbled; the communist regimes of Poland, Hungary, Czechoslovakia, Bulgaria, Romania, and (most remarkable of all) East Germany collapsed; the Berlin Wall came down and two Germanies, in the first free nationwide election since 1932, became a unified nation-state aligned with NATO. Before the end of 1991, the Soviet Union itself had disintegrated.

Largely unexpected, accomplished with minimal bloodshed and in some cases without so much as a shot fired, the events in Eastern Europe, most experts agreed, could not have happened without the acquiescence of the USSR. Although Reagan partisans were quick to assert that the Reagan defense buildup and Reagan's anti-communist resolve had destroyed the Soviet empire, George Bush prudently declined to declare victory in the Cold War. *Perestroika, glasnost,* and the "new thinking" of Mikhail Gorbachev, as well as longer-term internal developments within the Soviet sphere, ultimately sparked the communist collapse. Faced with rapidly deteriorating conditions within its own borders, the USSR apparently concluded that the costs of continued Soviet hegemony over East bloc nations were too high, that the USSR could address its own political and economic crises and ease tensions with the West only by allowing the democratic movements of Eastern Europe to develop unhindered by Soviet arms. For one seemingly eternal moment, a world that remembered Soviet repression of East European independence movements in the 1950s and 1960s held its breath. But the soldiers of the USSR did not march, and Gorbachev announced that Soviet forces would return to Soviet soil. Such restraint seemed the more remarkable because in June 1989 a pro-democracy movement in Beijing had been brutally suppressed by the Chinese government.

Once set in motion, however, Gorbachev's reform program inevitably threatened to bring down communist rule in the USSR. Sensing the danger to their power, hard-line communists within the Soviet government attempted in August 1991 to topple Gorbachev and reverse the processes of reform and pluralism. Badly planned and heroically opposed by the peoples of the Soviet Union and by Boris Yeltsin, elected president of Russia, the largest Soviet republic, the conservative coup d'état soon failed, and Gorbachev was returned to leadership over a failing central government. Within weeks almost all the Soviet republics declared their independence, and on December 26, 1991, the Soviet Union was officially dissolved. Forming a loose federation known as the Commonwealth of Independent States, Russia and eleven other former Soviet republics began the demanding and uncertain task of political and economic reconstruction. For the most part, Washington watched from the periphery as these events unfolded. Bush, who had more foreign policy experience than any president since Nixon, moved quickly in 1991 and 1992 to negotiate significant arms reduction agreements with Russia, but in general he was careful not to unbalance a delicate process. While Bush's hands-off strategy initially seemed judicious, the situation in the former Soviet Union grew increasingly complex. By the time the president left office, much of the region was engulfed in chaos and fragmentation. Seven separate ethnic wars were under way by the summer of 1993 in the former Soviet republics. And Boris Yeltsin's attempts to create a Western-style democracy and free-market economy from the ashes of the Soviet system proceeded slowly, generating economic hardship and a loss of national self-confidence. Ultranationalists and communists within Russia mobilized opposition to his leadership.

Nearly everyone understood that the end of the Cold War heralded the end of anti-communism as a primary engine of American foreign policy. But what would take its place? Most Americans seemed prepared to believe that the world was now a safer place; optimists even urged Congress and the White House to invest an expected "peace dividend" in the solution of domestic problems. But U.S. leaders argued that a strong military was still needed to assure America's foreign policy objectives — protecting American economic interests and American security — in a world still seething with regional conflicts, border disputes, and ethnic struggles. Strategists claimed the U.S. might now have to fight in more than one of these conflicts at the same time, as well as guard against any number of transnational threats, such as nuclear proliferation, terrorism, and drug smuggling.

Thus the military built to fight the Soviet threat would have to be maintained and even bolstered. Clearly there would be no peace. And no peace dividend either.

George Bush's primary approach to foreign policy in the post–Cold War era was to use maximum power to intervene in world affairs when the achievement of American objectives was clear and the outcome certain. This policy had first been proposed by Bush's chairman of the Joint Chiefs of Staff, Colin Powell — a lesson Powell had learned in Vietnam. The Bush administration demonstrated this strategy most dramatically by American military action in Latin America and the Middle East. As communism was crumbling in Eastern Europe, the U.S. flexed its military muscle to subdue the troublesome Latin American nation of Panama. General Manuel Noriega, a newfound ally of Castro's Cuba, one-time CIA informer, and reputed profiteer in the U.S.-Colombia drug trade, was the dictator of Panama, increasingly anti-American and a major embarrassment to the Reagan and Bush administrations. In December 1989, having tried to topple him by other means, Bush ordered a U.S. invasion of Panama to seize the offending strong man, transparently claiming the operation was designed to "restore democracy" in the country. The action stirred a new round of Latin American resentment and violated the charters of both the United Nations and the Organization of American States but installed a more pliant, pro-American government in Panama and, of course, was enthusiastically applauded in the United States.

A more difficult mission, requiring international acquiescence, came in the Middle East. On August 2, 1990, the tiny, oil-rich sheikdom of Kuwait (population 2 million) was invaded by the forces of Saddam Hussein, the ruthless dictator of Iraq (population 19 million). Ironically, Iraq had once enjoyed the favor of both the United States and the USSR. After the toppling of the shah of Iran by Islamic revolutionaries in 1979, Washington had looked to Saddam Hussein as a stabilizing force in a volatile Arab world. Notwithstanding its arms-for-hostages trade with Iran, the Reagan administration tilted toward Iraq during the Iran-Iraq war (1980–1988), supplying Saddam with military intelligence and advanced technology capable of both civilian and military applications. The Soviets, for their part, equipped Saddam with much of his armament. After Iraq's victory over Iran, the United States continued to fund the Iraqi military machine, seemingly oblivious to Saddam's ambitions for regional power. After Saddam's move against Kuwait, however, Bush privately affirmed Western geopolitical and economic interests, publicly warned of an impending Iraqi invasion of Saudi Arabia, and invoked the "lessons of Munich." He met the Iraqi dictator's aggression against Kuwait with Operation Desert Shield, a massive, well-orchestrated, and American-led international counteroffensive.

Prodded by the president, the United Nations Security Council, which had often been paralyzed during the Cold War when regional conflicts regularly became proxies for Soviet-American conflict, promptly condemned the invasion and imposed trade sanctions on Iraq; a subsequent UN resolution directed Iraq to evacuate Kuwait by January 15, 1991, or risk military action. As that deadline approached, the multinational allied force numbering some 500,000 American men and women and perhaps half as many additional troops from Egypt, Saudi Arabia, and twenty-three other nations was dispatched to the area, representing the largest and most expensive show of American force since Vietnam. Military experts noted that Saddam's army — some one million battle-hardened troops equipped with sophisticated arms, including chemical and biological weapons — was the world's "fourth largest." Many observers warned of an impending bloodbath in the Middle East. Saddam himself promised to wage the "mother of all battles" in defense of Kuwait, his "nineteenth province."

In the face of these fearsome prospects — and of mounting concerns that military action might undermine a fragile international coalition and perhaps win Iraq additional Arab friends — many experts counseled patience. A U.S.-sponsored war, critics noted, could inflame Middle Eastern sensibilities, triggering a new wave of Islamic fundamentalism and Arab nationalism. Most congressional Democrats favored continued reliance on economic sanctions — as did eight of nine recent secretaries of defense, two recent chairmen of the Joint Chiefs of Staff, such leading military strategists as Zbigniew Brzezinski, Paul Nitze, and Edward Luttwak, and (by one count) "90 percent of American and European experts on Arab affairs." In the end, however, the president had his way. Arguing that an embargo alone would not deter the desert warlord he likened to Hitler, Bush narrowly won congressional authorization for war against Saddam.

On January 16, 1991, Desert Shield became Desert Storm as allied bombers streaked toward Baghdad to begin one of the more one-sided wars in history. Quickly achieving control of the skies, the highly sophisticated allied air offensive in little more than a month destroyed an estimated 75 percent of Saddam's military capacity and virtually his entire command and control structure. A ground war, lasting scarcely one hundred hours, was won before it began. Dispirited by the unprecedented accuracy and destruction of the allied air campaign and by eight years of conflict with Iran, exhausted, hungry, and confused Iraqi soldiers simply refused to fight. Many thousands surrendered without firing a shot. By late February the war was over; Iraqi occupiers fled Kuwait; allied forces temporarily occupied southern Iraq; and Saddam, though he declared victory, signed a humiliating peace agreement and faced what American optimists believed to be certain political collapse. Unlike previous wars, Americans were able to follow the action from start to finish via television, though U.S. news reports, operating under a censorship nearly as complete as that imposed by Saddam Hussein, assumed a remote, impersonal, bloodless, mesmerizing quality that seemed more appropriate for a video game than a war.

Measured in allied lives lost, this was not a costly war. Although UN forces spent more than $1 billion each day the war lasted (most of this figure borne by nations other than the United States), fewer than two hundred Americans were killed in combat. Questions, however, lingered long after the armistice about a mysterious illness known as Gulf War Syndrome, which afflicted a growing number of veterans. The number of Iraqi military deaths was anybody's guess, but the figure surely numbered in the tens of thousands (casualty estimates ranged from 100,000 to 150,000). Compared with other wars in the twentieth century, civilian casualties sustained by Iraq in this "Nintendo War" of precision strikes with laser-guided "smart bombs" appeared to have been remarkably low. But much of Iraq was now a physical wasteland, its economic infrastructure reduced to rubble almost overnight. Kuwait was still more devastated; having looted its riches and terrorized its citizens, fleeing Iraqi soldiers torched Kuwait's oil fields, creating an unprecedented environmental catastrophe.

In the aftermath of an unexpectedly easy victory, Bush declared that the nation had, at long last, put Vietnam out of mind, a pronouncement sufficiently ambiguous to alarm a new generation of "doves" and to delight a new generation of "hawks." Jubilant Republicans, eager to capitalize on the mood of national triumph, looked forward to partisan conflict with Democratic "naysayers," while critics of the war (by no means all of them liberal Democrats) fell silent and watched uncomfortably as the president's public opinion ratings soared to new heights. Swept along on a wave of spontaneous, exuberant patriotism perhaps not felt in more than a generation, the American people celebrated the end of what many thought to be the first "good war" since World War II.

Whatever advantages the Gulf War had for boosting American morale, it soon became apparent that the war had done little to alter the internal politics of Kuwait or Iraq. Kuwait's undemocratic regime was quickly reestablished after the war, and despite Bush's claim that a goal of Desert Storm was the restoration of democracy in Kuwait, anyone familiar with the nation's politics knew the country never had any democracy to revive. The war also brought no end to the tragedy of multi-ethnic Iraq, a faction-torn "big Lebanon" in which the ruling Sunni Muslim minority (20 percent of all Iraqis) was outnumbered by pro-Iran Shiite Muslims (55 percent) and independence-minded, non-Arab Kurds (25 percent). The allied effort had effectively neutralized Saddam Hussein's threat to the stability of the Near East. But it stopped short of dismantling his military or toppling his unpopular Baath party regime. Immediately following the armistice with the allies, the Iraqi leader, threatened now by civil war, turned his guns on restive Iraqis. Apparently responding to Bush's appeal for a popular uprising against their dictator, Kurds and Shiites rose up, only to be slaughtered by troops loyal to Saddam. When this revolt was crushed, thousands fled to the unwelcoming borders of Turkey and Iran. Initially the Bush administration — wary of long-term entanglement in Middle Eastern political strife and apparently preferring a known and severely chastened Sunni regime led by Saddam to an unknown pro-Iranian Shiite successor — declined further intervention and thus allowed Saddam to reassert control. The U.S. had no right, Bush said, to meddle in the internal affairs of another nation, and, in any event, the international coalition Bush had assembled had agreed only to liberate Kuwait, not overthrow Saddam. Many close watchers of the Middle East agreed with the administration that prolonged civil strife and a power vacuum in Iraq could benefit a resurgent Iran.

Moved less by geopolitical considerations than by human concerns, however, the American public was deeply touched by graphic television coverage of mass death and homelessness among the terror-stricken Kurds. Belatedly Bush responded to popular pressure, and the United States began supplying refugees from Iraqi military terror with humanitarian aid. American troops soon constructed temporary shelters in northern Iraq for the displaced Kurds; under pressure from Washington, Saddam promised (as he had before) to allow democracy in Iraq and autonomy for the Kurds. In the end, despite the imposition of a ruinous trade embargo on Iraq — which perhaps caused as much suffering among the Iraqi people as the war itself — Saddam's murderous regime continued to survive long after his "defeat."

Although the war seemed merely to restore the status quo in Iraq and Kuwait, the United States emerged from the conflict as the major power in a region where the nation's interests were indeed great. While the Middle East remained a tinderbox of potential conflicts and unresolved ethnic tensions, the Gulf War demonstrated U.S. ability to assert its control, despite the continuance of a certain amount of surface chaos, over the pivotal region and its vital oil reserves. A sign of American dominance in the area could be seen in the increasing willingness of the area's Arab nations to move closer to developing a more lasting peace with Israel, a longtime American ally. This was capped by the signing of a peace accord between Israel and the Palestinian Liberation Organization in September 1993, which established a framework for ending the twenty-five-year struggle between the two groups. While ironing out the details of self-rule for Palestinians in Israel proved difficult — especially after the 1996 assassination of Israeli Prime Minister Yitzhak Rabin by an ultra right-wing Jew and the return to power in Israel of the more nationalist Likud party — most observers agreed that Israeli security had been strengthened in the post-Soviet, post–Gulf War world.

While Panama and Iraq demonstrated Washington's ability and willingness to act decisively in the post–Cold War era to protect its economic and security interests, Bush also faced more difficult foreign policy decisions. As the only military superpower left in the world following the breakup of the Soviet Union, questions surfaced about whether the U.S. military should be used (and whether American lives should be risked) in police actions to resolve ethnic fighting or to help those in peril around the world. For the most part, Bush declined to use American power for such operations except in the most limited of circumstances. In Yugoslavia, centuries-old ethnic tensions erupted violently in 1991 as the iron curtain dividing Europe rose, shattering the former Yugoslavia into several competing ethnic factions. As the breakup of Yugoslavia began, James Baker, Bush's secretary of state, declared that U.S. interests would be served by a democratic and united Yugoslavia and that the U.S. would take the necessary measures to ensure such a result. Bush and his advisers, however, declined to intervene when gruesome fighting (including so-called ethnic cleansing, or genocide of civilians simply because of their ethnicity) later broke out between Muslims, Serbs, and Croats in the former Yugoslavian region of Bosnia. The Bush administration ultimately concluded that U.S. armed intervention in Bosnia entailed much peril and little real advantage. In a somewhat different scenario, the administration wrestled with the question of whether to send American troops on a humanitarian mission to aid the people of Somalia after a civil war combined with a drought in the African nation threatened millions of people with starvation. Initially unwilling to act, Bush ultimately authorized a military mission, in part a response to pressure from the American public, who watched the catastrophe on television and increasingly called for American action. But Bush charged the sizable American force sent to Somalia with accomplishing only the limited objective of protecting the delivery of relief foodstuffs, not solving the larger problem of ending the country's civil war and ethnic fighting.

ELECTING A "NEW DEMOCRAT"

In the aftermath of the Persian Gulf War, George Bush appeared assured of a second term. In fact, as the 1992 presidential campaign began in the months after the war's end, many of the presumed front-runners for the Democratic party nomination looked at Bush's seemingly unassailable popularity — which had soared to an astounding 91 percent approval rating at the end of the war — and declined to enter the race. But as the glow of military victory began to fade and was even tarnished by the survival of Saddam's government, and as the economic recession that began in 1990 deepened, Bush's popularity nose-dived. While Bush had demonstrated his competency in the foreign policy arena, his inattention to domestic problems ultimately doomed his hopes for a second term. As the economy worsened, the president took little action, apparently confident that the problem would fix itself. To many Americans, however, Bush's approach seemed insensitive to the hardships brought to them by a sluggish economy. And when the president visited a supermarket and expressed amazement at the novelty of price scanners that had been a staple of checkout counters everywhere for many years, Bush appeared to be a member of the pampered elite, someone incapable of understanding the real economic anxieties of middle-class Americans.

The man who emerged from a lackluster field to win the Democratic nomination and eventually defeat George Bush in the presidential election of 1992 was Bill Clinton. The first president born after World War II, Clinton rose from humble beginnings in Hope, Arkansas, to acquire a first-class education (Georgetown, Rhodes Scholar at Oxford University, and Yale Law School). After a brief teaching stint at the University of Arkansas, he entered politics, winning election as governor of Arkansas five times. In the mid-1980s Clinton helped form the Democratic Leadership Council, an organization devoted to moving the Democratic party in a more conservative direction. And during the campaign Clinton sought to reassure voters that he was not the kind of Democratic candidate they had so emphatically rejected over the last several decades. Clinton billed himself as a New Democrat, a centrist who had forsworn the excesses of the New Deal and the Great Society — in short, as anything but a liberal. To bolster these claims, Clinton adopted a number of campaign positions designed to lure "Reagan Democrats" back from the Republican party: he promised to cut the deficit, "to end welfare as we know it," to support capital punishment, and to pass a "middle-class tax cut." Although Clinton did back some long-time Democratic initiatives, including reform of the health-care system and increased spending ("investment") in education, public works, and job training, he shied away from other typical Democratic programs, especially those that had alienated many white suburbanites in recent elections, such as efforts targeted to help inner-city minorities.

Trying to position himself squarely in the center, Clinton also capitalized on Bush's hands-off approach to the recession. Clinton reassured middle-class voters that he "felt their pain." Although President Bush tried to score points by attacking Clinton's character (alleging that he was unpatriotic, unfaithful to his wife, and unethical in his financial dealings), the Arkansas governor remembered the Democratic campaign motto — "It's the economy, stupid" — and stuck to his game plan of emphasizing the weak economy of 1992. In the end, many voters agreed with Clinton about the primacy of a candidate's economic policy over his personal behavior; others had their own lingering doubts about Bush's character, especially the president's role in the Iran-Contra affair. While Bush claimed to be "out of the loop" on Iran-Contra, other Reagan officials, such as Caspar Weinberger and George Shultz, continued to maintain that Bush was an early and strong advocate of arms sales to Iran.

The Republicans in 1992, in contrast to the Democrats' newfound moderation, seemed captive to their religious right wing. The New Right had never had total faith in George Bush's willingness to advance their conservative social agenda; consequently the president faced a surprisingly strong challenge in the Republican primaries from the conservative journalist Patrick Buchanan. Although his quest for the nomination fell short, Buchanan's candidacy mobilized the New Right. A minority within the party, it nonetheless dominated the party's August convention with talk of a "religious war" in America and engineered the adoption of a conservative platform. While Bush clearly remained a moderate, as did a large segment of the Republican rank and file, many Americans associated the Republicans with the extremism on display at the party's summer convention.

Another factor in the election of 1992 was the independent candidacy of Ross Perot, who mounted the most successful challenge to the two major parties since Theodore Roosevelt's Bull Moose campaign of 1912. A Texas billionaire who nominated himself to run (he had no party affiliation) and who financed his campaign with $60 million of his private fortune, Perot promised "to clean up the mess in Washington" and "restore a sense of ownership" to the American people. He pointed to the federal deficit as a key symptom of the irresponsibility of the elites who controlled government and declared that a balanced budget would be the "first priority" of his administration. He also promised reform of what he invariably called a corrupt campaign finance system. Perot was adept at identifying the range of problems that troubled the country, and he garnered support from millions of Americans who believed that Washington "insiders" had no idea how to (or no inclination to) fix these difficulties. But Perot himself offered no clear plan of how he would tackle these very complex problems, and some of his vague solutions indicated little understanding of how a president might actually formulate policy in a governmental system that also included a legislative and judicial branch. Despite his shortcomings, Perot won 19 percent of the popular vote, and his total might have been even greater had he not flippantly pulled out of the race in July, only to reenter in October. Perot drew voters away from both major party candidates, though his candidacy probably hurt Bush more. But perhaps the most important by-product of Perot's candidacy was that Bill Clinton entered the White House with the support of only 43 percent of the electorate, one of the smallest presidential mandates of the twentieth century.

THE CLINTON ADMINISTRATION

After his inauguration, Bill Clinton hit the ground running but tripped. During its first two years, the Clinton administration seemed plagued by controversy and miscues. One of the first issues Clinton tackled upon assuming office was the question of homosexuals in the military. His attempt to honor a campaign promise by lifting an armed services ban on gay men and lesbians caused an outcry from a public that had little sympathy for ending discrimination against homosexuals. A compromise was eventually worked out — the "don't ask, don't tell, don't pursue" policy — that certainly represented an improvement over the previous ban but that ultimately satisfied no one (the gay and lesbian community, the military, or the American public) and that raised doubts about Clinton's campaign renunciation of liberalism. The administration also fumbled as it tried to make political appointments. It failed to recognize potential problems with some appointees before confirmation hearings, and abandoned other nominees under pressure that they were too "radical," such as Lani Guinier, nominated for assistant attorney general for civil rights but unfairly dubbed by conservative critics as a "quota queen." Despite the initial difficulties he encountered in assembling his administration, Clinton ultimately succeeded in shaping an executive staff that "looked more like America," filling a number of cabinet positions with women, blacks, and Latinos. Questions about the president's character also continued to linger, especially after the White House used vague FBI accusations in 1993 to fire the White House travel office staff, apparently to fill the slots with Clinton friends and relatives, and when information began to surface in 1994 about the role of Clinton (and his wife Hillary Rodham Clinton) in aiding a failed real-estate venture called Whitewater, which was financed by a collapsed savings and loan institution. These and other problems weakened a president who had assumed office with only a minority of popular support.

Despite these setbacks, Clinton pushed forward with an ambitious domestic agenda. He seemed to have a plan for solving every problem and relished the details of domestic policy; friends and critics called him a "policy wonk." His two most important proposals were an economic plan and health-care reform. The five-year economic proposal he presented to Congress in 1993 promised $500 billion in deficit reduction, to be achieved through both tax hikes and spending cuts, and a small "economic stimulus" package of $30 billion that included government spending in areas such as public works projects, education, and social welfare services. After several important compromises and despite almost unanimous Republican opposition, Clinton did manage to get his economic program through Congress, though passage of the measure did not win the president many friends. Most of the tax increases fell on the wealthy, but a boost in the gas tax raised taxes for the middle class, undercutting Clinton's earlier promise to give them a tax cut. The economic stimulus package, which most liberals thought too miserly a government "investment" in human capital to begin with, was cut in half, including most of the money earmarked for social welfare programs. Although Clinton's economic strategy represented a real effort to downsize the federal government and reduce the federal deficit, few applauded his efforts beyond those who were associated with the financial markets, where deficit reduction helped keep interest rates low and stock prices soaring.

Clinton's other big proposal in 1993–1994, health-care reform, fared even worse. He appointed the First Lady to head up a task force to develop a health-care plan that would, at the very least, provide universal, affordable health care for everyone, a goal supported by a majority of Americans. The centerpiece of Hillary Clinton's plan — a seventeen-hundred-page proposal drafted with little input from potential opponents — called for government oversight and management of an already existing trend toward managed care, in which health-care providers organized in Health Maintenance Organizations (HMOs) competed for patients, thereby driving down overall costs. The Clinton plan called for a National Health Board to oversee regional networks of HMOs as a way of securing maximum reductions in medical costs under a managed care system. In addition, under the Clinton plan, all employers would be required to pay 80 percent of their employee's health insurance costs. Not surprisingly, small businessmen, many insurance companies, some parts of the medical community, a number of Democrats, and virtually all congressional Republicans hated the plan. Despite widespread popular support for health-care reform, opponents of the Clinton plan mobilized an effective lobbying campaign that killed the measure by portraying it as a bad reform, one that would merely create another big and inefficient government program that would limit people's choices in choosing their doctors. While the Clinton health-care plan would have created another sizable government bureaucracy, the medical choices of most patients were already being limited by the proliferation of HMOs.

Although Clinton's two major domestic initiatives faced difficulties, he pushed several noteworthy proposals through Congress during his first two years in office: a family-leave bill, a national service program (Americorps), and an anti-crime bill that included a waiting period for the purchasers of handguns and a ban on assault weapons. Clinton also reaffirmed executive support for the pro-choice position on abortion. Among other actions, he appointed two pro-choice Supreme Court justices and reversed a Reagan policy that had banned abortion counseling at family planning centers receiving federal support.

Clinton also worked for the passage of two trade agreements initiated by his Republican predecessors, the North American Free Trade Agreement (NAFTA) and the General Agreement on Trade and Tariffs (GATT). Approval of these two accords signaled U.S. acceptance of an accomplished economic fact: globalization. Spurred by the lowering of trade barriers worldwide and startling improvements in transportation and communication technology (most recently the Internet, which linked millions of individual computer users in a virtual marketplace), globalization had, beginning in the mid-1970s, gradually transformed the once-insulated American economy. The globalization of capital led American companies to downsize and streamline their operations or move their businesses overseas, where they could cut costs by taking advantage of lower wages and relaxed environmental standards. In the process, many American workers found they could no longer count on the kind of well-paying industrial jobs that had guaranteed prosperity for the post–World War II generation. By the 1990s America essentially had a three-tiered economy: a wealthy elite enjoyed unprecedented prosperity; professionals and managers held their own but were concerned about their long-term prospects; and industrial and service workers seemingly were losing ground every year. Statistical measures documented the resulting economic inequality. For instance, while at least 50 percent of the wealth created during the 1980s and 1990s went to the wealthiest 1 percent of Americans, by 1996 average real wages for nonsupervisory workers were more than 15 percent lower than they had been in 1973. Some commentators and politicians, on both the left and right of the political spectrum, advocated a restoration of American protectionism as a panacea for America's economic problems, but Clinton wisely rejected such isolationism as both impracticable and impossible. After all, American consumers overwhelmingly supported the increased variety of cheaper goods that flowed into the country as a result of globalization. At the same time, however, Clinton had little success in developing ways to assist those displaced by the economic changes. Nor did any of his policies do much to counter a growing sense that class lines in the United States were becoming more rigid than at any other time in American history.

As economic anxiety mounted, racial divisions also hardened. Many whites, no longer certain of a secure future for themselves and their children but seeking to maximize what advantages they still possessed, called for an end to affirmative action and the wholesale abolishment of aid to the "unworthy" poor. They also generally favored stricter limits on immigration. Since the 1960s the number of immigrants to the United States had risen dramatically; most of the new arrivals, including large numbers who entered the country illegally, hailed from Africa, Asia, and especially Latin America. As a result, in some parts of the country, such as California, the Southwest, and south Florida, the Latino population had become a sizable and often powerful presence. Faced with the possibility of becoming a minority in a number of locales, many whites called for tougher immigration measures, especially those directed at illegal immigrants.

Blacks viewed the increasingly uncertain economic climate quite differently. While many had advanced into the ranks of upper and middle-class America as a result of the changes wrought by the civil rights movement, approximately one-third of the black population remained trapped in inner-city ghettos in the 1990s, unskilled, poorly educated, and generally unable to find work in a post-industrial economy. The persistence of black poverty led many blacks to believe that most American institutions remained stacked against them and that black gains had been won only because of black protest and sacrifice or government prodding and oversight, which many whites now sought to abolish. These divergent perceptions of the realities of American life could be seen most dramatically in two events that occurred in Los Angeles in the 1990s. After four white Los Angeles policemen were acquitted in April 1992 for beating a black motorist, despite the existence of a videotape that detailed the brutal battering, black citizens in south central Los Angeles vented their anger at a criminal justice system seemingly hostile to black Americans by rioting for several days. The disturbance led to fifty-one deaths, thousands of injuries, and more than $700 million in property damage. Two years later, when a former black football star, O. J. Simpson, was acquitted of charges that he murdered his white ex-wife and another white man, reaction to the verdict further reflected the wildly differing opinions of America's criminal justice system and highlighted the depth of America's racial divide. Whites overwhelmingly felt that the black-majority jury had freed a guilty man on the basis of diversionary defense tactics that harped on the racism of one of the investigating police officers. For blacks, however, the charge of a racist cop harassing a black man rang all too true, and they saw little reason to question the weight that the jury had given to such testimony.

In addition to facing a population increasingly divided by race and class, Clinton also had to govern in an atmosphere of mounting popular skepticism toward the federal government. An anti-statist tradition had existed in the United States since the earliest days of the republic, but twelve years of Republican anti-government policies and rhetoric about the failures of big government had not only crippled the scope of federal power but heightened the belief among Americans that the federal government was their primary enemy (especially once the Soviet threat no longer occupied that position). Clinton had even acknowledged this new reality during his 1992 campaign, promising "to reinvent government" if elected. Popular animosity toward the federal government could be seen in the call for term limits for public officials, the widespread mistrust of political incumbents and

Washington "insiders," the various proposals to let the states take over most functions of the federal government, and, in the most extreme cases, armed attacks on the federal government. The existence of a growing anti-government militia movement became vividly apparent after two men linked to such groups were arrested for the April 1995 bombing of a federal building in Oklahoma City which killed 168 people. Although the American people often blamed their own government for all that ailed them, it remained unclear how dismantling the federal government would solve America's problems. As the historian Alan Brinkley noted, paralyzing the federal government would "weaken the only national institution capable of checking some of the other large organizations that dominate modern life," such as corporations, banks, the media, and lobbying groups, and leave Americans at the mercy of fifty state governments competing with one another to lower health, labor, safety, and environmental standards in the scramble to attract economic development.

Confronted by this uneasy, fractured, and often antagonistic populace, Clinton at times seemed unsure of how to proceed and vacillated on policy decisions. By the mid-term elections of 1994, he had spent most of the political capital he had accrued. The president was characterized by progressives as a chief executive barely distinguishable in his policies from his Republican predecessors, and by conservatives as an unprincipled and incompetent reincarnation of the classic tax-and-spend liberal. With Clinton's popularity lagging and anti-incumbent sentiment strong, Republicans swept the 1994 elections, capturing both houses of Congress for the first time in forty years and promising to fulfill what Reagan had started — dismantling the federal government. Although only 37 percent of the electorate participated in the election, New Right voters, especially members of the Christian Coalition, were highly mobilized. As a result, one-third of the Republicans elected to the House of Representatives were freshmen members, most staunchly conservative. Many of these new House Republicans had signed a document during the campaign called the Contract with America, pledging if elected to take action on a range of issues from a balanced budget amendment to tort reform to term limits for congressmen.

When the 104th Congress convened in January 1995, the House of Representatives elected voluble, intensely partisan Newt Gingrich of Georgia, the architect of the Contract with America, as speaker. Although only a small percentage of voters claimed to have ever heard of the Contract, the House moved quickly to adopt much of the Contract's agenda, approving within three months a balanced budget bill, a Congressional Accountability Act, tort and welfare reform, an anti-crime law, and legislation to prevent mandated programs to the states that did not also provide funds. House Republicans, however, failed to pass one notable Contract item, term limits, a change that would have perhaps gone a long way toward convincing Americans that the so-called Republican Revolution was something more than "politics as usual." The reason for not aggressively pursuing this part of the Contract was obvious: the Republicans had little desire to relinquish command of Congress after gaining control over the institution for the first time in decades. Despite the ambitious program of the House, the Senate, by nature a more deliberative body and not bound by the Contract, refused to enact many of the measures. President Clinton threatened to veto most of the others.

With work on the Contract stalled, attention turned to approving a budget for the upcoming fiscal year, due to begin October 1. Congress agreed on a budget plan designed to balance the budget in seven years (by the year 2002) through $900 billion in spending cuts and more than $200 billion in tax breaks, a proposal that seemingly sought to dismantle much of what remained of the New Deal and the Great Society. In all, eighty federal programs or organizations were targeted for elimination (including the Department of Education and the Commerce Department), while many more were slated for crippling reductions (everything from environmental regulation to public broadcasting to school lunches). President Clinton responded by reaffirming his commitment to the principle of a balanced budget, but he rejected the timetable and specifics of the Republican plan in favor of less severe cuts in education, health, and welfare spending. A fight over the budget ensued, and the absence of agreement resulted in a government shutdown of "nonessential services" during late 1995 and early 1996. Confronting locked museums, closed national parks, and the plight of unpaid federal workers during the Christmas season, Americans reacted angrily to this ultimate example of government gridlock, showering much of their wrath on the Republican Congress, whose budget proposals seemed too sweeping at best and mean-spirited and extreme at worst. Both sides eventually compromised, with Congress agreeing to spending plans more acceptable to Clinton and the president accepting the seven-year timetable for achieving a balanced budget.

In the wake of the budget debacle, the Republican Revolution forecast by many observers after the 1994 elections proved to be short-lived, or at least temporarily derailed. To their surprise, Republicans discovered that despite widespread dissatisfaction with the way government operated, the vast majority of Americans did not want a return to an era of limited government and were not willing to renew their reliance on an unrestrained free market, especially if the cost was reduced benefits, a damaged environment, hazardous workplaces, or the removal of the safety net for children and the aged. Quite simply, while Americans seemed to embrace the general idea that less government was desirable, they did not want cuts in programs that affected them or their families directly. As reaction to the Republican agenda turned negative, President Clinton's beleaguered administration actually got a boost as the president assumed the role of defender of middle-class programs and entitlements in the face of seeming Republican extremism. Ironically, as the nation prepared for the presidential election in 1996, the Democratic incumbent seemed to be a major beneficiary of the GOP's stunning congressional victory of 1994.

In foreign affairs, Clinton did little to modify many of the basic policies of his predecessor. For one thing, he made no attempt to undo Bush's maintenance of the vast Cold War military. Although flailed by liberal critics for failing to generate the much-anticipated "peace dividend" needed for domestic spending, Clinton, like Bush, embraced the thinking that a well-maintained military was needed in the post-Soviet era. Already vulnerable to attacks on his patriotism because of his earlier opposition to the Vietnam War, and aware of the positive economic impact of the military-industrial complex, Clinton advocated the continuance of high spending levels for the military. Although he cut overall military spending slightly, in real dollars his budgets for the Pentagon still consistently outdistanced the average for the Cold War years. Clinton also continued the Bush administration's support of Russia's Boris Yeltsin and his attempt to restructure his country along Western lines. While congressional support for Yeltsin began to weaken, Clinton continued steadfastly to back the Russian president, helping to arrange financial aid and other international support, despite mounting evidence that Yeltsin was not a model democrat, and despite his prosecution of a bloody war against the breakaway republic of Chechnya, where in a year and a half of fighting between December 1994 and September 1996 as many as eighty thousand were killed. Although Clinton had castigated Bush during the 1992 campaign for "coddling dictators" in China to advance American trade, once in office Clinton also acceded to Bush's China policy. The president concluded that the American economy could not afford to forgo China's lucrative market, and that a vibrant China trade would expose the Asian nation to the rest of the world and possibly force it to remedy its deplorable human rights record, its cavalier arms sale policy, and its penchant for allowing wholesale copyright violations. Although Clinton's China policy improved the U.S. trade balance, China showed little sign (beyond a vague promise in 1996 to crack down on copyright infringement) of modifying its totalitarian policies. Ultimately, however, Clinton recognized that promoting American commerce abroad was among the most important U.S. foreign policy objectives in the post–Cold War world, a realization highlighted by his creation of the National Economic Council within the White House, a group charged with coordinating foreign and domestic economic policy.

Despite these basic continuities with the previous administration, Clinton ultimately questioned the Bush strategy of engaging U.S. forces only when the advancement of American interests was clearly involved and when the outcome of intervention was certain. Clinton argued during the 1992 campaign that Bush had not done enough to end the human suffering in Somalia, Bosnia, and Haiti (where Bush had declined to aid the elected president, Jean-Bertrand Aristide, after his expulsion following a military coup, deciding instead to focus on keeping Haitian refugees from coming to the United States). Claiming the nation had an obligation to act in such crises, Clinton reversed policy in all three countries. Although his actions met with initial setbacks, he eventually achieved at least qualified success in Haiti and Bosnia. In Somalia he expanded Bush's limited food delivery mission into a police action to end the fighting between competing warlords and restore order to the chaotic nation. But after a group of American soldiers were killed in a firefight in October 1993, public opinion quickly eroded for such an expanded operation, and American troops soon returned home.

In Haiti, Clinton continued the Bush policy of repatriating Haitian refugees but pledged to solve the underlying problem by restoring Haiti's elected government. An initial attempt at intervention was repulsed in October 1993 when a Haitian mob prevented a Navy transport carrying two hundred noncombat U.S. troops from landing at Port-au-Prince. Clinton responded the following year by threatening to send, over the objections of Congress and most of the American public, a UN-backed armed invasion against Haiti. An actual clash was avoided when the military junta capitulated before the assault was launched. Although Clinton's action succeeded in reinstalling Aristide as president, the larger problems plaguing the Haitian people were not resolved by this transfer of power.

In Bosnia, after failing in 1993 to get support from America's European allies for a plan to use limited air strikes against the Serb aggressors and to lift an arms embargo on Bosnia to help the Muslims under siege there, Clinton backed off from his commitment to intervene in Bosnia to end the fighting. But after Serb forces continued their bombardment of Sarajevo and captured a number of UN-established Muslim "safe havens" in 1995, Clinton renewed his call for American action, despite a continuing widespread belief among Americans that no national interest existed to warrant American involvement in the conflict. This time Clinton succeeded in convincing his European allies to mount a limited air campaign against the Serbs. This policy pushed forward the peace effort, which culminated in the signing of the Dayton Accords in November 1995 by the three Bosnian factions — Muslims, Croats, and Serbs. Although the accords ended the fighting in Bosnia in early 1996 and led to elections in September 1996, the peace settlement was less than ideal. It effectively partitioned the country into three parts, with that of the Bosnian Serbs still effectively controlled by convicted war criminal Radovan Karadzic. And with most UN peacekeepers, including Americans, due to leave Bosnia in December 1996, the long-term prospects for peace in a Bosnia where ethnic divisions had not been eliminated but merely legitimized seemed less than certain.

As the presidential election of 1996 approached, Clinton appeared assured of reelection. Liberals were largely resigned to supporting a candidate who, though disappointing in many ways, had at least held off the Republican anti-government onslaught. Republican miscalculation of their 1994 mandate enabled Clinton to reposition himself as the same kind of moderate Democrat who had won election in 1992. And Clinton continued to disarm his conservative critics by embracing traditional Republican issues, leading some to dub him a "born-again Republican." In the months leading up to the election, Clinton sought to coopt Republican social issues by urging the adoption of a number of low-cost "solutions" to various problems (school uniforms to restore discipline in schools, curfews for teenagers to end juvenile crime, a national registry for sex offenders). He also signed a badly flawed Republican welfare reform bill, which he promised to "fix" at a later date. While questions about Clinton's character persisted, heightened by a number of indictments of Clinton associates in the White-water case, many voters ultimately found these flaws — which they assumed all politicians had in some form or another — less troubling than the apparent sharp turn to the right by the Republican party. The Republicans, for their part, sought to muzzle their right wing — the key constituency in their 1994 victory — by allowing the New Right to formulate the party platform but downplaying the existence of the document and lowering the visibility of Republican ideologues at their 1996 nominating convention. Their choice as standard-bearer was Bob Dole, a perennial Republican presidential hopeful, a longtime member of the Senate, and a bland yet competent moderate. To win the nomination and attract various factions of Republican voters, however, Dole was forced to sharpen his support of New Right social issues, deny his entire record of public service to satisfy anti-government Republicans, and promise a return to supply-side economics — in the form of a 15 percent across-the-board tax cut — to mollify economic conservatives in the party.

Clinton easily defeated Dole to win a second term, collecting a solid electoral majority (379 to 159) and securing almost 50 percent of the popular vote. The Republican Congress, however, was also reelected. Although expressing general discontent with American political leadership, the voters — at least that half of the electorate that bothered to cast a ballot — ultimately favored the status quo. Undoubtedly the strong, though not dynamic, economy of 1996 led many to decide for staying the course. But much of Dole's strategy during the campaign seemed to backfire. His endorsement of New Right causes, such as the anti-abortion stance, merely fueled an already existing Republican "gender gap"; indeed, Dole won only 38 percent of women's votes. And Dole's promise of a tax cut, a perennially popular issue, never seemed to resonate with voters who perhaps remembered the Laffer curve era of the 1980s and its consequences — short-term prosperity gained at the expense of long-term fiscal problems. In the end, Americans reluctantly embraced the vibrant yet flawed Bill Clinton to lead them into the uncertain future of the new century.

FOR FURTHER READING

Those who would chart the social contours of the very recent past should begin with newspapers and periodicals. Gerald Pomper, et al., detail *The Election of 1988* (1989). Early accounts of the Bush administration include Colin Campbell and Bert Rockman, *The Bush Presidency* (1991); Michael Duffy, *Marching in Place* (1992); John Podhoretz, *Hell of a Ride* (1993); and Charles Kolb, *White House Daze* (1994). An unprecedented number of books about Bill Clinton have already appeared. While useful as sources of information, most seem unlikely to have much lasting value. Among the better accounts are Richard Reeves's *Running in Place* (1996), Roger Morris's *Partners in Power* (1996), and James Stewart's *Blood Sport* (1996). This recent outpouring of instant political history even led to the appearance of an account of the 1996 presidential campaign several months *before* the November election: Bob Woodward's *The Choice* (1996). Dan Balz and Ronald Brownstein explore the 1994 Republican takeover of Congress in *Storming the Gates* (1996); Elizabeth Drew explains the aftermath of this election in *Showdown* (1996); Haynes Johnson and David S. Broder look at the battle over health care in *The System* (1996), as does Theda Skocpol in *Boomerang* (1996); the savings and loan scandal is treated by Martin Mayer in *The Greatest-Ever Bank Robbery* (1990); and Larry J. Sabato and Glenn R. Simpson offer a discussion of American political corruption in *Dirty Little Secrets* (1996). Examinations of American society and culture in the 1990s include William Julius Wilson's *When Work Disappears* (1996); Todd Gitlin's *The Twilight of Common Dreams* (1995); Kevin Phillips's *Boiling Point* (1993); Michael J. Sandel's *Democracy's Discontent* (1996); and John Fiske's *Media Matters* (1994).

Contemporary journals, including *Current History and Foreign Affairs*, are useful sources on recent foreign policy issues. Michael J. Hogan has collected essays on *The End of the Cold War* (1992); John Lewis Gaddis explores *The United States and the End of the Cold War* (1992); and Philip Zelikow and Condoleezza Rice offer a history of German unification from the perspective of two members of Bush's National Security Council in *Germany Unified and Europe Transformed* (1995). The Persian Gulf War is analyzed by Dilip Hiro in *Desert Shield to Desert Storm* (1992), by Micah Sifry and Christopher Cerf in *The Gulf War Reader* (1991), by Michael A. Palmer in *Guardians of the Gulf* (1992), and by Lawrence Freedman and Efraim Karsh in *The Gulf Conflict* (1993). Noam Chomsky provides a critical look at the foreign policy of the Bush and Clinton administrations in *World Orders: Old and New* (1994).

INDEX